Mlynov-Muravica Memorial Book (Mlyniv-Muravytsi, Ukraine)

Translation of
Sefer Mlinov-Mervits

Original Book Edited by: J. Sigelman

Originally published in Haifa 1970

JewishGen
מרכז עולמי לגנאלוגיה יהודית
The Global Home for Jewish Genealogy

A Publication of JewishGen, INC
Edmond J. Safra Plaza, 36 Battery Place, New York, NY 10280
646.494.5972 | info@JewishGen.org | www.jewishgen.org

MUSEUM OF JEWISH HERITAGE
A LIVING MEMORIAL TO THE HOLOCAUST

Mlynov-Muravica Memorial Book (Mlyniv-Muravytsi, Ukraine)
Translation of *Sefer Mlinov-Meryits*

Editor of Original Yizkor Book: J. Sigelman
Project Coordinator: Howard I. Schwartz, PhD
Layout and Name Indexing: Jonathan Wind
Cover Design: Rachel Kolokoff Hopper

Printed in the United States of America by Lightning Source, Inc.

Library of Congress Control Number (LCCN): 2022938244

ISBN: 978-1-954176-49-2 (hard cover: 572 pages, alk. paper)

About JewishGen.org

JewishGen, an affiliate of the Museum of Jewish Heritage - A Living Memorial to the Holocaust, serves as the global home for Jewish genealogy.

Featuring unparalleled access to 30+ million records, it offers unique search tools, along with opportunities for researchers to connect with others who share similar interests. Award winning resources such as the Family Finder, Discussion Groups, and ViewMate, are relied upon by thousands each day.

In addition, JewishGen's extensive informational, educational and historical offerings, such as the Jewish Communities Database, Yizkor Book translations, InfoFiles, Family Tree of the Jewish People, and KehilaLinks, provide critical insights, first-hand accounts, and context about Jewish communal and familial life throughout the world.

Offered as a free resource, JewishGen.org has facilitated thousands of family connections and success stories, and is currently engaged in an intensive expansion effort that will bring many more records, tools, and resources to its collections.

Please visit https://www.jewishgen.org/ to learn more.

Executive Director: Avraham Groll

About the JewishGen Yizkor Book Project

Yizkor Books (Memorial Books) were traditionally written to memorialize the names of departed family and martyrs during holiday services in the synagogue (a practice that still exists in many synagogues today).

Over the centuries, as a result of countless persecutions and horrific atrocities committed against the Jews, Yizkor Books (Sefer Zikaron in Hebrew) were expanded to include more historical information, such as biographical sketches of famous personalities and descriptions of daily town life.

Following the Holocaust, the idea of remembrance and learning took on an urgent and crucial importance. Survivors of the Holocaust sought out other surviving residents of their former towns to memorialize and document the names and way of life of those who were ruthlessly murdered by the Nazis. These remembrances were documented in Yizkor Books, hundreds of which were published in the first decades after the Holocaust.

Most of these books were published privately, or through landsmanshaftn (social organizations comprised of members originating from the same European town or region) that still existed, and were often distributed free of charge. Sadly, the languages used to document these crucial histories and links to our past, Yiddish and Hebrew, are no longer commonly understood by a significant percentage of Jews today. As a result, JewishGen has undertaken the sacred responsibility of translating these books into English so that the culture and way of life of these communities will be preserved and transmitted to future generations.

In 1986, a group of farsighted JewishGenners started a project to pool their efforts together in groups based upon their ancestors from each town and donate money to get the Yizkor books of their ancestral towns translated into English. As the translated material became available, it was made accessible for free at www.JewishGen.org/Yizkor. Hardcover copies can be purchased by visiting https://www.jewishgen.org/Yizkor/ybip.html (see below).

It is our hope that the translation of these books into English (and other languages) will assist the countless Jewish family researchers who are so desperately seeking to forge a connection with their heritage.

Director of JewishGen Yizkor Book Project: Lance Ackerfeld

About JewishGen Press

JewishGen Press (formerly the Yizkor Books-in-Print Project) is the publishing division of JewishGen.org, and provides a venue for the publication of non-fiction books pertaining to Jewish genealogy, history, culture, and heritage.

In addition to the Yizkor Book category, publications in the Other Non-Fiction category include Shoah memoirs and research, genealogical research, collections of genealogical and historical materials, biographies, diaries and letters, studies of Jewish experience and cultural life in the past, academic theses, and other books of interest to the Jewish community.

Please visit https://www.jewishgen.org/Yizkor/ybip.html to learn more.

Director of JewishGen Press: Joel Alpert
Managing Editor - Jessica Feinstein
Publications Manager - Susan Rosin

Notes to the Reader

The images in the original book were reproduced from photographs from the time of the first edition. These reproductions were already of poor quality, being pre-war and at least 30 or more years old. As a result the images in the book are not very good and the best achievable.

A reader can view the original scans of the book on the websites listed below.

The original book can be seen online at the Yiddish Book Center web site:

https://www.yiddishbookcenter.org/collections/yizkor-books/yzk-nybc313897/siegelman-yitshak-sefer-mlinov-mervits

Or the New York Public Library Digital Collection:
https://digitalcollections.nypl.org/items/460a3950-5b2c-0133-f63d-00505686d14e

To obtain a list of Shoah victims from Mlynow-Moravica the reader should access the Yad Vashem web site listed below; one can also search for specific family names using family name option. These lists are continually updated by Yad Vashem, so it is worthwhile to periodically search these lists.

There is more valuable information (including the Pages of Testimony, etc.) available on this website: https://yvng.yadvashem.org/

A list of all books available from JewishGen Press along with prices is available at: https://www.jewishgen.org/Yizkor/ybip.html

Credits and Captions for Book Cover

Front Cover:

Aaron Harari (right) boating on the Ikva River with other Mlynov friends, circa 1930–1933. Courtesy of Zev Harari.

Background Photo:

The Great Synagogue in Mlynov. Photo by A. Harari in the winter of 1937/38. Page 10 [11]. Original Photo - Courtesy of Audrey Goldseker Polt.

Background color and texture:

Rachel Kolokoff Hopper

Gone But Not Forgotten:
An Introduction

By Howard I. Schwartz, PhD

Buried under the rubble of time, forgotten by the vicissitudes of history, lie two small towns, both shtetls that until recently have been lost to memory, especially to the memory of families who ended up in the English-speaking world. They were sister towns, no more than a mile apart, and their economies, cultures, institutions, and families were so intertwined with one another that some residents later hyphenated the town names, as if they were one place. In the end, residents of the two towns were liquidated together in an area along the road between them.

The larger of the two towns, Mlynov (also spelled "Mlinov" among other variations), still exists on maps today as "Mlyniv," in what is now western Ukraine. The town today is nothing like what it was, once upon a time, when Jewish families lived and thrived there. There was a small Jewish community residing there not long after the area became part of Tsarist Russia in 1793 and Jews may have been there even earlier when it was still part of the Polish-Lithuanian Commonwealth.[1] According to an unverified belief reported in this volume, the name "Mlynov" was derived originally from a Slavic or Polish word for "mill" (p. 13, 47),[2] and writers testify to the town's character as a mill town as far back as anyone can remember. The smaller of the two towns, called Mervits ("Muravica," "Muravista," among other variations), no longer appears on maps today and its prior location is just outside the existing border of its larger and still existing neighbor. The meaning of the name Mervits has been lost along with the town that once bore its name.

Here in these two sister towns, a vibrant Jewish community once thrived. Their cemetery tombstones are now gone, the streets have been largely reconfigured and renamed, and only an odd building or two is still standing from that earlier period when the several synagogues were full, the shop owners sat on their steps and waited for customers, and kids skated on the pond they called a swamp in the middle of town. These are just a few of the many images that emerge out of the pages of this new, fully annotated translation of the Mlynov-Muravica Memorial volume, also known as a "Yizkor book." This new translation brings these two towns back to life for descendants who are searching for their family's roots and knowledge of their ancestors' birthplace.

What an extraordinary journey and honor leading this effort to excavate the past of these two forgotten towns. I am the grandson of first cousins, both born in Mlynov, who came at different times to Baltimore where they settled and eventually married.[3] Growing up, I never knew much about their lives. After my parents passed away, and as I grew older myself, I set off to learn about the history of my family and my family's past.

I discovered that my family journey was intertwined with the story of other families from Mlynov and Mervits who all knew each other and, in many cases, intermarried. The towns were so small in fact that many of the families were cousins of one degree or another. One essay in this volume, in fact, tells the funny story of how the rabbi in Mervits had difficulty finding "kosher" witnesses who were not relatives of the bride and groom (p. 157). Over the past several years, I tracked down and connected with more than 500 descendants of families that once lived in these two towns. Some of their ancestors came to the US before or after WWI. Others made aliyah (i.e., immigrated) to the Land of Israel (then still Mandate Palestine) in the 1920s and 1930s. Still others were survivors or descendants of survivors. I spoke to them by phone, exchanged emails with them and interviewed many by Zoom and in person. I asked them questions about their family trees and prodded them for family stories and photos that were passed down from the days of the shtetl. Each family had one or two pieces of the larger puzzle. Putting them together brought forth a more complete picture that amplifies the essays and photos in this volume.

When I first learned of this Memorial volume, I didn't realize the treasures it held. The essays, which were published originally in 1970 in Hebrew and Yiddish, were all authored by people who were born, lived, or visited these two towns during their lifetimes. Many descendants didn't even know that this volume existed, let alone what it said. Partial English translations circulated among a few families and was published in recent years.[4] Many descendants report that their immigrant parents and /or grandparents from these two towns were reluctant to speak about their birthplace, due in part to the trauma they suffered and/or because they were busy embracing their new cultures and identities in America, Canada, and Israel. For all these reasons, many of the English-speaking descendants know little to nothing about these birthplaces of their ancestors.

The essays in this first complete translation, replete with annotations about the authors and the individuals mentioned, help rectify this gap. The essays do more than mourn the loss of these places and the people who once lived there. In a vivid and magical way, they also nostalgically recall how residents lived life when these places were thriving and vibrant. While many of the essays recount the disturbing and incredibly painful experiences at the end, a number recall stories, anecdotes, and folklore which are nostalgic, funny, endearing and evocative. These moments touch the heart and provide a sense of what was good about life for a period of time in that place.

This volume thus has two streams that intermingle with each other. On the one hand, the essays tell the painful story of how these towns came to an end and the experiences of those who were viciously murdered or managed to survive. These firsthand accounts constitute the dark side of the story. They narrate the pain and suffering from the beginning of the Soviet occupation in September 1939 to the Nazi attack and occupation the week of June 22, 1941, through the erection of the Mlynov ghetto in April/May 1942, and its final liquidation on October 8, 9 or 10, 1942.[5] We relive the turmoil and horror of those who suffered through these events and the incredible stories of survival of the fortunate few. We learn too the names and characters of those who perished, memorialized by loved ones who left before the tragic events took place.

On the other hand, the essays capture the sights and sounds recalled from childhood including, the muddy streets in winter that sucked your boots in; the smell and beauty of lilacs in spring and the flowering of the cherry, apple and plum trees (pp. 40, 143); the sledding down hills in moonlight (p. 210); the teachers who were beloved and those who engaged in corporate punishment (pp. 147, 88); the first look by a young boy through the gate of the Church in town and the discovery of the figure hanging on the cross (p. 144); the folklore about how the Ikva River got its name (p. 13); and the disputes that arose among rabbis over who should have control over the community (p. 16). This stream of nostalgic memories is evocative, eye-opening, and even at times funny. This volume will be sacred for those who want to know what life was *actually* like where their families once lived.

***

Mlynov is characterized in this volume as a mill town that grew up along the Ikva River. The Ikva holds a prominent role in the childhood memories of those who once lived here. Residents boated on and swam in its cool waters during the hot days of summer (p. 210, photos pp. 171, 200) and the farmers and merchants from the nearby towns and villages took their horses there to drink and bathe on market days (p. 143). Sometimes, a child drowned tragically in the river (pp. 93, 378). Charred posts from several old mills that had once burned down stuck out of the flowing river and out of the ice when the river froze over (pp. 13, 35, 43). Folklore from the town indicates that the name "Ikva" came from the words of a Hebrew prayer that residents recited after blocks of ice caused the river to overflow its banks and flood the towns in the area. Their prayer caused the waters to recede. Even the gentiles supposedly liked the Hebrew-based name and adopted it too (p. 12).

Folklore recalls too how a very steep and memorable hill came into being across the Ikva River from Mlynov (photo p. 148). The young children called it "Mount Sinai" and played there (pp. 26, 48, 199). Teens and young adults called it "Greenik" (pp. 65, 144) and youth headed there to escape the watchful eyes of their elders (p. 199). One reached "Mount Sinai" from town by walking east across one of the bridges over the Ikva, which was at the crossroads leading west to Smordva and south to Dubno (p. 30, 199, photo of one of the bridges, p. 261). An old map below shows where Mlynov and Mervits (here called Muravica) were in relationship to one another and where bridges crossed the Ikva River.[6]

A 1925 Polish map shows the towns of Mlynov and Murawica on the bank of the Ikva River. Visible are the location of bridges, the approximate location of the Catholic church at the main square (large cross) the market square (a pentagon), as well as a cemetery (rectangle with crosses) east of town. A market square (a pentagon) is also visible in the nearby Mervits (Muravica).

Gazing east from the top of "Mount Sinai," one looked down on the town of Mlynov. Looking west, one could see the white walls of the nearby Count Chodkiewicz's palace, the local nobleman who owned all the property in the area including the towns and river. Mount Sinai was so prominent in the memory of Mlynov children that they wrote essays about it and went to see it as young adults when they later came back to town (p. 26). According to childhood folklore, "Mount Sinai" arose when a righteous man, a tzaddik, was attacked by the Count's dogs as he was walking by a church near the Count's property. Three times he uttered an incantation whereupon the Church was swallowed up by the earth and produced the hill (p. 144). Other legends attributed the origin of the hill to the soldiers of a Polish military leader and statesman who fought against Russia (p. 48).

One young girl named Silke, who was born in the nearby town of Lutsk and later was on the editorial committee of this volume, loved leaving her dirty, crowded hometown and going to Mlynov to visit her grandparents. Mlynov was rural and green, smelled wonderful, and everyone knew her name (pp. 249–53). She was there too for a beautiful wedding, when a young woman from Mlynov married a young man from Lutsk and when the town was filled with music and celebration (pp. 24–29). Even the Count pitched in, contributing horses and a wagon to carry the groom to the event. One summer holiday Silke traveled to Mlynov by coachman.

There her grandmother taught her to milk a cow and she first realized that cows were not the dumb creatures she once thought they were (pp. 252–53).

During one of those visits, Silke witnessed the annual pilgrimage to Mlynov, when devotees flocked there to the memorial of the Rebbe who had died suddenly near town (p. 80). His name was Reb Aharon of Karlin II. He was from the Stolin-Karliner stream of Hasidism, the first branch of this new religious movement to establish itself in Lithuania. Reb Aharon was the fourth in line of succession of this Hasidic dynasty of which his grandfather, Aaron the Great, had been the founder. There was a belief among some of the residents of town that the Rebbe's memorial would protect the town (pp. 109, 132), a belief that those in the younger generation doubted, prompting them to acquire rifles and organize self-defense (p. 111). Curiosity prompted children to ask their parents about the Rebbe's memorial and the man who guarded the eternal light inside (p. 55); one former resident nostalgically remembers the thousands of petitionary notes that were stuffed in a holy box in the memorial (p. 58).

Reb Aharon's sudden death near Mlynov in 1872 generated much folklore. According to one account, he was about to leave town when signs in the sky alerted him that he was about to die. He confessed his sins and returned to bed and was taken away (p. 80). According to another legend, he was traveling along the road nearby when he passed away and a tree grew into the shape of a menorah (candelabra) where his disciples buried him (p. 27). Looking back years later, one woman wrote a ballad to that tree (pp. 392–94). She recalled sitting under its shade as she and her girlfriend walked from Mlynov towards Mervits. She wonders if that old friend, the tree, is still standing there and hopes that the birds on its branches will recite a mourner's prayer (kaddish) for her family and the others who were senselessly murdered nearby along that road.

Silke's grandfather was one of the respected Hasids in town from the Stolin-Karliner dynasty (pp. 78–79). He attended one of the three synagogues (some essays say "two" synagogues and a study hall) that sprung up to meet the diverse religious inclinations of the Mlynov community (pp. 49, 55, 66, 210). In Mlynov, the largest synagogue of the Trisk Hasidim was built first (pp. 49, 55). The second synagogue was named for the Rebbe from the Stolin Hasidim. The third for the Rebbe of Olyka (p. 55). Before WWI, Mervits also had two synagogues (or three study houses) a bathhouse, two kosher slaughterers, a rabbi and a cemetery, but was otherwise heavily dependent on Mlynov for other functions (pp. 91, 93, 104). After War I, Mervits rebuilt on a smaller scale.

There were also two churches in Mlynov, a Catholic and a Russian Orthodox church (pp. 9, 48, 111, 116, 144). As one writer recalls:

> The focal point of the small town [of Mlynov] was the market square, at one
> end of which stood the Russian Orthodox Church. Along the river, opposite
> the palace of the Count, stood a Polish Church. On a number of narrow lanes
> around the market square stood Jewish homes. Behind the lanes of Jews were

streets of Ukrainian gentiles. These streets were called "The Village." Next to the palace there was a neighborhood of Poles, employees of the Count. Clerks and Polish businessmen lived among the Jews and Ukrainians (p. 48).

Some of the poorer residents lived in incredibly narrow alleyways of the shtetl (pp. 87, 166, 385). In these alleyways, young boys could hide away from the prying eyes of their parents (p. 144). On long nights, the young adults strolled from one end to the other (p. 385) and walked a little freer during summer when they could leave the narrow streets of the shtetl (p. 166).

The streets were so narrow in places that, if one safely passed through them, one essayist jokingly says one should recite "gomel," a prayer for surviving a dangerous situation or journey (p. 182). The streets were named after buildings or people who lived on them. Looking back many years later from Baltimore, the same writer described his memory of these streets this way:

> The Rabbi's Street, the Shochet's Street, Nasele's Street, Moyshe Toybe's Street [i.e., Moshe Fishman's Street], Chaim Leml's Street — all the little streets led to the marketplace — if you were able to cross the street without leaving a boot in the deep mud. On Khaykl's street [photo p. 160] there was much traffic. His street was known in the shtetl. Getting to the market was not so easy. Firstly, we had to go through a long, little street very carefully; it was the width of one person. On one side there was a wall from the stable of Wolf [Berger], Nute-Ber's son, and on the other side was a kind of separation with barbwire fencing in Ishtekhe's garden; if you finally made it out of the shtetl okay, you could recite *hagomel* the blessing for surviving.

> The little street had another good point: when you were busy making right turns, you quickly ended up in the Stolin synagogue where you could catch a prayer service, even if you had never been a Stoliner Hasid. But if you had to go out to the market, you needed to turn left. The street, which led to the market across from the Polish church, was called Tuvye's Street [Tuvye Berger]. In that street you needed a special strategy: namely, you had to hold onto the walls of the house — if not, you would fall, you should excuse me, into a mud of a different sort since there was always a mountain of manure in that street. As Tuvye's house was low, the windows reached to your feet, and you could see what was cooking in the fireplace. If you made it out of that street, there were cages. Again, you had to be careful and hold your body straight. More than once a heavy Jewish woman slipped into the mud with one foot; she would curse quietly to herself (p. 182).

Young people felt a comparable intellectual and cultural narrowness though a spirit of change began to reach the shtetls. One young man had his eyes opened and "was taken by storm" after reading a Yiddish book given to him by a friend (p. 240). But his widowed mother squashed his interest, fearing that his reading would seduce him to abandon her and his responsibilities to the family. Had he followed his heart, perhaps he would not have perished with his family.

By the 1920s, if not earlier, some young people were reading vanguard writers like Hayim Nahman Bialik, a pioneer in Hebrew poetry, and subscribing to newspapers and magazines that were reshaping their world view. In some cases, they were going off to study in larger cities like the sea-side town, Odessa (pp. 88, 200, 221). One young girl, a prodigy in town by the name of Chana Klepatch, knew the story of and memorized quotes from a Polish heroine, Countess Emilia Plater (1806–1831), the so-called Joan of Arc of Lithuania (p. 259). These external impulses tugged at the hearts of the young people, such as the young man, Solomon Mandelkern, who was one of Mlynov's most famous sons (pp. 493–96). Mandelkern was born in Mlynov in 1846 and his father prepared him from a very young age to be a traditional rabbinic scholar. At the age of 6, he was an expert in the Five Books of Moses and had memorized pages of Gemara by the age of 10. He left Mlynov at the age of 16 when his father died unexpectantly. Later, he abandoned his traditional studies along with his traditional wife. He was ordained a rabbi in Vilna, secured a PhD in Eastern Languages in St. Petersburg, and went on to write poetry and translate classic literature from Russian and German into Yiddish. According to folklore, when he came through Mlynov one day on the eve of the Sabbath and stopped in his sister's store, she didn't even recognize him with his top hat, his missing beard and his bushy moustache (p. 28, photo p. 493).

There were at least three different streams of Hasidism in town (Trisker, Olyker and Stolin-Karliner) and serious conflicts (p. 91) and even fisticuffs (p. 150) used to break out over the style of praying. Matters improved after 1903 when the large synagogue burned down and the Trisker Hasidim built their own separate chapel (pp. 91, 164). While most of the people in the towns observed the Sabbath, they were not as strictly observant as people in other places in Poland. No one wore fur hats (streimels) or have sidelocks, and women did not shave their heads when they got married as in some communities (p. 49). Not all the average folks were "so scrupulously devoted to observing" the Sabbath and some would instead leave town on the day of rest to enjoy the fresh air and grass of the fields and forests nearby (p. 172).

The most important and wealthiest men of town had seats in the synagogue facing the Eastern Wall (pp. 150, 205, 181, 227) where many also came to study traditional Jewish texts (p. 302). Following traditional practice, women were separated from the men during weddings (p. 25) and mention is made of a women's synagogue (pp. 152, 310, 319). Some of the husbands were so pious and focused on study and prayer that they forgot to eat, and they left the burden of raising the family to their wives, to the later criticism of their grandchildren (p. 243). Wives sometimes had to push their religious husbands to find an occupation, leading in one case to one man's botched attempt to sell kerosene on the black market (pp. 254–57). Some men, like the father of the famous poet, Yitzhak Lamdan, had a very rigorous religious routine of daily study and prayer (p. 223).

When the young people congregated at the back of the synagogue chatting and uninterested in the service, the elders hushed them and insulted them by yelling, "Outside you bums (*shkotzim*)." The young people periodically took their revenge, wadded up the wet towels that people used to dry their hands after relieving themselves and threw them on the heads of the elders (p. 150).

The synagogue was the place where emissaries lectured and where the most important and difficult community issues were aired, "such as the rising stench of the mikvah, or the gathering of money to buy wood for heating, to warm homes of the poor in town" (p. 113). These were resolved in contentious debates that took place before the Torah reading. "If not for that," one writer declared, "life would be too boring in the shtetl" (p. 173). Speakers during services sometimes provoked heated reactions from worshippers, one person even standing up and screaming, "Lies" (p. 154). Periodically, religious politics flared up. Disputes arose over which rabbi should lead the Mlynov Kehilla, a community governance structure which included and oversaw the other nearby shtetls of Mervits, Ostrozhets, Boremel, Demydivka, and Trovits (Torhovytsya) (pp. 15, 49). Apparently revenge kept Rabbi Gordon of Mlynov from winning such an election because he had earlier opposed the appointment of the Mervits rabbi. Instead, the rabbi from Trovits was appointed head of the Kehilla. "No conflict," one writer recalled, "creates as much diversity of opinions as the battle over the office of rabbi of the Kehilla" (p. 18).

Several essays recall youthful pranks and other memorable incidents that took place. When the young men reached 21, the age of military conscription, they felt they had nothing to lose and would go to great lengths to avoid duty. They would fast, cut off their trigger fingers, puncture their eardrum, among other efforts to render themselves ineligible, though the efforts often proved futile (pp. 169–70, 173, 247). One time, such a group of conscription-eligible young men pranked the well-to-do elders of the town. During the night, they gathered up all the wooden objects they could find lying around town regardless of who owned them. The next day, they instructed the man who managed the communal bathhouse (who was also the grave digger) to fire up the waters and provide the luxury of a heated bath to even the poorest in town who could not afford the fee (pp. 174–75).

Such evocative incidents open a window into life of the towns' residents. They include the story of residents rescuing a widow from seduction and conversion (pp. 163–64), the disappearance of the only gramophone in town with its music (pp. 181–83), and the story of how a teacher convinced a Jewish Communist soldier stationed in his home to have a proper Jewish wedding with the Jewish Communist woman with whom he was cohabitating (pp. 140–42). There are stories too about a ghost of a murdered Mlynov man who led residents to find his lost fur hat (pp. 178–79), and a religious man who became a teacher when his efforts on the black market literally fell apart (pp. 255–57). These humorous, ironic anecdotes illuminate the typical heartache and challenges of daily life.

Many of the towns' men were hard-working, eking out a livelihood as artisans, blacksmiths, carpenters, joiners, coachmen, grain merchants, inn keepers, teachers, fishermen, tailors, shoemakers, water carriers, masons, house painters, basement diggers, undertakers, and shop owners (p. 219). Most barely made a living, and during the winter many artisans and those in construction had no work at all (pp. 166, 217–218). Women sometimes ran shops themselves (p. 253), started nursery schools (p. 243) and were seamstresses (p. 218), especially those whose husbands studied all the time. Fabric making was a profitable and prominent industry in Mervits which one poor family aspired to enter (p. 192). Some shops sold beer to the German and Czech populations (p. 243). Even some rabbis had beer taverns, among other business activities, to supplement their meager income they derived from the kosher slaughtering tax (p. 16). As one writer remarked, "It was strange to see, from time to time, a Jew with a substantial beard standing behind the counter mixing beer for gentiles, and in addition, selling non-Kosher sausages to them" (p. 243).

Much of the economy in the area revolved around the Count's estate with its beautiful palace, gardens, and servants, which required a steady stream of farmhands to handle the animals, fields and forests (p. 214). The Count Chodkiewicz who owned the town and all the property in the area was descended from a well-known war hero Jan Karl Chodkiewicz, a prominent nobleman and military commander of the Polish-Lithuanian Commonwealth. The Count offered leases, for example, to use plots of land, the river, mills, to chop wood, and to catch fish (p. 214, 216). The palace of the Count served as an endless source of legends and tall tales for the children (p. 48).

A number of men in town were contracted by the Count (pp. 214), such as Hirsch Holtzeker, who oversaw the repair of Count's palaces which were damaged in WWI (pp. 226–27) and managed the alcohol, slaughterhouse and the river (p. 181). Hirsch was the eldest of the five Holtzeker brothers who came with their father to Mlynov in about 1891 after the Russian government expelled Jews from the rural villages following the assassination of Tsar Alexander II (p. 54). Though originally from Dubno, the Holtzeker family was given the nickname "Slobadar" (54, 181, 226, 236, 255), because they had been working leased land in the nearby village of Slobada (today subsumed in the nearby town of Uzhynets'). The Holtzekers are remembered as the largest family in Mlynov with many branches (pp. 236, 226). Each shtetl tended to have one large family that dominated the population. In Mervits, the Teitelmans were the largest family (p. 237).

Hirsch was one of the wealthy men in town; his home on Shkolna Street (p. 122) (also called Church Street, p. 182, and Synagogue Street, pp. 140, 142, photo p. 183), stood out and looked like that of a Polish nobleman with a fence, large yard, and fruit trees (p. 122). Hirsch was one of the few Jewish men in town who could go inside the Count's manor and "everyone in the shtetl talked about how Hirsch Goldseker kisses the Countess's hand when he says hello" (pp. 173, 48–49).

Prior to 1900, Count Chodkiewicz owned the large water mill which he would lease to local Jews (p. 214). Later the mill was owned by Yosef Gelberg, a wealthy Jew in town, who eventually brought electricity into the town in the 1930s (pp. 93–94). In an earlier period, the Count also leased a flour mill until it burned down (p. 55) in one of several severe fires that swept through the town (p. 164).

There are conflicting images of the Count which may testify to different periods of time. Some recall the Count sending his carriage and horses to support local Jewish weddings (p. 24) and riding to the Halperin brother's shop to buy tasty treats (p. 58); others note that Jewish residents feared strolling near the Count's park, afraid that the Polish workers and servants would sic their dogs on them or throw stones (p. 48). While antisemitism was present in the earlier period, essayists recall some trust and respect among the greatest part of the population and the relationship of Jews and Christians was in some measure loyal and even honest (p. 215).

***

The two shtetls of Mlynov and Mervits were located at the crossroads of two major roads leading to more populated towns with larger Jewish populations. Running north-south was a road that today still connects Dubno (just 13 miles south of today's Mlyniv) to Lutsk (22 miles north). That road intersects with a road running east–west which links Rivne (32 miles to the east) with Demydivka and Berestechko to the west (14 and 27 miles respectively). Most of the stories and narratives that take place in this volume lie along these axes and various small villages in between.

In 1850, Mlynov was a small town of 48 households and 201 souls.[7] By 1897, there were 672 Jews out of 1105 residents (p. 9), the Jewish population apparently growing by 10 persons per year between the two periods. In the 1921 census, there were reportedly only 615 Jews.[8] Writers recall that Mervits was substantially smaller than Mlynov and had only about 400 Jews (pp. 91, 356). Allowing for a natural growth rate, it is estimated that there were some 730 Jews in Mlynov by 1941 plus several hundred Jewish refugees, who arrived from Sokoliki (p. 353) among other places in western Ukraine. By the time of the liquidation, it is estimated that there were approximately 2,000 Jews living there.[9]

The area around Mlynov and Mervits was rural and there were many peasant farmers in the smaller villages nearby (photo p. 395). There was also a scattering of Jews in some of these nearby villages, such as the Grinshpun family in Peremilowka (pp. 390–91) and the Fisher family in Mantyn (p. 288). Often, farmers would come to Mlynov on weekly market days and during the four annual fairs to sell grain and produce and buy goods (pp. 91, 100, 143, 180).

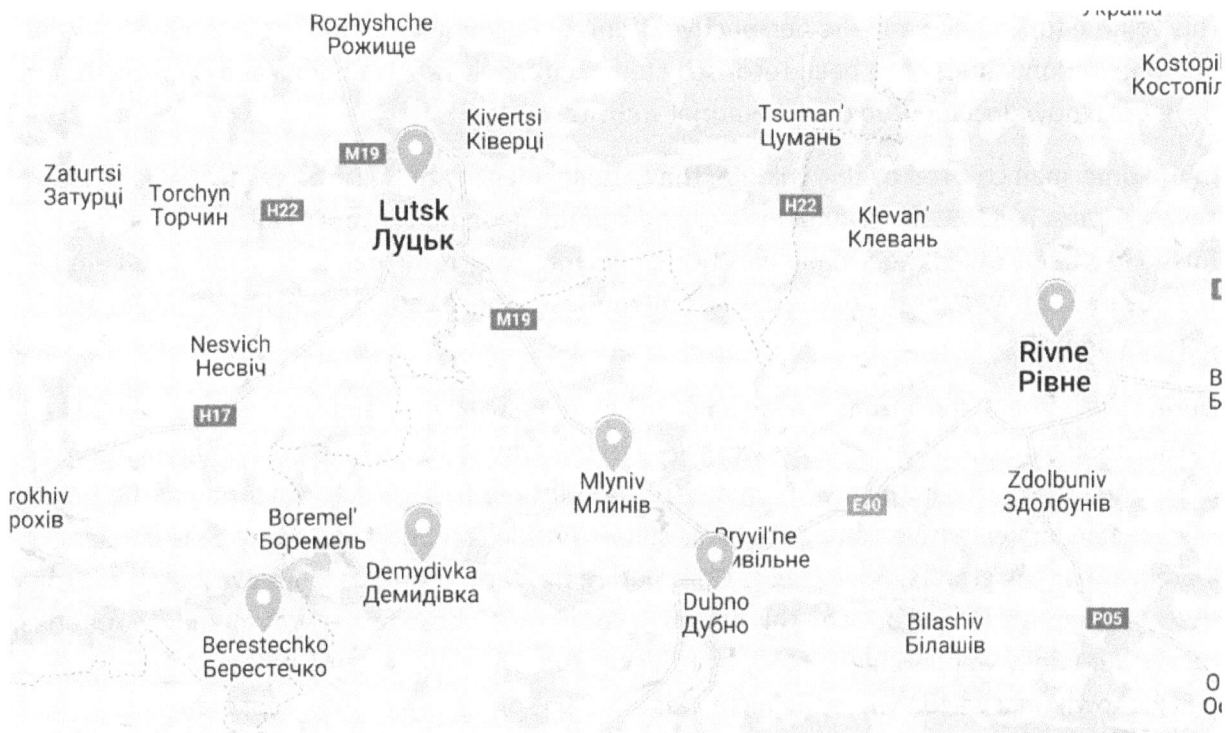

Contemporary map showing contemporary Mlyniv at the crossroads.

Several other ethnic groups lived in the area including not only Ukrainians, who were in the majority, but Poles, Czechs, as well as some Russians and Germans (pp. 100–101, 217). Despite the antisemitism fostered by the Catholic Church which grew worse during the 1930s, the Jewish men of town had good relations and became friends with some of their business contacts. These business relationships would later save the lives of some individuals and families. Ukrainians later comprised the police force that executed the violent German plans. Some of the Czechs and Poles were supportive and helpful to Mlynov and Mervits families

trying to survive (p. 217), though occasionally even a Ukrainian helped save a Mlynov family or individual (pp. 332, 344, 383). One writer comments that "we can openly say that thanks to the Czechs there was still a small trace of Jews remaining" (p. 217). And another survivor recalls one poor farmer named Bogdan who was "an angel in heaven" and who helped "all the Jews who wandered in that part of the woods." Bogdan never refused. He did it "not for riches but because of his kind character and goodness" (p. 315). Bogdan lived near Pańska Dolina, a village that no longer exists, but which at the time was in the hands of Polish resistance and where several Mlynov survivors found refuge at key moments in their survival efforts (pp. 286–88, 306, 326, 359–60).

The writers in this volume were born between 1875 and 1922 and thus have memories of the towns at different times and in different situations. Several of these writers left Mlynov and Mervits as immigrants to the US after WWI; some made aliyah to Palestine in the 1920s and 1930s, and some survived the Shoah. Only one immigrant to the US before WWI contributed to this volume (pp. 58–59) and the perspective of this early immigrant group is underrepresented. Their migration stories have been reconstructed from family oral traditions and US records and have been now documented on a memorial website.[10]

In the time span covered by this volume, the national identity of this area swung back and forth several times. In 1793, the two towns were part of the geographical area which became part of Russia in what is called the Second Partition of Poland. They remained part of Russia up until the outbreak of WWI. Many of the earliest memories in these essays recall life in this Russian period under the Tsars.

During WWI, the Eastern front moved back and forth near Mlynov and Mervits and several key battles took place nearby.[11] Mervits was razed to the ground (pp. 97, 103, 241) and fighting apparently took place in the town's cemetery, as indicated by an article published at the time.[12] Mlynov had less extensive damage but was still in terrible condition and many dead soldiers were lying on the streets (pp. 93, 103, 139). During this time residents were evacuated and/or fled as refugees. Looking back on this period, a young girl, whose father was already in America, recalls her family wandering the roads as refugees (pp, 137–38); a young boy remembers leaving town on a wagon when the night was lit up by spotlights (p. 145). Most families eventually came back after the War and rebuilt their homes and the communal buildings (pp. 93–94, 103).

In February 1919, the Russian Revolution overthrew the Tsar's government. Then in November that same year (October by the Julian calendar), the Bolshevik Revolution toppled the earlier Revolutionary government. With the rhetoric of "brotherhood for all," this was a period of new opportunity for Jews who could now enter previously forbidden professions. One former resident was even appointed judge in the Bolshevik government though he later returned to his hometown, apparently disillusioned, or dismissed (p. 221). During the period following the Bolshevik Revolution, the Tsar's armies still wandered the countryside and order broke down.

Self-defense was needed and organized in Mlynov (pp. 108–132). After one incident, the youth persuaded the town's elders they needed rifles and not sticks for defense, which one young man eventually acquired from a military unit stationed in nearby Smordva (pp. 97–99). To ensure that support did not wane, the young men carried out pranks to keep fear alive among the prominent men of town (pp. 121–23). The youth wore ersatz uniforms and gathered nightly for military style exercises at strategic locations around the town, especially at the homes with pretty daughters (e.g., Holtzekers, Shulmans) (pp. 123, 125).

In June 1919, the area became part of a newly created Poland which came back into being in the Treaty of Versailles at the end of WWI. The culture in the two towns began to change. Polish was now taught in the public schools. Immigration slowed to America as the US imposed strict quotas limiting the immigration of Eastern European Jews. A growing interest in Zionism flowered among the young people. At first, this Jewish nationalist movement inspired only a few young men in town who concocted a scheme to secretly send one of the poor boys to

Palestine as the town's first pioneer. The plan backfired in a humorous story that is as revealing as it is funny (pp. 191–201).

 In the 1920s, Zionist youth groups, like *The Pioneer* (HeChalutz) and *The Young Guard (Hashomer Hatzair)*, became the primary social outlet for young people in town (pp. 64–70). They also started a Tarbut ("Culture") school to teach Hebrew to children and even a kindergarten. The Russian and Yiddish library of the Shulman family, once the treasured hangout for the young people on the outskirts of the town, became obsolete as the interest among the youth shifted to Hebrew (pp. 61–62).

The Zionist youth groups also performed military style drills, spoke Hebrew, played volleyball and made trips to neighboring towns (p. 63, photo of volleyball p. 188). The youth involved in these activities yearned for Jews to become a normal people who could live off their own land. Several essays in this volume were written by such young people. They left the shtetl to prepare for kibbutz life on a training farm, and then made aliyah to the "Land of Israel," which was still under British control at the time and called "Mandate Palestine" (pp. 205–208, 228–32, 245–48, 384–86, 388–89). Not all the elders in town approved of their children's involvement in Zionist youth groups, viewing the movement as blasphemous for trying to force God's hand and representing a slippery slope away from religious observance (pp. 69, 197). In comparison to Boremel, the elders in Mlynov were apparently slow to get behind Zionism (p. 197), though over time there were adults in Mlynov took an active role in supporting Zionist causes (pp. 231, 377).

Yitzhak Lamdan, who in 1927 published the Hebrew poem "Masada," which made him famous, was the first Mlynov immigrant to reach Palestine. He headed there after his disillusionment doing a stint with the Red Army and after his brother had been killed in the civil wars. Those experiences and the memories of Mlynov would provide grist for his famous poem. In 1921, not long after Lamdan left, the Fishman family created a stir when they decided to sell off all their

belongings and make aliyah. Many thought they were crazy, as one man recalled from his younger years before his own family had perished (pp. 205–207). Other young people followed in the 1920s and 1930s as Poland lurched to the right and became less hospitable to Jews. By the late 1930s, the British restricted immigration quotas further and the youth had more difficulty obtaining certificates authorizing their immigration. Some like Sheindel Fisher (known as Yafa Dayagi in this volume) managed to get authorization just two weeks before the outbreak of WWII (p. 231) and a few like Baila Holtzeker managed to make aliyah even after the Soviets had taken over the town (p. 384–85).

During this Polish period between the two World Wars, some residents who previously left came back for a visit. Yitzhak Lamdan returned for a visit in 1931 in a perceptive and moving story told by a young man who hero worshipped the poet (pp. 28–33). In one of his own poems, Lamdan describes his own inner turmoil during that visit and wonders how revealing he should be with his aging father about the difficulties of his new life in Palestine (pp. 82–83). Then in the winter of 1937–38, Aaron Harari (born Aaron Berger) returned to Mlynov after four years living on a kibbutz where he worked raising sheep (pp. 75–77). Aaron told his parents he came back to Poland to investigate sheep rearing practices. In truth, he came back to fictitiously marry the sister of a kibbutz friend and help her leave Poland on his visa. Having substantially changed in his four years away, Aaron describes his feelings of alienation when first arriving in his birthplace (p. 75). On that visit, he brought a camera borrowed from a friend, and, fortunately for us, he had a sense that he should photograph his family, scenes around town, and the other typical characters who were still there. Many of the photos in this volume come from that camera and Aaron's trip back to his hometown.

***

Not much time remained for the two shtetls after Aaron's visit. The Zionist youth groups had fallen apart (p. 75). Many of the young people still there had all but lost hope for their future, as attested by a letter written by a young 16-year-old boy in Mlynov to his brother, Lipa, in Palestine during this time (pp. 184–85). On September 1, 1939, the Germans attacked Poland at the outbreak of WWII. Mlynov residents heard the news and quickly packed belongings, left town, and headed to gentile friends in nearby villages (p. 244). Within a few weeks, when the Red Army crossed the border and reached their area, they returned to their homes relieved. That Yom Kippur they were joyful (p. 244) knowing that they would be under the rule of the Soviets and not the Germans. They knew how to bear life under Russian rule.

Based on the non-aggression treaty between Russia and Germany (called the Molotov-Ribbentrop pact), the Soviets occupied Eastern Poland, where Mlynov and Mervits were located, during the third week of September 1939. They soon nationalized all businesses and poverty fell on the population (pp. 20, 266). The Count fled the area in fear for his life (p. 269). His palace was open for a few days to the general public, but it was empty, because everything inside was looted overnight by the farmers in the area (p. 48). The Soviets built an airfield outside Mlynov on the

Count's estate, and they billeted pilots in the homes of some Mlynov residents. They staged a political referendum to justify their annexation of the Polish lands, and they appointed a new governing council comprised of unsavory characters including a local Jewish woman who was released from prison. During this time, the local population lost most means of livelihood and with little choice, some turned to the black market. Residents stopped going to synagogue for fear of being seen as religious and thus enemies of the State. Many of those who had previously participated in Zionist youth groups were arrested even if they had subsequently joined the Polish Communist party (p. 266).

Though life was rough under the Soviet occupation, the suffering paled in comparison with what came next. On Sunday, June 22, 1941, Germany attacked Russia. The Germans bombed the Russian airfield outside of Mlynov and several homes in town. Some residents were killed and wounded (pp. 34–35, 269, 300, 322). The Germans occupied the town by Tuesday or early

Wednesday that same week (pp. 35, 269, 300) and one writer recalls the Germans entering her mother's home and demanding pork to eat (p. 269). Some of the young men in Mlynov fled east and survived the War in Siberia or the Russian army (pp. 244, 322–23). They left behind their parents and siblings, most of whom didn't survive.

The details of the German occupation emerge in painful detail from the personal accounts in this volume. Shortly after the occupation, young men and women were enlisted in forced labor; young women had to stand all day in the Ikva River cleaning German vehicles; young men had to make repairs to the Count's property (pp. 36, 303, 325). On July 12th, just weeks after the Germans first arrived, 10 [or more] people were killed including eight young people and two older men (pp. 301, 309, 312). The Mlynov Rabbi Gordon (photo p. 435), was interrogated and killed as well (pp. 271, 301, 311–12, 329). A series of official "Aktions" took place that summer confiscating gold and furniture among other valuables (p. 271). During those months residents had to fulfill increasingly impossible demands for various goods, such as soap, tea and cigarettes, on the threat of death (pp. 35-36, 303).

Residents remember the ghetto being established in Mlynov in the spring of 1942, between Pesach (April 1) and Shavuot (May 22) though one writer recalls its appearance on July 10th (pp. 36, 272, 329, 431). Mervits survivors recall being brought into the ghetto on Shavuot (May 22–23) (pp. 304, 313, 356). The ghetto was established in Mlynov on part of Shkolna and Dubinska streets and surrounded by barbwire (pp. 272, 313). Multiple families were crowded together "like herring" into houses, with reports of 7–8 or 10–12 people per room (pp. 36, 272, 313). Jewish residents from other nearby towns were also brought into the Mlynov ghetto. Sanitary conditions deteriorated.

People who were skilled and given work certificates were allowed to leave the ghetto during the day and a black market sprang up in such highly prized certificates. Fictious weddings also took place to maximize the impact and reach of these prized documents (p. 271). Work certificates enabled some people to stay outside the ghetto and hide when the news reached

them in September 1942 that pits were being dug nearby and that their own end was near. They already heard the rumors that Jews in other towns had been liquidated.

Trying to organize resistance, some of the young people acquired a few rifles which they hid in the Rebbe's memorial; they bought kerosene, too, intending to set fire to the ghetto and create confusion when the day of liquidation arrived (p. 272). After they were assembled in the streets, residents were taken out to a pit that had been dug between Mlynov and Mervits in an area called Kruzhuk (p. 273, 212), identified as a Ukrainian suburb by one former resident (p. 123) and a place near the town's slaughterhouse, according to a Jewish man who witnessed the mounds covering the mass grave when he was working in Mlynov disguised as a Christian (pp. 355). Gathered there, the ghetto residents were told to strip and then walk across a suspended plank; they were gunned down one by one by machine gun (p. 277).

Shortly after the liquidation, the Germans found Eliezer Mohel running around half-crazed. He had been absent the day his family was taken. According to his son, the Germans also murdered him not far from the slaughterhouse where he had worked as a shochet (kosher slaughterer) for so many years (p. 376). Ironically, the killing spot was not far from the "menorah tree" that had grown up where the famous Rebbe had died, as recalled by a woman who sat in the shade of that tree in her youth and wrote an ode to the tree in memorial (pp. 392–94).

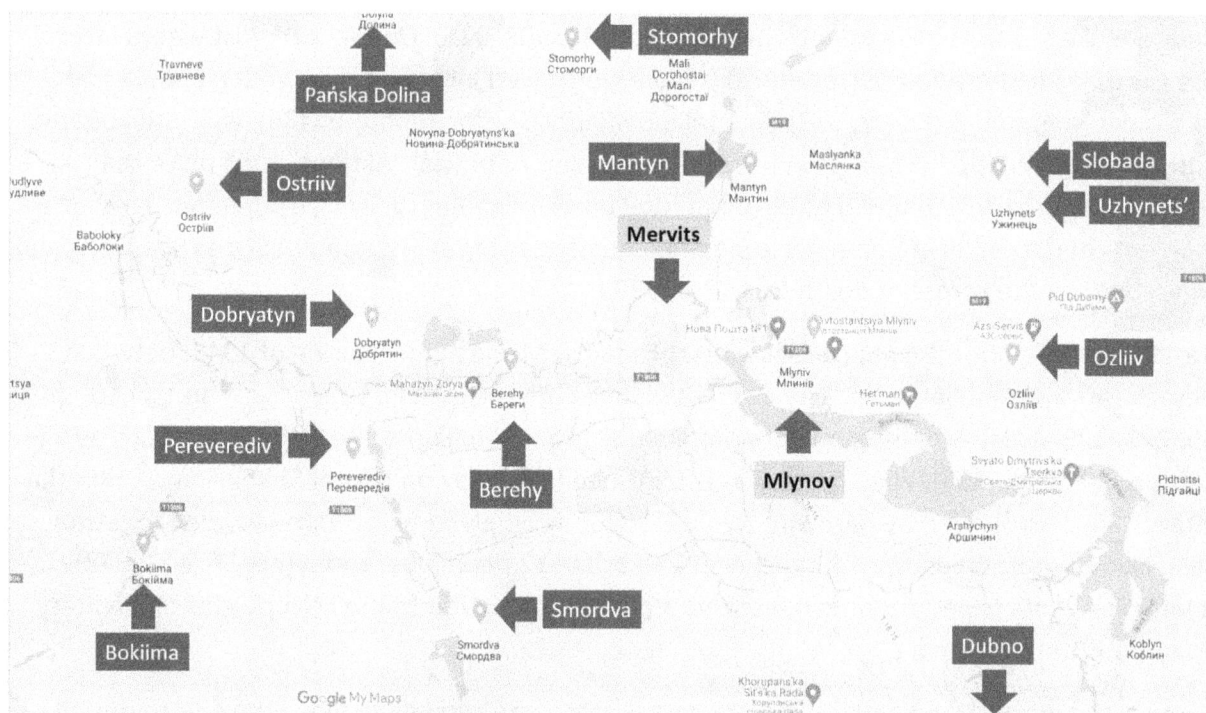

Some of the villages around Mlynov and Mervits that are mentioned in essays in this volume.

It is impossible to summarize the horrific experiences and suffering of those who survived. Readers looking for a single narrative which starts with the invasion and continues until survivors returned to their homes are encouraged to read the four-part testimony by the Mandelkern daughters and one of their husbands (pp. 269–297).

Those who escaped the liquidation at the end were mystified by their fortune and survival. Some husbands, like Nahum Teitelman and Getzel Steinberg, turned to trusted farmers to smuggle family members out of the ghetto (e.g., p. 306).[13] Nahum also leveraged a letter authorizing business activity outside the ghetto to get himself and his son Asher out (p. 306). Before the roundup, Moshe Mandelkern and his sister Yehudit took refuge in bunkers that had been dug in the nearby forests (p. 276). Arke (Aaron) Nudler somehow managed to get his wife and three younger children to other bunkers in the area, though only he and his daughter Yetka (Helen Nudler Fixler) managed to escape when the bunker was discovered (p. 279).[14] Others, like child prodigy Chanah Klepatch, turned down an invitation to the bunkers; she couldn't bear to abandon her widowed mother who was caring for several younger children (p. 260). She was shot trying to escape through the barbed wire at the end.

Days before the liquidation, Yaacov Tesler begged his daughter, Liba, to sneak out of the ghetto. It was the week of her 30th birthday. Liba dressed as a peasant girl and bribed the guard to open the gate. She was hidden by several different families until captured by the Nazis and eventually worked as a Polish slave laborer in Germany until the end of the war."[15] Icek Kozak, who had a work certificate as a wagon driver, took his family members out of the ghetto, one by one, covered under straw. The entire family survived (pp. 330–333). Fania Mandelkern bribed a ghetto guard and got out at the last minute with her sister, Rosa, but her mother refused to leave with them at the last minute (p. 276). Fania joined her siblings in the bunkers and lived to tell the story.

Bunia Steinberg put on a yellow sweater that disguised her yellow patches, threw her shoes over her shoulder, and walked out the gate past the unsuspecting guards who thought she was a Christian worker (p. 358). She survived as did two of her brothers, Getzel and Mendel. During the ghetto roundup, young Ezra Sherman, about 10 years old, told the guard he needed to relieve himself and, when given permission, went behind a building and climbed up into the top shelf of a shed and hid. He came out the next day and survived alone wandering the countryside.[16] A young woman named Sarah Neyter hid in a chimney for several days and got out after the Germans had stopped searching (p. 375). Her Mohel family friends who were hidden under floorboards were discovered and killed. Basye Blinder, a young girl under the age of 10, hid somewhere with her sister and came out a day after the Germans left (p. 346). After hiding in the cemetery and forests, she was eventually taken in by a caring Christian woman. These are only some of the stories of survival that emerge from these pages, some of which are now told in book-length accounts and recorded interviews.[17]

The stories of survival are heartbreaking, courageous, and miraculous. People survived in holes in the ground, in haystacks, under pigsties, in bunkers, behind stoves, in grain fields, scrounging for potatoes in the countryside at night, drinking green, putrid water, moving from one place to another when their hosts, afraid for their own lives, kicked them out or threatened to turn them in. Some passed for Christians. Others were hidden by former business associates. Reading their stories, one feels their shock believing what was taking place and trying to grasp the miracle of their own survival. Particularly poignant are the moments when survivors bumped into one another in hiding (p. 288) or emerged from their hiding places after the Russian liberation and discovered who else from their friends and family had survived (pp. 294, 277, 317, 339). Getzel Steinberg didn't even recognize his brother Mendel when they first met when they came out of hiding (p. 340).

As the War was ending, some of the young men who earlier fled to Russia and served in the Russian army, returned to their hometown for the last time. They discovered almost everything gone, even the tombstones where their ancestors had earlier been buried had been taken for sidewalks (pp. 212, 244, 324). Gentile residents were shocked initially to see a Jew alive (p. 244). Many, though not all, of the other survivors eventually headed back to Mlynov once it was safe to do so (p. 291–92, 319). One writer recalls 25 survivors present at the time (p. 291), though a stirring commemoration photo suggests about 45 survivors present (p. 297). The returnees shared rooms in houses where they or their neighbors had previously lived. In some cases, their homes were still occupied by non-Jewish families.

During this time, survivors managed to free several Jewish children who were still in the hands of Christian families. The Steinberg survivors managed to rescue Aviva Feldman who had been left with a Polish family for safekeeping (p. 297, 365–66). Young Rachel Fisher was discovered when she came shopping in town with her adopted parents and she was shocked when she met surviving Jews. (p. 295). So too, Basye Blinder was discovered by survivors during her visits to town (p. 348). These children initially felt divided loyalty having grown attached to their caretakers (pp. 348–49, 318). One case became a cause célèbre when a Polish family refused to return the child to her mother who survived. Eventually the court ruled in favor of the mother but not before thousands assembled at the court to protest on both sides of the case (p. 295).

The survivors who returned to Mlynov paid for and erected a monument on the mass grave of the martyrs and commemorated their loved ones. A photographer took a haunting photo of that moment and a percentage of the survivors in that photo have been identified (p. 297). With little left for them in Mlynov and too much pain to bear there, the survivors left for Displaced Persons Camps where they lived until they made their way to the US, Canada, and Palestine/Israel. They and their descendants lived to share their stories and memories of the shtetl life with us.

A Timeline of Major Events

1793	Mlynov and Mervits become part of Tsarist Russia in what is called the Second Partition of Poland.
1891–1914	A robust migration from Mlynov to the US and especially Baltimore takes place. A few of the immigrants settled in Jersey City, New York, Chicago, Providence, and Canada.
1914–1919	The Eastern Front in WWI moves back and forth near the two towns. Mervits is razed and residents of both towns become refugees.
1919 June	The two towns become part of Poland which is recreated in the Treaty of Versailles following the end of WWI.
1920–1939	Interwar Poland. Zionist youth groups develop and grow in importance in Mlynov and then Mervits. Young people make xxvliyah to Mandate Palestine. Immigration to the US gradually tapers off in the 1920s. Several young adults get into the US via Buenos Aires and Mexico; a few settle there.
1939 September 1	Germany attacks Poland, and Mlynov residents flee town. They return when they realize their area is under Russia control. The Soviets nationalize businesses.
1941 Sunday, June 22	Germany attacks Russia and bombs the airfield outside Mlynov. The Soviets soon abandon town. Some young men flee east to the Russian border.
1941 Tuesday, June 23 or early Wednesday, June 24	Germans occupy Mlynov.
1941 July 12	First persons murdered, eight young people and two older Jews. Actions that summer confiscate gold and other valuables.
1942 April – May	The Mlynov ghetto erected on two streets of town and surrounded by barbwire. Residents of nearby towns are brought into the ghetto.
1942 September	Rumors circulate that pits are being dug between Mlynov and Mervits for the liquidation.
1942 October 8, 9 or 10	The people in the Mlynov ghetto are taken to a pit on the road between Mlynov and Mervits and shot with machine gun.
1944 February 6	Mlynov liberated by the Russians.
1944 Spring	Survivors return to Mlynov. That fall they hold a commemoration for those who were lost.
1945	The last of survivors leave Mlynov for Displaced Persons Camps.

Where to Learn More

There exists a great deal more information about the families that once lived in Mlynov and Mervits beyond the present volume. Additional stories, photos, interviews and history can be found on the Jewishgen Kehilla site for Mlynov and Mervits:

The Mlynov/Mervits website:

https://kehilalinks.jewishgen.org/Mlyniv/

Biographical info on the Memorial book authors:

https://kehilalinks.jewishgen.org/Mlyniv/Mlynov-Yizkor-Book-Bios.html

Info on Mlynov and Mervits families

https://kehilalinks.jewishgen.org/Mlyniv/families.html

The 1850 and 1858 census from Mlynov

https://kehilalinks.jewishgen.org/Mlyniv/Mlynov-Revision-1850.html

The Migration from Mlynov and Mervits

https://kehilalinks.jewishgen.org/Mlyniv/documents/The_Mlynov_Mervits_Migration.pdf

Interviews
https://kehilalinks.jewishgen.org/Mlyniv/Mlinov_Interviews.html

Additional Resources

https://kehilalinks.jewishgen.org/Mlyniv/Mlinov_References.html

Book Committee for the Original Volume:

- Sylvia Goldberg (née Barditch)
- Lipa Halperin
- Yosef Litvak
- Shmuel Mandelkern
- Moshe Iskevitz
- Aaron Harari (née Berger)
- Yechiel Sherman
- Mendel Teitelman

---

[1] https://kehilalinks.jewishgen.org/Mlyniv/Mlynov-Revision-1850.html. An 1850 census (called a revision list in Russian) shows that a number of those residents were already in Mlynov by the 1835 census and likely were living there when the area became part of Russia in 1793.

[2] The page numbers in this Introduction and the Index refer to the page numbers in the English translation at the top of the pages. In the body of the translation itself, the page numbers that appear in the footnotes and cross-references refer to the page numbers from the *original* volume which are designated by square backets inside the translation, for example, *[page 15]*. The translators designated the original page number in brackets at the beginning of the first full sentence that appeared on the original Hebrew and Yiddish pages.

[3] My paternal grandfather was Paul Schwartz, son of Chaim Schwartz and Yenta (Demb). My paternal grandmother was Pepe Shulman (mentioned for example on page 118), daughter of Tsodik Shulman and Pearl Malka (Demb). Pearl Demb and Yenta Demb were sisters and born in Mlynov to Israel Jacob Demb and Rivka (Gruber).

[4] Mlynov family descendants, Irene Siegel and Gene Schwartz, commissioned an earlier translation of the Yiddish essays. David Sokolsky recently published some of these translations and supplemented them with paraphrases of some Hebrew essays. Had it not been for their earlier efforts, I would not have been aware of the value these essays held. This new translation builds on and completes their earlier efforts.

[5] Writers give slightly different dates for the liquidation in early October 1942: October 8th (pp. 273), October 9th (=28th of Tishrei) (p. 47). On October 10 (29th of Tisrhrei) news reached other survivors in hiding that the liquidation had taken place and graves were being dug (p. 315, 329, 333, 335). See also footnote 2 on page 52 for additional discussion.

[6] The Polish map reads in English: Print of the first edition of the Military Geographical Institute 1925. http://freemap.com.ua/maps/polskie/P46_S41.jpg?fbclid=IwAR0_ZZsHHQ45PJsGUXlO85L4WB4lXAVrIJ-Z34mpOeSktHT1W1dAx2AI_8s

[7] See https://kehilalinks.jewishgen.org/Mlyniv/Mlynov-Revision-1850.html and page 10 this volume.

[8] "Mlynow," in *Encyclopedia of Camps and Ghettos*. 1933–1945, Volume II, pp. 1428–1429. The United States Holocaust Memorial Museum. *Ghettos in German-Occupied Eastern Europe*. Bloomington: Indiana University Press. Ed., Martin Dean. 2012.

[9] Ibid.

[10] See https://kehilalinks.jewishgen.org/Mlyniv/documents/The_Mlynov_Mervits_Migration.pdf and https://kehilalinks.jewishgen.org/Mlyniv/families.html.

[11] See especially the Battle of Galicia and the Gorlice-Tarnow Offensive and discussion on the Mlynov website.

[12] Eugene Szatmari, "The Jewish Cemetery of Muravica." *Current History*. Vol 3, Issue 6 (March 1, 1916), New York.

[13] The information about Getzel was reported to me by his son, and survivor, Gerald Steinberg.

[14] See the Nudler family story on the Mlynov website.

[15] Recounted in David Sokolsky, *Monument*: *One Woman's Courageous Escape From the Holocaust*.

[16] Ezra recounted this story in an interview accessible on the Mlynov website.

[17] There are book-length survival accounts available about Liba Tesler, and the Steinberg, Teitelman and Mohel families, as well as video interviews with several survivors. See the list of resources at the end of this essay.

Acknowledgments

Being the editor and translator for this volume was a moving and daunting experience. The task was even more challenging than I first imagined. Every time I re-read the essays, some new insight or discovery emerged about the place from which my paternal grandparents came. I hope that this new translation does justice to the memory of these towns and our ancestors who once thrived there.

The Yiddish translation effort was generously supported financially by descendants of Mlynov and Mervits families whom I tracked down and whose names appear below. I want to thank all the many descendants who shared their family memories, stories, and photos with me. JewishGen staff, Lance Ackerman, Susan Rosin, and Jonathan Wind, were very gracious and helpful in what was a daunting effort to publish this volume online and in print.

The translation effort required understanding several historical periods, identifying foreign words in Polish and Russian, the location of various small villages that were near Mlynov and Mervits, not to mention the complex family trees and relationships that are implicit in these essays. To the extent feasible, I have tried to tease out these background assumptions and identify the individuals who are mentioned in the footnotes, tracking down their descendants, searching databases for their records, constructing their family trees, and cross-referencing information in this volume.

Because the Yiddish and Hebrew essays use a different language and idiom, we retained some variations in the translation of names and places to reflect the voice of the writers and the language they used. The footnotes draw attention to those variations. The names that appear in the text can often be rendered in multiple different ways in English. We followed the spelling used by descendants or that appeared in Yad Vashem records. Town and village names also have several original pronunciations with corresponding English variations depending on the period and the language. In general, this translation uses the current English spellings that appear on maps today to facilitate the reader's ability to follow along. Where in some instances we deviate from this practice, we try to footnote the current name.

For the Yiddish essays, we were blessed to have found and worked with Hannah B. Fischthal, PhD. Her sensitivity as a translator brought the Yiddish essays vividly to life. She worked on this effort as if she was one of the descendants herself and I am grateful for her support and impressive contribution. I personally translated the Hebrew essays with the support of Hanina (Charles) Epstein, whose mother, Bunia Epstein, was a survivor and a contributor to this volume. Hanina was born in the Pocking displaced persons camp and grew up in Israel. I had to brush up on the Hebrew that I once learned when I was ordained and later a professor of Religious and Jewish Studies. I translated each essay and then every Sunday I would review the translations with Hanina, a native speaker. Often, we would also discuss what we were reading and learn together. I am grateful to Hanina for devoting so much of his time to supporting this effort. He substantially improved this translation and helped me avoid some glaring mistakes. I ultimately own full responsibility for any of the mistakes that remain in this translation.

A number of additional people were critical to this journey: First and foremost, the Mlynov and Mervits born individuals who took the time to write original essays for the volume and to recall their towns. How fortunate for us they did this. Special thanks to Irene Siegel, daughter of David Fishman and Eta [Goldseker] who worked on earlier translations and keeping the memory of Mlynov and Mervits alive. Often as I would track down another Mlynov family or story I would find that Irene had already been there before me. Irene and her cousin (and my cousin), Gene Schwartz, commissioned an earlier translation of the Yiddish essays that circulated informally for a number of years. David Sokolsky recently published some of these translations and supplemented them with paraphrases of some of the Hebrew essays. Had it not been for their earlier efforts, I would not have been aware of the value these essays held. This new translation builds on and expands their earlier efforts.

David Sokolsky's book, *Monument*, on the survival story of his step-grandmother, Liba Tesler, was also important in my own journey back to Mlynov. When I found a photo of my great-grandmother, Yenta Schwartz with Liba Tesler back in Mlynov in 1930, I realized how tightly our family stories are intertwined. I am grateful to David's friendship and encouragement of me on this project. Audrey Goldseker Polt, daughter of Samuel Goldseker from Mlynov, and a family album creator herself, has become a close friend through this work. She was always willing to listen to my latest discoveries, share photos and stories, and offer helpful clarifying suggestions along the way. Joyce Jandorf, a Schuchman and Klepatch descendant, was the first to really open my eyes to the treasures the Yizkor book contained for retrieving an understanding of our families' histories.

I am especially honored and grateful for the experience speaking to and in some cases interviewing living survivors who were born in Mlynov and Mervits: Gerry Steinberg, Ezra Sherman, Karen (Kozak) Lowenthal, Helen (Nudler) Fixler, Aviva Feldman, and Tama (Hachman) Fineberg, as well as their children who shared their thoughts and reflections with me. How moving to meet people who were born in our ancestors' birthplaces before their communities were destroyed. I was supported as well by many Israeli-born descendants who helped me understand the role of aliyah in their family histories: Pavel Bernshtam, Dani Tracz (Issachar Mohel), Hagar Lipkin, Efraim Tomer, Zev Harari, Meir Litvak, Miriam Aharoni, Ziva Dar, Lior Wildikan, Rachel Gordon, Tamar Gahiri, Sari Fishman, among others. Many American and Canadian family descendants also shared their family stories and photos with me. Special thanks to my nearly 99-year-old new friend, Edith Geller (a Gelberg/Goldberg descendant), for all her memories about the Mlynov families who settled in New York. My cousin, Ted Fishman, passed away while I was working on this project. He was a consummate family historian, who regaled me on Sundays with stories of his Mlynov-born parents, Ben Fishman and Clara (Shulman). And finally, my wife, Carroll, deserves special credit for putting up with me and encouraging me while I obsessed over this effort, and my daughter, Penina, for always cheering me on.

I dedicate this new translation to the memory of my Mlynov-born paternal grandparents: Paul H. Schwartz and Pepe (Shulman) and to all the residents of Mlynov-Mervits who once lived there.

Howard I. Schwartz, PhD
(May 2022)

Financial Contributors

Descendants of families from Mlynov and Mervits contributed financially to the new translation effort. They include: **Adam Marcus** (Hirsch descendant) | **Amy Westpy** (Gelberg descendant) | **Anabel Fishman** (Fishman family relative) | **Andrea Carter** (Hirsch descendant) | **Arlene Polangin** (Demb, Gruber descendant) | **Audrey (Goldseker) Polt** (Fishman, Goldseker descendant) | **Barry Lerner** (Lerner descendant) | **Barry Stadd** (Polishuk descendant) | **Brooke Zigler** (Demb, Gruber descendant) | **Carol Engelman** (Rivitz /Hurwitz, Demb, Gruber descendant) | **Charles (Hanina) Epstein** (Steinberg, Upstein, Lerner descendant) | **Cheryl Lerner** (Lerner Descendant) | **David Sokolsky** (Tesler family relative) | **Denise Gelberg** (Gelberg descendant) | **Edith Geller** (Goldberg, Schuchman descendant) | **Eileen Reichenberg Sherr** (Demb, Gruber, Rivitz / Hurwitz descendant) | **Eileen Yoffe** (Fishman, Goldseker descendant) | **Ezra Sherman** (Sherman, Golisuk, Schuchman descendant) | **Galina Graber** (Berger descendant) | **Gerald Steinberg** (Steinberg, Wurtzel, Gruber, Lerner descendant) | **Harold Goldberg** (Goldberg, Schuchman descendant) | **Heidi Steinberg** (Steinberg, Lerner, Grenspun descendant) | **Helen Fixler** (Nudler, Polishuk descendant) | **Howard I. Schwartz** (Demb, Gruber, Schwartz, Shulman descendant) | **Josh Klavan** (Schuchman, Klepatch descendant) | **Joyce Jandorf** (Schuchman, Klepatch descendant) | **Larry Siegel** (Shulman, Steinberg descendant) | **Len Feldman** (Polashuk family descendant) | **Lillian Rosensweig** (Gelberg, Schuchman descendant) | **Marc Siegel** (Fishman, Goldseker descendant) | **Marlene Leffell** (Teitelman descendant) | **Miriam Berkowitz** (Gruber, Demb, Herman descendant) | **Miriam Litz** (Kozak family descendant) | **Richard Polt** (Fishman, Goldseker descendant) | **Robert Shulman** (Gruber, Demb, Shulman descendant) | **Ronald Gaynor** (Gaynor descendant) | **Saul Fishman** (Demb, Gruber, Fishman, Goldseker, Shulman descendant) | **Sheila Mandelberg** (Marder, Tesler descendant) | **Shelley and Sheldon Goldseker** (Fishman, Goldseker descendant) | **Sharna Goldseker** (Fishman, Goldseker descendant) | **Tamara Kirson** (Demb, Gruber descendant) | **Vivi Sadel** (Sherman, Golisuk, Schuchman descendant).

To my grandparents, Paul H. Schwartz and Pepe (Shulman),

first cousins from Mlynov who married in Baltimore.

And to the memory of all those who once lived

in the towns of Mlynov-Mervits.

GeoPolitical Information

Mlyniv, Ukraine is located at 50°30' N 25°36' E and 216 miles W of Kyyiv
Muravytsi, Ukraine is located at 50°31' N 25°35' E and 217 miles W of Kyyiv

	Town		District	Province	Country
Before WWI (c. 1900):	Mlinov	Muravitsa	Dubno	Volhynia	Russian Empire
Between the wars (c. 1930):	Młynów	Murawica	Dubno	Wołyń	Poland
After WWII (c. 1950):	Mlinov	Muravitsa			Soviet Union
Today (c. 2000):	Mlyniv	Muravytsi			Ukraine

Alternate Names for Mlyniv: Mlyniv [Ukr], Mlinov [Rus, Yid], Młynów [Pol], Mlinuv
Alternate Names for Muravica: Muravytsi [Ukr], Murawica [Pol], Marvits [Yid], Muravitsa [Rus], Mervits, Marvitz, Merovits

Nearby Jewish Communities:

Near Mlyniv	Near Muravytsi
Muravytsi 1 miles NNW	Mlyniv 1 miles SSE
Dubno 9 miles SE	Torhovytsia 8 miles WNW
Torhovytsia 9 miles WNW	Dubno 10 miles SE
Krasne 11 miles W	Krasne 10 miles W
Ostrozhets 12 miles N	Ostrozhets 10 miles N
Demydivka 13 miles WSW	Demydivka 13 miles WSW
Verba 15 miles S	Verba 16 miles S
Varkovychi 16 miles E	Olyka 17 miles NE
Kozin 17 miles SSW	Baremel 17 miles WSW
Olyka 18 miles NNE	Varkovychi 17 miles E
Baremel 18 miles W	Kozin 18 miles SSW
Ozeryany 19 miles E	Lutsk 19 miles NW
Lutsk 21 miles NW	Ozeryany 20 miles E
Berestechko 24 miles WSW	Kivertsy 22 miles NNW
Kivertsy 24 miles NNW	Berestechko 24 miles WSW
Klevan 24 miles NE	Klevan 24 miles NE

Jewish Population: 757 (in 1897), 167 (in 1921) in Muravytsi
                           672 (in 1900) in Mlyniv

MAP OF UKRAINE IN 2014

Map of Poland with **Mlyniv** indicated

Table of Contents

List of Photos

A Note to the Reader Regarding Page Numbers

There are two sets of page numbers in this volume.

- This English translation has its own page numbers at the top of each page.

- The page numbers from the original volume appear within the flow of the translation in square backets. For example, *[page 18]* from the original volume appears on page 16 of this new translation.

The page numbers referenced in the footnotes to the translation that follows refer to *the original page numbers* represented by a number in square brackets.

(Mlyniv, Ukraine)
50°30' / 25°36'

(Muravytsi, Ukraine)
50°31' / 25°35'

Translation of
Sefer Mlynow-Marvits

Editor: J. Sigelman

Published in Haifa 1970

Acknowledgments

Project Coordinator:

Howard I. Schwartz, PhD

Our sincere appreciation to the Mlynov Family Descendants group for helping to fund
the Yiddish translations.

See: https://kehilalinks.jewishgen.org/Mlyniv/Mlynov-Yizkor-Book-Effort.html#Funders

See also: https://kehilalinks.jewishgen.org/Mlyniv/families.html

See also: https://kehilalinks.jewishgen.org/Mlyniv/Mlynov-Yizkor-Book-Bios.html

---

This is a translation of: *Sefer Mlynow-Marvits* (Mlynov-Muravica memorial book),
Editor: J. Sigelman, Former Residents of Mlynov-Muravica in Israel,
Published: Haifa 1970 (H,Y 511 pages)

Note: The original book can be seen online at the NY Public Library site: Mlyniv

ס פ ר

מלינוב- מרוויץ

ערך יצחק זיגלמן

הוצא ע"יידי ועד יוצאי מלינוב־מרוויץ בישראל
ארויסגעגעבן דורך דעם מלינאוו־מערוויצער לאנדסלייט קאמיטעט
אין ישראל

תש"ל — חיפה — 1970

[Page 7]

There Were Two *Shtetlekh*

Memorial to the Towns of Mlynov-Mervits

The Editors

Translated and edited by Howard I. Schwartz, PhD with Hanina Epstein

Polish Jewry has been lost, including our beloved ones from our towns of Mlynov-Mervits. It has been more than 20 years since that ruthless and cruel people[1] cut away the cradle of our youth, but the blood of our brothers and sisters[2] cries to us still from the valley of slaughter.

We, therefore, can no longer tarry in the efforts to raise up this memorial to the martyrs of our two towns. And even though we also know that our language is not adequate enough to express and encompass the full horror of Shoah, we cannot release ourselves from the heavy responsibility that has fallen on us, to document and to bring to light at least the little that we can.

And it is incumbent upon us, the few of the remaining remnants, to raise a memorial to the town and its martyrs, so their memory will not cease. We are doing so in the form of the memorial volume before us.

Let these pages recount the active and vigorous lives, during the time when the two communities still stood on their foundations; the pure Jews who feared heaven, were upright and charitable; the Jewish workers and common folk, who put food on the table with the sweat of their brow; and the young people who breathed in liberty and sought improvement in our people and the world; and the dreams and desires, which were planned and realized — but ultimately were erased.

[Let these pages recount] the destruction and Shoah that befell these two towns, two communities that were cut out of the book of life, along with the destruction of the entire House of Israel. Therefore, let the agonizing path in which our beloved ones walked their last steps be revealed once more.

* * *

In our appreciation, we want to give thanks and recognition to all those in Israel and in the United States who supported and participated in the work of this book. May their reward be the recognition that they bestowed a final act of mercy on our martyred ones.

Editor's footnotes:

1. Quoting an expression from the prophet Habakkuk 1:6 in which God says that the Babylonians are being raised up to destroy the people.

2. The word in Hebrew is literally "brothers" but also carries the broader gender-neutral meaning of family and friends.

[Page 8]

The Shtetlekh Mlynov–Muravica: A Memorial

The Editors

Translated from the Yiddish by Hannah B. Fischthal, PhD

Edited by Howard I. Schwartz, PhD

Polish Jewry was annihilated, including our own dear ones from the double-town of Mlynov-Muravica. Even though more than 20 years have run by since that bitter time when an axe came down on the cradle of our childhood, the blood of our tortured brothers and sisters does not stop screaming to us from the killing fields.

Therefore, we few remaining ones have fulfilled our obligation to erect this monument to the martyrs of our two shtetlekh. We were fully aware that we were too deficient in language and in art to capture, portray, and express the entire width and depth of the annihilation and the horror, yet we still could not relinquish our responsibility to record and to write down at least this little bit of what we were capable of doing.

[Page 9]

May the pages of this book describe a blossoming, ebullient life of faultless, God-loving Jews; good and soft-hearted Jews; of workers and of plain people who earned their bread by the sweat of their brows. May it tell of a Jewish youth, of young Jews searching and yearning for ways to improve the world and to rebuild it for all people; of a youth struggling with dreams and desires, which were partially realized, and also partially dissolved and crushed.

May these pages describe the destruction and extinction which was fated to our shtetlekh, along with the entire house of Israel; may they describe two Jewish communities, which were erased from the Book of the Living. May these pages newly illuminate the painful journey of our dear ones' last steps.

* * *

Let us note with appreciation and gratitude all those who gave a hand, who supported and helped in the work for this book. They have earned the knowledge that they performed the last favor for our martyrs.

A group of young people in Tarbut in the company of the teacher Zilberg [H]
| A Youth Group [Y], 1933[1]

Editor's footnote:

1. Back left Aaron (Berger) Harari, front right Rosa Berger, next to her is Rachel (Shapovnik) Givol. This version of photo courtesy of Hagar Lipkin, daughter of Rosa Berger.

[Page 10]

Młynów 1.) mko nad rz. Ikwą i wielkim stawem, pow. dubieński, w 2 okr. polic. ołyckim, gm. w miejscu, o 15 w. na płn.-zach. od Dubna, 62 dm., 203 mk., w tem 38% żydów. cerkiew, kościół kat. par. pod wez. Wniebowzięcia N. M. P., wzniesiony w 1785 r. przez hr. Janusza Chodkiewicza; dom modlitwy żydowski, szkółka, browar, st. p., piękny pałac zbudowany w końcu XVIII w., ogród, most i przystań na Ikwie. Osada starożytna. Król Aleksander dawał M. i Piekielewo (Pakałów) Moskwicinowi Bobrowi, po bezpotomnej śmierci którego król Zygmunt I przywilejem z 1505 r. nadał go Jakubowi Michajłowiczowi Montowtowiczowi, namiestnikowi krzemienieckiemu, z obowiązkiem dawania 3-ch służb z M. a 1 z Piekielewa. Dziś własność Chodkiewiczów. Stan. August na przełożenie panów rady ustanowił w 1789 r. w mku dziedzicznem Józefa i Aleksandra hr. Chodkiewiczów, synów nieletnich Jana Mikołaja, ssty żmudzkiego, i Ludwiki z Rzewuskich, jarmarki na ś. Mikołaj, ś. Trójec, ś. Illią proroka i Przemienienie Pańskie podług kalendarza rus. W M. pracował i zmarł 24 stycznia 1838 r. hr. Aleksander Chodkiewicz, gen. brygady, senator kasztelan, chemik i poeta, który zebrał doborową bibliotekę. Par. kat. (od 1676 r.) dek. dubieńskiego, liczy 1072 dusz; filia w Koblinie, kaplica w Dobratynie. Ob. Pamiat. Kij. Arch. Kom., t. 4, cz. II, 74, 84, 108, 129, 140; Arch. J. Z. R., cz. VI, t. 1, 111, 114; Pamięt. kn. Kurbskiego, t. 1, 185, 187. 2.) M., ob. *Młynówka* i *Młynowce.*   J. Krz.

A paragraph from Slownik Geograficzny, 1885, Warsaw [Polish Encyclopedia]

Mlynow 1.) small town located on the banks of the Ikva, and a big pond, county Dubno in the second police region, 15 verst from Dubno, 62 houses, 203 inhabitants, of which 38% are Jewish. There is an Orthodox church, and a Catholic parochial church, founded in 1785 by Janusza Chodkiewicza; also a synagogue, school, brewery, post office, and a beautiful palace built on the river Ikva. An old settlement. King Alexander donated Mlynov and Piekielewo (Pakalow) to Moskwicinowi Bobrowi. After he died without leaving any descendants, King Zgmunt I gave the village, by decree in 1508, to Jakubowi Michajlowiezowi from Kremenez, with the obligation to provide three persons from the village and one from Piekieloewo to serve in the army. Now the village belongs to Chodkiewiczow. King Stanislaw August, in an assembly meeting in 1789, ordered that fairs should be held in the village on the festivals of St. Mikolaj (St. Nicholas), St. Trojee (St. Trinity) and St. Illia, the prophet, and others. Alexander Chodkiewicz, a brigadier general, senator, chemist and poet, gathered a splendid library. The Catholic parish has been there since 1676.[1]

Footnote:
1. Translation provided by David Sokolsky, ed., *Mlynov-Muravica Memorial Book*, p. 3

[Page 11]

Mlynov

Translated and edited by Howard I. Schwartz, PhD

(According to the Jewish Encyclopedia [in Russian], vol. 12, brought out by the Society for Jewish Scientific Publications, in partnership with Brockhaus–Efron,[1] St. Petersburg, at the beginning of the 20th century).

The town of Mlynov is in the region of Vohlyn,[2] in the district of Dubno. According to the 1847 population census, the number of Jewish persons in the community was 209. According to the census of 1897, there were 1105 residents in Mlynov and 672 of them were Jews.

* * *

(According to the General Encyclopedia [in Polish],
published by Orgelbrand,[3] Warsaw 1865, volume 18).

Mlynov is a town in the area of Vohlyn, along the Ikva River and large lake, with beautiful scenery. It was once a village that the King Alexander Jagiellończyk gave as a gift to a man named Bobr Muskvitin,[4] but after the death of the latter, the village reverted to a possession of the Crown. In 1508, the village was transferred by Sigmund I to Jacob Michelyovetch, the delegate of Kremenets.[5] Later the village belonged to the Chodkiewicz family. In 1789 Stanisław August, with the advice of his council, decided to hold four fairs each year in the town.

In his beautiful palace in Mlynov, the nobleman Aleksander Chodkiewicz worked and died. He was a well-known figure in Polish literature. Here, close to his many scientific collections and next to his large and rare library, he spent all his days and engaged in chemistry experiments.[6]

Mervits (Muravica)

(According to the General Encyclopedia, as cited on the previous page, volume 19)

The small town was in the area of Vohlyn along the river Ikva, a distance not far from the small town of Mlynov. In Mervits in the past, there was a defensive castle, that passed in the year 1560, with all of its wealth included to the possession of Grzegorz Chodkiewicz, as a bride price of his wife Katarzyna from the Wiśniowiecki family.[7] In a later period, the town was inherited by the children of the Krasitsky family; in 1790, the nobleman Michal Krasitsky, prince of the court, put on four new fairs.[8]

The Great Synagogue in Mlynov [H] The Great Shul in Mlynov [Y]
Photo by A. Harari in the winter of 1937/38
[Original courtesy of Audrey Goldseker Polt]

Editor's footnotes:

1. Brockhaus-Efron was a comprehensive encyclopedia published in Imperial Russia in 1890–1907, as a joint venture of Leipzig and St Petersburg publishers. The articles were written by the prominent Russian scholars of the period.

2. The area of Volhynia, (Volyn in Russian or Wolyn in Polish) is an area in the northwestern corner of Ukraine that was ruled by the Tzarist rule until WWI when it became part of Poland. During the Russian period,

1795–1919, Mlynov and Muravica were part of the district of Dubno and province of Volhynia. After becoming part of Poland after WWI, the towns were part of the district of Dubno and the province of Wolyn.

3. Samuel Orgelbrand (1810–1868) published a Comprehensive Encyclopedia in Polish of 28 volumes.

4. Alexander was King of Poland from 1501–1506. Buber Muskvitin is unidentified.

5. Sigismund I also called "the Old" was King of Poland and Grand Duke of Lithuania from 1506 until his death in 1548. Sigismund I was a member of the Jagiellonian dynasty. The identity of Jacob Michelyovetch is not known.

6. Appears to refer to Aleksander Chodkiewicz (1776–1838) who was arrested in Mlynov in on February 8, 1826, on the orders of Grand Duke Konstanty, and escorted to St. Petersburg and imprisoned there. Due to the lack of serious charges, he was released, and was to remain in Zhytomyr under police supervision for a year. After the November Uprising, he remained in Młynov until his death. In his villages (Młynov and Chernobyl), he established schools where Polish, Russian, arithmetic, moral science and catechism were taught. In 1830 he founded an Orthodox church in Mlynov to protect the local church from liquidation. Source Wikipedia.

7. Appears to refer to Grzegorz (also spelled "Hrehory") Chodkiewicz a Ruthenian noble and military officer of the Grand Duchy of Lithuania. In 1537 he married Katzarzyna from the Wiśniowecki family, a Polish princely family of Ruthenian–Lithuanian origin.

8. The figure Michal Krasitzki has not been identified.

[Page 13]

_____

"The Mill"

by Lipa Halperin, [Kibbutz] Yifat

Translated and edited by Howard I. Schwartz, PhD with Hanina Epstein[1]

The residents of the place, as befitting their nature and way of life, did not show interest in the past of the place in which they lived. The question did not occur to anyone — "what is the significance and source of the name of your birthplace?" or general questions that touched on the origin of this settlement, such as "where and when did the first residents, our Jewish brethren, arrive?" It was taken for granted that the events of family life were aligned to the events of the place. [For example:] — A person came here after the first fire. These houses and those houses were built after the second fire … and similarly, they knew how to enumerate a list of respected people who passed away during the epidemic.[2]

The events of the place were also depicted in relation to parallel events of the State or the period of Tzarist regime. [For example:] The road to Berestechko was paved during the Russo-Japanese War. The "Great Flood" from the river happened during the days of Alexander II; the immigration to America began here in the days of Nicholas II. So if a questioner wanted to know the time of an event according to a regular calendar, he had to know the history of the State … the time of antiques or very old remnants was captured in the idiom – "this is from the days of Khmelnytsky" [i.e., "a long time ago"].[3] You can also explain [that an object is from] a hundred years before Khmelnytsky. At one and the same time, knowledge of the past was at best limited to one generation's memory. From the more distant past, cloudy concepts remained that came to expression in folk sayings and proverbs.

In response to questions to which they didn't know the answer, they were accustomed to answer facetiously with this kind of language: "Go ask the Rabbi." The intention — the rabbi who was authorized to render a decision about Kosher rules, he will adjudicate your question. Let us imagine that in the beginning of the century an eccentric explorer appeared in Mlynov, seeking an explanation for the strange question "why is this place called Mlynov?" To whom could he turn? — "Ask your elders and they will inform you." (Deuteronomy 32.7)

The elder of the community, among those who were most respected, was Rabbi Hanich, may his memory be a blessing. He was known as "Rav" Hanich, because he had not been granted the authority as "the local rabbi of the place." Humble and modest was this man and far from the vanity of the world. Despite his weakness and pains, it was his custom to always fast on Monday and Thursdays, and say the prayer Tikkun Chatzos [each night after midnight][4] and he was satisfied with little to nothing.

He didn't preach musar (ethics) to the public, because he did not suspect that a Jew could sin [against God]....

[Page 14]

[Instead,] he rendered decisions on matters between one person and another, and the parties to disputes accepted his ruling without appeal. He spent most of his time in prayer and studying Torah.

That same eccentric man [mentioned earlier] turned one day, at a particular hour, into the poor home of Rav Hanich to seek an answer to his question, ["Why is this place named Mlynov?"]

He found him in his house, sitting on a low bench, his back bent and hunched over, submerged in a book of Gemara or in the Holy Zohar. As usual, Rabbi Hanich was occupied with questions of Kashrut (Jewish dietary laws), and they were not few. It was the way of women to strictly observe the dietary laws. Every blemish found in a slaughtered fowl required examination. And now he was being bothered with a strange question. A question like, forgive the comparison, what is written in our Holy Torah: "And he called that place Beth-el" (Genesis 28.19).

He examined the question with his tired eyes and a look of astonishment:

What is the point of this question, Mr. Jew? After all, our lives in this world are a passage before our entrance to the parlor of the Eternal in the world to come. And this place, this town, with our many sins, is only a stop in our wandering in exile (galut) until our righteous Messiah arrives. — What does it matter what the gentiles called it?

This was how Rabbi Hanich answered.

And no different would the answer to this question have been if offered by the well-respected Jews, who spend a great deal of time in prayer and studying Torah, and if the person answering the question were [from] average Jews, [such as] young shop owners toiling in their business, overwhelmed and anxious about supporting their family, [or] day laborers toiling with work that comes their way — their time is pressing and their minds are not free [to ponder] a question like this.

* * *

The Origin of the Names Mlynov and Ikva

With respect to the name of the town, it is possible to discern an answer from the testimony of the remains [of the mill], and because of this it is necessary for us to turn our attention to the Ikva River, on whose banks the town was built. The origin of the river is in Kremenets,[5] on its way to here, it passes Dubno and it twists along its way as it descends along Torhovytsia,[6] to the Styr River, the tributary of the Bug River.

My grandfather, Mordechai-Meir, may he rest in peace, told me once, that the name of the Ikva River came from [the verse in Genesis 1:9] "Let the waters (yikavu hamayim) be gathered."[7]

The relevant incident happened many generations ago. It was a difficult winter and snow fell in an unusual amount. The beginning of spring the water of the river rose dramatically, chucks of ice accumulated along the posts of the bridges, and "stood straight up like a wall" [quoting Exodus 15:8] and blocked the passage of the water. The river kept rising higher and higher, the towns in the surrounding area and the Jewish dwellings were inundated and the danger was great. This is why we were accustomed to say, "Water is more dangerous than fire" — from fire you can flee but from a flood, which comes suddenly, there is no escape or rescue. The Jews gathered for prayer and read in a chapter of Genesis (Parashat Bereshit) "Let the waters be gathered and behold the dry land appeared" (Genesis 1:9). The sun came out and melted the ice, and the water broke through in a tremendous stream, the pillars and the bridges were destroyed, "and behold the dry land appeared." This is the reason the river is called the Ikva. The name sounded good to the non-Jews and this became its name until today....

[Page 15]

The two bridges and the posts split the river into two streams.[8] Water from the first bridge reached Dubno, creating a waterfall, with turbulence of white foam, a noisy and raging tumult that does not end. From the second bridge, the water spread out into a wide stream. In the shallow water, black, charred stakes protruded. Their tips were sharpened in different shapes and of different heights. Thus, the partly burned wood remains today, the remnants of the mill, that burned many years ago.

If you ask: "when was the first mill built, the one before the one that was burnt down?", to this question, there is no answer. Nonetheless, it is clear, that the name Mlynov for the town was derived from the word "malin" which in Slavic languages means "mill."

Market day in the town [H]
On a market day in the Shtetl [Y], 1918

In the winter days, the remains of the mill could be seen like lumps of coal sticking up from the white snow. When spring came, they stood as obstacles to the blocks of floating ice, that hammered them furiously, but they stood firm for many years and did not get uprooted.

During summer months, oily decayed matter accumulated. The surface of the water was covered with a green mantle: a tangle of algae and water lilies and above the green cover the moss swirled like black scarves. The water flowed constantly with a soft, sad gurgling melody. Time passed by (heholef) and the events of the place flowed in parallel to the flow of the water. Thus, the generations passed (holef).[9]

The first fire, the epidemic, the second fire, wars. And in the end – the great fire.

Translator's and editor's footnotes:

1. We would like to acknowledge Lipa's daughter, Miriam Aharoni, for her help with improving the understanding and translation of her father's essay.

2. Probably refers to the pandemic of 1889–1890 sometimes called the "Russian flu" or the "Asiatic flu" which killed a million people worldwide. See also Moshe Fishman's discussion (p. 61) of the tragic events that occurred in Mlynov at the end of the 19th century. Insight courtesy of Lipa's daughter, Miriam Aharoni.

3. Referring to "Kmelnsytsky" was like saying "a long time ago." Zynoviy Bohdan Kmelnsytsky (1595–1657) was a Ukrainian character in the Polish Crown of the Polish–Lithuanian Commonwealth (now part of Ukraine). He led an uprising against the Commonwealth (1648–1654) that resulted in the creation of a state led by the Cossacks. Jews remember him as a mass murderer and it is customary to follow his name with the acronym, "may his name be blotted out."

4. This prayer was an expression of mourning and lamentation over the destruction of the Temple in Jerusalem, often popular among Sephardi and Hasidic Jews.

5. Kremenets is 64 km (40 mi) south of Mlyniv today.

6. Torhovytsia [known as Trovits in Yiddish] is 20 km to the northwest of Mlyniv today.

7. The full verse from Genesis 1:9 reads: God said, "Let the water below the sky be gathered into one area, that the dry land may appear. And it was so." The implication is the name Ikva (אקווה) was an allusion to the Hebrew verse "let the waters be gathered (יקוו)."

8. It is implied here that the split in the Ikva was caused by the collapse of the bridges which split the river into two streams.

9. Lipa is drawing an analogy between the flow of the river and the passage of time and the generations.

[Page 16]

Mlynov–A Kehilla[1] for Mlynov and its Surrounding Shtetlekh

by Sonia and Mendel Teitelman, Haifa

Translated from the Yiddish by Hannah B. Fischthal, PhD

Edited by Howard I. Schwartz, PhD

Mlynov–Surrounding Shtetlekh

The Mlynov kehilla included these shtetlekh: Mervits, Ostrozshets, Boremel, Demydivka, and Trovits.[2] In addition, there were some Jewish families who lived in the villages near each shtetl. Except for Mervits, which was not more than one kilometer from Mlynov, the shtetlekh were somewhat far from each other according to the possibilities of communication in those times. They were all independent. The villages surrounding every shtetl were the same distance away. For example, Ostrozshets was 15 kilometers from Mlynov; Trovits was 15 kilometers from Mlynov; Demydivka, 20 kilometers; and Boremel, 30 kilometers. The distance met the requirements for the shtetlekh in the area to belong to the Mlynov Jewish kehilla, although this was not a legal jurisdiction. All Jews from the above mentioned shtetlekh, and from their surrounding villages, were tied to the kehilla by annual taxes, by elections for the Jewish communal positions, and by other assorted details. Usually, regarding the citizens' duties to the local authorities, like to the regional governor, they belonged to the Jewish community.

From the inside Jewish point of view, however, the distance of the shtetlekh from the center in Mlynov lessened the feeling that they really belonged to the Mlynov Jewish community. Not all had real ties to the Mlynov kehilla. More than one person looked sadly at the luck of Mlynov, because both Demydivka and Boremel actually had larger Jewish populations than Mlynov. Mlynov was chosen only because of its geographic location.

[Page 17]

The anti-Semitic government desired it too, simply in order to have control over Jewish institutions, and Mlynov was the closest to Dubno, the central city. Every shtetl was independent, but each had to agree to be tied together into one Jewish community. There were also many family ties among the shtetlekh.

Elections to the Kehilla

Creating the Jewish kehilla in Mlynov, which would include the surrounding shtetlekh under its protection, was not easy.

Until then, nobody from the shtetlekh had had any Jewish elections. Jewish elections in all towns and in all times have had many issues. An entire structure with various divisions had to be created. For example, the kehilla had to handle issues of religion and rabbis, issues of weddings and divorces, issues of kashrut, social needs, cemeteries, and other subjects. It was always full of problems.

In a larger city, all the problems were concentrated in the same city, and the leaders of the congregation could control them more easily. That was not the case with the Mlynov kehilla, which consisted of distant shtetlekh and their surroundings. It had great difficulties with wanting to control all the issues.

It was necessary, for example, to begin voting for supervisors of the synagogues in the congregation. As usual, this election had to take place separately in each shtetl. Understandably, in every shtetl parties were created: Orthodox, Zionist–Orthodox, plain Zionists, and Bundists. Today we can imagine how the small number of voters had to elect supervisors. There was, of course, no shortage of volunteers for the positions, but how to choose? In such a small community, it was a large mishmash. There were great difficulties, and inexperience — because this was new for an important part of the Jewish population. All of this was carried through, and supervisors were elected.

[Page 18]

Then choosing the overall Rabbi of the kehilla first started. Here, you see, the thing was not so simple, because only the elected supervisors were able to vote, and not the general population. They could not come together with one voice, since there were a number of candidates for the rabbinical authority.

Who Will Be the Chief Rabbi?

The first candidate for Chief Rabbi of the kehilla was the Mlynov Rabbi, Rabbi Gordon, may his memory be blessed, and may the Lord avenge his blood. (By the way, he was one of our first victims, and he was brought for burial to the nearby village of Kutsa.) This candidate was very appropriate for several reasons. It would be frugal to have the chief Rabbi always in Mlynov, without having to pay traveling expenses, and without the physical difficulties of traveling. In addition, he was a highly learned genius. He had come to Mlynov from the big city of Lublin, and he had much experience in his life in business as well as in general worldly matters. He really was worthy of the position; but even though he had backers, he also had opponents from all levels, Orthodox as well as progressive. The orthodox parties could not agree on many things. Although they had never had such a sharp, educated person in the shtetl, they could not understand how such a learned man, an Orthodox Rabbi, could be so modern. According to the concepts of the Hasidism, he was modern.

Moreover, the modern and business–focused members of the population found another blemish that made him untrustworthy, and that finding was tinged with envy and hatred. The rabbis in Mlynov, and in many other shtetlekh, could not manage on their salaries, which until today I do not know who paid them. In every shtetl the rabbis needed additional income. Some sold candles and yeast, and they took a portion of the Kosher slaughtering tax. Other rabbis used to even keep little stores and beer taverns. The Rabbi of Mlynov, may his memory be a blessing, in addition to selling candles and yeast, was involved with interest–bearing loans (usually according to documents which gave permission to charge interest). Having contact with money matters, it was no wonder that envy and hate were by–products. His opponents decided that the democratic election would be the opportune moment to settle old accounts with the Rabbi, to get even with him, and in secret. Naturally, his chances of becoming Rabbi of the kehilla decreased after the first election.

[Page 19]

All the remaining rabbis of the other shtetlekh then came under consideration, and all were found to be untrustworthy for some reason or other.[3] But the Rabbi of Trovits, Reb Mordkhe Note Ackerman, may his memory be a blessing, had the greatest chances. He was a Jew who was popular with everyone, a man of the people, and in addition he was a brilliant, learned scholar. He was very often called on to important court trials, dealing with large sums of money, and with various general matters. Everyone was affected by his simplicity and cleverness. He acquired the position, and he remained Rabbi of the kehilla until the end. He attained even a greater reputation and also more honor than before.

The Rabbi of Mlynov

In addition to suffering financial loss, the Rabbi of Mlynov suffered a loss of honor. There was friction among the rabbis.

[Page 20]

There was also friction between the proprietors and the Mlynov Rabbi on various matters, which were matters belonging to the chief Rabbi of the kehilla. And I can say, as far as I can remember, that from those times on, no conflict in the shtetl created as much diversity of opinions as the battle over the office of Rabbi of the kehilla. Quite a number of misunderstandings had been created between the Mlynov Rabbi Gordon, may his memory be a blessing, and the Mervits Rabbi, because the brother–in–law of the Mervits Rabbi was the son-in-law of Peysakh the ritual slaughterer, may his memory be a blessing. And it seems to me that the Mervits Rabbi, as well as his brother-in-law in Mlynov, were also factors in the failure of Rabbi Gordon to attain the head title. They were retaliating from the time when the Mlynov Rabbi was opposed to the other's coming to Mervits as Rabbi. And the Mlynov Rabbi sensed that. In short, there was no peace among the rabbis from the beginning of the bloody war (then the kehilla with everything around it was destroyed).

As peace among the rabbis did not exist, so also did the peace among the local inhabitants diminish. Our relationship with the Christians in the area, with whom we had always been tied through business and income, also started to go downhill. Hitler's spirit, may his name be blotted out, slowly came to us in the small shtetlekh in Poland. It was an obstacle to our lives and ways of earning a living. And as the inhabitants were in need, this affected also the rabbis, who were supported by their congregations. Truly their earnings became constantly smaller.

The horizons of the Jewish population were covered more and more with black clouds. Everyone sensed it. Here it was heard that there were pogroms against Jews; over there Jews were beaten up in the high schools. There was picketing at Jewish businesses, so that the Christian customers could not buy from Jews. All these experiences affected, as already stated, the rabbis, the kosher slaughterers, and members of the clergy.

* * *

Here I want to mention a certain conversation that the Mlynov Rabbi led with his intimates from the town while sitting at a kiddush one Shabbat after prayer.

[Page 21]

He let himself into a discussion about Torah, like always, in holiness. It occurred a few weeks before the tragedy, about a month before the 22nd of June 1941. While the Rabbi was supposed to be talking on another theme, he declared this:

"I want to tell you, dear Jews, that you should know, that wherever a person dies, that spot is holy, and it is not necessary to exhaust yourselves for his honor by taking him to a Jewish cemetery...."

All those who were present looked at each other, and wonderingly thought what kind of a connection these words had to their group sitting at a kiddush. My brother-in-law Nakhman Teitelman, may he live, is a witness to these words.[4]

After that came the tragic event, with the Rabbi as one of the first victims. We have often repeated this with amazement, how our Rabbi prophesied and knew what he predicted.

* * *

Finished. The story of the Mlynov Rabbi is over. There is no more Mlynov Rabbi, with his illustrious family. There are no more heads of households, no more beautiful traditions of the past, which crystalized such a nice youth, especially in the last years. The closer the end came, all the more did the young people in Mlynov and Mervits blossom and grow. The same was true in all the shtetlekh which belonged to the Mlynov kehilla, and which had the same fate as Mlynov and the others. Even the youngest daughter of the Mlynov Rabbi, Dvoyre, suffered the same end as everyone else.

Children Coming from School
From the photos of A. Harari

[Page 22]

A remnant of the Mlynov Rabbi has remained. His daughter Toybeshe, who had the honor of hiding herself from the murderers, returned to Mlynov with us after liberation. A short time later, a young man from Russia, a relative of theirs, searching for remains of the Mlynov Rabbi's family, found Toybeshe and took her with him. They were married in Poland or Germany, and today they are in America. Two sons of the Mlynov Rabbi also survived. They were studying in a Yeshiva, and with the coming of the Russians to us in 1939, the Yeshiva boys were evacuated to Japan; from there they came to America, where they can be found today.

The Other Rabbis

The Mervits Rabbi, who was also the ritual slaughterer, was a young man with little rabbinical experience. He did not have a chance of being Rabbi of the kehilla, because in addition to having rabbinical knowledge, he had to also have rabbinical standing, and for that he was still too young. He went the same way as all the other Jews there, with his entire large family.

Regarding the Rabbis from Demydivka, Boremel, and Ostrozshets, I do not remember what happened, if their candidates were promoted or if they were fitting to the position. The Trovits Rabbi, who was finally elected, as already stated, was the most appropriate candidate. He held the title, "Rabbi of the Mlynov Kehilla and the Surrounding Shtetlkeh," with honor.

* * *

The Secretary of the kehilla was a Jew from Demydivka, with the name of Katsevman. Various people helped, whose names, unfortunately, I do not remember. I know that Lipa Halperin[5] who died in Israel, may his memory be a blessing, also worked there a while. The names of the sextons: from Mervits was Shamai Porizshok,[6] may his memory be a blessing; from Mlynov was Chaim–Yitskhok Kipergluz,[7] may his memory be a blessing; from Trovits was my brother, Nakhman Teitelman, may his memory be a blessing; and from Boremel, Alter Myoshever, may his memory be a blessing. The others I do not remember.

[Page 23]

The End

The demise of the kehilla began in the year 1939, with the marching in of the Soviet army into Mlynov. My wife Sonia and I, and many others, were walking around as if in the world of chaos; we benefitted from the Soviets, but we were also degraded. We benefitted from the secret Molotov–Ribbentrop Pact which, for a while, held off the Germans, may their names be blotted out. Degraded because that was the end of all the Jews there who were earning a living from business, and especially those who still owned something. This was also the fate of the Zionist organizations.

As Chairman of the Jewish National Fund for many years, I had quite a large archive. With the arrival of the Soviet army, I burned all the papers in the oven, so that not even a trace would remain. There were also other institutions which fell apart and disappeared by their own actions at that time. Being conquered by the Soviets, it is true, brought a temporary redemption, which is unnecessary to repeat. But at the same time, all Jews instinctively felt that they have to stop living their former ways of life, and they must begin everything anew.

And so we did. Every one of us started slowly to complete various jobs anew, and life was beginning to normalize. A few still could not quickly make peace with their fates, but nothing helped. Some earlier and some later. The worst was regarding the elderly, who all their days had lived the old way of life and done some small business; they had to quickly, in their older years, give their businesses over to the state, but still support their families. Of course, many did not give up their old businesses and they tried to continue as before in order to be able to exist. This brought a stiff punishment when the person was caught; it was not a light matter.

The members of the clergy suffered the most.

[Page 24]

The government did not tolerate them, and the population, who supported them in normal times, were, with their best intentions, not able to come up with a solution. There was not any hunger yet.

The same held true for all the shtetlekh which surrounded our Mlynov. We used to be able to travel from shtetl to shtetl, to relatives and acquaintances. Now it was extremely dangerous to use the trains. All the shtetlekh in the kehilla were in the same situation, and the same mood ruled everywhere–extreme pessimism.

It was not better in the bigger towns around us, like, for example, in Dubno, Rovno, and Lutsk. The important people from those large cities fell victim in the first days, when the Russians just came in. They were robbed in a delicate way; a short time later, many Jews were deported to a place nobody knew, and from which very few returned. The average and unimportant Jews did whatever they could.

* * *

The coming holocaust made an end to all of this; it did not differentiate between poor and rich, old and young, male and female; it only cared about who was a Jew. Our dear and beloved ones became martyrs with their Jewish faith. Interesting and sad is the fact that the enemy, may its name be blotted out, united and exterminated all the shtetlekh in the kehilla on the same day. Without giving details, the same things happened to all. The members of the kehilla lived together, they were tortured together, and they were also murdered together.

Editor's footnotes:

1. A Jewish congregation; a kehilla is a local communal Jewish structure. – HBF
2. Today: Muravytsi, Ostrozhets, Boremel, Demidyvka, and Torhovytsia, Ukraine. – HBF
3. The photo appears to be of a water carrier with two buckets suspended from wood that hung across his shoulders. Other essays in the Memorial book refer to this method of carrying water. – HS
4. Nakhman Teitelman is known later as Nahum Teitelman. – HS
5. Lipa Galperin in the Yiddish text. Note that the Russian language does not have an "h" and it does not distinguish between "g" and "h," so the confusion is common. – HBF
6. Dr. Howard Schwartz suggests the name may be "Polishuk" as he has traced a local family by that name. – HBF
7. Kipergluz also appears transliterated as Kipergloz. – HS

[Page 25]

_____

"The Cologia" [The Swamp]

By Aaron (Berger) Harari, [Kibbutz] Merhavia

Translated and edited by Howard I. Schwartz, PhD with Hanina Epstein

This was a large gathering of water ("mikveh") which during our time was called a pond or a pool, but we called this water "Cologia," and its meaning in the language of the gentiles was "swamp." The Cologia was in the center of the town and didn't bother anyone since it was part of the town forever. In the houses around the Cologia, lived most of the tradespeople such as: Mendel, the blacksmith, Moshe the tinsmith, Moshe the cobbler, and others. Even those "hourly" professions[1] had their homes on its banks. Mr. Moshe, the teacher, Mr. Pesach, the kosher slaughterer, Mr. Mendel, the scribe. North of it stood the Olyker synagogue and across from it the [ritual] bath house.

Who among us doesn't remember the croaking of the frogs during the summer nights, which could be heard even at a distance? On moonlit nights, it reflected shining, white light and in dark nights the stars appeared beneath the water. Who among the kids didn't enjoy the Cologia, during the winter months, when the water froze and they could skate on the ice — and this was the only sport for the children of the "cheder," who didn't dare, from fear of the rabbi [teacher], leave the boundary of the courtyard, and go to the wide open Ikva River? The cheder of R Moshe Melammed was in fact on the south bank of the Cologia and his pupils took advantage of every "kosher" moment to hang out on the ice and skate.

The swamp on Dinvinka Street. The Cologia.
On the left side: the Olyker synagogue.
From the photos of A. Harari

[page 26]

In the spring, with the melting of the snow, the water used to reach up to the fences of the houses, but the residents were never griped with a fear of flooding. And what did they do to get to the entrance of their homes? They put planks of wood, bricks, and boards and made something like a boardwalk — and thus they crossed until the Cologia water subsided.

And this is the origin of the Cologia. Many years ago, there was a grove of oak trees in this spot. They cut down these trees and, on that area, built houses. The walls of the houses they needed to plaster, and they found in this very earth that there was clay fitting for plastering the houses. Everyone would come[2] and take some of the clay. Thus, over the course of the years, a lowland was created and the water from the melting snow and rain would stream there and did not have an exit. Only on rare occasions in a year without rain would the Cologia dry up and the area take on the appearance of a dying swamp. The croaking of the frogs was silenced, and the ground used to crack into deep cracks, as if it was calling for renewal…

Market street
From the photos of A. Harari

Editor's footnotes:

1.   Hebrew uses the term "free professions" to refer to occupations like lawyer, accountant, and other labor for hire.
2.   Here Aaron uses the language from the Passover Seder "kol dichfin" (all are welcome to come as guests).

[Page 27]

A Wedding in Mlynov

by Sylvia Barditch-Goldberg, Jackson Heights

Translated by Hannah B. Fischthal, PhD

Edited by Howard I. Schwartz, PhD

It was after the holiday of Shavuot. A beautiful summer day. The whole shtetl was in a state of excitement. Chayeke, daughter of Ahron the blacksmith, is getting married today with her bridegroom from Lutsk,[1] Moyshe the cantor's son, who is also a cantor. The Count is sending out his carriage with two pairs of horses, decorated with ribbons and bells, to bring over the bridegroom with his parents. The Count does this for all the important people who marry off their girls. The bridegroom had *klezmorim*[2] come from Lutsk. The musicians from Ulik[3] were already there; they have the rights to perform here. The people are anxious to see a wedding with two klezmer ensembles.

I was, as is usual every year, visiting my grandparents for Shavuot. My grandmother tells me, "Silkele, wash up. I will put your new little dress and new shoes on you; I will comb your braids and put pretty ribbons in them; and you will go to the wedding with us." Afterwards, she orders me to not get in the way, because she and my grandfather needed to get ready themselves.

So I went out, all dressed up, in the street. I see in the house next door, in Chaim the miller's garden, men, women, children, and friends in white. Everybody wants to see the bridegroom, who is staying there. Near the steps at the entrance, the *klezmorim* from Lutsk are standing. I push through the big crowd and recognize, among the musicians, Isaac, our neighbor, with his flute. He puts his arm around me, kisses me, and says: "Silkele, dance for me like you do at home." I do not allow him to beg, and he tells the ensemble to play a cheerful tune. I dance, tapping my feet to the beat. The crowd is enthusiastically clapping, and I hear someone saying: "Here is a worldly child."

Someone screams out, "Make way, the bridegroom is going!" Two men show up who will lead the groom to the bride. The *klezmorim* play, the bridegroom is walking, and the musicians with the large audience follow the bridegroom to Chayse's house; the bride is staying there.

[Page 28]

Coming into Chayse's house, I see the bride is sitting on an easy chair, and the large room is fully packed with men related to the groom; the bride is surrounded by well-adorned women of her future husband's family. The *badkhn*[4] from Ulik, Reb Leyzer, a tall, big-bellied Jew in a black overcoat and high top-hat, gets closer to the bride and begins to sing a sad melody, in his own style with his strong bass voice: "Dear bride, dear bride." Then Itsik the fiddler from Lutsk, a deaf person, plays so artistically on his magical violin, making the strings cry, that everyone weeps out loud. Eyes are being wiped; noses are blown; the bride is crying with them.

After seating the bride, the girls stand outside with lit, colored candles in their hands. Boys, close friends of the bride, hold up the four posts of the chuppah. The Rabbi, Reb Henekhl, conducts the wedding ceremony. His beautiful voice resounds over the place. Afterwards the bride and groom are greeted—first in Hebrew, then in

Russian and in Yiddish. People scream "Hurrah!" and throw confetti on them. Suddenly a wide aunt with a braided loaf in her hands appears, dancing in front of the bride and groom.

In the house, the crowd sits at long tables on benches; men are separate from the women. Boys and girls sit together. A group of women serve the tasty treats, which the servers had prepared: they were Rokhl Paveshe's and Leybtsikhe, whose reputation and cooking were well-known. Gefilte fish is brought out, golden chicken soup, fatty kishkes, foods roasted and cooked. The men are brought bottles of 90 proof liquor. They smack their lips, and it doesn't take long until they become a little drunk. They dance the traditional *mitsva* dance with the bride.

Later, the Hasidim and the well-to-do from the town dance the Hasidic dances with enthusiasm. My grandfather, Itse Starosta,[5] a tall Jew with a handsome red beard, combed into two points, wearing a long *kapote*[6] and high boots — happily dances. And now Leybush Gershon's,[7] a Jew with a small beard and a wide smile, takes him into the circle. And here comes the *mashgiakh*[8] Itsik-Leyb, a tall Jew with a gray-white beard, in a black satin *kapote*, with high white socks, and with short half-shoes; he has a patriarchal appearance.

[Page 29]

The circle keeps getting bigger, the tapping with the feet, stronger. The men weave together, singing, in a holy chain. The *klezmorim* play louder, louder. People stand on the benches and watch the dancers.

Finally, they sit down, tired. The musicians now play for the women. Quadrilles, a lively sher dance, a *lenseis*, a cheerful *freylekhs*. Afterwards the boys and girls come and dance together: waltzes, mazurkas, *vingerkes, krakovyak, polyespans*. They dance until day comes.

It is fashionable for the musicians to accompany the in-laws to their home. The music is especially beautiful. It is heard over the entire street. Some neighbor women are awake, waiting to hear the music, which is long remembered.

And so ended the wedding of Chayke the blacksmith's daughter in the town of Mlynov.

* * *

The bride is led around the groom, she is turned around;
The groom, in his heart, follows her and accompanies her
Until he hears secrets from under the footsteps.

The *badkhn* suddenly finishes and becomes
The officiant of the marriage ceremony, and not for a joke,
And chants the blessings according to the laws and requirements.

(Excerpt from "The Chuppah" by Aleph Katz)

Translator's and editor's footnotes:

1. "Loyts" in the text, but I assume this is the town of Lutsk, Ukraine. – HBF
2. Jewish musicians who play klezmer music, usually including a fiddle, a clarinet, and other instruments – HBF
3. Probably Olyka, called Olik in Yiddish. – HS
4. Wedding entertainer who usually composes improvised humorous and sentimental verse about the bride and groom. – HBF
5. Head of the village. – HBF

6.   Long, black kaftan worn by Hasidim. – HBF
7.   Possibly a reference to Labish Gelberg from Mlynov. Sylvia later marries his grandson, Gershon / Joe Goldberg. – HS
8.   Supervisor of kosher laws. – HBF

[Page 30]

"My Hill"[1]

by Moshe Teitelman (later Moshe Tamari)

Translated and edited by Howard I. Schwartz, PhD with Hanina Epstein

At the edge of my town where I live, the river runs, and near it is planted a grove of Linden trees with thick tangled branches. Over the river is a rickety bridge, which is impossible to cross with a wagon, and therefore it is always quiet and restful there. Not far from the river there is one hill — in a corner that is lonely and quiet. When I was little, we used to hike there — I and some friends my age – once a year, on the holiday of Lag B'Omer. We used to call the hill "Mount Sinai," and there was no doubt among us, that this was "Mount Sinai" which we learned about in the 5 Books of Moses [*Humash*].

When I grew up, I treated this isolated hill as my most special place and on it I spent all my leisurely hours… There I dreamed the first dreams of youth. And when the time came to leave the town where I lived, I thought of the hill, and it was difficult for me to leave her …

* * *

Days and years passed, and I lived in other towns and walked among strangers, but my precious hill, I did not forget, and many, many times I longed for her. The ground was encased in green in summer and was enveloped in a shroud of snow in winter, I see her in my imagination and the scenery stood alive before my eyes …

When I returned home, my first stroll — to the hill. And my hill had not changed one iota. Then and also now, she was wrapped entirely in green.

"My hill was surrounded in splendor,"[2] — I thought, and my joy had no boundary…but after I sat there a while, I noticed a soft sound around me: with a wagon were coming pavers and bridge builders and they began to inspect and measure the area in that spot …

Every day the tumult grew, and the strangers began to come there frequently…the place became too confined for me and I left my cherished hill in grief and with a broken heart – – –

From that moment the question began to gnaw at my thoughts and didn't give me peace: if even here the tumult of the world penetrates and profanes the holy temple of my youth, where should I go with my soul full of dreams? …

Editor's footnotes:

1.   Published originally in "Eitoon Katan" [A Small Newspaper], Warsaw, 1929.

2.   A possible allusion to Psalm 145 speaking of God: "The glorious majesty of your splendor" (hadar kevod hodecha).

[Page 31]

The Tree That Resembled a Menorah on the Way from Mervits to Mlynov (A Legend)

by A. [Eliyahu] Gelman, Netanya

Translated and edited by Howard I. Schwartz, PhD with Hanina Epstein

It was the custom for the Tzadik[1] to circulate among the towns of Volyn to meet with the congregations of his Hasidim who were awaiting him. And even though he was an old man, advanced in years, nothing could prevent him from continuing on his way.

One Friday, the Tzadik went out, according to his custom, to visit in a nearby town, with those who were accompanying him. That same day, a winter day, the snow was falling and covered the entire face of the ground. The winter carriage[2] in which the Tzadik and his companions were traveling, made its way along the dirt road that was snow covered and went up a hill that was between Mervits and Mlynov. Suddenly, the wagon stopped at the direction of the Tzadik; strong pains attacked him, and he felt that the hour had arrived to take leave of this world. The Tzadik looked and saw the sun sending forth its bright rays in the approaching sunset, and in another moment the holy Sabbath would spread her wings [at which time transport and burial would be forbidden]. And he — how could he reach a Jewish grave?

Perplexed, the Hasidim stood around him without saying anything. The Tzadik with all his depleted strength, whispered towards his Hasidim, "Holy Shabbat is coming, and I am about to take leave of this world. Dig me a grave here and bury me on the main thoroughfare and you — go by foot to the nearby village and do not desecrate the Sabbath." And with these words, his lips began to move and he prayed, and while praying "Vidui"[3] [the deathbed confessional], his soul left him — at [the word] 'Ahat' [One]."[4] The mourning Hasidim did as they were instructed by their departed rabbi, and buried him in the grave on the main thoroughfare. At the place of his burial, they stuck a branch in the earth as a landmark and in memory.

Within days, the branch rooted, it grew and became a magnificent tree, with branches out to the sides, which formed the shape of a menorah, a witness and a monument to the one buried in the earth. In the winter, when a person passed that location, the wind blew through the branches with whimpering, the snow squealed under the steps of one's feet — and it recalled this legend [aggadah]: the legend of the grave on the thoroughfare and the headstone tree in the shape of a menorah.

Translator's and editor's footnotes:
1.   A term meaning "righteous one" used for a religious spiritual leader in the Hasidic world.
2.   Possibly with wheels removed and converted to sleigh, as told to Mlynov descendant Charles Epstein by his father.
3.   The prayer a traditional Jew recites during their final moments.

4.   The Vidui includes the Shema, "Hear, O Israel, the Lord is our God the Lord is one." When he got to "One," he expired.

[Page 32]

_____

In the Presence[1] of Yitzhak Lamdan in Mlynov

by Moshe Tamari

Translated and edited by Howard I. Schwartz, PhD with Hanina Epstein

Before WWI, Mlynov was known as a minor town in the western part of Great Russia, on the border of Austria. As is only natural, legends developed — beautifying and embellishing [life] especially for the routine days that were boring and depressing. The residents spoke with wonder —

- about the palace of the Count (Graf) Chodkiewicz and the hall of mirrors, and
- about the famous Polish doctor, and those who happened to meet him on the road would remove their hats in respect and honor, and at the moment the Russians forces wanted to execute him, all the Jews of the town came to plead for his life and saved him from a humiliating death;
- about the schnaps distillery, where there are red-carved bricks, and its small windows are well polished; and
- about Rabbi Aharon from Karlin, the grandson of Rabbi Aaron the Great [Aaron ben Jacob Perlov][2] who died there and in the cemetery they erected a "structure" [literally "tent"], that was a stone that attracted Hasidim, who came from afar and entered on "the Designated Day"; and
- ·about the town's far-flung son, who "left for bad [secular] culture," "Solomonle Mandelkern," shaven with a stiff mustache, the author of the poem, "Bat Sheva" and the concordance to the 5 books of Moses, called "Hechal Hakodesh" (the Holy Temple). There is a story that he happened by on his way from Vienna, wearing a top hat, and passed in front of his sister's store an hour before the start of the Sabbath and asked her the way to the study house — and she didn't recognize him…

This was what Mlynov was like, a fertile plain of Volhynia, built of wooden houses, tiled roofs, streets that extended in the shape of a pentagon from the circular market square, far from the railroad and from the intersection of the roads. The large Ikva River passed by her, and she was encircled by dramatic green hills and groves of oak and birch, and she was blessed with honest Jews who honored Torah, traded in grain, and from which derived a great diverse bounty.

* * *

During my childhood, people would talk about Itzi Yehuda Lebes, namely, Yitzhak Lamdan, who left via a nonexistent route for the Land of Israel, at the height of the raging war, at a time of uncontrolled pogroms. In the Land of Israel, he worked as a pioneer in every kind of hard work, hungry and sick with fever — and he became a literary giant. There are those who remembered him on markets days, when his father's house served as a lodge for many guests while Itzi, without a corner to himself, lay down with hands and feet outstretched on the wooden floor, and in the midst of great commotion, he would write his Hebrew poems and go back and copy them in his beautiful handwriting. When he reached 12 years, his first poem was published; after several years, he also earned the opportunity to publish in HaShiloah[3] and he received from Joseph Klausner a postcard written in his own hand.[4]

[Page 33]

The Jews of Mlynov were also tolerant in earlier generations. Yitzhak Lamdan, a man who instead of intending to be a teacher of knowledge in Israel, chose to write rhyming poems in the style of the gentiles – [nonetheless] they honored him. His father's merit was extended to him. What's so surprising, is he not the son of Reb Yehuda-Leib?

I do not remember him from the days before he made aliyah to the Land of Israel, but I attentively listened for anything said about him, as if he lived a long time ago. But the large house with the white front, in which a densely branched chestnut tree leaned over its windows, impressed me as more wonderful than other houses: He was born here in this house and from this treetop he dropped chestnuts[5] and here in the river he washed. When I went inside, I sidled up to the wall ("kotel"),[6] without realizing it, and turned my eyes to the floor, upon which he lay and wrote his poems. In the shining countenance of his father, I saw Yitzhak's likeness. And in the singing voice of his father at night when he read chapters of Psalms, I found the source of the son's poems. Although Reb Yehuda-Leib greatly loved the son of his old age, he never revealed his love or expressed wonder at [his son's] success in the Holy Land. What is the fuss all about– secular books? If he wrote, for example, a commentary on Psalms (tehillim) – that would be another matter. But the writing of poetry, it was no big deal.

In the right wing of the house, his eldest sister, Reva, dwelled. Attractive, a perfectionist, and beloved. To her house, which sparkled with cleanliness, even on the days that the mud was outside and came up to your knees, I used to come to read from the letters of Lamdan, and to see the books that he sent.

I don't know whether it was because of a special connection between Reva and my mother or because she knew my love of Hebrew literature that I was the only one to whom she would lend books that I could read at my house. When I returned [the poem] "Masada,"[7] I received the volumes, "Between the Islands" and "Reubeni, Prince of the Jews,"[8] which Lamdan had translated and after that [the volume] "In the Threefold Harness." She also let me in on the secret of letters he wrote to her. The days the books were in my possession, I would bring them to the clubhouse of [the youth group] Hashomer Hatzair, and the members would huddle together and read from them. Among my age group, there were a few who remembered him. Our hope that all of us would make aliyah to the Land of Israel never left us for a single day. Each one of us prepared him/herself to visit him after we merited going to The Land. That it might be possible he would come to visit Mlynov — this never crossed our minds. And there were many reasons for that.

It was known that Yitzhak longed to see his father, but it was also not lost on us that his visit was not in the realm of possibility, because he was a Russian citizen when he left [and Mlynov had become part of Poland after the war and as a result] the Polish government would not permit his entrance. Periodically, he would write from Berlin, [indicating] that he would try to realize his desire by going to Danzig, which was then a free city, and his father would go to him — and thus see him in person. After Passover, calendar year 5691 (1931), we learned that Yitzhak found a way to overcome the stumbling block [preventing him from visiting Mlynov].

[Page 34]

In a few weeks, he was about to arrive in Mlynov via Lithuania. When the rumor was verified, the excitement was palpable. And, in fact, there were signs of the pending visit. In his father's house, a room was set aside for him for which they installed new doors. In the meantime, letters and newspapers announced his lecture itinerary in Lithuania — about "The Fate of Zionism." When the day arrived, I was sent with a delegation of my friends on behalf of the Histadrut Hanoar [the Federation of students][9] to receive him personally at the crossroads where he was supposed to arrive in the evening.

As the bus from Dubno drew close, we stopped it and got on it. We looked for Lamdan but didn't recognize him. Indeed, we did see an elegant man sitting by himself on the last bench, his outer jacket spread on his knees, and his arm leaning on a briefcase, but we were confused and didn't know if this was our guest. Could this be the man of [the poem] "Masada?" It was not possible! According to his photographs, and our best estimates, we imagined meeting a pioneer dressed in a wide-open shirt, with unkempt curls on his head and a dreamy look, in the ways of a poet. And he looked at us, sensing our confusion, and did not introduce himself; only his eyes smiled kindheartedly: as if to say, 'look, how far do your sharp eyes reach, my provincial friends'. Better that you look to the heart and not rely on a person's clothes. Am I able to go across Europe in my work clothes from Ben Shemen and straw hat on my head?"– – When we approached him and timidly asked him his name, he smiled, but the barrier (*mehitzah*) did not fall away yet. We chatted on and off. We didn't tell him how much we looked forward to his coming, but he understood our emotion and it appeared to us that it pleased him. When we reached town multiple groups of young people waited. When we crossed the marketplace area — which hadn't changed at all since he left it — one couldn't detect excitement in him. The branches of the chestnut tree swayed quietly, the sun was setting in stages over the dam in the river and the grove across from it dripped summer coolness. It was approximately 12 years since his fleeing from the town which had gone up in flames.

We brought him to his home. His father didn't go to synagogue to pray Mincha [afternoon prayers] and was waiting for him. When he hugged him, we knew that we should slip away. Their meeting was a sacred and touching moment that was forbidden for us to see, just as we had been accustomed [to avert our gaze] in childhood and not look at the priests [the Cohanim] when they "rise to the platform" (ducan) and spread their hands [in the priestly benediction]…[10]

* * *

This was the month of Sivan, but the rains were pouring without let up. We prepared a welcome party for him and in the meantime, I visited with him morning and evening. During the morning, I would find him sharing a meal with his father who was positioned at the head of the table, and he was on a bench to his left, sitting modestly, as if he was still dependent on this table [for sustenance]. What subject was not spoken of during those days, when the rain poured heavily, and pounded the window next to them through which could be seen the scenery of the town, the darkened shops that surrounded the square and the rain, like dancing pins on the puddles.

[Page 35]

The river grew dark, and the grove became wrapped in fog. We asked about how Hebrew literature was faring in the Land, in the Kibbutzim and in Tel Aviv. We told him about the significant cultural activity in Poland, the network of Hebrew schools and the activities of the [Zionist youth group] Hashomer Hatzair. He recounted his days working in Sejera[11] and Ben Shemen.[12] As was his style, — he measured all his words with restraint, he smiled from time to time, shy and embarrassed. He also recounted that his apartment was close to the sea, and he washed in it every day. When the rain became intermittent, we sat with him on the bench in the shade of the chestnut and he chatted with his students, who came to him from Berestechko and Lutsk which were close, and where he had once been a teacher.

One time, we were going on a field trip passing by the grove of the Count [Graf], on the temporary bridge that was set up in place of the bridge that had burned during the First World War. To our right, the posts that stuck out of the river appeared blackened, burned posts left from the foundations of the "Mormon" (a large water mill in Mlynov) and the dam which had fallen into the lake; To our left were two banks covered with bent weeping willows. On the other side of the bridge was the hill called "Mount Sinai"[13] — by children — opposite the Count's estate. The façade of the white mansion, the colonnades and gravel walkways with flowerbeds. Only a few were privileged to enter the mansion, but the hill was the possession of this town's children for several generations. Lamdan paused looking at it and was silent. He was surely reminded of his childhood years, when he climbed up it on the Sabbaths, and at the same time, he was not able to take his eyes off the fields of birch that lined the way to the forest of Smordva. And then he suddenly turned his gaze. That very moment, my memories bubbled up with the lines from his poem Masada:

> The distant murmur of pine-forests caresses my ear.
> The ark of youth floats on the cool waters of the Ikva among the shady reeds Leave me, visions of yesterday! Why have you set on me?
> From your flourishing earth, I have pulled out all my roots…[14]

From here he sailed the ark[15] of youth; From here he fled and here he returned. But his sudden turning away hinted that his return was not as a poet of the people to his place of origin and town of his birth. Rather as if he was tempting and inciting the essence of childhood. Hebrew destiny followed in his footsteps to this same point of serenity…

As children of Volyn,[16] we were not normally used to confining our feelings, but he was used to distance and given to moodiness. Apparently, three cultures intermittently surrounded him: softness from the days of his childhood, hot [Hamsin] temperament of the people of the Land of Israel, and the restraint of European manners. It seemed that he had acquired for himself some of the ways of the Anglo-Saxons. All the times we attempted to get him to reveal his opinion on authors, he was cautious in his response. By contrast, he had much to say in general about literature and life in the Land — on the [literary] "responses" and books of "expertise." If my memory doesn't deceive me, also about the public reaction to the Dybbuk,[17] that was put on in the Beit Haam in Tel Aviv.

[Page 36]

The hours I sat in his presence were very enjoyable, without a separation between us and only once was I burned by his sparks. This was the time that he met with the members of the leadership of [the Zionist Youth group] Hashomer Hatzair. He was speaking about the Pioneer Movement and the difficulties of acclimation to the life of work in the Land. In the discussion, I revealed my thinking, that Tel Aviv expanded too much and that it was better for the Land and our Zionist future, that the Kibbutz towns expand and that the tendency for Jews to gather in cities required restraint.[18] In his reply, he rebuked me that there was no need for restraint against the Jewish city and I had no right to express my view before I saw the Land with my own eyes and before I was there. This was a decisive rebuke, and my complaint was finished. Nonetheless, I felt that justice was on my side. I thought to myself, what is this, to the poet of Masada, to spread his protection over Tel Aviv of all things.

The welcome reception went well, even though we couldn't find a fitting reception hall and it was held in one of the sections of the mill that was not finished, that was fixed up special for this, between exposed white walls and tin roof. Two days before, I entreated him to give the lecture "On the Fate of Zionism," the one he gave in Lithuania (from which good reviews reached us) but he didn't comply. The hall was full of youth from the town. He lectured on the challenges of Hebrew literature. As his lecture ended, he read his poem "Ivrit" (Hebrew), from the volume *In the Threefold Harness*.

Yitzhak Lamdan during his visit to Mlynov[22]

[Page 37]

His visit came to an end. He had to leave urgently for Basel [Switzerland] to the 17th Zionist Congress that was going to open at the end of the month, in its "world" mission. In the days before he left, the weather improved. It was moonlit nights, and we went out as a group across from the memorial tombstone along the main road outside the city.[19] The edges of the woods on the horizons were silver and the river slowly sang its song among the stalks of bullrushes and boulevard of willows, as it was swallowed up in the river that was larger still — the Styr. The dwellings of Israel dozed serenely on the soil that was held from generation to generation. It is only us who do not know rest, as if this land burned under us. It was hard for us to separate from him, and we didn't know why: the heart was full of longing and fear was concealed. The valley was immersed by the light of the moon along the small bridge in wonderous radiance, like an enchanted silver cradle. We looked at it and didn't know, not one of us, that not twelve years would pass, and this valley would be turn to a massive grave to our parents, our brothers, and sisters.

Published in "Gilyonot"[20] in memory of Yitzhak Lamdan, z"l, Chesvan-Kislev, 5715 [1954].

* * *

From the beginning of Yitzhak Lamdan's poem *Masada.*[21]

One Autumn night, on a restless couch far from our ravaged home, my mother died:

In her eyes, a last tear glistened as she whispered me a dying blessing. Before I went to campaigns on distant, foreign fields, with my army kits pressing on my shoulder…
On Ukrainian paths, dotted with graves, and swollen with pain,
My sad-eyed, pure-hearted brother fell dead, to be buried in a heathen grave.
Only father remained fast to the doorpost [mezuzah] wallowing in the ashes of destruction,
And over the profaned name of God, he tearfully murmured a prayer,

Whilst I, still fastening my crumbling soul with the last girders of courage,
Fled, at midnight to the exile ship, to ascend to Masada.

Translator's and editor's footnotes:

1. Tamari uses the word "bemehitzah" to refer to being in the presence of Lamdan, but he is punning on the meaning of the term which also means "a barrier." Later in the essay, he uses the same term to talk about the barrier between Lamdan and the Mlynov boys who greet him.
2. Rabbi Aharon from Karlin refers to the famous Hasidic rebbe, Rabbi Aaron Ben Asher of Karlin (June 6, 1802 – June 23, 1872), also known as Rabbi Aaron II of Karlin. He was one of the leaders of the Karlin-Stolin Hasidic dynasty. Rabbi Aharon reportedly died in Mlynov on a journey to the wedding of his granddaughter. Another essay in this volume, entitled "The Tree That Resembled a Menorah…" recounts the death of a Hasidic rebbe near Mlynov and alludes to this same story. Thousands of Rabbi Aaron's followers would visit him annually in Karlin around the Jewish New Year. A few years before his death, he quarreled with family members and moved to Stolin. Rabbi Aharon from Karlin was the grandson of the original Rabbi Aaron the Great [Aaron ben Jacob Perlov of Karlin] (1736–1772) one of the early founders of the sect who helped the rapid spread of Hasidism in Eastern Europe and was known for the fiery eloquence. Aaron the Great was succeed by his disciple, Rabbi Shlomo of Karlin, who was in turn succeeded by Rabbi Asher Perlov, the son of Rabbi Aaron the Great, who was then succeeded by his son Rabbi Aharon II, the one who died in Mlynov.
3. A Hebrew monthly founded in 1896 in Odessa by Ahad Ha'am, published in Berlin.
4. Klausner was a Jewish historian and professor of Literature from Vilna, active in Russia Zionist circles, who settled in Palestine in 1919.
5. The author uses the word "hsyr" which can mean to drop but may be a play on the word "poem" (syr).
6. The use of the word "kotel" for wall is a possible literary allusion to the Western Wall and to reverence the author felt towards Lamdan's house.
7. "Masada" was the famous poem Yitzhak Lamdan wrote in Palestine in 1927, which is quoted below.
8. David Reubeni (c. 1490–1538) was a Jewish traveler and adventurer who sought to create an alliance between Jews and Christians with the aim of establishing a Jewish state.
9. Appears to be a youth movement of Histadrut, the General Federation of Jewish Labor. The Histadrut was organized in 1920 in Palestine as a Labor Movement.
10. One is supposed to avert the eyes when the descendants of the priestly class go in front of the congregation and recite the priestly benediction called "raising of the hands" or "rising to the platform." The text of the blessing is found in Numbers 6:23–27.
11. A moshav in northern Israel also called Ilaniya. It was the first Jewish settlement in the Lower Galilee and played an important role in the Jewish settlement of the Galilee from its early years until the 1948 Arab–Israeli War.
12. Ben Shemen is a moshav in central Israel. The moshav was founded in 1905 and was one of the first villages established on Jewish National Fund land.
13. See the author's other essay in this volume called, "My Hill," describing his childhood memories of "Mount Sinai."
14. From Lamdan's poem "Masada," section "Outside the Camp." This translation from Leon Yudkin, *Isaac Lamdan: A Study in Twentieth-Century Hebrew Poetry*. Ithaca: Cornell, 1971, 218.
15. Possibly an allusion to the ark baby Moses was placed in.
16. The name for the Province under Poland, previously Volhynia under Russia.

17.   The Dybbuk is a play by S. Ansky, authored between 1913 and 1916. It was originally written in Russian and later translated into Yiddish by Ansky. The Dybbuk had its world premiere in that language, performed by the Vilna Troupe at Warsaw in 1920.

18.   The opinion Tamari is expressing here was also expressed by some members of Zionist leadership at the time and can be seen, for example, as aligned with the opinion of Chaim Weizmann as recounted in his autobiography.

19.   Possibly an allusion to the Rebbe who died along the road and/or the marker for the grave of Rabbi Aharon from Karlin. See footnote above.

20.   Gilyonot was a literary monthly that Lamdan founded in 1934 and edited. Its last issue was a memorial to him.

21.   Yitzhak Lamdan's poem, "Masada" was published in 1927 and played a significant role in developing the mountain fortress into a powerful symbol of identity among Zionist pioneers. Masada was a first century fortress where zealots held out in the war against Rome. For Lamdan, going up to Masada became a metaphor for aliyah to Palestine. This translation is from Leon Yudkin, *Isaac Lamdan: A Study in Twentieth-Century Hebrew Poetry*. Ithaca: Cornell, 1971, 199.

22.   The descendants of the Lamdan family believe Yitzhak is 4th from the left. It seems likely, based on a comparison to later photos, that the writer of this essay, Moshe Tamari, is the younger man without a tie in the photo, third from the left.

[Page 38]   _____

The Massive Disaster (Shoah)

Asher Teitelman, Haifa

Translated and edited by Howard I. Schwartz, PhD with Hanina Epstein

Thus it began . . .

With the breaking of dawn, the town shook from the sound of loud explosions. We thought it was just a military exercise, because there were military bases surrounding us, in addition to the large airfield on the Count's land on the other side of the river. That the war had broken out the day before between the two parties to the [Molotov-Ribbentrop] pact — no one believed this… but when we exited from our houses and the throng of residents gathered in the open areas of the town, and the situation was comprehended, the shock hit us like thunder on a clear day.

"War has broken out" — was heard from all sides. The Germans bombed the airfield, and the local Soviet army was thrown into shock, [but thought] this is nothing but a regretful skirmish. "It is not possible," the commanding officers responded, "that war has indeed broken out." But in the meantime, terrible news[1] arrived, each worse than the next.

Shocked and mortified, we stood, group by group, and discussed our situation. We had to plan what to do for the future. Who could have imagined that looting and destruction[2] were this close; that the walls of protection would be removed, that the mighty army of the Soviet Union would retreat completely along the length of the front?

In the meantime, the town and the airfield were bombed four-five times during the day. The large bridge that led to the property of the Count, was destroyed in the bombing, and the passage of vehicles was not possible; those going by foot endangered their lives and crossed it when it was broken up and its whole length was hanging by a thread above the water, but who paid heed to the danger? All the men were brought out by the Red Army to the airfield to fix what was possible to temporarily fix and I was among them. All the time there were sirens and bombings.

What was going on in the town, we didn't know. Only flames and stacks of smoke we saw from a distance and from this we guessed that here and there bombs had fallen. Towards noon, the airfield was bombed in a massive bombardment, and it was completely destroyed. There were dead among the residents of the townlet, Jews and gentiles both included, and some of the military men. Hundreds of people [took cover by] lying down along the shore of the river, by the meadow, and watched the aerial fighting taking place between the Nazi and Soviet planes. After the planes were driven away, a large surge of people fled to the townlet. The remnants of the bridge were going up in fire, and many succeeded to cross over to the town on the broken remains of bridge that still were floating.

[Page 39]

And the town? — most of the residents already had fled from it, and those who remained were waiting impatiently for the return of their loved one from the airfield. The town emptied quickly, the bombed houses burned, and the roads were destroyed. Towards evening, the Nazis took control of the airfield and on the next day they left again.

The second day passed quietly in the town that had emptied entirely of its residents, who had scattered to the rural villages and the fields. On the third day, rumors spread by the Soviet army, that they had repelled the invader, and that there was no immediate danger to our area. The rumors influenced [opinion] very quickly and the residents began to stream back home. Indeed, during the day it seemed that the danger had passed. But how astounded we were in seeing in the darkness of dusk German reconnaissance units wandering around between the houses. Panic seized the residents of the town and, in the blink of an eye, a strong flow began towards Mervits, and from there to Polish farming communities in the area. All night and during the fourth day, the migration occurred, and from afar the sounds of the Lutzk bombardment and its surrounding reached us; The burning town lit up the surrounding area.

During the night, the Red Army retreated after hard fought battles on the north side of Mlynov and evacuated the area. A number of buildings were damaged and among them the new flour mill of Rabbi Joseph Gelberg, z"l.[3] In addition, the supply of electricity to the town was damaged.

During the middle of the fourth day, the soldiers appeared in the area. An army that was large and numerous, with vehicles and by foot, gained control over everything. Tragedy fell upon us; we tumbled and couldn't get up. And that is the way it only started…

In Due Course . . .

Slaughter and robbery became a daily occurrence. These Ukrainians, who had been thirsty for Jewish blood for generations, experienced in theft and murder, were unleashed to pursue their iniquities. The first shots echoed already in the square of the town, blending well with the sounds of windows breaking and houses being destroyed. Farmers from the surrounding area wandered around with sacks laden with items that Jews had labored make. And following them their wives and child, laden with whatever came to hand. Under the protection of the soldiers, they passed from house to house, killing, plundering and destroying everything.

I remember how the people of the Gestapo gathered from the heads of the town, such as the Rabbi, z"l, and my father among them, and laid upon them a quota for ransom — a large quantity of soap, cigarettes and more. And if within twenty-four hours they didn't bring [the ransom] to the Gestapo building, their fate of death was assured. Mortified and chastened the good people of the town went out to gather the things, even though they knew from the outset that the matter was impossible. When almost all the residents gave all that they had, only a tiny bit was gathered and those designated beforehand for death stood with heads bowed before their murderers [as if] "to bring a gift to Esau" [i.e., to appease the enemy] (Gen. 33.11) … all the Jews of the town shook their heads [thinking all would be killed], but to the surprise of all, they all returned home, because there is a time for death and a time for life. But the grace period was not for long.

[Page 40]

The savagery continued. The murder and plunder continued; the Rabbi of the town, a magnanimous and honorable figure according to everyone, was among the first to be taken out to be killed. The angel of death did not discriminate among those who were available, older or younger, or in advanced stages of pregnancy. Each and every day, when day had dawned, the murderers and their accomplices charged around and expelled them from their houses to a large empty field in the center of the townlet, this marketplace ("Mark-platz") became the departure point ("Umschlagplatz"[4]), and after the assembly they were brought to places of labor, accompanied by the SS and a Ukrainian militia. With tears and blood, they saturated the roads, and not a day passed without murder and torture. The town's roads were sown with wounded, blood, and the dead. Day in and day out, the population of the town was thinned out. In the evening, we wished "if only it were morning" and in the morning we wished "if only it were evening"[5] … days of terror and fear overcame us, cold and hunger were our portion. All the inhabitants did hard labor, some in the fields of the Count, some in the airfield, in the vacated destroyed mansion of the Prince or in the estates nearby, like Smordva, and I also was among them. The torture was fully engraved in our minds and body. The order of the day began with an immersion at midnight in the pond next to the mill, in extreme cold, and after the immersion they ran us half naked for two full hours, "oy" if one falls or falters. Pistol shots would be a redeeming salvation for him, and for this each and every one yearned. The difficulties were unbearable.

* * *

The days of winter 5702 (1941) arrived. Rumors and futile hope began to spread and surge in our hearts: "General" winter would overpower them and with it would come our rescue. But our expectations were in vain. To be sure, in the arrival of the murderous troops to the gates of Moscow and Stalingrad, their advance was halted, the bitter enemy forces, may their names be erased, suffered heavy losses, and only then did their hand fall heavily upon us. In the town, the Judenrat was established, and the Jewish go-between was the execution arm for all the kidnappings of those sent for labor to the camps in Rovno, Studinka[6] and elsewhere. They seized warm clothing, furs, gold and silver and in the end also copper and everything made from copper. Life was difficult to bear in the town even before the ghetto was set up, and the fate of those who went to the work camps was no better, and not a small amount of their effort was invested in the holy work[7] of religious persecution and murder.

The Ghetto-the end

One of the days between Pesach and Shavuot, a decree was promulgated to gather up the inhabitants of Mlynov/Mervits in one ghetto. The ghetto was set up and the [plan] carried out. In two narrow and small streets, all the inhabitants of the two towns were gathered and from the surrounding villages. 10–12 persons — and sometimes more — were crowded together in every room, barbed wire fence was set up, with no entrance or opening, the trap around us was set.

[Page 41]

From here, through the entrance and exit gate, hundreds of men and women were taken to work each day. Early morning they would leave, and in evening return. Devastating news reached us from all the communities in the area, day after day, night after night, the Jewish residents were wiped out; the axe was poised. Rovno, Lutzk, Dubno and all the nearby communities were emptied of their Jewish residents. The mass graves were in the thousands, their blood saturating the accursed Ukrainian ground, the diabolical program of the Jewish oppressor went forward and was realized. One day, rumors spread that it was the turn of Mlynov, our town, to be counted. Several daring individuals broke through the ghetto fence and hid in the forests and the fields. But the incident was known to the Germans, and they postponed the day of the liquidation. Poor conditions and ravenous hunger tied them to the town, even the daring among them, and thus sealed their fate. The [fate of] the holy community was thus in the hands of heaven.

A large mass grave and around it dozens of grave sites and among them, my brothers Ephraim-Fishel and Shlomo, surrounded it. A few managed to escape and hide in the forests and fields but only a few were "brands plucked from fire [i.e., survived]."[8]

Mlynov, this is a small town in the Russian Pale of Settlement, most of its people were hard working men and a few of them were small merchants who, with integrity and by the sweat of their palms, earned their bread; in their moments of joy or sorrow, the older ones prayed but the younger ones through their activities lifted up their eyes to the land of Zion and longed for her redemption. Among the town's children [i.e., former residents] is numbered Dr. Solomon Mandelkern, the creator of the concordance to the Bible (Tanakh), Yitzhak Lamdan, among the great poets of our times; most of her children were educated on the lap of the national language [Hebrew], the town's go-getters and active members of the community worked towards a vision of returning to Zion[9] — this town, [including] all the inhabitants from Mlynov, from Mervits and its surroundings were annihilated with all the towns in the area. The ground of Ukraine is saturated with the holy and pure Jewish blood; cursed it will be forever, a disgrace forevermore. The memory of our loved ones shall be guarded in our hearts forever.

Listen up, a song rises and is exciting

With love and faith it erupts into the fullness of the world and lives —

Listen, Listen to the echo of a divine voice: she is powerful, free and uplifting

It will be sung in the choir of the Jewish people,

This is my eternity.

(Yitzhak Katznelson,[10] from Ghetto Fighters' House

Translator's and editor's footnotes:

1. Literally, "news of Job."
2. Quoting Isaiah 51:19
3. "z"l" is a Hebrew acronym for "may his memory be for a blessing," the equivalent of "may he rest in peace."
4. The term used during the Holocaust to denote holding areas adjacent to railway stations in occupied Poland where Jews were assembled for deportation.
5. This sentence alludes to Deuteronomy 28.67 which reads "In the morning you shall say, 'If only it were evening!' and in the evening you shall say, 'If only it were morning!' — because of what your heart shall dread and your eyes shall see.

6.   May refer to Studynka, Ukraine 238 m southwest of Mlyniv, Ukraine today.

7.   The term is used here facetiously, meaning the persecutions and murder were considered "holy work" by the Germans and Ukrainians.

8.   Quoting Zechariah 3:1—2.

9.   Alluding to Psalm 126.1 (also the first sentence of the blessing after meals (Birkat Hamazon): A song of ascents. When the LORD restores the fortunes of Zion — we see it as in a dream.

10.   Yitzhok Katznelson (1 July 1886–1 May 1944) was a Polish Jewish teacher, poet and dramatist. He was born in 1886 in Karelichy near Minsk, was involved in the Warsaw ghetto uprising and was murdered May 1, 1944 in Auschwitz.

[Page 42]

Kehilla Mlynov-Mervits: Eradicated

by Sonia and Mendel Teitelman, Haifa

Translated from the Yiddish by Hannah B. Fischthal, PhD

Edited by Howard I. Schwartz, PhD

We mourn the entire Jewish people that was destroyed, the house of Israel, and also our own Mlynov-Mervits which was small in number, but large in quality. Our dear brothers and sisters, from our shtetlekh from the Mlynov-Mervits kehilla which went down in flames, together with their old established nests,[1] our dear and beloved were torn away from us without mercy for eternity, for eternity. At the same time, our long-standing neighbors warmed themselves in the fires of our souls, and even poured fuel on our large fire. We, the survivors, will never in our lives forget this. Not us, and not our children, not in our freed Land of Israel, and not in the entire world!

How can we picture in our minds that the entire community of Jews from the Mlynov kehilla [which included] — Mervits, Trovits, Boremel, Demydivka, Ostrozhets, the survivors of Turka-Sokoliki,[2] and the few Jews from the villages — are no longer there, and they will never be there again?! How can we imagine that the well-trodden footpaths, on which our brothers and sisters walked, covered with sweat and blood, are now overgrown with grass, and that no Jewish feet will ever step there again?! How can we imagine that the dear children, brought up tenderly with great efforts, are no longer there, and will never be there again?! Never again will we celebrate in the Mlynov kehilla and the shtetlekh Jewish sabbaths and holidays; never again will the shabbat and holiday candles shine out of the Jewish houses; never again will we hear the happy laughter and Zionist songs of the Jewish youth over there.

[Page 43]

We will not meet Jews who, in the freezing dawn, run while carrying their prayer shawls to the beautiful, warm, large synagogue. And no more will we hear their heartfelt prayers and tears when they weep while requesting their various needs; no more will we see Jews getting up before dawn for Selichot,[3] preparing themselves for the Days of Awe. We will never again see them dance with religious ecstasy, singing, hand in hand, after the large collective "l'chayim!" Never will there be a Jewish celebration of bride and groom there. There will never be a gathering from all the distant neighborhoods to the Karliner Tsodik's grave,[4] where anguished Jewish hearts were poured out.

There are no more toiling wagon drivers, who used to get up in the cold winters before daylight, driving the grain from the local merchants to Dubno, Lutsk or Rovno; never again will they get there. There is no longer anyone to visit the graves of our ancestors in the cemeteries where our fathers and grandfathers and other generations were hidden. And there is not even a possibility for survivors of the destruction to be able to visit the other graves, which God alone knows if any signs have remained, because the assisting murderers certainly wanted to erase everything that marked their shame. There is no trace of the footpaths, which our dearest had stepped on for hundreds of years, from generation to generation.

And also gone is a strong hand that would defy the masses of murderers and their helpers for the needlessly spilled blood. What person could carry through an appropriate eye-for-an-eye punishment? And with what can we comfort the orphaned Jewish people even when we have the satisfaction of the establishment of the land of Israel, for which our former generations, for thousands of years, with so much blood and tears, prayed, but did not live to see? And we, survivors, did live to see it.

The Mlynov kehilla is finished and eradicated.

Translator's and editor's footnotes:

1. The term "nest" was used to describe groups of the Zionist Youth group, Hashomer Hatzair. – HS
2. Sokoliki in Turka powiat (county). – HBF For background, see the essay, "Murder of the Sokoliki Refugees," with notes pp. 384–385. – HS
3. Penitential prayers asking for divine forgiveness. – HBF
4. Rabbi Aaron Perlov (1802–1872) was a Hasidic Rebbe of the Karlin-Stolin dynasty and buried in Mlynov. – HBF See also the essay in this volume about the legend of "The Tree That Resembled A Menorah." – HS

[Pages 44]

Our Small Town Is No More

by A [Eliyahu] Gelman, Netanya

Translated and edited by Howard I. Schwartz, PhD with Hanina Epstein

The Jews of Mervits were tied to their town with every fiber of their being and only a few solitary individuals immigrated[1] to the United States during the large migration of Jews of Poland and Russia — or made aliyah to the Land [of Israel] with the wave of immigration between the two wars.

Meanwhile, significant changes began in the towns of Volyn in our area. The youth established branches for each pioneer movement, established secular schools, which educated jointly with the pioneer movements, for aliyah to the Land [of Israel], but to our small town, these new winds [of change] barely arrived. The town continued the way of life that was customary before the War. At the center of life stood, of course, the small traditional study-hall [Bet-Hamidrash], which served as a place of worship and for the study of Torah. Also, [it served] as a meeting place both for elders and youth together for discussions of politics, and general subjects, during the secular days of the week but especially on the Sabbath and festivals.

[The hall would be used for] every holiday and for its particular purpose, for joy, or for sadness. Festivals of spring, Passover and Shavuot, would bring joy to everyone's hearts, and would banish their sorrows, that were not lacking all the days of the year. Lilac shrubs flourished and the smell was intoxicating, the flowering of the cherry, apple and plum trees and the first sprouting in the village fields around the town merged together so nicely with the verses of spring in the Song of Songs,[2] which was recited during the evening of the [Passover] Seder, and with the exalting melody of the Akdamut[3] prayer on the Festival of Weeks (Shavuot). In contrast to the spring festivals of Passover and Shavuot, the atmosphere of the fall holidays, of Rosh Hashanah [New Year] and Yom Kippur [Day of Atonement] were different. Deep sadness encompassed the people of the town; Heaven and hearts would be broken open by the mother's blessing in lighting the candles the evening of Rosh Hashanah and Yom Kippur, the prayer "All Vows" (Kol Nidrei)[4] and the prayer Yizkor[5] during Yom Kippur, and they expressed the fear of what was coming in the new year and of hope that it would be good. With the prayer, Neilah,[6] and the Tekiah[7] note of the Shofar — only then does hope begin to surge, that their prayer would be accepted and only good would come and comfort for the heart.

The festival of Sukkot [Feast of Tabernacles] was a truly joyous holiday. Young and old joined together in the building the sukkah and in dwelling in it; the study hall [used for prayer services] was completely packed. The circling [of the synagogue] and the flags in the hands of children, the festivities and shaking of the etrog and lulav, preparing the branches of the willow, — the Shoshana prayers — engaged everyone and filled every heart with joy. And at the peak of the holiday — Simchat Torah[8] —there was joy with no restraint or limit. Being called up to the Torah everyone from old to young; the dances and various melodic songs, and especially drinking, of wine and vodka according to religion, and in the end of the day every restraint and inhibition was removed.

[Page 45]

One of the Jews would go to the roof of his own home wrapped in his prayer shawl, with the lulav and citron (etrog) in his hand.[9] And he sings from the heights of the roof the prayer melodies of the holiday prayers, accompanied by the words and tunes with Yiddish, and their contents are silly words, but also filled with sorrow, anticipating the winter that is on its way.

Last but not least — the day of Sabbath. This day is like a [bus or train] station [where one rests] — after six days of work and exertion without stopping, in order to earn a livelihood for their households. Washed and attired in Sabbath clothing, they welcome the Sabbath. The whole family tries to prepare better food to honor the Sabbath and spends most of the day in rest and sleep after a week of work.

Enjoyable but filled with sadness is the completion of the "three meals"[10] with the end of the Sabbath, a candle before it is lit.[11] A sad Hasidic melody emerges from the poor study hall [Bet-Hamidrash] — where a number of Jewish prayer quorums [minyanim] have gathered, to continue and prolong the holiness of the Sabbath.

Also, another song is heard from the distant fields in the Ukrainian village — a song of the farmers daughters and sons. A song of nature and the soil, but also on occasion a song of loathing and hatred, which the first Nazis adopted to fan the fire, which consumed our town and its Jewish population.

Students in school for Hebrew.[12] Original photo courtesy of Miriam Litz.

Translator's and editor's footnotes:

1. In fact, a large immigration from Mlynov/Mervits to the US took place between 1890–1925 of which this author apparently was not aware.

2. It is customary to read the Song of Songs on the first night of Passover at the end of the Seder. The Song of Songs is one of the "scrolls" (megillot) found in the third part of the Tanakh and celebrates the sexual love between a couple blossoming in spring. The text was given an allegorical interpretation by the Rabbis as indicating God's love of Israel.

3. The liturgical poem which starts with the word, Akdamut, is a song of praise to God for having chosen Israel and granting the Torah.

4. An Aramaic declaration, named after its first words, said at the start of Yom Kippur, which asks to proactively annul all upcoming vows made to God, to preemptively avoid sinning against God.

5. Yizkor is a special memorial prayer for the departed, recited in the synagogue four times a year, following the Torah reading on the last day of Passover, on the second day of Shavuot, on Shemini Atzeret and on Yom Kippur.

6. Neilah is the concluding service on Yom Kippur, the Day of Atonement, and the time when final prayers of repentance are recited.

7. Tekiah is one long blast on the shofar and is sounded at the conclusion of the Day of Atonement.

8. Simchat Torah is the holiday that commemorates the completion of the annual cycle of Torah reading and the beginning of the new cycle.

9. The citron (etrog) and lulav are waved during the holiday of Sukkot (Tabernacles). The lulav refers specifically to the closed frond of the date palm, but the word has been generalized to include the other species of plants (myrtle and willow) that are waved together.

10. It is considered a commandment to honor the Sabbath by eating three meals.

11. A candle is lit marking the end of the Sabbath.

12. Survivor Genya Kozak (later Jean Litz) in front row seated on the far right, 5 years old. Survivor Helen (Nudler) Fixler believes she may be next to her.

[Page 46]

Prayer for Revenge

Yitzhak Lamdan

Translated by Shirelle Maya and Dina Feldman

Not death, God of retribution! Could it alone constitute
That utmost of reprisals and avenge all, all?
Only death and no more?
Oh, no and no!
Give them life, unbearable life,
In which every moment, to its depths is
By knives of dread and horror
Slashed and punctured!

Within their lives, deepen their hellish grave,
And let them feel day in and day out, hour by hour
Fear devouring them like maggots,
Shivers of horror pricking their flesh!
May they never experience even an ounce of repose--
Without mercy, oh, rob them rob
Of even the strength to moan
And dam up their eyes from shedding a tear!

May their life's morsel stick in their throat like a bone
Unable to be swallowed or spat out!
Because the innocence of childhood's springs
Was murdered by their defiled hands--
May death not rush to redeem them!
May they be thrashed by scorpions of terror days upon days,
And be held in the nights
In a prolonged vampire's embrace!

[Page 47]

Sick the dogs of their hearts to chase them unceasingly
From dead end to no end,
From present to present,
And anywhere they turn their gaze--
A reflection will burst forth and pounce upon them
--like a wild beast in an ambush--
Their own reflection, that horrific image
Erased of the likeness of man!

Do not let them be charmed by the land's renewed beauty,
Do not let their eyes caress tree and grass
And wind, do not bring them perfumes from afar!
They who enjoyed the mortifying cries of mourning
For whom the screams of children inspired laughter--
May the universe withhold from them even the slightest of its smiles,
Let it be to them a cruel stepmother,
Oh, God of Vengeance!

Life, life grant them--of nightmares and pain,
Of silence laced with the poison they fed us,
So in their flesh they will see, and in their souls know
What their heinous hands did unto us!
They will feel, as we feel now,
What is the point of life that is doomed by the agony of hate
And a helpless orphan, what is he--
May they feel this as we do!

And also this: I know, we will forgive again
As we forgave time after time
Oh, this rushed, criminal forgiveness--
Oh God, do not let it succeed!
Distort their mind so they will not understand her speech
And in every utterance, every call of hers and echo
Let them hear nothing but the gnashing of angry teeth
And the roar of joy at their demise!

[Page 48]

Not death, God! Would it alone avenge
That which our whole nation could not?
How merciful is this punishment, how easy
For those who scattered death around them
Effortlessly, like a pleasure seeking eagle![1]
Life please give to them, God of vengeance and retribution,
In which you multiply by seventy seven
All that they have done to Israel!

Translator's footnote:

1. This might be a reference to the Nazi's eagle insignia.

[Page 51]

Life and Youth

Bear a Melancholy Blessing

Yitzhak Lamdan

Translated by Shirelle Maya and Dina Feldman

Bear a melancholy blessing, sad childhood abode,
Open your door to this visitor, a remnant of your past!
I may have not removed my shoes before entering--
But my heart, in a barefooted tremble, will bow at your threshold.

A dozen years like a dozen heavy curtains
Will darken, dim, and deepen the gap between us,
Oh, how much bitterness has flowed since
And how much of life's dust was shed by the saw of time!

Would your bosom still provide warmth, could repose still be found
Within the shade of your roof, like once in the days of dawn?
Away from the street and the market, overlooking the river and meadow,
You stand wounded in ruin, proud like a fallen aristocrat.
Your cracks have not been mended since those evil days,
Barren is your destruction, exposed, without cover:
The fence uprooted, the garden trees cut to the roots.
Where is the cherry's shade, the redness of the strawberry bushes?

(Only the chestnuts still stand at your entrance
--Guarding with wounded trunks and tangled tops--
Of all the multitude of trees only these two survived,
Dutiful invalids, faithful guardians.)

It seems every one of your walls recounts its woes:
"Much evil I saw and scores of dreadful blows,
I will never be what I once was--
So why heal? For what? For whom? It isn't worth it!

[Page 52]

Here is where the Don's horsemen raged, Austrians, Germans battled,
Petliura's savages, ḥamil's great-grandchildren, scum of the earth, rampaged,[1]
The pentagram turned red,[2] and as of late
Poland's wealthy landlords, with their twisted pride, staked their claim here.

You have known my story. In your own flesh you know. Oh, these are
The chronicles of the houses of Israel at times of revolution and repulsion!

No longer am I a restful dwelling but a house of pain,
With my head down between my cracks I wallow in tears!"

Bear a tearful blessing, childhood's pained abode,
Receive the gift of heavy sorrow from a visiting descendent,
I may have not removed my shoes before entering--
Yet my heart, in a barefooted tremble, will sob at your threshold.

A Group of "The Pioneer" (HeHalutz), 1931[3]

Translator's and editor's footnotes:

1.   Refers to a series of pogroms committed in Ukraine between 1917–1920, during the leadership of Symon Petliura, and to pogroms carried out in 1648 under the leadership of Zynoviy Bohdan Khmelnytsky (called "ḥamil ha-rasha," ḥamil the wicked, by Jews). – SMDF

2.   This might refer to the pentagram shape formed by the streets coming out of the circle of the town market. See the essay in this volume by Moshe Tamari, "In the Presence of Yitzhak Lamdan," p. 32. – HS

3.   Aaron Harari stands in the back row, second from the left. HeHalutz was the Zionist Youth Group for the older youth who graduated from Hashomer Hatzair. See Aaron Harari's discussion in this volume in "The Youth Movement," p. 69. – HS

[Page 53]

The Town of Mlynov

Yosef Litvak, Jerusalem[1]

Translated and edited by Howard I. Schwartz, PhD with Hanina Epstein

After 3–4 years of wandering, our family settled down in the small town of Mlynov near Dubno, the district of Volyn, in Western Ukraine, which during the period 1918–1939 was part of the Polish state. In this town lived my grandfather — my mother's father, Rabbi Judah Leib Lamdan, an exceptional Jewish person and human being, worthy of mention and special description. In this town I grew up, was educated and was personally molded. Here I passed the years of my childhood and youth and became a man. I left in August 1940 — two years and two months before they covered over the mass grave, which contained the entire Jewish congregation, including my parents, my cousins, all my friends, the day of slaughter, the 28th of Tishrei, 5703 (1942), August 7, 1942.[2] Not one of the few survivors of the destruction returned to dwell there and the small town was erased from the map of the Jewish communities forever.

I will dedicate the lines that follow to this small town — which was typical of many others in the Jewish Pale of Settlement in Western Ukraine, and in which generations of Jews grew up rooted and full of life, faithful to the house of Israel, adhering with their entire souls and might[3] to their people and its tradition and with a vision of its redemption.

The Small Town

The small town of Mlynov was situated a distance of 4 kilometers from the intersection of the Rovno-Berestechko and Dubno-Lutzk roads. The distance to the close towns: 20 km to Dubno, 35 km to Lutzk, 50 km to Rovno, 40 km to Berestechko. The district seat was Dubno, to which the towns were tied from an administrative perspective both in the period of the Russian Tzarist government until 1918 and also in the Polish government (1919–1939). Its commercial ties were with two "large" towns in the district: Dubno and Rovno. Dubno served as a center for trade of grain and convenience items, Rovno — [served as a] wholesale center for textiles and sewing. Occasionally, the merchants of Mlynov would go by train to the distant town of Levov ("Lemberg", in Yiddish and German), 153 km distance from the town of Dubno. (The closest train station was in Dubno).

The small town was situated in the center of the estate of the Count Chodkiewicz, descended from the well-known war hero Jan Karol Chodkiewicz.[4] It was by the Ikva River.

[Page 54]

The town [of Mlynov] was established in the beginning of the 19th century or at the end of the 18th century. The source of the name Mlynov was from the Polish word "Malin" which means mill. In the river there were still, in the period I am writing about between the two Wars, columns and posts — remnants of four flour mills, near where the town was established. These mills were consumed in a great fire in the second half of the 19th century.

On the other side of the river, in a large, fenced park, the palace[5] of the Count was situated, only very few honored individuals from the Jews of the town were entitled to see inside, because the entire family of the Count had an extreme hated of Jews. For various kinds of dealings, indeed, the Count needed Jewish merchants, but they came into contact only with managers of the estate [not the Count]. They would say that the Count himself would only rarely come out to speak to a Jew. In addition to the hatred from the Count's family, Jews were afraid to stroll near the park out of fear of Polish workers and servants, who worked on the estate of the Count and in his household economy, who would always sic their dogs against Jews, stone them with rocks and, more than once, lash them with whips. The palace served, therefore, for the Jews of the town, and especially for the kids, as an endless source of legends and tall tales about the Count's family, his father the old Count, their parents and their parents' parents, and about the precious and rare ornaments that were in the palace. With the Soviet conquest in September 1939, the palace was open for a few days to the general community, but it was empty, because everything inside was looted and destroyed overnight by the farmers in the surrounding area.

Not far from the park near the main road to the Count's fields was a man-made hill, which according to legends was set up by soldiers of Kosciuszko[6] who stayed in this place for a number of days. Jewish children who imagined scenes from the Five Books of Moses (Humash) in all places, called the hill, "Mount Sinai."[7] On the hill and around it grew thick trees and its loose soil during spring sprouted dense and tall grass, and it had a strong pull on Jewish youth during Sabbaths and festivals. In contrast, no Jewish foot dared to draw near during Sundays and Christian holidays from fear of non-Jews ("shkotzim"[8]).

The whole area was beautiful: the river valley, and the pasture meadows along it, fields extending to the horizons, orchards, extensive and thick woods and forests dozens of square kilometers, which in the past were filled with gangs of legendary robbers and in the future would serve as a hiding place for Soviet partisans and national Ukrainians bandits and "White Poles."[9] Many of the Jews who sought hiding in these forests from the Nazi invader, died at the hands of various murderers and only a few in number managed to find a place to hide in them until the day of liberation.

[Page 55]

The Town's Residents and Livelihood

The focal point of the small town was the market square, at one end of which stood the Russian Orthodox Church. Along the river, opposite the palace of the Count, stood a Polish Church. On a number of narrow lanes around the market square stood Jewish homes. Behind the lanes of Jews were streets of Ukrainian gentiles. These streets were called "The Village." Next to the palace there was a neighborhood of Poles, employees of the Count. Clerks and Polish businessmen lived among the Jews and Ukrainians.

In the small town as a whole, there were two thousand souls, about 800 of them Jews, about the same number of Ukrainians and the rest were Poles. Most of the Jews were small grocery and pub owners, artisans and waggoneers, who engaged in transporting grain from the small towns to cities nearby and transporting back needed goods from the cities. Once a week, a large market day was held and was attended by thousands of farmers from the many villages in the area as well as hundreds of Jewish merchants also from the nearby towns. These Jewish families made a living by selling drinks [alcoholic], cakes and sweets from stalls in the market, and from this day alone they made their meager living for the entire week.

On the Sabbaths and during the Jewish festivals the entire town rested, and the market square was empty of people. By contrast, the town bustled with life during the Christian holidays, during which many farmers came from the surrounding area. Even though commerce during these holidays was forbidden by the Polish government, it flourished behind closed doors and shuttered windows.

Most of the Jews of the town lived with difficulty and barely earned a living. Artisans worked hard from early in the morning until late evening hours. One segment of the artisans, namely the builders, carpenters, plasterers would circulate during the week to the villages and return home on the Sabbaths. During the winter, they were without any work. Before the festivals, tailors and shoemakers would work until midnight. The shop owners would also extend their store hours up to the Sabbath with the expectation of sales. Two small groups[10] of merchants, namely those in grain and textile, were "wealthy" relative to the generally low economic standards. Only one Jew was a "rich man" — owner of a large flour mill, which sold flour to distant places, and the return on his efforts, according to rumor, were a million gold Polish [currency] a year. The same man, Mr. Yosef Gelberg, repaired wooden wagon wheels in the past — he was, as usual, a miser. The Soviet government expropriated his wealth in September 1939. Three years afterwards, he was brought to slaughter with all his sons and all the Jews of the small town. (One grandson of his, who fled to Russia, survived and is now living in Israel).[11]

In the small town were three synagogues: The large one of the Trisk Hasidim, the "kloyz"[12] [house of study] of the Stolin Hasidim and the "kloyz" of the Olyker Hasidim.

[Page 56]

All the older people were strictly observant, but this observance was not extreme in comparison to that which was true of Congress Poland[13] and Galicia.[14] In the small town, there was not anyone who wore fur hats (streimels)[15] and they didn't have long, curly sidelocks (peyot).[16] Women did not shave their heads[17] upon entering the marriage canopy (chuppah). The religious did not belong to religious parties and related in general with tolerance to the younger generation, who in turn did not publicly injure the feelings of the religious persons.

In the Jewish cemetery, there was the grave of Rabbi Aaron, the grandson of Rabbi Aharon "the great," from Karlin. This rabbi expired suddenly at the end of the 19th century while visiting his Hasidic followers in Mlynov and was buried there. One of the days in the month of Iyar became the anniversary of the Rebbe's death. On that day, hundreds of Stolin-Karliner Hasidim would "ascend" to the grave of the Rebbe and would finish the day with a great festive meal (kiddush).

When the communities (kehillot) were recognized, at the start of the 1930s, as autonomous religious organizations, in other words, as authorized legal entities, and among other things able to impose taxes on the members of the community, Mlynov was joined by 5 additional small communities in the towns nearby: Muravica (Mevits), Boremel, Demydivka, Targovista (Trovits) and Ostrozhets; Mlynov served as the center for this unified community (kehilla). The head of the Kehilla was generally chosen from the residents of Mlynov which is where the Kehilla office was located. During the period the Kehilla existed until its destruction, they appointed two heads of the Kehilla — R. Yosef Berger, z"l, sexton (gabbai) of the "large" synagogue, a wealthy man in the past, but whose fortunes diminished after WWI, and he sustained himself from a small store for kitchen wares. A smart man with an honorable appearance. He died in 1935. The second was Mr. Chaim Kipergluz,[18] sexton of the study/prayer house (kloyz) for the Stolin Hasidim, an owner of a clothing store, a Zionist who inclined towards [the religious Zionist organization] Mizrachi,[19] a supporter of The Pioneer (HeHalutz) youth movement. His daughter, Rachel, made aliyah to the Land [of Israel] as a Pioneer in 1935 and lives today in Hadera. The last Rabbi of the congregation was Rabbi Yehuda Gordan.[20] This rabbi was taken out to be killed by the Nazis shortly after they occupied Mlynov. As the last head of community, who served during the Nazi period, and a member of the Judenrat, he was taken out to be killed during the day of general massacre.

Zionist Movements

The whole town was penetrated by the Zionist spirit. The Zionist activities were concentrated almost entirely among the youth movements. The adults, the fathers of the children, were preoccupied in their minds almost entirely with worries over a living and were not organized into parties. A few mover and shakers were active in raising money for financial endowments, sold shekalim[21] before Zionist Congresses, and served as representatives towards the governments. But most of the "average persons on the street" related with great love towards everything connected to the Land of Israel (Eretz Yisrael) and looked favorably on the activities of the pioneer youth movements.

[Page 57]

It was not within the capability of the small and poor community (kehilla) to establish a Hebrew school, but all parents, even the poorest among them, including shoemakers and waggoners, sent their children, if they so desired, to a private teacher to study Hebrew. The (importance) of studying Hebrew was not questioned, just as it was self-evident that every child needed to learn how to pray. There was no house that refused for ideological reasons to have the blue [charity] box of the Jewish National Fund (Keren Kayemet) for Israel.[22] In the Zionist rallies of the people before the election of the Zionist Congress, or in relationship to the important events in the Jewish world and in the Land of Israel — for example, the protest over the "White Paper"[23] and also for Zionist festivities — all the residents of the small town participated except for a few of the elderly and infirmed.

For Simchat Torah, most of the people younger than 40–45 joined the Zionist quorum (minyan) and many older folks as well. Basically, there was no group established that was anti-Zionist.

A small group of communists was only organized in the last years before the destruction who almost did not dare to appear in public. This group was established under the influence of two families of "strangers" who came to the town from the close town of Dubno. They were joined by a number of young men and women who were disaffected and who had left the youth group, The Pioneer (HeHalutz) (member of this group, who survived the destruction, returned [to Zionist commitments] and afterwards made aliya to the Land [of Israel]).

The Zionist activities of the town began in fact some time before WWI during the Tzarist reign. Already there was a group of young educated people, experts in Hebrew literature, who saw themselves as aligned with "Youth of Zion" (Tze'irei Zion).[24] In 1919, moreover, the first immigrant to make aliyah from Mlynov, when he was 19 — the well-known poet Yitzhak Lamdan (the brother of my mother, the person writing this essay), who became very famous in the later part of the 1920s in Israel because of his poem "Masada."

Only when life returned to normal after War World I and the Polish-Russian War, in the years 1921/22, were the youth movements, "The Pioneer" (HeHalutz) and the "Young Guard" (Hashomer Hatzair), organized. In 1924/25 all the local youth, ages 18–30, were signed up in The Pioneer (HeHalutz) and in the local "Palestine Office"[25] — of which my father was the director and which set up our small apartment for no fee on its authority. These youth had serious intentions, and all were ready to make aliyah with no additional prompting. There were many younger people who "forged" their age and registered as age 18 with the hope they would be able to make aliyah. The most substantial activities were brought to light by "The Pioneer" (HeHalutz) branch, which had majority and best of the youth involved. During the decade from 1926–1936, the youth clubhouse bustled every day from late afternoon until late in the evening, and alone served as the center of light and hope for Hebrew youth in a cruel and depressing reality, which already by then hinted of the coming destruction which was imminent.

[Page 58]

Besides "The Young Guard" (Hashomer Hatzair), The Pioneer and Betar[26] groups were active. In the years 1931–1932, a training kibbutz (hachsharah) of the Betar movement was established in the small town [of Mlynov].

The activities that were blessed were brought to life by the Tarbut[27] ["Culture"] branch, which was established by Samuel Mandelkern,[28] one of the first pioneers of all the local Zionist activities and one of the first to make aliyah to the Land [of Israel] (1925), who lives today in Israel in Tel Aviv and continues his fruitful public activities. In fact, this branch failed to establish a local Hebrew school officially recognized [by the Polish government], but he managed, with the help of the youth movements, to spread knowledge of Hebrew with great success. Every young local Jewish person knew Hebrew. The activities of the youth movement were conducted almost entirely in Hebrew.

Fröbel-School[29] (kindergarten) and Public-School "Tarbut" in Mlynov
Original courtesy of Zeev Harari

After a few years, the branch established a Hebrew kindergarten. The entire time, until the destruction, a large library was established that had Hebrew, Yiddish and Polish books. This library served as the only source of knowledge for the local youth, because in the small town there was only a government-sponsored grade school and not even one Jewish family sent their children to high school outside the small town. Under the rubric of "Tarbut" (Culture) along with the youth movements, they put on question-and-answer evenings, literary judgments, and dramatic plays.

[Page 59]

The Zionist activities and influence on the Zionist youth movements diminished in the last three years before the outbreak of the War, principally because most of the activists with leadership ability made aliyah to the Land [of Israel].

* * *

The seniors set up groups for: Mishnah, Psalms, and Ein Yacob.[30] During the winter months and Sabbath afternoons, there were always groups of Jews in the synagogue studying Torah. Likewise, charity (tzedakah) groups were active: "Supporters of the Poor" and "Visitors of the Sick" (Bikkur Holim). In addition to Supporters of the Poor, which established an organized monthly collection, and gave steady support to those in need, there were men and women movers and shakers who organized collections of "Anonymous Gifts" for the needy who were ashamed to receive open handouts. The feelings of solidarity and charity (tzedakah) were highly developed. It happened more than once that the head of a comfortable family got sick for a prolonged period and the family was left with no provider, or that one of the family members got sick and the recovery required paying a large sum, greater than the ability of the family, or that a Jew violated some law of the State and was expected to be punished with incarceration and was not able to pay a lawyer, or someone was going to make aliyah to the Land [of Israel] and didn't have the means for the trip – in all of these and similar situations, they would organize collections from house to house and everyone donated according to his capacity. In addition, they would organize receptions, raffles, plays and the income would be "holy" [dedicated] to an actual goal.

There was also a "Committee on Orphans" that was supported by the American JOINT (Distribution Committee) and also by the "Charity Treasury" which was supported by the same organization. This treasury was well respected in helping small shops, who were always very hard-pressed by a shortage of cash. In addition to the treasury mentioned above, the practice of charity was very developed. Jews of the town always helped each other by giving small, short-term loans, which were regarded as a life-line.

In the city of Baltimore in the United State, there was a committee of immigrants from Mlynov, which twice a year before Rosh Hashanah and before Passover would send a sum of money to be distributed among the needy.[31]

Editor's footnotes:

1. Joseph Litvak was son of Motl-Meir Litvak and Dvora (Lamdan). Dvora had been born in Mlynov (1884) but moved to Kiev in 1911 where she met and married Motl. Their photos appear in the Mlynov Yizkor book (p. 454). Their son Yosef, the writer of this essay, was born in Kiev in 1917 as was his sister, Pnina. After the Communist Revolution, the family fled Kiev and went to live in Mlynov where Dvora had been born. Yosef's sister, Pnina, made aliyah in 1937. Yosef was away studying at a teacher's college in Rovno when the Nazis invaded. He fled east and survived in Russia and eventually made his way to Palestine. His parents were both killed in the liquidation of the Mlynov ghetto. – HS

2. Survivors in Israel and US recall slightly different dates when the Mlynov ghetto liquidation took place. Here, Litvak recalls the date as the 28th of Tishrei 1942 which was October 9, 1942, though Litvak here gives the date apparently mistakenly as August 7, 1942. The Steinberg family survivors who went to Israel also recalled the date of liquidation as October 9, 1942. (See *A Struggle to Survive*, p. 29 footnote, by Shoshana (Upstein) Baruch). The Steinberg family in the US commemorated the date as the 29th of Tishrei, which was October 10, 1942. Itzik Kozak identified Oct. 1st as the day they learned that graves were being prepared (p. 356) while Shaulik Halperin identified October 10th as the date they learned the ditches were being dug (p. 352). In David Sokolsky's book, *Monument: One Woman's Courageous Escape from the Holocaust*, 3rd ed. (pp. 1–2) about Liba Tesler's survival story, he quotes Liba as identifying October 8 as the liquidation date, 3 days after her October 5 birthday. – HS

3. A possible allusion to the Shema prayer in which one is commanded to love God with all one's heart, soul and might. – HS

4. Jan Karol Chodkiewicz (c. 1561–1621) was a military commander of the Polish-Lithuanian Commonwealth army and one of the most prominent noblemen and military commanders of his era. His coat of arms was Chodkiewicz, as was his family name. – HS

5. The Hebrew term is translated as "palace." From paintings of the Count's abode, it appears more like a large mansion, though from the perspective of Mlynov residents it probably seemed like a palace. – HS

6.   Andrzej Tadeusz Bonawentura Kosciuszko (English: Andrew Thaddeus Bonaventure Kosciuszko; 1746–1817) was a Polish-Lithuanian military engineer, statesman, and military leader who became a national hero in Poland, Lithuania, Belarus, and the United States. He fought in the Polish-Lithuanian Commonwealth's struggles against Russia and Prussia, and on the US side in the American Revolutionary War. – HS

7.   See also the essay in this volume called "My Hill," by Moshe Tamari, describing his relationship to the same hill.

8.   A derogatory word for a non-Jew derived from the word "abomination." – HS

9.   Perhaps a reference to the "White Army" that fought against the Red Army, but the meaning is not clear. – HS

10.   The Hebrew reads, two "minyanim" (two quorums of 10) which is interpreted here as small groups.

11.   Yitzhak Gelberg survived, married and eventually made his way to Israel. The saga of the Gelberg family is recounted on the Mlynov website. – HS

12.   Yiddish for house of study. – HS

13.   "Congress Poland" or Kingdom of Poland is a term that refers to an area of Russia that had formerly been Poland before the Partitions of Poland. Congress Poland was created in 1815 when the great powers reorganized Europe following the Napoleonic wars. Congress Poland was created on part of the Polish territory that had been partitioned between Russia, Austria and Prussia. During Russian rule it was generally a puppet state of the Tzarist regime. – HS

14.   Galicia was a historical and geographic region at the crossroads of Central and Eastern Europe. The nucleus of historic Galicia lies within the modern regions of western Ukraine: the Lviv, Ternopil and Ivano-Frankivsk oblasts.

15.   A fur hat worn by some Jewish men, mainly members of Hasidic Judaism, on Shabbat and Jewish holidays and other festive occasions. – HS

16.   Growing the sidelocks was based on the biblical verse, Leviticus 19:9–10, in which God tells Israelites they should not cut the corners of their fields. The rule was symbolically extended to the four corners of the face.

17.   Some Hasidic women not only cover their hair out of modesty but shave their heads to ensure their hair is never seen. – HS

18.   The surname is rendered as Kipergluz in the Yad Vashem database in records filled out by the author of this essay. The name is also rendered there as Kiperglaz. – HS

19.   Mizrachi (an acronym for Merkaz Ruhani lit. "religious center") is a religious Zionist organization founded in 1902. Mizrachi holds that the Torah should be at the center of Zionism and also sees Jewish nationalism as a means of achieving religious objectives. – HS

20.   See page 433 for a photo of Rabbi Gordon. – HS

21.   The Zionist shekel was the name of the certificate of membership in the Zionist Organization given to every Jew who paid annual membership dues. The name comes from the unit of weight and currency used in the First Temple period. Purchasing the Zionist shekel expressed identification with Zionism and its goals. The revenue from the sale of the shekalim (plural of shekel) was used for Zionist activities. The number of delegates that each country sent to the Congress was determined based on the number of shekalim sold in that country. – HS

22.   The Jewish National Fund was founded in 1901 to buy and develop land in Ottoman Palestine for Jewish settlement. – HS

23.   Refers to the 1939 White Paper, a policy paper published by the British government responding to the Arab revolt in 1936–1939. In the eyes of Zionists, the paper reneged on the commitments of the Balfour Declaration and abandoned the idea of Partition. – HS

24.   Tze'irei Zion was a popular movement, founded in Russia in 1903, of young Zionist Jews who emphasized practical Zionism of aliyah, pioneering and Hebrew. Most members of the movement also carried socialist aspirations. After a split in which a considerable number of its members resigned in order to form the Zionist-Socialist Party (ZS) in 1920, the movement joined the Hapoel Hatzair party. The movement was an active member of the HeHalutz movement. – HS

25.   After World War I the "Palestine Office" was the term for local Zionist offices charged with the organization and implementation of Jewish immigration to Palestine. They were subordinated to the Jewish Agency under the provisions of the Mandate and were run in every country by a commission composed of representatives of various Zionist parties. – HS

26. Betar was the youth movement started by Ze'ev Jabotinsky and affiliated with the Revisionist movement. Jabotinsky advocated for the recreation of the ancient Jewish state of Israel, extending across the entirety of both Palestine and Jordan. Youth activities, in addition to learning Hebrew, included military drilling. – HS

27. Tarbut was a network of secular, Hebrew languages schools established in newly independent Poland during the period between the world wars. – HS

28. Mandelkern was married to Malcah Lamdan, who was sister of the poet Yitzhak Lamdan. In some sources, the surname appears as Mandelkorn. – HS

29. Friedrich Fröbel (1782–1852) was a German pedagogue who recognized that children have unique educational needs and created the concept of and coined the word, "kindergarten." Aaron Harari, back row, second from the right. – HS

30. The Mishnah is the first major work of rabbinic literature, comprised mainly of laws derived from Scripture. Ein Yacob is a 16th century compilation of non-legal sources (aggadot) from the Talmud with commentaries. – HS

31. Records of this group which called itself the Mlynov Verein are available in the Jewish Museum of Maryland https://jewishmuseummd.org/ms-36-mlynover-verien-and-maryland-free-loan-society-records/ – HS

[Page 60]

Mlynov in the Past

(From the answers to a questionnaire of an elderly person from Mlynov)

Moshe Fishman, Balfouria[1]

Translated and edited by Howard I. Schwartz, PhD with Hanina Epstein

I was born in Mlynov, but I lived for 25 years in Sloboda.[2] Afterwards, I went to live in Mlynov until I made aliyah to the Land [of Israel] in 1921.

I studied with three teachers: Natan, Yosel, and Artzi. The latter was brother-in-law of Zechariah and his house was next to Aaron Putchter.[3] I studied until age 16, and afterward, I started to work in road construction; this continued until the First World War.

I remember all the heads of households in Mlynov for two generations. For example, Yosel's father and Chaim Berger, and the father of Moshe Ares' [son], of Itzikel Bulmas and Putcher and so on.

Abraham Slobodar [Goldseker][4] came from the town of Dubno, I estimate in the year 1870, and lived in Slobada with his family, which included 5 sons and one daughter, whom you, the younger generation, will also definitely recall. Until 1891, he would lease land from the Count and work it with his sons, and with a few hired laborers until 1891, as I said, – until that period when the Russian government expelled all the Jews from the villages.[5] At that point, he moved with his family to Mlynov and engaged in construction contract work for the Count. The family grew and branched out and this is the Goldseker family.

Aaron Putcher was easy going and popular with everyone. There were three sons and three daughters in his family. His brother, Benjamin, was the Rabbi in the town of Ostrozhets. The wife of the Rabbi Benjamin was my aunt, the sister of my father.

The year in which the Rebbe from Stolin died, I do not remember exactly. I only remember, because when I was ten, I asked my parents about the building that stood in the cemetery. And they told me that the Rabbi from Stolin came to Mlynov to visit and died in a sudden fashion. They set up a memorial monument and around it a building – [called a] "tent" (ohel).[6] In the tent was an eternal light and there was a man, Abraham Khollis,[7] who watched over the eternal light so that it would not go out; The son of this Abraham, Asher Khollis, you also undoubtedly remember. On the anniversary (yahrzeit) of [the Rebbe's] death, many from cities and towns would gather in Mlynov; they could even come from the Land of Israel (Eretz Yisrael).

[Page 61]

The large synagogue was built first and next to it the small synagogue, which was named for the Rav from Stolin. The third synagogue was named for the Rabbi of Olik [Olyka, Ukraine today].

The flour mill belonged to the Count Chodkiewicz. In the early years, a Jew from Mlynov leased it and his name was Rabbi David – the father of Shintzi Maizlish. He held the mill for a number of years and then passed away. Afterwards, merchants from Dubno leased it but apparently were not successful with their enterprise. They insured the flour, the grain and even the sacks — and the mill burned down – "the owners" received the insurance sums and that ended the matter. This was in the year 1893.

With respect to the large fire in Mlynov there was the following incident. One Jew from the town of Lutsk came to Mlynov and rented a house from [or next to][8] a Goldseker and opened a pharmacy. He insured his wealth, including the medicines, with an insurance company. During a month of festivals, he traveled with his family to his parents in Lutsk, and he "entrusted" his holdings to a young man in Mlynov — and the house burned down. This fire burned two-thirds of the town. The wind was strong, and the fire reached even to the village of Kerychuk[9] and overtook several houses there. With the sum of money that he received from the insurance company, he built a large building for himself next to the building of Dr. Vislotsky.

After the large fire, the Count Chodkiewicz refused to permit the building of new houses before renewing their contracts. Additionally, he also demanded large sums [of money] in addition to the prior sums [imposed]. There were lawsuits and judgments that were favorable for the town's residents. After [the fire], building began and continued for two years — 1892/93.

I didn't have disputes with gentiles during those days. During the War period (the First World War), they helped me a great deal. Before I made aliyah to the Land [of Israel] one gentile came to me and offered me a [conditional] gift for the festival of Passover, 2 pods of wheat if I didn't go to the Land of Israel …

The large pandemic[10] broke out about the year 1894/1895 and 50 people died in Mlynov.

The period of the Revolution broke out about 20 years before the War and continued until the War. Many were killed and imprisoned and the suffering was great. After the War, all the force was organized, and they toppled the government of [Tzar] Nicholas II. This began the Communist reign.

How did I make aliyah to the Land [of Israel]? I worked with a contractor. He was a major Zionist. It was he who influenced me and planned a program for me in the Land [of Israel]. When the War [WWI] began, he fled with his family to the Russian interior, and I fled to Rovno. Frequently I got from him letters and invitations to visit. In

1921, I made aliyah to the Land [of Israel]; The contractor followed in 1934 with his family. He settled in Rehovot and died there.

In arriving in the Land [of Israel] I went to Petah-Tikvah. There I was given a good place of work. My son David and I, worked in an orchard. Shortly afterwards, the bloody clashes between Jews and Arabs occurred and somehow, we were not harmed. In 1923, I moved to Balfouria.[11] In 1929 the unrest began again — thank God I survived this danger.

Moishe Fishman and his grandson Aaron [Slivka]. Moshav Balfouria
Original courtesy of Irene Siegel, dated April 1953

Editor's footnotes:

1.   Moishe Fishman (1873–1968) was the son of Berel Dov (also Dov Aryieh) and Toba Fishman. In 1921, Moishe with his wife, Chaya (Gilden), and two of his children, David and Chuva, made aliyah to Palestine where they eventually settled in Balfouria. They were the first Mlynov family to make aliyah. Their other son, Benjamin Fishman, left Mlynov for Baltimore in 1920 and settled in Baltimore where he married Clara Shulman also from Mlynov.

2.   The town of Sloboda appears on old maps slightly northeast of Mlynov and is now incorporated into today's town of Uhzynets'. This location is consistent with descendants' memories of the distance to the town and with the identification of the town's location in the essay by Shmuel Mandelkern, "Self-Defense in Mlynov," pp. 118, 128, 135, 137, 138.

3.   It is not possible from the Hebrew to determine here whether the surname should be pronounced "Futchter" or "Putchter."

4.   As noted by Sonia and Mendel Teitelman in this volume, 256–258, "Sloboda" became synonymous in Mlynov with the Goldsekers because the family came from Sloboda. In this essay, the Goldseker patriarch is known as "Abraham Slobodar" and in another essay in this volume, one of Abraham's sons, Hirsh, is referred to as "Hirsh the Slobodar" (see "The Goldsekers" by Baruch Meren, 245-246). According to Goldseker oral history, Abraham and his wife, Baila, had five sons: Hirsh, Moishe, Yankel, Yoel, and Shimon. This is the only story in which a daughter is mentioned. As recorded by Goldseker and Fishman descendant, Irene Siegel, the family surname "Goldseker" or "Holzhaker" was linked to the family's occupation as "woodchoppers." Irene's grandfather, Moishe Fishman, is remembered as the one who brought the Goldseker family to Mlynov and who introduced his sister, Anna Fishman, to her future husband, Shimon Goldseker, one of the five Goldseker sons mentioned above, and the ancestor of the Goldseker family who settled in Baltimore.

5.   Alludes to the repressive restrictions that followed the assassination of Tzar Alexander II and began with the May Laws.

6.   Perhaps an allusion to the biblical "tents" in which God's presence followed the children of Israel.

7.   Perhaps related to the mother of Gitel Goldberg who is called "Pesye Khoyle's" daughter (p. 507 and p. 147).

8.   The Hebrew is ambiguous whether the house was a possession of a Goldseker or next to Goldseker's house.

9.   The identity of the village is uncertain, perhaps Kozyrshchyna, Ukraine, 20 km from Mlyniv today.

10.   Referring to the pandemic of 1889–1890, sometimes called the Asiatic or Russian flu, which killed about 1 million people worldwide.

11.   Balfouria is a moshav in northern Israel, south of Nazareth, located near Afula. The moshav was founded in 1922, the third to be established in Palestine, and was named after the 1st Earl of Balfour, writer of the Balfour Declaration, which embraced Zionist plans for a Jewish "national home." According to a census conducted in 1922 by the British Mandate authorities, Balfouria had a population of 18 Jews.

[Page 63]

Shtetele Mlynov

by Yisroel (Sol) Berger[1], Chicago

Translated from the Yiddish by Hannah B. Fischthal, PhD

Edited by Howard I. Schwartz, PhD

I thank you shtetele Mlynov, my dear shtetele in which I spent my childhood years, for giving me the opportunity to learn in your cheder, in your school, and in your study house. I left you on the eve of the first World War, when I fell into the huge melting pot of the United States of America. I have, however, sworn to never forget you.

I cannot forget: —

- The resounding, hearty outbursts during the Stolin Hasidic prayers in the Stolin prayer house…
- The rebbe's visit. We celebrated with a meal in the prayer house, and Hasidim grabbed the remnants of the rebbe's food.[2] As they repeated "L'chayim"[3] and started to dance, who could worry about the future? …
- The many thousands of petitions that were tearfully thrown into the holy box in the room at the cemetery[4] …
- The many Hasidim who came from faraway places and from Palestine.[5] Hasidim with their white socks, in their shiny kapotes and fur hats, celebrating in the Stolin prayer house, having meals there, and visiting the grave every year on the anniversary of the rebbe's death.
- The weeping and cries when someone in the family passed on, and the sad sounds of, "charity saves from death."[6]
- The meeting between bride and groom with their parents on the day of a wedding; the musicians, the entertainer, the wedding ceremony near the house of study.[7]
- The school assistant with his broad shoulders carrying the children to cheder.
- Itse the water carrier with two huge pails of water, and the yoke over his worn shoulders.

[Page 64]

- The Mlynov bathhouse. We used to ask Peysi the bath attendant for a small broom rubbed with fat; we would climb on the highest bench and scream out, "Padovi, another bucket!" We beat and rubbed and scraped our backs until they were red.[8] Afterwards we would go up to cool off in the ritual bath.
- The deep mud in Mlynov.
- The freezing winters, when our fingers "fell in love with" the doorknob when opening the door.
- The Halperin brothers with their tasty, imported products. The Count used to ride there with his two horses in tandem, one behind the other, and shop.
- The speaker with his sermons. The intellectuals swallowed every word. Once a Litvak came and gave a sermon using his "s" and his "oo" — who understood his language?[9]
- Peysi the ritual slaughterer. When he took the shofar into his hands during Rosh Hashana, the windows really trembled. He did not blow a single incorrect note.
- Spreading out fresh–smelling hay the night before Yom Kippur, and then flagellating ourselves with the "holy whip."[10]

- The many backs that were warmed in the winter at the study house oven.
- Chanting *maftir*[11] and praying at the eastern wall.[12] How many respectable men did not receive these honors?
- The outdoor scenes, when Passover paraphernalia was made kosher.[13]
- The pharmacist who prayed only during the high holy days.
- The small stores watching out for customers; their owners were running around somewhere creating interest-free loans.
- The sons of Aharon with their horses–and–britzkas,[14] which drove Polish functionaries to their appointed places.
- The tones of the organ and bells from the Christian church in the middle of the market.
- The pretty melodic folksongs which the peasants used to sing coming home from harvest.
- Walking to Mervits on the Sabbaths; the fair in the marketplace; the Polish doctor; the Mlynov Count with his estate; the beautiful river; the bridges; the post office; Pinkhasovitsh the lawyer; the Goldseker family; the butcher shop – – –

Translator's and editor's footnotes:

1. See the Mlynov website for the background on Sol and the Berger family that migrated to Chicago. – HS
2. It is an honor for Hasidim to take the rebbe's leftover remnants. – HBF
3. A toast: "To your health!" – HBF
4. It is customary to write *qvitlkeh*, petitionary notes, and place them at a rebbe's gravesite, so that he will intercede with heaven on the hasid's behalf. The Karliner-Stolin Rebbe has his ohel [resting place] in Mlynov. – HBF
5. Israel after 7 May 1948 – HBF
6. Chanted at funerals – HBF
7. For a detailed description of a wedding, see the essay in this volume by Sylvia Barditch-Goldberg.
8. The Russian bathhouse was like a sauna. The men would sweat and beat themselves with branches to improve circulation. Padovi was the name of the attendant who would pour heated water on the hot stones. – HBF
9. Litvaks, Jews from Lithuania, confuse the "s" and "sh" sounds. They also say "oo" while Ukrainian Jews say "i." This is a source of much humor. – HBF
10. Some Hasidim would flagellate themselves 39 times on their backs the night before Yom Kippur for atonement; they would use a special whip. – HBF
11. Reading of the haftorah in the synagogue (lessons from the prophets). – HBF
12. Jews pray facing east, under the assumption that they are facing Jerusalem. The most prestigious seats in the shtetl synagogues were those at the eastern wall; they were reserved for important, highly learned, and wealthy men, who paid for the privilege. – HBF
13. According to one Mlynov survivor memory, Passover dishes were made kosher for Passover by being buried between uses. They were dug up and cleaned for the holiday. – HS
14. A britzka was an open carriage with a foldable top over half of it. – HBF

[Page 65]

There Was Once a Shtetl Mlynov

by David Fishman, Baltimore

Translated from the Yiddish by Hannah B. Fischthal, PhD

Edited by Howard I. Schwartz, PhD

Maybe there is still a trace that can be found of our shtetl. If there is, it stands ashamed, weakened, and defiled from all the evil perpetrated there. No Jew is there anymore who can rekindle the *Ner Tomid*.[1] The Shabbat "*lekho dodi*"[2] and the weekday "vu rakhem"[3] are no longer heard there. The moon does not have any Jews to bless it every month when it first appears. The river, where even our fathers and grandfathers observed *Tashlikh*[4] — is also not there.

The pine tree forest, once the scene of the youth of Mlynov and Mervits, alive with songs and discussions and also love, is no longer there. And don't forget the weeping willow trees which provided the branches used during the Sukkot prayer service. Also remember the Mlynov shopkeeper with his fire pot, who used to sit, worried and waiting, for a good Christian customer. Remember the Mlynov market with its passengers going to Dubno (across from Brukhe-Batya's store). I am reminded now of the busy market fairs.

Nu, not only our religious Jews are gone, but also the non-believers, who used to, excuse me for saying it, desecrate the Sabbath. In general, our small-town boys with their dream-filled eyes, who used to look up to the large, wide world, are also gone.

The Christians in the villages cannot throw any more stones into Jewish sukkahs.

It is difficult to take in and to imagine that our Mlynov is really without Jews, really dead, deceased. I would like to know if even our sacred cemetery with the graves is still there.

Translator's and editor's footnotes:

1. A flame burning perpetually in the synagogue before the holy ark. – HBF
2. [Come my Beloved], a song in the Jewish liturgical service that welcomes the Sabbath. – HBF
3. [And He is compassionate] First two words of a request recited during everyday prayers. – HBF
4. An atonement ritual in which Jews write down their sins and throw the scraps of paper into the river on the first afternoon of Rosh Hashana. – HBF

[Page 66]

Culture, Education, and Social Life in the Small Town

Aaron (Berger) Harari[1], Merhavia

Translated and edited by Howard I. Schwartz, PhD with Hanina Epstein

After the First World War, when most of the residents returned from their locations of exile as refugees and the small town had recovered from its destruction — the house of Shulman[2] served as a cultural (tarbut) center in the town. This was a meeting house for all those seeking culture (tarbut). There was the library where they rehearsed plays and in a large-covered patio next to the house, performances were held.

A group of educated [persons], teachers and those engaged in culture

The teacher Reichman (top right), Shohet and his wife (front right), Miriam Maizlish (standing 2nd from right), Malcah Lamdan (standing 3rd from right), Dvorah Berger (standing left), Samuel Mandelkern (seated left), Clara the dentist (seated center)

Since all of them were absorbed and influenced by Russian culture, the language spoken was peppered with Russian, and most of the books in the library were in Russian, and a few in Yiddish; there was not a trace of Hebrew books. The club, that centered on the Shulman house, was far from Zionism; and those that shied away from Russian culture, in the club mentioned above, were forced to look for another hangout.

Very slowly a Zionist club crystalized which espoused Hebrew culture and at its center was Samuel Mandelkern.[3] A modern Hebrew school, "Tarbut" (Culture), was established. Many children, who previously studied in cheder, transferred to study in the school.

[Page 67]

They were led by an instructional system that was adopted in the schools of the cities and towns. They brought two teachers from outside. Jacob Eisenberg from Rovno (today – [surname] Eshed, in Ein Harod Meuchad[4]) and the teacher Penina from Varkovitchi. In addition, the local teacher was Malcah Lamdan, sister of the poet, Yitzhak Lamdan, z"l, and wife of S. Mandelkern.

Around this school, educational and cultural work was concentrated and flourished. In the evenings, there were lessons for adults, a foundation was put in place for a Hebrew library, and a choir was organized and conducted by Pesach Zutelman.[5] We organized parties in which students dressed up in costumes [drawn from] lives in the Land [of Israel] and choirs with songs from the Land [of Israel]. This was a shining period in the lives of the shtetl youth. The animating spirit in all these activities was again Samuel Mandelkern, without him nothing would have gotten started. He was a person of energy and his initiative had no limit.

I remember the day that the Balfour Declaration was celebrated. There was a large parade in the streets of the shtetl in which all strata of the people participated. The shop owners closed their shops, the artisans left their workshops, the women left their housework — and they all came out to the streets. At the head of the parade was a company of youth riding on horses with flags of blue-white in their hands.[6] Following them, marching in order, the choir, singing Hebrew songs, students from the school, and after them the bulk of the public. The gentiles came out to the street and with surprise watched the Jews in their Palestinian celebration. The chief of police, who was friendly with the local movers and shakers, supervised the order.

We celebrated nearly every Zionist and national event which took place with a very impressive appearance and a large participation. I also remember the banquet, that was put on for the dedication of the Hebrew University on Mount Scopus (Har HaTzofim).[7] This was organized in good taste, and participation included local government officials and honored individuals who were invited as well as educated gentiles. In addition to the gastronomic program, there was an art program that enchanted all those present.

To be sure, there were ups and downs in the cultural and educational activities. The Hebrew school sometimes closed and opened again, whether due to a lack of teachers or the small number of students. But the study of Hebrew continued all the time, even with a reduced class size.

In order to create the foundation for first grade (kitah aleph) [Samuel Mandelkern] had the idea to create a kindergarten that would serve as a natural transition to the school for the children and parents alike. Mlynov parents had never sent their children to kindergarten, and this was the first attempt in the shtetl. We had to make an intensive effort to convince the parents to send their children to the kindergarten. The parents first convinced to do so were few in number and had a relationship of some sort to Zionism and Hebrew culture. The rest of the parents from the regular folks, one by one, sent their children to the kindergarten; the idea enchanted them and they were convinced. A parental committee was chosen that joined us in attending to all the technical and organizational arrangements for the kindergarten. The female kindergarten teacher and the children together prepared the celebrations [lit.

"spirit"] of Hanukkah and Purim and this introduced vigor and life to the shtetl, which was entirely lacking sources of amusement and recreation.

[Page 68]

By the way, the female teachers that worked during the years of the kindergarten's existence and the teacher Zilberg — they had been educated by [the youth group], The Young Guard (Hashomer Hatzair).

For many years, a drama club existed in the shtetl, from the effort of and during the time of Samuel Mandelkern, which put on the best of Jewish repertoire. The club operated on a very high artistic level. All the people of the shtetl would come to the shows except the religious extreme and the elderly. The actors were of the same generation as Samuel Mandelkern, and when [Samuel and Malcah] married and Samuel made aliyah to the Land, we continued the tradition: Lipa Halperin, z"l,[8] Yehuda son of Eliezer,[9] and the writer of these lines. The income was dedicated to the goal of education and culture. Periodically, a drama troupe came from outside of town, and we contributed the organizational help required. Thus, there was a continuous series of plays and receptions.

With a group of youth, we attempted to organize an orchestra of wind instruments without borrowing. We bought new instruments and brought a Czech teacher from the Czech settlement of Maslianka[10] but the attempt failed. After a number of months, they were fed up with the effort and the instruments turned to junk.

Sport activities which the youth engaged in were: swimming, boating, volleyball, cycling, and ice skating. There was no group organized for the purposes of municipal sporting competition. Both Jews and gentiles, office workers and teachers, played volleyball. The playing field was on the bank of the beach, near the river. The beach was busy in summer with many of the youth, especially in the afternoons and the Sabbaths.

A "Tarbut" school during the festival of Lag B'Omer, 1919

Translator's and editor's footnotes:

1.   Aaron Harari was born Aaron Berger (1908–1984), one of five children of Wolf Berger and Golda (Kentor). Aaron played a leadership role in the Zionist youth group, Hashomer Hatzair, in the 1920s and participated in a training kibbutz (hachsharah) in Slonim, Russia before making aliyah in 1934 with the Planty group and settling in Kibbutz Merhavia. He later became a well-known expert on sheep breeding. On the history of the Berger family, see the Mlynov website.

2.   The Shulman house refers to the home of Tsodik Shulman (1863–1947) and his wife, Pearl Malka (Demb) (1865-1933). Tsodik was the nephew of the famous Kalman Schulman, a maskil and Hebrew writer whose work was significant in the development of modern Hebrew literature. Tsodik was recalled in family memories as being responsible for overseeing the Count's forest. The Shulmans had seven children, five of whom accompanied them in 1921 to Baltimore. The Shulman library was also remembered by Mervits-born, Benjamin Fishman, as the place where he was able to meet and court his future wife, Clara Shulman. On the history of the Shulmans, see the Mlynov website.

3.   The Hebrew sometimes is rendered in English as "Mandelkorn."

4.   The kibbutz Ein Harod split in the 1950s into two kibbutzim distinguished by those who supported Stalin loyalists and those who followed Ben Gurion and his preference for the US.

5.   Pesach Zutelman or Settleman migrated to Baltimore with the Shulman family and became Paul Shulman in the US.

6.   A precursor to the blue and white flag of Israel was made in 1891 for the Zionist movement. The basic design recalls the Tallit, the Jewish prayer shawl, which is white with black or blue stripes.

7.   The Zionist movement envisioned a Hebrew University in Palestine, and the dedication of the original stones took place on July 24, 1918.

8.   Lipa Halperin is a contributor to this volume. See his essay, "The Mill," 15–16.

9.   Referring to Yehuda Mohel. On the Mohel story, see Dani Tracz, Riva and Yehuda: *Life Story of Trancman, Mohel, Tracz and Ben-Eliezer Families*, 2015. Trans. from Hebrew by Lynda Schwartz. D.C.P. Haifa, Tel Aviv, Israel, 2017.

10.   The settlement has not been identified.

[Page 69]

The Youth Movement, "The Young Guard" (Hashomer Hatzair)

by Aaron (Berger) Harari[1], Chicago

Translated and edited by Howard I. Schwartz, PhD with Hanina Epstein

The initial establishment of "The Young Guard" (Hashomer Hatzair) in the small town was in the summer of 1920 by a young man from Rovne[2] by the name of Lemel Rosenfeld, who visited as a guest with the family of Chaim Berger. As himself a member of The Young Guard, he organized around him a number of friends his own age and he led them in activity; afterwards they continued on their own.

In the "nest,"[3] at that time there were two groups, one of older youth — ages 15–16, and the second younger, ages 12–13. The two groups were comprised of boys only. I belonged to the younger group, which numbered 10 boys. I remember the first meeting, that took place one evening in the classroom of the Hebrew school. David Maizlish, z"l, spoke to us and explained to us the essence of The Young Guard and its true ethical significance for Hebrew youth. His words kindled sparks in our hearts and breathed new life in us. A sacred trembling and an adult seriousness passed over us even though we were still young lads.

A "Hashomer Hatzair" nest in Mlynov in 1926[4]
Original courtesy of Dani Tracz (Issachar Mohel)

[Page 70]

This took place during the summer months as we gathered twice a week outside the shtetl on "the Greenik,"[5] a place so called by everyone, which was a small hill next to the Count['s estate], at the intersection of the dirt road to Dubno. The main activity that we engaged in was orderly exercises. We marched as a group according to military formation and according to the commands: "Listen," "Attention," "At Ease," "Left Face," "Forward March," "March in Place" and so forth, all the commands being given in Hebrew, and also the communications were conducted in Hebrew. We also sang songs of our homeland, and our greetings were: "Be strong" and "Be strong and courageous."

The summer passed, and the rainy days of fall began, and the activity outside completely ended. Occasionally, we would go into one of our houses on Shabbat afternoon, and the guides[6] would read a book or newspaper for us. But after a time, this ended too [because] the guides emigrated to Argentina,[7] and there was no organization in the shtetl or initiator who could do something to organize the youth. Samuel Mandelkern led a club to read the legends [aggadot] of Bailik and Rawnitzki.[8] Due to a lack of participants even this group did not last long. In the small town, a complete cultural wilderness prevailed. This situation continued for several years.

The sign reads: "Hashomer Hatzair nest in Mlynov, Poland.
The leadership during its deliberations."
Original courtesy of Dani Tracz (Issachar Mohel)[9]

During the summer of 1925, I wrote a letter to the headquarters of The Young Guard (Hashomer Hatzair) in Warsaw and I requested help to establish a nest for the movement. I received a shipment, that included diverse instructional booklets, but, to be honest, I had no idea how to implement the efforts of organizing the youth and what to do with them afterwards. As a first step, I decided to announce the matter widely. The publicity spot in the town was the synagogue. I made an announcement with the following approximate language:

[Page 71]

"The organization of 'The Young Guard' is organizing and all boys and girls who want to belong to the organization should come sign up with Aaron Berger."[10] I hung the announcement on the Sabbath eve (Erev Shabbat) in all three of the synagogues. During the week, dozens of youth signed up from all ages. I involved several of my friends in this effort and I split those who registered into two groups.

Every Shabbat we would go in a forest at a distance from the town. We sang songs of the homeland, played sports, read booklets about what was happening in the Land of Israel (Eretz Yisrael) and we felt a sense of unity among the youth. This is how the summer passed but since there was no place to gather [at the end of summer] the activity ceased.

In the spring of 1926, I took a course for leaders in Rovne, where I stayed for a week and met for the first time with dozens of guides from other nests, from the towns of Volyn and its various towns. I heard lectures on educational and organizational challenges from members of the principal leadership. My eyes were opened, and I returned home crammed full of knowledge and enthusiastic about the practical value that I had derived from the course.

I invited Yehuda Mohel (son of Eliezer) and suggested a working partnership to organize the nest again. I read to him the notes from the lectures I had heard, and with energy we once again tackled the work with the youth. Since we now had some guidance in our hands, we were able to accelerate momentum with greater confidence. We established a quorum of local guides, rented an apartment for the nest — and the activity began.

Group HaTikvah 1927
Original courtesy of Hagar Lipkin[11]

[Page 72]

The members of The Young Guard stood out in the small town with their special dress and scarfs symbolic of the movement. The activity started in the summer outside, under the dome of the heavens. We had designated places to meet: by the May 3rd monument,[12] the Greenik,[13] the hills on the way to Mervits, the "Young Guard Grove" across from the palace of the property owner [the Count], etc. In the winter, we gathered in the clubhouse, which was filled late into the night with youth who were joyful and happy, spoke pure Hebrew, and sang new songs of the Land of Israel (Eretz Yisrael).

We, the guides, visited periodically those nearby [groups] in Dubno, because from an organizational perspective, we belonged to the Dubno chapter of the movement. There we would meet with members and guides of the nest, and we learned from them the methods of doing educational work with the youth. In addition, we were visited by representatives from the principal leadership in Warsaw and representatives of the movement from the land of Israel (Eretz Yisrael). We participated in rotating national conventions in summer camps and in leadership meetings. All of these expanded our horizons and we saw ourselves as part of a flagship "Guard" group in Poland.

The text in the photo reads, "Festival of the flags, Passover, 5689 (April 1929)."

The nest carried the yoke of the Zionist and cultural activity on its shoulders. Apart from The Young Guard (Hashomer Hatzair), there was no other Zionist organizations or youth movements. Subsequently, "The Pioneer" (HeHalutz) was established, and all the graduates of The Young Guard became members automatically. A few members also joined who had not been members of "The Young Guard."

The nest organized parties and plays which many of the population attended and the income was dedicated to cultural activities. The youth in small towns like ours, which was enclosed in 4 walls [literally in "4x4" cubits], and was isolated from the outside world, found in the walls of the nest the information for what needed to be done in the land [of Israel] and first knowledge of Jewish culture.

[Page 73]

In group discussions, they covered material and subjects that were not taught in school. The guide would prepare by studying books before bringing his thoughts to the group. The youth would come to the library and exchange books, and a lively educational and cultural operation was noticeable among the youth.

As the nest reached its full momentum of activity, harassment began. From one side, the local rabbi, preached in his sermons in the synagogue against "The Young Guard" (Hashomer Hatzair) …. according to him, the educators [of The Young Guard] were leading the youth away from Judaism, mercy upon them. From the other side, the principal of Polish school forbade the students to belong to the nest and this was a very difficult period for the guides who carried the responsibility for the activity. But despite all the difficulties and persecutions, our activities continued, some clandestinely.

We sent a delegation, drawn from the best of our guides, to the Rabbi, and we tried to convince him that there was nothing harmful in our activity to the youth because we didn't teach against the religion. Of course, the rabbi didn't agree with us, but the visit and conversation reduced the severity of the attack a bit. Furthermore, we presented ourselves to Mr. Veinstock, who was influential with the local government and requested his intervention with the principal of the school on our behalf. Indeed, the persecutions from this side ceased.

Nest of "Hashomer Hatzair" – 1929.
Going away party for the aliyah of Yehuda Mohel.[14]
Original courtesy of Dani Tracz (Issachar Mohel)

* * *

The older mature members began steps towards fulfilment [of aliyah]. Some went to preparatory training (hachsharah) and dreamt of aliyah to the Land, and the nest made aliyah in purposeful bands. The first person to make aliyah from the nest was Yehuda Mohel. After him — Moshe Chizik (or Tzizik),[15] z"l, Moshe Teitelman (Tamari),[16] Tzipporah Holtzeker,[17] Rosa Berger.[18] Rachel Kipergluz ([married name] Kleeman), the writers of this essay, and others. With the aliyah of the senior guides to the Land [of Israel] and with the young guides going to preparatory training (hachsharah), a difficult setback befell the nest, and all activity was silent.

Most of the townsmen who are present today in the Land [of Israel] in the city or kibbutzim, were members of The Young Guard (Hashomer Hatzair) who had absorbed the culture of the youth movement. They surely remember the days and nights of their childhood and youth, which they spent in an atmosphere alive and animated, which gave them purpose in life and the [desire to] pursue the pioneering ambition.

From "Masada"

by Yitzhak Lamdan[19]

The chain is still not broken,
The chain still continues,
from father to child,
from bonfire to bonfire,
the chain still continues…
The chain is still not broken,
the chain still continues,

from night of Simchat Torah
to nights of Simchat Masada:
the chain still continues…

Thus danced our fathers;
one hand on a neighbor's shoulder,
the other holding a scroll of the Law–
a people's burden raised with love–
thus danced our fathers…

So let us dance;
one hand gripping the circle,
the second clutching the load of a generation,
a great, heavy book of sorrow–
so let us dance……

Translator's and editor's footnotes:

1. See the previous essay for Aaron Harari's biographical background. – HS
2. Today, Rivne, Ukraine. – HS
3. "Nest" (ken) is the Hebrew term for a Zionist group or club. Nest was used in the English to capture this original terminology. – HS
4. Aaron Harari, the author of this essay, is back row, 3rd from the left. Yehuda Mohel is in the back row, second from the right. – HS
5. The Hebrew here reads "Agreenik" but appears to be the same hill called "Greenik" in the photo of the young people standing on the hill on p. 158 in this volume. See also the essay in this volume, "My Hill," p. 30, by Moshe Teitelman, probably about the same hill, known by the young people as "Mount Sinai" and which held a special place in the life of the town's youth. – HS
6. The Hebrew term can be translated as either counselor, leader or guide. Guide seems most appropriate since counselor makes it sounds like a summer camp and does not seem to capture the serious goal of the activities.
7. The author's older brother, Kalman Berger, was among a group of Mlynov boys who made their way to Buenos Aires on the way to the US between 1923–1926. Other Mlynov young men who followed the same route included Frank Settleman, Samuel Goldseker, Julius Deming, and brothers, Morris and Isadore Wallace. On the Mlynov boys in Buenos Aires, see the Mlynov website.

8.   Hayim Nahman Bialik (1873–1934) was born in Volhynia and was a pioneer of modern Hebrew poetry. Bialik and Yehoshua Hana Rawnitzki (1859–1954) together published *Sefer Ha-Aggadah* ("The Book of Legends"), a compilation of legends from the Talmud.

9.   Yehuda Mohel is seated second from the right and Aaron (Berger) Harari is third from the left. The story of Yehuda Mohel is told by his son, Dani Tracz (Issachar Mohel) in *Riva and Yehuda: Life Story of Trancman, Mohel, Tracz and Ben-Eliezer Families.*

10.   Aaron Berger was the birth name of the author.

11.   Rosa Berger, front center, Rachel Shapovnik, middle row right, Chuna Goldseker, middle row, second from the right.

12.   May 3rd is a Polish national and public holiday that celebrates the declaration of the Constitution of 3 May 1791.

13.   See note 4.

14.   Yehuda Mohel is seated in the third row, center, with the white shirt. Aaron (Berger) Harari is in the same row, (third row, 4th person from the left). Others in row three: Moshe Chizik (or Tzizik) (Rosa's future husband) (3rd from left), Yehuda's sisters, Bayta Mohel (5th from left), and Dvorah Mohel (1st from right with dark tie). In row four standing: Rachael (Shapovnik) Givol (4th from left in dark dress), Aaron's sister, Rosa Berger (5th from left in white shirt and tie), Yaakov Mohel (Yehuda's brother) (2nd from right in dark shirt and white tie). Back row: Saul Halpern (3rd from right), and in second row from front: Yitzhak Gelberg (first on left).

15.   Moshe Chizik (also Tzizik) (1909–1959) made aliyah and eventually married Rosa Berger from Mlynov. He died prematurely of a snake bite.

16.   Moshe Tamari was born in 1910 as "Moshe Teitelman," in the town of Varkovytchi but his family moved to Mlynov to make a living and Moshe spent a good part of his youth growing up there. He contributed two essays to this volume, "My Hill" and "In the Presence of Yitzhak Lamdan." He became Moshe "Tamari" sometime after making aliyah in 1933 and wrote and published a number of books and stories in Israel. Moshe's father, Anshel, was an older brother of Nahum Teitelman from Mervits, who also published an essay in this volume. Moshe lost his parents and his brother in the liquidation of the Mlynov ghetto in October 1942.

17.   Tzipporah Holtzeker (1910–1986) was second eldest of twelve children of Yaakov and Rosa Holtzeker and made aliyah in 1933 with the Kibbutz group Wahlinia B and settled first in Rishon LeTzion and then Givat Keren Kayemet and eventually Kibbutz Negba. Most of her family was killed in the Shoah. A sister, Baila, and brother made aliyah and joined her in Palestine. Another brother, Hanoch, escaped the Mlynov ghetto liquidation, made his way to Palestine, but was killed defending Negba, in the War for Independence in May 1956.

18.   Rosa Berger (1910–1994) is the sister of Aaron (Berger) Harari, the author of this essay. She made aliyah in 1933 with the Planty Group and eventually married Moshe Chizik (or Tzizik) who also made aliyah from Mlynov.

19.   From Yitzhak Lamdan's poem, "Masada," from the part called Night Bonfire, section 3. Translation from Leon Yudkin, *Isaac Lamdan: A Study in Twentieth Century Hebrew Poetry*, p. 213. Ithaca: Cornell, 1971.

[Page 75]

_____

Jewish Farmers in Mlynov

by Aaron (Berger) Harari[1]

Translated and edited by Howard I. Schwartz, PhD with Hanina Epstein

Not many in Mlynov engaged in real agriculture. I knew only of my uncle Faivel and my father, z"l.[2] The two of them loved agriculture and found meaning in their life by fulfilling the commandment, "bring forth bread from the earth" [hamotzi lehem min haaretz].[3]

My uncle had a large vegetable garden that was spread out over an area of approximately 5 dunams,[4] as well as dairy cows. Our family also had dairy cows and in cooperation with my uncle we worked large fields that we rented them from the owners of the property in Smordva.[5] The fields we received needed first to be prepped for agriculture, by removing roots from the forest trees and burning shrubs, and bramble, and filing up ditches. My father and uncle thus invested much effort even before they were able to work the land. Afterwards, they grew wheat, barley and seeds for making oil. In addition, we had fields of hay for feeding the cows. These fields were harvested twice a year.

Batia, daughter of Faivel Berger, milking the cows
From the photos of A. Harari

My father and uncle would rise early in the morning, hurry through the morning prayers (shaharit), and go out to work. Most of the work — plowing, sowing and transporting — they did themselves, and only during the harvest and threshing season would they get help with hired workers. At the busy time, household members would be enlisted to help. During the summer, during free time from studies, I would work with the hay, hauling it, threshing it, and so forth.

[Page 76]

Nevertheless, working the leased land did not last many years. Once the owner of the property realized that the cultivated fields were producing a good crop, and there was apparently no contract in place related to working the land, he reclaimed the land and no longer leased them to us to be worked. Thus, we were left embarrassed by all the agricultural equipment that we acquired: threshing machines, plows, an [agricultural] harrow, sickles, scythes, and more. From that point on, the agriculture was reduced in favor of raising dairy cows only, and therefore they had to acquire an independent supply of hay which we bought from the owner's holdings for which we paid in hard cash. We also continued to grow potatoes on the land that we received in exchange for manure. In addition, my uncle continued to grow vegetables on the personal plot next to his house.

We would sell the milk to regular customers, who came daily to the house to get it. From the surplus milk, we would make butter and cheese. I remember how Father would awaken me every morning, before sunrise, in order to take the cows out to pasture. I would take a book to the pasture with me and prepare my lessons and return home before I went to school.

* * *

It is a pity Jews such as these did not at the time make aliyah to the Land [of Israel] and settle in some agricultural settlement (moshav) and invest their life energy here, instead of preparing the land for strangers….

During my visit to Mlynov in 1937,[6] my uncle, Faivel, implored me to try to help him make aliyah to the Land, so he could engage in agriculture here, which was his desire — but the matter was not realized.

Faivel Berger (center right), Wolf Berger (center left) – and their families[7]
Original courtesy of Zeev Harari

Translator's and editor's footnotes:

1. See above page 66, footnote 1, for Aaron (Berger) Harari's biographical background.
2. Aaron's father was Wolf Berger.
3. These are the words said during the blessing before eating bread.
4. A measure of land area used in part of former Turkish empire including Israel, where it is equal to about 900 square feet.
5. 12 km from Mlynov.
6. In the next article, Aaron relates his trip to Mlynov was in 1938. His son believes it took place the winter of 1937–1938.
7. Part of Aaron's family who perished in the Shoah. In the list of martyrs, p. 431, Faivel Berger is also called Sharga. His wife's name is Matil. His daughter, Batia, is seated front right. She was the one milking the cow on the previous page. Wolf's wife, Golda, seated left, and his daughter, Hannah.

[Page 77]

Visit to Mlynov in 1938

Aaron (Berger) Harari[1]

Translated and edited by Howard I. Schwartz, PhD with Hanina Epstein

Only four years passed since I made aliyah to the Land [of Israel], and what a great chasm was created between me and the people whom I had left in the town. What a different feeling I had getting off the bus and passing down the main street. When the shop owners saw me, they indeed stared at me with great curiosity. In truth they were the same Jews — but in my eyes they seemed different. And when I met acquaintances, close and dear friends, I no longer had a common language with them. Every one of them was odd to me, as if I was hurled into another world … their gait, their ways of speaking, and their activities, aroused pity in me. I believe it was not from excessive arrogance that I felt this way but rather from an expression of an internal transformation that occurred in my personality during the 4 years of my acclimation in the Land [of Israel], with a full and intensive life in work, in the workers' movement, in the kibbutz, in agriculture and in defense. All of these left their mark on my soul and character such that I was not able to find my place in the suffocating social and cultural atmosphere that I found in the small town.

The few older members of The Young Guard (Hashomer Hatzair) were waiting for their aliyah and the nest no longer existed. The youth sought out questionable entertainment spots, and the older ones spent their time in the billiard hall, that had been opened in the home of Shimon Schechman.[2] Out of curiosity, I visited the clubhouse mentioned above and I was shocked by how the youth were spending their time. No cultural activity was conducted in the town and also no one was initiating any activity.

My visit aroused curiosity in the town. I was, in fact, the second visitor from the Land [of Israel] after Yitzhak Lamdan. In personal meetings and conversations, I was asked a great deal about the Land, and I was talking nonstop. Even the gentiles who recognized me from earlier days came to visit me and were interested in Palestine — the Jewish State — and the educated among them asked pertinent questions.

My father,[3] may his memory be a blessing, insisted I go with him to the synagogue on the Sabbath –although he knew that I was not in the habit of praying. To prevent my being called to the Torah, which made me uncomfortable, I refused him. In the end, I agreed with an explicit condition, that before the reading of the Torah portion for the week, I would leave. It was a great honor for my father that I accompany him to the synagogue. Many of the homeowners grabbed my hand with the greeting "Peace be upon you" (shalom aleichem) and grabbed my coat and smelled it, perhaps there is something special from the smell of the Land of Israel (Eretz Yisrael) … Father prayed from a prayerbook bound in a fancy olive wood cover that I brought from the Land, and many looked at him with envy.

[Page 78]

After that, I indeed regretted what had happened — because what, really, did it matter to me to go up to the Torah, to be honored with the "maftir" and to read the haftarah in the Sephardic congregation with the cantillation notes?[4] … Then my father would have been radiant with joy and happiness. Therefore, I had regret about this, but what was done couldn't be undone.

That same Shabbat, father invited his friends to the house for "Kiddush"[5] and he honored them with wine from the land of Israel, "Carmel Mizrahi"[6] wine, which I brought from the Land and with cake from the Kibbutz, that I received as provision for the journey which had held up in spite of the bumps along the way. As is the custom in small towns when a guest comes, friends and relatives send "treats" (mishloah manot) to him at the house. That same first Sabbath of my visit, we received as gifts: bottles of liquor, cakes, various pastries, and especially one gift, which is worth mentioning: the children of the ritual slaughterer (shochet),[7] Eliezer Mohel, sent a traditional Jewish stew (cholent) which included stuffed entrails and stomach.

The goal of my visit was to help a sister, of one of the Kibbutz Merhavia members, make aliyah. Since I had come on an individual passport, and I had Land-of-Israel[8] citizenship, I would be able to add her to my British passport via a fictious marriage and bring her to the Land without a certificate,[9] which in those days was hard to come by. Out of fear of bad luck and from what people would say, I told a different story entirely. Most in the small town knew that I was engaged in raising sheep in the Land [of Israel], and [understood] that my visit was related to business involving sheep and wool. My parents, in their naivete, also believed this story. Until one day clear day, I revealed to them the secret. I told them that in the coming days a young woman would visit in our home, and she was the sister of a member of my kibbutz, and it had fallen on me to help her make aliyah to the Land of Israel, but that there was nothing between us. To carry out the plan, I needed to arrange a fictitious wedding. My parents had a hard time understanding the meaning of a fictitious wedding. In their view, there was only one special meaning of a marriage: bride and groom, in-laws, with rabbi under the canopy (chuppah) and betrothal (kiddushin).[10] I struggled a great deal until I succeeded in explaining this to them. They only relaxed when I said that all this would not take place in our shtetl but by the British ambassador in Warsaw.

My visit home continued to bring my parents satisfaction. In the evening, special friends visited as well as neighbors. Parents, who had children in the Land [of Israel], came to ask about their well-being, who thought, in their innocence, that the Land of Israel (Eretz Yisrael) is a "colony," and everyone lived together, and I met, at least daily, with all of them. From the stories I told about the Land of Israel, what made an impression on them was that rain didn't fall from Passover to Hanukkah, [that] herbage could be harvested almost all year long for the cows, that oranges were cheaper than other necessities, and so on and so forth.

I had the feeling that this was my first and last visit to the town and I said to myself, it is worthwhile immortalizing the scenery and the different typical characters. I had with me a cheap kind of camera, that I borrowed from a member of my kibbutz, from which it was difficult to get photos deserving to be so-called, due to the winter weather and my own inexperience with photography.

[Page 79]

To my bad luck, it was necessary to convince people that I was interested in them, in all the ways I could think of so they would let me photograph them — but I was not always successful.

I found many changes in the town. New paved roads and much work on fortifications going on all around, as defense against the Soviet Union. Therefore, the many foreigners involved in these fortifications, wandered around in the streets.

Herschel "Duetino,"[11] drawer of water, near the house of Yaakov Holtzeker[12]
Photo of A. Harari, 1938

Translator's and editor's footnotes:

1.   See page 66, footnote 1, for Aaron Harari's biographical background.

2.   This probably refers to Shimon Schechman, son of Noach Moshe Schechman and Faiga Beshe Wolk. A photo of S. Schechman appears on page 220 of this volume. The list of martyrs, p. 433, lists a Shimon Schechman, his wife Pesia and daughter Sara. Shimon was one of five children of Moshe and Faiga. Shimon's father, Noach Moshe Schechman, was a brother of Joseph Schuchman who came to Baltimore in August 1913. Shimon's brother, Shlomeh (Shlomo) Schechman, survived the war with the partisans after being shot and wounded several times. He later met and married Liza Sabirowicz in Lutsk. Their son, Morris Schechman, was born in 1945 in a train on the way to the displaced persons camp Föhrenwald. They joined relatives first in Waterbury, Connecticut before moving Baltimore to join their Schuchman relatives there.

3.   Aaron's father was Wolf Berger. See the previous essay describing his farming efforts.

4.   The maftir is the last person called up to say the blessing over the weekly Torah portion and who then reads the designated selection from the Prophets, called the "haftarah," which is sung with cantillation notes.

5.   A blessing over the wine to sanctify the Sabbath.

6.   Carmel Mizrahi was an older name of the Carmel Winery, the largest winery in Israel. Two of its wineries were established in 1888 by Baron Benjamin Edmund de Rothschild.

7.   One who is trained to slaughter an animal properly according to a prescribed method so the meat is kosher.

8.   It was still Palestine at this point under the British Mandate.

9.   Jewish immigration to Palestine was limited by the British and one had to be issued a certificate in order to legally immigrate.

10.   The first stage of the Jewish wedding.

11.   Possibly a reference to the word "duet" in Hebrew, Yiddish or Polish since he carries a pail on each side suspended from wood across his shoulder.

12.   There were at least two Yaakov Holtzekers/Goldsekers in town who were related. A photo on page 245 of this volume shows a Jacob Goldseker with a large family that included several children who made aliyah in the 1930s and a son Hanoch who survived the liquidation. There was also another Yaakov Hotlzeker /Goldseker (son of Moshe, son of Yankel), who survived the War in the Red Army, and contributed an essay later in this volume called, "My Hometown Mlynov."

[Page 80]

Stoliner Hasidism in Mlynov

by Sylvia Barditch – Goldberg

Translated from the Yiddish by Hannah B. Fischthal, PhD

Edited by Howard I. Schwartz, PhD

Reb Yitskhok Staroste[1]

As is known, Jews from Volhynia used to be Hasidim. They voted Hasidic because Hasidism ruled Volhynia.

In the town of Mlynov, the Hasidim followed a few rebbes. The rebbes would come on occasion to visit the shtetl, and the Hasidim would regularly travel to their rebbes. The largest number of Hasidim in Mlynov were drawn to the Stoliner – Karliner *Tsadik*.[2] Among them was my grandfather, Reb Yitskhok Staroste,[3] as he was called in Mlynov. A handsome, erudite Jew, and an expert in music, he was one of the distinguished members of the community in the last century in Mlynov. He was also known and respected in the surrounding areas.

Reb Yitskhok Staroste

[Page 81]

Reb Yitskhok was a strongly passionate Stoliner Hasid. Even when he was a father of six children, he would travel to the rebbe in Stolin for holidays, leaving his family alone. Returning home, Reb Yitskhok would relate stories about his rebbe, about the miracles he had performed, and about the rebbe's celebrations. He would talk for a long time about his stay in the rebbe's court. Hasidim listened to Reb Yitskhok and copied him; they also traveled to the rebbe to drink knowledge from the righteous source.

Reb Yitskhok was additionally blessed with an additional gift of a wondrous voice and the ability to share emotion in prayer; his audience loved it when he would lead them in the prayer service. From Lutsk and Mizoch he would be invited to lead during the Days of Awe[4] as an intercessor for the community. Reb Yitskhok, with all his energy and feelings, prayed for the people and sang the melodies of Rebbe Arele Karliner and his son, of blessed memory.[5]

That is how Reb Yitskhok lived in his Mlynov: quietly, Hasidic, and satisfied with his God-given blessings.

When Reb Yitskhok married off his oldest daughter Basye,[6] he took his son-in-law Yekhiel to his home to live. He took him to the Stolin *shtibl*,[7] and afterwards he also took him along to his rebbe for the holiday.

Reb Yekhiel was strongly inspired by the Stoliner rebbe and became one of his devoted Hasidim for all of his years.[8]

Reb Arele Karliner's *yortsayt*[9] in Mlynov

Mlynov had the honor of having the gravesite where the bones of the famous *Tsadik* Reb Aharon rested. His name was Reb Arele from Karlin,[10] the grandson of Reb Aharon the Great, who was one of the students of the *Magid*[11] Reb Dov-Ber from Mezritsh and Rovne. On his grave was an *ohel*,[12] a grave for a *tsadik*, which drew thousands of Hasidim every year so that they could be inspired by and be alone with the remains of their *tsadik* – – until the Nazi extermination. The old Hasidim Reb Avrom Holtse's and Reb Yitskhok Leyb took care that the *ner – tomid*[13] was never extinguished.

From my grandfather Reb Yitskok, I heard what righteous old men related about his passing:

[Page 82]

Once, after Shevuos, the *tsadik* came to Mlynov, and as usual, stayed with Reb Chaim Leml's. The rebbe spent about a week in the shtetl. He greeted the Hasidim, who came to welcome him and have the honor of his blessing. The Hasidim would incidentally pay money according to their circumstances, as it was done. In the shtetl there was a great excitement from the many Hasidim who came and stayed in practically all the houses because of the *Tsadik's* visit.

When the rebbe was ready to depart from the shtetl, he ordered his carriage harness. As soon as he went out of the room — the sky became cloudy. The *tsadik* turned back, calling out, "My sky became cloudy; the time has come." He prayed, confessed his sins, and went to bed. It did not take long until he was taken away to God and his angels. A commotion followed immediately, and the shtetl was wrapped in mourning. Telegrams were quickly dispatched to the rebbe's court and his family. A large funeral was ordered with a memorial speech.

Many legends are told by the Karlin-Stolin Hasidim about this funeral.

I remember my visit as a child to my grandfather Reb Yitskhok in the days of Reb Arele's yahrzeit,[14] which falls on the 17th day of the month of Sivan. The young rebbe from Stolin arrived with God's angels; they stayed in my grandfather's house. At sunrise we started to go to the grave of the *tsadik*. We sang psalms, and we wrote notes, in which we expressed requests and pitiful appeals. Among the mourners were also Jewish mothers who cried and prayed. People came and people left the shtetl. We sat, telling stories about signs and wonders of the *tsadik*, which were true. The belief and faith among the Hasidim was so huge, that even non-Jews were affected and influenced by the Jewish *tsadik*.

While talking, they would drink a little liquor and have a bite to eat. Afterwards they went again to the *ohel* until it was time to go back home. All departed with the certainty that the honor of the *tsadik* would be helpful, and that their requests would be realized.

Is the *ohel* still on the *tsadik*'s grave? – – Who knows!

Translator's and editor's footnotes:

1. Reb is a form of address, similar to Mr., used with a first name. Reb Yitskhok has the honored Russian title of "Staroste [старосте]." According to the *Internet Encyclopedia of Ukraine*, "In the Russian Empire the village starosta was the head of … the village community. He was for three years by the village assembly." See http://www.encyclopediaofukraine.com. – HBF

2. A righteous, holy man – HBF Also a term for a Hasidic rebbe who had a court. – HS

3. Sylvia is writing about her grandfather, Icik Ferteybaum, whom she used to visit in Mlynov. See Sylvia's other essay in this volume, "A Wedding in Mlynov," describing one such visit to her grandparents during the festival of Shavuot. The family name Ferteybaum became Teitelbaum in the US when the family migrated. See "The Story of Sylvia Barditch Goldberg," on the Mlynov website. – HS

4. The 10 holy days between Rosh Hashona and Yom Kippur, when Jews pray for forgiveness and the blessings of a new year. – HBF

5. To enjoy hearing an audio clip of a Stoliner nigun [melody], see https://yivoencyclopedia.org/article.aspx/Karlin – Stolin_Hasidic_Dynasty. Click on "See Media Related to this Article."

6. Basia is Sylvia's mother. – HS

7. Hasidic house of prayer – HBF

8. Sylvia's father, Yekhiel Borodocz, immigrated to Baltimore in 1910 where he became Isidore Barditch. – HS

9. The anniversary of someone's death – – HBF

10. Aharon II Perlov of Karlin (1802–1872). During his rule, Karlin-Stolin Chasidism experienced the "height of its growth and popularity" in Lithuania and Volynia. Nadler, Allan. "Karlin – Stolin Hasidic Dynasty." *YIVO Encyclopedia of Jews in Eastern Europe* 17 August 2010. 16 July 2020 see https://yivoencyclopedia.org/article.aspx/Karlin – Stolin_Hasidic_Dynasty. – HBF

11. Preacher; Dov-Ber was "the foremost leader within Hasidic circles after the death of the Ba'al Shem Tov in 1760." Green, Arthur. "Dov Ber of Mezritsh." *YIVO Encyclopedia of Jews in Eastern Europe*. October 27, 2010, 15 July 2020 see https://yivoencyclopedia.org/article.aspx/Dov_Ber_of_Mezritsh. – HBF

12. A structure, usually a small building, on an important person's gravesite. – HBF

13. Eternal light. – HBF

14. The annual ritual after the loss of loved ones to remember and commemorate them. – HS

[Page 83]

Selected Poems

by Yitzhak Lamdan[1]

Translated and edited by Howard I. Schwartz, PhD with Hanina Epstein

Internal Turmoil[2]

You grew exceedingly old and slowed down,
good father, how deep in you is the poignant sadness of plowing season, but you are mute
about it!
My throat is choked up, no word is on my tongue,
but I make my face merry, against its will, ha, I make it smile.

My eyes are clouded with tears and my lips are forbidden to smile,
Because of this I know: after years of much suffering,
minimizing reconciliation, downplaying the countenance of fate,
the father looks forward in his heart to the coming visit of his son

In the end, I merited [a visit][3].… [after] twelve years and more…
Now tell, my son, every little discrete detail…
Your letters were always short: "Praise God, hello"— and that's it …
Now let me merit hearing everything at length.

Tell me about your life in Eretz Yisrael there
Is it really good to you and are you happy in your portion?[4]
And I become talkative, I tell him the following:
"It is good for me there, Abba. It is good for me, very good!"

How could I do otherwise for father, loaded with grief,
expecting now, from his son, relief and consolation?
Will I expound on the part of our life, that is hard and very bitter?
That is not dripping with honey and not spread with butter.[5]

Should I say that the doorpost of this journey
has confined and restrained me
with wretched love, even great despair?
Because like a stumbling gazelle, I was caught in the brambles of the scenery
whose sky is copper and whose earth is ablaze

Shall I speak of the appointed wagon, weighted with the burden of the generations,
which near the edge the abyss advances with a heavy burden?

Should I speak about my homeland, lacking the loving caress of a mother,
who gives her child a breast depressed and lonely.

[Should I speak] of the small number of fists, closed tightly with anger and bitterness,
which knock on the locked gate, sealed for a long time[6]
or the gloomy cavern of life, full of fear and darkness-
the dwelling of alchemists with a vision of a daring rebellion?[7]

Should I speak of the great daydream that was a swamp
that swarms with little fish that crisscross with much yearning?
About the murky waters of dispute, with no sail or mast,
the rocky disputes that shatter the hopes of babes?

Should I speak of the lack of rest that follows me like a shadow
and that my path was thwarted as I came and went,
past the concealed threat (which I will always see![8])
the tearing of the silver screen,[9] between all that is there and here?

Am I able to tell of it all, to rip away the mask of a smile
To shout out[10] a man's truth, embarrassed in the middle of his way:
"How great is the burden on his back, the burden of your son,
I am not able to carry it, my father, nor do I dare remove it!"

My father's look cleaves to me, thirsty for a bit of illumination.
I know: to lighten his burden, my depressed father expects me to say something
And my face restrained with a smile, my lips forced to speak,
"My situation is good, my father, things are good with me, very good."

[Page 84]

In a Boat Torn to Pieces[11]

Father,
Given that you don't know, ha, you don't know
where the boat of your son was flung, on the frenzied waves
if you only knew ….

[Page 85]

The sea didn't guard your blessing which you delegated to me.
since I forgot the prayer for a journey which you taught me
and now –
Broken are my oars which cause trouble at the opening to the sea route
and with uncooperative hands shaking opposite the shore: "Not this, Not this"– –
The sails are torn which were spread
before the sky's four winds
I blessed my ship which is torn to pieces, I will kneel
but I won't pray,[12]

Because it is all the same, whether sea or dry land–
The arm of the mast is broken, reduced to nothingness
Next to my despairing eyes – – –

Lost Diamond[13]

The diamond of your devoted tears, father,
that you set in my heart at separation,
as a good luck charm for me along the way
Alas, even this is lost!
Because the waves consumed my entire heart
along with your diamond tears – –
And where, father, will your diamond go and land,
will the depths of the sea
dredge it up?
There are no fishermen by the shore anymore. The storm made
them flee…
The markets are empty on the eve of the Sabbath,
And the others who honor the Sabbath
they too have to take up a collection
and who from the deep waters of the sea, will dredge up the
diamond?
Whither will it go and reach,
if your son doesn't know how to protect it?

Without Shabbat[14]

In palaces[15] destroyed,
the hand of charity has disappeared,
The details of the past harps are hidden,
And music was stolen from my ears –
The music of your playing:
"Peace be upon you ("shalom aleichem"), angels of the Sabbath, angels of peace!" [16]
Father, Father, the angels of peace have not visited my home.
The claws of the profane tear through the window of my holy pupils:
Sabbath candles– –
From dark holes they watch over the world of orphans[17]
thirsty for rest, and dressed in rags[18] –
Like me, orphans of the world, like me,
And will the angels of peace bring me baskets of rest
And a gift of mercy to an orphan?
Where is a mother who will light the Sabbath candles for him,
wash his head of unkempt hair,
And change his filthy garments?
Along their paths, convoys are wandering lost
and seeking the Sabbath:
Where, oh, where is the mother of mercy who gathers the wanderers of night

to a dwelling of rest?
Where is that purple robe of her kingdom[19] whose edges covers
our nakedness shivering from the cold?
There is no answer to the night wanderers and no gathering,[20]
And I will advance in their steps[21]
On my neck – arms always bent
and its[22] Kiddush[23] [sanctification] on my mouth–
for the Sabbath that is assembled – –

[Page 86]

My Days and My Nights

And how do the days and nights pass for you, my son?
In the words of your letters, I read
Alas, father, come let me tell you
My days and my nights –
The wounds in the body of the afflicted generation
Open wide their mouths and spit out blood with a roar
when there is no cure– –

[Page 87]

With cloth flags I bandaged myself and new synagogue curtains
And it was made into a bandage to heal
The greats of the generation have been weakened with pain
And the future problems have been dripped on them
But there is no healing for them—
And with what, father, shall we close up the opening to these wounds
without screaming?
I was drugged by the moments of youth, and the youth–
a gleaning dropped on the ground and its mercy to the poor who go upon her,
[24] _
before me a caravan is rolling and behind me a fence is found[25]
(from a small charitable penny to the distant dinar
the delight of a woman) [26] – –
one by one I will gather the scattered youth
and their open wounds I will close up
and their roar will cease for a moment, and afterwards –
with spitting bunches will be discharged with contempt for their despicable
healing
And they will be ashes of a blaze a roaring that arises anew– –

* * *

And what father, can you fix for my days and nights
The wounds in this body of the afflicted generation
Which open wide their mouths and spit out blood with a roar
for which there is no cure? – –

For Forgiveness[27]

And where, father, have I gone, alas, where am I
Is the path to God, is it to the house of prayer
Behold you know!–
The hand of night is heavy, and the threat is pressing my eyes,
And I forgot how to say Shema[28] …
And the fingers of Tishei[29] knock on my window
And I am alone and impoverished, without a mezuzah[30] …
Father, father, give your lamp to me–
I will get up and go to Selichot[31] – – –

Editor's footnotes:

1.   Yithak Lamdan was born "Itzik Yehuda Lubes" in Mlynov in 1899. After the civil wars that followed WWI, when his parents' home was destroyed and his brother killed, Lamdan made aliyah to Palestine in 1920 where he became a well-known poet, particularly for his poem, "Masada." The source and date of the selections published here is not provided. However, all of them speak from a place of anguish and lost hope and appear to recall the difficult early years when the Lamdan was living in Palestine. Touching in particular is the imagined conversation with his father whom he has left back in Mlynov and whom he had finally come to visit. The translators want to acknowledge that this poetry is particularly difficult to translate with its metaphoric nature and built-in ambiguity.

2.   This poem is about a boy who returns to see his father and his dilemma about how revealing and honest he should be in answer to his father's questions. We know the author, Yitzhak Lamdan, went back to his hometown Mlynov and saw his father in 1932. This visit is described in the essay in this volume by Moshe Teitelman called "In the presence of Yitzhak Lamdan in Mlynov," pp. 32–37. It is possible to read this poem of Lamdan as a reflection on that visit.

3.   According to the Teitelman's essay about Lamdan's visit, Lamdan was not able to come back to Mlynov for a period of time because Mlynov had been part of Russia when he left and had become part of Poland when he wanted to return. Polish authorities would not issue a passport or visa for a period of time.

4.   The expression "happy in your portion" has traditional resonances and is a possible allusion to Pirke Avot 4:1, which says "Who is rich? One who rejoices in his portion."

5.   An allusion to Exodus 3.8 which describes the land as one of "milk and honey."

6.   Possible reference to the British reducing the flow of immigration to Palestine in the 1930s.

7.   Possible reference to thoughts about rebelling against the British.

8.   Possibly an allusion to his brother's death during WWI.

9.   Possible reference to a large movie screen and the ripping up of the beautiful images of life in Palestine on the big screen.

10.   The Hebrew term here is not recognized in this form and may be the poet's creation from the Hebrew word sa'ak meaning to shout.

11.   Like the first poem, this poem probably also alludes to the hardship Lamdan suffered making his way to Palestine or his early years there. The torn apart ship represents his aliyah or the hardship of living in Palestine in the period he arrived.

12.   The poem ironically contrasts the blessing which his father gave him and he forgot, with the blessing he is uttering here to save his life. Though he kneels, he won't pray indicating he has lost faith in traditional devotion.

13.   The lost diamond appears to be a metaphor for the keepsake given by a parent to a child and may allude to the tradition of Judaism itself that is handed from a father to a son.

14.   Lamdan is here reflecting on the absence and loss of Sabbath from his life in the secular, non-religious life he is living in Palestine. The poem alludes to a person coming home from the synagogue on the Sabbath eve, when the poem Shalom Aleichem is sung, the words of which welcome the angels who accompany a person home. The liturgical poem was written by mystics.

15.   A possible allusion to the mystical concept of the palaces of the King of Kings who is alluded to in the Shalom Aleichem poem.

16.   A partial quote from the poem Shalom Aleichem. The words have been altered slightly. A number of other words from the liturgical poem appear throughout this poem which despairs about getting help from the angels of peace who accompany a person home on the Sabbath.

17.   Lamdan thinks of himself and his generation as orphans since he and they left parents behind in the shtetl.

18.   A description of what life is like without the day of rest, the Sabbath.

19.   Using royal imagery for the Sabbath, the queen.

20.   Night wanderers are those who don't have the light from the Sabbath candles and appears to refer to those in the Yishuv.

21.   Possible allusion to the stems of goblets used for drinking wine on the Sabbath. The word for stem and legs is the same.

22.   The masculine possessive "his sanctification" makes it appear that the blessing is not for the Sabbath which is gendered feminine. What is being sanctified is ambiguous, perhaps intentionally so.

23.   Kiddush is the name of the blessing over wine said before the Sabbath meal.

24.   Apparent reference to the custom that the gleanings that fall from a reaper's hand or sickle should be left for the poor, as described in the Mishnah Tractate Pe'ah. An analogy seems to be with the days of youth.

25.   The sentence seems to imply he is following or being pulled forward by those ahead of him and there is no turning back to life in the shtetl from which he came.

26.   The intent seems to be that the poet doesn't have money but he has the love of a woman.

27.   The Hebrew word for forgiveness is Selichot, the same word used as the name of such prayers of forgiveness said during the Days of Awe.

28.   The prayer "Hear O Israel" which is a centerpiece of the evening and morning prayers.

29.   The month in which fall the Jewish Days of Awe including the Day of Atonement.

30.   Here referring to a mezuzah that traditional Jews affix to the doorposts of their house to commemorate God's activity in Egypt.

31.   Communal prayers for forgiveness said during High Holidays and Jewish fast days. Traditionally they are said between midnight and dawn.

[Page 88]

———————————————

Impressions and Memories

by Moshe Iskiewicz (Isakovich), Haifa[1]

Translated from the Yiddish by Hannah B. Fischthal, PhD

Translated and edited by Howard I. Schwartz, PhD with Hanina Epstein

To the memory of my dear parents, who were tragically killed in the Shoah in Mlynov.

I remember in our tiny town the impoverished residents and houses; every path and every garden is inscribed in my memory despite my being barely a lad. The images of their faces are engraved in my memory, as I saw them with my own eyes through the windows of our house which faced the narrow alley, "Hagasel."[2] I used to watch how most of the Jews of the town would lace up their legs with cumbersome boots [on the way] to the study house, during the early morning hours of cloudy days, full of cold and snow, some walking hastily because time was pressing, others walking at a relaxed pace and even with a certain indifference. Every one of them had a gloomy and sad look on their face, their livelihoods being the main worry on their minds. There were also some, whom I called "righteous ones" (tzadikkim) or "the 36ers" (the lamed vav [niks]),[3] who had almost no interest in what was around them. They would walk in early morning to the worship of the Creator with a joyful countenance. They were calm and all their thoughts were directed to matters of the above.

I also remember how those Jews would in fact change their appearance on the Sabbath and holidays, as if they unloaded the burden of the world and an atmosphere of festivity and joy encompassed them. But after the "three meals" of the Sabbath, and the Havdalah,[4] a changed feeling returned to them. A new week began and again the same worries and problems. Today all this belongs to the distant past. The final solution came, and all was destroyed. There are no Jews any longer in Mlynov, only the mass grave remains in the valley of death, along the way to Mervits.

I remember also the youth before WWII, the days of their childhood and adulthood. My dear boyfriends and girlfriends were killed in the midst of their lives. Remember their advancement in educational "ulpanim"[5] of our shtetl, a place they spent most of their time, and perhaps all their time, where they began the cheder[6] of Rabbi Neta which took place in the kitchen, around the thick stove, sitting on low benches. We absorbed the aleph-bet (the Hebrew ABCs), amidst the daily arguments with his wife Perel, may she rest in Eden.

I remember too in the autumn days, when the streets of Mlynov were covered with a swampy mud, we would be carried on the back of the teacher's assistant ("bayhelfer")[7] and he would transport us across the mud in his giant boots.

And from the cheder [we transferred] to our rabbi, Ben Tzion [Gruber],[8] z"l, to learn Talmud.

[Page 89]

We did not easily digest the endless debate with no end between the House of Hillel and the House of Shammai, and the misdeeds of the ox of Shimon and Rueben.[9] And the Rabbi did not excel in pampering his students much and more than once we felt the slap of his hand. All of this was after we returned from our studies in the Polish school, where the teachers did not excel at sympathy for their Jewish students; there were also many disputes between us and especially the Ukrainian students.

I will point out also the names of the teachers with whom the students felt enjoyment studying. They were our teacher Motel Chizik (Tzizik), z"l,[10] and the teacher and educator Ben Tzion Gruber, z"l.[11] The first excelled in teaching Tanach, and he was the first who implanted the yearning and love for our land in us through his interesting explanations. I would say, we were "like dreamers"[12] for all knowledge that came out of his mouth about our great past and all its manifestations. I remember him — his short stature, with a cigarette in his mouth, he would smoke, and smoke and…cough.

And last but not least, our teacher and educator, Ben Tzion Gruber, z"l, from Mervits, who roamed to far-off Odessa to learn in a well-known Hebrew high school (gymnasium). He was not only a great teacher, but also, in essence, an outstanding educator to his students, whom they totally venerated. I remember he dressed meticulously, walking stooped with his walking stick and all of him evoking honor.

Winter in the shtetl
From the photos of A. Harari

And we, the youth, reached adulthood. Suddenly we stood at the crossroads. Each and every one of us began to seek his path in life, some turned to handicrafts, others to commerce, and some continued their studies. And then, like thunder on a clear day, the Shoah came and severed the branches of the tree. Our tiny town is still there, but most of her Jewish residents were slaughtered. A few returned after the suffering and hardships from [their hiding places in] the forests, from the bunkers and the Russian wilderness. A few isolated brands of wood remained [after the fire][13] who can console us.

And perhaps our sole consolation is that we were fortunate to establish the State of Israel.

Translator's and editor's footnotes:

1.	Moshe Iskiewicz (also spelled Isakovich) was one of four children born to Eliezer and Chaya / Faiga Iskiewicz and the only one of his family who was not killed in the Shoah. The four siblings were: Shlomo (1921–1942), Raizel (1927–1942), Szeindel (1935–1940), and Moshe, the author of this essay. Two photos of the family appear on p. 464 of this volume and another of his father "Leazar" on p. 477. According to the list of martyrs in this volume (p. 431), his brother Shlomo was missing after the battle of Stanlingrad in August 1942. The Yad Vashem records filled out by Moshe provide some additional information. Moshe's father, Eliezer, born in 1896, was the son of Sheindel and Shlomo Iskiewicz and was a textile merchant. Moshe's mother, Chaya Faiga, was also born in 1896, part of the large Grin family in Mlynov. Her parents were Leib and Dvorah Grin. It is unknown at the time of this writing when or how Moshe made aliyah.

2. "Hagasel" means small street in Yiddish and was apparently the name they use for the alley he is looking at through the window.

3. The Hebrew letters Lamed Vav equal 36 and has come to represent the traditional Jewish idea that there are 36 righteous men in every generation whose lives justify the purpose of humankind in the eyes of God. Jewish tradition holds that their identities are unknown to each other and that, if one of them comes to a realization of their true purpose, they would never admit it.

4. It is traditional to eat three meals on the Sabbath and the Havdalah is the ceremony marking the end of the Sabbath.

5. Ulpanim (plural for) ulpan comes to mean a school or institute for the intensive study of Hebrew.

6. Traditional elementary school in which Hebrew and traditional knowledge is taught.

7. Using a Yiddish word here.

8. See note 11 below.

9. Alludes to the Talmudic discussions about what to do when one man's ox gored another's. This section of the Talmud is often the first that students learn. For example, Talmud Baba Kama 33a.

10. Motel Chizik (or Tzizik) (1909–1959) made aliyah in the 1930s where he married Rosa Berger from Mlynov. He later died of a poisonous snake bite in 1959.

11. Ben Tzion Gruber was one of the brothers of Rachel (Gruber) Teitelman and Sonia (Gruber) Teitelman, the latter one of the prominent contributors to this volume. Ben Tzion died with his wife, Gitel (Margulis), and daughter Yehudit in the Mlynov liquidation.

12. An allusion to Psalm 126:1 a passage that also became part of the blessing after meals, called Shir HaMaalot.

13. An allusion to the verse, "For this is a brand plucked from the fire" [Zechariah 3.2] referring to a high priest who was saved from Satan.

[Page 90]

People in a Shtetl

Sonia and Mendel Teitelman ("SMT")[1]

Translated from the Yiddish by Hannah Berliner Fischthal, PhD

Edited by Howard I. Schwartz, PhD

At the shores of the Ikva and Styr, in the part of Polish Volhynia among the cities Kremenets, Rivne, and Dubno on one side; and Lutsk, Kowal [Kovel], and Volodymyr-Volynskyi[2] on the other side; were found shtetlekh [plural of shtetl] which belonged to the Mlynov kehilla, like Mervits, Trovits,[3] Ostrozhets, Boremel, and Demydivka. The principal one was Mlynov, near Dubno. In addition, the small number of Jews who lived in the villages outside of the shtetlekh also belonged to the Mlynov kehilla. The Rabbi from Trovits, Horav[4] Ackerman, z"l,[5] was the Rabbi of the kehilla. The president was Yoysef Berger, z"l.[6] He passed on before he finished his term of office. After him, Chaim Yitzhak Kipergluz, z"l, took over the position as president. He served until the beginning of the Second World War. At the marching in of the Soviet troops in our neighborhood 17 September 1939, he collapsed.

I, Mendel Teitelman, son of Avrohom-Leyb and Rivke, and my wife Sonia, daughter of Yoysef and Shifre,[7] were born the beginning of 1900 in the shtetele Mervits, which was separated from Mlynov by a narrow stream and an unpaved highway of about one kilometer. Mervits and Mlynov also were divided by a macadamized highway, which stretched from Rivne to Berestechko, through Demydivka, in the direction of Brody, which was, until the end of the first World War, an Austrian city.

A Glance at Mervits

In the small shtetele Mervits, in which I went to cheder and in which I was brought up, there were no official buildings like a post-office, community center, church, and so on, because all these were found in nearby Mlynov. Yet it still had a character of a shtetl. Until the First World War, there were three study houses, a bathhouse with a mikva,[8] two kosher slaughterers, a Rabbi and all other clergy, a voluntary burial society, and a Jewish cemetery. And although the shtetl was very small (about 400 Jewish souls), there was still a marketplace in which the main stores were concentrated.

[Page 91]

Every couple of weeks fairs would take place there. They were a principal source of income for a larger part of the Jewish population.

The Jewish population of the shtetl was divided into two groups of Hasidim — Trisker and Olyker. The larger and the so-called richer part of the local Jews belonged to the Trisker Hasidim; the smaller part to the Olyker. There were many conflicts, which more than once led to serious fights and even to beatings, over the styles of praying, and so on, until a nice morning in 1903, when the general large synagogue, famous for its beautiful structure, burned down from a fire in a neighbor's house. That led the Trisker Hasidim to build a separate chapel, and from then on peace reigned in the shtetl. There were now a Trisker synagogue, an Olyker synagogue, and also a small synagogue, on the place of the burned large, beautiful synagogue.

Income for the local Jewish population came from various sources. Some people had various stores, for example iron, or manufactured or colonial goods, for the local population and other villagers. A small number sold grain, cows, and various other village products. About half of the population lived from construction work, which was only seasonal (summer). A very small number were home manufacturers (shoemakers, tailors), and there were a few who worked on the earth. There was no professional intelligentsia. The Mlynov medical doctor Vislotsky served the local population together with the entire surrounding village population. In the shtetl there was only a healer, Reb Zaylik Rufa, who, for his trade, also had to be a barber. His daughter Chana helped him in order to increase his income.

[Page 92]

The great poverty that ruled most of the shtetl did not prevent some important young people from growing up and making a reputation in the world, as, for example, Aharon Firer, z"l, and Sender Shokhet's son and his brothers, my friends, Shmarye, Arye and Yoyne. Aharon and Shmarye were murdered in Denikin's pogroms[9] in Moscow and in Kiev, and the last — from followers of Hitler, may his name be blotted out. Also growing up were my brother-in-law Ben-Zion Gruber, z"l, a student of Bialik; and Mayerke Kubilensky, z"l; Kahat Gekhtman, Melekh Zider, and Hersh-Leib Margulis, z"l; and also others whose names, unfortunately, I no longer remember.

The school system was on a very low level. Until the first World War, the only student who attended the elementary school in Dubno was Hersh-Leib Margulis; others had to learn on a small scale. But the main subject and education was strictly Orthodox, held in the cheders by the local teachers, and in the yeshivas in the outside world. I attended them with my brother Nachman, z"l, and with my other friends. We did not reach a higher and more worldly education and upbringing, which had been the desire of our parents. Yet even though thick poverty ruled in the shtetl, the mood was happy for the most part, especially when celebrating engagements, weddings, circumcisions, high holy days, and Shabbat.

There also were several organizations dedicated to charities, for example, an organization that loaned money without interest, organizations for Rabbi Meir Baal HaNes's pushke[10] for the Land of Israel, organizations providing lodging for the homeless and sick, organizations providing brides with wedding dresses, and organizations who purchased holy books. All this led to a friendly brotherhood, and very often friends would celebrate good deeds.

I also want to mention the industry that was found in the shtetl at that time: the so-called oil presses, driven by horses. The largest oil press was Zeylig Wurtzel's[11], z"l. The next largest presses were owned by the brothers Tali and Gedalye Helman, z"l, Yankev Ranis, z"l, and Yankev Khorwits, z"l. Pinkhas Matis, z"l, also attempted to work such a press, but without success and for a short time. Moyshe Shchna's, z"l, dealt in wool. There also were a few kosher butchers, who did their butchering in the local stalls and then sold the meat in the houses.

[Page 93]

There were a few horse and buggy drivers; they never could earn a living with their work, and they always had to search for additional jobs, which varied.

During the First World War

In 1914, the beginning of the First World War, I was in the yeshiva in Baranovitsh.[12] I was very young, but that did not prevent me from having been sent very far from home, learning two years in other yeshivas in Rovno[13] and in Stolptsy.[14] My beautiful childhood years in Rovno and Stolptsy I will never forget for my entire life, because they are always fresh in my memory. Clearly my parents, may they rest in peace, were then comparatively well-off. By an order from the Trisker Rebbe, I was the first in the shtetl to be given specified eating "days" with the well-to-do in the town, the way it was practiced in all Jewish communities at that time.

In the early years of the First World War, when I was in Baranovitsh attending the yeshiva, I was captured by the Germans in Kaiser Wilhelm's Army. The German army had established itself in the Baranovitsh neighborhood, on the length of the White Russian neighborhood. The occupation encumbered the movements of the civil population. Because of security and concerns about espionage, the military power, in agreement with the civil power, decided to evacuate a considerable part of the population into further areas which they had earlier occupied, like, for example, Poland. As usual, the first scapegoats were the weak and the lonely. I fell into that category together with my friend Simcha Zutelman,[15] now in Russia. After wandering for two days and traveling in cold freight trains, we were brought, on 1 January 1916, half-frozen from the cold, to Ostrów-Mazowiecka, near Warsaw, and we were quartered in the abandoned barracks of the Russian army in Kamarab near Ostrub.

The poor food we received from the military power led to various sicknesses, like typhus, pox, and so on.

[Page 94]

This lasted about 6 months. One early morning all of us who had been deported were taken to the train. We were divided, 15 men in a group, and sent to the nobility in the area to work on their estates.

The nobleman managed our work. At the same time, he allotted us rations from the poor food for nourishment. We faced a new time of hunger and need and hard work; but still we did despair, knowing that our day would come when we would be free. My friend Simkha Zutelman and I were the youngest in the group, and we had to suffer through the hunger the same as the older men. This lasted until 1918, until after the Russian Revolution. Then we started to think about turning back home to Mervits, which had undergone difficult metamorphoses during our time away, when the ruling powers had changed every Monday and Thursday. We came into our shtetl Mervits, which, after the war, had only three Jewish houses left…

After the War

My parents, may they rest in peace, barely survived to see me after despairing of it. In addition to the fact that the war had completely ruined them, it also happened that my younger brother Note, z"l, had drowned while bathing in the Ikva. When they saw me, they hugged me hard, with tears in their eyes, and without words; the celebration was indescribable. My friend Simkha Zutelman found his two brothers Peysakh and Efrayim (now in Baltimore, United States)[16] and also several family members in Mlynov. Mlynov was barely harmed by the war. Almost all the houses there remained standing. The shtetl, except for all the experiences deriving from the constant change of power among Petliura the Hetman, Bolsheviks, and Poles,[17] remained in quite a good situation regarding livelihoods. It can be said that from that time on Mlynov became the center of the surrounding shtetlekh, and especially of Mervits. Mervits, which had been entirely erased from the map during the war, had to rebuild itself from the beginning. It was entirely dependent on Mlynov. Mervits rebuilt itself on a small scale. It had already two Zionist parties, a left and a right, two synagogues, a Rabbi, and a ritual slaughterer. These lasted until the Second World War.

[Page 95]

However, Mervits no longer had all the important qualities of a real shtetl; everything, everything went to Mlynov. The school, the post office, not even talking about official state positions and livelihoods — everything was in Mlynov. Therefore, there were few families in Mervits with incomes; the larger part had incomes that were tied to Mlynov. Mlynov itself also started to rebuild itself from new in the time of the Polish normal rule, which first began in 1921.

* * *

Until that very year there had been no scarcity of evil decrees and fear. There had been no scarcity of attacks by local groups who very often robbed and murdered. The same was also true of the not yet regular Polish army, who always found the Jew, and mostly the Jew from the small, unprotected shtetl, as its victim. From that year started the so-called, alas, good time. Actually, a very few Jewish businessmen and artisans did well.

My parents, may they rest in peace, had built an oil press, although they were never suited for this kind of work. Their lives were ruined, but as though the press had been inherited from successful businessmen, they prospered and started to change to the modern industry: namely, a mill with an oil press driven by the energy of a motor. That flourished at first, but, as I noted earlier, because they were not appropriate people for this, the entire business started to go downhill. Afterwards the business was divided up, and a part was carried to Ostrozhets … In addition, the anti-Semitic [Polish] government started to strongly oppress the Jews with the high taxes, from which the entire Jewish population in Poland suffered so much. The miserable personality Finance Minister Grabsky was not affected by the pain. And because the small incomes of many Jewish merchants ended, whoever had saved a little money put it into investments, and mostly into mills. For example, in Mervits, Zelig Wurtzel,[18] z"l, constructed a mill with his partners.

[Page 96]

The Fisher brothers, z"l, also. In Mlynov, Yoysef Gelberg, z"l, deserves to be complimented. In addition to his oil press, which had prospered well, he also put up a mill. Because he and his son, Gershon, were so efficient, they prospered in a big way, better than any of the others in the entire area. At first, they build a wooden building on the place of the oil press. In a short time, they had built out a four-story, large, beautiful building, in which they established a large, beautiful mill, as well as a beautiful house in which to live next to it. And the mill truly prospered more and more every day.

Economic Blossoming and Ruin Politics of the Government

This mill was the first to give electrical lighting for the shtetl. A few Jews had, in a certain measure, trade ties with the mill. The family Gelberg with their son-in-law Shike Goldseker, z"l, prospered very much, but at the same time, the small mills lost most of their value. As much as life was beginning to normalize, all the more difficult it became for the Jewish population to earn livings. There certainly were differences from family to family. For example, the family of Chaim Nekunchinik (Chaim Dants's) prospered very nicely with their wooden warehouse, which had, after the ruinous war, generated nice profits from building materials. The family of Noach-Moshe Schechman,[19] headed by his son Shimon, z"l, also did well. After his marriage to Pesi Ranis, he himself built out nice walls for living and for his oil press. I especially want to mention that he was also a local businessman with social welfare interests from the Joint Bank; he helped voluntarily, and not in order to receive a reward. I will also mention that such a Joint Assistance Bank existed in Mervits too, under the leadership of Israel Vortsel, Shammai Parizshak, Chaim Neyshtayn, and Mendl Lumer, everyone z"l. (I also took part in it.) It all fell apart with the coming of the Soviets. Shimon Schechman was also a Zionist adviser. I still remember when he came to me with Yudl Matoyk to cash in the foundation money, because the Jewish National Fund was also in Mervits, and I was permitted to help until the Second World War.

[Page 97]

This way a few businessmen prospered, like, for example, Avrohom Gelman (Avrohom Batye's), z"l, with his son-in-law Dovid, z"l; Yankev Goldseker, z"l, with his children; and Moyshe Goldseker (Moyshe Yoyal's), z"l, with his soda factory; Beynish Shvarts, z"l; Chaim Geler Rabinovitsh, z"l; Mayer Kwasgalter; and a few more, like Shloyme Morer, Chaim Goldseker, sons of Valach [Wulach], sons of Lipa Halperin, and so on. A medical doctor moved to Mlynov then, Dr. Fink z"l, from Sanek, and led a nice life. In addition, there were smaller businessmen and artisans from various classes; some were a little better situated materialistically, and some worse.

But there was no lack of poor people who very often were supported by loans from the so-called American Bank which was in Mlynov. My brother-in-law Nokhum Teitelman,[20] may he live [a long life] (today in Israel) was its President. They also received some help for the needy. There was even a certain time in which the bus was a Jewish possession of the Fisher brothers. By the urging of the strangers, the Polish Osadniks,[21] it was torn out of Jewish hands, and it became owned solely by an Osadnik with the name Shidlovsky, who had, by the way, a Jewish wife from Ostroh.[22] He was befriended by the Jewish population in the shtetl, but it did not improve the mood of the local Jews. When the anti-Semitic decrees from the Endecja[23] power grew more virulent, his relationship with Jews helped very little. The closer it came to 1939, when Hitler, may his name be blotted out, had already put his paws on the Western countries of Europe, the Jews in Mervits and Mlynov felt it more and more.

There was no lack of anti-Semitic provocations against Jews, which always ended fatally for the Jewish population. The situation of the Jewish businessman became very oppressed on at least two fronts. On one side was the government with its "owszem" politics,[24] which with the help of executors extracted not only the gains from the businessman, but actually the last possibilities of existence, so that in a short time, people were ruined. From another side came the terrible anti-Semitic treatment on the part of the Christians.

[Page 98]

So, for example my brother Shike, z"l, was ruined and he had to leave Mervits. Also my brother Nakhman, z"l, became similarly ruined. In addition to his own horrible experiences from a tragedy that had happened to him, he was further bankrupted by the ruling power with its tax-system. My uncle Chaim-Mayer and his sons, z"l, were entirely ruined by the taxes. The same situation took hold in Mlynov and in the entire surrounding area. The only people in Mervits who still supposedly were doing well, were Shamay Parizshak, z"l, Shloyme Sherman, z"l, jubilee couple Getzel and Mendel Steinberg,[25] and also myself. A few other numbered individuals in Mervits and in Mlynov, if not for the oncoming war in 1939, would anyway have been bankrupted, some earlier and some later, because of the decrees from the ruling power regarding Jews.

The politics of ruin took on a mass character regarding the Jews in all of Poland. Terrible ideas came from every corner of the country. It was said everywhere that Jews were forbidden to continue their livelihoods, and sometimes they received horrible beatings and were further oppressed. And if this were not enough, Mrs. Fristor[26] decreed a ban on kosher slaughter. In Kartoz-Breza[27] a concentration camp was established which was arranged practically solely for Jews. The Jewish situation colossally worsened from day to day, and the depressed mood sunk lower and lower.

The Ukrainian population, although itself in a certain measure oppressed by the Polish powers, became a willing partner in harming the Jews. They sat with crossed arms while the recent bruises of Petliura[28] were still on our bodies. The panic took hold until the sad, famous date 1 September 1939, when the war with Poland started through Hitler's troops, may his name be blotted out. The idiotic anti-Semitic politicians did not want Jews to take part in the resistance against the German beast. Even in the last days of Poland's destruction, we heard the foolish sounds of anti-Semitism: "Not with Jewish help for Poland," until the hugely disastrous Polish anti-Semitic politics descended together with the destruction of the Jewish population.

[Page 99]

Poland was smashed and occupied by the Hitlerite troops, may his name be blotted out, in just a few days.[29] For the Jewish population, true hell started, which I am not in a position to describe.

Translator's and editor's footnotes:

1. On Sonia and Mendel's background, see their bios on the Mlynov website. – HS
2. *Ludmir* in Yiddish. – HBF
3. Torhovytsia, Ukraine. – HBF
4. [the Rabbi] title preceding the name of a respected Orthodox Rabbi. – HBF
5. May his memory be blessed. – HBF
6. Also known as Yosef Gelberg. On his background, see the Gelberg family story on the Mlynov website. – HS
7. Yoysef (Yosef) Gruber married Shifre Teitelman. – HS
8. Jewish ritual bath. – HBF
9. Anton Denikin was Deputy Supreme Ruler of Russia during the Russian Civil War of 1917–1922. His army carried out the White Terror, which included pogroms against the Jews, as well as mass executions and plunder. – HBF
10. Well-known charities in memory of the Jewish sage (139–163 CE). Observant women place coins into the tin can alms box (pushke) before lighting Sabbath candles. – HBF
11. Alternative spelling, Wurtzel. – HS
12. Today Baranavichy, Belarus. – HBF
13. Today Rivne, Ukraine. – HBF
14. Today Stowbtsy, Belarus. – HBF

15.   The family name variations in English include Zutelman and Settleman. – HS
16.   Pesach Zutelman immigrated to America with the Mlynov Shulman family in 1921, married Sarah Shulman and became Paul Shulman in Baltimore. His brother followed via Buenos Aires and became Frank Settleman. – HS
17.   Symon Petliura was head of the Ukrainian General Army Committee from 1917. The Hetman was chief of the Cossacks. The Ukrainians, Cossacks, Bolsheviks, and Poles were deadly enemies and battled constantly. – HBF
18.   Another variation of the family name is Wurtzel, who married into the Steinberg family.
19.   Schuchman, Schechman or Schichman is a variation. – HS
20.   Also known as Nahum Teitelman. – HS
21.   Veterans of the Polish army who were given land on which they settled in Belarus and Western Ukraine. – HBF
22.   Town in Ukraine – HBF
23.   Right-wing, anti-Semitic, populist party in Poland. – HBF
24.   "Yes, by all means; why not?" was the Polish government's well-known response to Polish boycotts and other transgressions against Jews. – HBF
25.   Refers to Getzel and Mendel Steinberg both survivors of the Shoah. – HS
26.   Fristor was a representative to the Polish sejm who demanded an end to kosher slaughter. – HBF
27.   Today Byaroza, Belarus – HBF
28.   Szymon Petliura was President of the Ukrainian People's Republic 1918-1921. Under his command, close to 500 deadly pogroms against the Jews were carried out, leading to tens of thousands of deaths. – HBF
29.   In 1939, when WWII started, Mlynov was in the area occupied by the Russians, per the agreement with Germany. The Germans broke their non-aggression pact with Russia on June 22, 1941. Mlynov was occupied by Germans almost immediately. – HS

Different Times in the Shtetl

S.M.T.[1]

Translated from the Yiddish by Hannah Berliner Fischthal, PhD

Edited by Howard I. Schwartz, PhD

In the Old Days

The total number of Jewish men, women, and children in the shtetl Mervits near Mlynov, in the district of Dubno, was about 350–400. While births and deaths were recorded in larger cities by the civil authorities, in Mervits it was different. Mervits never had an independent administration. It never had a Jewish kehilla; and after the First World War, Mervits became tied to Mlynov. Actually, both became one town.

Sender Shoykhet[2] was ordered to report the births of newborn boys every month according to the date of the Parsha of the week. Crown[3] Rabbi Margulis entered this information into his official books according to the civil date. Because of that, the authorities knew when the boys would need to fulfill their military duty. This happened, understandably, regarding sons. It was different for the births of girls; they did not have military responsibilities, so therefore nobody registered them. Similarly, deaths of the elderly, people without military duties, were not required to be registered; only young men were listed.

[Page 100]

These procedures held until about 1914–1915; twenty years earlier, as much as I can remember, practices were entirely different. Until that time, there was a kind of merging of Jewish shtetlekh into the larger towns. So, for example, Mervits belonged to Olik,[4] 25 kilometers from Mervits. And when people needed birth certificates, they turned to the civil authority in Olik.

It was different, again, after 1920, when the Poles ruled. Then all legal procedures were carried out by the community in Mlynov, with the help of the village magistrate, who now had to report both genders, births of both boys and girls, and deaths of people regardless of age, without exceptions. The magistrate in Mervits was, until the Second World War, my brother Yankev-Yoysef, z"l.[5] He had full responsibility for everything that was done in the shtetl in connection with the ruling power, like taxes, birth certificates, and so on. The local authorities even demanded that the magistrates wear uniforms (caps), but almost nobody wore them. They were used only during official parades. The magistrate also received a minimum wage. I still remember the same functioning Jews in our shtetl during Tsarist rule, Noyach-Staroste[6] and Shloyme-Koval-Staroste.[7]

After the War

The new generation, which grew up after the first world war in our shtetlekh, breathed more progressive air, which affected both their outside appearances and their inner contents. That came about during wartime, when they were refugees in large Tsarist Russia, acquiring from other places the atmosphere that influenced Jews from the small villages. Practically all of our shtetl inhabitants were refugees. Returning home after the First World War, the Jews, unfortunately, saw that not a trace remained of our shtetl Mervits.

[Page 101]

There were only trenches the length of the River Ikva and reserve trenches a little further from the river. All the houses in the shtetl had been used by the military as protective ditches; therefore, the entire shtetl had been erased from the map.

My parents,[8] may they rest in peace, in 1918, after the war, began to think about rebuilding. The Mlynov general population was already back in their homes because their houses had not been ruined. But my parents did not think of building in Mlynov. There were many reasons for that and maybe the most important — they did what the Rebbe ordered. What he said was holy and dear to my parents, and as he actually told them to search for what they had lost, they did not ask why. An historical reminder of how far the belief in the Rebbe's words extended: My parents had buried a large sum of gold coins before they ran away from Mervits. Coming back, the first thing they did was to search for the treasure-cache. After much searching, it was not found. They turned to the Rebbe, who lived then in Rivne. After a prayer enabling them to find the treasure, he assured them their search would be successful. They returned, renewed the search, and found it. Understandably, the Rebbe secured his redemption money, and the experience left a strong impression on my parents to rebuild in the ruins of Mervits.

And if the town's wealthiest man rebuilds on its ruins, it is a sign that it is a good idea. So little by little others started to copy my father. Among the first to build was my brother Yankev-Yoysef, z"l, with his then small family, and my uncle Mordkhe, z"l with his famiy, and Note Raykhman, z"l, with his family. There were oppositions by local anti-Semitic Christian neighbors, our enemies, against the rebuilding of the Jewish community. But the power of strong will and good promises from the Rebbe conquered everything. Little by little, more and more former residents of Mervits started to build houses in their former hometown.

[Page 102]

All who resettled in Mervits had to deal with assorted troubles and difficulties more than once. The assorted post-war diseases, like typhus with its rash and accompanying stomach pains, was epidemic in all countries after the war. It did not wipe out Mervits, but it tore away dear victims, like Arky Tsvik, Asher Sherman, and others. Practically everyone suffered through the diseases, some slightly and others with more difficulty.

The change of power to the Poles, which in our neighborhood changed all the time from Bolsheviks, Petliura, and Poles, started to stabilize by 1920, lasting until the beginning of the Second World War. Health and income situations also began to stabilize. My parents, for example, made an oiler, which later turned into a motor mill. In the end it was entirely shut down, and my parents found themselves in a critical situation their last few years.

It must be noted that the oppressed economic situation, existing in Mervits with few exceptions from the Jewish population, became a deciding factor in having to remain in Mervits until the extermination. Effective people like my cousin Ben-Zion Gruber,[9] may he rest in peace, and others — if they had not been blocked with the obstacle of not having even the slightest financial possibilities to leave, would surely have thrown everything away and gone out into the wide world. Instead, the best and most honorable people were rubbed out as though between mill stones.

Translator's and editor's footnotes:

1. Abbreviation for Sonia and Mendel Teitelman. – HS
2. A *shoychet* (also spelled shochet) is a ritual slaughterer, an esteemed profession which requires specific knowledge of anatomy – HBF
3. The Crown Rabbi was a position in the Russian Empire given to a member of a Jewish community appointed to act as an intermediary between his community and the Imperial government, to perform certain civil duties such as registering births, marriages, and divorces. Because the main job qualification was fluency in Russian, crown rabbis were often considered agents of the state by members of their own communities, not true rabbis, and they often had no education in or knowledge of Jewish law. – HS
4. Today Olyka, Ukraine. – HBF
5. Mendel Teitelman is speaking here about his brother and appears to be the one speaking in the first person throughout the essay. – HS
6. A *staroste* was the chief of the village or one who had administrative duties. – HBF
7. A *koval* is a blacksmith. – HBF
8. It appears that the Mendel, not Sonia, is the one speaking in the first person. – HS
9. It appears that Mendel is speaking in the first person here. Ben-Zion Gruber was Sonia's brother. He was also a first cousin of Mendel. – HS

[Page 102]

Sources of Our Existence

S.M.T.[1]

Translated from the Yiddish by Hannah Berliner Fischthal, PhD

Edited by Howard I. Schwartz, PhD

We want to give an overview of the sources of our spiritual and physical strength. As everyone knows that "if there is no flour, there is no Torah;"[2] we will try to describe the origins of our physical nourishment, which were the bases of our spiritual strength.

[Page 103]

In our small shtetlekh, almost without exception, were the same ways of life. As usual, not everyone was in the same situation, but the sources — practically the same. Those were commerce and skilled handiwork; agriculture played a very small part. Here I must add that farming was not a main source of income, but a supplemental income. The Jews were not born farmers; their possessions came mostly from industriousness and diligence.

Commerce

The majority of Jews in our shtetlekh lived from other sources, mostly from trade. Out of everybody from the Mlynov kehilla, there were just a numbered few, and I stress few, of whom it could be said that they were making a living. While there were many who did earn a living, life was not easy, and it was full of uncertainties. There were also Jews who, after all their suffering, were still without an income.

As we are speaking about the source of income from trade, we will here point out some of the differences. Later we will describe the skilled artisans and the farmers. The differences among the three classes of traders were almost in all areas. The main reason was the competition which was so large that even today I do not understand how even the so-called stronger businessmen could exist. It was only with the secret of various combinations, because logically I absolutely cannot fathom how the Jewish population at that time had any income at all.

Take for example the grain business, which was the largest source of income in our neighborhood. I remember that the merchants should have made only large deficits, but there was always a complicated approach. The local grain merchant, for goods that were worth 100 zloty, paid 110, and so on. And where he left room for profit I do not remember today. For all the days of his life, any profits came like miracles. And that was after hard labor with his entire family, day and night, which nobody today could endure.

[Page 104]

And more than once a merchant would say that he was sure that his neighbor had a loss, and the neighbor's loss was profit for him.

All merchants, without exception, had a large partner, a merciless tax.

Heavy Taxation and Expulsion Politics

Taxes on capital were etched into the body and soul of the Jewish merchant. There were not only taxes on profits, which was understandable, but also on possessions and on sales. The Jewish merchant was in competition with all factors, both with his friends and with the anti-Semitic government, whose goal consisted mainly of a desire to ruin the Jewish businessman. So with the competitive rush the Jewish merchant had to work hard and earn little. The government had more motivation to take more sales tax, because if the Jew made large sales, it was a sign that his income was also large. So was there a bigger motive for a Jew to sell more, so the government could extract the very last bit of marrow from his Jewish bones?

The Christian merchant was not treated like that. He was treated completely differently. The government supported him. There were no picket signs put at his stores. He was, instead, supported in all directions. From this alone, one can see how hard the Jewish merchant's situation was in general, and how hard it was for the Jewish merchant from the small shtetl in particular. Only through miracles could the Jewish businessman survive. We are not talking about the end of the 1930s, when the war was already on the threshold, and Hitlerite agents, may their names be blotted out, had already poisoned all of Europe with their venom, and especially in Poland. The situation simply became without a way out. The general Jewish population felt it, and the Jewish merchant felt it even more.

It was like that in other areas, too, as, for example, in iron manufacturing. The anti-Semitic government gave concessions of all kinds of iron and lead to the Christian employees, and thus robbed the Jewish merchant of his bread. The situation became intolerable. Jewish merchants throughout the country felt this. Spiritual and physical oppression hit the general Jewish population in that time, and especially the Jewish merchant.

[Page 105]

The situation of the Jewish skilled artisan was no better. The Jewish artisan was little by little pushed out of his positions. There were constantly more and more Christian artisans in all professions, and in all places, in the city and in the village, with the intentions of pushing the Jew out of his livelihood. Usually, the Jewish artisan was not pushed out as quickly as the Jewish businessman, but neither one was excluded from the anti-Semitic treatment.

I want to add another thing that was a factor in a certain measure for competition, and that was the market fair. The fairs in Mlynov, which were famous far and wide from the first years after the First World War, provided Jews work and livelihoods. Those opportunities also had shrunk for the Jews. It went so far that the Christians could already make fairs without Jews. Christian businessmen grew like mushrooms after a rain, in all fields. We are not even talking about horse and cow merchants, the majority of whom were lately Christians.

Evil Edicts

The evil edicts did not suddenly grow and pour themselves onto Jewish heads; in truth, they started to come in the first years of this century. They surely came more slowly and with periods of interruption, which gave the impression that these were very nice times. The truth is that the nice times were short, and, for the most part, they were dark degradations, in various shades, since the entire Christian population was not yet in charge. We had a mixed population of Jews, Ukrainians, Russians, Czechs, and Poles. Because there was strong antagonism among them, in the confusion it was possible to find a good friend, perhaps not because of love for Mordechai, but because of hatred for Haman.

[Page 106]

The friction between the Ukrainians and the Poles was very frequent. The Ukrainians, as the overwhelming majority, always looked at the Poles as foreign occupants, and until the end Ukrainians did not agree to their ruling over them. As the rule is, where two are fighting, the third one benefits. In this case the Jews benefitted somewhat, and perhaps it helped our possibilities to exist, since, according to all details, it was a mystery how the Jewish businessman and artisan could have existed altogether.

I remarked in the beginning, that there were exceptions, although very few. For example, there was a mill owner. Even though there were Christian mills, around the shtetlekh Jewish mills were still the leaders, and as a matter of course contacts were created.

Also, there were Jews with larger funds, which the Christian population needed more than once. We will here note that Jews loaned Christians money with interest, which enabled them to buy fields and forests from the larger property owners, and to make weddings for their children, and to build houses. In the end, the Jewish bread-givers remained with all the poverty. In the beginning of the 1930s, a kind of commission was created, meaning a prolonged and on-going commission, for debts for farmers. The anti-Semitic goal was to target the Jew, and to free the poor farmer, who had so many heavy debts due to dealing with many fields, forests, and so on. The aim of the commission was to unburden the farmer of his heavy yoke, and thereby impoverish the Jew, and that was accomplished. When a Jew had IOU notes from a Christian for a debt, the Christian merely had to announce that he had been given such IOU notes to sign, and then nobody could help the Jew collect his money.

A flood of evil decrees and rulings poured over the heads of the Jewish population, and that included the largest part of Jewish population, which was impoverished after the decrees.

[Page 107]

There were even instances in which the debtor demanded punishment or a refund for the interest that he had given the Jewish moneylender. He did not have to certify this with witnesses or other proofs; it was enough to slander a Jew with a few warm appealing words for help, and the verdict was already in his favor. And thus, the edicts strengthened from day to day through various ways.

In the year 1939 the situation worsened every day, and then we did not talk anymore about earning a living, because we had already seen worse things than not having an income … And how this ended is unnecessary to repeat here.

In addition, the few Jews who had little pieces of land could not earn any money from them, apart from the fact that there were not many. In Mlynov was the family Kolton, the tinsmith farmers, sons of Fayvl Kritser, and the farmer sons of Nekunchinik. In Mervits: Shmuel Lokrits, a tiny bit of land, his brother-in-law's, z"l, small pieces [of land], Getzel Steinberg,[3] a small piece of land in the perished village, the Shpiros a piece of ground, Ayzik Volf a larger possession, and a few others, whose names I do not remember, but that was not their main source of income, just a supplement. Not to be forgotten as farmers, Fayvl Berger[4] z"l, Avram Grin z"l, Beynish Shvarts[5] z"l, and also the sons of the perished villages, Smardive,[6] Notshicz, Fiyna, and so on.

And so the jewels of the crown of the Jewish population in our shtetlekh lived their entire lives primitively and with illusions, and they were mostly satisfied, even though their sources of income seldom had a healthy basis. And how these people raised children, who with their abilities and little knowledge, did not stand lower than others, is still a puzzle to us. From what roots have these people sucked, outside of the house of worship, and from the Gomorra [the Talmud]?

They took the secret of existence with them when they were sent so tragically from the world. And as their lives were bad and hard, so their ends were also tragic and hard.

[Page 108]

The angry, murderous hand had no mercy on the precious flowers of our people, who were raised with such difficulty, and in the end, shone so beautifully…

Translator's and editor's footnotes:

1.   Sonia and Mendel Teitelman. – HS
2.   Pirkei Avot (Ethics of the Ancestors) 3.21. – HS
3.   Getzel Steinberg and his family survived the Shoah and their story is written about in *A Struggle to Survive,* by Bunia (Steinberg) Upstein.
4.   Aaron (Berger) Harari, in his essay on "Jewish Farmers," tells how his uncle Faivel Berger was a farmer with Aaron's father Wolf Berger and how he asked Aaron for help making aliyah but the opportunity never arose. Faivel and his family was killed in the Mlynov liquidation. More on Faivel Berger and the Bergers family from Mlyniv, on the Mlynov website. – HS
5.   A photo of Beynish Shvarts appears on page 478 of the Mlynov Memorial Book. The exact relationship to the Schwartz family from Mlynov is not known. – HS
6.   Probably the village of Smordva. The other village names are not identified. – HS

Community Buildings in Mervits

Sonia and Mendel Teitelman ("SMT")[1]

Translated from the Yiddish by Hannah Berliner Fischthal, PhD

Edited by Howard I. Schwartz, PhD

How, in normal times, did one construct a building for the community in Mervits? This portrayal and description will surely surprise many people, even former residents, who still remember the hidden tales about our hometown. This subject can only be discussed from the first years of the present century up until 1939, the beginning of the Second World War. With the start of the war, nobody thought about public things. All levels of the population were already restless, and everyone felt that something was coming in the near future.

First and foremost, Jews aspired to build a synagogue, and after that other holy places. They could not concern themselves with cultural institutions because of the inappropriately high expenses involved, which they could not afford. In addition, they would just suffer more obstacles from the anti-Semitic government, which would certainly have put rocks on the way with an assortment of excuses, sometimes supposedly humanitarian, and sometimes supposedly sanitary. In short, they could not think about these things. So, what could they do? The main thing was to construct a synagogue! The anti-Semitic government had already announced the opinion that religious people are those who are praying for the well-being of the government officials. So, are better people needed? Is a person with culture needed? And Jews yet.[2]

[Page 109]

It was good to focus on building holy shrines. Mlynov, which had not been totally ruined in the first World War, just needed to make small repairs on public buildings.

Mervits, in contrast, which had been entirely erased from the map in the First World War, had to rebuild from new. While Jews were building their houses, they also started to erect a synagogue. Although the opportunities were very small, Jews felt great pressure and a need for it, because in that time a synagogue was not only a place of worship, it was also an important location in which to meet; a place where, between prayers, one could talk a little bit about everyday concerns. There was no better club than a synagogue at that time; in addition, our parents had made it holy with their praying and learning. The first of those who wandered back after the war started to realize this thirst for a synagogue, and they took steps towards reaching their goal despite their limited resources.

The kind of buildings were not like those today in the wide world; they were more primitive. Private apartments were primitive, and public buildings were primitive. The first task was to clean up the base of the remains of the old, burned synagogue, and to lay the foundation for the so-called floors, and then to build. Heads of households at that time numbered six, but more came over to help. They really did everything with their own strength. They dug, carried, smeared, everything. We took Ivan Tsarik to help. He had been recommended by Moishe Fishman, leader of the road workers. Moishe knew him, and he praised him as a person who does the work of three. And actually, he worked well and honestly, and helped us in our hard work until the poor building was such that we could gather under its roof and pray. On Rosh Hashana we already prayed in the synagogue with a closed roof over our heads, although the sanitary improvements were still missing.

It took quite a bit of time until the entrance was a little fixed.

[Page 110]

That was the first community building. A small group of people built it with few resources and opportunities.

In time, the former inhabitants of Mervits, as in other shtetlekh after the First World War, started to return to their old homes after being wanderers during the war. They built small huts, and Mervits once again had the appearance of a shtetl. As usual, the growing population started to concern itself with a second synagogue, because the first was already too crowded, and there simply was not enough air to breathe …

As is known, our shtetl had many types of Hasidim. Being in such a tight place created so-called differences more than once, due to various Hasidic traditions, until, through the initiative of a smaller group, a decision was accepted to take steps to build a second synagogue. Said and done. Jews threw themselves with enthusiasm into the job and conquered all the financial and physical difficulties, and the synagogue building was constructed. (This was in addition to the first, which the few families, like my father, Reb Avraham Aryeh Teitelman z"l,[3] my uncles, Reb Chayim Mayer Teitelman, z"l, Reb Mordkhe Teitelman, z"l, Reb Yoysef Gruber z"l,[4] my brother Yankev-Yoysef Teitelman, z"l, and Note Raykhman, z"l, had built earlier). Many of the worshippers surpassed their own efforts and abilities to complete it.

The entire shtetl took part in helping, and the worshippers there did more than what was possible. I remember a Jew, Yoysef Shamash z"l. That Jew used superhuman strength in order for that little synagogue to exist. Trisker Hasidim and Olyker Hasidim already had their own synagogues in the shtetl. Among all the other worshippers, I remember the local prayer chanter Reb Moti Fines, z"l, a concrete worker who labored hard for an income for his entire family. But he chanted the prayers and the psalms for the community with such a sweetness, that I still feel it and cannot get it out of my thoughts. There were others who outdid themselves there at that time.

[Page 111]   ***

One more community building was to be built in Mervits, and with great sacrifices — that was a bathhouse. A bathhouse, for the sake of sanitary and Jewish ritualistic reasons, existed in Mervits until the First World War, after which it was destroyed together with all other buildings. Wanting to establish a bath for the shtetl, in order not to be dependent on Mlynov in that regard, Mervits searched for a source for building expenses, and found it. Near the former bath was quite a bit of property which belonged to the kehilla. Moyshe Shvartsman, z"l, had grabbed up part of it for free. The congregation decided to take back part of the property from Moyshe, and to sell it. And so it was done. A piece of Moyshe's garden was reclaimed and sold to Mendl Vayner z"l; he paid full price for it. Unfortunately, he could not even use it, because of various stumbling blocks. The money, which had been taken from Mendl Vayner, was not used either. An anti-Semitic hand was preventing the establishment of the bath. The government employed sanitary excuses, but the real reason was plain anti-Semitism. The poor shtetl of Mervits was not strong enough to meet 100% of the standards, and all the expenses that had been paid with difficulty were for nothing.

This is how poor Jewish shtetlekh lived and suffered. Seldom did the light shine in the Jewish houses. One could not even think about youth clubs. Sometimes young people used the synagogues for meetings. There we got together in larger groups, and there we discussed various issues. Zionist meetings, too, usually took place in the synagogues.

This was the life in the poor shtetele Mervits, as it was in many small shtetlekh throughout Ukraine and Poland.

Translator's and editor's footnotes:

1.   Sonia and Mendel Teitelman – HS
2.   The intent of these questions is not entirely clear. The language seems to suggest that nobody (neither Jews nor the Tsar) had a need for cultural institutional buildings. – HS
3.   z"l is an acronym for "zikhroynu livrokho," may his memory be blessed. – HBF
4.   Yosef Gruber was Sonia Teitelman's father. – HS

[Page 112]   _____

Song

By Alef Katz, New York

Translated by Hannah B. Fischthal, PhD

Song,
Boil!
Scream—don't be silent.
Sing with every letter and limb.
Cry, and sing your melody.

You must cry, all is lost,
A curse is sown in you:
The bitterness of ten times 600,000
Burns in your intestines.

Ten times 600,000 roots
Call, remind: "Do not forget!"
Wrap them up in your flames,
In the lines of your miracle.

You have inherited the calls—
Carry the screams in front.
Give the sounds—words, souls,
Carry the pains in front.

You are a relative of prophets,
In your catastrophe comfort is blossoming—
Cry the cry, but sing of continuity,
Because that is what was created, song.

October, 1945

[Note: The Yiddish poem was written in ABAB rhyme-scheme. The Zohar says there are 600,000 letters in the Torah, corresponding to 600,000 Jewish souls. – HBF]

[Page 115]

This Is How We Lived

An Old Portrait

by Aleph Katz

Translated by Hannah B. Fischthal, PhD

On a wall in a museum, an old portrait,
After years of silence, suddenly started to talk
When it was stirred by a warm glance
And a sense of youth from the past.

The portrait speaks and discloses on the wall:
My hand was mirrored on linen,
The brush dipped into colorful springs,
Afterwards sent with yellowish rays
To the empty linen, with a quick touch,
With spots and tiny pieces of my form.

I look out of the frame onto a strange-wild world
And everything that I see is obscured with fog.
No more is the hand here that formed me;
No more is the person whose heart stormed
When he crumbled, lined my face,
And created me from shadows and light.

Also he whose smile is mirrored now
Right here on the linen—rounded, pointed—
Is not here anymore; and I do not hear anymore,
Also I do not see those who with tears
And words cried for him when he departed,
Looked at my face, searched for his days.

I now remain a stranger, alone,
A blitz from a second that cannot pass away,
A lonely hero of a wordless drama,
A shadow-character of a disturbed world,
A secret of the past, a foggy pane,
A nobody forgotten in dust.

[Page 116]

Self-Defense in Mlynov

by Shmuel Mandelkern,[1] Tel Aviv

Translated and edited by Howard I. Schwartz, PhD with Hanina Epstein

The Russian Revolution and the Jewish Reaction

With the fall of the Tzarist regime in Russia and the establishment of the Revolutionary government, there was happiness and joy in all the towns of Russa. The Jewish and non-Jewish populations all together espoused the slogan "brotherhood of peoples, love and fraternity between individuals and among peoples." All the racist discriminations were annulled going forward, as if they never existed.

The Jewish population in that same period related in different ways to the Revolution, aligned with their social composition.

The Jewish bourgeois, among them, captains of industry, heads of large businesses and others, did not embrace all the nice slogans with great enthusiasm, and especially, it goes without saying, the slogan "what is mine is yours and what is yours is mine …" because immediately they had partners in their sizeable possessions, which had passed to them as an inheritance from their ancestors. But with no choice, they choose silence and hoped for the future.

The situation of the young people was different, and most of all, the youth who were studying, the "externals"[2] as they called them, who were thirsty for study their entire youths, for science, for different types of continuing [secular] education, [because] all the doors to higher learning, the universities, and academics, which had been shut in their face until now — were suddenly thrown completely open, and all the Jewish youth drank thirstily from the secular teaching (Torah) and wisdom (Hokmah).[3] And this segment of youth was not distinct from the all youth who studied.

The Jewish workers, who were scattered and dispersed with no organization all over Russia, suddenly found themselves as free people, unfettered, and master of themselves and their own opinions. All the slogans about brotherhood of nation, freedom, peace and friendship, rang nicely in their ears, and they embraced the slogans of the Revolution with great joy. It is perhaps notable, that in all the cities of Russia, in the establishments of industry and all the other workplaces, their happiness was very conspicuous; their participation, awakened in rallies and assemblies, in different celebrations of worldwide workers — was recognized.

The situation was completely different in small towns, like Mlynov and similar ones.

[Page 117]

The bourgeois here … were not [true] bourgeois … their entire property was a 4 by 4 [store], with shelves for merchandize, but with no merchandize … and all shop owners had in fact two worries: one — to support his family, and the second — perhaps the situation of his neighbor was much better than his, and this would bring hatred and jealousy between Jew and Jew. Nonetheless, he was happy in his portion,[4] he didn't complain, he was satisfied with little, and some say that he didn't even know what he was lacking … this same Jew didn't distinguish between the repressive Tzarist regime and the liberated Revolutionary regime. All the matters of the Revolution, [namely], the ousting of the Tzar, and spilling of blood (of course, not in Mlynov), didn't bother him whatsoever. What occupied him were the partially empty shelves which were shrinking daily,[5] and not knowing what will happen each day.

The apples don't fall far from the tree. The youth of the town grew up without education (Torah) and work, and their lives were completely idle and empty. Most didn't learn a trade due to a paucity of workshops and parents unwilling to teach their children a trade, like shoemaking, tailoring or carpentry, lest that work damage the "reputation" (yihus) of the family, that they had continued for generations. And thus, they would reside in their parents' home and live off them. Just as they didn't care about their way of life, so too they didn't care about change of government. And like their parents they continued to be idle and wait for what was come. This was the situation in small towns and those like them in all the areas, and they thought that their work would be done by others.

"Strike the Jews and Save Russia"

After some time, however, things turned upside down,[6] and the matter started at the top, in other words among the leaders of the Revolution. Each one of them thought that only he was capable and suitable to stand at the head of the people and Revolution. That's when they started overthrowing each other. Yesterday, so and so deposed so and so, and he had his reasons, and the next day it was reversed — and he had his reasons. And all the removals were accompanied by the spilling of blood, and, of course, Jewish blood. And here in this case too they had their reasons and excuses. When a new regime was established it lacked the labor force and management in all the government institutions, [including] the military and municipal, and the "external"[7] Jewish youth, who were knowledgeable and aware, grabbed the work openings mentioned above and filled them with great success in all areas — it was this phenomenon that was like thorns in the eyes of the anti-Semites, who remained left over from the days of the Tzar, and when they saw in all the institutions mentioned above Jewish youth vigorous and working and filling responsible roles, they found (an opportunity) in every change of regime to lay the blame on the Jews, and take vengeance and spill their blood. And the slogans of brotherhood of peoples and the like quickly became the slogan, "Strike the Jews and you save Russia."

At that time, there was no Jewish institution or body that would raise its voice and express the sentiment that Jewish blood is not a "free for all"[8] and cannot be spilled without consequence. The Jewish bourgeois worried about its capital and wealth and the enthusiastic youth stood powerless and helpless.

[Page 118]

Thus, a chaotic situation was created in which violence prevailed — and the pogroms began against the Jews. One liability in this was that Jews in every place thought that the pogroms would not reach there or their town. In other words, the Jews from Odessa thought that the pogroms would be in Kiev and not Odessa, and therefore there was nothing to be agitated or alarmed about, and the Jew from Odessa thought the opposite. In the final analysis, both turned out to be deceived. This was more or less the thinking of all Jews in every single place. For example, a Mlynov Jew was sure, that tragedy would not reach Machiper[9] from Slobada, and the pogroms would be in Zhytomyr, Zvyahel,[10] Berdychiv and so forth. In other words, [they would occur] there, that was far, far, away but in Mlynov? Who would dare?

Especially in Mlynov they did not believe that someone would do something bad to them, after the death and burial in the Mlynov cemetery and in the unique "tent" of the Admor Aharon Karlin from Stolin.[11] Jews of Mlynov had complete faith that his merit would protect the Jews of Mlynov and the surroundings. In fact, nothing bad happened to the Jews of Mlynov. There are those who believe that it was the result of the Rebe's merit, while others believe it was due to capability of defense. The believers will believe.

At that time, there were two different kinds of pogroms with many variations: namely, political or anti-Semitic forms. In places where there was a regime change — each and every regime which came to power, one day the Whites and the next the Reds arising to govern, would go on a rampage against the Jews with murder, plunder and rape. Reverberations of these pogroms came from afar and crushed the spirit, souls and independence of every Jew who was there. The depression was great, not knowing what would happen daily, and every small town waited for the bitter fate of its Jewish residents. This was the situation in around Kiev, Berdychiv, Zhytomyr and Zvyahel. The situation was different in our area: Dubno, Rovno and Lutzk, places where the non-Jewish population was not nourished from anti-Semitism and national politics, but from local anti-Semitism exclusively.

And this is how matters began: since a substantial segment of Jewish youth even in our areas recognized that it required only a short time to master the Russian language inside and out, it grabbed government positions thanks to its intellectualism. By contrast, the non-Jewish students were not able to attain government positions, lacking education and knowledge– [thus it] created national jealousy which ate at each and every one of them. In every place and time, they heard the cry: the "Jewish government" – a day will come and we will slaughter all the Jews, and their end will be like the Jews of Zhytomyr, Zvyahel, Berdychiv[12] and so on. This slogan was on the mouth of the youth and seniors alike.

And thus very slowly, with the bad rumors the tragic deeds also reached our area … but in spite of this our situation was different and matters developed differently: From the area between Kiev and Zhytomyr until the Russian Carpathians, a large army of the Tzar was based, with its senior elite officers and equipment. And they were living there separated. Without participating in the different uprisings.

[Page 119]

They seized encampments in the large estates of the Polish nobility and relaxed there without worrying about their families or the regime. A battalion like this with a large and vast army, with all the different types of equipment — I remember, they even had even a private train — found a place to station itself in the village of Smordva close to Mlynov, in the massive estate of the Count Liudochowski. And since the Ukrainian population from the villages close by like Berehy, Smordva, Bokiima,[13] and others, suffered heavily from a lack of food and clothing, they befriended the soldiers of the battalion just mentioned in order to enjoy the abundance of food, the footwear and clothing that were under military control. Not much time passed before the residences of the villages were wearing Tzarist military uniforms, until you couldn't distinguish between a military man and civilian … In exchange for all this, the farmers in the surrounding areas would incite the encamped soldiers to attack the Jewish population, with the goal of plunder, rape and even murder. And since the village Smordva was in total 6 km from Mlynov, and therefore "the prerogative of being the first born"[14] was bestowed on Mlynov….

The Attacks

Among the soldiers encamped in Smordva was a battalion of calvary on white horses. They began to visit Mlynov during the night, with the goal of plunder and rape. Their activity was as follows: They would knock on the window of a certain house and request [the occupant] to come outside to show them the road that goes to Lutsk. Those who believed them and opened the door — they would break into the house and take whatever they found.

In the morning, when the Jews would gather in the synagogue to say morning prayers (shacharit), each would tell a neighbor about the events at night, and he would say the prayer of survival (birkat hagomel)[15] that it ended the way it had. Of course, these appearances greatly worried the Jewish population not knowing what would happen daily. In addition to the attacks that happened locally, there were other attacks by other remnants of the Tzar's military that wandered from place to place, directed by the anti-Semitic Ukrainians, who followed behind them with wagons and empty sacks in order to participate in the looting.

In the meantime, rumors arrived from nearby towns about attacks by "the Drifters" that were accompanied by plunder, rape and murder. I remember that most of the deeds mentioned above were carried out by the Sixth Division whom they called "the Sixers" (zekserlekh).[16] And if the local anti-Semites wanted to instill fear in the Jews, they would say, "Just you wait, the 'Sixers' will arrive and do to you what they did to the Jews of Mizoch,[17] Shumsk,[18] Kuniv[19] and others. Regarding the visit of the Sixers who stayed in Mlynov opposite the Ukrainian church (tserkva)[20] (the Russian Orthodox church) — this matter [to be discussed] separately. There were also Jews that were ashamed to admit that these plunderers visited them in their homes.

[Page 120]

The Idea of Self-Defense

If you asked yourself and wondered, "From where did the idea, or original suggestion, come to establish self-defense in Mlynov?"— I too asked myself this question, since my father and grandfather were not men [who embraced] defense. And my answer will be to meet that obligation.

The idea was born one Sabbath at sunset and the answer is easy to understand. One thing I knew, that to establish a force like this it was necessary to establish it in the local minds and community, and while Mlynov, in truth, was a community comprised of young people, middle aged and older people — but the opinion followed the head of the community, like Rabbi Avraham Moshe Ahrones,[21] Rabbi Yehuda Leib Lamdan,[22] Rabbi[23] Mordechai Meir, the sexton (gabbai) of the synagogue, Rabbi Shlomo Zalman, Rabbi Efraim-Fishel,[24] and others. I knew full well, that if I would go to the synagogue with idea of establishing a defense, their response would be as it is written, "unless the Lord watches over his city, the watchman keeps vigil in vain …"[25] Therefore I turned to each person individually, to implant the idea and convince them that they needed to lend their support to the defense establishment effort, because they were shop owners, whose entire possessions were first in line in the danger of plunder, along with all the other related dangers.

The direct petition was to Israel Halperin.[26] Nute Iskiewicz[27] (the two of them committed themselves entirely to any activity that was called for), Yehoshua Goldseker, Yaakov Goldseker, Moshe Goldseker,[28] who was called "Moshe with the beard," and so forth and so on. And they made a direct appeal to the heads of the community in the large synagogue. They accepted the idea without great resistance from their side. But there was a catch to it. Their condition was that firearms not be used, but only … walking sticks. In other words, a defense unit would go out with sticks against the plunderers who were armed with firearms … and this is how they explained the matter.[29] If we had firearms, and during the attack we, God forbid, killed one of them — the following day they would come with the instigators and wipe out the Jewish residents from beneath the heaven …

It is worth pointing out the origin of the idea of sticks: this is how "defense" was conducted inside of Mlynov. The administration of defense in essence began in an ordinary[30] way with two policemen, and for their reinforcement there was an obligation every night that a man take his turn from the residents of the town. This man did not, God forbid, go about empty-handed, but with a large, stout walking stick, the height of a person, and on it was stamped the municipality with red wax. From its heavy usage over the years, you in fact could no longer see the stamp or the wax, but they knew that this staff, which came to you from your next-door neighbor, obligated you to guard duty that night. And on the following day you passed the staff to your next-door neighbor. I remember that this inanimate staff was not received warmly. But what could one do? — the law of the land was law.[31]

That's where the idea of defense with sticks came from. Of course, there was general resistance to this idea, but who could disobey the elders of the community (kehilla)?

[Page 121]

We also knew that we would obtain firearms only with difficulty from the civil government in Dubno without agreement of the community leaders. Meanwhile, a state of disagreement developed between the obligatory nay-sayers and those in favor, in the synagogues, in the bathhouse, in the street, and in every place.

It is interesting to mention one episode that occurred: since the youth had gathered and were arguing near the home of R. Fishel[32] and Abraham Gelman, R. Fischel, who was hiding behind the wall of his house called out to us and said, "Friends, look, from here we can see the house of Yehuda-Leib [Lamdan], for example. If the attack is there — we will be standing here, and we will see and hear what is done there, at which point from here we will yell, "Help! Help!" and will begin to run in the direction of that house with the sticks — will the plunderers not be afraid of us and will they not flee?! If so, why do we need weapons? …

After the arguments, which lasted a few weeks, with no apparent movement or concession from the leaders of the community, and we knew that they were going to stick to the [rabbinic] saying, "Once [a witness] gives testimony, he cannot retract and give [contradictory] testimony,"[33] — we started suggesting to them that we get firearms in a symbolic way only: we reduced [our request] to 10 rifles for all the "defense." We knew that if they gave approval for firearms, they would not go further and count them. But their response was a forceful "no." Since the town, its people and its honor were precious to us, we agreed in the end to a "defense" with sticks and whistles, all means to summon help from all the residents of the town, in other words, even from those who were sleeping in their homes.

Defense with Sticks

The key turning point came with bad tidings that reached us about the plunder, murder and rape of Jews in nearby towns. Much of it was done at the hands of Ukrainian anti-Semites, the future partners of Hitler, who were spreading all sorts of false rumors, [for example,] that in such and such a town they had slaughtered all the Jews, and in another — they had killed, burned and the like. All of this inclined us towards concessions and to start activities. And while I said above that the *idea* of defense was born during the Sabbath eve at sunset, the activity of defense itself was born literally on a Friday night. One Friday afternoon, a tumult arose from the youth who were obliged to present themselves after the Sabbath meal in the large synagogue corridor ("Palush").[34] We chose the "corridor," because there was not a home that agreed to accommodate us, the young people and future members of defense, for this purpose, since it smelled like explosives.[35] It should be noted that at the time in Mlynov there wasn't a spacious enough house in which to accommodate all the youth, and therefore, the most fitting location we found was the "Palush" [corridor] of the large synagogue.

It is interesting, that the heads of the community at that time, who were all God-fearing observers of commandments, did not pose the issue of desecrating the Sabbath, in line with the saying, "Saving a life overrides the rules of the Sabbath."[36] Immediately after each one finished the Sabbath meal at home, the youth starting streaming without exception to the corridor ("Palush") mentioned above.

[Page 122]

And the organization was as follows: We broke into 4 brigades. The role of one brigade was to guard Shkolna Road, which began at the corner of the house of Yoel Goldseker, and ended at the last house on the street, at the home of Yose Meir's (son).[37] The role of the second unit was to guard the road that began from Yoel Goldseker to the Shulman house, after that the house of Muti Lieberman. Since this road was short, the duty of this unit was also to keep an eye on the town center, the square next to the house of R. Judah Lieb, and R. Muti Meir Shrentzel.[38] The third unit guarded the second square that began at the home of Beynish Schwartz[39] to "Kruzhuk"[40] and they also had responsibility to keep an eye on the entire surroundings, including the bridge over the Ikva, that lead to the estate of Count Chodkiewicz. The fourth brigade remained in reserve in the corridor ["Palush"] to help in time of need for any of the brigades that needed its help.

The enthusiasm was great, and everyone wanted to join the brigade that had the most dangerous spot. As a matter of fact, it was not known from where the trouble would arise, and which place was more or less dangerous. Since the first enemy during that time were the horsemen from the army stationed in Smordva, and they were the ones coming to plunder at night, the brigade had to keep an eye on those riders whose telltale sign were white horses. Upon spotting one of the gangs mentioned above, the brigade was to shout for help from the other units by means of whistles that they received and in general make a racket and awaken the residents of town for help.

The First Defense Incident

The first incident happened at one o'clock at night, when the first brigade from Shkolna Street returned from its patrol of the road next to Yosel Gelberg's. When they reached the synagogue, they detected at a distance, from the other end of the same street, next to the home of Mr. Fishel Teitelman,[41] the recognizable white horses were tied across from it, by the fence of Mendel Mandelkorn. Immediately they made alarm signals and all the units came quickly to the vulnerable spot. Fate ordained that it began with a good deed (mitzvah), would you believe, in the home of Mr. Fishel?[42]

The event unfolded as follows: The riders approached the home of Mr. Fishel and broke into his home. The horses were tied, as previously mentioned, by the fence of Mr. Mendel Mandelkorn. Since Mr. Fishel's son, Anshel, bought and sold manufacturing remnants, they pounced on the discovery, and gathered up whatever was possible to gather with their hands, among other things the underwear of the men in the household, and when they heard the hullabaloo outside, they thought, God only knows what force was coming to attack them, and they began to quickly flee from there mounted on the horses, and left behind all the possessions that they had stolen.

[Page 123]

Since the brigades received orders not to draw close to a vulnerable spot, but to create noise from afar since they had no weapons, they acted accordingly during this incident, and in the meantime, intentionally at the start, they gave the plunderers time to get on their horses and flee … their retreat by Shulman Street.[43]

In the meantime, all the units gathered around the spot of the incident. Those retreating smelled [a trick, namely,] that the noise was loud, but the hands were empty without weapons, and the proof was that that there was no shooting at them, [and thus] they regretted their retreat, turned around, and opened fire on the defenders. There were no casualties, but because of the noise, all the residents had awakened and come out of their houses in their underwear; finally, the plunderers left.

Even the Ukrainians in Mlynov were happy, among them Dominic [the priest][44] and others, apparently because we succeeded in expelling the horsemen; this was like the situation where [Moses' father-in-law] "Jethro rejoiced,"[45] they patted us on our backs for the great success, and their primary interest was in how many shots were fired from our side … obviously, we had not revealed to them the secret [that we had no weapons]. Meanwhile, dawn was breaking. Every mother with rising panic sought out her son. No one went back to sleep, and as was the custom on the Sabbath, the entire community, went to the synagogue to pray, and especially with curiosity to hear about the events that transpired during the night.

It was a custom in small towns, and Mlynov among them, that for every important communal matter: such as the rising stench of the mikvah, or the gathering of money to buy wood for heating, to warm the homes of the poor in the town, or on the eve of Passover the "flour of Passover"[46] [i.e., the charity for needy families to buy matza and other Passover necessities] — they would delay the reading of the Torah until the matter was resolved, obviously after lively debates. This is the way it happened this time, after morning prayers (shacharit): they delayed the reading of the Torah, and the members of defense announced that they would no longer guard without firearms in hand, and the proof was provided by the events of the prior night. But that time too there were the obligatory nay-sayers. Their claim was that if we had firearms, we would certainly kill one of them, with that result that they would gather all the soldiers in the area, and among them all the anti-Semitic farmers nearby and wipe the town off the face of the earth. The debate ended with no immediate result, but with the assurance that after Shabbat they would do something.

The First Rifles

In order to squeeze an agreement to buy firearms from the leaders of the community, we began again to negotiate and offer proof about the importance of weapons for us. We wrung out of them an agreement to accept weapons from the militia in Dubno, which was called P.P.[47] and we traveled to Dubno with the documents in hand, in order to receive the weapons. At the head of the delegation was Israel Halperin,[48] and when we got to Dubno, the men of the P.P. did not look favorably on the request and their objection was that they also lacked defense and that this would cause us trouble. We argued that while technically speaking they didn't have a defense, the men of the P.P., most of whom were Jews, owned personal firearms and they had the strength to defend the Jewish population of Dubno.

[Page 124]

Since they could not convince us, a negotiation commenced about how many weapons we would receive from them. We insisted that we needed a minimum of 10 rifles, as we had told the leaders of the community in Mlynov. After arguing, they squeezed us down by three rifles and we received only seven. When we returned to Mlynov in the evening with seven rifles, waiting for us by the home of Israel Halperin, was not a small group, and every one of them had to feel a rifle in his hand, as if this was a Torah scroll that they received from Mount Sinai …

Indeed, with the reception of the weapons there was great joy among the group, and by the same token they were happy about getting a smaller number of P.P. insignias, although some difference of opinion emerged related to the distribution of the weapons every evening among the units. Every unit claimed that the area it was guarding was the most dangerous and should take precedence, and that precisely that unit was isolated among all the other units. Each claimed that it had the expertise to care for the weapons and therefore should be the one to shoulder the guns … for these reasons and for reasons of self-defense, we felt a need for additional weapons.

There were different opinions and suggestions about how to obtain additional weapons. Among the best was the suggestion to buy weapons from the Drifters, who were ready to sell not only weapons, but all kinds of goods which they had — anything to make money. However, they were liable to sell you the weapons today and the following day send authorities or just their friends after you who would threaten and demand the return of the weapons, even without returning what was given in exchange. Furthermore, they were capable of selling you weapons with one hand, and with the other shooting you on the spot. Therefore, it was the general opinion that this was not the way to buy weapons needed to arm all the defenders, which was our goal: everyone capable of carrying a weapon — should carry a weapon.

I Looked to Buy Additional Weapons

Just as the idea of defense was born on Sabbath eve at sunset, so too the idea about where we could purchase weapons came to me on at sunset on a Sabbath eve. I made the decision — without asking, because had I asked, neither those at home nor my friends would not have given permission, because of the grave danger involved in this — to enter into the jaws of the lion and purchase the weapons from the large army that was in Smordva, from which all riders had come, our known nighttime visitors. No trivial thing! Therefore, one morning I got up and dressed in a military hat and uniform, I saddled the beautiful red horse of my brother, Isaac, and rode straight to Smordva. When I arrived, I asked the soldiers who were around the village, for the location of the Colonel's[49] residence. They showed me the house from a distance; I arrived there. I encountered two sentries, who stood by the gate of the Church with rifles with bayonets, and I requested permission to go into the Colonel because I had an interview with him; they requested that I wait a minute, so they could enter and confirm with him.

[Page 125]

I received approval to go in, and upon entering his room, I said to him, "Hello, comrade!"

He responded, "Hello, what do you have to say, young man?"

At that moment, a heavy sense of dread came upon me, and I could not finish my sentence, and I said to him, "I came to you to buy something," but I didn't specify what I wanted.

He stood up quickly from his spot, put on his overcoat, approached the door and said, "Come, let's go." And he went outside. He walked and I followed. He didn't say a word to me. In the moments that passed as I was walking behind him, I was reminded of the [biblical story about the] Binding of Isaac (Genesis 22), in which it is written, "And the two of them walked together."[50]

We walked through the village and after a few minutes of walking came to the area which belonged to Count Liudochowski, which the years of reform[51] had turned the grounds into a place of horse stables and a dairy barn for cows. Since the period of revolutionary chaos, the farmers of the area stole everything without receiving punishment — and perhaps this was the cause of the great appetite to plunder possessions of Jews — all these areas were renovated, cleaned and served as different storage areas for the large army, which encamped in the village. When we reached one of the stables, he took me inside, and told the sentry who was standing there to open the curtain and revealed to me a vast storeroom of military coats. He pointed to them: "Buy as much as you want."

I answered him, "I don't need this."

"Fine," he said, and called me to follow. By the way, from the suggestion he made, I understood that he thought standing before him was a Jewish boychik, a speculator, who wanted to get rich reselling merchandise. When I left there with him, he brought me to storage unit 2 and told the sentry exactly what he said to the first. The latter opened the curtain and showed me a storage unit filled with dress military uniforms of a very exceptional quality. And when I told him that I also didn't need these, he brought me to storage unit 3 and there I was dazzled by chrome boots of exceptional quality, the like of which I have never seen. But all this abundance did not attract me or tempt me, because my heart was set on weapons exclusively.

When I said to him, "I also don't want this," he called me back to his room, sat down and asked me, "If so, what do you want?" I answered that I wanted to buy weapons.

I said to him, "You know that the entire Ukrainian population in the area exploits the new regime as a means of personal benefit, and after they plundered the vast wealth of the Polish upper crust,[52] the wealth that was supposed to fall to the workers' government, fell into their hands; and since with food comes an increase of appetite — they turned to robbing and plundering the belongings of the Jewish population. All the 'good deeds' they did they lay the blame on you and the Bolshevik army, which does not enhance your standing. On the contrary, this makes you stink and be hated by the Jewish population in particular, and by the non-Jewish population in general. Therefore, we decided to organize a local defense with weapons in hand, in order to repel all the attempted attacks on us for plundering and robbing. And for this reason, I came to buy weapons from you."

[Page 126]

Then he immediately asked me, which weapons I wanted. I said to him, "Rifles."

Responding to me he said, "I'm willing to sell you not only rifles, but machine guns and canons." I responded that we were not interested in attacking anyone, and therefore machine guns and canons were not necessary, and furthermore, I didn't have any place to store them. Just the rifles, therefore, were sufficient. He asked me what price I was willing to pay for a rifle. I answered that I wouldn't quibble on price, and I would pay him what he asked. He answered in jest, that since a Russian rifle weighs 13 pounds, therefore, you pay 13 rubles for each rifle.

I agreed to the price. I consulted with him regarding the transport of the rifles from the storeroom — to Mlynov. I explained to him, that since I needed to ride with them past the villages of Smordva and Berehy, and since the non-Jewish population is hungry for weapons, therefore there is danger that may befall me on the way, and they may kill me and take from me the weapons. Therefore, I am planning to take only 10 rifles each time and to put them 5 at a time in each sack, and to tie the sacks on both sides of the saddle, so they won't be visible to the eye. But because of the long length of the Russian rifle, and the length won't fit inside the length of the sacks, therefore I request [the following] of you — "Since I see a large welding workshop under your authority, please give an order to shorten the barrel of the rifle as I request."

He enlightened me about this request, "Listen, if you shorten the barrel of the rifle, it will cease to hit its target." I responded that I understood this but since our goal was not to attack or kill, but only and exclusively for defense, we would be satisfied with them missing their target.

Immediately he walked with me to the welding shop, and commanded the supervisor as follows, "when this man comes with rifles and wants to shorten them, do this for him." Immediately, he said to bring 10 rifles, to shorten them as I requested, so that I wouldn't return home empty-handed.

I Got Rifles!

With the completion of the transaction, I rode homeward on the red horse, and on the two sides of the saddle were bound two sacks with rifles. On the way home, I felt great relief, as if I was bringing the Jews of Mlynov complete salvation. The company [of defenders] received me with great joy. From then on, I went daily, and each time brought 10 rifles, that were snapped up among the members of the defense, and each became like private property of each member, since everyone paid voluntarily from his own funds, and we didn't need a general fund raising campaign. In a short time, we had acquired 200 rifles for the town, even though the members of defenders numbered 70 young people. From this we determined that apart from the weapons in the hands of the young people, there were domestic weapons for every man in every home.

Once the weapons were acquired, the seat of the defense [organization] was in the streets of the town, and in particular in the central square by the Russian orthodox church (tserkva).[53]

[Page 127]

Every member of the defense knew that from 5–6 o'clock in the afternoon his place was outside and especially in the central square, and there was no need to draw up a personal list or to make a special announcement [to get members there].

Until the establishment of the defense, the lives of the Jews of Mlynov were paralyzed. In other words, tradesmen engaged in almost no work; they were nourished with difficulty from [the things grown or purchased] in the past; the shop owners did not open their stores, essential goods could not be found; the focus of their effort was to gather, one time here, then there, and especially in the synagogue between afternoon and evening prayers, to hear the news, what was known in advance of the bad tidings from the towns close and further away, some which were correct and some not, and life was full of predictions without knowledge.

But with the establishment of defense — a new light began to shine on the Jews of Mlynov. All the "bubba meisas" ceased, and each and every person went back to his work. The shop owners opened their stores. They threw open their shutters and their two doors and way of life returned to normal. The key business was salt, which at that time was scarce, and kerosene. It is interesting that kerosene flowed from the same source from which I purchased the weapons, since among all the assets in the hands of the army units which were stationed in Smordva, there was also tens of thousands of barrels of kerosene, that during that long period supplied the Jews of Mlynov, Mervits, Demydivka, Berestechko, on the one side [West], and on the other [East], a flow to Varkovychi, Mizoch, Konov[54] and until Ostrera.[55] This entire flow passed through the hands of Yitchak Smordebeer, brother-in-law of Mr. Eisik Leib Klepatch[56] and even though I knew the source of the distribution, and the sellers, it never occurred to me to seek "good fortune"[57] from them and get rich. When I finished the weapons business with them, they did not see me there again.

After we purchased the rifles — the human capital, in other words, the volunteers from the community, came on their own. As previously noted, the place for the youth each and every evening was in the "Church" (tserkva) plaza, which was in the heart of the town. There was no need for any call [to duty], mobilization, and so forth. The volunteers came out of feeling [of wanting] to protect the honor of the town and its people, and it all happened automatically.

I must give special praise to the memory of Moshe Gitelman, who was called Moshe — Ruchel Feivesh's [son]. He was the lead supplier of rifle bullets especially for the defense and for the men of the town in general. It is worth pointing out the means for purchasing the bullets. Since Moshe — Ruchel Faivesh's [son] was a "carefree" young man, he would put himself in danger nearly every day, and would connect with the remnants of the army units, who would pass nearly every day, back and forth past Mlynov, who were called "Drifters;" he would approach them directly with the words [in Russian] "Kerus Tovarishchi" ("Throw it friends") and he would show a crate of bullets. The comrades understood the hint and without negotiating would throw a crate or two with bullets and make the exchange. Not once was negotiation required, and he answered [in Russian] "[word unidentified] spasibo," "thank you very much."

[Page 128]

Thus, we also had no lack of bullets. As a result, all the material required for defense was found in abundance: the will, people, and equipment.

The format of guarding and inspection was conducted in the following way: the gathering place that had once been the corridor ["Palush"] of the synagogue moved completely outside, by the square. From there, the units would go out to Bathhouse Street, by the main road that goes to Lutsk, to the primary road that goes to Kruzhuk and Mervits. One unit went to the two bridges that go towards Keretz,[58] one unit was along the road that goes to

Ozliiv[59] and last but not least, the road to Rivne; there a large unit gathered, and the place they were stationed was the home of Mr. Tzodik Shulman. It is possible that this came about because of … the daughters of Shulman, Sorke, Chaika, and Pepe; all of them live today in the United States.[60]

Since this house was the last house, encircled by a large expanse of fields, which leads towards the villages of Slobada, Ozliiv and the main road that regularly was busy with movement 24 hours daily, and because there was suspicion that attacks and malicious events would arrive to the town from this direction — therefore all the training was conducted by the Shulman home as if facing a battle front. There, every evening, they would defensively shoot tens of thousands of bullets. The noise of the shooting would reach all the farmers near and far, and it was accompanied by all different kinds of Russian war songs; this put great fear into the people of the villages, so they wouldn't dare try any type of hostile action towards the people of Mlynov.

Not much time passed and the reputation of the Mlynov defense was praised in the whole area, and the fear that arose spread and grew among all the villages in the area and all the various kinds of plunderers among them.

There were days that "friends" from the nearby villages would come to me, intending to spy, and ask, "Every evening we hear reverberations of your defense with massive shooting at a distance, but where is your force and how big is it? During the day, in fact, we don't see anything, so where are they? What is their strength? And more …"

I had one answer for all of them, "We have great strength in people and equipment, and we lack nothing needed to keep away all those with malicious intent towards our town. In the day we rest and at night are alert to anything happening …" I thought to myself of the [biblical story about] torches in tails [of foxes] that Sampson sent to the Philistine camp, which caused great fear and consternation in the camp of the enemy (Judges 15:4).

Organizing Defense in Demydivka

"And he saw that it was good"[61] and that everything was organized for the benefit of the entire population, [at which point] I extended my influence to the neighboring town of Demydivka, which was a distance of 18 km [11 mi] from Mlynov. I traveled there to organize the youth, who also understood in that time of need that they needed to defend themselves by having weapons.

[Page 129]

As an example, I showed them the defense in Mlynov and with the intention that they "see and faithfully adopt"[62] the model. It was apparent that that I didn't need many words or persuasion and in the house of Gelikel Kolton (apparently here too the impetus [to gather here] was the beautiful daughters) the youth gathered, from the very best[63] of Demydivka, among them Moshe Firer, Moshka Liter, Shemoah the teacher, and Issachar "the idler," Eliyahu Kolton, and so on and so forth … They bought weapons and their reputation was also known in all the surrounding villages.

One fact from those days: one day at sunset, a special representative came on behalf of the Demydivka defense and announced that a murder had taken place. What had taken place was as follows: In Demydivka, there was one Jew named Moshe, who would go door to door to gentile homes, and he would lend some rubles on interest, on a small margin, and he lived his life in great poverty. One day he entered the home of a borrower in the village of Admuvka[64] and requested his money, which then amounted to 3 rubles. The borrower asked him to the forest near the village, on the pretext that his money was hidden there and that he would repay the debt. Instead of the debt repayment, he swung an axe and killed him.[65]

News spread quickly throughout the town, and the eyes of the Demydivka's residents turned to the young men of the defense, and they hoped to hear from them their opinion about how to respond to this act of murder. For this purpose, they summoned us — the men of Mlynov — to caucus together about what to do about this incident.

The news reached Mlynov at 4 o'clock towards evening. Immediately, I ran to Shimon — Noach Moshe's [son] Schechman[66] — and I said to him, "Bridle the horses to go to Demydivka;" I related the whole matter to him. Since it was winter, we traveled in a winter wagon,[67] and after an easy hour we were in Demydivka. In the homes and on the streets, they were speaking of the incident, and when they saw us, men of Mlynov who had come to help them, they were very happy and surprised we had gotten to them lightning fast. Immediately we organized a meeting, and the following was decided: Since the praiseworthy reputation of the Mlynov defense had been established in the area, and the region knew that a defense had been established in Demydivka, it was imperative that we not delay in responding, because if we did, they would think that we were weak — and this would harm us in the future. Therefore, it was incumbent on us to travel immediately to the village of Admuvkah and insist they hand the murderer over to us. Of course, there were also other opinions. There were those who thought that this step too hasty and that we should wait a few more days. But we held our ground. We included a number of members from the Demydivka defense, and we headed out to the road.

When we headed to the road, most of the town was outside. They accompanied us with a sorrowful doubtful gaze: "Who knows," they said, "If they will return alive."

When we reached the village of Admuvkah, we entered straight away to the "Soltice" (the town head)[68] and we said to him: "Since in the area of your jurisdiction they killed a Jew from Demydivka, therefore, we, men of the Mlynov and Demydivka defense, come to you, not for war and quarrel, but with the modest request to hand the murderer over to us." After several answers and different excuses, which did not make sense, we said to him forcefully, "Let it be understood, that the blood of Jews is not taken freely[69] and we won't budge from here without receiving the murderer."

[Page 130]

When he heard the forcefulness of our request, he told us, that he alone is not able to take full responsibility [for the decision], and therefore he requested more time from us until he would go consult with the village committee, but since we were afraid that the consultation outside the house would be hostile towards us, we therefore advised him to call the members of the committee to his house and in our presence we would sit together to consult jointly. He accepted the advice and went out to call the members of the committee. When he left the house, each one of us individually thought to himself, "who knows what they are liable to do to us" … after some time, the owner of the house appeared with a number of the town's committee, and we again began to reiterate our request to them directly. Of course, they also were not eager to fulfill our request, and we therefore realized that we needed to engage them with greater forcefulness, and we told them that we didn't intend at all to withdraw our demand and return from the town empty-handed, because by doing so, we would be strengthening the hands of the criminals and murderers, and on account of them innocent and hardworking people would suffer. We added, "Let it be understood that we are just emissaries of the defense, and in fact your village is surrounded by members of the Mlynov and Demydivka defense, and we are not responsible for the harm they are likely to cause you; they are likely to burn your houses, cowsheds and barns — and if so, why should peaceful folks thereby suffer on account of some irresponsible murderer?"

When they heard these words, one stood up spontaneously and said [with a Polish curse], "Let him get cholera,"[70] [translated to Hebrew]: (Let this crazy man go to hell [azazel]). "Come and we will go to his house and hand him over to you, and you can do what is good in your eyes."

After several minutes we were at the house of the murderer, who made a very pitiful impression upon us, and he began to beg us: "A demon attacked me and incited me to commit the crime."

We responded that we were neither judges nor interrogators. "We will take you now to Demydivka; you will stay overnight with us, tomorrow we will send you to the county seat of Dubno, and there you will go before the court. Since in our eyes you murdered a person, we cannot bring you unrestrained, and we need to tie up your hands and feet." Without waiting, we took rope, we tied up his feet and hands, and put him in a wagon and hurried to Demydivka.

Logically, we assumed that all the people of Demydivka, men, women and children, would be waiting for our return in peace. And thus it was. When they saw that we had returned with a gentile (goy) in the wagon, they understood that this was the murderer, and they all broke out in joyous shouting. The joy was twofold: a) that we returned in one piece and had not been injured and b) that we succeeded in bringing the murderer. But something happened which pointed to the pessimistic and depressed spirit that prevailed among the Jewish population in every location without exception: When we wanted to bring the murderer with us into a house [in town] in order to recount the negotiations that had taken place with the town's committee which had delivered the murderer to us — every single person was afraid to bring us into his house, lest his house and name would become known to the people of the village and they would harass him and his house.

[Page 131]

And since Moskeh Firer, son of the kosher slaughterer (shochet) Rabbi Meir Firer, was active among our circles, and because in the small town the house of the kosher slaughterer and Rav was in the "communal home"[71] (public house) — therefore without asking and against his will we entered his house — [namely], all the members with the murderer …

The house of Rabbi Meir the shochet filled in the blink of an eye until there was no room, and all the men of the town, including their children and infants, filled the plaza in front of the house, which was in the center of market. All of them shouted out together, "Give us the murderer, and we'll give him what he deserves." But those inside the house, refused to send "the great discovery" outside, and, as a matter of fact, set upon the "find" [i.e., the murderer] with walking sticks, shovels and anything else at hand. Only then did a number of those present intervene with Rabbi Meir the shochet at the lead, and with tears actually in their eyes, they implored [everyone] to leave him alone, and that his blood not be spilt in Demydivka, because after [such a] deed, the residents of Admuvka will come and take vengeance against us. When they saw that their cries and requests were for naught, they covered the murderer with their own bodies, and created a barricade between the fired up young people and the murderer. I remember that Rabbi Meir the shochet turned to arguing that if we, the men from the Mlynov defense, finish "the work," and return in peace to Mlynov, then the response of the Admuvkah residents and all the trouble bound up in this, would fall on the leaders of the Demydivka men, and especially on his house. The members continued the beating of murderer, but at the same time knew to keep him alive, in order to send him alive to the authorities in the county seat of Dubno. The night of guarding continued until daybreak, and then we brought him half dead to the authorities in Dubno.

Thanks to this activity, which made a great impression on all the residents of Mlynov and in particular on the members of the defense, the stock of the defense increased, and we were appreciated, not only by the Jews, but also by all the people in the area, and they obeyed and listened to everything that the defense said.

This operation doubly increased the energy, especially of the youth who were active in the defense, and its leaders, and they continued to guard the property and especially the lives of the Mlynov Jews.

The guarding continued perfectly organized on its own; without [the need for] ordering or mustering [anyone], each of the young people knew that at twilight[72] his place was in the square outside the Church (tserkva). For purposes of strength, they also enlisted, so to speak, men for reserve duty who were more senior and had families, like: Israel Halperin,[73] Nute Iskiewicz,[74] several of the married yeshiva students from the Goldsekers, Meir Kwasgalter,[75] and more. And after the arrangement in town, almost everything was restored to normal, namely, the shop owner opened his store with no fear or worry that he will be plundered, the tailor returned to his needle, the cobbler returned to his awl, and the merchants returned to villages, with all kinds of merchandise, and everything was being conducted properly. And by their knowing that the guard of Israel did not slumber or sleep, these married yeshiva students very gradually began to be tired after their day work and they began to lag in their guard duty participation as before …

[Page 132]

The breach [in commitment] grew day to day until in the end the young people were affected and they began to whisper complaints among themselves — why was it on them to guard every evening the possessions of Abraham Batya's [son], Yosef Halperin,[76] Yaakov Holtzeker,[77] and so on and so forth … then I asked myself how to restore the prior momentum, to evoke fear, as at the beginning, of the horse riders who would visit each and every night in our town to burglarize and plunder and such. Since turning back the wheel was just good advice, we therefore established a unit of men from the defense as an intimidation mechanism for the shirkers, those who allegedly were sleeping in their beds in the afternoon instead of participating in guard duty, and who thought that their work here and there was being done be done by others …

The "Intimidation" Unit

The creation of an intimidation unit, came about as follows: Oh well,[78] [we would need] "soldiers" for the unit, instead of plundering horsemen from Smordva, we had our own [soldiers] … but horses where could you get them? The proverb says the cure comes before the injury [meaning, a solution appears before the problem presents itself].

And what occurred happened this way: Who doesn't remember one of the Mlynovers and folks from Mervits, Mr. Abisch Shapovnik z"l,[79] the son-in-law of Mr. Yosel Shachna's [son][80] from Mervits and father of Levi Shapovnik z"l,[81] who was tragically killed in the Shoah. Mr. Abisch was a classic beggar, in line with what's written [in Scripture], "Without food for sustenance, without clothes to wear, naked and lacking everything."[82] Everything by him was "lacking," and for some reason he thought that if he bought a horse and a wagon these would serve as a means of livelihood for his family. But in the end, this added just another ravenous being (on four legs), which suffered sharp hunger with the rest of the family.

According to worldwide custom, a poor and hungry person visits homes to request bread to eat and clothes to wear and so on. Progress had produced great results [i.e, getting the horse], but before the four-legged creature needed to go begging to the houses of the two-legged creatures, the blond horse of Mr. Abisch found a big "meadow" for his sustenance:[83] Since the farmers who would come to the town for trade would place their wagons with horses in all the empty lots of the town — and there were many like this — the farmer would bring them food in a feeding trough ("Oflakis" in a foreign language) [and] they filled the food from all quality stuff befitting their [word uncertain][84] during their stay in town. When they left the town, remnants of the food were left in the middle of the streets, and this was more than enough to sustain the horse of Mr. Abisch.

And since the horse wandered most of its days in the open areas of Mlynov and sustained itself from abandoned property (hefker), we deduced a comparable rule,[85] that the horse also was [by technical legal standards] abandoned (hefker) and belonged to the public, and we had permission to use it for our holy purpose … what did I do? Under the cover of night, I mounted the horse with khaki clothes, as was custom then (all the people wore military khaki clothing at the time).

[Page 133]

Surrounding me walked ten members of the defense Unit One, trained well to imitate the neighing of horses. About 50 meters from us defense Unit Two was ready; their role, if the need arose, was to draw near to the weak spot, to drive out Unit One and grab its place.

And here [is how it was carried out]: I was at the head of Unit One, riding our horse, [and] and would draw near to the window of some average person,[86] and begin to knock on his window and request that he come out to show me the way to Lutsk, exactly the way of the real attackers before the defense had been established. The [chosen] person, who was scared and terrified, came to the window to explain to me the way to Lutsk, because he was afraid to come outside, and in the meantime, I would hear him standing [on the other side of the wall] opposite me commanding his wife [in Yiddish], "Khaye, quickly take the money, and throw it into the oven …" And while he was afraid and trembling, the unit of two-legged horses entered, and began to kick their feet and neigh like horses, and some of them would imitate the voices of calvary, like "Sty, Sty!" (Stand Still) — thus, the typical person wondered to himself how many riders would attack him.

During the back and forth between me and that person and the noise of horses, Unit Two would begin to charge with whistles and Russian songs. All of this with loud voices, and then the head of the first unit would say in Russian: "Comrades, the men of the defense are drawing near, let us flee!" When the typical person saw with his own eyes that the riders were fleeing from fear of the defense, he would run outside half-naked and in great joy thank the group for saving him from the attack of the marauders.

And during the following morning, when he came to the study hall, his story was on the lips of everyone, and all of them were unanimous in saying that it was forbidden to shirk guard duty and would go to join the activity with the young people. Thus, after a number of such operations like this during several nights, one evening in this street, and the following in another street — the sloppy participation reverted to the way it used to be and there were no further incidents of refusal.

Episodes

All the fuss mentioned earlier with fictitious riders and horses, which in the beginning was created as a means of deterrence against the waning interest in defense activities, became over time a means of amusement, good and joyous entertainment with diverse, unusual episodes. And here are a few of them:

Clearly, the young defenders were only human, and the guard duty, which began from 5–6 in the evening until five in the morning was a heavy burden — they therefore needed to seek out different forms of entertainment. "And he saw that it was good"[87] the people [of defense] began requesting from time to time to continue the bogus attacks and "the sacrificial victim" was [selected] by majority choice. Of course, the lot fell to families that had beautiful daughters.

[Page 134]

The home of Mr. Hirsch Holtzeker, which was in the middle of Shkolna street, was a house that stood out from the other houses on the street, with a fence and large yard, with fruit and fruitless trees; it was similar in fact to the house of a Polish nobleman, and fate decreed that in this house there were beautiful daughters, "beautiful in appearance and full bodied,"[88] a true delight to the eyes, and whoever saw them was reminded of one of the dreams of Joseph in Egypt[89] … and it was not surprising, therefore, that one evening the lot fell on the house of Mr. Hirsch Holtzeker with the beautiful daughters.

I remember the very night we advanced to the yard of Mr. Hirsch [Holtzeker] with a loud racket on horses with their riders. I stood opposite his window and I demanded that they show me the way to Lutsk … Since Mr. Hirsch was already old, and the daughters, as noted, were too beautiful to reveal themselves[90] when showing the soldiers the road to Lutzk,[91] that responsibility fell on the son, Yantil, to represent the family. (His name was Yankel and not Yantil, but because he could not pronounce a "k" nor "g" we also were not obligated to).[92] While this Yantil stood opposite us, without opening the door to come outside and show us the road to Lutsk, he gestured with his hands and with a variety of different expressions the direction to Lutsk, and then I heard Menucha, one of the daughters, say, "Oy va-voy, what will I do if, God forbid, if they enter the house?" And her sister Gitel answered her [in Yiddish]: "Be mute"[93] [then translated in Hebrew]: (Be silent), "They will recognize the voice of a woman and then we are lost … " As usual, the back and forth continued about ten minutes and finished when, as usual, the members of the defense arrived and drove us away and the gag broke up with wails of laughter from each member …

The following day, when this Yantil bumped into me, he said to me, "Shmuel, I am certain that you spoke to me last night, but one thing I don't understand, where did you get so many horses?" … Participating in this conversation was also Eta, the daughter of Shimon Holtzeker,[94] who had returned from Kursk,[95] and who was lodging with her uncle Mr. Hirsch [Holtzeker], and she continued with a pat on the shoulder: [in Yiddish], "May you be stricken with apoplexy, Shmulik," then [continuing in Hebrew]: "Out of fear, my uncle soiled his pants." And then after her, Yantil let slip: [in Yiddish], "Yes, yes, father shit his pants … " [then in Hebrew] I don't envy you if he knows that it was you."

And thus the group continued with this fun entertainment for a long time. And so that they [the town's people] wouldn't become suspicious that there was favoritism for anyone, or a vengeful side of anyone, we also didn't skip the houses of R. Yosel Maizlish and of R. Aharon Kubal.

This last person was the only one who recognized us, and courageously yelled to us from the house: [In Yiddish], "Shmuelik, are you leaving? If not, I am coming out with a pole to crack open your head" [then translated to Hebrew:] (Shmuelik, go away, otherwise I'll come outside with a 2x4 and split your head). Needless to say, we didn't keep negotiating with him and we left.

[Page 135]

Military Maneuvers and Exercises

No less interesting were the maneuvers, that we organized nearly twice a week. As noted, our central meeting place was in the Church (tserkva) square; we chose this place for two reasons:

1. Because it was in the middle of the small town, and from this point there was an opportunity for us to observe the bridge over the Ikva, and to the road that goes towards the villages of Smordva, Berehy, and others; the road that goes to Ozliiv and its environs; the road that goes to the main road of Slobada and Uzhynets'; the road that goes to Pecherneda,[96] Dorohostai[97] and more. And thus, there was the opportunity to keep an open eye on the substantial part of the town, which was opposite the Catholic Church and the Ukrainian suburbs called Kruzhuk.
2. Since the remnants of the Russian army, whom we called "Drifters," chose this as the place for gathering. These "guests" would go from place to place, with no objective, except to kill time, and without belonging to any kind of military combat unit, they had gotten accustomed in the meantime to enjoy

124

Mlynov-Muravica Memorial Book

anything that was good which they found in the fertile Ukrainian fields and villages, and this was very convenient. Sometimes [they also] enjoyed something in the small towns from a murder, plunder, or rape. As noted, they chose for themselves to spend the night here [in the Church plaza], and broke down their horses and equipment, to arrange their field kitchen for a rich nighttime dinner, and in general, to watch just as we did, what was being done in the town, in hopes that an opportunity will come their way to grab something. Almost daily, at 5 towards the evening, the honored guests would appear, and in agreement with their predecessors[98] would organize here.

And we, as agreed the day before, gathered in that very same place. We organized a large bonfire, and we baked potatoes for the company, which in the rainy and cold nights were savory to their palate. The main thing was that we observed all the movement of our guests, the small as well as the large. We would not lessen our watchfulness the whole night until they left the town toward morning. Then we knew that time had come that we could rest in our beds in peace, everyone in his own house, with his own family.

And neither [company] "drew close to each other all night" [alluding to Exodus 14.20].[99] I thought of that legend (midrash) when standing each night with our bonfire opposite our uninvited guests in front of their own bonfire. I don't recall one incident from all the nights of guarding, when one of us drew near to them for any conversation, or vice versa that one of them drew near us for any purpose, even though the space between us was negligible. The impression was, that on one side was a force that intended to plunder, rob, and so forth, and on the other side stood a resisting force, and it is very possible that this force of ours was the reason they didn't contend with us.

[Page 136]

If some of these Drifters got up after eating from the bonfire and took leave from the rest of the members, the members of the defense began to follow them immediately, out of suspicion that their intention was to separately carry out some scheme.

For important and essential operations, there were different military exercises and training. Among them: marching, standing correctly, and others. The activity was conducted under the supervision of Mr. Nuta Iskiewicz z"l,[100] since he was a Russian military man and perhaps also successful, even though his age and family situation was different completely from our situation, that of younger men. It is worthwhile pointing out that he dedicated himself completely into this work with all his energy and devotion. He was like one of the young men, and perhaps even more so.

Whoever saw or heard Nuta Iskiewicz marching in front of the unit, marching correctly, a whistle in his mouth, was seeing, not volunteers or men [called up from] reserve, but a real, regular military … I don't recall even a single evening from all the days of guarding when Nuta Iskiewicz was absent, even though he was very busy day to day in his shop of glass items. Mr. Nuta conducted activities in the evenings that were [planned] for improvement, not less than twice a week. And in evenings that were not [planned] for improvement, namely when the Drifters, the uninvited guests, suddenly stayed the night, about whom we got intelligence in advance from our friends, namely, men of the towns around us — then [on those nights] his operation was full of much needed momentum.

One morning, female farmers from nearby villages appeared to buy what they needed from the Jewish shops, and they leaked information, including terrible news: some town was plundered, another [had] a murder, and they warned us that now it was our turn, so to speak; as a reward for the good news, they requested different discounts on their purchases and the like.

Even though we didn't regard this news as completely trustworthy, because we knew that some of the information was intended to scare people of the town, nonetheless, some of the news we necessarily took seriously. In preparation Mr. Nuta Iskiewicz implemented an additional routine activity, a special activity which was like a spectacular display.

And his usual method in "special" operations went like this: In the central place (in the square of the Church [tserkva]), he would station a unit of 15–20 men, and he would take one unit to be a formation in the road that goes Dorohostai[101] to Mlynov, and the second unit he stationed by the municipality[102] and thus similar to an aerial formation, they formed one line, and via signals with different whistles which were prearranged, the two units would begin to march at the same time, and with Russian marching songs, such as "The girls are in the forest and we follow them" and such. The sound of the marching, whistles, and singing made an impression like hundreds of trained marching soldiers. The two units would unite into one large unit by the synagogue and [by the house of] R. Chaim Berger, and they would march together to the house of Beynish Schwartz,[103] and then return in the direction from which they came. The intention was to confuse "the guests" and make an impression and the critical thing was that they would not see our miniscule numbers. This maneuver was very successful, making the required impression and would be repeated all night long.

[Page 137]

Another maneuver which we initiated nearly every evening, and was no less important than the first [was as follows]: since we definitely knew that 90% of our friends didn't know how to use a rifle, and the men on reserve duty were almost afraid to hold a rifle in their hands, so much so that the wives of these men would warn their husbands when they left for guard duty: "Yukal, for God's sake, be careful with the rifle" — therefore, out of caution, we would go out each and every evening, in separate units of about 20 men, to the field by the road towards Uzhynets' and Sloboda, by the house of Mr. Tsodik Shulman, and train there in the handling of rifles, shooting practice and the like. This activity was also accompanied by song, and the noise of the shooting and song made an impression on the people of the villages mentioned above and they thought that in Mlynov — who knows how many soldiers and defenders are there.

The location of training mentioned above was chosen for several reasons: 1) the field opened toward the surrounding villages. 2) [We could visit] in the meantime with the beautiful daughters of Shulman: Sarah-keh, Chiya-keh and Pepe, who live in America to this day.[104] 3) The house of R. Tsodik and Pearl Shulman was the only house in Mlynov, that was beloved by all the Mlynover youth, thanks to their support for youth engaged in cultural activities and such. Therefore, it was unanimously agreed that the maneuvers should be done close to their house, in order to bring the girls out of their isolation, since this house was the last at the end of the town. Each evening, the shooting practice would begin at 8 and ended at midnight — no trivial thing on behalf of those who lived in the house. And thus because of three things: defense, the [location of] Shulman's house, and Shulman's daughters, some men from Dubno, who also feared for the Jews of Mlynov, would visit us in Shulman's house, at night no less, for a meeting, tactical instruction, and the main purpose was the encouragement of our men.

Among the men of Dubno, I remember, there was a Georgian,[105] who was not Jewish, who remained in Dubno, a leftover remnant[106] of the Drifters, with the goal to help in the defense of lives and property of the Jewish population, and it was he, among others, who gave us instruction as follows: 1) don't be the first ones to initiate a battle with men of the regular military, 2) avoid meeting face to face in war. His reasoning was — that we are not able to withstand this, and we will always be the underdog. He taught [us] to scatter in the streets nearby, behind every fence and house, and from there rain fire without stopping.

"But don't act that way," he said to us, "in the event of an attack by the anti-Semites from the villages. With them," he said to us, "conduct the battle face to face, because they will not hold a position, because their fear is great and after some shots from our side they will flee for their lives."

It is worthwhile pointing out, that this Georgian friend was very sweet, very handsome, beloved and cherished, by all and in particular the Jewish girls.

[Page 138]

May his memory be blessed wherever he is. With him a young man from Dubno visited us by the name of Vilner. He was one of the beloved actors from the Dubno theatre, who lives now in one of the cities in the United States.

The trainings under the direction of Mr. Nuta Iskiewicz, the visits to the house of Shulman and the firing practice across from the villages of Sloboda and Uzhynets' to the east of the town — all these were like an occupation and entertainment for the young and the long night passed by pleasantly. All that is related above truly became a routine obligation, and no one thought to avoid participating in guarding even one night.

Robbery Attempts

Guarding was 99% concentrated at night, but also small incidents, of less significance, occurred by the light of day. I — the writer of these lines — I was a witness to what was happening in town during all the hours of the day. My partner and companion was Moshe Gitelman[107] who was called Moshe Ruchel Feivish's [son]; I mentioned him above as the purchaser and supplier of bullets. And it happened, one day, when we were strolling about the streets, we saw from a distance that a man, in a uniform which we didn't recognize, was coming closer, clearly with a rifle in his hand, and at first glance the very beautiful boots [of Moshe] caught his attention, leather chamois, the work of the hands of the shoemaker Shlomo Kreimer.[108] (It is worth pointing out that he was as his name implies: His family name was Kreimer and he in fact had crooked legs, in Yiddish "Krimer"[109]). The soldier mentioned above turned without hesitation and barked an order to Moshe: "Take off your boots, comrade!"

Since the two of us were not frightened children, I said to him, "You will get the boots, but not in the middle of the street. Let's go into one of the nearby houses, he will remove [them] and you can put [them] on, and everything will be settled, and he can go in peace." We entered by chance into the house of the shoemaker, Shlomo Kreimer, and the man was close on our heels. As expected, the owner of the shoemaking workshop did not receive us with great joy, from fear — perhaps something else from his handiwork will appeal to the unknown soldier … but in those days and in that situation at that time one did not refuse. Moshe sat on the shoemaker's bench, took off a boot, and I, as mediator, suggested to the uninvited comrade to put on and wear the boot, [to see] if it was his size.

The fine boot of Moshe fit the foot of the soldier, as they say in Yiddish "on the tip of the nose." He made an effort to put his foot in the boot, but it wouldn't happen. I said to him, "Friend, take off the boot please, since it doesn't fit your foot." He obviously didn't want to give up the windfall, but in the end, when he wanted to relinquish the boot, this also wasn't possible. The effort to remove his foot from the boot was accompanied by known, spicy Russian "blessings" [i.e., curses].

When I offered my help, to extricate him from the situation, he rejected my help and said, "No, no, let him give me the second boot and I will manage … "

[Page 139]

When I heard his refusal of my help, I seized the opportunity, with him in an uncomfortable situation and unable to pursue anyone, and turned to Moshe and said, "Take the opportunity and flee with one boot!" Moshe didn't hesitate. He opened the door and he fled … when the soldier saw what happened he began to shout, "The son of a bitch, where did he flee?"

I said to him, "I am not responsible for him, chase him if you are able …" In the end, with great difficulty he got the boot off, and with a curse peppered with "sons of bitches" he left the house in disgrace and went on his way.

And here is the second [incident] — also involving boots. In those days the most elegant clothing of the young people was French.[110] Etched pants and shiny boots. I also desired boots like these. While the color of most boots was black, I was very lucky to have brown boots the color by which all the military officers adorned themselves. I had a big daily argument at home with my father, z"l, when I put on the boots, "You'll see what those boots are going to cause you …" I obviously paid no heed to his words. Each and every day I would put on those aforementioned boots.

Thus one day, when I saw in the street there was some movement of mounted soldiers, I went outside out of curiosity to see what was happening. And while standing innocently by the fence of our house, three of the military riders drew near and turned to me with "advice:" "Friend, remove your shoes." Having learned from experience I told them that they should accompany me to my home, and I would willingly give them the boots. Since they didn't know that I was standing beside my house, I took the opportunity and told them to follow me a bigger distance. After a number of steps, I got the idea to bring them to the smithy of Aharon the blacksmith (Koval),[111] for two reasons: 1) he was a courageous man, 2) he was my uncle, and 3) it was a workshop. When I drew close to the smithy, I went in, took off my jacket, and approached the bellows they used to stoke the coals, and began to work, as if I was one of the workers there. Aharon Koval immediately understood the situation and did not say a thing, but simply waited to see what would happen.

At that moment, the soldiers stopped in the gate of the smithy on their horses and yelled to me: "Friend, take off your boots."

I replied, "Friends, I am the blacksmith's apprentice and only with great effort do I earn enough for clothing; and you are going to take my boots?"

My words, apparently, made little impression on them, and one of them got down from his horse and approached the place where I was and said to me, "Show me your hands!" When he saw that my hands were those of a "gemara boy,"[112] he called out jokingly to his friends, "Look, comrades, at the hands of a blacksmith," and showed them my clean, white, hands.

I said to them, "Friends, the period of the Tzarist regime has passed when all workers are dressed in dirty torn rags, with blackened faces and hands, etc. Now we wash well, dress well before we go outside and we look like everyone else."

Then the third [soldier] said: "Come let's leave him," and they left …

[Page 140]

The "Sixers" Are Coming!

The men of defense in Mlynov at that time were gaining more and more self-confidence; they neither feared nor were impressed by the rumors that were spread by the anti-Semitic farmers from the villages in the area. We knew and were confident [that] in the event of an attack upon us by independent forces, that we would prevail. The main preparation was for the unexpected, for we didn't know — when and from where the surprise would come from the "Drifters" who were moving about here and there, from place to place.

The main fear was from the men of the Sixth Division that they called the "Sixers." And if a Jewish shop owner, for example, did not agree to the price for herring, a kilogram of salt, etc. — immediately the threat would come from the buyer, who was a farmer: "Just you wait, soon time will come when the Sixers will fall upon you and do to you what they did to the other towns nearby." This is how it was in the convenience shops, textiles stores, haberdashery, etc. This refrain was repeated day in and day out. Of course, this influenced the members of the defense to be motivated and prepared.

Then we received word that finally the Sixers would come to us to spend the night. Since the place designated to spend the night and for dinner was opposite the Church (tserkva), we expanded the guarding that same day while it was still daylight; we organized a large bonfire, and around it was a large segment of the defense members, singing different songs that inspired cheerfulness and raised the spirit; that was on one side. On the second side, marching under the direction of Nute Iskiewicz, which included Bathhouse Street and Kruzhuk Street, they too were singing different songs, and on the third side — trained shooters by the house of Shulman. All this together made an impression like you were in a battlefield. At night, clearly, the impression was very striking. Our "Sixers" indeed came for an overnight stay during the expected evening, as was their custom in every little town. But their situation was different than in other small towns. They were impressed by all the commotion mentioned above, and they didn't leave their spot all night. Obviously, we followed them with great alertness, their numbers I don't remember, but they were armed properly, and there wasn't an incident in which one of them left the group for a stroll at night about the town. Towards morning, when they got up and began to gather their belongings to leave the town — we breathed easier and knew that the fear was behind us. It is worth mentioning, that the news of the Sixers overnight stay flew throughout the town, and all the Jewish inhabitants were at the ready in their homes all night long. During the first "quorum" (minyan),[113] for praying at dawn in the synagogue, the first conversation of the worshippers was about the overnight stay of the Sixers in town, which passed without any loss of life or property.

[Page 141]

New Threats

The overnight stay of the "Sixers," which passed peacefully, did not satiate the palate of the anti-Semites in the area, who had hoped in vain for something "happy." After several weeks of rest after the threat of the "Sixers," farmers from the area came with a threat and another story. Rumors spread that a unit of soldiers was going to attack us one night soon, and the attack would be sudden. They even indicated from which road they would come. They said the marauders were going to come from the side of the main road of the cemetery, in other words, from the east side of the town. Obviously, not all the guarding was directed to that side, but instead towards all the roads leading to Mlynov, but preparation and special attention was nonetheless directed towards the eastern side.

Whenever preparing for special incidents, including this one, we adjusted the method of meeting and preparations. For this incident, we decided to meet those [soldiers] who were not familiar to us, not as defenders against an army, but as army against army. But how could we do this? — We knew that the top of certain kinds of trees falls regularly year to year, and decomposes on the ground, and at night gives off a light like phosphorous. Therefore, we sent several of the defense members to the forest of Uzhynets' and they brought back the material that sparkles at night, and it occurred to me, that we could give the material to the women of the town, who could make all kinds of military symbols, like stars, honorary ribbons, and more, and we could attach them to the shoulders and chest, and suddenly, overnight, we would be transformed into a regular service of military men (only at night …). This [wearing of badges] was also included in the different entertainment activities and the group didn't want to remove them even for a regular night during the week. It is worth pointing out that all the different kinds of ribbons, and badges of distinction, were apparently made with such discernment that it was not possible to tell the difference between them and the honorific badges received by the regular military.

Indeed, as noted, the work on stars and ranks was done by the girls of the town, but the oversight was done by Moshe Grenspun z"l,[114] from Parmilovka,[115] who, by the way, encountered his tragic death in Russia. If I am not mistaken, also Ahron Berger (now Harari)[116] who is living in Kibbutz Merhavia, was a great help in the work mentioned above.

The preparations continued for the encounter with the unknown [soldiers] who, according to the reports of the farmers in the area whose words we didn't fully trust, were supposed to come via the forest of Uzhynets'. And of course, every evening we paid special attention to that side. And I remember that one Sabbath eve when the company was in high spirits, we saw from the main Rivne road that the riding soldiers had turned off onto the dirt road that came towards town. We had no doubt that finally these were those unknown ones who were heading towards us to execute their scheme. The only question among us was whether they were the scouts ahead of the arriving camp, or the perpetrators themselves; from the distance we noticed only a small number of riders.

[Page 142]

I don't know who gave the order but, as in all the incidents, the order arose spontaneously. We organized in rows one behind the other, with rifles on shoulders, the officers with whistles in their mouths, and the rows began to move towards them. The space between them and us grew closer from moment to moment. And when we advanced in the direction of the main road to Rovno, they advanced in direction of the town.

Suddenly we saw that they had stopped in the square that was in front of "Dikan"[117] (the priest's assistant) which was northeast of the church (tserkva). At that exact moment the order was given to the column of defense to halt. It is worth pointing out that the column moved at the pace of Russian soldiers, organized in Russian military formation, "One, two, three!" Immediately, they took their rifles down from their shoulders and the formation stood at "ease," and the area that separated us was about 50 meters, a very small and limited space. But the situation was already impossible to change, and we were primed for what would go down. Given the closeness, we could hear their words [and] one asked another, "Which army is this?" The question arose, apparently, from the impression made by the organized marching and clothing with the honorary emblems. The answer came immediately, "the Devil knows them." And immediately followed the suggestion, "You know what, comrades, come let's turn back." And immediately they arranged themselves and returned the way they came. We followed behind them in their footsteps, of course at a good distance, and when they got to the main road that goes to Rovno, we reached the house of the beautiful daughters — of the Shulman house. The girls saw what was happening through their windows and they welcomed us joyfully, which was customary almost every night.

After this evening and the prior evenings involving the "Sixers," including the frequent meetings with the Drifters — if, after all this, no disaster occurred, it was a sign that all the terrible things that were likely to happen in our town were behind us and we felt a kind of respite. Thus, almost all the members of the defense returned to their work and daily lives, whether assisting in a shop, with trade, or in labor. Obviously, we didn't neglect the defense, and we nourished it almost every evening as a valuable asset. It is noteworthy that the defense united and drew the youth close together, something that didn't exist in Mlynov before its establishment.

* * *

Since there was no industry or even small workshops in Mlynov, everyone was dedicated to trade and commerce blossomed then, and since this was in essence a time of war, the essential necessities, like salt, kerosene, and more, were not to be found, except in the underground. But the profit in the commodities just mentioned was great, and provided the temptation to engage in this trade, which in my opinion was not an appropriate thing to do.[118] For example: the farmer from the village would need to pay a large portion of his wheat or barley for one kilogram of salt or a bottle of kerosene and so on.

[Page 143]

Not infrequently we heard resentment about these unreasonable exchanges, and I am sure that this bitterness continued to leave its mark in the days following the war.

As noted, the core commerce was in salt and kerosene, work that was easy with a very large profit. But I admit without shame: that in order that others not view me as an "unsuccessful" man, [who was] negligent and so on, which was not a great advantage for [a good] matchmaking, to support a family, etc., I also engaged in this trade … My area for this commerce was in the west [of town] until Berestechko, and east to Mizoch, even though the roads were dangerous due to the Drifters, since, on the one hand, all the roads were in their control, and on the other hand, since the farmers were angered about the large profiteering in essential goods. They would attack on the roads and knew, that if a Jew passed by — one of two things was the case: that his pockets were full of money so he could buy goods or because he had sold goods, and this would induce attacks of robbery. Their slogan was: "Stick 'em up." And for refusing to obey, not a few paid with their lives. They would attack their victims in two [types of] places: in a dusty place during the summer and a muddy place in the winter, or on a slope up a hill, two places in which it is not possible to flee or travel quickly. There were those among the Jewish youth who, in the places previously mentioned, were accustomed to [proactively] confront the evil and scare the robbers with gun shots. This possibility was presented to nearly all the youth, since almost all of them were members of the defense and went nowhere without their rifle.

The flourishing commerce, the meetings with friends, and occasionally parties with a drink of alcohol, did not weaken the devotion to guarding of life and property in our town. On every trip, near or far, towards evening an invisible force pulled you home to happily take part. And just as a religious Jew would hurry during the late afternoon leading up to the Sabbath to reach his town before the Sabbath began, so the defense members would hurry and be punctilious to arrive home, in order to be present at the appointed time, and not be late even by a little.

* * *

In those days, without a newspaper or news by telegraph, the population was nourished by word of mouth,[119] in other words, news from the synagogue shared behind the warm stove and more … and it is worth pointing out that though most of the news was from nonofficial places, most turned out to be true.

Among the previously mentioned news was a whisper that the Germans had made an agreement with the Ukrainians, that they would gain independence under a German Protectorate and somewhere they had already established a government called "Hetman," at whose head was a fellow by the name of Skoropadsky.[120] But in exchange for the deal mentioned previously, Ukraine was obliged to help the invading German army with men, with equipment and most importantly with food, which was so depleted in Germany, after the military defeat.

[Page 144]

Jews in the area greeted these rumors with great joy, since they had faith that the Germans would destroy all the local gangs, drive out the remnants of the Russian army, that had caused the Jewish population grief and fear of the future.

The rumors about the establishment of a new reign, a Messianic kingdom as it were, that to the Ukrainian Jews would resemble a German protectorate, passed from mouth to mouth, from person to person, from town to town; and what accounts for all of them expecting the coming of the Righteous Redeemer? There was no doubt that the matter would surely come to pass. The only question was the timing, in other words, when? Following the suffering of the Ukrainian Jews, the constant fear without end, the Jewish population wanted to receive and live under any government, as long as, obviously, change would come to the unruly situation that had previously victimized the

Jews, and they adopted the Ukrainian idiom, "It could be worse, but it will be different."[121] These rumors, indeed, to a great extent unburdened, psychologically speaking, the general population and in particular, the members of the defense, but the defense regiment, guarding etc. continued as before and the young people had commerce and work in one hand, and in the other hand — the rifle.

Attention then turned towards what was going on in Ludmir,[122] Kovel, and Lutsk etc, since we knew, according to our reckoning, that the conquerors would come from there. There was general interest — how the Germans would execute the invasion of Ukraine. Would there be resistance from the crumbling Russian military, [what would be] the reaction of the local population and especially the Jewish [population], and the opposite – the behavior and relationship of the invaders to the population in general and Jews in particular. Not much time passed when we heard that the Germans were advancing towards us in giant strides.

Then on a clear day we learned that the Germans were already in Kovel, and on the following day, we heard that they were already in Lutsk, and since we already knew that that area didn't have any regular or non-regular Russian military, we estimated that in another day or two, they would be in Mlynov.

During that time, exactly in fact the day the changing of the guards occurred,[123] I was spending the day outside of Mlynov. During the evening when I returned to town, I found in the courtyard opposite the Church (tserkva), where we had invested so much planning and energy, a large number of German canons. I went into my house, so they could see that I had returned safely home and then I ran straight to the synagogue, the place of the "slipper post" [i.e., word of mouth news], in order to know how the guards had changed and what tomorrow would bring?

In the entrance to the corridor known as "Palush," the place where initially the possessions of the defense had been kept, exactly in that place, a German officer came towards me, accompanied by Pochbar Prystufa[124] (the Ukrainian who became notorious in the days of Hitler. They told me about him, that in the period when they put up barbed wire around the ghetto of Mlynov, he was the one who checked and found that the space between the wires was too large, and that it was possible to find a way for food to enter, God forbid, to those living in the ghetto), he pointed towards me, [indicating] that this is the very same man who heads the defense in town.

[Page 145]

There on the spot the commander asked me if I was that man who led the defense. After my affirmative answer he asked me if we had weapons, how many and what type? I answered him, that I didn't know the precise number but apart from the rifles we didn't have any other weapons and I added, "Since the goal of the defense members was purely to guard the lives of the town's population, we did not need weapons apart from the rifles."

Then he said to me, "Tell the Jews, that they should bring all their weapons to the Commander, so I don't need to send my men to gather the weapons, otherwise matters will be far worse …"

After this instruction they brought me to the apartment of Moshe Aharon, the sexton, which was part of the synagogue, and I found young Ukrainians inside who were being guarded by German sentries. No one knew the intent of imprisonment. I was extremely angry since I was the only young man from the youth of the town, among the non-Jewish boys (shkotzim). After several hours, about 8 in the evening, I turned to the head of the sentries and explained to him, "Since I was on the road traveling, I didn't eat all day, and I am thirsty and hungry; I beg you to accompany me to my house, so I can prepare dinner." He asked his supervisor and with his agreement went with me to my home; I ate and drank and returned to the place of imprisonment.

The development of these events was very difficult for me. It was clear that all of us were imprisoned — I being the only Jew from Mlynov — in order to help the Germans, according to an agreement the Germans had with the Ukrainians. We were brought to Lutsk — and after many adventures after many days of wandering, I had a chance to escape from this entire situation. I returned with the help of my father to Mlynov and from there they transferred me, for the sake of additional security to the town of Mizoch, where I stayed with my relative.

And in summary, the agreement between the Germans and Ukrainian to give independence to the Ukrainian plunderers, and the ban by the German governing bodies on weapons that were in the hands of the defense members, determined the fate of the defense, and thereby ended the magnificent matter of defense in Mlynov.

And if your child asks you in the future[125] — "what was the strength of the defense in Mlynov, which succeeded in all its operations and which retained its position for an extended period?" — I don't have a specific answer. One thing is worth mentioning: the most important factor was the unanimity, indeed the will, the great discipline without supervision and without arrogance, without authority or commanding officers, neither big nor small. It seems to me, that this was the biggest success of all. I don't remember even one tiny, small incident in which a member of the defense refused to fulfill his role or obligation and so forth. At the beginning of this essay, we mentioned that those opposed to defense were principally among those who sat in the study hall (beit midrash). Their claim was: since the remains of Rabbi Aharon from Karlin, the Admor,[126] is in the ground of Mlynov — his merit will protect us from all evil, and there is no need at all for defense, rifles and the like … Those who believe will believe, for the fact is that during this entire period, there was not a small town that did not taste of plunder, rape or murder, but only in Mlynov nothing bad happened through the merit of the Admor, let [one who believes that] live by his faith … But it must be added that the principal cause nevertheless was the defense.

Translator's and editor's footnotes:

1. The author's surname appears at times as "Mandelkern" and "Mandelkorn" in Hebrew and in Yad Vashem records. Shmuel Mandelkern married Malcah Lamdan (sister of the famous poet, Yitzhak Lamdan) and the couple made aliyah in 1924. Their individual photos appear in this volume, p. 482 and they appear in the group photo on p. 66 this volume. Mandelkern played a leadership role in the development of the Zionist Youth Groups in Mlynov, as described in the essay by Aaron Harari in this volume, "Culture, Education, and Social Life in the Small Town," pp. 66-69. He was also a town prankster described in the essay by Boruch Meren, "An Event in the Shtetl," pp. 188-195. From the list of martrys, it appears that Shmuel's mother was named Nekhama. His father's name is not listed. His mother, sister Perel, and brother Moshe, were killed in the Shoah. Shmuel's other siblings, Yitzhak and Yosef, made it to Israel.

2. Using a non-Hebrew word here for "externals" and probably referring to "outsiders" or those who are studying in secular studies in the universities.

3. The author ironically uses the terms Torah and Hokmah, terms for traditional Jewish learning, as descriptions of the new secular studies that had opened up.

4. An allusion to Pirkei Avot 4:1: "Who is rich? One who is happy in his portion."

5. It is not clear here if the worry was the lack of merchandize because of the economic situation or the fact that he wasn't selling briskly enough (i.e., clearing the shelves).

6. Literally, the "pot turned upside down."

7. See note 2.

8. The term "hefker" is a legal concept in Jewish Law meaning "ownerless" or "abandoned" and used most often to describe abandoned and unclaimed property.

9. The term appears to be a name, but the meaning is not certain.

10. The Yiddish name of Novohrad Volynskyi.

11. Referring to Aharon of Karlin II (June 6, 1802 – June 23, 1872), the grandson of the founder, who died suddenly in Mlynov. See the folklorist account by Eliyahu Gelman in this volume about the tree that looked like a menorah (pp. 31–32) which grew in the spot where he died. A number of other contributors to this volume, like Sylvia Barditch-Goldberg, p. 80, and Moshe Fishman, p. 60, recall the memorial in town as well as the memorial yahrzeit that would bring many people to Mlynov.

12. The text appears to say Rogachev, but probably was meant to be Berdychiv, which is consistent with the towns listed above in the Zhytomyr district.

13. These villages are all west of Mlynov and close by.

14. Meaning, that since Mlynov was closest, it took precedence.

15. One says the prayer, "birkat hagomel," when one has survived an event or after one has traveled.

16. From the Yiddish for "six," alluding to the 6th division name.

17. Today Mizoch, Ukraine, 52 km east of Mlyniv.

18. Today 100 km south of Mlyiv and a bit to the east.

19. Not far from Shumsk, Kuniv is 107 km from Mlynov.

20. A Ukrainian word for church structure.

21. Also referred to as Moshe Arelas (literally meaning Moshe, Aaron's [son]) was the son of Aharon Hirsch. He is the brother mentioned in the ghost story of Daniel Hirsch's murder by Shirley Jacobs, "A True Event in Mlynov from 96 Years Ago," pp. 196–197. The Hirsch children were all referred to as "Arelas." Aleph Katz's mother was called Henia Arelas for the same reason.

22. Father of the poet Yitzhak Lamdan.

23. The writer is using the full term "rabbi" for these names, but it is probably an honorific title like Mr. even in these cases.

24. Efraim-Fishel from the Teitelman family, one of the six children of Asher Teitelman.

25. Psalm 127:1 being interpreted to mean that defense was in vain if God was not watching over the city.

26. Father of Lipa Halperin, one of the contributors to this volume.

27. Surname also spelled "Isakovich." Yad Vashem records indicates that Nute was born in Mlynov in 1872 and was a housewares trader. His wife's name was Rachel and they had a daughter Zlate (or Zlata) and they lived in Luck where they were all killed during the War. A daughter Sarah lived in Israel and a son Avigdor lived in Canada.

Nute was related to the family of Eliezer Iskiewicz, possibly his brother, whose photo appears in this volume, p. 464. Below, the author tells us that Isakovich had a military background and helped with the drills for the defense units.

28. There were five Goldseker brothers who were the sons of Avraham and Baila Goldseker in the oldest generation in Mlynov: Hirsch, Moishe, Yankel, Shimon, Yoel. The three Goldsekers named here were likely among their sons: Yehoshua and Moishe (sons of Yankel Goldseker) and Yaakov (son of Moishe Goldseker).

29. The term "hafstal" appears to be Yiddish for "the abstract" and the meaning appears to be "summarize" the matter.

30. The term "ordynik" does not appear to be either Hebrew or Yiddish and perhaps is Ukrainian or Polish for "ordinary."

31. Quoting a rabbinic expression in Aramaic.

32. Possibly Efraim-Fishel Teitelman who is mentioned earlier.

33. See Babli Kebutot 18b, meaning here that they were not going to change their decision.

34. "Palush" is a rare term in Hebrew for entrance way or corridor.

35. It appears this is meant figuratively, "it smelled of danger," since they had not yet purchased rifles.

36. The town elders did not suggest that meeting of the defense members violated the Sabbath restrictions in line with a rabbinic principle (Yoma 85a) that treats saving a life ("pikuah nefesh") as superseding the restrictions of the Sabbath. Defense activity was interpreted as "saving a life."

37. Referring apparently to Yosef Gelberg, Pinhas Meir's son, who is remembered elsewhere in this volume as the wealthy owner of the mill in town, and the one who first brought electricity to the town. Read more about the Gelberg family on the Mlynov website.

38. The grandfather of Liba Halperin, who told him the folklore about how the Ikva River got its name, in the essay called "The Mill," pp. 13–15. Mordechai-Meir Shrentzil's photo appears on p. 458 in this volume.

39. A photo of Beynish Schwartz appears in this volume, p. 478. His home is mentioned again below.

40. The valley between Mlynov and Mervits where later the ghetto liquidation took place. Referred to below as the Ukrainian suburbs.

41. Efraim Fischel Teitelman, father of Nahum Teitelman.

42. Mr. Fishel was one of the men who had turned down the use of rifles earlier. The incident near his house helped change his mind. He is calling it "a good deed" here because it helped change opinion.

43. Below, the Shulman house is described at the east end of town on the road that leads towards Uzhynets' and Slobada.

44. Possibly a priest in town based on the analogy with the following quote from Scripture.

45. In Exodus 18:9, Moses tells his father-in-law, Jethro, a gentile priest of Midian, all that God had done to Pharoah for the sake of the Israelites. Jethro rejoices. By analogy even the priest in Mlynov was happy with the defense.

46. An Aramaic term meaning literally "flour of Passover" but referring to charity on Passover for the purchase of matza and other necessities.

47. The PPS or Polish Socialist Party (Polish: Polska Partia Socjalistyczna, PPS) is a left-wing Polish political party. It was one of the most important parties in Poland from its inception in 1892 until its dissolution in 1948.

48. Probably, Israel Halperin, the father of Lipa Halperin, a contributor to this volume. The surname is here spelled "Galperin" with a "gimel," but the surname is typically spelled as "Halperin" in English and thus rendered that way in this translation.

49. "Polkovnik" is a military title in Eastern armies.

50. Mandelkern is thinking of himself as the biblical Isaac who is walking with his father Abraham, not knowing that Abraham is intending to bind him for a sacrifice at God's command (Genesis 22).

51. The Communist Revolution had repossessed the estates of the large landowners.

52. The term appears to be "yacht" in Yiddish and is here interpreted as "the upper crust."

53. The Hebrew uses the Polish term, "Cerkiew," which means church structure.

54. The identity of the last two town names is not certain. The enumerated towns appear to be going in an eastern direction, but the last two towns are unclear, perhaps Koniv and Ostriv to remain consistent with directionality, though the Hebrew names appear more like "Kunow" and "Austria" which would be a great distance in the other Westerly direction and do not appear to fit the context.

55. See previous note.

56. Klepatch descendant Joyce Jandorf indicates that Rabbi Yitzchak Leib Klepatch, who lived in Smordva, used to be involved in Mlynov with cemetery maintenance and other activities. His son Moshe lived in Mlynov and raised a family there.

57. Using the Yiddish word "glikn."

58. This town is not identified unless Kivertsi is intended though that seems too far away to explain its use.

59. A small town just outside Mlynov today to the east and south.

60. Tsodik Shulman and his wife Pearl Malka (Demb) and his daughters Sarah, Clara, and Pepe immigrated to Baltimore in 1921. There, Pepe Shulman married her first cousin, Paul Schwartz from Mlynov, and is the grandmother of Howard Schwartz, the editor of this volume. Clara Shulman married Ben Fishman from Mervits and Sarah Shulman married Paul Settleman from Mervits, who retained the name Paul Shulman since he had immigrated with the Shulman family.

61. Allusion to the language in Genesis (1:4, 1:10, 1:18) in which God "saw that it was good" after various acts of creation.

62. Using the rabbinic expression "see and sanctify it."

63. Literally, "semolina and oil."

64. The location of a village by this name near Demydivka has not been identified.

65. For a similar story involving a Mlynov man, see the story of Daniel Hirsch in Shirley Jacob's essay, "A True Event in the Shtetl," pp. 196-198.

66. Referring to Shimon Schechman, son of Noach Moshe Schechman and Faiga Wolk. Shimon's photo appears in the group photo on p. 226 this volume and he is mentioned in the essay by Aaron Harari in "Visit to Mlynov in 1938," pp. 77–80. His brother, Shlomo, survived WW2 and later made his way to the US and eventually to Baltimore.

67. The wheels removed and turned into a sleigh according to oral traditions in the Epstein family.

68. The second word, "muchtar," is a Turkish term used for the head of a village.

69. The term "hefker" is a legal term that typically refers to abandoned and ownerless property. Here the term means that you can't take Jewish blood without consequences.

70. The expression represented in Hebrew letters appears to be a Polish curse (Do Tsyenshkay Kholyery Vyaryat). The word "cholera" (kholyery) is a nasty curse word in Polish.

71. Expressed in Yiddish, "khlisha shtuv."

72. Perhaps an allusion to Haim Nachman Bialik poem called "In the evening of the day."

73. Father of Lipa Halperin, a contributor to this volume.

74. Also spelled Neta Isakovich. Nute was a cousin of Moshe Iskiewicz who is a contributor to this volume. According to Yad Vashem records filled out by Moshe, Nute was born in Mlynov in 1872 and was a housewares trader. He died in Luck during the Shoah as did his daughter Zlata, who was 30 years old and single. A daughter Sarah lived in Israel and a son Avigdor in Canada, according to the Memorial book list of martyrs.

75. According to Yad Vashem records filled out by his daughter and survivor, Rachel (Kwasgalter) Rabinowitz, Meir Kwasgalter was born in Mlynov in 1896. Meir died in the Shoah at the age of 48 and was killed in the forest of Mlynov by the Soviets. His parents were Faivel Kwasgalter and Leah (surname unknown). He married Sheina (also called Sheintzi) who was born in 1900 in Rovno, maiden name Gonik or Genik. They also had a son Chaim born in 1931. Sheindel and their son Chaim died in the liquidation of the Mlynov ghetto.

76. Probably referring to Saul Halpern's father, Yosel or Joseph, who was the brother of Israel Halperin.

77. Probably referring to Yankel, one of the five Holtzeker sons of Abraham and Baila, whose large family photo appears on page 245 and whose home appears on page 79 of this volume.

78. The Hebrew construction here is not clear but the gist is that they could make a unit of their own soldiers.

79. From the martyr list, p. 133, and Yad Vashem records filled out by daughter Rachel (Shapovnik) Givol, Abisch Shapovnik (1882–1939) was born in Lutsk but lived in Mlynov. He died in the Mlynov ghetto in 1939. He was married to Khaia Friedman. In addition to Rachel, they had two sons Levi (1911–1942) and Moshe (1930–1942), and a daughter, Brakha. Rachel Shapovnik appears in a photo on page 9 in this volume.

80. Abisch's wife's name per the previous note is Khaia (Friedman) so it seems reasonable to conclude that his father-in-law R. Yosel's last name is Friedman as well.

81. See note 74.

82. Part of the expression appears in Deut. 28:48.

83. The structure of the sentence is confusing but seems to imply that he got the horse before he had the wherewithal to feed him and thus pastured him in the open fields.

84. The word does not appear to be Hebrew unless it transposes letters for "kevodo" (befitting their honor).

85. Evoking a Talmudic expression of reasoning by analogy (gezerah shava).

86. The Hebrew is "peloni." In English the closest expression is "Joe Shmo" or "the average Joe."

87. See note 57 where the same expression is used and is an allusion to God's approval in Genesis of what has been created.

88. A humorous allusion to the language of Pharoah's dream which Jacob successfully interprets in Genesis 41:2 in which seven "handsome and plump" cows are grazing in the Nile.

89. See previous note.

90. Literally "in their nakedness."

91. The Hebrew is a bit confusing, but the intent seems clearly to be that to avoid the daughters exposing their presence to the soldiers, the responsibility fell on their brother.

92. Yantil appears to have a speech impairment called primary dyslalia, which today is considered a very simple problem to correct in 2 or 3 speech therapy sessions.

93. It may be the writer intended the Yiddish to be "aynshtiln zikh" "be quiet."

94. Shimon Goldseker was one of the five brothers who came to Mlynov. His daughter, Eta Goldseker, subsequently married David Fishman in Palestine and the couple later moved to Baltimore.

95. Eta's descendants remember a story that Eta would pretend to be part of the Red Army and would make trips across Russia and smuggle contraband back to Mlynov in a teapot.

96. Perhaps Puhachivka which is just beyond Mali Dorohostai on the same road.

97. Probably [Mali] Dorohostai which is on a road not far from where the Ikva reaches Mlynov.

98. The intent seems to be that these roving bands would tell each other where they had encamped, and one would follow another.

99. Quoting Exodus 14:20 in which the cloud / angel of God stayed between the Egyptian and the Israelite camps and "one did not draw close to the other."

100. See note 27 for notes on his background.

101. The text says "to Dorashti," "to Mlynov," but is understood as the road between the two since the units were already in Mlynov. Dorohostai is assumed to be "Mali Dorohostai" on contemporary maps.

102. The term "gmina" refers to a principal unit of the administrative division of Poland, like a municipality. It appears he is referring to a building in town for administrative purposes.

103. The home of Beynish Schwartz, p. 122, is mentioned earlier as at the beginning of the square. A photo of Beynish appears in this volume, p. 478.

104. See note 60 on the Shulman background.

105. Referring to the ethnic group native to Georgia and the South Caucasus, also called Kartvelians.

106. It is not entirely clear if he was originally a Drifter himself or a refugee from the Drifters.

107. The list of martyrs, p. 433, lists Moshe Gitelman, his wife Sal, and their daughter Yehudit (~1926–1942). A Yad Vashem record submitted by Moshe Isakovich indicates there was a second daughter, age 12, whose name is no longer remembered.

108. Family name spelled "Kreimer" in Yad Vashem records. The family is included in the list of matyrs, p. 438: Shlomo Kreimer, (Shlomo the shoemaker, with disability), Teltzi his wife; [children] Yaakov, Rachel, Aharon, and Shmuel.

109. In Yiddish meaning someone with a limp. – HBF

110. The term "frnttze" is not Hebrew and appears to be "French" in Russian.

111. His surname Kowal means blacksmith in Polish.

112. Delicate like one who studies a lot.

113. Quorum of at least 10 required to say certain prayers.

114. A Moshe Grenspun appears seated second from the right in a photo on p. 203 labelled "educated ones." The same photo includes Shmuel Mandelkern (seated left) who is the writer of this essay.

115. Unidentified village.

116. Aaron (Berger) Harari is one of the other major contributors to this volume.

117. Possibly Yiddish or Russian for "deacon."

118. Boruch Meren tells the story of his father Ben-Tzion Meren attempting to work and ultimately failing in the black market in kerosene in "The Treasure That Ran Out," pp. 272-276.

119. Literally "slipper post." – HBF

120. On April 29, 1918, the Rada government was overthrown in a German-supported coup by Gen. Pavlo Skoropadsky.

121. Anything different would be better.

122. Volodymyr-Volynsky 75 km east of Lutsk.

123. Referring to the Central Powers advance and occupation in the summer of 1918 following the Brest-Litovsk Treaty.

124. An identification of this person has not been established.

125. An allusion to the children who ask four questions on Passover.

126. An acronym for the honorific title "Our Master, our teacher, our Rabbi."

[Page 146]

My Dove

Translated and edited by Howard I. Schwartz, PhD with Hanina Epstein

A multitude of doves making love to lovers (ahavim)
Among the branches of the oak in the thickness of the forest (hayar)
There we sat also slaked our lovers' thirst (dodim)
On the trunk of a tree, we carved our names with a blade (be-taar).

While still day the trees there are animated
The doves on it during the day make love (yitalsu)
And names of both of us, as of now have been erased
There on the trunk where they were (yitnossu)

How my dove is making noise and rebellious
I didn't know where she was carried by the wind (ruah)
To the oaks she will no longer come
in the spreading shade, a day that the wind will blow (yafuah).

Dr. Soloman Mandelkern[1]
(from his book, "Hebrew Poems")

Translator's and editor's footnotes:

1.   Shlomo Mandelkern (1846–1902), a poet, rabbi, Haskalah writer, was born in Mlynov. He went to Dubno after his father's death at the age of 14 and spent time with the Hasidim of that community and the son of the rebbe Menachem Mendel of Kotzk. He subsequently left and studied in Vilna where he became a rabbi and later studied Oriental languages at St. Petersburg University. In 1873 he became assistant rabbi at Odessa, where he was the first to deliver sermons in Russian, and where he studied law at the university. The degree of Ph.D. was conferred upon him by the University of Jena. About 1880 he settled in Leipzig and occupied himself with literary works and with teaching. In 1900 he visited the United States. He returned to Leipzig in 1901 and was visiting Vienna when he suddenly became ill and died in the Jewish hospital there. He was most famous for the Concordance to the Bible that he compiled.

[Page 147]

In Pain from the First World War

by Helen Lederer[1], United States

Translated from the Yiddish by Hannah B. Fischthal, PhD

Edited by Howard I. Schwartz, PhD

It was during the time of the first World War. A cold winter day, a burning frost, a deep snow. The Germans are getting closer to our town Mlynov. All of us are taken out of our homes. The soldiers intrude into the synagogue sanctuary and pack us inside, like sardines. We are lying in great anxiety — not knowing what to expect. 2:00 a.m. An angry wind howls, like devils dancing. A banging is heard. Soldiers are standing with guns. They order everybody to go out into the street.

The soldiers have brought wagons, which are standing there: "Pack what you can on the wagons, and you — walk." The horses can barely drag themselves in the deep snow. Women and children shlep after the wagons on the way to Varkevetsh.[2] Everybody's hands are busy grabbing provisions for the children to eat. My mother, Gitl

(Pesye Khoylye's daughter),[3] has four small, crying children shlepping along with her. Also my Aunt Soreke (Pesye Khoylye's daughter) is going, carrying something in both hands, with her little girl Dvoyrele. After having walked a few versts,[4] Soreke looked around – the child is not there! … She screamed; there was a commotion; Soreke ran back. The soldiers with their rifles drove on and said that the Austrians use searchlights on us; they will see her walking, and they will shoot. Soreke crept back and found Dvoyrele in the snow, passed out!

It is day. We get to Varkevetsh. We come to our relative Nakhman Leyb.[5] There is not even room for a pin. There is my grandfather, Leybush Gershon's;[6] both his daughters Chana-Gitl[7] and Chaye[8]; and other refugees — there is no place for us. And there is no place to go to. Frozen, tired … at last we see a cover over the cellar-- the only empty spot. We put a feather bed on it, and we lay down, exhausted.

The next day we were on the way to Oziran.[9] Until we managed to get there is another chapter.

[Page 148]

In Oziran we learned that we had to walk from there to Rovne.[10] With great effort and suffering, a few people with us made it to Rovne. However, not a single house in Rovne had room for more people; all the houses were filled up with unlucky refugees.

So we stood, my mother with the children—[aunt] Soreke, her little girl, and Basye-Chaye (Malke's daughter),[11] a pregnant woman during her time who was pitifully shivering from the cold.

It is said: a gentile makes the exile longer … Imagine that near us stands a coachman and speaks Yiddish the same as we do. A lover of Jews. He even gives money to the rabbi, to help the poor … And this angel in a human image takes all of us under his protection. Namely, he took us to his home through an underground door — so that his anti-Semitic wife would not see us. Over there we stretched out our tired bones.

Coming out into the street, we learned about the Joint Help Committee from America; they gave out packages of food to every refugee.[12] So my mother stood in line and, thank God, we now had what to eat.

Basye-Chaye (Malke's daughter) suffered labor pains, and after much anguish she gave birth to a child in the cellar. The coachman kept us four months and provided for us. His name will always be on my lips.

In the summer the Austrians left, and most of us from Mlynov returned home. I remained with a cousin, Gitel Sotiver; I studied from the same teacher as her children. When my mother wanted to have me near her in Mlynov, I returned home.

We went through much fright and suffering until we made it to America. Thank God that this all happened in my young years, and I was able to overcome it. May the future generations know of better times with peace spread over the entire world. Amen.

Translator's and editor's footnotes:

1. Helen Lederer was born "Chultzie Gelberg", daughter of Moishe and Gitel (Weitzer) Gelberg. Helen's father, Moishe Gelberg (later Morris Goldberg) migrated to New York in 1911. Helen's family was separated from her father during WWI. This essay tells the story of the family's evacuation from Mlynov during the War. After the War, Helen migrated to the US with her mother and siblings in 1921, where she later became Helen Dishowitz and subsequently Helen Lederer. Helen's siblings were: Sura Gelberg (Sara Lewbel), Jack Goldberg (Gershon), and Abraham Goldberg. See the Gelberg/Goldberg story on the Mlynov website. – HS
2. Varkovychi, Ukraine. – HBF

3.   Helen is referring to her mother Gitel (Gelberg). A photo of Gitel appears on page 507 of this volume where she is described as "Gitel Goldberg, z"l, Pesya Khoylye's daughter." Pesya Khoyles may be related to a man mentioned earlier named "Abraham Kholis" (spelled slightly differently in Hebrew) (p. 60) who was responsible for keeping the eternal light lit in the Stolin Rebbe's memorial in Mlynov. – HS Note *Khoyle* is someone who is sick; perhaps the mother of Gitel and Soreke was ill. Yiddish names are often in the format of first name, then a possessive of their parent. Here Gitel is possibly the daughter of a sick woman – HBF

4.   A verst is about .66 miles. – HBF

5.   Nakhman Leyb is Nathan Spector, father of Samuel Spector. Sam fell in love with Helen's aunt, Sura Gelberg/Gelberg (Helen's father's sister) and they married in the US. – HS

6.   Leybush, Gershon's son -- HBF This is Labish Gelberg who married Eta Leah (Schuchman). – HS

7.   This refers to the "Labish Gelberg" who married Eta Leah (Schuchman). Their children became Goldbergs in the US. "Leybush, Gershon's" is a possessive construction in Yiddish indicating this is "Gershon's Leybush." Since Labish's father-in-law was Gershon Schuchman, the assumption is that it is this Gershon who is being referenced. The Yiddish linguistic construction would be the same if Labish had a father named Gershon. In the Gelberg/Goldberg family oral tradition, Labish's parents' names are not known and Labish is remembered as an orphan. – HS

8.   Helen's aunt, Chaye, refers to Ida (Gelberg) Gevantman who later migrated to the US and settled in Baltimore.

9.   Ozeryany, Ukraine, according to Jewishgen.org Gazeteer. – HBF

10.   Rivne, Ukraine. According to Google Maps, the walk from Mlyniv to Varkovychi to Ozeryany to Rivne was a distance of about 65 km or 40.4 miles. – HBF

11.   Basye-Chaye, Malke's daughter. –HBF

12.   American Jewish Joint Distribution Committee. – HBF

[Page 149]

A Good Deed (Mitzvah)

Episode

by Boruch Meren[1], Baltimore

Translated from the Yiddish by Hannah B. Fischthal, PhD

Edited by Howard I. Schwartz, PhD

It happened in 1921, in Mlynov. Those were restless years. The First World War was actually over, but bloody battles between the Bolsheviks and the Polish armies were still continuing. The small shtetlekh, mainly the Polish-Ukraine shtetlekh, went through the frights of having opposing armies continuously coming in and getting out — the Bolsheviks would come and leave, and immediately the Poles would come in. The power could change several times in one week just like that …

Mlynov, as it turned out, was strategically important in the Great War. The Austrian-Russian battles left the shtetl in a terrible condition with ruined, burned houses. The shtetl was unrecognizable. High, black chimneys had been knocked down. The number of fallen soldiers in the middle of the shtetl was frightening.

Nevertheless, many Jewish families courageously began to come back to the shtetl and they started, with hard work, to build over the ruins and to re-establish a normal life. Enough being a wanderer among strangers!

And now to the plot of the story, attesting to the character of those abnormal times:

It was in the summertime. For two weeks, the shtetl was empty, meaning, there was no government. Our "strategy experts" predicted that the Bolsheviks would come back, and so it was. On a nice morning — the enemy is here. The Bolsheviks were in the shtetl again on the two main streets, Market and Synagogue Streets. They put out their wagons and horses — starving, tired, and wearing dirty, torn clothes.

[Page 150]

They started to make themselves at home in the shtetl. Odors of sweat from the soldiers and horses carried through the air. The cauldron, in which the soldiers' soup was cooking, gave a separate smell …

Many soldiers were distributed into the houses. It so happened that a soldier who was assigned to our house was a Jewish boy from Rivne, whom my father immediately recognized. As it turned out, we had been neighbors of his parents two years ago in Rivne. He, the soldier, had been a student then. His father was cantor in the city. When my father questioned what he was doing in that Russian echelon, and how does a cantor's son become a Bolshevik, the young man answered briefly:

"There is a revolution in the world. We need to fight for a better and more beautiful world. My girlfriend is with me too, in the same echelon. She works in the office."

"Like that?" my father asks. "You are engaged? Is she at least a Jewish girl?"

"Yes, she is also from Rivne, totally devoted with body and soul to our struggle."

"If you would listen to me, Grisha, you would marry your girlfriend! Really, here by us, with familiar people, who know your parents," my father says. "What, it is no big deal, Moyshele the cantor from the large synagogue? Believe me, it will not hurt your revolution. Instead of shlepping around with a girlfriend, is it not better with your own wife?"

"Now is not the time to devote oneself to these incidental matters, Reb Ben-Tzion," answered the boy, "And it is also forbidden. You know how that smells?"[2]

But my father did not want to hear about it. For two days my parents worked on the soldiers, gave them food and drink, almost took away the last crumbs from us children, all with the hope that they would maybe agree to my father's proposal and get married.

[Page 151]

And actually, it helped. It was agreed to have the wedding as soon as possible, because who knows, either the pair could regret the decision, or the echelon could leave.

The ceremony had to happen quietly, so that no soldier would see nor hear it. It could not come to the Commander's attention. That the wedding would be "quiet," the cantor did not need to be afraid, because no musicians played, no jester performed, and no large noise of spoons and plates were heard. It was truly a "quiet" ceremony.

In a small, dimly lit little room, the floor recently scrubbed with yellow sand in honor of the celebration, the Red soldier and his girlfriend were standing under the chuppah and reciting the vows, with shaky voices, word by word: "Behold you are consecrated to me" (hare ot mekudeshet li…).[3]

By the stores of Kipergluz and Holtzeker
From the photos of A. Harari

My father, may he rest in peace, was the officiate. He was dressed in his black, Shabbes kapote.[4] His face was shining … Reb Peysakh Shoykhet[5] and other important people were present. My mother, with a few other neighbors, set the table with a clean, white paper, and they served a fine supper — two herrings with a bread, and tea to drink. In those circumstances that was a meal fit for a king.

After supper everyone dispersed happily — a small thing, to accomplish such a good deed! The couple was also happy; their faces were witnesses. The bride especially could not control herself, and she left a tear under the chuppah.

[Page 152]

The newlyweds heartily thanked everyone, said good-night, and went out of the room into the dark night, arm in arm, quietly. They had to sleep on the wagons, because any minute they could get an order to depart. And so it was.

The next morning, we looked out of the window. Synagogue Street was empty, quiet, not a trace of any soldier ... no Bolsheviks, no Poles.

We were informed from Dubno, that the Poles were already in charge there. Jews were afraid to go out into the street, because Poles cut off Jewish beards. The same week, around 200 Polish soldiers came to us in Mlynov. Jews were afraid for their beards … How could a Jew not have a beard on his face in that time? But a miracle happened. Not a beard was touched. My father said that he was sure it was only because of the wonderful mitzvah, the good deed of marrying the Jewish Red soldiers, that the shtetl was protected from harm. And the Jews in the shtetl remained with their beards.

The local council hall, an assembly of area marksmen

Translator's and editor's footnotes:

1.   Boruch Meren (1908–1996) was son of Ben-Tzion Meren (1867–1942) and Miriam Goldseker (1870–1942), daughter of Hirsch and Ida Goldseker. A photo of Boruch's parents and his sister Seril, who all died in the Mlynov liquidation, appears on page 456 of this volume. Boruch's father, a teacher and observant Jew, forbid Boruch's participation in the Zionist Youth groups popular in the 1920s and 30s. Nonetheless, Boruch had a romance with Rosa Berger, who made aliyah from Mlynov in 1933. The two corresponded between Mlynov and Palestine until 1938 when Rosa was able to secure a scarce British immigration certificate for Boruch and he made aliyah. Boruch's love relationship saved his life. Unfortunately, Boruch and Rosa's romance fell apart because life in Palestine had changed Rosa substantially. In a later essay in this volume (pp. 220–225), Boruch writes about his visit during this period in Palestine to Moshe Fishman, in Balfouria, among the first to make aliyah and another contributor to this volume. In 1938, Amelia "Milka" Shargel, a young Mlynov woman who immigrated to Baltimore in 1929, came to Palestine to meet Boruch and the two got married there. Amelia secured Boruch a US passport and in 1940, he traveled from Naples, Italy to New York, arriving on April 11, 1940. He settled in Baltimore with Amelia and they had a son Allen J. Meren. To see the photos and postcards Boruch sent to Rosa during their romance, see the Mlynov website. – HS

2.   It appears the young man is referring to fact the when the Bolsheviks came to power they viewed the family as a bourgeois institution. – HS

3.   The traditional words of bethrothal in Hebrew. – HS

4.   Kapote is man's long coat of medieval origin worn especially by Jews of eastern Europe. – HS

5.   Kosher slaughterer. – HBF

[Page 153]

When I was a lad ... [1]

by Lipa Halperin, [2] z"l, Yifat

Translated and edited by Howard I. Schwartz, PhD with Hanina Epstein

[When I was a lad] … and I first climbed up on a chair on my own, I stood to look out at the world through the window of our house. It was a spring morning, and my gaze was draw to the fields of lilac shrubs, purple flowers along the length of Church's fence. A distance across the river, in the thicket of trees, shined the whiteness of the estate palace. Close to [my] house was a road that led down to the river. Along this road, each and every day — in morning and evening time — passed pairs of horses of different colors: brown, black, white and gray and with each pair, a single rider. There was a rider who passed at a gallop, with a delicate, darling foal hurrying behind him. And another, an old farmer, his hat sloping towards his ear, his two legs on one side of the horse, and he relaxes the reigns and sings softly to it. A young rider holds the reigns in one hand and with the second tosses sunflower seeds into his mouth and the shells fall from his mouth with astonishing speed. This is how the farmers and coachmen routinely brought their horses to the river for watering and immersion. And upon their return from the river, the crowd grew larger and the calls of coachmen spurring on [the horses] mixed with the whinnying of the horses into a terrible commotion, swallowed by clouds of dust. Man and horse, horse and man — this pair rooted itself in my consciousness in those days as inseparable. Our most beloved toy was the horse, and the most beloved game — playing horses. One lad would grab the rope between his teeth — and he was the horse, and the other grabbed the ends of the rope and snapped the whip.…

* * *

In the center of town there was a market square. There was a plot of land for parking the many farmers' wagons that would come here from the surrounding villages on days off work and went to the two churches, the Catholic and the Russian Orthodox.[3] With their wagons weighed down they would go to the intersection of the roads to the towns of Dubno, Rovno, and Lutzk.

The flow increased especially during the fairs. Appearing already early in the morning were the heavily laden wagons of the merchants who set up stalls filled with a rich variety of goods. The market days during the summer are remembered: voices of the merchants announcing their wares and the music boxes of the jugglers[4] drowned out by the tumult of crowing roosters, mooing cows, squealing pigs, and whinnying of the horses. A complete mixture of human and animal sounds, a combination of sweat and dust– – –

[Page 154]

When I got older I would run to the home of my grandmother Pesya and uncle Yosel.[5] There was a narrow alleyway there in which the "naughty boys" (shkotzim)[6] spent time in games and mischief, evading adult scolding. They were all there: Yosele, Shelomoleh, Benzi, Pinchasal…

Yosele and I had hiding places known only to the two of us. In the barrier of the fence around the church was a narrow gate of iron, which was always closed. When I peeked inside the first time, I saw the statute of the cross on the wall. The hands and feet bound to the cross and the head leaning sideways. At twilight, it seemed like he was alive.

"Who is this?" I asked Yoseleh in fear.

"Be quiet. It is forbidden to look."

"But who is this? Who is this?"

"This…jeez, it is forbidden to say; this is their God."

"Why is he hanging there?"

"Don't talk so loud. You know, he flies but he doesn't have wings. Come on, let's escape quickly, they…"

We ran to the length of the street and reached the wood fence made of planks. We peeped through the cracks. Inside, large, fattened pigs moved about, pressed together and sniffing around. In the corner of the square, on a tree stump was stationed a strange character, like a monster. It had a sleepy expression; its miniature eyes were sunken and the bones of its jaws protruded. The body was covered in a gold cloth shirt and its legs extended forward. The hand carelessly moved around with a feather and the head fell alternatively right and left.

"This is the son of Shelilkah Bazirnik," Yosele whispered to me. "And it is a kind of man-pig golem,[7] and always thirsty for blood…"

Suddenly, this golem moved from its place. We quickly fled – – –

* * *

On the Sabbath, we walked to Hagranik[8] — that hill along the river, from which there were views of the entire town. We stood there, and Yosele told a story:

"Many years ago, a large church stood in this place. One time a great tzadik (righteous man) from Dubno traveled here, and when he passed by the magnificent church, the Count's large dogs attacked him, which guarded the palace which was opposite it. It was similar to the Jews who fled Egypt — in front of them was the sea and behind them the Egyptians and on both sides animals of prey. The tzadik ran towards the church and cried out [an incantation]: "Abominable thing, we abhor; detestable thing, we detest, you are banned."

That's what he said, repeated a second time and a third time … and the earth opened its mouth and the church and all that was in it was swallowed by the earth and was covered by soil [creating the hill] —

[Page 155]

* * *

One time, at sunset, Yosele quickly burst into our house.

"Look, the sky … How red! …"

"It is like a flame of fire," I said.

"Like blood, like blood and fire," I heard people talking — they said there will be war. "Blood and fire, is a sign of war …"

From morning until night, the convoys went by. Soldiers with guns and bayonets were marching and laden down wagons traveled behind them. Wagons harnessed to six horses carried the canons. And there were also calvary. All of them walked on the main road of Berestechko.[9]

We stood full of wonder watching the spectacle. The dukes[10] especially captured our hearts. They were more wonderful in our eyes than even the calvary. During my sleep I would continue to hear the unceasing marching of the horses and men.

I was exceedingly happy. Everyone bought horses and wagons, even Father. "Kashtan" was a sweet horse and they even permitted me to ride him.

Every day Yosele would appear and with emotional news to relate:

"Come quickly to look. Boznikim[11] (refugees) are passing by … they say they are Jews from Brody[12] …" I saw Mother wipe away tears, but Yosele and I were happy. These were Jews who were also gypsies …".

"Perhaps we also will travel like gypsies," I whispered to Yosele. "Gosh, how wonderful that would be …"

One morning I stood along the front of the house, looking forward to the arrival of Yosele. Not an hour passed, and he came running and yelling from afar: "The bridges are on fire!"

We ran to look. We yearned to look at the burning bridges, and we were angry that flames were not rising from them. But that same night, when I woke up, I saw Father and Mother packing up everything. Light was in the room, and it appeared Mother was crying. I fell back asleep again.

When I opened my eyes a second time, a dark night was above me. I was sitting in the upper part of the wagon and the cold wind whipped my face. A sea of fiery sparks burned.

"Mother, fire! Fire is in my eyes! M–o–t–h–e–r ——"

"This is only a spotlight," mother reassured with a quiet voice. "They will not shoot us, we are refugees. Do not ask why everything is burning and red. These are the fires. And there, also our house is burning. Everything is no more ——."

Translator's and editor's footnotes:

1.   Apparent allusion, likely with irony, to the verse in Palms 37:25: "I have been young and am now old, but I have never seen a righteous man abandoned, or his children seeking bread." Lipa would pass away before this essay was published.

2.   Lipa Halperin, a descendant of the Hirsch and Halperin families, was born in 1907 in Mlynov, made aliyah in 1937 and passed away in Israel in 1969 after writing this essay but before the Yizkor book was published in 1970. He contributed a number of other essays to this volume. More details about his life on the Mlynov website.

3.   The Russian Orthodox Church has diverging doctrinal views particularly around the pope's role that differentiates it from the Catholic tradition from which it split in the 11th century.

4.   Could also be magicians.

5.   Pesia (Hirsch) Halperin, his paternal grandmother, and Uncle Yosel, his father's brother, Yosel Halperin.

6.   A derogatory term from the Hebrew Bible meaning detestable things sometimes applied to non-Jewish boys, applied here as a term of endearment to Jewish boys who misbehave.

7.   A golem is a kind of monstrous creature in Jewish folklore created entirely from inanimate matter.

8.   This hill is called Grinik or Greenik elsewhere in the essays, which Aaron Harari mentions as a place where Zionist youth groups met (p. 70), and which the younger children called, "Mount Sinai." See especially the essay by Moshe Teitelman, "My Hill," p. 30.

9.   The road to Berestechko heads due west and then somewhat south from Mlynov.

10.   Perhaps viewing the captains as "dukes" through childhood eyes.

11.   Meaning of word uncertain, possibly a foreign word meaning "refugees," possibly in Russian.

12.   The city of Brody was part of Austria from 1772–1919. It is south of Berestechko and it would be natural for refugees from Brody to head north to Berestechko and then east along the road to Mlynov. Possibly refugees from the Battle of Galicia (Lemberg) the first major battle on the Eastern Front in August-September 1914 which was near Lemberg (Lviv).

———————————————

[Page 156]

Our Former Way of Life in Mlynov

by G. Goldberg[1], Jackson Heights

Translated from the Yiddish by Hannah B. Fischthal, PhD

Edited by Howard I. Schwartz, PhD

Memories. I imagine friends and acquaintances, radiant and smiling, lively, happy, joyous. With songs on our lips, we walk together in the count's forest to pick green gooseberries, strawberries, and grapes. All our hearts beat together, rhythmically and full of hope. And here Shmuelik-Mendele's [son],[2] full of aspirations, who had just returned home from a distant yeshiva, proposes creating a troupe of amateur actors. We eagerly take steps to form such a troupe.[3]

The troupe consisted of Dvoyre Berger, Feygel - Sholem's [child], Peyse Zutelman,[4] Henye – Khaye-Malke's [daughter], Gershon Goldberg,[5] Pese - Ranye's [daughter], Itsik –Yente-Brayndl's [Shargel],[6] Saul the bookbinder, Soreke - Shulman's [daughter][7] and Malke,[8] a daughter of Yehuda-Leib Lamdan, from a very prestigious family, the brothers Hertsik and Shimon [Shulman], the sisters Khayeke and Pepe [Shulman].[9] Shmuelik – Mendele's [son] himself, the director without a crown, began to assign and edit roles for every member. As makeup man, Yankl Tsirulnik was outstanding in the group. Revenue was dedicated to the poor and the sick.

* * *

The cheder. Our generation established strict teachers who really sacrificed for their students. They planted in their pupils' hearts the most beautiful ideals and the finest ethical principles, based on the holy Torah. Their methods were old-fashioned, mostly based on the long wooden pointers they used to help push Torah into the heads of the students. I remember the actions of the rabbi who used to hit naked backsides with his pointer, while the other students used to stand opposite, clapping their hands, and singing:

[Page 157]

> Whipped
> With all the beautiful blessings
> On one head,
> What is pride
> Should be driven out of another head.

The young students did not make any boycotts, nor did they know from any protests; instead, they quietly swallowed their running tears. They crushed the shame inside themselves, and … they continued learning. These teachers produced brilliant scholars and geniuses who made their way in the world.

How can children forget a week visiting a woman who just had a baby boy, where they were taken to say *Krishme*[10] before the bris, and the Bobe[11] Leybtsikhe used to give every child a little honey cake or cookie? Nobody ever succeeded in getting two cookies by lying, for example by saying that his little brother was sick. If a clever boy would succeed in untying the Bobe's wide apron, where she held the treasures, and the cookies then fell on the floor — then the children grabbed them…

* * *

Gutkele the teacher was very strict with the children; he used to whip, pinch, hit, punch without mercy. Moyshe the Pentateuch instructor and Hershl the Gemara instructor were also quite strict. They did not spare any slaps and hits with open hands. The elite, the cream of the shtetl, learned with Aharon Glezer, an outstanding scholar of the Talmud. These boys included the writer of these lines, Shike Moyshe-Nakhman's [son], Dovid Nisele's [son], Khayim Itsikl's [son], and so on. Boys also learned under Reb Ahron-Shmuel. Motl Chizik (Tzizik)[12] was really a "murderer," a strict disciplinarian: he used to teach the bible by heart, and for the slightest sin, he would slap a student's face. I had to learn with him together with Aleph Katz[13] and Yitzhak Lamdan,[14] may he rest in peace.

I only remember two aristocratic teachers — they were Shmuel Katz— Henia Ahrele's [son],[15] and Nokhum Schwartz —Chaim Peretz's [son].[16] They punished the sinning children not on their bodies, but on their little fingers and hands with a wooden ruler.

[Page 158]

Remarkably, with their tough discipline and physical punishments, these teachers raised a generation of proud and worthy Jews, Jews concerned with social issues, people who with their culture and intellect reached the highest levels of the societal ladder, people with an international reputation on many subjects of culture and civilization — among them: Shloyme Mandelkern,[17] Yitzhak Lamdan, Aleph Katz, and so on.

Yes, I miss the beautiful bride — Mlynov. Over there was my baby carriage; there I took my first steps in the wide world. In my great struggles and wanderings, through all the stages that my family and I went through — I carried Mlynov in my heart. You, my shtetele, were my eternal light that lit up and warmed my long exile, like the pillar of fire for the Jews in the dessert. I have respect for you, my beautiful Mlynov, my comfort and consolation.

A group of youth on a fieldtrip on the "Greenik."[18]
Original photo courtesy of Hagar Lipkin.[19]

Translator's and editor's footnotes:

1. George (Gershon / Joe) Goldberg (1896–1984) was the youngest child of Labish Goldberg and Eta Leah (Schuchman). He followed a number of his siblings to America arriving in April 1921. He subsequently married Sylvia Barditch who is an editor and contributor to this volume. Find more on the Goldberg family history on the Mlynov website. – HS
2. People were known by the name of a parent or spouse. This was probably Shmuelik, Mendele's son. – HBF

3.   See also Mendel's recollections of returning to Mervits after WWI from yeshiva in Baranovitsh in the essay "People in a Shtetl," 90–99. See similarly, Aaron Harari's discussion of the plays put on in the Shulman house after WWI in "Culture, Education, and Social Life in the Small Town," 66. – HS

4.   He became Paul Shulman in Baltimore. – HS

5.   The author of this essay. – HS

6.   Probably Yentel Brendel Shargel's son Julius (Itsik), who immigrated to New York in January 1911 and later Baltimore. – HS

7.   Likely the Shulman sister, Sarah, who later married Peyse Zutelman in Baltimore. – HS

8.   Referring to Malcah Lamdan who was a teacher in Mlynov and subsequently married Shmuel Mandelkern [also Mandelkoren] and made aliyah. – HS

9.   Referring to the other Shulman siblings, Simon and Hertz, Clara and Pepe Shulman. They all arrived in Baltimore in 1921. – HS

10.   The prayer that begins with "Hear O Israel." – HBF

11.   A midwife, called a Bobe [grandmother], was usually hired to deliver the baby, and if it was a boy, she would stay until after the bris. – HBF

12.   Refers to Mordechai Chizik (Tzizik). His son, Moshe, made aliyah and married Rosa Berger. – HS

13.   Aleph Katz (1898–1969) was the pen name of well-respected Yiddish poet, born Moshe Katz in Mlynov, who arrived in New York with his mother and siblings in 1913. His father was Chaim Yerukhim Katz and his mother was Henie (Hirsch) Katz. For the Hirsch family story, see the Mlynov website. – HS

14.   Yitzhak Lamdan (1899–1954) born in Mlynov was the author of the famous Hebrew poem, "Masada." See the essay about Lamdan's visit back to Mlynov in this volume, "In the presence of Yitzhak Lamdan in Mlynov," written by an admiring Moishe Teitelman, 32–37. – HS

15.   Shmuel Katz was the brother of Aleph Katz and the son of "Henia Ahrele" [Annie (Hirsch) Katz]. A photo of Henia Ahrele appears in the Yizkor book, p. 500. – HS

16.   Refers to Norton Schwartz, son of Chaim Schwartz (who was son of Peretz). Norton arrived in Baltimore with his family, and his sibling, my grandfather, Paul Schwartz, in 1912. On the Schwartz family, see the Mlynov website. – HS

17.   On Shmuel Mandelkern's activity invigorating the Zionist youth groups in Mlynov, see the essay by Aaron Harari, "Culture, Education, and Social Life," p. 66. – HS

18.   This hill, called Greenik here, is probably also the one the children called "Mount Sinai" and described in "My Hill," p. 30, by Moishe Teitelman. Greenik is also referred to as a place the Zionist youth group met in the essay, "The Youth Movement," 69–74, by Aaron Harari. – HS

19.   This photo has a story. It was sent to Hagar's mother, Rosa Berger, in Palestine from Mlynov by Boruch Meren during their courtship. On their love story which saved Boruch's life, see the Mlynov website. – HS

[Page 159]

———————

Local Color of the Synagogue

by Aaron Harari[1]

Translated and edited by Howard I. Schwartz, PhD with Hanina Epstein

In addition to communal prayer and the study of a Mishnah chapter, the large synagogue served as a center for meetings and secular discussions. During the weekdays they would assemble only in the large synagogue, which in the evenings filled with visitors. During the break between afternoon (Mincha) and evening (Maariv) prayers, the erudite teachers would spread out, one to a table in this corner and another to different corner, and they would study the holy books. Others gathered in various circles and discussed the issues of the day. What wasn't discussed there?

Business, taxes, politics, and just gossip. These matters were very interesting. There were many who came, not to pray, but just to meet friends. On the Sabbaths, usually before the reading of the weekly Torah portion, they would break for a period of time in order to take up shared communal concerns. The head of the community would bang on the table, announce something — and calls from the different corners of the room could be heard and the noise would continue to get bigger. The community would argue without order, and it was possible only with difficulty to hear and understand what was "going" on there. Occasionally, the air would become so heated that it led to fisticuffs.

Twice a week, after the evening prayers, there was a study group on the books of the Chofetz Chayyim[2] etc., for Jews who didn't know [how to study] a chapter of the Mishnah;[3] the leader of them was Rabbi Eliezer [Mohel],[4] the shochet, z"l, the father of Yehuda, Yaakov, Devorah and Chaika, who are living in Israel. This study group was modeled on the discussions of the older youth group in the nest [group] of The Young Guard (Hashomer Hatzair). Since Rabbi Eliezer's home housed the leadership committee of the movement, where meetings and preparations took place and occasionally continuing education discussions of the older youth, and he related to us with much friendliness — I have a reason to conclude, that he borrowed the [educational] model from us ...

The synagogue served also as a hall for the people's gatherings; there emissaries of the national funds gave addresses, [as did] sermonizers of various kinds, cantors [performed] who came from outside [town] for concerts, [as did] election gatherings for the Zionist congress as well as various elections.

During the Sabbath and festivals, the synagogue was packed shoulder to shoulder. Each homeowner sat in his established place, and the most esteemed sat along the Eastern wall.[5] Opposite them were many praying people who did not have established places and who sat on regular benches or stood and moved about without a spot. The average Jewish folks sat in the back. The teenagers and crowded together by the entrance and the hallway ("the Palush")[6] and would talk loudly and raise a rukus, an occurrence that regularly annoyed those sitting at the eastern wall. Not infrequently calls could be heard from the benches on the eastern wall directed towards the youth, "Outside, you bums (shkotzim[7])!" But this was not very effective.

[Page 160]

The youth couldn't stand the insults and responded to the homeowners with acts of "vengeance:" they would take a towel, from the sink [designated for] a visit to the restroom[8] ("asher yatzar") that was always wet, roll and fold it, and throw it indiscriminately on the heads of those seated along the eastern wall. Tempers flared but the thrower was not revealed. This was executed quickly and was difficult to detect in a crowd. There was also no snitching [on the perpetrator]. Yechiel Sherman[9] told me that in his youth he was among those youth who gathered by the corridor ("the Palush") and those who sat at the eastern wall attempted to keep in order and he [Yechiel] also absorbed [the reprimand] "You bums, outside!" Among those who shouted [this way] was my father, z"l.[10] And one time when he [Yechiel] passed by our house and saw the samovar boiling and ready for tea, he snuck up, opened the tap ... the samovar emptied out and of course broke down. This also was an act of "revenge" for the insulting call, "You bums, outside!"

Sometimes some rebbe would come to town, whose Hasidic pedigree I didn't know. Many Hasids came from Olyk,[11] Trisk,[12] Stolin[13] and so forth. Meals on Sabbath eve, the three meals of Sabbath were arranged in the large synagogue for everyone. People from all the strata and ages would come to watch and to listen to words of Torah from the Rebbe and to earn some leftovers from the meal. Every evening, during the week, the Rebbe would receive the community in his room in the guest house, and the synagogue manager (gabbai) would write notes the content of which were requests for health, livelihood, a wonderful match for a daughter, a pregnancy in the near future, and so on. In addition to reading the notes, the Rebbe would speak personally with the visitors (male and female) — and this was for sure a great psychological influence on the visitor. For the Torah processions (hakafot) on Simchat Torah, children, women and infants would come to kiss the Torah. The congregation crowded together for a long hour until the processions ended. On Simchat Torah after prayers, small repasts (kiddushim) were organized that were fitting for the occasion.

Jews drank schnapps to drunkenness, and to fulfill the [Scriptural] obligations that "You shall rejoice in your festival" (Deuteronomy 16:14) and that "wine will gladden the heart" (Psalm 104:15), happiness and celebration surpassed all bounds. They danced on the tables, sang and until the throat was horse. The youth in the group would gather in the home Mr. Hirsch Holtzeker and organized a modern style kiddush of their own, with the fairer gender in attendance, who arranged the table and worried over the gastronomic aspects.

On Sabbaths at sunset, pleasing Hasidic songs burst forth, which were Hasidic songs for the "three meals" [required on the Sabbath]. The song was harmonious, quiet, and not offkey. Some of those songs are song today in Israel, in new arrangements and in different styles.

Translator's and editor's footnotes:

1.   Aaron (Berger) Harari (1908–1984) was a member of the Book Committee for this volume and contributed several essays about life in Mlynov as well as many of the photos from his trip back to his birthplace in 1937–38, pp. 77–79. Learn more about his life on the Mlynov website.

2.   Yisrael Meir Kagan (1838–1933), known by the title of one of the books he wrote, was an influential rabbi of the Musar movement.

3.   A compendium of law and foundational text of rabbinic Judaism, which forms the basis of the Talmud. The Mishnah is much easier to learn than the give and take discussions in the Gemara.

4.   Rabbi Leizer Mohel (1872–1942) and his wife, Hanna Beila (Kaszkiet) (1882–1942) came to Mlynov from Boremel in 1924–1925 when Rabbi Eliezer, a shochet and mohel, was hired for a position in town. His son, Yitzhak Mohel, contributed the essay "A Murdered Family," pp. 410–412. A photo of the Mohel home and the Mohel sisters appears on page 411 of this volume. The son Yehuda Mohel appears in several photos in the essay about the Zionist Youth Movement, "The Young Guard," pp. 69–74. The amazing life story of Yehuda Mohel is told in a full length book, by his son Dani Tracz (Issachar Mohel), *Riva and Yehuda: Life Story of Trancman, Mohel, Tracz and Ben-Eliezer Families*, 2015).

5.   Rabbinic law (Berakhot 30a) indicates a person should face towards Jerusalem during prayer and that synagogues should orient themselves in that direction. "Facing east" was normally associated with facing Jerusalem among Jewry west of Jerusalem. However, Jerusalem would be in a southernly direction from Mlynov. The fact that the most respected Jews of Mlynov were along the eastern wall of the synagogue seems to imply that prayers were facing in that direction, though that is not ever explicitly stated. If that were the case, it is not clear why they weren't facing in the southerly direction. There are other opinions in rabbinic law that allow for prayer to be facing in other directions.

6.   Shmuel Mandelkern identifies this same hallway called the "Palush" as the place where meetings of the self-defense units would take place, p. 116.

7.   The term used is "shkotzim" (plural of sheygetz), which comes from the biblical term for a detested thing and is used as a term for naughty children or unruly youth and as a derogatory term for non-Jewish youth.

8.   According to Jewish law, "asher yatzar" ("who created") is the blessing over the wondrous workings of the body that is said after use of the bathroom. It is not clear if there was a lavatory inside the synagogue, but apparently there was a sink with towels for washing the hands after bathroom functions.

9.   Yechiel Sherman is a contributor to this volume. He was survived WWII in the Russian and Polish armies and reunited with his brother Ezra Sherman, who survived as a young boy in the countryside.

10.   Aaron Harari's father was Zeev Berger (1878–1942). His photo appears in Aaron's essay "Jewish Farmers in Mlynov," pp. 75–76.

11.   Olyka is 34 km (21 m) northeast from Mlynov and was the cradle of the Olyker Hasidic dynasty that was founded by the famous Rabbi Hersh Leib Landa, the first Olyker rebbe.

12.   The Trisk dynasty is a Hasidic dynasty, a branch of the Chernobyl dynasty, originating in Turiisk, Ukraine, 121 km (75 m) north of Mlynov. According to other essays in this volume, the largest synagogue in Mlynov was oriented towards the Trisk Hasidim.

13. Karlin-Stolin (today Karolin and Stolin, Belarus) is the name of the Hasidic dynasty originating with Rebbe Aaron the Great of Karlin in present-day Belarus. Karlin is 247 km (153 m) north of Mlynov today. Karlin and Stolin were one of the first centers of Hasidim in Lithuania. The rebbe who died in Mlynov was the grandson of the founder.

[Page 161]

Days of Celebration in the Shtetl

by Sonia and Mendel Teitelman, Haifa

Translated from the Yiddish by Hannah B. Fischthal, PhD

Edited by Howard I. Schwartz, PhD

In our shtetlekh in the Mlynov kehilla, as in all the other kehillas in the diaspora, practically 100% of the men, from the youngest to the oldest, were religious, and they observed the Jewish traditions, some more and some less. All men, from school-age children to grandfathers, came to pray in the synagogue. Most of them prayed every afternoon for the afternoon and evening services. At the same time, some would study a page of the Talmud. Others would enter into a little conversation about daily matters, including business, professions, and all kinds of local concerns. That was during the weekdays.

In Mlynov and Mervits, and in all the surrounding shtetlekh, Shabbes and holidays had an entirely different appearance, as though there was a presence of Jerusalem. In our shtetl, like in all surrounding shtetlekh, Jews populated the streets, but surrounding them was a much larger majority of Christians. On Shabbes, however, there was complete rest in the shtetl. Only on a rare occasion could one see a wagon driven by a non-Jew. In the shtetl, everything was strictly locked with keys; everything rested on Shabbes. Everyone, according to his means, dressed in Shabbes clothes. Men spent the early morning hours, until noon, in the synagogue. The women's synagogue, similarly, was full during those times.

Returning home after the prayers, everything was holiday-like. Tasty treats had been prepared. It was an honor, according to tradition, to bring a poor man home as a guest for lunch. The lunch was mostly cholent with fatty treats. Sometimes a kiddush[1] was made in the synagogue, or in a private room, for a happy occasion like a bar mitzvah, a calling up of a prospective bridegroom to the Torah, a bris,[2] and so on.

Every holiday had its specialties. Preparations for Passover, for example, included whitewashing the walls, koshering, baking matzas, preparing shmaltz[3] and eggs, and more.

[Page 162]

New clothes were almost always made for holidays. In our old home with its cold climate, Passover would often be cold and wet.

In contrast, Shavuot had no equal, as we used to say. The weather was beautiful, warm, sunny, and dry. Greenery was all around. All kinds of tasty treats were eaten, both dairy and meat; traditional blintzes were a popular treat. In short, this holiday was a happier one than all the others, including even the longer holidays.

As is known, in the diaspora, every holiday, without exception, is held a minimum of two days. After **Shavuot** and a long break came **Rosh Hashanah**, the **Days of Awe**, **Yom Kippur**, and **Sukkot**. Already from the beginning of the month of Elul, a penitential mood was felt. Penitential prayers, the treasure of the days of repentance, the sacrificial ceremony, and fasting were brought into the shtetl with the first trumpet of the shofar.

This was all stricter in the beginning of the century, when my parents and my grandparents, may they rest in peace, were still alive. The Day of Judgement in our shtetl was very serious.

The Days of Awe were regarded differently in the thirties of this century, that is, not with such fear and anxiety, but still within the framework of religious order and tradition.

In contrast, **Sukkot** and **Simchat Torah** were celebrated by most people with splendor. Outside of the traditional sukkah, which was different for everyone, a good mood ruled, as though we had actually taken the abundance from our fields to enjoy God's generous gifts. Unfortunately, many families sadly and anxiously feared the cold winter coming, since they had no wood, nor warm clothes, nor potatoes. In general, however, there was a good mood, and we celebrated Simchat Torah in splendor, with drinks and good pastries and assorted meats. The celebration started right after carrying the Torahs in synagogue. Most of the community, after synagogue service, sat down at tables spread with honey cake and liquor. Shoulder to shoulder, hand in hand, we made a large circle around the stage, singing and dancing for hours.

[Page 163]

Our true devotion and love for Judaism is indescribable.

I still remember from my childhood days, when my grandfather, Reb Asher,[4] may he rest in peace, used to celebrate Simchat Torah magnificently, and everything was done in the Russian language. (Until today I do not understand why only in Russian?) He used to grab Hershl Goldenberg's long beard, may he rest in peace, with his left hand; he kept his right hand ready to slap him. For every inexact repetition, my grandfather slapped his face and said in Russian:

"Take your tallis and tefillin under your arm, put your white shirt in your bag, and walk to Trisk."[5] He repeated this several times with conviction. We all stood around him, enjoying the happy play. We only regretted that we had to wait an entire year for such fun. (It seems as though we had no other worries).

When we became older and less religious, we were able to make up a Zionistic quorum for Simchat Torah, with vows honoring the Jewish National Fund. When the celebration was already in progress, we all went from house to house, usually singing and chanting various slogans, like "Next Year in Jerusalem!" And before ending the holiday, we all got together again in the synagogue. The cantor dressed up in disguise, anything to make it jolly! One thing that is important to remember, is that this was the only holiday in the year in which men and women celebrated together. It was different the rest of the year, when men and women were strictly separate.

Also years ago, at the end of the Sukkot holiday, a Jewish man wearing a prayer shawl and carrying a lulav[6] would go up onto the roof. He would sit on the chimney and shake the lulav and sing out various arias made of his own prayers: "I have enemies in the east, west, north, south, I hope to you above, that they will all be buried." He referred to the evil governments of the Tzars with their anti-Semitic edicts.

Throughout the year there were more usual, minor holidays.

[Page 164]

Hanukkah was celebrated in the synagogue, but a happy holiday mood was created in homes, too. Firstly, there were the popular delicious latkes, which we used to eat on Hanukkah. There was also the tradition of playing cards (but not everywhere).

On **Tu BiShvat** (new year of the trees), it was a good deed to eat fruits of the earth, like carob pods and figs. Purim is also a minor holiday, but it felt important. During all the minor holidays there was a collection of funds for charity; Purim took top place in raising money. As usual, Purim started with a fast, but in the same evening, we read the megilla[7] and booed Haman[8] with all our might, feeling that we made all the Hamans in all times disappear. Coming home from synagogue, we felt a Purim holiday mood in all the houses. The next day, we went again to the synagogue to hear the megilla, and we came back home to a holiday table. And before night — the Purim feast. I want to mention and praise here the sending of food gifts from one to another, as it was a beautiful tradition in those times. In addition, practically the entire Jewish population in the shtetl went to gatherings devoted to raising funds for all kinds of needs. Jews gave with open hands, to the best of their capacity. This was a tradition in all of the Eastern European diaspora.

Tisha B'Av is a sad day. However, in the synagogue, along with public mourning, there was a kind of odd situation: A little laughter crept in on the lips of the young people from the tradition of throwing sticky burrs onto one another. Woe to the Jew with the long beard who had done something not honorable to a young person. Everybody threw his burrs on his beard, and it was not possible to get them out … Nu, whether you want to or not, you must give a smile.

The beadles in our synagogues in our shtetlekh were born to the job, which was, by the way, never with a decent salary.

[Page 165]

They were generally supplied with an apartment in the synagogue but with a reduction in salary for it. And until this day I do not know how they managed to live, and still raise children, and among them also good children. With what they nourished and raised them I do not know.

* * *

There were a few more celebrations in relation to the synagogue, which were held irregularly, such as when Rebbes used to come to the shtetl, or when a new Torah was brought into the synagogue, or when there was a bar mitzvah or the calling up of a bridegroom to the holy ark. In addition, from time to time, there were political speeches about Zionism and courses which I still remember; they also brought joy into my life.

And with that I want to mention a course in Mlynov, on a certain Shabbes, when a speaker from Mizoch[9] came during the time of the trial of Stawski-Arlozorov.[10] Standing in a tallis at the Holy Ark, so that in case of danger he could claim to be giving a religious sermon, Ribe Litvak,[11] may his memory be a blessing, heatedly screamed, "Lies!" This was only an interjection, but the audience became aroused, and sides were soon created. It took a while until people quieted down. The revisionist[12] speaker did not continue any more.

Such courses were given quite often. In addition to overviews and various opinions, which were conducted in various places of the shtetl among friends of the Zionist parties, right, left, and so on, there were talks led by older Jews in the synagogue next to the warm oven, on the same themes; the audience never came to an agreement.

* * *

Another of the celebrations in which all sections of the local population took part, was the calling up of the groom-to-be to the Torah. On Shabbes, a kiddush was given in the synagogue. There was also a kiddush at home for close family and friends. The same was true for a bris. A Torah being led to the synagogue was celebrated in high style. But that was rare, just one time in several years.

[Page 166]

The celebration was accompanied by drums and dances, in which the largest portion of the local population took part.

When their Rebbe used to come for his yearly visit to the shtetl, his Hasidim would celebrate. He would stay with Feivel Berger.[13] During the course of his stay in Mlynov, the Hasidim used to visit him, and a few also invited him to visit their homes. My brother-in-law Nahum Teitelman did this. And usually, wherever the Rebbe used to be, Hasidim came in order to sweeten his evening, and it was entirely interesting and jolly. It is appropriate to note here, that in a certain discussion with the Rebbe, which I myself heard, he was in favor of making aliyah to Palestine. Not like other Rebbes, who were opposed. The Rebbe also paid a visit to Mervits.

* * *

This is how the Jewish community in our old home celebrated happy occasions during the course of their lives. There was no entirely happy occasion, as it was for our Christian neighbors, in my opinion. Seldom-seldom was an occasion celebrated that was not mixed with tears. And there was always a reason for the tears. The Jew did not need to swear, "If I do not go up to Jerusalem I will be happy," because he never had a perfectly happy occasion. Even in his best times, the occasions were accompanied by fear and oppression. And out of familiarity, we used to, for the most part, not emphasize such things, but just continue on …

Translator's and editor's footnotes:

1. A small meal, such as herring and challah, after services. – HBF
2. Bris means "covenant" and refers to the rite of circumcision of a Jewish male on the eighth day after birth. – HS
3. Rendered chicken fat. – HBF
4. Mendel is speaking about his grandfather Reb Asher Teitelman. Reb here is likely a title of respect like "Mr." and may not signify he was a rabbi. – HS
5. This phrase, a mix apparently of Aramaic, Yiddish and Hebrew, was translated with the help of Mlynov Schwartz descendant, Jack Nudelman. Trisk today is Turiisk, Ukraine, 120 km from Mlyniv today. – HS
6. A bouquet of palm, myrtle, and willow branches used in the synagogue service during Sukkot. They are shaken in a special way to send blessings to all creation. – HBF
7. The Book of Esther. – HBF
8. Evil antagonist in the Book of Esther who planned to kill all the Jews in ancient Persia. – HBF
9. Town in Ukraine, 50 km east of Mlynov. – HS.
10. Abraham Stawski was an activist member of Betar, the Zionist youth group. On June 18, 1933, Stawski was arrested by British police in Palestine for the murder of Chaim Arlosorov. He was convicted and sentenced to death June 8, 1934. This decision was condemned by the Jewish community. The conviction was overturned in 1934. – HBF
11. Probably refers to Motel Litvak, father of the writer Yosef Litvak in this volume, p. 53. – HS
12. Revisionist Zionism was an ideology developed by Ze'ev Jabotinsky, who advocated a "revision" of the "practical Zionism" of David Ben-Gurion and Chaim Weizmann. Revisionism differed from other types of Zionism primarily in its territorial maximalism. Revisionists had a vision of occupying the full territory and insisted upon the Jewish right to sovereignty over the whole of Eretz Yisrael, which they equated to the whole territory covered by the League of Nations Mandate for Palestine, including Transjordan. – HS

13. Faivel Berger was the uncle of Aaron (Berger) Harari, one of the contributors to this volume. Learn more about the Berger family on the Mlynov website. – HS.

[Page 167]

Joys and Sorrows in Mervits

by S. M. T.[1]

Translated from the Yiddish by Hannah B. Fischthal, PhD

Edited by Howard I. Schwartz, PhD

Celebrations and mourning in Mervits took place in an entirely different way than in other Jewish communities. I want to say here that there were individual celebrations, as, for example, an engagement, a wedding, a bris, and other family celebrations (We used to say: "They eat honey-cake — a daughter is getting married"); and there were community celebrations, like Shabbes, ushering out the sabbath feast, holidays, leading a new Torah into the synagogue, and so on. I do not remember any other special opportunities to celebrate. There were more similar community celebrations, like fundraising parties dedicated to the Jewish National Fund, to United Israel Appeal, and to local needy inhabitants.

Similarly, there were individual moments of sadness, as, for example, difficult illnesses, funerals, and conversions. The attempt to convert a person occurred once in my life. The sadness and willingness to sacrifice oneself for God's name, and the facing of danger to save a Jewish soul, was also grief for the community. We will begin with celebrations.

Engagements

In Mervits before the First World War, as I remember, nobody fell in love, God forbid. To get married for love, God forbid — that did not happen. If anyone really did love someone, marriage without a matchmaker was against the law, or just plain not Jewish. Matchmakers were sent for, and most of them came from the initiative of the bride's family.

First there was bargaining over the dowry; not a thing could be settled without the dowry. It was said, "For a pretty girl, a dowry helps." After a lengthy bargaining session, when both sides came to an agreement, they set the engagement for a good and a lucky hour. The wedding was usually a year later. There were instances where the bargaining over the dowry took a very long time, and after lengthy negotiations, the mother of the groom said finally to the matchmaker: "Listen Reb Moyshe to my final decision: if this and that total is not given, then let him suffer another year.

[Page 168]

OK, he will be sick of wandering. But he will not become any cheaper."

And that is how the couple was matched up. This does not mean that there never were any nicer ways. Quite possibly, but seldom, and mostly not until after the First World War. Then the youth of Mervits started to adopt more pleasing paths to love. It even happened that a marriage took place without a dowry. The parents, who adhered to the older way of life, looked very askance at this, but they lost.

"What a world we have today!" they used to say with a sigh.

When it was time for the engagement, the bride's family started to bake honey cakes and all kinds of egg cookies. The *shames*[2] was sent to invite the entire shtetl, from end to end, without exception, regardless of relationship or honor. All gathered in the home of the bride, with the Rabbi at the head. The bridegroom was told to be seated, similar to the king, by the eastern wall. The commotion in the home was enormous. Everybody came dressed up in Shabbes clothes, the women in the most beautiful and best dresses.

The Rabbi sat with a goose quill in his hand, which he kept dipping into the inkwell next to him, and he wrote and wrote.[3] Finally, he started to search for two kosher witnesses who were not related to either side, and that was very rare, because by us everyone was a relative, some further and some closer, but everyone without exception. So a search started for pure witnesses who were not related to each other, until the Rabbi finally decided, that an eighth of an eighth [relationship] may be a witness.[4] So he found witnesses, but they could not write well. The rabbi put his hand over where the witness needed to sign, and he said all the time: "Reb Yukl, draw with the quill a small line, and afterwards a longer one, and afterwards a little bit until"... until it is good. "Kosher, kosher, a kosher signature," the rabbi ruled. The same procedure for the second witness, and all was kosher and honest.

Now the rabbi slowly pulled out of his pocket, from under his frock coat, the red handkerchief, which was used more than once on a cold day as a shawl around his throat. He gave the groom a corner of it, and he held the rest himself, and said to him: "Nu, dear groom, receive the property, in a good and lucky hour!"

[Page 169]

And the groom took the handkerchief, and he felt in it a little dampness from tobacco, but anyway, if the Rabbi says do it, probably it has to be like that. He took the handkerchief, and he sent it to the bride. She also needed to take a corner of it in agreement.

The *shames* pushed himself through the crowd and screamed loudly, "Let me through, let me through to the bride. She needs to take the handkerchief in agreement; the Rabbi ordered it."

The wives, who were separated from the men, concentrated around the bride. Hearing that the Rabbi sent the *shames*, they started to wipe their wet eyes with their aprons, shaking their heads, and praying to the heavenly father, "Oy, sweet Father, may it only be in a lucky hour."

And the *shames* pushed through to the bride, and said to her: "Nu, bride, take the handkerchief in agreement; the Rabbi orders this."

Hearing that the Rabbi ordered it, there is no argument. Probably this is the "contract."

With a trembling hand, the bride touched the red handkerchief with the scent of tobacco. The *shames* wound back through the crowd, screaming, "Let me through, I must give the Rabbi the 'contract' that I took from the bride. Let me through, let through, let through!"

All in the audience, with great respect and with a smile on their lips because of the occasion, listened to the Aramaic words that the Rabbi read, as though he would be sending a telegram to the Lord of the Universe: "Dear God, I am marrying another Jewish couple for You, and I pray here with my Aramaic words, that You bless them with all kinds of good things and with children and with sustenance.-- And may the groom with this maiden soon rise to greatness today, Amen."

- Reb Yokl son of Ksyal Naftali, witness
- Reb Tsvi Hirsh Volf, son of Yekhiel Mikhl, witness, the kehilla of Mervits.

At this the Rabbi raised a plate high, and quickly let it drop with the shout, "Mazl-tov, mazl-tov!" Then came real sobs as well as good wishes, an entire dictionary of good wishes, an ocean of all kinds of blessings, kisses, hugs, and hot tears. And again and again good wishes, may it be in a good hour, with luck and with income, with health and with children and grandchildren. Amen selah. And all the good wishes together with the crying and wiping eyes take up quite a bit of time --

[Page 170]

Then they start to do something really important, which means, to put something in their mouths. They toast "L'khayim"[5] with wine, Wishniak (cordial), and liquor. And now the mouths are put to work to sing, sing, and sing until daylight, and not stop. Singing and talking took up the entire evening. We ate, we snacked, who needs it; the main thing is the singing and being joyous, and our townsfolk knew well the art of singing.

The engagement evening, during which the bride had a good time with her friends, and the groom celebrated with the clergy and townspeople, until the light of day was over. The crowd started to say good-bye. It was already daytime and time for prayers, and the parents of the groom of course needed to go pray, in order to give praise to the Creator of the world, who sent their son his true match.

And so, the week went slowly. The first Shabbes afterwards, everyone sent the groom drinks, and everyone sent drinks to the prospective bride; and she sent liquor to her fiancé, and he sent it to her. The drink consisted, mostly, of a saucer of preserves, covered on top with a shawl. Those who did not own this (there were many) sent two bottles of beer. And with that came another series of good wishes.

The family of the couple started to prepare clothes and bedding. Furniture and apartments were seldom given.

A Wedding

This is about the wedding of a couple before the First World War. A wedding was a happy attraction. It could stretch out to a week, meaning, over the *Sheva Brokhes*.[6] And usually the preparations started much earlier than the wedding. I stress this because the preparations alone were an entire matter by themselves. It was not the same in all houses, in all families, because the poor families did not have the same opportunities as the rich. The preparations took place up until the *chuppah*[7]... and, God willing, up to the bris. In those days, that practically meant that one needed to rely on the Creator of the Universe —probably He would not neglect them, and He would nourish them the same as all Jews.

[Page 171]

An apartment is also not a problem — an attic in the home of parents is good. What more does a couple after their wedding need than a separate alcove? You see, clothes and bedding — that yes, that is a problem, that must be managed as well as possible. I remember that my grandmother, may she rest in peace, even in her extreme old age, for whatever celebration it was, would put on her wedding dress with her wedding cape. People had to worry about clothing, in case, God forbid, one could not make clothes later for oneself, because soon the little children will have to be taken care of, one after the other.

This is generally describing well-to-do families. Poor families also prepared up until a short time before the wedding, but, unfortunately, they prepared entirely differently and not as much.

Well, the preparations for the wedding. First of all, for the year after the engagement until the wedding, geese were raised, killed, and plucked for their feathers, in order to make several pillows and covers; that was done by both sides. Having already a mass of feathers which had been plucked, with great efforts, during winter nights by the shine of a lit naphtha lantern, they started to think about linens; those were generally purchased while buying the general clothes for the bridegroom and the members of his household, and especially for the bride-to-be and members of her household.

The travel to Malke Stul in Dubno to buy dresses for the wedding is a chapter in itself. As usual, neither the prospective groom nor the prospective bride went with their parents to make the purchases. Everything was done by the parents, with the help of specialists and with the advice and trust of Reuven and Malke Stul, may they be remembered with praise. The manufacturing businessmen of the Stul family were honest and dependable people; the entire area trusted them.

The first thing was the bed cover, and afterwards the underwear. For a well-to-do groom-to-be, two dozen pairs were made, meaning shirts with undershorts, apart from body coverings and other details, because nobody wore any other kind of underwear. And the overclothes, meaning a *kapote*, a robe from alpaca, and several overcoats: a winter one with fur, and an autumn one with a velvet collar, and sometimes also a dust coat, or a fur coat; for the wealthiest, a European polecat or a fox coat.

[Page 172]

And whoever could afford it took along a tailor from home who measured the centimeters. The tailor would use all his expertise and he sweated. Usually, he did not receive a reward for the journey, because he was, after all, the tailor hired for the year, the family tailor, who more than once had sewed a pair of pants or a robe for the family over the past months.

All purchases were packed up with a straw mat and with an iron hoop, and Reb Reuven Stul wrote out the bill. Either everything was paid for immediately, or the parents made payments for many years after, depending on how well off they were. And in the several weeks before the wedding, the tailor was taken into the house, and he sewed everything from A to Z. The same was happening with the bride-to-be.

Shoes were also bought for the wedding, including a pair of boots with thick rubber. There were instances when grooms, having a desire to dress up more for the wedding, and regardless that the weddings were taking place in the summertime, they donned their new thick rubber boots, wishing to look good and wealthy.

If the bride was from another shtetl a distance of 15, 20, or 25 kilometers away, then, in addition to all the wagon drivers in the town who were mobilized for the day, several village farmers were hired to harness their horses and wagons. They were happy to drive to a wedding, because in addition to the payment, they also benefitted from a good Jewish meal with a white roll, as well as a drink of liquor.

The Bridegroom is Coming!

About two kilometers from the shtetl, the entire traveling convoy stopped, and one of the foremen rode to the town to announce that the bridegroom and his parents were not far away. Hearing this news, a delegation from the bride's side rode out to meet them. With great honor, the groom and his parents were led to the shtetl. They went to the prepared area, where they were joined by people and musicians for the *badeken* ceremony, when the groom put the veil on the bride.

[Page 173]

After that, they went to the *chuppah,* the wedding canopy.

The place which had been prepared for the groom with his in-laws was called the bridegroom's station. They stayed there until after the wedding, and from there the parents rode back home, leaving the groom. Going to the chuppah was not talked about until the groom was in his station, because it sometimes happened, that due to complications like huge mud puddles or snowstorms, there would be a delay, and the groom either was late, or he could not get out altogether, and he could not even send a messenger. I do not wish on my friends such an obstacle to the celebration.

If everything was in order, the joy was of course huge. And as the groom, with his family, got closer to the town, a band of musicians, as well as everyone in the entire shtetl, greeted him. After completing the preparations for the ceremony, they went to put the veil on the bride, and then they went straight to the chuppah. Before the ceremony there was, as usual, crying upon hearing the wedding *badkhen*[8] whose job it was to seat the bride and groom, and to provide witty songs. Tears poured like water; if the bride were, God forbid, an orphan, then the *badkhen*'s smart material was especially tear-jerking. Everything finished, they went to the *chuppah.* Most times the ceremony took place at the synagogue. The bride and groom with their parents were brought in separately. Some walked with burning candles in their hands, and some with kerosene or oil torches. Sometimes there was even fireworks, which kept on showering sparks. The entire procedure to and from the *chuppah* was accompanied by the musicians. And there were endless good wishes! It is indescribable.

After the ceremony, the couple was quickly given something to eat after the long fast. They were served golden soup and other good things, accompanied by music. After the meal and the blessings, the dancing started. There was a row of wedding gifts. The gifts, who gave what, were announced separately by the *badkhen*, and humorously. In general, the *badkhen* worked hard the entire evening, making everybody happy at the meal and after the meal.

When all the formalities were over, the custom was to sing and dance.

[Page 174]

Only a few knowledgeable women could dance. And men danced themselves, because dancing with women cannot even be mentioned! God forbid, men and women dancing together, nobody heard of it. They danced until the second half of the next day. At the end, everybody danced a parting song, the so-called Retshke. This dance was the precursor to the end of the wedding night.

After the Retshke dance, everyone, all tired, packed everything up and went back home to their regular weekly lives. There were weddings where even after the out-of-town in-laws left for their homes, the celebration continued. I still remember, in my childhood years, the wedding of my Uncle Zelig's daughter Ester, z"l.[9] The wedding itself lasted an entire week, with all kinds of attractions, with dancers riding on horses, and the horses coming into their home. We children had never seen a bigger celebration in our lives. The wedding was talked about for many years. Life continued from generation to generation almost in the same form.

A Bris[10]

A *bris* was also a very nice celebration, because almost everyone in the shtetl came together. And even those not well off exerted themselves to make a nice feast. The celebration was usually without musicians and without other attractions which were necessary for a wedding. After all, there was just one wedding, but baby boys----

So, they were a small celebration, but beautifully observed. It is well known that in those times births took place at home. A midwife delivered the child. When the woman felt labor pains, her husband ran to call the midwife. If this happened in the night, he had to wake up the midwife, who was usually an old woman. In a great rush, she did not dress exactly correctly, or her face had become smeared with soot while searching in the dark near the chimney for matches. When she came running in like that, the woman in labor had to laugh through her pains, and that was a happy remedy.

[Page 175]

Other Celebrations

When the Sabbath was ushered out, it was often celebrated with a feast. And if God had helped to make it a good week, there was also a goose, not to mention herring with white challah.

And when a new Torah was led into the synagogue, or a new ark — that was equal to a wedding celebration. There was music and a *chuppah* for the Torah. People danced, and the musicians played. All enjoyed themselves throughout the evening until full daylight. There was no difference if the Torah were given by an individual or by a group; it was the same celebration.

As, for example, I remember when a new Torah was given by the family of Hirsh Moliner, in memory of their daughter Feyge, who had died young; that was before the First World War. The celebration began with the scribe writing letters in the Torah. Everything took place in the home of Vigdor Zisyen, because he had a large house and an inn. The celebration was taken from Hirsh Moliner's home, which was a large business house, into his son-in-law Vigdor's house which had enough room for many guests.

I still remember quite well how my grandfather, Reb Asher,[11] z"l, went first to the *mikve,* the ritual bath, before he would inscribe a letter in the Torah, and so did many other elderly Jews. (By the way, my grandfather also had sponsored a Torah, but that happened before I was born). And when they finished inscribing the letters, the chuppah was brought over and it was erected in front of the door of Vigdor's house. Berke the *shames*, may he rest in peace, called out all those with honors to the Torah. All the youth of the shtetl, with torches in their hands, and all the musicians, who were especially brought in, came to the *chuppah*. The musicians began to play; the drumbeats were a sign of celebration. And even though the synagogue was nearby, just across the way, the Torah was led to the *chuppah* with song and music throughout the marketplace, and up to the other synagogues, which were all lit up with lanterns. We carried the other Torahs out in our arms, and we introduced the new Torah to them.

[Page 176]

We returned it to the Trisk Hasidic synagogue,[12] where it was supposed to reside forever. The cantor and the congregation recited the blessings for Simchat Torah, and they paraded around like on that holiday. With every procession we danced and sang, and the musicians played, until the late hours of the night.

When the synagogue procedure was finished, then there was a feast. All participants washed their hands and made the blessings over challah. Meat, fish, liquor, and beer were served. We danced to the music until daylight. I, like many others, thought then that those who have never witnessed this joy were unfortunate. This was how a wealthy person donated a Torah.

On the other hand, soon after the First World War, a society called "No Workers Party" (because workers – yes, union – no) donated a Torah. It was a big celebration, with practically all particulars, but not with the same religious spirituality. The leader of the artisans was Shaye Miler,[13] may he rest in peace. Everything was concentrated in his house, the inscribing the letters, and starting the parade. But it was not the same as Moliner's celebration. It had more of the character of a demonstration against the rich, than a celebration of writing a Torah.

The poor workers of the small shtetl wanted to make this kind of celebration quite often, because they always felt that they were not given the same honors as more esteemed Jews, such as rich businessmen, scholars, important Hasidim, and so on. Practically every artisan felt this, and he always carried a hidden hatred towards the non-artisans. When they celebrated a Torah, they made sure to invite the entire shtetl without exception, both in honor of the Torah, and as a statement, as I have already written, to express their equal rights.

I remember, before the First World War, I was led up to the ark in the synagogue. The ark was given by Leyzer Upstein,[14] may he rest in peace, and his family, called Leyzer-Eli Moyshe's [son]. The ark was decorated by his son Hanina, may he rest in peace.

[Page 177]

Then it was very joyous too, with musicians and with songs up to the synagogue and inside it. That also was etched into my childhood memories. The musicians playing, the singing, and the dancing while carrying the holy ark as though it would be carried into the large synagogue in Jerusalem. Then we ate a whole night until daylight. I will never forget it!

Celebrations For the Sake of the Land of Israel

In addition to the monthly gatherings for various land of Israel funds, in which my wife Sonia and I and others participated, we also made parties from time to time.

The earnings were dedicated to the Jewish National Fund, and so on. Younger people than us also participated in the work. Mostly they carried through the technical work. They were: Malke Lokrits, z"l, Yitskhok Epshtayn,[15] who celebrated a special birthday,[16] Chaim Grinshtayn, z"l, Mayer Kleynbord, and others.

We also had a right-wing party which did not participate in the fundraising, and that was Betar.[17] More than once fights broke out on principles, and there even was hitting. I remember an evening when Betar people hid in a place on the way to Mlynov, near the house of Yankev Kiniver, and they wounded Yitskhok Blinder, may he rest in peace, with a stone; the differences of opinion went that far.

I will mention another institution which demanded frequent fundraisers, and that was the women's union, in which my wife Sonia actively participated. From time to time this union had entertainment which always brought in money. All the women used to bake assorted sweets which were auctioned off. The customer who received it divided it among his friends. Everyone had to put aside money, and all this brought in a total that increased the earnings of the union.

On such evenings, women and men in the entire shtetl would have a very good time.

[Page 178]

Mourning in the Shtetl

If something sad happened in the shtetl, practically everyone took part. Every person shared in the mourning. If someone got sick, he or she was never abandoned. There were continuous visits, every day. Whatever could be done to ease the family and the patient was done.

There were examples of sleeping with the sick person, or financial help, or traveling with the patient to a large town to see an important doctor; such help was always available. For a funeral, the entire shtetl participated, without exceptions.

* * *

In my childhood years there was a conversion plague, and someone was rescued from conversion. To make this rescue, the entire shtetl stood ready, even to the point of martyrdom. I do not remember all the particulars, but I will mention a few. May this praise the residents, who were ready to sacrifice their lives, as long as they could save a Jewish woman from conversion.

That happened around 1908, when Khayke, daughter of Avrom-Yankev Brizgal, was a young widow of 36–37. In her best blooming years, she was a pretty woman who was caught in the net by the compliments of a Christian, about 10 years older than she, from a neighboring village. The Christian, with his nice words, tricked her. She was going to pick cherries with him, and for payment, she would be permitted to bring home half. Not having an occupation and staying with her three children at the home of her not wealthy parents, this seemed to be an easy job for her. She had no suspicions. Once there, the Christian did not spare any compliments until she fell under his influence, and meanwhile she stayed for another day of cherry-picking. Their relationship became more and more romantic, and she finally agreed to stay with him. The Christian, who was more cunning than she, foresaw that her family would certainly resist, so he took her away a few dozen kilometers from his home in an unknown direction.

My mother, may she rest in peace, and my wife's mother, may she rest in peace, being sisters-in-law[18] and then young, capable women, went to that village.

[Page 179]

They went to a neighbor, a trustworthy one, and begged him to spy. They had the thought that she would be taken in the direction of Pochayiv,[19] the well-known holy place for Christians, where conversion ceremonies took place.

When they returned home with this notion, it became *Tisha B'Av*[20] in the shtetl. All, without exception, mourned. It was decided that the next day before dawn all the men would ride out on a rescue action. In the morning, all the men, without difference of age and social standing, prayed and went out on the road in the direction of Pochayiv. And they rode with the determination that the woman would be grabbed out of whatever place she was. I remember, being tired from riding on the distant and dusty road, we stopped in a nearby village not far from Pochayiv to feed the horses and dust ourselves off a little. By accident, a local peasant found out that the entire group, wearing their *kapotes* and their long sideburns, were riding in order to kidnap a Jewish woman who wanted to enter his God's faith. From jealousy and disappointment with the unbelieving Jews, he alarmed the entire village. The incited Christians all came out wielding sticks, and they beat up the Jews going by. With great efforts, the Jews barely succeeded in tearing themselves out of the murderous hands.

The Jews who went to Pochayiv were met with the same terrible pogrom-like welcome. With great effort and suffering, they succeeded in coming home, broken and beat up, insulted, and the end with empty hands, without the so-called convert.

[Page 180]

So, what do Hasidim do, injured, insulted and robbed of the convert? -- To the Rebbe! The Rebbe advised, that as the woman had an 18-year-old son, who worked in Kyiv as a clerk, the son should come as soon as possible. Only the son and his uncle from Lutsk should ride to Pochayiv, without words and without entreaties. They should stay around for a day, just walking among the laurels. In short, this method helped. The same day, when she, being stuck in the closed rooms of the monks for a long time, and looked out of a window from boredom, she noticed her elegant, handsome, blonde son from Kyiv walking near the church with her brother Yehoshue. She did not look at anything, but she went out and threw herself on her son's neck. With hot tears, she swore regret over everything, and in the same day they came home with her to Mervits.

All the Jews in the shtetl were very happy with the good deed. The end was, that her brother Shaye took her away to London. As of today, nobody knows where her body is lying.

It is in order here to mention the measure of sympathy in the community during the mortal danger posed by fires, which were very frequent. This plague lasted a long time. The reason for this is quite simple: the poor Jews seldom covered their roofs with sheet metal, tiles, or shingles. Their roofs were covered with straw, which did not cost much, and that burned very easily and caused fires. As is known, fire drags fire. Once it started, the entire shtetl could be burned up. I remember many such fires. The last one happened after the First World War, when a spark came out of Zelig's mill from the steam machine, and it burned down Leye Sherman's house, and Benyomin Grinshpan's house. There were not many houses then in the neighborhood after the war. Usually, if it had happened before the war, then certainly the entire shtetl would have been in flames. By the last years before the First World War, people started to live more modernly, so that the apartments were all the time becoming more covered with tiles.

That led to the creation of factories in Mervits.

For many years, people talked about the fire of the large, beautiful synagogue. The fire began from a certain Khane-Rokhl Yusele-Smalikops' house, and spread to nearby houses covered with straw, and then it ended with the large, beautiful synagogue.

Translator's and editor's footnotes:

1. Abbreviation for Sonia and Mendel Teitelman. Sonia and Mendel Menachem Teitelman were among a number of Shoah survivors from the Teitelman family. Mendel was born in Mervits, the son of Abraham Teitelman (1850–1922) and Rivka Halperin, and one of nine siblings, most of whom died in the Shoah. His year of birth is given variously as 1900 and 1905. Mendel married his first cousin, Sonia Gruber (1900–1980), daughter of Yosef Moshe Gruber and Shifra (Teitelman). Sonia and Mendel had no children but remained close with the family of Sonia's sister, Rachel (Gruber) Teitelman and her husband Nahum, who are also contributors to this volume. – HS

2. Multi-tasking synagogue aide. – HBF

3. Apparently writing the ketubah, the marriage document. – HS

4. Rabbinic law required that the ketubah be signed by two witnesses who are not related to each other. This was difficult in the small shtetls since all the families had intermarried and were related. The expression here seems to suggest two witnesses who share great-grandparents (3rd cousins) or more distantly related could be witnesses since one has eight great-grandparents. – HS

5. "To Life." – HS

6.   Seven Blessings recited during the wedding ceremony, after the wedding feast, and for seven days following a festive meal. – HBF

7.   The chuppah refers to the wedding canopy when the actual wedding took place. – HS

8.   The wedding *badkhen*, the entertainer, acted like a master of ceremonies. He also composed songs in rhyme about the couple. – HBF

9.   Possibly a reference to Mendel's first cousin, Ester, daughter of Abraham Teitelman, who married Meir Gruber. – HS

10.   Ritual circumcision of a baby boy when he is eight days old. – HBF

11.   Asher Teitelman, grandfather of both Mendel and Sonia, since they were first cousins. – HS

12.   The largest synagogue in Mlynov. – HS

13.   Likely referring to the person remembered as Saul Meiler (or Malar) who married Nechama, one of the Shulman daughters. – HS

14.   A Yad Vashem record filled out by Mendel Teitelman indicates Eliezer Upstein, son of Eli Moyshe, was born in 1865 in Mervits and died in Mlynov or Dubno in the Shoah. He is the father of Hanina Upstein and the grandfather of Yitzhak Upstein (1910), who survived the Shoah while in the Russian Army and who subsequently married Bunia Steinberg, another survivor. Yitzhak and Bunia made aliyah after the War. The family story is told in *A Struggle to Survive*, which is published on the Mlynov website. – HS

15.   Possibly "Yitzhak Upstein," grandson of Leazar Opshteyn in the previous paragraph. – HS

16.   The Yiddish appears to have an acronym "Yb"la" which appears to be a misspelling of yoyvel (Jubilee), signifying reaching a special birthday or wedding anniversary. – HBF

17.   A revisionist Zionist youth movement founded by Jabotinsky in 1923. – HBF

18.   Mendel and his wife Sonia were first cousins. Mendel's father, Abraham Teitelman, was a brother of Sonia's mother, Shifra (Teitelman) Gruber. Therefore, their mothers were sister-in-laws. – HS

19.   Likely Pochaiv (or Pochayev), Ukraine today, a town 93 km due south of Mlyniv. The monastery there, belonging to the Ukrainian Orthodox Church, has been a spiritual center in Ukraine. – HBF

20.   Saddest Jewish holiday, a fast day of mourning the destruction of both Temples in Jerusalem. – HBF

[Page 181]

Baking Matzas

by S.M.T.[1]

Translated from the Yiddish by Hannah B. Fischthal, PhD

Edited by Howard I. Schwartz, PhD

Before the great tragedy, matzas were baked in Mlynov. There was a machine which was always used, from Passover to Passover, for that purpose. All the Jews from Mlynov and Mervits and the surrounding villages bought their matzas from Mlynov. The profits were used to support the surrounding villages with matzas for Passover. At the same time, several unemployed artisans earned enough for their own Passover expenses from their work with the matzas. For a few of them, these were their first earnings in the spring; most of them probably sat through the entire winter without earning anything, which was quite usual for a part of the population.

They baked matzas and *shmura*-matzas![2] The Vaynshtok family and a few others also made a few egg matzas for Passover. All these preparations were an annual celebration for the entire Jewish population in all houses.

When the matzas were brought into the Jewish home, cheer was brought inside with them. People kept wishing for each other: "May we live until next year with happy hearts, with, with, with …"

And when the first seder night approached, one could feel everyone's joy, which reigned in every house without difference. And so stretched an entire eight-day holiday with happiness. We investigated whose matzas were more successful, thinner, fresher, tastier, not burned, and not raw. We even discussed the wine used in the four cups at the seders — who received wine from the land of Israel for Passover, and who had raisin wine. The main points were the taste and color. We talked about prospective brides and grooms, and who was going to the bride-to-be after the first two days of the holiday. There was never any talk about a man riding to visit his fiancée in another town on the first two days; that was simply a sin.

[Page 182]

I do not remember that ever happened.

There was talk about preparing for Passover in general, how difficult it was. Firstly, whitewashing the houses, which was a tradition from ancient times. Being kosher for Passover had many difficulties, especially if it was a late spring and the snow was still an obstacle, or if there were large mud puddles. So, the whitewashing came with bitterness, and therefore the joy after that was large.

Then dressing up for Passover! That is an entirely separate chapter. Not all Jewish families could afford this luxury. It happened quite often that the tailors could not afford new clothes for the holiday for themselves, unfortunately. Those, though, who could have special clothes made for the holiday, talked about the quality and beauty of the clothing in various meetings, at the synagogue, or visiting. It was this way with shoes and other small things. We had quite a lot of laughter in celebrating the seder, which was different in all Jewish homes. In more than one Jewish house entire histories were related, and very often happy ones.

The dear, warm summer would be approaching, and everything would blossom and grow, and the hard winter with its cold difficulties would leave. The livelihood of many toiling Jews would, with the coming of summer, improve. Bricklayers and carpenters would revive with the coming of summer because their jobs were unsteady in the winter because of the cold. The young people would walk out a little freer from the narrow streets of the shtetl. And so, all areas would improve with the arrival of summer.

Also, our shtetele Mervits, both separately and often together with Mlynov, made all the above-mentioned preparations with small exceptions. Until the First World War, for quite a few years, matzas were baked in the so-called "meadow": girls and women from the shtetl gathered, and from early in the morning until the evening, they kneaded and rolled out the dough for matzas. The men were more active in carrying the matzas to everyone's home. Shoveling and measuring meal was done by the young. I do not remember exactly how much a matza worker earned in 3–4 weeks, working 12–13 hours a day, but in the shtetl people talked that this one and that one would already earn enough for Passover.

[Page 183]

That is how it was until about three years before the First World War. There were no other ways of baking matzas outside of a "meadow" until Peysakh Rimer brought a machine, paid the rabbi to certify it was kosher, and baked matzas with it. And usually, who provided the power to turn the wheels of the machine? People. We, pranksters, kept running out of the cheder to at least look through the window, to see how the new wonder makes matzas, which used to be the job of 20 women. And when Peysakh Rimer could not drive away the curious cheder-boys, he teased his little dogs. His was the only Jewish house with dogs. That stopped us from leaning on his windows to see the miracle machine.

After The First World War, people in Mervits did not bake any more matzas. They bought them in Mlynov.

* * *

I will mention mainly how we baked matzas that first year when the Hitlerite criminals, may their names be blotted out, were already in our shtetl, in 1942; and how we baked them one time before we left Mlynov in 1945 after the winter.

There could not be any talk about baking matzas in 1942, because that was simply life endangering, if it would, God forbid, be discovered. As we know, people strive to do what is forbidden, and so it was also in this instance. We kind of thought that the honor of the good deed, and maybe also good wishes, would maybe help, and our wishes would be realized. We baked and we wished, but our good wishes did not come true. To cover up our baking, we, not yet being in the ghetto, gathered in a house which was not on the main road from Mlynov-Lutzk. That was at my brother-in-law Note Gruber,[3] may he rest in peace. His house was slightly hidden by trees on Mikhalovske's land. Several of my relatives baked matzas there, like my Uncle Chaim-Meir,[4] z"l, with his family; my brother Yankev-Yoysef, z"l, with his family; and my Uncle Yankev Gruber, z"l; and my brother-in-law Yankev and Khayke,[5] z"l with their families.

[Page 184]

And so it was in other houses. Several people got together — and they baked. I acquired meal from the mill where I worked. Also, we were able to trade with a "better" Christian. We would exchange a dress or a shoe for meal. The baking took place during the day, so that the night shine would not, God forbid, ever interest our enemies who would ask, "What is shining over there?"

While rolling out the dough and baking, everybody wished each other well. Yet in truth bloody tears poured out of our eyes by themselves, as though everyone had a premonition: God knows if next year I will still bake matzas …

Despite all the difficulties, somebody would get an egg, somebody a piece of meat, we wiped away the tears, and we held a seder.

I cannot describe what took place at the seder tables. This could only have taken place in Spain during the Inquisition, and in other similar circumstances. Tears poured out like water. We all had the feeling that we were celebrating the last seder in our lives. Old and young, everyone had the same premonitions.

The sad days of Passover went by as usual. There could not be any talk about observing Passover as a holiday. Everybody who had what to do worked, because the enemy's hand did not drop its baton on Passover. Right after Passover, they [the Nazis] started to demand that people go to work in Rovne. Work was bitter enough at home, but we survived Rovne with only a few victims, among whom were Gershon Peysi's two sons, twins. They did not return from the hands of the murderers. Others, though, managed to run back home, like, for example, Asher–Nokhum's [son],[6] Avrohom–Khayke's [son], and others. That was a great victory.

* * *

We who survived the great fire returned to spend about 15 months in Mlynov. We decided we would bake matzas with the consciousness that even though we had been freed, and we could bake the matzas freely, we knew that in Mlynov matzas were being baked for the last time, and nobody, nobody, would ever bake matzas here again.

[Page 185]

We baked in my home, where my wife Sonia and I and the three children of my cousin resided,[7] at the house of Yankev Tesler, [8] z"l. We had the remaining survivors of Mlynov, and a few outside of Mlynov who had come there for various reasons after their liberation, and a few Jewish officers in the Russian army. We were not short of anything then, like meal, wood, and all necessary things which were needed for baking matzas. But missing were the best and the most beloved Jews!

When we baked the matzas, we sang whatever came into our mouths, to jab our enemies who were around us. Previously, when they were important people at the top, they did us much harm, not less than the Germans.

Our only form of revenge was to bake matzas freely, to pretend our hearts were okay, and to sing a song, even though bloody tears were still covering our faces. And in addition, we knew that in a few weeks we would leave Mlynov altogether.

The second of Tamuz 5705 [13 June 1945] we left Mlynov forever.

Rovno Street

Translator's and editor's footnotes:

1. Acronym for Sonia and Mendel Teitelman. – HS
2. Matzas made with extreme strictness and supervision. – HBF
3. Brother of Mendel's wife, Sonia. – HS

4. Mendel's uncle Chaim-Meir Teitelman. – HS

5. Mendel is referring to his wife, Sonia's, siblings: Yitzhak Gruber (later Hofri) and Chaika (Gruber) Schichman. – HS

6. Referring to Asher Teitelman son of Nahum. See his story of survival on the Mlynov website. – HS

7. Probably referring to his cousin Nahum Teitelman and their children Asher, Shifra and Yosef. Nahum was married to Rachel (Gruber), the sister of Mendel's wife, Sonia (Gruber) Teitelman. All of them were first cousins. – HS

8. A photo of Jacob Tesler appears on p. 478 in the current volume. His children Golda, Hinda, Itzhak, and Peretz all died in the Shoah. His daughter, Liba Tesler, escaped and survived and her story is told in David Sokolsky, *Monument: One Woman's Courageous Escape from the Holocaust.* A photo of Liba and her sisters appears on page 469 standing center behind Yetta Schwartz, great-grandmother of editor, Howard Schwartz. – HS

[Page 186]

The Military Recruits

by Aaron (Berger) Harari[1]

Translated and edited by Howard I. Schwartz, PhD with Hanina Epstein

From time immemorial, Jews avoided serving in a foreign military: they would bribe the enlistment officials to obtain a certificate of release, and a person who did not obtain one tried to produce a bodily deformity. They would amputate the trigger finger from the right hand, burrow an iron wire in the ear to deafen it, or jump from a height in order to create a fracture in the foot. Shika Shechman,[2] for example, adapted a cough that sounded frightful to the ear, and when he stood before the medical military committee and he produced his fake cough — they were all afraid and thought him to be sick with tuberculosis. Shika received an exemption immediately, even though he was entirely healthy and didn't have a cough at all….

During my time, when people my age had to present themselves, abstentions from physical pleasure were routine. Two weeks before their appearance they would abstain from sleep and food, walk around at night and "make merry," and during the day ride a great deal on bicycles until physical depletion. The essential food was sunflower seeds and biscuits baked from dough with castor oil as a means of getting diarrhea, all of these caused weight loss and organic pains. But, actually, these activities didn't have an influence during the military medical exam. Apparently, the doctors knew that the Jews prepared themselves for their appearance, and this only caused confusion with the medical findings.

Winter — against the background of the Count's garden

[Page 187]

And even those whose health was deficient for real, didn't receive an exemption but only a postponement for a year. Only a few received exemptions, in exceptional circumstances, after another return examination.

Moving about at night and making merry was like an obligation. If one of the recruits was absent, they would gather by his house and sing by his window [in Yiddish] "When a man is called, one must go, it does not help to laugh or cry" [translated in Hebrew:] (when they call you must go, it does not help to laugh or cry) until he was willing to get up from his bed and join us. More than once, we encountered cursing and swearing from the parents and neighbors whose rest we had disturbed. But none of this intimidated us, since they were [done] with a military exam that was pending.

There was a specific group of youth that was unorganized, did nothing and were bored, who would gather in the evenings in the central square and invent all kinds of practical pranks. For example, they took a thin, long string and tied it to the window of one of the houses and the group hid in the bushes at a distance from the house and plucked the string with their fingers like stringed instruments. This would make a humming sound in the house which the residents couldn't explain it. Occasionally, when they went outside to explore the reason, the [pranksters] would stop what they were doing, and when the inhabitants went back inside, they would renew the plucking … Afterwards they would shift to another house. Or another "prank": they would introduce confusion into business signs. The sign of the barbershop they hung on the butcher shop, and vice versa … And they would do this on several streets. Or, for example, they would gather all kinds of junk, furniture and ladders and build a tower out of them in the center of the town.

Boating on the River Ikva[3]
Original photo courtesy of Zeev Harari

All this activity was done Sabbath night without interference, and on Sabbath morning, when the congregation was going to the synagogue, they couldn't believe their eyes … there were some who thought it was the work of demons and spirits. It was never revealed whose hands were involved in these deeds, lest revenge be taken against all of them. And if suspicion fell on someone, they were afraid to pay him back for fear of revenge. The police did not get involved in this, because they didn't regard the deed to be criminal.

Translator's and editor's footnotes:

1. For Harari's background, see footnote 1 in his prior essay.
2. Possibly referring to Shimon Schechman, son of Noach Moshe Schechman. In an earlier essay, "Visit to Mlynov, 1938," pp. 77–79, Harari mentions Shimon Schechman who had a club house for the Zionist Youth Group where they played billiards.
3. Aaron (Berger) Harari, the author of this essay, is standing on the right.

[Page 188]

An Event in the Shtetl

Boruch Meren[1], Baltimore

Translated from the Yiddish by Hannah B. Fischthal, PhD

Edited by Howard I. Schwartz, PhD

Whoever was born and raised in a small shtetl in Volhynia, like my little shtetl Mlynov, will never forget the childhood years: the cheder, even the slaps from the teacher; the school; the bathhouse, pardon the comparison; the happy and beautiful holidays, like the spring holiday Passover, and Shavuot; all of which gave so much meaning to our lives. And of course, we cannot forget the beautiful countryside around the shtetl with its wonderful, fresh air in the summer.

To tell the truth, the air in the shtetl was not so clear and fresh, because Moyshe the teacher's green puddle attracted ducks which flocked there, spoiling the air. In addition, whenever a Jewish woman wanted, she would open the door from her kitchen and pour the dirty water out into the street in front of the door. So, when we wanted to revive ourselves with truly good, fresh air, we would take a walk outside of town where fragrant green fields and lawns were spread out in front of our eyes.

As in all small villages, the shopkeepers were standing in their stores looking out for customers. The shopkeepers would often fight over a customer. But when it came to Yom Kippur, they would all make up. Right after Yom Kippur they started the old business again, exactly like before. Even among the artisans there was competition.

The number of rich people in the shtetl could be counted on one's fingers. Most of the Jews were respectable paupers who praised the Lord of the Universe for the little they were given. Shabbes brought rest for the body and the soul. Every Jewish man during Shabbes was like a king in his home. The house was spotless, the wife and the children dressed in clean, nice clothes in honor of Shabbes. The poorest woman baked challas for Shabbes, cooked fish and put up cholent.

[Page 189]

During the day, after napping, a well-to-do Jew would sit comfortably at his table, his greasy yarmulke on his head and the *arbe-kanfes*[2] over his white undershirt, and enjoy drinking a hot glass of tea while looking into his prayerbook. On the other hand, the artisans and plain people were not so scrupulously devoted to observing Shabbes. They took their wives and children and walked out of the shtetl, lay down on the grass, and breathed in the wonderful air of field and forest.

The fields during the month of Tamuz[3] were wonderful when the high ears of corn with their golden color shook in the wind like ocean waves, their heads bent due to the weight of the ripe grains. The Jews from the shtetl, especially the grain merchants, used to walk here, think about the field, tear off several ears, rub them, think about them, and make a prediction that soon the grains will be ready for harvesting. The shopkeepers and the artisans waited with impatience for when the farmers would harvest the grains from the fields, and then they would be able to buy things and pay off their debts. We, the Jews, furnished salt, sugar, and manufactured items for them, and they made the beautiful wide fields grow. I was always jealous of them. Why do they live like a normal people on their land? And we, Jews, live from the wind? As a small boy it occurred to me, not from cheder, that we Jews also once had a land with our own farmers. Even today I feel the tragedy of the saying: "Because we sinned, we were exiled from our land, and we moved far away from it."[4]

The attraction of the shtetl was the Count's manor, although nobody was permitted to go inside. The proverb, "What comes out of my speaking Polish, if I am not permitted in the manor," was correct in our case. Of all the Jews in the shtetl, only my grandfather[5] had the honor to go inside the manor, because Hershko was a useful *Zhid* (Jew). He was a contractor and he worked for the Count. When Jews needed a favor from the Count, my grandfather, Hirsh Goldseker, was the intermediary. Everyone knew that he found favor in the eyes of the Count and the Countess. Everyone in the shtetl talked about how Hirsh Goldseker kisses the Countess's hand when he says hello. My grandfather used to tell us grandchildren wonderful histories of life on the estate.

[Page 190]

As the summer used to end and fall would start, the shtetl looked sad. Because of the rains and the deep mud, we had to sit home, and it gnawed at our souls. Nature became unrecognizable. Sadder and more naked, the trees shook in the wind. The gardens were already empty. The last to go were the potatoes, which we dug out of the ground and put into the cellars for the long winter, since the earth would soon freeze, and a white snow would cover the fields for the entire season. Poor families would be frightened. The expenses became larger because wood had to be prepared for heating, and people had to buy warm clothes, mainly boots, which were very necessary.

The Jews in the shtetl spent more time in the synagogue in the winter, sitting on chairs around a long table near the warm oven, studying well in the long evenings. Even the plain Jews used to sit on the side and listen to a word of Torah.

In the synagogue people could also find out the prices of wheat, which was the main business; they rented wagon drivers to drive the grain into the city. In the synagogue we used to also talk about world events, and in general find out the news of the world. An argument would often break out in the synagogue regarding community matters. In such conflicts there were always two sides, and the shtetl went into battle. Young and old took part in the arguments. If not for that, life would be too boring in the shtetl.

* * *

And now I want to relate an episode that excited the entire shtetl.

In Mlynov, when boys turned 21 and needed to enroll in the military, their parents would be extremely worried. What parents wanted their son to be a soldier and eat non-kosher food from the soldiers' kitchen?

[Page 191]

Fathers would groan quietly, and mothers wrung their hands. But not us, the boys, the recruits, because when one is young, one can make a comedy out of a tragedy. We did not take it so much to heart. To get out of serving there was one way: not to eat and not to drink enough, to live only on dry crackers and drink tea without sugar. Then one could hope to be completely freed from duty. The self-torture went on for four weeks. To help pass the time, the recruits got together every night and worked out a plan on how to spend the night. That usually consisted of going around singing under windows, especially where there were girls. Or pranking certain bosses. Recruits could do it and be forgiven because they were almost soldiers.

One night, when we recruits did not have anything planned but we wanted to do a special prank so the shtetl would remember us, we went to Shmuel, the joker of the shtetl.[6] (A brother-in-law of Yitzhak Lamdan), Shmuel was then a young man old enough to get married. He was known as being versed in books; he brought Zionism into the shtetl; he founded a library; in general, he tried to modernize the shtetl. He was respected. He loved to play tricks on the big shots and that is why we called him Shmuel the joker. (He now lives in Israel). We went, as I said, to Shmuel. We woke him up from sleep, got him out of bed. He rubbed his always red eyes, put on his glasses, and he said in a sleepy voice:

"Nu, friends, you don't have to tell me what you want. I see in your inflamed cheeks and shiny eyes that you want to do something tonight, and certainly you want my advice?"

"You got it," we all answered at the same time.

"I have a plan for you," Shmuel the joker said. "Today is Thursday night and tomorrow is Friday before Shabbes. And Jews have to go Friday to the bath to steam their bones and to wash in honor of Shabbes. I want you to heat up the community bath, and to let all the craftsmen and the poor to come in for free, without money.

[Page 192]

They also deserve a little happiness in this world. They should enjoy the steam and then wash in honor of Shabbes to spite all the fancy bosses, because even in the bathhouse the wealthy Jews take up the highest benches. Such social injustice!" Shmuel screamed out with wrath.[7]

"Correct!" we all say, "but where will we get wood to heat up the bath?"

"There will be wood," Shmuel said. "You yourselves will go through the streets and yards (in front of every house was a piece of land) and gather together everything that you can: chairs, tables, blocks, old boards which are lying around near the houses, old doors, everything that can burn. I tell you, comrades, it is for a good purpose! 'The fearful and tender-hearted will go and return home.'"

His warm words worked strongly on us, and we started, with the flame of youth, to heat up the bath. We collected everything, whatever came into our hands, and threw it on a mountain near the bath. We woke up the bath attendant, who was also a shammes in the Stolin synagogue as well as the gravedigger in the shtetl; after receiving all his salaries, we still had to send him something for Shabbes. We ordered him to get right to work and heat up a hot bath. We helped him fill up the mikveh with water, threw in the wood in the two large ovens. The attendant frightfully obeyed our order, and he promised us he would fulfill our orders: to positively let all the artisans and poor Jews into the bath for free.

Before daybreak, the tired recruits each went home to take a nap.

The next day, Friday morning, the shtetl learned what the recruits had done. One told the other. People were missing a chair, a table, a piece of wood that was lying for years near the door. They cursed. The children in the cheders, who were dismissed, as usual, a half day Friday, also learned the news, so they ran around the streets and screamed:

"Jews, go into the bath for free!"

Craftsmen, who had just arrived all muddy from the villages, quickly grabbed their white, clean laundry and hurried to the bath. The Jews had pleasure from the hot steam, sitting on the uppermost bench of the sauna, and screamed:

[Page 193]

"Give it! Give it!" That meant to pour more hot water on the hot stones and increase the heat.

"Thrash yourselves, Jews, to spite Reb[8] Yosel Berger," screamed Shloyme the lame shoemaker.[9]

"Ay, ay, it is good," screamed red Shaye. "It has been a long time since I had such a wonderful bath! Moyshe, thrash me again on the right side."

"A blessing on the group of recruits; for this good deed may they be freed and be Jews at home," all screamed.

The wealthy bosses from the shtetl boycotted and did not go to the bath that Friday. From that we understood that it would be "jolly"[10] in our Trisk synagogue. And so it was.

Saturday morning, right after the morning prayers, the Shammes went up to the platform and announced that Mr. (Reb) Yosel Lemel's [son], the trustee, had something important to say, therefore be quiet, and he gave the lectern a slap. Soon three Yosels came up onto the platform: Yosel Mayer's [son], Yosel Lemel's [son] and Yosel Lipekh's [son]. They were the committee that took care of the congregation's needs.

The first to speak was Yosel Lemel's, the biggest and devoted advisor, a handsome, tall Jew, with quite a stomach, which garnered respect from the Jews. Angrily, he banged the lectern, and his deep bossy voice let out a sound like thunder.

"Gentlemen, Jews! Be informed, that the 'heathens,' the recruits, practically burned down our bathhouse. We had toiled so much for it; have you heard of such unruliness? I would send them to prison for stealing wood."

Immediately voices and wildness were heard; it was deafening. The parents of the recruits felt guilty, and it was maintained that they should take the blame, because we, the "guilty," had immediately left. In short, it came to slaps. The artisans and the healthy boys stayed together in the small room, ready to apply their healthy fists. But then Mr. (Reb) Yehuda Leib Lamdan (father of the famous Hebrew writer Yitzhak Lamdan) mixed in. This Jew, whose name was appropriate, was a big scholar and a God-fearing man.

[Page 194]

Everyone respected him. He interrupted his learning, straightened out his tallis over his head so that only a piece of face looked out, spread out his arms, and started to beg the crowd for mercy:

"Gentlemen, I beg you, be quiet! It is a desecration of God's name for Jews to fight like this, especially in a holy place.

A group of friends

Brothers, if they already did it, then it's too late! After all, they are still Jewish children, and they accomplished an important thing: poor Jews washed themselves in honor of Shabbes, and that is a very good deed. For that honor, God will help and free them from service, and they will become devout young men in their parents' homes."

The well-to-do Jews immediately quieted down, and they forgave the recruits for their "heathenish" piece of work. If Mr. (Reb) Yehude Leib Lamdan orders, one must obey.

Translator's and editor's footnotes:

1. For Boruch Meren's bio, see footnote 1 in his essay "A Good Deed," p. 149 this volume. – HS
2. Fringed ritual garment worn by boys and men. – HBF
3. June-July on the Gregorian calendar. – HBF
4. The Hebrew verse apparently is from the prayer tradition of Mizrachi ("Oriental") Jews. It is part of the Amidah prayer during the Musaf service on the three festivals. – HS
5. Boruch's mother was Miriam (Goldseker) and her father was Hirsch Goldseker. – HS
6. Apparently referring to Shmuel (Samuel) Mandelkern, who married Yitzhak Lamdan's sister, Malcah Lamdan. This same Samuel Mandelkern is the one who helped organize the Zionist Youth Groups and who made aliyah in the 1920s. In other essays in this volume, he is remembered as a serious organizer among the youth. On Mandelkern's role in establishing The Young Guard, see Yosef Litvak's essay, "The Town of Mlynov," p. 58, and Aaron Harari's essay, "Culture, Education, and Social Life in the Small Town," p. 67. Mandelkern also contributed an essay to this volume on "Self-Defense in the Shtetl." – HS

7.   The viewpoint expressed here reflects the socialist world view embraced by The Young Guard youth group (Hashomer Hatzair) that Mandelkern helped establish in town. – HS

8.   Reb typically is used like "Mr." in English. – HS

9.   The statement here seems to reflect the class tensions in Mlynov, between the poor lame shoemaker and a wealthier man, Yosel Berger, and may also reflect the impact of socialist ideas on the town's residents. The young men appear to be stoking class tensions in town through their prank pitting the poor against the well-to-do. "Thrashing" seems to refer to therapeutic thrashings of the body with soaked branches, a practice still found in some bathhouses today. – HS

10.   In other words, that the situation would be serious during the Sabbath services. – HS

[Page 195]

Bread and Wood

Sonia and Mendel Teitelman

Translated from the Yiddish by Hannah B. Fischthal, PhD

Edited by Howard I. Schwartz, PhD

Our brothers and sisters were constantly plagued their entire lives trying to obtain the bare necessities of life. In this regard, there was not even a big difference between the richer people and the poorer ones. Even for those who were better off, buying four or five wagons full of wood to enable cooking in the winter was a big expense. It could not be ignored. Without wood, nobody could survive the very cold winters. To be unable to provide heat was life endangering. People could simply freeze to death. For children, as usual, it was much more dangerous.

Once people were able to get a wagonful of wood, there was still the problem of sawing and chopping. Finding a place to put the wood was another problem. Also, the ovens were a problem. Everything in the shtetl was primitive. Well-constructed cooking ovens were very rare here. We had to be satisfied with the *Khrube*[1] that stood in the middle of the room to warm up as much as possible around it. It was used for heating and for cooking. It had a small built-in area to keep the food warm. A Christian woman heated up the stove on Shabbes. The cholent was put inside to keep warm. As usual, every family made a cholent in their baking ovens which were in every house for baking bread and challah.

The baking took place, as a rule, on Friday — challah for Shabbes and bread for the whole week. The bread was the main food in the house. According to the folk saying, "If bread and water are here, there is no hunger here." Everything was baked Friday so the holiness of Shabbes would be more noticeable. Nobody needed tasty foods during the week, when it was enough to just be able to drive away the hunger, but for Shabbes, that was already something else. Everything good was in honor of Shabbes.

This conduct more than once aroused the jealousy and hatred of the Christian neighbors. Why? Where does the poor neighbor, who has many children, get a white challah?

Translator's footnote:

1.   Probably some kind of cast-iron, pot-bellied stove. – HBF

[Page 196]

A True Event in Mlynov from 96 Years Ago

Shirley Jacobs,[1] Bronx

Translated from the Yiddish by Hannah B. Fischthal, PhD

Edited by Howard I. Schwartz, PhD

My mother, Itse Starosta's[2] oldest daughter, Basye,[3] told me:

In Mlynov there was the Ahreles family, very respected people. There was a Henye Ahreles,[4] Khaye Ahreles, Zelde Ahreles, Moyshe Ahreles.[5] The oldest son was called Daniel. He had an iron store; later, Moyshe Ahreles took his place.

This Daniel used to loan material to the Czechs, who lived in the nearby villages. In the winter they would buy on credit and pay the debt after harvest-time. One day a Czech came to Daniel and asked him for a cash loan. The Czech was not a poor man, and Daniel loaned him the money.

Not long after that, the Czech came on a cold winter day to Daniel and said to him: "If you want your debt repaid, come with me to my house, and I will pay you everything I owe you." Daniel's mother Libe[6] begged him to not go; his wife Dvoyra, pregnant, fell on his chest and tried to stop him from going.

"It is terribly cold."

But Daniel wrapped himself up, put on his fur cap, and set out. The Czech had promised he would bring him home the same day.

There was a dead silence in the house. Both the women were uneasy. They kept looking at the door … The day was over. It was night and Daniel was not there. In the morning — still not there …

So, they took a horse and sled and left to find the Czech. On the highway, they found Daniel, murdered.

The entire shtetl was in mourning. They performed the necessary rites for the body; they had to bury him in his clothes. The fur hat, however, was missing.

A few days later, an alarm spread through the shtetl that Daniel had been seen in the street. Daniel was wandering around in the world of ghosts. Later another person said that Daniel came to him in his dream, and he told him to go to a certain place where his hat was lying.

[Page 197]

Daniel told him to take the cap and put it into his grave.

For a while, people were afraid to go out at night; my grandfather was led to the synagogue. It was decided to take the Rabbi with a minyan of important householders to the place Daniel had mentioned in the dream. And the hat was found there!

They did what Daniel had told them to do. After that, Daniel no longer appeared on the street or in dreams.

(His wife Dvoyra gave birth to a son. He was called "brother."[7]

Savka, tree cutter

Later, she married Motye-Mayer. Everybody from Mlynov knows him. They had children. One son is here — he is called "Zun" (son). And a brother died not long ago in America.)

Translator's and editor's footnotes:

1.   Shirley (Barditch) Jacobs, originally Sura Borodacz, (1905–1983) is one of four children of Isidore Barditch (originally Borodacz) from Lutsk and Bessie Teitelbaum (originally Bassa Ferteybaum) from Mlynov. Shirley's sister is Sylvia (Barditch) Goldberg, an editor of this volume and another contributor. Both Shirley and Sylvia were born in Lutsk. Their grandfather from Mlynov was Samuel Yitzchak Ferteybaum, whom the family recalls as "Itse Starota" in this essay. Sylvia also wrote fondly about their grandfather in "Stoliner Hasidism in Mlynov," pp. 80–82, and indicates that their grandfather got their father involved in Stoliner Hasidism. Sylvia also discusses visiting their Mlynov grandparents in "A Wedding in Mlynov," p. 27. The Barditch (Borodacz) family came to the US in October 1921 and settled in Baltimore before a family tragedy led the family to move to New York in a story recounted on the Mlynov website. In the US, Shirley married Benjamin Jacobs and they had three children. A photo of Shirley's eldest daughter, Marilyn (Jacobs) Israel, appears as a young girl on page 500 of the original volume with Shirley's sister Sylvia (right) and their mother Bassa (left). –HS

2.   A *Staroste* was a government official. – HBF See also the essay about Itse Starosta written by granddaughter Sylvia Barditch-Goldberg in this volume, pp. 80–82. – HS

3.   A photo of Basye Barditch appears on page 500 of this volume. – HS

4.   Henye Ahreles appears in the photo on page 500 and is also called "Aleph Katz's mother" there, which provided the clue as to her identity and those of her siblings mentioned here. – HS

5.   The name "Ahreles" is a diminutive for "Aaron" and thus refers to Aaron Hirsch, patriarch of the Hirsch family. Anna (Hirsch) Katz is called "Henie Ahreles" in a photo in this volume with the author's mother, sister and daughter. The Hirsch members referred to here are Henye Ahreles [=Anna (Hirsch) Katz], Khaye Ahreles [=Clara (Hirsch) Newman), Zelde Ahreles [=Zelda (Hirsch) Berger] and Moyshe Ahreles (Moishe Hirsch) and Daniel refers to Daniel Hirsch. The majority of these Hirsch individuals came to America. On the Hirsch family saga, see the Mlynov website. – HS

6.   Liebe Hirsch, matriarch of the Hirsch family, wife of Aaron. – HS

7.   I suspect that Dvoya's son referred to here was the young man named Daniel Hirz/Hirsch from Mlynov who arrived in New York in November 1926 and is listed as a cousin of the other Hirschs. On this Daniel's manifest, his mother is listed as Dwoira. If this interpretation is correct, he was given the name of his father, Daniel, who passed away before he was born. I suspect he was called "brother" by his father's siblings who saw their brother in his son. – HS

[Page 198]

In the Shtetl

David Fishman[1], Baltimore

Translated from the Yiddish by Hannah B. Fischthal, PhD

Edited by Howard I. Schwartz, PhD

If you would ask me what I had for supper yesterday, I definitely would not remember — but I do remember exactly our shtetele Mlynov of more than 40 years ago, especially the entire winter until Purim time: the mud, the snow with the cold, the market people, the shopkeepers wearing kaftans and fur coats, boots on their feet, with their fire pots and wool gloves without fingers. The two-week long fairs, including the drunken Christians after the fair — that is a separate chapter. The others in the shtetl kept inside near the hot grease that was cooking, where potatoes and herring were being prepared.

In the evenings, after the Mincha-Maariv prayers, the shtetl was practically empty, sleepy, and dreaming. But nobody felt as good as we boys who used to go to cheder at night carrying lanterns. While walking, we sang to drive away our fears of coming across a Christian or an angry dog.

Years later, more grown up, Yitzhak Lamdan, z"l, and I studied together under Motl Chizik.[2] We told each other scary, fantastic, and superstitious stories about insane people, clowns, and evil people. We talked about corpses that rise up out of their graves exactly after 12:00 at night and fill up the House of Prayer. Sometimes a dead body would be found in the mikveh, exactly when a young wife was going to immerse herself.

I see it in front of my eyes: Yitzhak Lamdan would sit, leaning over to hear every word, and then he would say: "I do not believe any of those silly tales."

The more frightening the story, the more we moved closer together to hear about thieves, robbers, Gypsies, forest-robbers, wolves, wild boars, angry dogs, and the black cats and witches who controlled women in childbirth.

Translator's and editor's footnotes:

    1.   David "Dudek" Fishman, born in Mlynov in 1899, was the eldest of three children of Moishe Fishman (1873–1968) and Chaya Gilden (1880–1927). His father Moishe is also a contributor to this volume. The Fishmans made a significant stir in 1921 when they became the first Mlynov family to make aliyah to Palestine where they soon settled in Balfouria. That story is told below by Boruch Meren in "The First Immigrant to the Land of Israel," p. 220. In 1924, David was joined in Palestine by his first cousin from Mlynov, Eta Goldseker, and the two were married in July of that year. Eta and David had their first daughter, Selma Ann, in Palestine in 1926. In 1927, they made the difficult decision to leave Palestine and settle in Baltimore. Their second daughter, Irene Siegel, was born in Baltimore in 1929. Irene became a consummate family historian. – HS

    2.   The surname is also spelled Tzizik. – HS

[Page 199]

Khaykl Shnayder's Gramophone

Boruch Meren,[1] Baltimore

Translated from the Yiddish by Hannah B. Fischthal, PhD

Edited by Howard I. Schwartz, PhD

People said my grandfather, Hirsh Slobadar,[2] had a gramophone before the First World War, and that made sense. He had been a rich Jew. He had been a postman; he managed the alcohol, the slaughterhouse, the river, and he had a prestigious place by the eastern wall of the Trisk synagogue. But how did Khaykl, the ladies' tailor with many children, get a gramophone? He inherited the gramophone from his father Shloyme Shnayder.[3] So again the question: How does a gramophone come to Shloyme the tailor? What tailor could afford such a luxury?

You should know that the gramophone was old. How the gramophone survived the First World War was simply a miracle. Maybe the Lord of the universe wanted a poor tailor to have something to be proud of, something to spite all the rich Jews? Apart from that, Khaykl wanted his poor neighbors to have the pleasure of enjoying a piece sung by Yossele Rosenblatt,[4] even if only on vinyl; not too many good cantors who gave concerts dropped into Mlynov.

Khaykl Shnayder's house, you need to remember, stood on Shkolner[5] Street, namely Church Street, three houses away from the Trisk synagogue. The right wall of Mr. (Reb) Khaykl's house was leaning on Leyb Stoler's[6] house. Maybe that is why Khaykl Shnayder's house did not fall down. Going through the First World War left it weak. On the other hand, Leyb Stoler's house was stronger. A carpenter himself, with a board here and a piece of wood there, and not being thrifty with nails, he made it sturdier and thus lengthened the years of both huts. But a tailor, who could hold only a needle in his hand, what could he add to strengthen his house?

Between his house and Mr. (Reb) Shimon Slobadar's (Goldseker)[7] house was a small and muddy street; the shtetl in general consisted almost entirely of little streets.

[Page 200]

The Rabbi's Street, the Shochet's Street, Nasele's Street, Moshe Toybe's[8] Street, Chaim Leml's Street — all little streets led to the marketplace — if you were able to cross the street without leaving a boot in the deep mud. On Khaykl's street there was much traffic. His street was known in the shtetl. Getting to the market was not so easy. Firstly, we had to go through a long, little street very carefully; it was the width of one person. On one side there was a wall from Mr. (Reb) Volf, Nute-Ber's [son's][9] stable, and on the other side was a kind of separation with barbed wire fencing in Ishtekhe's garden; if you finally made it out of the shtetl okay, you could recite *goyml*.[10]

The little street had another good point: when you were busy making right turns, you quickly ended up in the Stolin synagogue where you could catch a prayer service, even if you had never been a Stoliner Hasid. But if you had to go out to the market, you needed to turn left. The street, which led to the market across from the Polish church, was called Tuvye, Nute-Ber's [son's] Street.[11] In that street you needed a special strategy: namely, you had to hold onto the walls of the house — if not, you would fall, you should excuse me, into a mud of a different sort since there was always a mountain of manure in that street. As Tuvye, Nute-Ber's [son's] house was low, the windows reached to your feet, and you could see what was cooking in the fireplace. If you made it out of that street, there were cages. Again, you had to be careful and hold your body straight. More than once a heavy Jewish woman slipped into the mud with one foot; she would curse quietly to herself: "Whoever thought this up should not get a taste of the other world!"

Yes, where are we with Khaykl Shnayder's gramophone? Saturday nights during the summer, when it was hot and humid and the flies were tearing you to pieces, the entire household would gather outside under the free sky. The parents used to sit on a bench, and the children would lie on the ground and listen to the choir of frogs.

[Page 201]

On such an evening, Khaykl Shnayder would open his windows and turn on the gramophone. The sweet voice of a cantor carried through the yards and streets. Little by little, people started to come to his windows. The harm was only that the gramophone became old, and the records were worn out. The gramophone began to just groan and the voices of the cantors became weaker and weaker. It was a pity on Khaykele.

One Saturday night, a group started to clown around and make fun of the worn-out records, and they called out assorted insults, like: "Reb Khaykl gave the cantor a gogl-mogl,[12] so unfortunately he is hoarse."

This made Mr. (Reb) Khaykl very sad.

So he went to the window, stuck his head out, and screamed: "Barefoot swindlers! What do you think — I need to get you cantors?! What did you want, I should travel to Lemberg to buy new records for you? You would not live so long!"

And with terrible anger he shut his window. That was the last gramophone concert in the shtetl; Khaykl Shnayder's gramophone disappeared forever---

Synagogue Street. Khaykl Shnayder's residence
From the photos of A. Harari
Original courtesy of Audrey Goldseker Polt

Translator's and editor's footnotes:

1.   For Boruch Meren's background, see his earlier essay, "A Good Deed (Mitzvah)," p. 149, footnote 1. – HS

2.   Hirsh Slobodar is the nickname of Hirsh Goldseker. Slobadar was a nickname for the Goldseker family who was named after the town where they lived before Mlynov. For a discussion, see Moshe Fishman's essay, "Mlynov in the Past," and particularly footnote 4. Regarding the Goldsekers being called "Slobodar," see Sonia and Mendel Teitelman's essay in this volume, 256–258. – HS

3.   A *shnayder* is a tailor. The martyr list (p. 436) indicates that the actual family name of Khaykl Shnayder was Nudler and from this essay we know his father was Shlome. Based on Yad Vashem records, it appears that Shloyme Nudler and his wife Leah were also parents of Aaron/ Arke Nudler (1888–1948) who survived the Shoah in the Smordva forest with his daughter, Helen (Nudler) Fixler and whose two sons, Morris and Harold, survived in the Russian Army. The martyr list indicates Khaykl and his wife Bat Sheva, and his children, Avraham, Yaakov, Alta and Faiga, all perished. – HS

4.   Josef "Yossele" Rosenblatt (May 9, 1882–June 19, 1933) was a Russian-born chazzan (cantor) and composer. He was regarded as the greatest cantor of his time. – HS

5.   Pronounced Shkolna in the Hebrew essays. – HS

6.   A *stolyer* is a carpenter. – HBF

7.   Shimon Goldseker married Anna Fishman and had eight children, several of who migrated to Baltimore including Ida (Goldseker) Fishman/Gresser, Eta (Goldseker) Fishman, Morris Goldseker, and Samuel Goldseker. Later in life, Shimon's son, Samuel, in an interview with his daughter in Baltimore, recalled one of his fondest memories as listening on weekends to the music from his uncle's gramophone. For more on this family of Goldsekers, see the Mlynov website. – HS

8.   Moshe Toybe is Moshe Fishman, a contributor to this volume. His mother's name was Toba and he was called "Toybe's" meaning her son. – HS

9.   Referring to Wolf Berger, son of Nute-Ber. Wolf is the father of Aaron (Berger) Harari who wrote in this volume about his father and uncle as farmers in Mlynov in "Jewish Farmers in Mlynov," 75–76. – HS

10.   *Birkat hagomel* is recited by people who have survived a life-threatening trauma. – HBF

11.   Tuvya Berger was the son of Nuta-Ber Berger and a brother of Wolf Berger. – HS

12.   A cure-all drink usually made with hot milk and honey. – HBF

[Page 202]

A Young Man Writes to His Brother in the Land [of Israel]

Avraham Halperin[1]

Translated and edited by Howard I. Schwartz, PhD with Hanina Epstein

To my dear, brother, Lipa,[2]

Lipa, you made a mistake. You wrote that I am a 14-year-old boy; that's not true because father says that the 18th of Tamuz I will have reached 16 years old.[3]

And thus, I took an account [of myself] and I realized that the best of my years is gone with nothing [to show]. Because my teachers they cut off my head without knives.[4] All they want is for the month to pass by quickly so they can get their salary … true, Mordechai Chizik[5] still knows how to teach, but the one who is teaching me lately is completely killing me. He teaches with no organization, with no vitality. He plugs up the spirit of poets that crouches inside me. I stopped hanging with my friends because they are among the Hasids of Mlynov and only Moshe Shalyn is my friend.[6] He is also a good Hasid, but is at least with us. Strong but shy, as the verse says, "the arrogant is headed to Hell and the blushing to the Garden of Eden" (Pirkei Avot 5.20). Since I am fed up with my friends, I'm fed up with Mlynov, because I know that I am sinking in Mlynov and the best years of my life will amount to nothing.

Then a month ago, I went to sleep in the first hour and got up in the third hour.[7] And during the night while the whole town was already asleep, I sat by myself opposite the moon on a bench next to our house and took a personal reckoning. When I realized I was almost 16 years old and that the best years of my life were lost here in this accursed Mlynov, emotions stormed inside me, and I thought: the world is wide and I want to flee to a place that will sustain the spirit ... Then suddenly I'm reminded: yes, the world is wide, but not for you, small loathsome Jew, Jew among the Jews of the Diaspora (golah). For sure you read about how the eternal Jew who goes knocking on all the doors of the nations, [asking] that they give 4 cubits of space, which is needed for a corpse, and then they give him the same answer in every place: "There is no space for the loathsome and inferior Jew, be on your way." Then I awaken in my place and want to run in all the streets and shouting for help ("shouting hamas"[8]): Where is the justice? How can one who moves about in a forest with animals of prey, protest or sing, afraid that he will arouse the wild animals who will prey on him? Then I go to bed, but I am unable to sleep. The thoughts penetrate my mind. I'm reminded of our ancestors, who died sanctifying God's name (kiddush hashem) in Spain and Portugal[9] and who went like calves to the slaughter, is this the sanctification of God's name? Sampson, the hero, who said, "Let me die with the Philistines," [when he was about to topple the pillars of the building] (Judges 16.30), died for the sanctification of God's name, and sanctification of his people and his homeland. And our ancestors (it is forbidden to say this) died sanctifying the disgrace of the Jew.

In my future, I will remember that this [the land of Israel] is [my] homeland. I decided — when I go there, during the day I will do hard work, with the sweat of the brow[10] I will build our homeland, and at night I will stand guard, and I will not fear death.[11] But if death [is my fate], three hundred Arabs will first die, and I will be a parable for my people, so they will not say, in poems he said he would die for his homeland but when alone he hid in the attic of the roof.

[Page 203]

And even here, where I am a despised Jew, and when I stroll with Moshe in the middle of the night, we walk strongly, like military men, and when a murderer walks [towards us], we don't flee but instead walk towards him with fists at the ready, and he doesn't dare touch us, but instead turns aside. Only when light appears outside in the third hour do I get up. First of all, I open the windows, put on tefillin, because the tefillin are my weapons. Is a military man who stands guard going to throw away his weapon? Thus, I am not able to abandon the tefillin. Afterwards I go outside and begin collecting the trash and everything that needs to be done, I do. Thus, the day pointlessly goes by. Day follows day, the wheel of the world keeps turning, and these are [the passing days] of life.

A group of educated ones,[12] next to the waterfall on the Count's property:

Sitting [front], from the right, Moshe Grinshpan,[13] Meir Grinshpan, Pesach Zutelman,[14] David Apithoker[15] the teacher Eisenberg-Ashed,[16] Shmuel Mandelkern.[17]
Standing from the right, Ephraim Zutelman,[18] Yitzhak Grinshpan, Bat-Sheva Grinshpan,[19] Malcah Lamdan.[20]

Translator's and editor's footnotes:

1.   Avraham Halperin (1924–1942) was the younger brother of Lipa Halperin, a contributor to this volume.
2.   Lipa Halperin (1907–1969) was on the book committee for this volume. Lipa made aliyah to Mandate Palestine in 1937 and his brother Avraham wrote to him there. Avraham perished in the Mlynov ghetto liquidation.
3.   The letter, written by Lipa's brother, Avraham, who was born in 1924 is not dated. He would have turned 16 in 1940.
4.   Figuratively cut off his head by not teaching him anything.
5.   A photo of the teacher Motel Chizik (or Tzizik) and his family appears on p. 457 below. David Fishman and Yitzhak Lamdan studied with Chizik (p. 198). Gershon Goldberg recalls him as a "murderously strict disciplinarian" (p. 157), Moshe Moshe Iskiewicz (Isakovich) describes him (p. 89) as one of "the teachers with whom the students felt enjoyment studying" and that he "excelled in teaching Tanach, and he was the first who implanted the yearning and love for our land in us through his interesting explanations. I would say, we were 'like dreamers' for all knowledge that came out of his mouth about our great past and all its

manifestations. I remember him — his short stature, with a cigarette in his mouth, he would smoke, and smoke and … cough." Chizik perished with his wife and daughter in 1942. His sons, Moshe and Meir, made aliyah in the 1930s. Moshe married Rosa Berger (Aaron Harari's sister) in Mandate Palestine and died of a snake bite in 1959. Meir married and had five children.

6.   Moshe Shlayen is included in the list of Mlynov matyrs along with his family. He was the son of Yaakov and Sara Shlayen. He had a sister Henia.

7.   He is using the rabbinic concept of a relative hour which broke daylight and nighttime into 12 fixed periods. He went to bed early in the night at, for example, 8 pm and arose at 11 pm.

8.   An expression that is used in Job 19:7.

9.   Referring to the Inquisition.

10.   Using the language from God's punishment in Genesis 3:19 that man will get his food "by the sweat of your brow" as a result of Eve eating the fruit.

11.   Alluding to Psalm 23:4 and not fearing to walk in valley of the shadow of death.

12.   The term maskilim alludes to those educated in secular studies who embrace enlightenment (haskalah). The photo was taken before 1921 since Pesach Zutelman in the photo left with the Shulman family for Baltimore in that year.

13.   Also spelled Grenspun and Greenspun. There were several Grinsphan families listed among the Mlynov martyrs (p. 434), and one in nearby villages (p. 446). The woman called "Bat Sheva" Grinshpan in this photo is listed among the martyrs from one of "the nearby villages." Her father is listed as "Yoel-Leib Grinshpan from Parmilovka," (possibly Peremylivka, Ukraine today). Her mother had already passed away. Two of her siblings, Yitzhak and Riva, were also martyred. The list indicates that "a son is in Israel, a daughter Tovah is in Israel, their son Micael is in France and a daughter Mania is in Canada." It thus seems likely that the other Grinsphans are family or related. The Yitzhak is in this photo is probably her brother. The man named Moshe Grinsphan in this photo is probably the one recalled by Shmuel Mandelkern in "Self-Defense in Mlynov," p. 141, who recalls a "Moshe Grenspun z"l, from Parmilovka," who oversaw the production of fake military badges for the uniforms of the self-defense in Mlynov. Mandelkern comments that Moshe "encountered his tragic death in Russia." No other mention is made of Meir Grinsphan and it seems likely he may be the "Micael" who is mentioned in the martyr list as living in France.

14.   Pesach Zutelman (1895–1988) from Mervits traveled with the Shulman family in 1921 to Baltimore under the identity of their son Hertz Shulman. He subsequently married Sarah (Sura) Shulman. He retained the name Paul Shulman, the surname he used on his passenger manifest.

15.   Alternative spellings Apoteiker, Apotheker, Apteykar. A woman by the name of Sonia Apteiker is listed in Yad Vashem records for Mlynov matyrs but no other information is known about this family.

16.   Jacob Eisenberg-Ashed is mentioned as a teacher brought from Rovno in the essay by Aaron Harari, "Culture, Education, and Social Life in the Small Town," p. 67

17.   Shmuel Mandelkern is one of the other contributors to this volume. For his background see footnote 1 in his essay, "Self-Defense in Mlynov," p. 116. Mandelkern married Malcah Lamdan also in this photo. They both also appear in the photo on page 66.

18.   Efraim Zutelman became Frank Settleman in Baltimore. He migrated to the US via Buenos Aires in 1923 and used his brother's name (Pejsach Zutelman) on his manifest to the US since his brother had snuck in using a Shulman name. He subsequently married Chaja Blomenkranz (Helen Blum) from Kovel and they had two sons.

19.   See note 7.

20.   Malcah Lamdan (?–~1980) was the sister of the poet Yitzhak Lamdan. She married Shmuel Mandelkern (also in this photo) and they made aliyah in 1924. She is remembered as a teacher and appears in a photo on page 66 and was part of a troupe of amateur actors in Mlynov (p. 156), before 1921.

[Page 204]

Poem

Dr. Shlomo Mandelkern

Translated and edited by Howard I. Schwartz, PhD with Hanina Epstein

***

This is your portion, poet, because you cleaved to your people
To [your people] you dedicated your heart and also sacrificed your soul
Your spirit is for its sanctity and your life for its future.
Its trouble is your enemy, on a bad day you will weep bitterly
Your poor daughter will flow by a bursting stream of an alien people
Where is the captain of song, thus his tears were shed!

From "Hebrew Poems," 1901

[The Youth Group] Hashomer Hatzair — on a fieldtrip in the area of Demydivka

[Page 207]

People and Landscapes

To My Little Town

by Eliyahu Gelman[1], Netanya

Translated and edited by Howard I. Schwartz, PhD with Hanina Epstein

My little town,
   I will hold you from afar
      days and days
The image
   Of father who perished
      and alongside his gravestone, in the cemetery
[saying] "Kaddish"[2]
   In a choked voice a son is praying
      (Woe to me — your gravestone is shattered from before and is no longer)
Mother's appearance
   for the sake of her children
      is sacrificed day by day
[so too] the appearance
   of brothers, sisters and children
      the whole community of Israel
(alas – they are no longer living, with no trace and no marker for the grave)
            *

Time lengthens from the days of their wounds
The remaining are brand plucked from the fire[3] — its last days will fade.
And you will be forgotten by the human heart and the world.
A person will no longer say

"there used to be a little town"

      12.10.65 [October 12, 1965][4]

Translator's and editor's footnotes:

1. Eliyahu Gelman (1913–2008) contributed "My Father's Home," pp. 259-260 to this volume with additional notes there on the family.
2. The prayer during mourning and in commemoration.
3. Allusion to Zechariah 3:2 which refers to a brand plucked from the fire.
4. The date format in Israel is dd/mm/yy indicating that this poem was written very close to the anniversary of the Mlynov ghetto liquidation which took place on the Gregorian date of October 8th, 9th, or 10th, 1942.

[Page 208]

In those days ...

Yaakov-Yosi[1] goes to the Land of Israel (or doesn't go...)

by Shmuel Mandelkern,[2] Tel Aviv

Translated and edited by Howard I. Schwartz, PhD with Hanina Epstein

In those days,[3] when the Zionist idea was not widespread, even as a presumptuous dream by the Jewish people in the Diaspora (golah), and the idea was especially considered an abomination (terefah) in the eyes of the orthodox stratum — then, in that period, there might be one [Zionist] in a town and literally two in a family, of course in the small towns. But in Mlynov there were four boys, who were drawn, God save us, to the Zionist idea.[4]

[First:] The writer of these lines was captivated by Zionism following his studies in the yeshiva and with the Rav, Rabbi Moshe Avigdor Amiel,[5] then the Rav and head of the orthodox secondary school (mesivta) of the town of Swieciany where he was Zionist (towards the end of his life he was chief rabbi of Tel-Aviv-Yaffo.) Of course, all his students, about 450 young men, held fast to the Zionist idea.

[Second:] My friend was Yermeyahu Maisler,[6] son of Mr. Mendel the writer (schreiber) from the Jewish community of Mlynov: He held fast to Zionism after being a student of the Rav Yitzchak Yaacov Reines[7] (who merited a number of roads in Israel being named after him), [and] was the Rav and head of the orthodox secondary school (mesivta) of the town of Lida, in the area of Vilna.

[Third:] Berel Lovshis, son of Aharon the blacksmith.[8] He also studied in the study house (kloyz) of Rav Malis[9] from Vilna, and it is no wonder that one who studied in the cultured city of Vilna, embraced the Zionist idea.

[Fourth:] Last but not least, "the Benjamin" [i.e., the youngest][10] that was in the group, the poet Yitzhak Lamdan, then young, weak, pampered by his family and especially his father, Rabbi[11] Yehuda Leib Lamdan, who protected him from all harm. As evident by his literary future, it was as if he was born with Zionist idea.

The activities of the four boys mentioned above relied on activities for Keren Hakayemet [Jewish National Fund] which was relatively speaking "very limited." And since the minor activities didn't satisfy us, we sought out bigger and more substantive Zionist activities.

Sending a Pioneer to the Land of Israel

One operation like this, the idea of which totally captivated us, was to actually send a young person from Mlynov to the Land of Israel, in the capacity of a pioneer who would go ahead of the group.

[Page 209]

We choose for this good deed (mitzvah), for various reasons, Yaakov-Yosi Gruber, son of Mr. Yisrael Mordechai's [i.e., son of Mordechai's son Yisrael][12] from Mervits, one of the Hasids "burning with passion" for the Maggid from Trisk[13] who was from a very venerated and famous family.

Why did we specifically choose this Yaakov-Yosi, and not one of us, to be the first pioneer from our town in Israel? — the choice was for the following reasons. Yaakov-Yosi was a young man not from the group of friends. He did not dress nicely[14] and this stemmed from the pressing [economic] situation of his father. For the same reasons he didn't continue in his studies among other things. Among our friends he was like "the gopher" [lit. luggage carrier] of the group. We would say that he was left in the dust behind the smart students, so to speak. Thus, we planned to save him from the poverty of his father's house and help him to set some sort of a goal in his life. We decided, therefore, that the best solution for him would be — aliyah to the Land of Israel.

And from talk, we moved onto action. Since we knew that aliya to the Land of Israel required specific preparation in order to pass the examinations that were set up then in Odessa, the place where all the immigrant pioneers had to take the tests, we thus began actual preparations implemented via daily lessons and instruction that he received from us.

Superficially, all was on track, but — there was a fly in the ointment [lit. a thorn in it]. In those days, when the livelihood of most of the small towns' population was under severe pressure, there was a small portion that was doing well, with no pressure — and this was the small industry of fabric makers, an industry that occupied for some reason most of the people of Mervits, which was close to Mlynov.

Mr. Israel [son of] Mordechai hoped one day to realize this respected livelihood, both because the young lad Yaakov-Yosi was growing up, and when it came time, they would say he was a respected person and he would marry a daughter of a good family who had a substantial dowry, and then he [Israel] would be able to realize his dream of establishing a fabric shop. To achieve this goal everything was in place, meaning — there was a groom … because he was 18 years old. A specific location for this industry was also already prepared. Thus, to carry out an operation like this [namely,] — sending his only son to the Land of Israel, and robbing him of hope to better his situation — involved much risk, if the matter were made known to his parents. For these reasons, each of us was truly afraid and didn't want the preparatory lessons to take place in his home. Casting lots determined that the intensive Hebrew school (ulpan) would take place in the home of Yeremiah Maisler,[15] son of the teacher in Mlynov. To avoid the evil eye, the place of instruction would be in the roof attic in the house of Mr. Mendel the writer (schreiber), a place that was designated for the chickens of Mr. Mendel. Each day Yitzhak Lamdan in particular would come to give him the required lessons. From time to time, we would gather in the attic to listen to his progress in the studies. On occasion, we would even arrange examinations. If my memory does not deceive me, I was the only one who said that our effort was a waste, because he would not pass the tests in Odessa. The only one who had a positive opinion in this was Yitzhak Lamdan.

[Page 210]

Funds for Aliyah

After a substantial time and a complete winter, we met to solve the financial challenge to fund the travel expenses, a matter that was not easy in our circumstances then. We decided to turn to personalities, Zionist wheeler-dealers in the area, to bring our program to their attention and request financial assistance.

With respect to collecting funds we adopted a system – we took every opportunity that came to hand. For example, our friend Yermeyahu Maisler had a cousin of the family in Trovits [today Torhovytsia],[16] named Shlomo Fuksman, a senior clerk in the flour mill of Richter. He had two sons and an only daughter, and like children of the wealthy, they would lag in their studies, as it is written [in the Talmud, B. Nedarim 81a] "Be careful with the education with children of paupers since from them Torah will issue forth".... Since Yermeyahu had graduated the Lida yeshiva[17] and had much knowledge in Talmud, and especially Hebrew, his cousin gave him an appointment as teacher and mentor of his children; in this way our friend Yermeyahu was popular and respected by the local youth.

And the following custom came first during joyous occasions in particular at weddings, when hearts were partaking fully in wine and all sorts of alcohol and food, they would donate favorably to all applicants for donations and charity (tzedakah) such as: helping the poor, bringing a [poor] bride [to the canopy],[18] visiting the sick and so forth. In the latter years the youth also exploited [this time] during wedding parties — among other opportunities — to gather donations for Keren Hakayemet. And we thus were the smart ones who saw what was going down, and we followed the advice of our friend Yermeyahu to capitalize on the eve of the wedding, that was going to take place in Trovits, for our goal. At the outset, we were confident in our success because of the participation of our friend Yermeyahu in the donations since he was known locally.

The Trip to Trovits [Torhovytsya]

The first opportunity, during the winter days, in the first wedding to take place in the town, I, the writer of these words, and friend Yermeyahu took the mission upon ourselves. We rented a winterized wagon,[19] and went on the road, in order to arrive in time for the wedding. We made the following estimation: since the wedding meal began about 8 o'clock in the evening, and the fundraising took place, obviously, during the meal, as noted above, "when the participants in the meal were merry with wine"[20] — we were sure that we would arrive exactly on time, since our town of Mlynov to Trovits was a distance of 15 km [9.3 mi], about a two hour trip at the time … therefore we decided to leave at 5 in the evening, in order to arrive before the time of donations, so that the local young men of the town could join us in this important Zionist fundraiser, since among them was Avramel Ackerman son of the well-known Rav Rabbi Mordechai Neta [Ackerman], [21] z"l, the sons of R. Meir Feldman,[22] and others.

[Page 211]

However, the distance between talk and action is vast … when we left Mlynov about 5 o'clock, and when we passed the town of Mervits, a small storm began, accompanied by large flakes of snow, and the storm grew bigger from moment to moment. The road was obstructed and we saw only a white surface in front of us, with no road, no sky, and with no sign of a nearby settlement … and this despite the fact that there were several villages along the road, like Stomorhy,[23] Dobryatyn, Ostriiv and others. We noticed another thing, [namely] that we were traveling and traveling but remaining in one spot with no possibility of continuing or going back. In truth, we had not anticipated endangering our lives, since we were wearing good winter clothing, but at the top of our concerns was the worry that we would be late for the meal, and after traveling in the chaotic storm for several hours, the sound of barking dogs reached us from afar. We realized that we were finally close to a settlement. We turned our steps towards the barking dogs, and we reached the town of Pańska Dolina (the valley of the noblemen) at 8 o'clock at night. The upshot was that instead of a typical trip of one hour, we traveled three hours …

When we saw a faint light that came from one of the houses, we didn't wait for an invitation; we knocked on the door and entered inside. By chance, the homeowner was the village head (muktar). We told him what had happened to us, and we asked for his help, to facilitate us reaching Trovits as quickly as possible. But our homeowner didn't hurry and began to change his tune (literally "sing a new song").

"You say that you are from nearby Mlynov, your request is fine, but I don't believe you …" (due to the tense political situation that prevailed then between Russian on one side and Austria on the other[24]). "I suspect you of being spies for Austria and your goal to spy out the area. Because it is not possible that young people from Mlynov don't know the way to Trovits, which is so close." And furthermore," he asserted "I have never in my days seen young people of Mlynov wearing such beautiful clothing" (since we were in-laws of the wedding party [and thus dressed for a wedding]) …

Treating us like Spies …

As a government official (muhtar of the village), he believed he was obliged to act in an official capacity and obligated to transfer us to the district seat of Dubno. We thus had to spend the night in the village jail, and in the morning everything or everyone would be restored to normal …

When we heard what he said we were furious: a: we would lose the fundraising opportunity during the wedding, and b: this was the key point, when they would bring us, as he said, to Dubno, it would be necessary to pass Mlynov, and suddenly the people of Mlynov would see us tied up. And then, obviously, an inquiry will start — what is the purpose of our traveling to Trovits, and there would be a significant risk that the whole "story" of sending Yaakov-Yosi to the Land of Israel would become widely known.

[Page 212]

We, obviously, held our ground and asked him, literally with tears in the eyes, not to cause us this kind of shame, by bringing us the next day as prisoners past Mervits to Mlynov.

Our words apparently made an impression on him, and he said, "One thing I'm able to do for you, in spite of the late hour, and that is — to call together the village committee to my house to take counsel on the matter and hear their opinion. He sent a member of the household to the committee, and we were sitting on pins and needles [lit. sitting on hot coals], because the time for fundraising was passing. After some minutes, some of village committee members appeared. The head of the village (muktar) introduced us to them by saying "the fish were caught in the net," and he suspected us of spying. Their opinion was no different than his and emphasized the point that they never had seen youth from Mlynov so dolled up. The entire time I conducted the discussion and maintained that our words were truthful, that we were Mlynov young people and not spies. During the discussion, an idea came to me, and then the proposal to which they acquiesced. The proposal was: "If I list for them all the business men from Mlynov and Mervits, with whom you have business ties, in other words, from whom you buy all necessities and clothing, and to whom you sell your products, and the market days in Mlynov that you visit every two weeks, selling your horses and your cows, and buying from the men of Berestechko your winter boots and from the men of Chavlykah[25] your rustic furs – will this satisfy you that we are not spies?" After saying this, we saw a positive response in their faces and for their part they began to ask additional different questions about the men of Mlynov and Mervits, and in the end they asked us what we needed from them. When we explained that we were headed to Trovits, and we were requesting help getting there, they took us outside (the storm in the meantime had abated) and they pointed us in the direction, "Look, you can see sparkles of light in this distance, this is the town of Trovits — you can go safely along this road, and in another half hour you'll reach the area you are seeking.

And so it was. We continued on the way and after a bit of time we were in Trovits, near the house where the wedding was taking place. There we found all the Trovits youth outside, peeking inside via the windows, as was customary in small towns, waiting for our arrival and worried about our delay. When we arrived, there was great joy and before we had time to recount the detailed story of our difficult trip, we decided first of all, because of the late hour, to carry out the fundraising among the wedding guests. The fundraising was a great success due to the participation of the golden youth of Trovits. [It was a success] from the perspective that no one refused.

After the fundraiser, we gathered together and told them the details of getting lost on the snowy roads and the suspicions of the Pańska Dolina village leader that we were spies and came to check out the area. Thus, after succeeding in carrying out the mission completely and with success, we were very happy, and we spent all night in song and singing and it was like a mini-Zionist evening.

[Page 213]

The Youth of Trovits

Among the youth, several stood out who didn't submit to the will of their parents' whose sole goal was "at age 18 the wedding canopy," [namely] to make a good match with the daughter of a good family and to receive a hefty dowry, and ultimately open a store for herring, salt and more; and the main purpose to continue the tradition of the grandfather and parents. Among those who refused to continue in this faltering tradition was Avramel, son of the Rav [Ackerman], several sons of Mr. Meir Feldman, and their desire was to continue with their studies and leave the small town, and travel to places of Torah, like the Lithuanian yeshivas, the Odessa yeshiva, which was conducted by "Young Rabbi" (Rabbi Chaim Tchernowitz[26]) and even complete their education in Kishinev in the yeshiva of Rabbi Tsirelson[27] and this was no small thing. But all these wishes encountered and were shattered by the wall of their parents who objected: a) "how can I abandon my son to someone else's education?" b) "Heresy," the reputation of agnosticism sticks like it came from heaven to those educated in the yeshivas mentioned above since they carry one towards Zionism. They realized that continuing education in Talmud, in Tanakh, and in Hebrew, is the start of the road that leads to Zionism, and, heaven forbid, the repudiation of God, by failing to wait for the redeemer and for the coming of the Messiah.[28]

In most cases the parents had the upper hand. When Avramel son of the Rav met us that night, he had identified a good [kosher] time to convince his father, the rabbi Mordechai Nute Ackerman, that the devil is not so bad, and that you can look [at Zionism] and not get hurt, and he invited me to visit in his house for an lowkey conversation with his father at two in the afternoon of the following day. I asked the group about its views of the spiritual leader, the Rav, of Zionism, Hebrew and more; they answered that their Rav was mostly neutral and in my eyes, this was a significant accomplishment by the local youth, since most of the rabbis in the small towns of Ukraine were strongly against Zionism, Hebrew culture, and all things Hebrew. I did not accept very heartily the opportunity to visit mentioned above since there were rabbis and students of Talmud among them whose goal was to trip up the youth in [their] knowledge of Talmud and so forth. But out of mutual respect, I agreed to the visit.

In the House of Rav Ackerman

On the following day, at exactly two o'clock, I entered the house of the Rav and found him in a well-ordered room. He engaged me respectfully, befitting an honored guest. His personality was pleasant,[29] he was clothed elegantly[30] and organized meticulously. Everything about him said "honorable." He received me with a big "Shalom Aleichem" [Peace be upon you], invited me to sit and asked me. "What's on your mind?" I told him that yesterday I came to Trovits for a short visit. Obviously, I did not reveal the purpose to him and he didn't ask. "My intention had been to return to Mlynov today," I said to him, but since his son Avramel invited me to his house, I made good on the saying, 'one may not decline the request of a great man.'[31]

[Page 214]

Since Avramel was really short in stature, the Rav answered me half in jest [in Yiddish]: My son Avramel "is just a small boy," so how are you interpreting "one may not decline the request of a big man"? I answered him [explaining that] the sages didn't mean a big person from an athletic perspective but a person great in wisdom and thus [moreover] "the acts of fathers are a sign to the sons."[32] And he ended [the conversation with]: "Good."

The conversation continued for about two hours. We talked about this and that and the key matter of interest was the study methods in the Lithuanian yeshiva. "What is the difference," he asked me, "between a boy's study hall, one who is studying between the walls of the study hall in a small town and the students of a yeshiva in Lithuania?" Similarly, he was interested in the lives of Lithuanian Jewry, their situation, livelihood and so on. And he especially pressed me to explain to him how a young lad, who has no supervision from his parents in a foreign location among hundreds of teenagers, what impels him to continue his studies. With this question, he reminded me of a Russian proverb which says, "No father, no mother, there is no one whatsoever to fear." On this point, I answered him that: first, there are some teenagers who have a diligent character; this type of youth is capable of coming at 8 o'clock in the morning to the "yeshiva"[33] and to sit until one in the afternoon and not move from his spot, and they pull along with them another large segment of the students, and are the "envy of scribes" [i.e., because they can sit so long without moving]. Second, in the study ulpan during the entire time there is constantly more than one eye supervising, watching over the course of studies. I told him, to my embarrassment, they even put in place detectives, who track each and every student, and monitor their behavior in the streets, in the home, and each and every place, and they report "violations" to their superiors — thus all the activities of students are documented in a book, a practice most students opposed.

"I admit without embarrassment," I continued, "that I am not one of the studious ones because the Vilna students are not able under any circumstances to be diligent for six continuous hours in one spot. On my own I encourage myself this way by saying to myself — that I have already sat in study for much time, and it seems to me that I haven't advanced in my studies, and God forbid (oi va voi) if I return home empty-handed. In the end, each and every student, must try to acquire knowledge and wisdom on his own, according to his ability and his own idea. Obviously, there are those who are exceptional, but their numbers are insignificant. Most students exemplify [the saying] "[such is the way of a life of Torah]: you shall eat bread with salt and rationed water shall you drink, you shall lie[34] on the ground and in Torah shall you labor" [Pirkei Avot 6:4].

"And what about the subject of Zionism in the yeshiva?" he asked me. I told him that there are two streams among the youth. One is enthralled by socialism and the second Zionism. And how is it possible to avoid being Zionist, at the time the yeshiva was established, Rabbi Moshe Avigdor Amiel and Rabbi Yitzhak Yaakov Reines, the Rav of Lida, and more, trained hundreds of students and each had study partners." I continued, "The hint is sufficient for the wise man."[35]

In the meantime, 4 o'clock approached, the time for going to the synagogue to study a chapter of Mishnah and say afternoon and evening prayers.

[Page 215]

The Rav took leave of me and while departing his son Avramel said to him, "Father, why don't you bring him, [give him] 'a large portion of gemara' and examine his character." He answered him, "there is no need, I already know the whole story" [indicating Mandelkern had earned his respect].

The Visit with Mr. Meir Feldman

In the meantime, our reputation preceded us in the town, and towards evening we were invited for dinner to one of the town's wealthy men, Mr. Meir Feldman.[36] In Mr. Meir Feldman, there was a mixture of Torah and wealth in one place, he was being cared for by sons, who also faced the problem of leaving parents and the town in order to be educated in the world at large.

The meeting in the home of Mr. Meir Feldman was different from that in the home of Rav Rabbi Mordechai Nute. While in the home of Rav, Rabbi Mordechai Nute, the meeting was conducted in a question-and-answer style, [whereas] in the home of Rabbi Meir Feldman this was an evening of disagreement among a group of friends about different subjects. Of course, in particular, the discussion [literally, the axle] turned on boys of the yeshiva, Hebrew culture, and Zionism, God help us. It was interesting that that each and every person saw Zionism as [inappropriately trying to] force the Messiah's arrival.[37]

R. Meir Feldman was a successful forester, among the rich in the area, and there was a custom among such traders, obviously also a convenient practice, to go from forest to forest and from place to place not with a rented wagon, but rather in a private vehicle, that took the form of a nice carriage and in the winter a nice winter sled with two noble horses. The person in charge of the vehicle was a gentile, and he would perform all the trips at the order of his superior. When the parents were in a good mood, they would permit their children, from time to time, to organize a fieldtrip for enjoyment. At the end of the discussions that evening Mr. Meir got up and said, "You see, children, when you have a strong will [to do something], you succeed." And he concluded with the expression, "There is nothing that stands in the way of the will." He ended with [the statement] to Asher Lemel, his son, that he would instruct the person in charge of the horses to pull together a fieldtrip for about an hour. As an aside, he asked us, "Where are you supposed to be tomorrow?" From his question, we realized that his son told him our goal in coming to Trovits. We told him that we had been referred to Mr. Chaykl Weitz, who lives in Boremel, by his cousin David Lerner, a brother of Artzi (who, by the way, is living now in Israel, a member of [the kibbutz] Meshek Kfar Giladi), to brief him on our goal, and since we already had left Mlynov, and the distance from Trovits to Boremel was short, we were headed the following day to Boremel. Because R Meir was feeling good about the whole evening, he instructed the coachman to take us the following day to Boremel. This was the very pinnacle of our success. It is interesting that during the evening fieldtrip not one of the girls from town participated, and it was left to the boys to interpret [its meaning].

In the Town of Boremel

The following day we were taken to Boremel, straight to the house of Mr. Chaykl Weitz.

[Page 216]

A Jew of medium height, he spoke Hebrew with us, a typical educated character (maskil) of the time. He was well-dressed, had a well-kemp beard, such that I didn't know who copied [the beard] from whom — Mr. Chaykl Weiss from professor Chaim Weitzman[38] or the reverse … and when he heard about the purpose of our visit, he told us that he would invite us that evening for a meeting in his house with participation of the local Zionist committee, which he presided over as the chairman. When we left his house, we remarked jealously[39] to one another, "Boremel has Jews up in age who support the Zionist Committee, and Zionism is not considered to be a matter for young men and woman, who are idlers and so on."

At 7 o'clock in the evening, the members of the committee, who were advanced in years, gathered together and after the chairman introduced us to them, he said to us, "Young men, say what you want to say." We told them all the details about the mission sending a pioneer to the Land of Israel before the rest of the group and the essential challenge we faced finding funds for the journey. And due to the secrecy of the matter, we took upon ourselves to collect money for this goal exclusively from "birds of a feather" who live nearby. After very tangible questions, and not just "klutz questions," he asked us, "How much do you want and how much has been given to you?" I, who apparently was one of the lead speakers, responded that during the building the Temple [in Jerusalem], the people brought gold, silver and copper, and they would choose on their own [what to give] from one of those three items. Then the chairman, M. Chaykl Weitz, said to the members of the committee: "Give them gold in the largest coin." This was then 15 rubles of gold. And he provided a justification for his instruction, "I see in these young emissaries the golden youth [who will work] for the establishment of the Land of Israel." The treasurer gave us 15 rubles and wished us complete success. The chairman, full of excitement over us, got up from his table and went towards one of the rooms, opened the door, and called to his daughter, "Sara, come and meet the boys of Mlynov and enjoy the beautiful Hebrew which they speak and even with a Sephardic ascent!"[40]

After light conversation about current events and matters related to the Land of Israel, they asked us, where we were headed the next day. We told them that we hadn't crystalized our plan yet, but we needed more money to cover the expense of the trip. Then they said to us, "there are many Jews like us, in other words Zionists, in Berestechko, which is close to Boremel, and we therefore recommend you head to the Zionist committee in Berestechko, and obviously we will recommend you." The following day we traveled to Berestechko. Even though Berestechko was bigger and better organized in matters of Hebrew culture such as the Hebrew school, library and more — the Zionist committee was less organized. Nonetheless, they welcomed us and we didn't leave them empty-handed.

The following day, our friend Yirmeyahu returned to Trovits to teach Torah in the Fuksman home and I returned to Mlynov.

Among those who knew our secret [goal], who were also completely in on the secret matter [of the trip], was also our friend Chaim Yitzhak Kipergluz.[41]

[Page 217]

Since his education which he received from the Hasids of Stolin, it was hard for him to be in public with the four boys [mentioned at the start of the essay] who were enthralled by Zionism and he was considered a "Zionist prisoner" in other words: [he was] a "closeted Zionist."

Upon my return from the trip, he was first to meet me and said to me, "Shmuel, don't worry, everything will be okay, since here, in our small town, a rumor[42] circulated and said that the yeshiva boys, Yermeyahu and Shmuel went to Trovits for a wedding, following in the footsteps of the beautiful daughters of Hirsch Goldseker who were invited to this wedding. That's good since the real secret is not known by most ..."

I want to point out here the great faith that my parents placed in me. Despite my absence that entire week from the home they neither interrogated me nor investigated where I had gone. They believed that if I traveled, it certainly involved something of importance.

Preparations for Aliyah

In the first meeting of the four [friends after the trip], it was decided to continue with the efforts to raise the amount needed to reach the total expenditure required for the journey and to quickly tackle the implementation of our program's first stage, namely, to send Yaakov-Yosi to Odessa with the goal of his aliyah to the Land of Israel.

Not much time passed before the needed sum was fully in hand. Since we were afraid that something might happen on the train trip to Odessa, that was full of pickpockets and swindlers of all types, and that these pickpockets might also visit the pockets of Yaakov-Yosi, and he would be at risk of arriving in Odessa empty-handed, and all our efforts would have been in vain — [for this reason] we sent 40 rubles to the committee in Odessa and to Yaakov-Yosi we gave only six rubles, the expense money for the trip from Dubno to Odessa.

At this point, two important problems stood in our way: (A) since the trip from Mlynov to Dubno took place only via coachmen, such as Kalman Fishman[43] and others, and the trip left from the center of town, where the travelers were accompanied by their wives and others, the question was — how would we secretly integrate Yaakov-Yosi among the other travelers and for what purpose is Yaakov-Yosi suddenly going to Dubno? A question not simple at all. (B) how could we send Yaakov-Yosi to Odessa, who was, as it were, our representative to the Odessa Zionist committee, with him in torn and worn-out clothing, since he was a son of poor parents who with great difficulty supported themselves?

The two problems were resolved with a better approach. We decided not to send Yaakov-Yosi on the main road, in other words, with a coachman who traveled to Dubno, but rather, we, the whole group, would go together with him along the dirt road that goes to Dubno across from the Count's estate. There was a hill there covered in greenery where the youth used to gather as a pastime and for conversations with friends, especially on the Sabbaths; this hill was called "Mount Sinai."[44] This hill stood in fact at the crossroads, that leads from Mlynov, [starting] from the village of Smordva, Berhy and others, to Dubno, and we knew that a wagon from one of the nearby farmers which were going to Dubno would occasionally happen by and would take him to Dubno, and in our town no one would be the wiser about the scheme.

[Page 218]

As to the second question [regarding his worn out clothes] — we decided that each one of us would pilfer from his home, without parental knowledge, one taking shoes, another pants, a jacket, hat, a nice shirt and more, and in that spot, on "Mount Sinai," and in spite of the cold that had reached its [winter] peak, we would strip off his worn out clothing and dress him in a really nice outfit. And when we completed this effort, we suddenly saw before us a nice looking and healthy young man, with ruddy cheeks, his entire being announcing youth and vitality, and we almost didn't recognize him, and we asked one another "Is this Yaakov-Yosi?" . . .

Boating on the Ikva River

In order to coverup the traces of our last activity, we left Mlynov for Mount Sinai in the following manner: Three of us walked the road to Kruzhuk,[45] made a turn across the big bridge by the horses[46] and arrived at the designated place, while two would go straight from the town across the bridge over the Ikva and also reached the designated place. And after we changed his clothes, we took his torn clothes, put them on the banks of the Ikva that passed nearby — and if in the coming days a commotion would be made by his family, because Yaakov-Yosi, their only son, had disappeared without a trace, we will participate in the search for him and we will find his clothes on the bank of the river, and this will be proof that he had drowned in the river … [47]

It was not a trivial problem how to stay in touch via letters with Yaakov-Yosi in Odessa. The delivery of letters was done by the non-Jewish mailman, and in every house that he entered with a parcel of letters, they [the residents] would out of curiosity search through his bundle. There was a danger, therefore, that due to such searches, they might find out who sent the letter and who received it — and reveal the secret of Yaakov-Yosi …

[Page 219]

Not one of us was willing for the correspondence from Odessa to Mlynov to come to his address, because each saw great danger in this. Yitzhak Lamdan was especially afraid — that he would disappoint his father who held him in very high esteem. Therefore, I took this danger upon myself. Since the mailman brought me the newspaper Ha-Tsfira"[48] daily, and frequently some brochures about forthcoming books, like Tushiah ["Sound Knowledge"][49] and Moriah[50] and others — he could also bring me the letters from Yaakov-Yosi among the rest of the items.

In those days, a trip to Odessa lasted three days, and a letter from Odessa took three days, which meant that for [the first] news from Yaakov-Yosi, it was necessary to wait at least six days.[51] Nevertheless, by the third day of his trip, my colleagues were already asking me "Have we still not gotten a letter from Yaakov-Yosi?" …

On the seventh day, we received a letter from him — but, oh no! The letter was written entirely in Russian, and this was after all the efforts we invested in him in the roof attic of Mr. Mendel the writer (schreiber), to teach him, among other things, the Hebrew language. Of course, I immediately ran as if bitten by a snake to Yitzhak Lamdan, to bring him the bad news of his betrayal of the Hebrew language, and the key thing was that it said nothing of substance about the trip to the Land of Israel, apart from his visit to Ussishkin.[52] Quickly, we sent him a letter indicating that the key item that interested us was when he would make aliyah to the Land of Israel, and with a light rebuke for his betrayal of the Hebrew language.

In the second letter that we received from him, he wrote that as far as his betrayal of the Hebrew language is concerned, who among us was as great as Ussishkin, and even in his house they spoke exclusively Russian … and with respect to his journey, it was too early to clarify the matter. His cousins, who lived in Odessa, did not agree with this trip and he still did not know how it would go down … and he continued with the following statement: "What are you all thinking, that Odessa is Mlynov? In Odessa, there are big, beautiful houses and there are large establishments of commerce and many other nice things that you have never seen. And there are boulevards and I sat there on one bench with a young woman …" After a short exchange of additional letters, we were convinced that our labor had been in vain, and we gave up on Yaakov-Yosi …

Immediately we notified the Odessa Committee, that the money we had sent them as funds for the aliyah of Yaakov-Yosi, we were transferring to the credit of Keren Hakaymet of Israel [The Jewish National Fund] and with this we put the final nail in the coffin [of Yaakov-Yosi's aliyah].

Our Yaakov-Yosi remained in Odessa. He married, participated in WWI, was wounded and was left with a physical disability, and we said to ourselves that God had punished him for his betrayal of the Zionist idea. And if one asks, "what became of the commotion that Yaakov-Yosi's family was supposed to make in Mlynov over his sudden disappearance?" — the answer is this: this schlemiel was smart enough to catch the wise in a trap … apparently, matters had all been agreed with his parents that he would exploit this opportunity to go forth into the world at large, and go to Odessa, without it costing him a penny. Perhaps he also thought that he would emerge from the affair with great wealth …

Translator's and editor's footnotes:

1. Below, the author identifies Yaakov-Yosi as the son of Yisrael Gruber, who was the son of Mordechai Gruber. Mordechai Gruber is known from family trees in the Teitelman family to have had a son Yisrael, and this "Yaakov-Yosi" is apparently Yisrael's son. Yaakov-Yosi was thus first cousins to Rachel (Gruber) Teitelman and Sonia (Gruber) Teitelman, other contributors to this volume. Yaakov-Yosi's father, Yisrael, was therefore a sibling of Yosef Gruber (who married Shifra Teitelman), Rikel (Gruber) who married Gedaliah Gelman/Alman, Leah (Gruber) who married Azriel Kleinberg, and Sura (Gruber) who married Zelig Wurtzel.
2. Shmuel Mandelkern contributed the earlier essay, "Self-Defense in Mlynov," pp. 116–146. See the first footnote for his background.
3. Based on several details that emerge in this story and at the end, it appears the incident described occurred before 1919 and apparently before the outbreak of WWI (1914). Yitzhak Lamdan (1889–1954), who left Mlynov in 1918–1919, is still present in Mlynov in this story. The Zionist youth movement has not yet taken off in Mlynov which would happen in the 1920s under the leadership of this essay's writer who made aliyah in 1924. The story also mentions that Menachem Ussishkin was present in Odessa during the events of this story, and he made aliyah in 1919. The Hebrew publishing house Moriah is mentioned which had a revival in 1917–1918 before it shut down under economic and Bolshevik pressures. Finally, the story ends indicating that one of the characters ended up being injured later in WWI suggesting this took place sometime before 1914.

4.   On the development of Zionist youth activity in Mlynov, see the essays by Aaron Harari, "The Youth Movement," pp. 69–74, and "Culture, Education, and Social Life in the Small Town," pp. 66–68 which also talks about the role of this essay's author (Shmuel Mandelkern) in its development. On the first aliyah of a family, and the consternation it caused in Mlynov, see Boruch Meren's essay, "The First Aliyah from the Shtetl," pp. 220–225.

5.   Rabbi Moshe Avigdor Amiel (1883–1946) was a religious thinker and rabbi who studied in Vilna and became rabbi of Swieciany at the age of 22 where he had a yeshiva and many students. He was one of the first rabbis to join Mizrachi, the religious Zionist movement. He was appointed chief rabbi of Tel Aviv in 1936.

6.   Alternative spelling Meizler. The background of this young man has not been determined. A Yad Vashem record filled out in Russian by a Mikhael Maizler, indicates that his father Elke /Elya Maizler was born in 1896 in Mlynov and married a woman Gisya from Dubno. The family settled in Dubno and perished there. There was also a family named Shraiber (alternative spelling Shrajber). Yad Vashem records submitted by a Moshe Shreiber indicate his family was living in Mlynov during WWII but the names don't include either a Yermeyahu or a Mendel.

7.   Rav Yitzchak Yaacov Reines (1839–1915) was a Lithuanian orthodox rabbi and founder of the Mizrachi Religious Zionist movement and a correspondent with Herzl. He was born in Karolin (now part of Pinsk, Belarus).

8.   In his earlier essay, p. 139, Mandelkern identifies Aharon Kuval (or Koval), the blacksmith, as his uncle and tells the story of hiding in his shop when he and another boy are accosted by Russian renegade soldiers. Kowal means blacksmith in Polish suggesting that he was known as Aharon Kuval but that that was not his formal surname. Here we learn that Aharon son's last name was Lovshis (alternative spellings: Luwiszes Luvishes). A list of Jews in the Rowno ghetto compiled by the Judenrat on 01/15/1942 lists Shlioma Luvishes who was born in Mlynov to Aaron. A Yad Vashem record submitted by Fridel Piatigoretz identifies Moshe Luwiszes, a blacksmith, as born in Mlynow, Poland. He married Rachel (Piatigoretz). During the war the family was in Dubno, Poland. It seems reasonable to assume the boy Berel referred to here was part of this family.

9.   Since he says that Berel "also" studied with Rabbi Malis, perhaps "Malis" is here a shortened form the same teacher the author studied with: Rabbi Moshe Avidgor Amiel (see footnote 3).

10.   "Benjamin" here means youngest alluding to the biblical Benjamin, the youngest of twelve sons of the patriarch Jacob.

11.   Yitzhak Lamdan's father was very pious and respected, but it is not clear whether he was actually a rabbi or the term here is honorific like "Mr."

12.   See note 1.

13.   Rabbi Avraham Twerski of Trisk (the Magid of Trisk) (1806–1889) was one of the eight sons of Rabbi Mordechai (Twersky) of Chernobyl (1770–1837), the second rebbe of the Chernobyl Hasidic dynasty.

14.   Using language from Isaiah 63:1.

15.   See note 6 above.

16.   Torhovytsia (alternative spellings Torgovitsa and Targowica) is (15 km / 9 mi) northwest of Mlynov.

17.   A city in west of Minsk in western Belarus today. Yitzchak Yaacov Reines, founder of the Mizrachi Religious Zionist Movement, founded a modern yeshiva in Lida which attracted many students throughout Russia.

18.   Considered a mitzvah in Jewish law to assist a bride and groom so they can get married especially helping a young woman raise a dowry.

19.   A wagon with wheels removed and turned into a sleigh, per oral communications to Hanina Epstein from his father.

20.   Language that appears to allude to Esther 1:10 in which "the king was merry with wine."

21.   Rabbi Modechai Neta Ackerman is described lovingly in essays in the Trovits Yizkor book, 139–140, which has not yet been translated. The essays mention his only son was Avramel. In an earlier essay in this volume, "People in a Shtetl," p. 80, Mendel Teitelman indicates that Rabbi Ackerman from Trovits had been elected rabbi of the Mlynov kehilla (community) which included Trovits and other towns; the Trovits Memorial Book concurs.

22.   The writer of this essay, Shmuel Mandelkern, contributed a short memory to the Trovits Yizkor book in which he recalled Mr. Meir Feldman as a successful forester and learned man. He indicates that three of Feldman's children survived: Yitzchak-Leib, David, in the US, and a Miryam in Israel. A portrait of Meir

Feldman is also included on (page 163 of that volume) by a nephew Reuven Raberman. He describes Feldman as one of the most esteemed persons in town and the leader of congregation in prayer (shaliach tzibur) and chazan.

23.   A map below shows the typical route from Mlynov to Trovits and on to Boremel and Berestechko and the approximate location of the town of Pańska Dolina (near today's Dolyna) where the boys ended up by mistake in the storm.

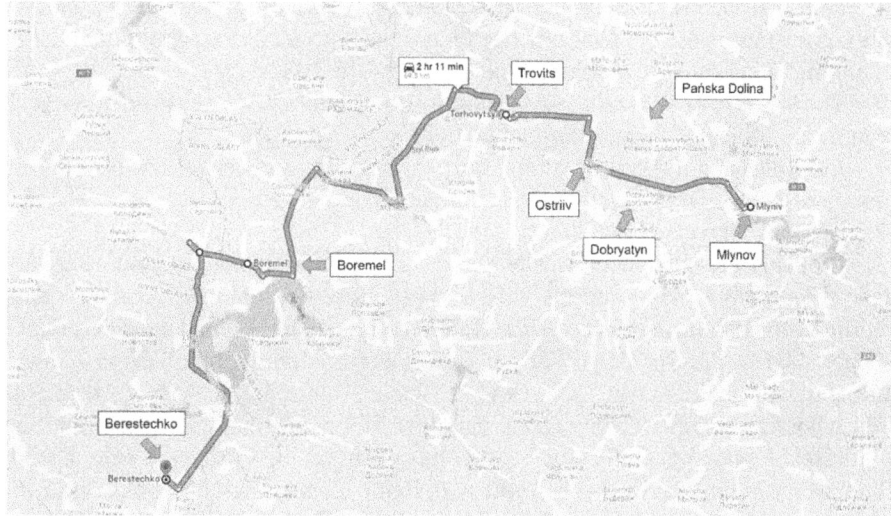

24.   See note 3 on the estimate when this story took place. In 1914, Russia had entered WWI when Austria-Hungary declared war on Serbia, Russia's alliance partner.

25.   Unidentified place name of "חווליקה".

26.   Chaim Tchernowitz (1871–1949) was a Talmudic scholar and Hebrew author who opened a yeshiva in Odessa in 1897 which later became a rabbinic seminary in 1907.

27.   Yehuda Leib Tsirelson (1859–1941) was appointed religious and crown rabbi of Kishinev.

28.   Religious critics initially believed Zionism represented heresy by relying on human efforts to hurry the results God had promised at some distant point in time with the coming of the Messiah.

29.   The language comes initially from the Talmud Bavli, Taanit 16a.

30.   Drawing on language from Isaiah 63:1.

31.   A rabbinic expression as, for example, in Talmud Bavli, Bava Metzia, 87a.

32.   Quoting a saying of Ramban to indicate that the Rav's greatness would rub off on his son and his son too could be classified as a great man.

33.   Punning on the word yeshiva which derives from the word "to sit."

34.   Mandelkern slightly misquotes the Hebrew which says, "you shall sleep (tishan) on the ground."

35.   Mandelkern is apparently here quoting a rabbinic saying from the Midrash on Proverbs 22:6 which says "educate a boy according to his way," and is interpreted to mean that you use the rod for a fool but need only a hint for the wise. These quotes demonstrate to Rav Ackerman the extent of his education. Mandelkern's final comment here is subject to various possible interpretations and is left to the reader to determine his intent. One possibility is that he is arguing that education should be tailored to the character of the student. He may also be hinting that the embrace of Zionism was inevitable in the world of the yeshiva at that time.

36.   See note 22.

37.   This was one of the original religious objections to Zionism, which was viewed initially as a secular movement which undermined traditional religious commitments.

38.   Chaim Weizmann (1874–1952) a Russian born biochemist and Zionist leader who served as the president of the Zionist organization and later as the first president of Israel.

39.   They were jealous that the senior members of this community supported Zionism in contrast to Mlynov where Zionist youth had much less support among the older members. This was the period before the Zionist

youth movement began to flourish in Mlynov in the 1920s. For example, Boruch Meren, a contributor to this volume, mentions the consternation of residents when the Fishman family decided to make aliyah in 1921 (pp. 220–221). Various family oral traditions indicate that that some of older generation continued to disapprove of and forbid their children's involvement in the Zionist youth activities. For example, Boruch Meren's father forbade him from participating, as recalled in the essay, "The Love Story of Rosa Berger and Boruch Meren" on the Mlynov website. Similarly, after Bunia Steinberg's father died, her grandfather forbade her to be involved in Zionist youth activities, as told in the Steinberg family story. Other essayists in this volume apparently had parental approval such as Yafa Dayagi (pp. 247–250). The attitude towards the Zionist youth movement in town probably grew more positive over time as the groups became more popular and the opportunities for education and economic opportunity dwindled in the Poland of the 1930s.

40.　The boys spoke with what was becoming the modernized Sephardic pronunciation of Hebrew in contrast to the more traditional Ashkenazi pronunciation.

41.　See notes about the Kipergluz family in the essay by Mendel and Sonia Teitelman, "Tragic Tales," p. 327, footnote 11).

42.　Literally, "an echo of a divine voice."

43.　Probably the nephew of Moshe Fishman, a contributor to this volume (p. 60). Moshe's brother, David Fishman (died before 1904) and his wife Sivia (Goldseker) had a son named Kalman (or Calman) Fishman. According to the list of martyrs (p. 437), Kalman, his wife Chaya and sons Pesach, David, Shimon, Asher, and Yosel, perished in the Shoah. A Yad Vashem record submitted by Yaakov Goldseker, a contributor to this volume, indicates that Kalman's son, David Fishman, married Nuna (Goldseker) Shkolnick (1912–1942) from Mlynov who also perished. Nuna was a daughter of Chaim Shkolnick and Liba (Goldseker), the daughter of Yoel Goldseker, and apparently was his second cousin on the Goldseker side. David and Nuna's children who perished were Avraham, Hasia, Eliyahu and Batia. A handwritten family tree by Moshe's son, Benjamin Fishman, records Kalman's wife as Beile Gitelman (not Chaya) and suggests they had 8 children.

44.　The same hill is the subject of the essay, "My Hill," p. 30, by Moshe (Teitelman) Tamari in this volume.

45.　The Kurzhuk valley was where the mass murder took place later.

46.　The Hebrew term is uncertain but appears to derive from the word horses.

47.　The story has an interesting similarity to the story of the biblical Joseph (Genesis 37:23–36) in which his brothers sold him to slavery and brought his blood-stained clothing to his father to explain he was killed.

48.　A Hebrew language newspaper published in Warsaw Poland from 1874–1931 and included coverage of news and politics.

49.　Tushia was a press that published original and translated works in Hebrew including essays, popular science books, travel books and biographies. It was founded in 1896 by the writer Ben Avigdor (Abraham Leib Malkovich) a pioneer in publishing modern Hebrew.

50.　A Hebrew publishing house, founded in 1901–1902 in Odessa by poet Hayim Nahman Bialik and others in Ahad Ahad Ha'am's circle. Under Bialik it became the premier Hebrew publishing house in the period before WWI. It ended after a revival in 1917–1918 amid economic crisis and Bolshevik suppression. The press was known for its adaptations of texts for students in modernized Hebrew-Zionist schools.

51.　He had to travel there for 3 days and then send a letter which would take another 3 days.

52.　Menachem Ussishkin (1863–1941) was a Russian born Zionist leader and appointed head of the Jewish National Fund in 1923. He made aliyah in 1919 to Mandatory Palestine. He was part of the B'nai Moshe society founded by Ahad Ha'am. He was one of the Jewish delegates to the Paris peace conference after WWI.

———————————

[Page 220]

The First Aliyah from the Shtetl

by Boruch Meren[1], Baltimore

Translated from the Yiddish by Hannah B. Fischthal, PhD

Edited by Howard I. Schwartz, PhD

In 1921, when Reb ("Mr.")[2] Moshe Fishman (we called him Moshe Toybe's [son][3]), an energetic Jew with a red, short beard in his middle years, disclosed the secret to one of his friends that he had decided to go (or as it was called in that time, "make aliyah") with his wife and children to Palestine, the news immediately spread throughout the shtetl.

At first, nobody wanted to believe it.

However, when it was discovered that Moshe Toybe's already had the necessary papers, his passport with all permissions, and he had started already to sell out his household goods, then the shtetl started to believe it. This amazing event was talked about in the synagogue, in the market, even among the Christians from the village Slobada,[4] with whom Reb Moshe had dealings. One expressed surprise to the other that "Moshka is going to Palestine," to become a Jewish worker on the land.

Children in the cheders talked with enthusiasm and they were jealous of the Fishman family that was going to Palestine and would be treading on the holy ground about which they had just learned in the Bible. And they would be eating oranges, carob, and figs.

The adult Jews in the shtetl thought differently.

"You have to be crazy, heaven forbid," they argued. "How does a Jew with a family, with a nice house, with a barn, a cow and horses, in addition to a small grocery store, a Jew with an income, a decent Jew with a seat facing the center of the eastern wall of the Trisk synagogue; how does he go and break himself away to go to a distant, empty land, where wild Arabs attack, kill and rob?"

Friends argued with him: "Is it possible, Reb Moshe, what are you doing? You are not allowed to break away."

But Reb Moshe was not among the people who allow themselves to be talked out of something.

[Page 221]

"We are sick and tired of the Pollacks and all the Christian hooligans, the peasants. I cannot tolerate the businesses made in the air," he said, "I feel pity for the poor Jewish storekeepers, who stand in the stores and keep looking for a customer. I can work on the field. I will become a *moshavnik*, (earth worker) and with God's help we will live and have what to eat. I will work harder, as long as I can live in our free country," was his argument.

Reb Moshe Toybe's had a family consisting of five people: himself, his wife Khaye, two sons, and a daughter.[5] The younger son Berel had been taken by friends to America a year earlier,[6] and the oldest son Dovid, a young man of about 20, used to take care of the store. His head however was not into it. He hated the store and neglected it.

Going every day into the house of study I would walk by the little store, and I often went in to buy something. Dovid always used to sit with his head in a Hebrew book or journal. It was a sin if a customer interrupted him. The shtetl knew that he was a Zionist. His father could depend on his physical strength if hard work was needed.

* * *

I will never forget the goodbyes to our first family of pioneers. The night before they departed, their entire house was lit up all night long. All the Jews in the shtetl came to say goodbye. The house was packed with people. There was a big commotion. People kissed and cried.

All the baggage, in a separate room, was packed in large baskets and in sacks. I looked at a large basket and I thought how that very basket was going to Palestine. I wanted to get into the basket that minute and go along to the land that had so teased my young fantasy; I longed for the land of our fathers.[7] A group of students from the house of study, I among them, with our teacher Ayzenberg (he is now a friend in Kibbutz Ein Harod, near Balfouria, where our Moshe Toybe's is a resident), stood and sang Hebrew songs, and at the end, the Hatikva.

[Page 222]

The crowd dispersed little by little, shrugging their shoulders, "What Moshe Toybe's can think of!"

The next morning, not looking at the bitter cold and deep snow, curious people again gathered around his house. A few helped carry out the baggage and put it onto the wide, Christian sled, as the Christian driver was standing dressed in his thick fur coat with a bashlyk on his head.

Reb Moshe with the children wore thick, warm, furs. They went onto the sled. The Christian whipped the horses, and the sled started to move from its place. The crowd called after: "Go in good health. Shalom! Shalom!" The sled headed out towards Dubno. In Dubno they embarked on the train, and from there they went more quickly.

The crowd dispersed. Only a small group of people remained standing in the small, paved yard and pondered the house and the barn, which now looked so empty and sad. I got closer to the group of people to hear what they were saying.

"And I tell you," Yankele, Moyshe's [son][8] interrupted the silence, "that he will regret it forever. Look what a household a Jew sold out."

"Certainly," the rest agreed while they tapped their feet as if dancing to warm up a little.

"The one thing we need to be jealous of Moshe and his family — they are going to a warm country, and they will not freeze like we are," Yankel, Hirsh's [son][9] called out.

"That, yes," they all admitted while touching their pockets to see if they had the keys to their stores. They left to open their stores.

* * *

A few years passed. The strength of the pessimists who promised Moshe Toybe's would run away from Palestine and come back to Mlynov was not realized, not even considering the first difficult years that he and his family went through.

[Page 223]

The shtetl received regards and word that Moshe had settled in Moshav Balfouria (in the Jezreel Valley) and was working very hard. Everyone added that Moshe was a Palestinian Jew and would not come back to Mlynov.

In 1938, when I arrived in Palestine, I decided that I must see Reb Moshe. When he had left Mlynov in 1921, everyone in the shtetl, sad he was departing but thinking he was insane to go so far away, had accompanied him to the sleigh.

In Balfouria it was not difficult to find him. I stood in the middle of the village and thought about the yards on both sides of the road. I saw small, white houses with red roofs and concrete barns behind each house, and white chickens in coops. I looked inside every yard and said to myself: I will search for the best-looking and richest yard, because Moshe Fishman's yard was the richest in Mlynov. I went into the first yard that I liked, and there I saw Reb Moshe dressed in working clothes. I recognized him immediately, although he was already almost white and had aged a great deal. He was standing next to his barn, and he divided groups of hay for the animals. It was lunch time.

"Shalom, Lord Fishman," going closer to him.

"Shalom and blessings. Who are you? What is your name?" he asked me, sticking the fork into a mountain of hay. He extended his lucky hand.

"I am Hirsh Slobodar's grandson, Bentsye's son,[10]" I said to him.

"Really!?" He was happy. "Hirsh Slobodar's grandson? If so, we belong together. Your grandfather and mine — well then, what's the difference? Come inside the house, grab something for your mouth and tell me about Mlynov, how they are there."

He lived then with his daughter and son-in-law, who helped in the field.[11]

[Page 224]

His wife was no longer alive. We sat and talked for a long time. He asked me about everyone. I reminded him about what the shtetl had thought about his going to Palestine. He smiled, but soon his face changed, and he became almost angry.

"Such scoundrels! Why are they still sitting in the stores? Why don't they run away? What are they waiting for, for Hitler to kill them, heaven forbid? Who knows, maybe it is already too late," he added with a sigh.
He looked at the clock and noted it was almost time to milk the cows.
"Come with me now to the yard, so I will show you my farm," he said with pride.
I went after him and thought to myself: How correct and wise he was in 1921, and how unwise were his critics. There is so much truth in Reb Moshe's simple words. Maybe it is already too late?
"You see the white hens," he pointed with his finger, "they lay more eggs than the Christian hens in Ukraine, and our cows cannot be compared to the Christian ones. Ours are fatter and better looking and give more milk. They are also smart and understand Hebrew."

He convinced me and said to one of his cows in Hebrew, "Pick up a foot," and she actually did it.
"I am telling you, even a cow is smart in the land of Israel."

* * *

In 1952 I met again Moshe of the moshav of Balfouria in America. He flew over to visit for three months with his two sons, daughters-in-law, and grandchildren, who live in Baltimore. He was then about 78. He begged his children to show him American farms. He seriously studied them and added, "Very nice farms, but ours in Israel are nicer."

Moshe of Balfouria did not want to stay longer than three months in America. He was drawn to his home. Without him, he argued, his management will not be in order.

[Page 225]

Soon the hay will have to be gathered, and he must be there, he explained.

He took with him a gift for his synagogue in Balfouria — a Torah.

"Learning and devotion are needed in Israel," he said with a smile.
He said a heartfelt goodbye and asked us to come to Israel.

A group of young people[112]

Translator's and editor's footnotes:

1. For Boruch Meren's background, see his earlier essay, "A Good Deed (Mitzvah)", p. 149, footnote 1. – HS

2. Reb is a term of respect like the English "Mr." and does not imply he was a rabbi. – HS

3. The name means "Moshe, Toba's son." Moshe Fishman's mother was Toba, and he was so called because his father had apparently already passed away. – HS

4. On Slobada, see Moshe's earlier essay in this volume, "Mlynov in the Past," p. 60, footnote 2. – HS

5. On Moshe Fishman's background and his family, see "Mlynov in the Past," 60, footnote 1. – HS

6. Moshe's son, Berel / Ben Fishman, joined three families from Mlynov heading to Baltimore in 1920 to be reunited with their husbands there after the war. They included the wives and children of Aaron Demb, members of the Marder and the Lerner family. Ben Fishman subsequently married Clara Shulman in Baltimore who arrived from Mlynov in 1921 with the Shulman family. See the Fishman story on the Mlynov website. – HS

7. Boruch Meren made aliyah in 1938 through the help of his sweetheart, Rosa Berger, also from Mlynov. Rosa had made aliyah in 1933. After their relationship didn't work out in Palestine, he married Milka Shargel, also from Mlynov and she brought him to the Baltimore where her family had already settled. On Boruch Meren's story, see "A Good Deed (Mitzvah)," p. 149, footnote 1 in this volume. The story of Rosa and Boruch's relationship is told in, "A Mlynov Love Story," on the Mlynov website. – HS

8. Possibly Yankel, son of Moishe Goldseker. It is possible this refers to the same Yankel who wrote the next essay in this volume, and who survived the Shoah. – HS

9. Possibly Yankel, son of Hirsch Goldseker. Hirsch was also the grandfather of Boruch, this essay's writer. – HS

10. Boruch's father was Ben-Tzion Meren. His mother was Miriam Goldseker, daughter of Hirsch "Slobodar" Goldseker. – HS

11. Of Moshe's three children, only his daughter still remained with him in Balfouria. His son, Ben, had gone to America in 1920 before the family made aliyah. His son, David Fishman, another contributor to this volume, had been with him in Balfouria but left Palestine for Baltimore in 1927, with his wife Eta (Goldseker) and their daughter. In 1938 when Boruch made aliyah, Moshe had only his daughter and son-in-law helping him. – HS

12. Morris Nudler (1921–2004) is seated in the front row, second from right. His family indicates this photo was a photo of a Hashomer Hatzair group. Morris was one of five children. His parents were Masha Eatta Polishuk, who was from Mlynov, and his father was Arke (Aaron) Nudler. He and his brother Harold survived WWII in the Russian Army. After the War, they rejoined their sister Yetka (later Helen Fixler) and their father who had survived by hiding in bunkers in the Smordva forest. The rest of the family was shot in the forest. The family eventually made their way to the displaced person camp of Pocking where they stayed for three years. Morris subsequently migrated to Canada where he had a relative and eventually brought his sister Helen and brother Harold there to join him. – HS

[Page 226]

My Hometown Mlynov

by Yankev Holtzeker,[1] Tel-Aviv

Translated from the Yiddish by Hannah B. Fischthal, PhD

Edited by Howard I. Schwartz, PhD

Mlynov was extremely beautiful. The streets were clean. Leafy trees grew on both sides of the road. In May, when the flowers started to blossom, we actually became drunk from the aroma. The shtetl looked like a forest in bloom. We also must remember that in Mlynov all Jews used to plant a couple of trees near their houses or in their gardens.

The River Ikva flowed through Mlynov, adding to its beauty. Young and old used to come and bathe in the river or warm themselves in the sun after a hard day of work. There were various sports games, which the young people enjoyed. The bridge which crossed the river and led to the count's palace also added to the shtetl's charm.

Culturally, Mlynov was on a high level. In addition to the public Polish school, there were several cheders as well as a Tarbut School,[2] where every youth in Mlynov could learn. As already mentioned, young people had the possibilities of benefitting from various sports clubs and competitions with groups from other surrounding shtetls.

In Mlynov there were several Zionist movements, like The Young Guard (Hashomer Hatzair), Betar, and others. We used to get together to have a good time, read books, and hear various Zionist speeches. There were also excursions. On Lag B'Omer, for example, we used to go into the nearby forests and have fun a whole day, returning home at night. In the winter young people would take sleds down the mountains in the moonlight. The political parties used to organize various events and plays.

Mlynov owned two synagogues: the Stoliner Synagogue and the Olyker Synagogue, as well as a House of Study, where all people would come and learn Torah until late in the night. Every Shabbes, the synagogues would be full of enthusiastic Jews.

[Page 227]

During holidays the synagogues were even more crowded. The study house is especially engraved in my memory. It was the place where I used to pray with my father, may he rest in peace. With his high and sweet voice, he led the congregation. I remember also how he used to sit and learn until late at night with other Jews of the Mishnah[3] Society.

* * *

And Simchas-Torah, I remember that we used to organize Simchas Torah night at Nokhum Teitelman's,[4] may he be celebrated with a long life. The entire party was there. He was also in the Mishnah Society. We used to dance out of the synagogue with the holy books and with music, locked by our arms into a long chain. We danced until we reached Nokhum's house. There we made a real feast. Afterwards, with the same joy, we would go again to the synagogue.

* * *

A group of young people
Pesach Mendelkern, Dovid Holtzeker, Rayz, P. Kleper, Y. Lieberman, Sh. Schechman[5]

[Page 228]

The Jews of Mlynov were virtuous and ethical. Their high moral standards resulted in being kind to guests, and in helping one another in every need. They led modest lives. The Jew in our shtetl was a worker who realized he must "Eat bread by the sweat of your brow (Genesis 3.19)." I take this opportunity to remember my Uncle Avram Gelman, z"l, with his fine qualities. He sacrificed himself for everyone with whatever he could, whenever someone was in need. My Rebbe Meren,[6] too, used to exert his greatest efforts onto all the children so that they could learn.

Moreover, I remember all the honest Jews, like Yankev Holtzheker,[7] whose house was open for every needy Jew, even though he himself had a large family. All the Holtzhekers were like that. In my father's family, each person separately used to sacrifice for all. And I note my mother Toyva, Reuven Ostriyever's daughter, a pious woman with a good heart.

And in general, all the Jews, the artisans, businessmen, traders, and a large percent of farmers, were good. Everyone made his living with honor and honesty.

* * *

I will tell a little about Mlynov after my return from the Red Army, after the Holocaust, in 1945. Broken physically and spiritually, I still had the great privilege of taking revenge for our dearest brothers and sisters, fathers, and mothers.

The shtetl looked like a catastrophic graveyard. Every little footpath was saturated with Jewish tears and blood. I got frightened as soon as I approached my shtetl. Everything was blocked and ruined. All the streets were a mountain of stones. The only Jewish houses remaining were occupied by Christians. Not a trace remained of the Study House and the other synagogues. Everything had been destroyed. Wild grass grew on the streets.

I went only to my brother's grave,[8] located on Kruzshak, between Mlynov and Mervits. I wept heartily because of the dark fate that had befallen us.

Translator's and editor's footnotes:

1. There were several men named Yankel in the large Holtzeker/Goldseker family tree. This Yankel Holtzeker (who later became "Yaakov Golceker" in Israel) was born in Mlynov and survived WWII in the Russian army before making his way to Palestine. He was the only one of his immediate family to survive. Based on the Yad Vashem records which he filled out, it is possible to reconstruct his family line. This Yankel was grandson of Yankel, his namesake, one of the original five brothers to arrive in Mlynov. This Yankel's parents were Moshe Golceker and Toba. Toba is recalled in this essay and in the list of martyrs as "Toyva, Reuven Ostriyever's daughter." The Yad Vashem records indicate she was from what appears to be Ostrog (Ostroh today). Moshe and Toba had six children including Yankel (Yaakov): Chaya Bejla (1905–1942), Yojna Reuben (1907–1942), Rywka (1912–1942), Genia (1915–1942), and Pesia (1918–1942). Yankel's uncle, Yehoshua Golceker (Yeshea in some family trees) also married a woman named Toba and they had four children: Baila (1903–1942), Chaja Baila (1905–1942), Rywka (1910–1942) and Abram (1912–1942) all murdered in the Shoah. – HS
2. The Zionist Tarbut schools became popular throughout Poland and Russia in the 1930s. As opposed to the cheders, which were always Yiddish and religious, the Tarbut Schools were secular and taught Hebrew. – HBF On the development of Tarbut in Mlynov, see the essay in this volume by Aaron (Berger) Harari, "The Youth Movement, 'The Young Guard,'" pp. 66-67. – HS
3. The Mishnah is the first compendium of rabbinic laws and comprises the foundation of the Talmud. – HS
4. Nahum Teitelman is a contributor to this volume and was married to Rachel (Gruber), the sister of Sonia (Gruber) Teitelman, one of the main contributors to this volume. – HS
5. Possible identifications: Pesach Mandelkern (1911–1987) son of Rivka (Nudler) and Abraham (Mandelkern). Sh. Schechman is Shlomo Schechman (1910–1969), the father of Morris and Ruben Schechman. He fought as a partisan in WWII and returned to Mylnov to help rescue hidden children. He met his wife Liza Zabirowicz after the War in Lutzk and their first-born son, Morris, was born on a train on the way to the displaced person camp Föhrenwald. The family eventually made their way to the US and after a stay in Connecticut settled in Baltimore. – HS
6. Probably referring to Ben-Tzion Meren, whose wife was Miriam Goldseker. Their son Boruch Meren, another contributor to this volume was a third cousin to the author of this essay. Boruch writes about his father Ben-Tzion in "My Father, Ben-Tzion," p. 255. – HS
7. Possibly referring to this writer's own grandfather for whom he was named. – HS
8. The Yiddish reference to "brother's" is in the singular, though Yankel lost several siblings and he is referring to the location of the mass grave where the Jews of Mlynow ghetto were liquidated. In Hebrew and Yiddish, the idiom for "mass grave" is "brothers' grave." – HS

[Page 229]

Poor Lives

by Sonia and Mendel Teitelman

Translated from the Yiddish by Hannah B. Fischthal, PhD

Edited by Howard I. Schwartz, PhD

Jewish families in our shtetls and the surrounding villages generally felt satisfied.

However, we remember very few people of whom we could say that they were truly happy with their lives. The very small number of Jews who were surviving without strenuous physical and emotional exertions cannot be compared to the happy Christian population.

For example, in the Mlynov area, there were quite a few so-called princes, counts, and similar aristocrats. That was a class of people who played a very prominent part in our neighborhoods of Mlynov, Smordva, Ostrozhets, and many other places whose names we barely remember.

Fradl, [one of the] typical characters in Mlynov
From the photos of A. Harari

[Page 230]

Every one of us knows and still remembers how these people lived until 1939, in their beautiful palaces, with beautiful gardens surrounding them, with all the comforts that could be found, with servants, and with steady farmhands to handle the animals, the fields, and the forests. A number of Jews derived their livelihoods from the prince with his estate by handling production, and by buying and selling. It was not unusual for a Jew to be despised and humiliated in order to eke out his little livelihood. It was similar with various leases of the aristocrat's properties, like rivers, mills, and also with leases to catch fish, chop wood, and many other things that had a connection to business.

Income from Noble Estates

Count Chodkiewicz of Mlynov, until the beginning of the twentieth century, owned a large water mill together with the Ikva River. The mill was always leased. Jews had leased it for many years until it burned down in the first years of the century. People talked for a long time about the beautiful, large mill which, by the way, had generously supplied an income for several Jewish families.

A locksmith's shop, which had several hundred workers, was also on the Mlynov estate in those years; I don't remember any Jews working there. We used to say that on the one hand, they provide jobs for the Jewish population, and on the other hand, they would very often perpetrate damages and get drunk. A drunk Christian, in general, hit Jews. But what does a Jew not tolerate in order to earn some money? So, they accepted everything with love. Also, there was a smoking room[1] at the Mlynov Count's estate. I do not remember if Jews had an income directly from the Smoking room or not, but anyway it counted as a part of the local large industry.

In Tsarist times, the whiskey factory was a monopoly; the entire fortune and the raw materials belonged to the Count.

[Page 231]

However, production was strictly measured by the Tsarist government, and a tax collector had control over every drop manufactured. Right after it was produced, it would be transported to the distillery center somewhere far from Mlynov, and from there poured into bottles. It was sold retail in the so-called *Hurt* [group] monopolies. A monopoly owner could only have been a Christian, not a Jew. A royal whiskey monopoly was in Mervits, also owned by Christians. A few Jews also kept liquor secretly and sold it in smaller quantities, such as in quarter-bottles and in glasses, and they received their income from that. I remember such a barkeeper in Mervits, Menditshekhe. In addition to selling quarter bottles to Christians, which was naturally not enough for her to live even in poverty, she had another supplemental income: teaching girls how to pray, how to read the *Shema* prayer, how to make the blessings. That was the highest education that a girl was permitted and could get in Mervits at that time. Even in the last years, teachers started to sprout. We can imagine the standards, but that was in the very last years, before the First World War in 1914. Usually there were individual exceptions to the rule, which was how our people grew up.

A good farm was located on a part of the Mlynov estate in Mervits. The field was hundreds of hectares large. There was also living inventory and an ox field; that was for oxen raised specially for meat, nourished with the malt grains from the distillery. The malt grains were stored in large barrels, especially for this purpose. Then it was taken from the distillery in Ozliiv,[2] through Mervits, to the Mervits estate. The oxen were harnessed two in the front and two in the back, and in the great mud of the unpaved road, the strong oxen would shlep masses with difficulty, and bring them to the farm.

Another livelihood provided by the Mervits estate was the leasing of a dairy farm. My wife Sonia's grandfather, Mordkhe Matis [Gruber], may he rest in pace, had maintained one.

[Page 232]

Futi

Leibish Preziment

From the photos of A. Harari

Afterwards it was managed by my Uncle Yankev Gruber,[4] may God revenge his blood. The milk was brought by Oyzer (Tomish). In my grandfather's house, they kept the milk in primitive earthen milk-pots until they made butter and cheese, also primitively, and the products were brought to Dubno. As usual, the workers from the estate were also consumers in the Jewish stores. The farmhands also sold their poor products to the Jews. Even though they displayed their anti-Semitism whenever they could, still, in various times, among various families, there was an ideal of some trust and respect among the greatest part of the population. The relationship between Jews and Christians was still in some measure loyal, even honest. We cannot say that an anti-Semitic attitude was missing in our lives, because that was always there, but it was far from what it was just before the Second World War. The greatest anti-Semite and murderer would not have dared to use such a tone as did our Christian good friends in the last years.

[Page 233]

In short, lawlessness did not rule in the earlier years.

Fishermen

Another prominent livelihood that Jews had as lessees from the princes was fishing. Until the end of the First World War, the princes owned many of the rivers (during the Polish rule the rivers became nationalized), and the aristocrats used to lease them to Jewish fishermen for a certain time frame. The lessees of the rivers mostly caught their own fish and traded them; they would only rent help from time to time.

Mayer-Yankev and Zekhraye and others whose names I do not remember were fishermen in Mlynov. Usually, there were also Jewish fishermen in Mervits, who lived from that. Their grandchildren are today in Haifa and in Kiryat Binyamin near Haifa. As to how many Jews from our neighborhood, businessmen and craftsmen, labored hard and bitterly for their piece of bread, is well known. But the Jewish fishermen labored much harder in their profession, summer and winter. The work was mostly night work, by the shine of fire. In the biggest snowstorms, when it was cold and windy, they remained in their boats on the river, searching for fish. The work made more than one sick. I remember also a tubercular Jew from Mervits, a fisherman, who died young from his job. And yet, volunteers for this difficult income were not missing. I remember how the neighboring Christians used to make fun of the fishermen when they would go to greet the Count at the New Year. They made fun of their appearance and expressions at the Polish blessings, because Polish was strange to them. Making fun of a Jew was a usual thing.

For the prince on the estate, in addition to business, there were carpenters, harness-makers, and so on. Also, animals needed to be taken to pasture for the entire summer, for a price. There were other various connections to an income with the counts and their goods, which the Jews in our area needed very badly in order to make a living. Even though the profits were not big, and even through the gains were not large, and even though they were often humiliated, still, necessity ignores everything ….

[Page 234]

Financial Relationships with Christians

There were also a smaller number of well-to-do Christians with whom Jews always had negotiations, as for example Pakhiluk from Perverediv[5] who also had a small fortune in Mervits, and similar one in Dorostoy,[6] and so on. Regarding the Christian Pakhiluk, it is appropriate to remember him as one of the Righteous Among the Nations, who should not be deprived of praise, which he earned [by] quite kosher [means]. There were, however, suspicions of ugly behavior from his grandchildren in the time of our great tragedy. Pakhiluk had a tradition of sending packages every Passover to poor Jews who had sat practically the entire cold winter without possibilities of earning an income. Pakhiluk did this until the end of his life. He also made a few Jews happy with an inheritance; one of them lives in Haifa. Jews in the area had trade relations with him — he himself was clever, he had been a Justice of the Peace, and he knew outstandingly well the Jewish situation. He ruled according to his own understanding and not according to the governmental laws. And that was really the best assistance, for he humanely and nicely supported Jewish needy families.

There were also lesser aristocrats in other villages, who were also in various connections with Jews, but I do not remember any good deeds they may have performed …

Czech Colonies

In our neighborhood there were a few villages that were populated entirely by Czech people. It is also appropriate to stop here too, and to say that the largest part of these Czechs deserve praise for their behavior in the time of our tragedy. These Czechs started to wander into our neighborhood in the beginning of the 20th century. Their development started with a very intensive colonization, beginning with buying fields with forests. Coming from poor Austria which became Czechoslovakia, they settled in poor huts the first year.

[Page 235]

They worked hard and sold trees to exist. They took out the stumps themselves. They made brickyards and made their own bricks, and they constructed beautiful houses with them. Thanks to their efforts, their value of the houses rose every year. My father, may he rest in peace, financed them until they stood on their own feet. Through all the years, he had a good trade relationship with them.

In our area of Lutsk, Dubno, and Rivne, there was a heavy Czech colonization. Under Polish rule, there were a quarter of a million Czechs, with a Czech Consulate in Kvasiliv near Zdolbuniv.[7]

As better people from the western lands, everyone listened to them. In the war, we can openly say that thanks to the Czechs there was still a small trace of Jews remaining.[8] For those few Jews who survived, it is thanks to their help. There were a few exceptions, because they also had a few bad people, but a small number.

* * *

Regarding the general Christian population with whom Jews came into financial contact, some were better, and some were worse. That means in general there were a few Christians who were decent, and the Jews working for them earned money and they were happy. But the larger part of the Christian population, even in the good times, was not decent to Jewish merchants or craftsmen.

So many Jewish craftsmen, from all branches, gave the Christians credit in order to have them as customers. It was very difficult to collect the money from them. They made all kinds of excuses in order to not repay their debts to the Jews, who badly needed their payments to exist.

The Jewish craftsmen, like masons, carpenters, joiners, and others, received most of their earnings from the surrounding villages.

[Page 236]

With great effort they labored long hours in the day at their difficult tasks. It can be said that the larger part of their salary for their hard work still remained with the Christians, who used various excuses again and again to not pay.

Struggle for the Piece of Bread

I remember the hard labor of the toiling merchants and craftsmen in their difficult conditions in the village. Poorly nourished, partly for reasons regarding keeping kosher, and working from dark to dark, resting in the farmer's barn in dirt and in dust; and then, after finishing his hard work, the Jewish craftsman's pay was postponed until the end of the summer, when the farmer would be free of his fieldwork. When it was already winter, when the poor craftsman had no work to do, he used to run around to his debtors, and with great difficulty collected portions of the debt. As long as there would be dough for Shabbes to make bread--

When I remember all the particulars with which I was well acquainted, my heart cries within me. Dear God: Jews lived like that from generation to generation, and never examined their poor, shameful lives, not striving for anything better. How painful it is to remember that life of the Jewish merchant and craftsman, how many days and weeks they and their children sat around actually with no bread, without a piece of wood, to warm their apartment! And that is how they suffered their entire lives, from generation to generation. In the meantime, they had to swallow the treatment from their clients, from better to worse. I remember the majority of such families whose entire lives were a struggle for that dry piece of bread. Little, very little, brightness shone in these houses. Every day, up until today, I see them in front of my eyes.

* * *

And when a mental account is made of those lives up until the catastrophe, the account is terrible. It is unfathomable. What kinds of sins did those people do to be so tortured all the days of their lives?

[Page 237]

I could reckon long columns of such abused people, who in their entire lives did not see a light shining and, in the end, were still so tragically murdered.

As an example, we will bring here a few families, and from them we will be able to imagine the lives of the supposedly better-off families.

In poor Mervits lived Menashe Shteinshneid. A clumsy Jew, a son of a water carrier, himself an undertaker, and more such. Had once a wife, but then became a widower. After the First World War, he returned to Mervits with an illiterate son and a hunchbacked daughter. They lived the first years in an earthen hut. A few years later they built another hut, with quite recognizable patches. The son had his father's trade, but certainly with even fewer blessings. In addition, he was an animal driver. And from all the work he was able to save enough for a calf, in order to have a little of their own milk. The son married, and he continued with his trade. The daughter was a housewife until the catastrophe. She fed the cows, and in addition, a few chickens. Year after year, sometimes they were happy. They never felt that they lacked anything. If one can call this a life, even this very life the murderers of the world took it away by force. The victims had kosher souls and kosher bodies.

And now another image, a little clearer. There was a Jew, with the name Shaye Nudler. He was called Shaye Eli Mordkhe's,[9] may he rest in peace. The father Eli Mordkhe was a basement-digger, and possibly a house painter, and in addition to these two jobs, for Passover he would bake matzas in his house. How this very Jew could afford to have a house, even one like that (with a straw roof), I do not know, but he had it. In this very house sons and daughters were born. Practically all had one source of income: they were masons and seamstresses; we can say they were skilled artisans. The son and his brothers worked for good artisans in Lutsk, and they were first class in their profession. All the brothers and sisters married, and led separate lives, all similar.

[Page 238]

I was closer to Shaye's children; a few were practically my age. They were working people, good artisans, and laboring under the same conditions mentioned above. And in the winter, there was not enough bread in the house to satisfy them. They had a house full of children. All learned skills. A few of them, up until the Holocaust, were already independent and good artisans. The measure of distress, they all together and each one separate lived with, cannot be described! And in the end, all murdered, unprotected by their honors and by the fact that they built up the entire area, built the best houses. Many of them were never paid until this day. What artisans would now rebuild the ruined world, from which our enemies would surely profit? And the same question comes up, why?? Whom did this family hurt??

Take my brother Yankev Yoysef Teitelman,[10] may he rest in peace, and family, and my sister-in-law Chaika Shikhman,[11] may she rest in peace, and family, and many similar to them. Until the First World War they were raised in so-called richer houses. They married. Then the First World War came, and they had to wander around, homeless. When they returned at the end of the war, they were already without wealth. They struggled to make a living; they labored hard and lived in poverty; but they raised very successful children. Nobody could have given their children a better education with their resources. They barely finished public school, and the children grew up needy, but smart. And their end? Bitter and sad. Their good relationships with the surrounding neighbors in the villages did not help; just the opposite: the neighbors helped to murder them.

We could publish here a large list of various merchants and artisans from Mervits and Mlynov and from the area who seldom complained about their suffering. Old men and women, honest, who were impoverished their entire lives in spite of working hard. And all were killed so tragically with their children, who had never seen anything good in their entire lives. A few of them — the so-called grain and animal merchants, who possessed horses and wagons, then the means of communication, formed a class of strong people who knew much and toiled hard.

[Page 239]

And they did that — they labored hard. They were very competitive; they rushed and worked long years. Woe on all of them in their lives …

We could, understandably, mention very many names in assorted occupations, but you will see in all of them the same pictures and the same kind of life, in practically all details the same, with small differences. The end was also the same for everyone …. Take, for example, the Mlynov tailors, shoemakers, carpenters, joiners, and blacksmiths. We portrayed these craftsmen earlier, whose work was in the area, seldom at home, and how difficult their lives were. And yet, they were satisfied with their arduous work. Now the artisans who worked at home, as much as I can remember, used to work 12–15 hours a day. And how did they benefit from it? Who from his toiling had the possibility to live better? And in more comfortable apartments? To give children a better education? Or afford to go on a two-week vacation, which was necessary for all of them for their health? Except for Moyshe Zider, may he rest in peace, and his older son Zelig, that is how it was with all craftsmen: they worked hard, and their lives were hard.

Regarding the storekeepers, with small exceptions, most worked hard, long hours. They were as competitive as they could be, and more than they could be. They satisfied themselves with small earnings, as long as they could exist. Additional competition came from a giant store founded with the *Ovshem*[12] title, established not so much to earn money, because that was unnecessary, but to ruin the Jews. To maintain a client, one had to work long and hard, and earn little. How in those times could one think about improving one's life?

Grain merchants, wagon drivers, and innkeepers — if each one would be mentioned with his details, it would make a thick book. The wagon drivers— Yoysef Wurtzel, Kalman Fishman, Arke Nudler,[13] Fishl Kritser, Yekhezkel Liberman, and Yitskhok Kozak[14] — they also worked 18 hours a day carrying heavy burdens on their backs!

[Page 240]

With the paths and bad highways, I think that today none of us would be able to make such journeys. They shook more than the lulav… and what did they gain from their efforts?

A few from Mervits came to them, Aharon Kalir and Meir Wurtzel, not even talking about those like Borukh Likhter, Arki Shamesh, or Fishel Kleinburd, who officially had a different income. This was additional income, when the other was insufficient. I only remember their hard labor and impoverished lives, even though there was happiness sometimes also. Naturally, nobody could hope for better.

The Mlynov hotels — a chapter by itself. They were a continuation from old times, when nothing was motorized yet, and people with their loads could move only by horse and wagon to other places. On the journey, the horses needed to rest and eat. In Mlynov, Khayim Berger and Yehuda Leib Lamden,[15] may his memory be a blessing, had such inns for people and their horses. For that purpose, they had large houses, with a few rooms, as well as large barns for their horses and wagons. That lasted until the Second World War, although towards the end there already were a few buses. How the inns earned enough for existence, I do not understand up until this day.

There were some celebrations for holidays; we danced a *freylakhs* happy dance at joyful occasions. On Simchas Torah, who could equal our joy? We felt we could be happy until eternity. A plague on our enemies! Did they have Hanukkah, Purim, Simchas-Torah?

Yes, a satisfied but a poor, very poor life.

Translator's and editor's footnotes:

1.   We have been unable to determine the meaning of this word since it is not a Yiddish word. The translator suspects it may Ukrainian, Куралнье, Kuralnye, meaning smoking room. Other descendants suspect it may be Polish for hill country (górzysty) and refer to hilly areas in the Count's estate where non-Jews labored. – HS

2.   Ozliiv, Ukraine is only 4 km east of Mlynov. – HS

3.   Leibish Preziment is the son of Yankel Preziment and his wife Chana-Gitel (Gelberg/Goldberg) daughter of Labish Gelberg and Eta (Schuchman). Leibish was apparently named for Chana Gitel's father. A photo of the family is on p. 473 and Leibish is the young boy in that photo. The list of martrys (p. 437) reads as follows: Preziment, Jacob (=Yankel), Chana Gitel [Goldberg] his wife; [their son] Leibish and their daughters. Assistance with research provided by Joyce Jandorf. – HS

4.   The identity of Yankel Gruber is not clear. In this essay, it is Mendel who is speaking in the first person. It therefore appears to refer to his uncle. As far as we know, Mendel didn't have an uncle by the name of Yankel Gruber, though he did have an uncle named Yosef Gruber (who had married his father's sister, Shifra Teitelman). – HS

5.   Pereverediv, Rivne Oblast, Ukraine, 8 km west of Mlynov today. – HS

6.   An alternate name for Puhachivka, Rivne Oblast, Ukraine, just north of Mlynov and/or reference to the nearby town of Mali Dorohostai. – HS

7.   Zdolbuniv is 62 km (39 mi) east of Mlynov today. – HS

8.   Several Czech families helped the Teitelman family survive as documented as recorded in the book-length survival story of Asher Teitelman, published on the Mlynov website. – HS

9.   This probably refers to Yeshayhu ("Shaye") Nudler mentioned in the Mervits list of martyrs (p. 443). No other information is known about him. – HS

10.   Mendel's brother. – HS

11.   Chaika (alt. Khayke) Shikhman/Schechman was the sister of Mendel's wife, Sonia, and born Chaika Gruber. Chaika married Yaakov Schichman/Schechman. The story of Chaika is included in the survival story of the Asher Teitelman. – HS

12.   In the 1930s, the anti-Semitic Polish government successfully impoverished Jews through boycotts and more violent means. The official response was *Owszem*, meaning "yes, indeed." The authors are no doubt referring to the government supported Christian cooperatives established to compete with Jews. – HBF

13.   Arke Nudler (1888–1948) was the husband of Masha Eatta Polishuk (1898–1942). They had five children: Moshe (Morris) Nudler (1919–2004), Yehiel (Harold) Nudler (1918–1992), Yetka (Helen) (Nudler) Fixler (1927 –), Iszhok (1924– ~1943) and Feigale (1930– ~1943). Moshe and Harold survived WWII in the Red Army. The rest of the family escaped the Mlynov ghetto. Only Helen and her father survived the shooting

of the family in the Smordva forest. Arke later died of a routine surgery in the Pocking displaced person camp. – HS

14.   See the essay by Itcik Kozak below, 354. The Kozak family escaped the Mlynov ghetto and survived intact and later came to Philadelphia to live. – HS

15.   Well-respected father of poet Yitzhak Lamdan. – HS

[Page 241]

The Two of Them

by Eliyahu Gelman,[1] Netanya

Translated and edited by Howard I. Schwartz, PhD with Hannah B. Fischthal, PhD

I want to record memories of two people of our small town who perished in the Shoah. Two who left our town for the enlightened[2] Odessa[3] but came back and put down roots in her.

The first:

Bentzi (Bentzion) Gruber[4] — he and his friend from Mlynov, who later in life was the well-known poet Yitzhak Lamdan, were students of Bialik.[5] Later they said that Bentzi preceded his friend — the poet of the future — in writing stories that were sponsored by Bialik but which nonetheless he did not publish, and they remained handwritten in his possession. He returned to the small town and settled there. He married the beautiful Genia Margulis and his life was no different from that of other people of the town. He was a grain trader. But I always saw him as the classic enlightened Hebrew man (maskil), a man of much knowledge, in Tanakh and its interpreters, in Hebrew and Yiddish literature, Russian and general [subjects]. He was brighter and sharper than all the others.

Why did he stay and not get carried away with the aspirations of his friends [to go to the Land of Israel or pursue other dreams]?

This is a mystery that has no answer.

The second:

Hersch Leib Margulis.[6] Hersh Leib was completely different. He went to Kiev to teach in a Russian school. The winds of revolution also swept him up in their orbit. And in the first days of the October Revolution, he was appointed a judge in the new regime.

But he also left Kiev and returned and settled in his birthplace. What moved him to do so — I do not know. But he was so very different from the other people of the small town, in his mannerisms and clothing, in his behavior and humility.

He was first to greet the elderly and young, with a smile full of good will that lit up his face.

May their memories be a blessing.

Translator's and editor's footnotes:

1. Eliyahu Gelman (1913–2008). A photo of Eliyahu with his family appears on p. 473 of this volume. Notes on the author and family appear in the poem by the same author, "To My Little Town," p. 207.

2. The Hebrew term "haskalah" can mean "educated" and have more of a technical meaning of being involved in the Jewish enlightenment movement that was embracing secular literature and studies.

3. Odessa was a port city on the Black Sea and a center of Jewish cultural activity in the period. In his essay about sending "Yaakov-Yosi to the Land of Israel," p. 219, Shmuel Mandelkern writes that it was a three-day ride at the time by coach from Mlynov to Odessa.

4. The two men described here appear with their families in the photo on page 457. Ben-Tzion Gruber (1900–1942) was born in Mervits, the son of Yosef Gruber and Shifra (Teitelman). He was a brother of Rachel (Gruber) Teitelman and Sonia (Gruber) Teitelman, both contributors to this volume. "Bentzi" was remembered elsewhere in this volume as a teacher in Mlynov. His wife, Gitel Margulis, was the sister of Hersh Leib Margulis, who is described next. Ben-Tzion and Gitel and daughter Yehudit perished in Lutsk.

5. Hayim Nahman Bialik (1873–1934) was a pioneer of modern Hebrew poetry also born in a small town in the Russian empire and raised in Zhytomyr. Bialik left for Odessa at the age of 18 where he studied Russian and German languages. He lived in Odessa until 1921 when his publishing house Moriah was closed by Communist authorities.

6. Hersch Lieb Margulis and his wife Reizl (Margulis) Naishtein (1910–1942) appear in a photo on p. 457 with notes. They are listed among the martyrs of Mervits (p. 442).

[Page 242]

Portraits

by Yosef Litvak[1], Jerusalem

Translated and edited by Howard I. Schwartz, PhD with Hanina Epstein

Mr. Yehuda Leib Lamdan,[2] may his memory be a blessing

A learned man, God-fearing, righteous, a lover of humanity and beloved by all, shy of accolades, but esteemed by the people of the town, including the Christians.

Until the First World War, he made a dignified living, more or less, with a convenience store, that was managed by his stepmother and his daughters; the store was destroyed and burned during the War. In the period between the two World Wars, he earned a livelihood with greater difficulty from his home serving during market days as a restaurant for the Jewish merchants who came from elsewhere.[3] Periodically, a "guest" would come to stay overnight during non-market days.

During the First World War, one of his sons [Moshe] was killed by the gangs of General Denikin.[4] His second son, Yitzhak Lamdan, made aliyah. With him in his home — he had become a widower in 1917 — was a married daughter, with her husband but no children.[5]

All his life, he was dedicated to the work of the Creator. At 4 o'clock in the morning, — in summer and in winter — he would rise and begin by reciting Psalms and [the section of morning prayers called] "Korbanot"[6] after which he studied Gemara. At 8 am, he would go to the synagogue for morning prayers (Shacharit) and remain there in prayer and study until 12. After a meager midday meal, he grabbed a nap for a short hour and again returned to his studies. Afterwards, he would return to the synagogue for afternoon prayers (Mincha), evening prayers (Maariv) and group study. At a late hour he would return home, eat a light meal, continue in his study[7] (Mishnah) until midnight. Only when he was confined to his bed would he not visit the synagogue. Otherwise, nothing deterred him, not even the worst weather — hard rain and snowstorms, mud, and dark nights in the town that had no lights or sidewalks — from walking to the synagogue, which was relatively speaking far from his house, he being older than 70 and frail.

He led the congregation in prayer (shaliach tzibur) and read the Torah (baal korei) all his life without thought of compensation. His prayer and singsong Gemara reading were full of feeling, pleasing to the ear, and sacred trembling would penetrate the heart of those who heard it. Despite his challenging troubles and personal suffering, he never complained, and he lovingly accepted his lot. No one was happier than him during [the festival] Simchat Torah. His sincere joy infected and inflamed the congregation, and no one compared in spilling sincere tears and merit through [the prayer] "Tefila Zaka"[8] and in the recitation of "Lamentations" (Eicha) during Tisha B'av.[9]

[Page 243]

Many preferred to go to him with "questions" in matters of kashrut [the Jewish dietary laws] and with requests to resolve disputes. The elderly gentiles also honored him and thought him a holy man. He was nice to everyone, adult, child, very religious and nonreligious, ally and non-ally. He served as a supreme moral authority, and he would render decisions periodically in public matters and between one person and another and he would pursue and make peace.

He lived long and died at a ripe old age of 76, in the month of Cheshvan 5701 (November 1940), six months before the Nazi conquest. He was fortunate[10] to die in peace in his bed, before the invasion of the Nazi troops, and he went to his grave, accompanied by all the Jews of the town with crying and in bitter eulogy.

During the months anticipating death at the hands of the Nazis, many Jews of the town prostrated themselves on his grave and implored him to intercede to annul the evil decree, but the gates of mercy were locked.

Mr. Mordechai Meir Litvak

My father, Mordechai Meir Litvak,[11] of blessed memory, (1881–1942) — educated, modest, a trusted community worker and active Zionist. Though he was weighed down by worries about livelihood, which came with great difficulty (a small fabric store), he dedicated a lot of his time to public activities.

In the first years after World War I, he organized and administered welfare activities in the town on behalf of the American government fund and the JOINT [American Joint Distribution Committee]. He set up a kitchen to feed children and to distribute necessities and he organized the committee for assisting orphans. After this, he set up and administered, without renumeration, "a charity fund" to help shop owners and tradesmen. Similarly, he set up a bank for the same purpose, which lasted only two short years. In the domain of Zionist activities, he managed the local Palestine Office[12] which organized the aliyah of the first pioneers in the years 1923–1926. He served as established chairman of the elections committee for the Zionist Congress, and he was one of the essential active members in all Zionist activities: the distribution of shekels,[13] funds, culture and so on. His home served over the course of years as a center and as a home for the committee for the local active Zionist members.

During the period of the Nazi occupation, he was appointed as secretary of the Judenrat in the ghetto. He carried out this obligatory and wretched role, with integrity, dignity and decency. He was cruelly beaten a number of times by the Nazi rulers for his refusal to fulfill the extortive demands. He died a holy death, with my mother, of blessed memory, at the murderous hands of the Ukrainian police during their attempt to flee from the ghetto a few days before the mass murder of the community, near the end of the month of Tishrei 5703 (beginning of October 1942), and their burial spot is not known.

May their memory be a blessing. May their souls be bound in the bonds of everlasting life.

[Page 244]

R. Mordechai Chizik[14]

The teacher Mordechai Chizik z"l was *the* teacher with emphasis placed on the word "the." And thus they called him R. Motel the Lerner (teacher). The fact that the youth and children of town all knew Hebrew, was due exclusively to great merit of Mr. Mordechai Chizik. It was he who imparted to them all the foundations of the language. Some continued independently with reading and study and reached a serious level of language mastery; others did not expand their knowledge. But thanks to the knowledge their teacher imparted to them in childhood, there was not one young person in town who didn't know how to read and write elementary Hebrew. For about 35 years he instilled Torah into the children of Israel and was fortunate to teach the children of those who had been his students. He didn't teach just Hebrew, but also Bible, the history of the people Israel, and Gemara. In large measure, his virtue should be credited with the Zionist atmosphere in the town. His two sons made aliyah to the Land [of Israel] as pioneers to the Kibbutz Beit Alpha. The younger son died in 1959.[15]

In addition to his educational efforts, he was also an active community participant and during his life served as chairperson for the branch of Tarbut ("Culture") and as authorized representative of the Jewish National Fund (Karen Hakayemet of Israel).

May his memory be a blessing. May his soul be bound up in the bond of everlasting life.

Batya Mohel

Batya Mohel[16] (1906–1942), of blessed memory, daughter of kosher butcher and inspector, R. Eliezer Mohel, of blessed memory, — a moral and spiritual figure, refined and pure. She dedicated many years to the activities of [the Zionist youth groups:] The Young Guard (Hashomer Hatzair), The Pioneer (HeHalutz), and Tarbut. She served as the highest authority for the local Pioneer youth. They abided by her counsel and her guidance in public and in private matters.

Unfortunately, she was never authorized to make aliyah to the Land [of Israel], even though she had spent years in Pioneer preparatory training (hachshara), because of a physical deformity (she was lame). Because of this deformity,[17] she was not able to join her two brothers and two sisters who succeeded in fleeing by foot from the town before the arrival of the Nazis.

She was cruelly murdered with her parents and two smaller sisters in their house trying to hide on the day of the slaughter.

May her memory be a blessing. May her soul be bound up in the bond of everlasting life.

Translator's and editor's footnotes:

1.   Yosef Litvak (1917–2001) was son of Motel Litvak and Dvorah (Lamdan) and one of the eight individuals on the committee that oversaw the Memorial Book and also a contributor to this volume.

2.   The author's grandfather. A photo of the author's parents and grandfather appears on page 454.

3.   A description of the house being used this way is included in Moshe Tamari's essay "In the Presence of Yitzhak Lamdan in Mlynov," p. 32, recalling the poet's return to Mlynov in 1931 to visit his father.

4.   Referring to Moshe Lamdan, whose photo also appears on p. 454 of the photos. He was killed by the gangs of General Anton Denikin who led the White Army against the Bolsheviks in the Civil War following WWI.

5.   Moshe Tamari, "In the Presence of Yitzhak Lamdan," p. 33 recalls visiting with Reva Lamdan when he would go to the Lamdan house and borrow writings of her famous brother.

6.   A section of the morning daily prayers devoted to recitation of legal passages relating to sacrificial offerings in the ancient Temple.

7.   The Hebrew term used here can mean either "in his recitation of Mishnah" or "in his studies."

8.   A personal purifying prayer asking forgiveness traditionally recited after final meal before fasting for Yom Kippur.

9.   Eicha is the first word in the biblical book of Lamentations, a series of laments over the destruction of the first Temple in Jerusalem. Eicha is read in synagogue on Tisha B'Av, the 9th of Av, an annual day of mourning and fasting.

10.   The Hebrew term zch can mean "fortunate" as well as "merited." Both meanings fit here.

11.   A photo of Mordechai "Motel" Litvak and his wife Dvorda Lamdan appears on p. 454.

12.   The Palestine Office ("Eretz Yisraeli") was the name of local Zionist organizations outside of Palestine that were charged with the organization and implementation of immigration to Palestine.

13.   Membership in the World Zionist Organization was open to all Jews, and the right to vote for delegates to the congresses was secured by membership dues called the shekel after the ancient Hebrew coin. Any person who turned 18 and acquired the Zionist shekel could elect delegates to the Congress for a year.

14.   Mordechai (also called Motel Tzizik) (1882–1942). A photo of the family appears on p. 457 with notes.

15.   The son Moshe, who had married Roza Berger from Mlynov, died from a poisonous snake bite.

16.   Batya Mohel appears in the photo of Hashomer Hatzair youth on p. 73 and with sisters in front of her house on p. 411. Batya was the eldest child of the Mohel family. Notes on the family appear in "My Lamentations," 408–409 and in "A Murdered Family," p. 410–413, written by her brother Yaakov Mohel.

17.   According to the longer book length account by the son of Yehuda Mohel, Batya's brother Yaakov tried to convince Batya to join them when leaving Mlynov after word of the Nazi invasion. But she refused and decided to stay with her mother. See Dani Tracz (Issachar Mohel), *Riva and Yehuda: Life Story of Trancman, Mohel, Tracz and Ben-Eliezer Families*, 2015, 225.

[Page 245]

The Goldsekers

by Boruch Meren,[1] Baltimore

Translated from the Yiddish by Hannah B. Fischthal, PhD

Edited by Howard I. Schwartz, PhD

The Goldsekers[2] and their branches were well-known in the shtetl and in the area. They were honorable people, and everyone respected them. Who did not know Hirsh Goldseker, or, as we called him, Hirsh Slobodar, since at one time he lived in the village Sloboda?

Each of the five brothers[3] had sons and daughters, as many as God would give. As it is stated in the Scriptures: "And they multiplied and increased" (Exodus 1:7). There were sons and daughters, grandchildren and great-grandchildren. All followed the righteous ways of their parents. They accepted matrimonial matches, and they celebrated weddings. The wives had children while some of the men stood in the grocery stores and sold kerosene and salt to the Christians. Others dealt with grains. Business was not bad.

My grandfather, Hirsh Slobodar, was a clever contractor. He employed bricklayers.

Yankev (Yaakov) Holtzeker and his family,[4] may their memories be a blessing

[Page 246]

He worked mainly for the Count (Chodkiewicz). He was always repairing the two large palaces, which had been damaged in the First World War. The estate was the pride of the shtetl. It was surrounded with tall acacia trees as well as with angry dogs, who did not permit Jews to go inside. But the Count respected Hershke. If any Jews needed to see the Count, it was my grandfather Hirsh who was the messenger, the ambassador. If anyone needed feed or pasture for the cows in the shtetl, Hirsh Slobodar handled it with the Count.

All the brothers had nice, respectable houses, with yards and with orchards of fruit-trees. In the Trisk synagogue, they had seats of honor with oak reading stands at the eastern wall. And they had influence! They also helped repair the Study House that was destroyed after the First World War; they erected a fence around the Holy Place (cemetery); and they fixed, pardon the comparison, the bathhouse.

By the way, I want to remember here two important established families, known in the shtetl and in the area: the Lipekhes[5] and the Bergers, who donated much money and advice to all the Jewish institutions in the kehilla. Khayim Berger was the treasurer of the synagogue, and his brother Yosel was president of the Jewish kehilla in the shtetl under the supervision of the Polish community — which was *practically the government, and that is no small accomplishment!*

Translator's and editor's footnotes:

1. Boruch Meren was the son of Ben-Tzion Meren and Miriam Goldseker. For more on his background, see his essay, "A Good Deed," p. 149, fn. 1. – HS
2. Descendants adopted variations on the English spelling of the family's surname including: Holtzeker, Hotzheker, Golceker, among others. – HS
3. The five Goldseker brothers refers to the sons of Abraham and Baila Goldseker: Hirsch, Moishe, Yankel, Shimon and Yoel. On the Sloboda connection, see also the essay of Moshe Fishman, "Mlynov in the Past," pp. 60-62. – HS
4. Yaakov is one of the five Goldseker brothers mentioned earlier. Yaakov and his wife Risia are seated in the center. Their children around them. Several of the children made aliyah to Palestine in the 1930s and after. Tzippora Sulovsky-Holtzeker (1910–1986) stands between her parents with hand on her mother's chair and Baila (Holtzeker) Wildikan (1914–1990) stands with her hand on her mother's chair as well. Nachman stands between them. Hanoch is thought to be seated front left. Tzippora was involved in Hashomer Hatzair and made aliyah in 1933, followed by Baila in 1941. Nahman's date of aliyah is unknown. Hanoch (1930–1948) was a young lad when the Nazis invaded. He managed to survive and eventually make his way to Palestine in September 1947 after being retained in British camps in Cyprus. He joined his siblings in Kibbutz Negba. He tragically died May 25, 1948, defending Negba in the battle with Egypt. See Baila's essay, "To the Memory of My Dear Ones", pp. 420-421. A photo of Hanoch as a young boy appears this volume, page 455 top left. Information courtesy of descendant Lior Wildikan. – HS
5. Lipekhes or Lifekhes – HBF

Reb Noyekh-Moyshe[1]

by B. M. [Baruch Meren]

Translated from the Yiddish by Hannah B. Fischthal, PhD

Edited by Howard I. Schwartz, PhD

He was a quiet, decent Jew. A respectable head of the household in the shtetl. His sons and daughters helped him with the oil mill, which provided a good income; he was regarded as a wealthy man in the shtetl. He generously gave charity to all needy institutions. Poor people, who used to come from out of town to gather donations, received a good meal in his house as well as a good donation.

The entire family was murdered by Hitler, may his name be blotted out. The only one in the family who survived was Shloyme.[2] He died in Baltimore in 1969, leaving a wife and children.

Translator's and editor's footnotes:

1.   Referring to Noach Moshe Schechman/Schuchman. Noach Moshe was son of Gershon Schuchman and Shaindel Bluma. His siblings included Eta Leah (Schuchman) Goldberg, Joseph Schuchman, and Hanah (Schuchman) Golisuk. Noach Moshe married Faige Beshe Wolk and they had four children: Shlomo (1910–1969), Gershon, Zlotye and Shimon. – HS
2.   Shlomo fought as a partisan in WWII and returned to Mlynov to help rescue hidden children. He met his wife Liza Zabirowicz after the War in Lutzk and their first-born son, Morris, was born on a train on the way to the displaced person camp Föhrenwald. The family eventually made their way to the US and after a stay in Waterbury, Connecticut, settled in Baltimore. In addition to Morris, they had another son, Ruben. Shlomo's photo is the furthest to left of the young men on page 227 of this volume. – HS

[Page 247]

Home and Youth Movement in Mlynov

Yafa Dayagi,[1] Kibbutz Ramat David

Translated and edited by Hannah B. Fischthal, PhD with Hanina Epstein

I remember Mlynov starting in 1926, the year I entered first grade. Until then the whole family lived near our flour mill, which we expanded after the First World War. The place was called Mantyn, after the name of the village[2] nearby. Our house and the flour mill stood alone on a wide area with fields, grasses and water. In the beginning, we utilized the water to turn the flour mill, and later we used the water also for a fishpond. Parallel to the river rose mountains and hills that were partly covered by woods and vegetation. Truly, the place was beautiful beyond belief. During the summer the place was truly a vacation spot. As children we loved to hike in the forest, to gather strawberries, to gather flowers, and to dip on the warm summer days in the chilly waters. By contrast, life during the winter was hard; then it was as if we were cut off from the world by snow and rain. Mlynov was about 3 km [1.8 mi] distance from us.

Along the road to Mlynov was the very small town of Mervits. My parents lived there before the First World War. After the War, a few dozen families returned there and established themselves. Their livelihood was typical of the traditional livelihoods of Diaspora Jews.

A photo of children in the people's grade school in Mlynov (Class 7)
In the middle from the right Rabbi Gordon[3], the Russian Orthodox priest, the principal of the school, and the Catholic priest.

[Page 248]

The children continued in the path of their ancestors and thus from generation to generation. By contrast, Mlynov was completely different. The effervescence of the youth was like that of the larger world; later this awakening began in this smaller town of Mervits. The children began to attend the school in Mlynov. The youth began to participate in the [youth] movement and thus began the contact between the smaller number of youth in Mervits and the youth of Mlynov. I remember that when I first began to attend the Polish government grade school, we still didn't live in Mlynov and when I passed the town [of Mervits] I disseminated the news — the children of Mervits began to follow in my footsteps to the school [in Mlynov].

A group of friends in Mlynov. Young Friends[4]
Original courtesy of Miriam Aharoni

Before then, Mervits children would go to cheder and to private teachers who, of course, were not certified. Given that we had a large family of children and all were of a young, educational age, we moved our residence to Mlynov. Our parents built a big, spacious house and during the course of the years it became a center of [the youth group] Pioneer activities. All the youth older than me belonged to The Pioneer (HeHalutz), except for [my brother] Tzvi, of blessed memory, who belonged to The Young Guard (Hashomer Hatzair). I belonged to the "The Young Pioneer" at the beginning of its formation. My sister, Miriam, took up the mantle of responsibility for The Pioneer and The Young Pioneer, devoting herself to the movement with fervor and dedication — later, when she passed it on, I assumed the movement's mantle of responsibility. This is what the atmosphere in Mlynov was like that influenced us. The youth were lively and tempestuous. The movement was the center of life, and perhaps even more than this – the Holy of Holies.

[Page 249]

The Polish government looked unfavorably on us. More than once the police chief called our father to warn him to cease the gatherings in our house. To them the activity looked like Communist activity.[5] On the other side, my principal at the Polish school called Father — concerning why I belonged to the "organization" (the movement), and more than once he warned that he would expel me from the studies. The area where we lived was an area of Polish and Ukrainian gentiles which is where their "gmina" was (the regional council) and my grade school. It is not surprising, therefore, that we were always under prying eyes. But none of this prevented our home from being a center of activity. Our parents were willing to risk endangerment and they didn't want to hinder us.

Ultimately, the movement required self-realization. Two of my sisters, Miriam and Baila, and also [my brother] Tzvi went for preparatory training (hachshara);[6] Baila was in general the first of the Mlynov youth who went for preparatory training. A short time after they left — I was still very young — I also left my parents' house and went for preparatory training. This was before Rosh Hashanah. The work before the holidays was exhausting. I was not familiar with any kind of work, but the strong will gave me the strength to endure it. Later, I specialized in the saw and cutting wood. After a hard day of work, in very poor conditions which prevailed then in preparatory training, I was pulled into local social activities. My preparatory training was in Radyvyliv,[7] near Brody in Galicia. I loved the location of preparatory training very much and leaving was hard for me when I was approved for aliyah in 1936.

The dream didn't materialize quickly. At that time, aliyah had ceased[8] and a significant crisis swept over the Pioneer and Kibbutz movement. The branches [of the movement] dissolved and preparatory training was finished and only a few, small central kibbutzim continued to function. I remained stuck in my parents' house and looking forward to aliyah for three years. The whole time I kept up a connection with the kibbutz in Będzin[9] that I belonged to. Every so often I prepared for aliyah, and each time it would be canceled due to a shortage of certificates. But I didn't despair. Many quit but I remained impatiently waiting for aliyah — in 1939 I was fortunate to make aliyah to the Land [of Israel] as part of Aliyah Bet,[10] exactly two weeks before the outbreak of the War.

The trip was one of a kind. About 6 weeks we were traveling on a ship carrying livestock, with a number of people that exceeded what it was supposed to carry. Instead of 180 people, there were at the start 800 immigrants, all members of the Pioneer movement, from Poland, from Lithuania, from Romania, and from Bulgaria. In the middle of the trip, in the heart of the ocean, another couple hundred immigrants joined us from Czechia, who had spent months scattered on the sea and in hospitals. I remember that night while I was standing on the deck, seeing a terrifying sight: in the middle of the night, in the middle of the ocean, they were transferring broken and shattered Jews from ship to ship — which is the moment I began to feel and see the massive tragedy of the Jewish people.

[Page 250]

On the boat there was an unbearable crowdedness with the joining of these immigrants. A person could not move from the place in which he or she was standing. There was no food or medical means. The consequences did not tarry. An epidemic of terrible dysentery broke out, the heavens and seas decided our fate. As a result, a female friend from Lithuania died in the middle of the sea, whose sister waited for her in Kibbutz, who I went to see in Tel Yosef. Another female friend [died] already within sight of the shores she longed to see with her own eyes …

And if these sacrifices of the epidemic were not enough, two young men fell from British bullets: The first, during an attempt to reach the shore of the Land [of Israel], was attacked by a British guard. The young men were standing watch by the top ship officer when they fell. Later, after much suffering and hardship, our boat entered the harbor of Tel-Aviv and ran aground on a shoal, as planned. Of course, we were incarcerated by the British, and after many efforts from the Jewish Yishuv [settlement], we were freed after 10 days from the detention center.

Question: from where does the strength come to bear suffering like this and to overcome all obstacles? And the answer: Mlynov and other towns like these kindled in the heart of many of her young residents the great fire of faith in the Pioneer ideal and thanks to this we were fortunate to remain alive and be here. The heart aches that most of them, and among them our large family and extended family members, were not so fortunate.

And these are the names of my sisters, brothers, and parents who perished: (parents) Shimon, Tova; (brothers and sisters): Tzvi, Benjamin, Shmuel, Ester, Brendelah. And also my maternal grandmother Pesia, of blessed memory.[11]

Only one sister, Rachel, and two relatives, survived the nightmare of the eradication and were fortunate to come to the Land [of Israel] and rebuild their family. The wounds still will not heal forever. Only one comfort remains, that we fortunately have a State of Israel. And a prayer is on our lips for peace between us and our neighbors so that we are able to continue to build and be prosperous.

Translator's and editor's footnotes:

1.   Yafa Dayagi Dashut (1916–1998) was born Sheindel Fisher (also spelled Fischer) to Shimon Fisher (1871–1942) and Toba Guz (1879–1942), who were both born in Mervits. Sheindel was one of nine siblings. Three of the family's daughters, Miriam, Baila (Fisher) HaLevi, and Sheindel (i.e., Yafa) made aliyah, and a fourth, Rachel, survived the Shoah. The other siblings perished: Tzvi Fisher (1908–1942), Benjamin Fisher (1913–1942), Ester (1918–1942), Shmuel (1924–1942), Bronia (Brandla) (1926–1942). Tzvi Fisher had married Rivkah (Holtzeker), daughter of "Moshe Nahmanis" according to the martyr list and Yad Vashem records. After her aliyah, Sheindl married Avshalom Dayagi-Dashut in Mandate Palestine in 1943 and they had two children.

2.   Mantyn is just 6 km (3.6 mi) north of Mlynov today.

3.   Rabbi Gordon's photo also appears on p. 453 below.

4.   Lipa Halperin standing on the left, a contributor to this volume, with several of his siblings. Next to him is Yosef (Gertnich) Ganon, who contributed the essay "Memories from Home," 261–263. According to Lipa's daughter, Miriam Aharoni, who contributed the original, this is a photo of first cousins in the Halperin and Gertnich families. Sorke Shrentzel, the sister of Lipa's mother Miriam, married Moshe Gertnich. You can see other photos of these families on page 458.

5.   Reflecting the tension in the 1930s between Poland and the Soviet Union.

6.   Preparatory training involved living on a training kibbutz, learning agricultural and vocational skills to prepare for agricultural life in kibbutzim.

7.   Radyvyliv is 73 km (45 mi) south and west of Mlynov today.

8.   The British, under pressure from the Arabs, curtailed immigration as the 1930s progressed and the number of certificates available to immigrate dropped dramatically. In this same period, for example, Aaron Harari, a contributor to this volume, recalls coming back to Mlynov in 1937–1938 to fictitiously marry the sister of a kibbutz friend and get her out of Poland.

9.   A town much further away from Mlynov, today about 580 km due west, past Krakow.

10.   Aliyah Bet is the Hebrew code name that refers to the clandestine immigration of Jews to Palestine between 1920 and 1948, when Great Britain controlled the area.

11.   Yafa's grandmother, Pesia, was born in Mervits with the maiden name of Fridman. She married Alter Guz. Their daughter Toba (Oz/Guz) was Yafa's mother.

———————————————

[Page 251]

Poems[1]

by Sunny Veiner[2], Haifa

Translated from the Yiddish by Hannah B. Fischthal, PhD

Edited by Howard I. Schwartz, PhD

In the Whirl of Battle

In difficult days of despair and fright–
From where does the poet now get his poem? –
Evening twilight uncovered the silence,
How the horror and pain lurk.

Something happened today in the world.
A firebrand rolls from land to land.
People spill blood on the mother earth
When a brutal hand waves a sword and shame.

The day has not yet made an account,
Who remains alive and who dead.
Shattered and numb bodies lie around,
Lips whisper for help, water and bread.

May 1942

In the Chaos of Life

I accompany today.
Tomorrow comes to me.
Yesterday, which is gone,
Left traces on my paths.

Life is a storm-wind;
It runs quickly and all of a sudden stops…
The storm laments with strange tones–
And does not let me go further…

I remain standing alone in the whirl of life.
Many thoughts rotate in front of my eyes,
And accurately as a devil's-game,
And I do not know where to go.

[Page 252]

I feel a warmth is hugging me
And calling me–come, come…
Do not stay on one place - - -
This is not the last card…

June 1945

Fate In Dream

To you who strove and dreamt,
To you who changed my youth into dream,
With your light I will forge my future
And not allow more empty space to hang around.

The bullet will not scare me
That carries death with it.
My way will not be blocked
When enemy brings me need.

I discovered my eastern land,
In all its paths.
I will between light and shadow
Weave my dreams further…

1948

A Little Bird in the Early Morning

Today someone knocked
On the window of my room.
Someone brought me by mouth
Music and song of spring.

A little bird in early morning
Clearly sang,
Heartily, happily, without any worries
Jumping in my window.

In the blue morning
It made me drunk in my little room,
As though it would have said:
Sing also the song of spring…

Translator's and editor's footnotes:

1. The poems were originally written in rhyme--HBF
2. There are various English spellings of the writer's surname in online records: Veiner, Weiner, Winer. His full name from online family trees appears to be Nathaniel Sonny (probably Zyn in Yiddish) Winer (1918–1995). He was the son of Yaakov Veiner and Brendel (Freeman).
The list of martyrs, p. 434, has his other siblings as Abraham and Feiga/Tzipporah. Yad Vashem records filled out by Sonny's widow, Dina (Mikel) Veiner, seem to indicate there may have been other siblings as well: Mordechai, Henya (Anna/ Chana), Chaia Leah, and Rivka. It appears from other Yad Vashem records and the list of martyrs that Henya (Anna/Chana) Veiner may have been born in 1896, married and lived in Kursk, Russia (USSR), and may have had a daughter, Beracha, who married and had children, Hannah and Yehudah, whose their families made aliyah from Russia to Israel. – HS

[Page 255]

My Father Ben-Tzion z"l[1]

Boruch Meren,[2] Baltimore

Translated from the Yiddish by Hannah B. Fischthal

Edited by Howard I. Schwartz, PhD

Was a religious Jew, may his memory be blessed,
Always reminded me to recite a prayer…
"Go to cheder, study, pray—be a Jew!"
With every step he took---
Worked for a living, during the day and during the night,
My mother was weak, did not sleep.
They complained, "Woe and bitter…
"There isn't any wood, and winter is coming soon…."
That is how I remember them, troubled and sad,
Always afraid of tomorrow…
Yes, my father, rest in peace,
I just saw you yesterday in my dream…
Your starry eyes toward heaven, your beard white,
And I look at him with wet eyes.
"Father, tell me—where is my mother, sister Serl?
"My Uncle Azshe and my Aunt Perl?" …
But my father is silent, he does not speak anymore …
I get up and wipe off a tear.

[The original Yiddish poem was written in rhyming couplets.—HBF]

Translator's and editor's footnotes:

1. Ben-Tzion Meren (1870–1942). A photo of Boruch's parents and sister Serl appears this volume, p. 456. – HS

2. Boruch's background is in his essay, "A Good Deed," pp. 149—152, fn. 1. – HS

[Page 256]

Small Shtetls, Large Families

by Mendel and Sonia Teitelman

Translated from the Yiddish by Hannah B. Fischthal, PhD

Edited by Howard I. Schwartz, PhD

The shtetls in the Mlynov kehilla, which were all destroyed, had been blessed with a valuable quality — solid friendships within the families. This influenced the sons of the families to always concentrate on keeping their family ties as strong as possible. At that time there was a contrast of opinions. For example, according to the proverb, a rebbe is worse than an apostate, because he associates only with an Orthodox Rabbi or a state rabbi, but never with a Jew. However, I am of the other opinion, that because of their limitless devotion to one another, families were bound together more and more.

For the main example of that opinion, I want to write about the multi-branched, honorable family Goldseker (Holtzeker),[1] the largest family in Mlynov. I greatly doubt that there was such a large family in the kehilla of another shtetl. Thanks to its sizeable numbers, this family had the luck of having a few surviving remnants. Very many other families did not leave the slightest trace of their existence; they were literally wiped out.

The family Goldseker had another nickname, and that was the "Slobodyantses." It was likely that their grandfathers, or great-grandfathers, lived in the nearby village Sloboda, and it was enough to call out the name the "Slobodar" to indicate that somebody from the Goldseker family was meant.[2] And as I already said, it was the largest and one of the most respected families in Mlynov. Because of their size and honor, I will make an effort to note some names. As residents of Mervits, my report will not be exact, but it will be true for the most part.

I will begin with the old man, Reb [Mr.][3] Moyshe, z"l, the father of Yankev, Ben-Tsiyon, Shike, and all z"l, from the family.[4] Yankev Goldzeker z"l,[5] the oldest son of the family, had a large family himself, which, thanks to its size, had a few survivors. Those survivors were Baila in Kibbutz Rukhama, Tzipora in the Negev, and Nakhman in Kiryat-Hayim, all with their families.[6]

[Page 257]

In addition to the parents, who were murdered in the Holocaust, one of the successful children, Hanoch, z"l, was killed in the Negev during the War for Independence. [Another son] Menashe z"l was spared during the Holocaust; he was together with us near Mlynov.[7] From there he was mobilized into the Red Army, and he did not return; he probably died.[8] A few other descendants were with a group in the Smordva forest, where they were killed.[9] The parents Yankev and Risia z"l died in the ghetto. They were a part of the large Goldseker family. It will not be an overstatement to designate them with the title of "tribe," because even for a tribe, they were not small in number. "It is a pity for those who are gone and no longer to be found!"[10]

Further, there was Nokhum Goldseker with his family, Beni Goldseker with his family,[11] Shike Goldseker with his family, Peril Basis Goldseker with a son and family,[12] Yankev-Kalmen-Moyshe Yoel's-Risl,[13] and a few others, whose names I do not remember, and they all had large families.

It is not for nothing I call them a "tribe," because they were.

After them there were other large families, but smaller in number. There were the Berger families:[14] Yoysef Berger, Khayim Berger, Faivel Berger, and Wolf Berger, with their families. There were a few other Berger families, whose names I do not, unfortunately, remember. Survivors from the Bergers are: Ahron Harari, a veteran in Israel, and his sister [Rosa/Reisel Berger];[15] Pinkhus Berger, and his sister Liza, in Brazil, who endured the terrible time in the forest with us.[16]

* * *

Another group of families, although smaller in number, yet large enough and having branches, were the Mandelkerns. A few of them are in Israel.[17] Additionally, there were smaller families, smaller in number. In addition to their great importance, the numbers there were larger than can usually be found today. And in a certain measure we can say that the entire shtetl was divided into tribes. Small families were, for example, Halperin,[18] Schechman,[19] and so on. All this gives the impression that a few families owned the small shtetls.

[Page 258]

Small shtetls, with large families. That applies to Mlynov.

It looked like that also in Mervits. For example, the Teitelman families: Khayim-Mayer z"l,[20] the family Mordkhe Teitelman, z"l, the family Yankev-Yoysef (my brother), z"l, and my family — Shmuel Teitelman, Avrohom Yankev Teitelman,[21] Motil Teitelman. The street on which we Teitelmans lived was settled densely only by us, and also by Anshl[22] z"l. And may the Lord avenge his blood, Nakhum Teitelman[23] was from Mervits.

Following in number was the family Epshtayn,[24] z"l, a large, many-branched family; The families Steinberg,[25] Sherman,[26] Raykhman, Gruber[27] and others followed.

Also I remember Ostrozhets was similar. For example, the Garber families z"l had the largest number of families in that shtetl. That was my brother-in-law Mayer Garber and sister's husband and family. And in general, the Garber family was the largest in Ostrozhets. There were a few more large families in Ostrozhets, but I have forgotten their names.

Avromke – A typical Mlynov character
From the photos of A. Harari

In Trovits,[28] the Feldman families were large in number. Boremel and Demydivka had the Fuks families; all had many branches. So it was in almost all the small shtetls where we had been born: small shtetls, large families.

Translator's and editor's footnotes:

1.   The Hebrew spelling of the surname in the Memorial volume sometimes begins with a "heh," as in Holtzeker, and sometimes with a "gimel" as in Goldseker. This variation in the Hebrew, which carried over to the English, reflects the fact that a "h" was not pronounced in Russian and some Slavic languages. There are many other variations of the surname in English records. – HS

2.   See the essay by Moshe Fishman in this volume, "Mlynov My Hometown," which indicates the Goldseker family came to Sloboda from Dubno, pp. 60–62 and then followed Moshe to Mlynov. On the location of Sloboda, see footnote 2 in that essay. For another essay on the "Goldsekers," see that of Boruch Meren, a Goldseker descendant, 245–246. See also the essay by Yankev Holtzeker, "My Hometown Mlynov," 226–228. – HS

3.   Reb is an honorific title like Mr. and does not signify the person was a Rabbi. – HS

4.   Moshe Goldseker was one of the five sons of Avrum and Baila Goldseker. For a list of the five Goldseker sons, see Boruch Meren's essay, "The Goldsekers," 245-246, note 3. According to oral tradition among the Baltimore descendants, the Moshe Goldseker referred to here and his wife Ida had ten children: Yankel who married Risia, Benne, Pinchas, Nachum, Goldie, Yehea, Baila, Ruchel, Tchize (also spelled as Shisha or Sivve)

and Rivkah. Some of Yankel's children survived as described below. Tchhize married David Fishman and one of their sons, Morris Fishman, came to Baltimore." – HS

5.   A photo of this Yankev's (or Yankel's) family appears this volume in the essay by Boruch Meren called "The Goldsekers," p. 245. He is to be distinguished from the Yankev who wrote the essay in this volume, "My Hometown Mlynov," pp. 226-227. – HS

6.   Tzipporah Sulovsky-Holtzeker (1910–1986) made aliyah in 1933. Baila (Holtzeker) Wildikan (1914—1990) made aliyah in 1941. Nahman (Holtzeker) Israeli (1920–1986) made it to Israel at some unknown date and lived in Kiryat-Haim. Their younger brother, Hanoch (1930–1948) survived the ghetto liquidation and made aliyah in September 1946. He was killed defending Kibbutz Negba on May 25, 1948 by an Egyptian shell. – HS

7.   Menashe is listed in Yad Vashem records as another child of Yaakov and Risia. – HS

8.   He was seen one more time after he was mobilized. Mendel and Sonia's nephew, Asher Teitelman, who had enlisted in the Red Army and was wounded tells of meeting Menashe once more in the hospital when they both were wounded in battle. That was the last time anyone saw him. See Chapter 4 of Asher Teitelman's life story published on the Mlynov website. – HS

9.   Other Mlynov families in the Smordva forest include the family of Asher Teitelman and the family of Helen (Nudler) Fixler. See note 1 for the Teitelman story and for background on Helen Nudler's family story, see the Mlynov website. – HS

10.   The quotation comes from the Talmud in Tractate Sanhedrin 111a. Basically the expression laments the great loss of the deceased persons who are irreplaceable. – HS

11.   Nahum and Beni are other children of Yankel and Risia. – HS

12.   Based on Yad Vashem records, probably Peril Shokhet who married Aisik Goldseker. They had a son Srul (Israel) who married Shifra Kotch. – HS

13.   We are not able to identify these other Goldsekers. – HS

14.   Wolf and Favel were brothers. See the story and photo of them as farmers and a photo in this volume, by Wolf's son, Aaron Harari, in "Jewish Farmers in Mlynov," 75-76. It is not known whether or how Yosef and Khayim Berger were also related. – HS

15.   Aaron and Rosa were Wolf's children. Aaron is a contributor to this volume and took many of the photos in this volume. – HS

16.   Pinchas and Liza were children of Tuvia (also Tevel) Berger, another brother of Wolf and Faivel. Pinchas survived the Shoah in the Red Army and Liza writes about her survival experience later in this volume, pp. 347–350. – HS

17.   Shmuel Mandelkern, who was a leader in the Zionist Youth Groups, made aliyah. See Aaron Harari's reflections on Mandelkern's role in "Culture, Education, and Social Life in the Small Town," pp. 66—68 and "The Youth Movement, 'The Young Guard' (Hashomer Hatzair)," pp. 69–73. – HS

18.   Lipa Halperin is a contributor and editor of this original Memorial volume. He was born in Mlynov (1907–1969) and made aliyah to Palestine in 1938. All of his immediate Mlynov nuclear family were killed in the Shoah. Lipa's father was Israel Halperin and his mother also from Mlynov was Rivkah Shrentzel (also spelled Shrenzel / Shrentsil). Lipa was named after his grandfather, Lipa Halperin, who had married Pessia Hirsch from Mlynov. Lipa's siblings can be seen in photos and in the 1935 home movie taken when Lipa's cousin A. D. Hirsch visited from the United States. See the Hirsch family story on the Mlynov website. – HS

19.   There was a large Schuchman family in Mlynov and the descendants of one line transliterate their surname Schechman. – HS

20.   Chaim Meir and Mordkhe (Mordechai) were brothers of Mendel's father, Abraham. – HS

21.   Possibly Abraham, son of Chaim Meir Teitelman. – HS

22.   Possibly Anshel Eliezer Teitelman, a brother of Nahum Teitelman. – HS

23.   Probably referring to Nachman Teitelman, a brother of Mendel, who died in the Shoah. – HS

24.   Yitzhak Upstein (1910–2004) was one of five children of Raizel and Hanina Upstein. Hanina's father was Leazar Upstein. In the family, only Yitzhak survived WWII in the Red Army. He married Bunia Steinberg after returning to Mlynov. See Bunia's essay, "Wandering During the Terrible Catastrophe," pp. 387–404 After a stay in the Pocking displaced persons camp, Yitzhak and Bunia made aliyah. – HS

25.   Getzel (George) Steinberg (1907–2003) was one of seven children of Asher Anshel Steinberg (1881–1923) and Chaya Lerner (1881–1942). Getzel married Pessia (Paula) Wurtzel (1907–1994) daughter of Zelig Wurtzel and Sooreh Gruber. They survived the Shoah with their son Zelig (Gerald) Steinberg (1937–) and two

of Getzel's siblings, Getzel's sister, Bunia (Upstein) and his brother, Mendel and his wife. After the liberation, the families made their way to the Pocking displaced persons camp. Getzel's family eventually moved to Springfield, Massachusetts; Bunia and husband Yitzchak Upstein made aliyah with son Hanina, who was born in Pocking. Mendel and his wife Shaindel Grenspun settled in Cleveland with their daughter Susie who was born in the Lechfeld displaced persons camp. – HS

26. Ezra and Yechiel Sherman were sons of Moshe Sherman and Etel (Ester) Golisuk (who was a daughter of Hanah Schuchman). Yechiel is a contributor to this volume (p. 415) and survived WWII with the Red Army. Ezra escaped the Mlynov ghetto as a young boy and survived wandering from place to place in the countryside. After the brothers were reunited, they made their way to Palestine where they settled. You can listen to Ezra speak about his experiences in an interview posted on the Mlynov website. – HS

27. There were a number of Gruber lines in Mlynov and their exact relationship is not known. Sonia, one of the authors of this essay was born Sonia (Gruber). Her sister was Rachel (Gruber). The two Gruber sisters and other siblings were daughters of Yosef Gruber, son of Mordechai Gruber. Their siblings were Yitzchak (Gruber) Hofri, (1910–2008) who made aliyah in the 1930s, Bentzion, Chaika (Chaya) Schichman, and Nuta Gruber. Another line of cousins included four sisters: Riko/ Rikel who married Joseph Gelman/Alman and migrated to Springfield, MA, Sooreh (Gruber) Wurtzel, Rachel (Gruber) Feldman, and Ester (Gruber) Boronstein. In addition, there was a line of Grubers descended from Moshe Gruber's daughter, Rivka, who married Israel Demb. Most of the Demb descendants migrated to Baltimore between 1900–1925. There was also a Shmuel Gruber who married Charna (Goldseker), both killed in the Shoah. – HS

28. Today Trohovitsya, Ukraine. – HBF

[Page 259]

Mr. Avraham-Shlomo Teitelman[1]

by Eliyahu Gelman[2], Netanya

Translated and edited by Howard I. Schwartz, PhD with Hanina Epstein

From the abyss of oblivion of more than half a Jubilee generation of years [25 years] from the Shoah — the images of the town's people rise up and appear as if they are standing alive before our eyes. Here is one of them: Avraham Shlomo son of Mordechai and Freida from the multibranched Teitelman family. His father died and the burden of worry for the home's livelihood fell on his shoulders and strong hands, [including:] worry over a sick mother, younger and older brothers and sisters.

He circulated among the villages in the area — and returned home on cold winter nights and on days of summer rain, on snowy roads, and muddy, dusty trails. He brought with him cattle which he bought.

More than once he would encounter a gentile hooligan, who attacked him, but Avraham Shlomo did not recoil and was not afraid, and would display his relaxed [muscular] arm.

This way of life continued day and weeks, months and years, except for the days of Sabbath and festival, on which he rested and slept, prayed in the congregation, and learned a chapter of Mishnah.

One time he found me with a book of Sholem Asch[3] in Yiddish. He read one [essay] and then continued to read a second and third and the world of books that opened before him took him by storm. And when he returned home tired and worn out from trading in the villages, he found a source of enjoyment in reading.

But he found not only enjoyment in books — The depths of life in the small town became too narrow for him and it seemed as if he would break out of the circle of sorrow and join the youth who were seeking new paths. But it was not to be. His mother, who felt the change that had begun in her son, did not permit him to follow these paths. "You, my son — the burden of the family is entirely upon you, and you are forbidden to confuse your head with stories and tales which who knows where they will take you and where you will go."

Avraham Shlomo, the traditional good son, obedient and responsible, listened to his mother's words and accepted them. Eventually, he married a woman and had a family; they perished in the Shoah with all the Jews of the town.

Translator's and editor's footnotes:

1. Avraham Shlomo Teitelman (1903–1942) was born in Mervits, one of seven children of Mordechai Teitelman and Freida (Horowitz), five of whom perished. Avraham was a first cousin of Nahum and Mendel Teitelman, contributors to this volume (their parents were siblings). Avraham's sister Sarah (Teitelman) (1924–1983) survived and married Rabbi Yisrael Feldman in the displaced persons camp of Bad Gastein. They subsequently moved to Milwaukee in the US. Avraham's brother Naftali Hertz Teitelman (~1912/1915–2002) died in Israel. The siblings who also perished were: Moshe Lipa, Chaya Dvoira Schwartzkopel, Yosef Aryeh, and Shmuel Teitelman and their families.
2. Eliyahu Gelman contributed a number of essays to this volume. See the following essay about his family for more details.
3. Sholem Asch (1880–1957) was a Polish Jewish novelist and essayist in Yiddish who settled in the US. Originally trained traditionally he was exposed to Enlightenment ideas and Yiddish literature. He arrived with his family in the US in 1914.

My Father's Home

by Eliyahu Gelman[1], Netanya

Translated and edited by by Howard I. Schwartz, PhD with Hanina Epstein

World War One, which razed Mervits to its foundations, caused the residents of the town to flee to towns in the area, and with the cessation of fighting at the end of the War, a large part of them returned to the destroyed town, and rebuilt the destroyed houses anew.

My father and the members of his household, and also his brother Joseph[2] and Moshe[3] and the members of their households fled to the nearby Varkovychi[4] which was not damaged severely during the war.

[Page 260]

In this town my father continued his occupation from before the War, teaching Gemara, Bible (Humash) and Rashi.[5] My sister, Esther, married my cousin Benjamin during those years and went back to live in Mervits. In 1928, my father decided to return to [Mervits] the town where he had been born. He was 70 years old and felt, apparently, that his days were numbered, and he wanted to be buried in the place where his father, mother and relatives were buried from previous generations. And truly he didn't live long.

In the stormy winter at the beginning of 1929, my father died a painless death. I remember that evening the day before his death, we were sitting by the stove and warming ourselves. My father sensed that his strength was leaving him, even though he had begun going again every day as was his custom to the study hall, sighed and said, "Ah, if only I was able to extend my life at least five years, to raise my children, and guide them and marry them off …" but the following night, after a day bedridden with illness, he called me to him. When I drew near, he asked me to bring him a bit of water in a jar. He extended his hands, said a short prayer – apparently the Vidui confession [said for the final moments of life] — his head dropped on the pillow and his soul departed. My mother, my sister Yenta and myself, remained living in the house of aunt Brendl, who had gone to live in a village, where she opened a convenience shop. Our married sister Ester joined us with her husband Benjamin, and her three loveable children, Leahle, Perele and Hershele.

In 1938, I made aliyah to the Land [of Israel] with the hope that I would succeed in bringing the members of my family there. But I was not so fortunate, nor were they, and thus came their cruel end.

* * *

The family members of my uncles, Joseph and Moshe, perished in the ghetto of Varkovychi. The family members of my father's sisters, Hannah and Brendl were killed in Mervits and its surroundings. My aunt Belumah and her family remained alive and made aliyah, and she and her husband Ben-tzion lived fortunately for years in Haifa, and passed away at a good old age several years ago. They were fortunate to see children and grandchildren, who live in Haifa to this day. My sisters Freidel and Dobrish — my father had succeeded some time before the First World War in sending them across the Austrian border on their way to the United States. There they live to this day. From my uncle Moshe's family, [his son] Meir Gelman and his family remained alive, living in Beit Eliezer near Hadera.

These are the generations of my father's family in Mervits. One family among many others in the town, which had a bitter end. It is a shame that so few remain, to record the history of their family. And their memories will join with the memory of that small town, [in which] generations came and went, as the tapestry of village life was spun until annihilation and destruction.

It is a rule and custom in Israel to rend one's garment after a death [called keriah], and the tearing is not only a religious symbol, but also a tearing pain in the soul of those bereaved. Children and grandchildren established year after year a day of remembrance, a "yahrzeit" and a "zicharon" to the memory of the departed.

But there were murdered women, men, babies, children and elders, who had no keriah [i.e., no one was left to rend a garment for them] and had no gravestone in remembrance.

Translator's and editor's footnotes:

1. Eliyahu Gelman (1913–2008) was the son of Pesach Gelman and Raisi/ Raisel. Eliyahu made aliyah in 1938. In this essay, he describes what happened to his family whose photo appears on p. 473 of this volume. The family is listed in the Mervits martyr list, p. 441. Eliyahu had four sisters, Ester, Yenti, Freidel and Dobrish. This essay indicates that two of his elder sisters, Freidel and Dobrish, were sent to the US before the War and were still living there when this essay was published. Their married names are unknown at the time of this writing. It is unknown if or how this Gelman family is related to Gedaliah (Gelman) who took the surname Alman in the US or Tola Gelman, both of whose photos appear on p. 477. The Pesach Gelman listed in the Mlynov martyr list as a scribe and shochet is not Eliyahu's father, Pesach, according to family descendants. Eliyahu married Yehudit Rhyber (or Reiber) (1922–2000) in 1944 and had three children.
2. Yad Vashem records of those who perished in Varkovychi indicate Joseph Gelman (1876–1951) married Leah (1880–1942) and had the following children: Fejga (1914–1942), Ester (1918–1942), Machla (1916–1942), Elia/ Elijahu (1920–1942) and Ephraim (1922–1942).

3.   Yad Vashem records from Moshe's son Meir Gelman indicate his father Moshe was born in Mervits (1877–1942) to Avraham Gelman and Gitel and married Sara (née Torchin) who was born in Warkowicze in 1881. They perished along with Meir's siblings Sprinca (1924–1942), Feiga (1902–1942), Herschel Tzvi (1906–1942), and Genesja (Gelman) Raber (1904–1942).

4.   Varkovychi (alternative spelling Warkowicze) is east and a bit south of Mlynov today 31 km (19 mi). See also Helen Lederer's essay "In Pain From the First World War," pp.147–148, about the Gelberg family's experience as refugees from Mlynov during WWI and their experience reaching Varkovychi.

5.   Rashi is the acronym for Rabbi Shlomo Yitzhaki (1040–1105), the French rabbi who wrote a comprehensive commentary on the Bible and Gemara, often credited staying closer to a literal reading of the texts.

[Page 261]

Memories of Home

by Yosef [Gertnich] Ganon,[1] Kiryat Ata

Translated and edited by Howard I. Schwartz, PhD with Hanina Epstein

When I was a boy of 8, my family came from Rovno to Mlynov to settle there. My first impression was that most of the town's houses looked likely to fall down, only there and there did one's eyes alight on a house that stood [firmly] on its foundation …

During spring and autumn seasons, the mud in Mlynov was so deep and so sticky that even today I imagine that you would need to operate a bulldozer in order to extract pedestrians from it. Although the Jewish population of this town was relatively meager, the center of the town was comprised almost exclusively of Jews. In the front of every Jewish home was a shop, sometimes a business on a larger scale. I was impressed especially by the multitude of shops selling beer in the small town like this, but the reason for this was that nearby were many villages with German and Czech populations — and they loved to drink beer. It was strange to see, from time to time, a Jew with a substantial beard standing behind the counter mixing beer for gentiles, and in addition, selling non-Kosher sausages to them.

My father, Moshe Gertnich[2] was a native of Mlynov, as were his parents and their parents for generations. From the stories I heard from my father, uncles and aunts are engraved in my memory, especially the character of Grandmother, peace be with her, Faiga-Hinda, mother of my father. She was an exemplary woman in her generation. Beautiful, sparkling and polished; a wise woman, righteous, a pure soul. On her and her superior female shoulders was placed the burden of support for 9–10 souls. Grandfather, who was learned, sat day and night at the house of study on his bench and repeated his chapters [of Mishnah]. If not for Grandmother, who would remind him, that there is a need to eat sometimes — he would skip even this … Not once did he come on his own requiring a portion of the meager food. All of his effort was invested in holy books to the extent that he didn't set aside time for raising his children. This burden too Grandmother assumed.

With respect to this: Grandmother adapted a profession for herself that was like teaching. In her small home — where ten toddlers "roamed about" — she set up a kind of "cheder" [i.e. nursery]. Daily the children of Israel heard Torah from her lips, and she based her livelihood on this activity for families with many children. Additionally, she found free time to get involved in the charitable causes (tzedakah): helping brides get married (hachnasat kallah), assigning the poor to families for the Sabbath [meals], and more.

My two [paternal] uncles,[3] Shayiah and Yitzhak, them and their families and descendants were born, lived and died in Mlynov. I remember when I was a lad of 12, I studied in the traditional grade school (cheder) of Ben-Tzion (Bentzi) [Gruber][4], and already by then I was studying Gemara. Each and every week one page of Gemara. Each Sabbath my father would return, with my uncle Yitzhak, from the synagogue after the afternoon meal and my parents would nap.

[Page 262]

My uncle, who lived close by, would not eat his meal immediately but would sit first and review his studies. Afterwards I would go to his house, settle down by his table, take down a volume of Gemara from the bookcase that stood opposite me in the corner, and would begin to read aloud a page of Gemara, that I had studied during the week. It was incumbent on me to interpret with all the commentators that I learned (Bartenora[5], Rashi[6] etc.). If I succeeded in satisfying my uncle, I would receive pears which grew on the old pear tree in his garden, and praise in my presence or not, but if, God forbid, I didn't succeed and I hesitated a bit — on the spot I would receive a ringing slap. And if this wasn't sufficient, I had to tell Father the whole truth and not hide, God forbid, any little thing …

Thus the serene life flowed until the Great War, which was followed by the terrible Shoah, unlike anything humankind had ever known.

* * *

September 1939. The War broke out and many people temporarily fled the town because of the bombardment. Our family also headed to a nearby village for several days to non-Jewish friends. The terrible days approached and on the horizon the Germans could be seen advancing to the Bug River, which served as a natural boundary between Volyn and the western districts of Poland.

The holiday of Rosh Hashana passed with a tense atmosphere and sense of foreboding. But, as is known, suddenly there was a turning point, and the Red Army crossed the border and penetrated to our area.[7] That's when we returned to our home.

The joy was great. Yom Kippur was at that time a great festive day for us. We indeed thought that we had been saved from the Nazi claws. We especially increased our celebration and rejoicing on the festival of Simchat Torah. We rejoiced over the rescue effected by the Russians, even though austerity had already begun with the privatization of commerce, which the Jews suffered first.

* * *

In June 1941, when the Nazi military attacked the Soviet Russia, I left Mlynov with a group of young people.[8] By a difficult route and after many adventures and wanderings, I arrived very deep into Russia — and I was then a young man of nineteen.

After the War and the terrible Shoah, on a day of heavy rain, gray and gloomy, I arrived back at my town. I passed along her streets and I found only debris. It is true, here and there a house stood on its foundation,[9] but I saw no Jewish soul …I met some gentiles and the sight of me provoked amazement, "From what planet does a Jew now appear? … "

Truly, every gentile was certain, and not without good reason, that all the Jews had been liquidated.

The day drew to a close and I turned my back on the town of my birth forever.

Translator's and editor's footnotes:

1. Yosef Ganon (also referred to as "Kuftzia") was born Yosef Gertnich (alternate spelling Gertnikh) in Mlynov. His father was Moshe Gertnich (1900–1942) son of Mordechai Shmuel. Yosef's mother, Sorke (Sara), was the sister of Rivka (Shrenztel) Halperin, both daughters of Mordechai-Meir Shrenztel. Yosef was thus first cousin of Lipa Halperin whose essay "The Mill," pp. 13–15, talks about their shared grandfather Mordechai-Meir Shrentzel. Yosef had two siblings: Shmuel and Feiga. A photo of the family with the young Yosef appears on page 458 of this volume and a photo of him as a young man appears on page 248 standing next to his cousin Lipa Halperin. Yosef was the only survivor of his immediate family.

2. Here the last letter of the surname is spelled with the Hebrew letter Qof as in "Gertnik" but in the martyr list and in Yad Vashem records spelled with a "kaf" like "Gernich."

3. Yosef's father had two brothers, Yehoshua (Shaye) Gertnich and Yitzhak Gernich. His uncle Yitzhak was a glazier and Yehoshua was a rabbi according to Yad Vashem records.

4. Ben-Tzion Gruber, son of Yosef Gruber and Shifra (Teitelman) was remembered as a beloved teacher in Mlynov. A short profile of him is provided in "The Two of Them," p. 241, by Eliyahu Gelman and a photo appears on page 457 with his family.

5. Bartenura refers to a commentary written by a 15th century rabbi, Obadiah Bartenura, best known for his commentary on the Mishnah.

6. Rashi is the nickname and acronym for Shlomo Yitzchaki (1040–1105) who wrote a comprehensive commentary on the Gemara and Hebrew Bible.

7. The Soviets and Germans had signed a non-aggression pact, agreeing to split Poland between the two powers. The Germans invaded Poland on September 1, 1939. The Soviets delayed their attack until September 17, 1939. During those intervening days, the residents of Mlynov were terrified they would be occupied by the Germans.

8. See also the essay by Yechiel Sherman, "Departure from Home," p. 344, who left Mlynov with the same group of young men.

9. With this image, the author poignantly returns to his very first memory of Mlynov when his family moved there, in which most of the houses were unstable and only a few secure on their foundation.

[Page 263]

The Home That Was Lost

by Bat-Sheva Ben-Eliyahu (Ribetz)[1]

Translated and edited by Howard I. Schwartz, PhD with Hanina Epstein

A memorial candle to my beloved ones. To Mother, to Father, to Sister, Brothers and their families and to all those who have no one to write a eulogy for them.

On Tisha B'Av 1939 [July 24, 1939], I left my beloved family forever. [I am] mentioning the time when mother, of blessed memory, hugged me and I felt in her hug and embrace, that this will be a separation forever.

* * *

For years I didn't believe that such an awful thing happened. I was not able to imagine that there are human beings who are worse than animals of prey. Until … until one day I found out, first about you, my beloved sister Freidl (Penni), that you were so cruelly and brutally uprooted by Hitler's troops. And Mommy (imaleh) you continued to live in grief until the redeemer [i.e., Death] came and with all town's residents you were destroyed with the ghetto of Mlynov.

For years I was not able nor wanted to be consoled. How terrible I felt ... what you wanted while alive was to merit hearing a bit of satisfaction from me. But you weren't so fortunate, my beloved [Mother]. However, as long as there is life in me,[2] — your faces and memories will not leave me for even a moment. And during days of grief and joy, all of you are with me. With me, day and night and in everything to which I turn.

I continue to uphold your testament and walk in the ways of Father, of blessed memory — upholding the three pillars of commandments [upon which the world stands Pirkei Avot 1:12]: Torah Study, Worship (Avodah[3]), and acts of lovingkindness (gemilut hasadim).

Therefore, it is hard to put on paper all that a person feels, about a time when everything one regards as precious is lost; and lost with so much cruelty. Nevertheless, I want our children and the future generations after us to know. They should know, first of all, that we, those still alive and living here, we also had parents. A house. There were brothers and sisters and large families. We want our children to know that they also had grandmothers and grandfathers, aunts and uncles.

I want those who turn these pages and read these lines to know that there was once a town Mlynov in which lived Jewish residents — old and young, children and infants. And we had a youth movement, "The Young Guard" (Hashomer Hatzair), thanks almost entirely to which we survived and are living here in the Land [of Israel].

[Page 264]

And they should know to be proud of these grandmothers and grandfathers even though they never met them. They were cultured and noble people, and they bequeathed to their daughters and sons what is good and refined in the human soul; and that from our town came people of the pen and the book and industrious people.

* * *

A bit about my family

Father, of blessed memory, died before the Shoah. And those here with us among the living or across the ocean do not remember my father. Everything that is humanly good was in my father. Anyone who came and spilled their inner troubles to him — he would immediately extend help and assistance.

Mother, did she not always go to any home in need? — and that's how they always were. To one [who needed it], she would go with a pitcher of sour cream, for did we not always have a female cow or goat? And this was the way she would feed all in need. And we, the children, would also help her. And after this [assistance of food], [there followed] "the donation of sleeping quarters" (linat tzedek) and "acts of lovingkindness."

* * *

About the Town

Many were surprised. "What, you all know Hebrew? They learned Hebrew?" It was difficult for them to believe that there were educated and learned people in our town who had a strong desire that their children should also study and learn [the language]. For this reason, there was a school where Hebrew was taught and spoken fluently. And there was a kindergarten, which I together with Miriam and Alice supervised; certainly, many still remember that period and its experiences. There were drama clubs and choirs. And Zionist quorums (minyanim) during Simchat Torah. I have a memory of my mother, of blessed memory, preparing treats and baked goods that the Zionist activists could enjoy after prayer.

On the eves of Rosh Hashanah and Yom Kippur, the time when all the friends and relatives greet one another with "A Good Year" (Shanah Tova) and "May you be inscribed well" (gemar hatimah tovah). And [the prayer at the start of Yom Kippur] (Kol Nidrei) ("All Vows") and [the festival] Simchat Torah, a time for getting drunk and dancing, and grabbing from the Sukkot anything that is there ... the days of Hanukkah, a time when we go from house to house and count the windows, pasting Hanukkah stickers, and [collecting] money for Keren Kayemeth LeYisrael (the Jewish National Fund). On every window a lit candle and we acknowledged the Festival of Lights. On Tu BiShvat with small bags of fruit from the Land [of Israel]: carobs, figs, and raisins — donations went to Keren Kayemeth LeYisrael. And the holiday of Purim with costumes. And Lag B'Omer ...

How did they bake matzah in the communities? — Until Father went up on a trip to Dubno, and brought back a matzah machine, and everything changed ... people would come to sign up, like in an employment office ... they worked [making matzah] in shifts, because matza was ordered from us for the whole area.

* * *

Recruits[4] during the period of self-denial would eat [in Yiddish:] flat bread with poppy seed, [then in Hebrew:] (dry cakes with poppy seed) and sometimes caused various defects and deformities, all in order to avoid serving "the Government" ("the pony"[5]).

[Page 265]

The unique characters. Avrahamke, the teacher.[6] He was a righteous man (tzadik). And Futi, the unfortunate one, who cleaned houses and talked and cried about her only son who remained in Russia. The water drawers and wood cutters. Herschel Datina,[7] as he was called by the residents of the town. And many other good Jews, who appear as if living before my eyes.

My uncles and aunts from village Peremylivka[8], who came periodically to town during the month of Elul[9] with a wagon weighed down with goodies, fruit of the vine and fields, to distribute to the poor. And this they did also in the [spring] month of Nisan, on the eve of Passover.

* * *

And you, Rivka and Tzvi,[10] my dear ones ... it never occurred to me that only I would remain from our quadruplets, as we called ourselves. Were we not so connected during our lives, never believing it possible we'd be torn apart in so cruel a fashion. And it happens, that at night I can't sleep a wink, and I see you in your joys and sorrows, and your aspirations to make aliyah to the Land [of Israel] which is what we all wanted.

Bat-Sheva Ben Eliyahu (Ribetz) by the grave of her father

Translator's and editor's footnotes:

1.   Bat Sheva Ben Eliyahu (née Riwic, alternative spellings Ribitz/Rivitz/Rivetz) (?-1998) was born in Mlynov, the daughter of Nute Rivitz. Her mother Chana (née Braker / Beraker) was born in Klevan to Yehiel and Sara. A photo of Bat Sheva with her family appears below, p. 470, and a photo of her cousin, Pesia Rivitz, appears on page 462. From Yad Vashem records, Bat Sheva's father, Nute, appears to have been the son of Yaakov and Sheva Rivitz and had at least one brother, Abram, who was married to Rivka (Klaper) with three children who also perished. In this essay, Bat Sheva indicates that she made aliyah in July 1939 shortly before WWII broke out. Her parents and sister Freidl (also Fania) (1921–1940) are listed among the Mlynov martyrs (p. 438), though her father died before the War; her sister Fania was taken by the Germans before the ghetto liquidation. Yad Vashem records indicate her brother Mordechai Rivitz (1906–1942) married Dvora (Kupferman) and had three children, all of whom perished in Beresteczko. A second brother, Yitzchak (1908–1942), his wife Batia (née Gonik) and two children, Ronia, age 5 and Nute, age 3, also perished. Bat-Sheva Ben-Eliyahu married Efraim Ben-Eliyahu in 1949 in Israel and it appears from records she ran for the Histadrut in 1959. She was buried in Beer Sheva. It seems plausible that the street in Beer Sheva called "Bat-Sheva Ben-Eliyahu" may have been named for her.

It also seems possible that as a "Riwic/Rivetz" descendant, Bat Sheva may be a relative of survivor Shaulik (Saul) Halperin, also a contributor to this volume, whose mother was remembered as Cipa Rywiec (another English variation on Rivitz). This Rivitz family may also be related to the two Rivitz siblings who were early immigrants from Mlynov to Baltimore. They were the children of Mordechai Rivitz. His daughter, Chaia

(Rivitz), married Getzel Fax and they were the first family from Mlynov to migrate to Baltimore and the US. Chaia's brother, David Rivitz, married Pesse (Demb) from Mlynov and migrated to Baltimore where they settled and became the Hurwitz family. See the Mlynov website for additional background on Rivitz/Hurwitz line in Baltimore.

2.   A possible allusion to Job 27:3–4 in which Job says, "As long as there is life in me, And God's breath is in my nostrils, My lips will speak no wrong, Nor my tongue utter deceit."

3.   Following the implied modern understanding in which Avodah means "worship" and not the more technical meaning of Temple ritual.

4.   Young men who came of age for the military. On this same topic, see more details in Aaron Harari's essay, "The Military Recruits," 186–187.

5.   A Hebrew term analogous to the English expression "serving Uncle Sam."

6.   In the martyr list (p. 434) Avrahamke is listed with the surname Veiner, is described as a bachelor and Stolin Hasid. His photo appears on page 258.

7.   A photo of Herschel Datina carrying water is on page 79.

8.   20 km (12 mi) east and slightly north of Mlynov today.

9.   The sixth month of the Hebrew Calendar and the month traditionally for searching one's heart and drawing close to God in preparing for the sacred days of Rosh Hashanah, and Yom Kippur.

10.   It appears that Bat-Sheva is here speaking to her friends in the Zionist youth movement.

[Page 266]

Visiting My Grandparents

by Sylvia Barditch-Goldberg[1]

Translated from the Yiddish by Hannah B. Fischthal, PhD

Edited by Howard I. Schwartz, PhD

I was always attracted to the small shtetl where nature's beauty was serenely spread over the lawns, gardens, and orchards; I wanted to be away from the crowded city streets of my hometown Lutsk.

I was thrilled when my mother's parents from Mlynov, with their wagon driver Itsik Ulinik, sent a note to my mother, asking her to be sure to send her children to them for summer vacation.

"As the air is clean, fresh, delightful, the children will also blossom after languishing in the house all winter. They will certainly enjoy drinking milk right from the cow; eating fresh sour cream, cheese, and butter; they can even churn butter. They can stay for as long as they want, if they don't get homesick and want to return."

The question was — which of the children to send? My older brother Alter attended the city school, so he could not go.[2] My younger sister Sorele[3] would get homesick. The smaller two brothers, Benyomin and Mayerke, were too young to leave their mother. My mother could not afford the pleasure of coming too. My father was in America,[4] so she needed to be in the store. So whom, you ask, does she send? Yes, you guessed it; I was fated to go.

At the time arranged with Itsik Ulinik, I came to the place where passengers were boarding the wagon. They were merchants from Mlynov. I looked around, and I saw the familiar, long wagon bedded with a lot of straw. Two giant horses were harnessed to it. A thought ran through my head that they would take me to a distant, pretty world; I was enveloped in a feeling of delight. When I sat with everyone in the straw in the wagon, and Itsik Ulinik gave a snap with his horsetail whip and sang "Viyo, viyo, viyo," it was melodious music to my ears. I closed my eyes, and my childish imagination took me far away over the dusty roads.

[Page 267]

Everything in me sang happily.

Having ridden about 12 versts,[5] we stopped in the village of Kripe.[6] The driver unharnessed the horses, fed them oats from a linen bag, and brought them water from the well in a linen pail. We passengers happily came out of the wagon, straightened out our legs which were stiff from sitting, and went into the inn for goat's milk.

Everyone sat around a wooden, uncovered table, on narrow seats by the wall. The innkeeper's wife came out with disheveled hair, with an unbuttoned, dirty dress, and barefoot. She turned to us good-naturedly with an embarrassed smile.

"What should I give you, goat's milk or cow's milk?"

Tending Goats[7]
From the photos of A. Harari

Everyone ordered goat's milk for a change. Her husband the innkeeper came in right after her wearing linen pants and a worn shirt. He greeted the men with "Sholem" and the women with a hello. He asked about city things and was surprised by every answer, as though it would have come from a distant world.

Finally, we all went back to the wagon. As soon as it started to move, I closed my eyes, and my thoughts carried me far away. I saw myself in various places with various people. My young heart was happy.

[Page 268]

A few hours later, we arrived in the shtetl of Mlynov. The wagon stopped in the middle of the marketplace. Everyone, dusty, climbed out of the wagon and left. Some went home and some went to a store. Holding my bundle, I headed towards my grandparents' home. A small Jewish woman came over to me; she had a wide basket in one hand and a long knotty stick in her other hand. She was a trader.

Smiling, she threw everything down and grabbed me and kissed me and asked about everybody at home.

She commanded me, "Stand here. Don't move! I will run and announce to Male [Malia], your grandmother, that you are here, and I will have performed a good deed."

As soon as she left, I was surrounded by the market people. Yente Brayndl's,[8] my mother's friend, came out of her food store. She was a redhead with a pleasant, laughing face; she spoke heartily, dragging out everyone's name like her children's: Malyenyu, Idele, Itsikl, Berele, Elkele, Milkele.[9] She turned to me, hugged, and kissed me.

"Silkele, how are your mother and Alterl and the other children?"

And then came good-natured, lovable Yose Brayndl's, her husband, a tall and thin man, who almost always wore a small shawl around his neck. He hugged me, tenderly stroked me, and begged me to come and play with his children. Most of his time he devoted to his children.

And here is the wide Mayer Yankekhe, near me, who almost got up from the step. She could not sit on a chair outside.

She asked about everybody, and she called out to her girls Toybe, Nekhe, and Sime: "See who we have here!"

Her unlucky daughter Patye, who wheezed and was practically impossible to understand, was also there. I felt such pity for her. I wanted to answer her, but I didn't know what she was asking. The other sisters just wanted to know when my brother Alter will come. And here is Henia Arele's,[10] another of my mother's friends. She hugged me and kissed me.

"How is your mother?" she asked.

And here is Soreke with Gitel-Pese Khlie's [daughter].[11] More kissing, again the same questions.

I saw my grandmother. A pretty woman with a white scarf on her head. A little shawl over her shoulders. A sweet little smile on her pretty, white face. When she came closer and saw the large crowd, the smile disappeared, and she screamed out with fright:

"Where is my child? What happened?"

I pushed through the large crowd, and I gave her a hug.

[Page 269]

She held me close with love, and said, frightened, "Come already, babbler."

She took my bundle from me, and we went to the house. Coming in, my grandfather was walking back and forth over the large dining room. He was a tall Jew with a long, red beard, which was divided into two parts.[12] His appearance demanded respect from everyone. He was dressed in a long *kapote* with a belt holding it closed; a hat with a visor; tall boots. He was a true genius. He was known in the shtetl for his learning. He led the prayers for the Stolin Hasidism in their synagogue.

In addition to that, he was the town starosta,[13] and also the official shtetl scribe. He was very strict with his children. I was a little frightened of him.

But how surprised I was, when he, with his arms outstretched, came closer to me, gave me his hand, and smilingly asked me:

"How are you, Tsutsik?"

He used to call his grandchildren Tsutsik, Putsik, Nyutsik. Not by their names. He asked about my mother, the children, if I am learning, where I am in my studies, and if I obey my mother.

My grandmother mixed in: "Come, Silkele, wash up, then you will eat something."

She led me into the kitchen; on a large oak shelf, in a corner, hung a snow-white linen bag with three points — that was fresh cheese for me, the guest.

"This," said my grandmother, "is for you."

After eating I was taken to a basement room where a ditch had been dug out. There they placed earthen jars with milk, which became sour cream and sour milk. From the cream my grandmother said she would let me churn butter if I would be a good little girl and not ask to go home. When I heard "churn butter," I promised her everything.

Late afternoon the shepherd drove the cows home from pasture. I was shown a red cow with a large udder.

"That," said my grandmother, "is our cow."

Remarkably, she went away from the herd and straight to the stable. I could not believe it: a cow, I used to think, had no intelligence.

[Page 270]

A bucket of bran is mixed. My grandmother took a small stool and a large pail and told me to take a glass. Together we went into the stable. The cow was already standing bent over the bucket of feed, as though nothing affected her …

My grandmother went energetically to work. She milked and milked. The pail kept getting fuller. I was surprised, and I could not understand what was going on around me.

Suddenly I heard my grandmother's voice: "Silkele, take the glass. Put it under right here. Milk her like this."

With a beating heart, I went over closer, as though I were afraid the cow would not recognize me. When I touched the cow, it turned out she recognized me and immediately greeted me with her tail. It got dark in front of my eyes; out of fright, I jumped backwards.

My grandmother, a quiet person, said: "Manka, stand!"

Amazingly, the cow stood and looked guilty, her head down, and let me do my work. A thought went through me that the beast understood and was not a beast.

The next morning, my mother's younger brother Benimke,[14] who was the same age as my older brother, but who treated me a lot better, showed me around the small garden: "Here will be red radishes; here – white radishes; here – beans; here will grow shallots; here, young onions."

The orchard consisted of two flower gardens and one thin little tree. In the middle was a scarecrow. That was a stick, dressed in torn men's clothes and a cap, so that the birds would be afraid to come and eat the miserable little garden. In the flower garden on the left, the thin little tree was standing orphaned with a bent rose on it. It seemed to me that it was embarrassed in front of the rose bushes standing opposite, in the priest's large orchard, where the fragrances of the flowers, the fruit trees, and jasmine aromas wafted over the entire shtetl.

How happy I felt, when Benimke gave me millet in the fold of my dress, and said to me, "Here, you feed the hen with the chicks, and the goose with the goslings, and the turkeys."

[Page 271]

I threw the bran and called "Tyu-tyu." The chicken and geese ate; that gave me a strange pleasure. I was especially proud when I was given the wooden butter churn. I raised and lowered the stick and saw how pieces of butter formed; little by little they became one large piece. It was put into cold water, and we had butter.

"Akh," I thought to myself, "If my city friends would see me now! I would show them how important I am!"

Benimke thought about various things that would bring me pleasure. He took me to Khaye-Malke (a widow), who maintained a small store that consisted of one cylinder of soda-water, several little pieces of candy, a few cooked peas, and rotten, small cherries. I was thinking.

Benimke said, "Khaye-Malke, this is my sister Basye's little girl. Give her whatever her heart desires. Every day she can come and take as much as she wants. I will pay for it."

In my head I compared her to our Brayndl, the fruit-seller in Lutsk. She had a smaller store. But she had whatever a mouth could pronounce and whatever a child's heart desired. She had large cherries, small cherries, red cherries, and black cherries, grapes, raspberries, many large and small berries, green apples, red apples, kvass apples with all flavors, broad beans, cooked peas, strawberries, cooked cabbage, old after the season. Now the candies: colored chocolates with gold and silver, and candies grouped according to various prices, as much as one could afford. And if one did not have the money at the time, Brayndl talked her into borrowing.

So I stood and looked and did not know what to pick, while Khaye-Malke begged me: "Silkele take, take."

So I finally settled on soda-water. I was happy with all the attention that was given me.

Translator's and editor's footnotes:

1. Sylvia was one of the editors of this Memorial volume. For her background, see her essay about her grandfather, "Stoliner Hasidism in Mlynov," note 3, as well as her essay about her visit for, "A Wedding in Mlynov," pp. 27–29. Photos of Sylvia appears on pages 494 and 500 of this volume. – HS
2. Referring to her older brother known later as Paul (Peretz Borodacz) Barditch (1895–1961). – HS

3. Referring to Shirley (Borodacz / Barditch) Jacobs (1905-1983). – HS

4. Sylvia's father "Jechiel Borudocz" (Isadore Barditch) immigrated to Baltimore in July 1910. The rest of the family followed in November 1921. – HS

5. About 8 miles, – HBF

6. Probably Krupa today, 11 km from Lutsk on the road to Mlynov. – HS

7. It is interesting to note that Aaron Harari took these photos of goats in the winter of 1937/1938. By this time, he had begun breeding sheep in Palestine. When he went back to Mlynov, he pretended the purpose of the trip was to study breeding techniques. In fact, his actual purpose was to fictitiously marry a sister of a fellow Kibbutz member and enable her to make aliyah. See Aaron's narrative in "Visit to Mlynov in 1938," pp. 77–79. – HS

8. Yentl Braindl (Weiner) Shargel (1872–1956) married Joseph Shargel (1870–1954). Some of the children migrated to the US followed by their parents and several came later via Mexico in order to avoid quotas. Yentl Braindl's uncle was the famous Solomon Mandelkern, who developed the concordance to the Hebrew Bible, pp. 484-487. More on the Shargel family on the Mlynov website. – HS

9. The Shargel children are Malyenyu (Mollie Shargel Feingold), Idele (Earl Shargel), Itsikl (Julius Shargel), Berele (Bernard Shargel), Elkele (Elka Shargel Yakobovitz), Milkele (Amelia Shargel Meren, future wife of Boruch Meren). Yentl Braindl and Joseph's photo appears in this volume, p. 507. – HS

10. Also referred to as Henya Arelas (and Ahrelas), (Annie Hirsch) Katz the mother of Aleph Katz. Her photo appears on p. 500 of this volume with the mother of Sylvia, the author of this essay. On Henya's background, see the Hirsch family story on the Mlynov website. – HS

11. Likely Sorke Gelberg (Sarah Lewbel) (1906–1987) daughter of Gitel (Weitzer) (1880–1939), wife of Moshe Gelberg (Morris Goldberg). The latter is called Gitl, Pesye Khoylye's [daughter] in a photo on page 507 and in an essay by Moshe's daughter, Helen Lederer, "In Pain from the First World War," p. 147. Sylvia, by the way later married Morris's younger brother, George Goldberg (Gershon Joe Gelberg). – HS

12. See the photo and essay by Sylvia about her grandfather on p. 80. – HS

13. A lower government official in Ukraine. – HBF

14. We know that Sylvia's mother had a brother Usher (later Harry Teitelbaum) who migrated to Baltimore in March 1911 along with the two other Mlynov men, Israel Schwartz, and Nathan (Chaim) Fischman. It is unclear here whether she is referring to him or another brother. – HS

[Page 272]

The Treasure That Ran Out

by Boruch Meren, Baltimore

Translated from the Yiddish by Hannah B. Fischthal, PhD

Edited by Howard I. Schwartz, PhD

What I want to tell here brings both tears and laughter, but mostly tears.

It happened to my father,[1] may he rest in peace, in my former shtetele Mlynov near the city of Dubno, neighborhood of Volhynia, right after the First World War.

Poland had just become an independent country. The country was poor. Artisans had no work. Farmers first started to cultivate the fields. The stores in the marketplace were empty, and Jews searched for ways to make a living but did not find them. The few bits of merchandise that were still found in the marketplace were passed from hand to hand, and by the time the little bit of food reached the customers, the price was sky high.

Only a few people could come near it. Is it a wonder that one had to go a little hungry? It was lucky that the blessed Ukrainian earth gave an abundance of potatoes. Potatoes always helped the needy poor. In the summer, during the season of cherries, grapes, and other assorted fruits, life became a little easier. Summertime, mothers would say they only have half their troubles. They could fill a mouth of a child with a handful of cherries and crust of bread, which was enough to quiet the child's hunger. And who could complain if one had a little garden behind the house? Or a cow that gave milk? We sold a little and left a little for ourselves, so it was almost a half income. We had to do a little trading — which in those abnormal times was called smuggling. Jews used to do it secretly since trading was not kosher in the eyes of the government. Because of the struggle for necessary products, a black market developed with all its characteristics. Police searched, caught, and put merchants into prison. It did not prevent further trading.

[Page 273]

Jews risked their lives and fortunes. After all, they had to support wives and children.

*

And now I come to the episode that happened to my father when he was persuaded to become a "speculator."

My father, may he rest in peace, Bentsye – Hirsh Sloboda's[2] that's how he was called — was a refined Jew who was an expert in the holy books. He was a prayer leader, he read the Torah for the synagogue, and he prayed with the last minyan of respectable Jews. Yet out of all this there was no income. The earthly world, my father would say, is only a corridor where the Jew needs to prepare good deeds, the more the better, for the true world. With such an approach to life, one could not feed a wife and children.

One time my mother, may she rest in peace, said to my father (both were killed by the Hitlerite murderers):

"Bentsye dear, what will be the end? You need to find an occupation! Go also out in the market, give a sniff! See what others are doing. We cannot just let the children starve. Sitting late in synagogue and studying does not bring bread into the house."

So my father saw that my mother was right. He went out to the marketplace to find out with what he could trade. There he learned that Jews risk their lives by traveling to Rivne. That was a town about 40 miles away from our shtetl. There one could buy secretly a gallon of kerosene or a sack of sugar, which was in those times practically a treasure. Getting the merchandise was dangerous. Robbers used to befall the wagons and take everything, and often also murder. And if the police caught them, it was lucky if they took them to a designated area. If the merchants managed to return home from such a journey, they recited the blessings for escaping danger.

With a heavy heart and with much fear, my father became a "speculator." He rented a wagon driver with two healthy horses, so that in an unlucky time they would be able to go back. The driver himself was young and strong, so he could deliver blows if needed. But my father did not rely on them completely.

[Page 274]

He relied on the Lord of the universe. He, the Guardian of Israel, will protect him from harm and bring him peacefully back home to his wife and children.

He made up with the wagon driver that they would depart in the evening, between the Mincha [afternoon] and Maariv [evening] prayer services, and drive the entire night. My mother, with a heavy mood and eyes wet from tears, put a loaf of bread, and something to go with the bread, into a bag. Mainly she did not forget to put in his tallis and tefillin.

Meanwhile her lips murmured: "Lord of the universe! Have pity on us and bring my husband back home in peace. He is, after all, a father of children. And I pledge a pound of candles for the synagogue."

I was then a young man of 16 and understood the situation well.[3] I pitied my mother very much, and I told her I will recite psalms every day, and I will heartily pray to God for my father. The younger children promised her also that they will not annoy her by begging all the time for food.

As soon as it got dark, the wagon driver came noisily with a long wagon, bedded with straw. He stopped across from our house. He climbed out of the wagon and with his whip in his hand, angrily came into our house: "Nu, there is no end! Finish already! Finish the evening prayers! Get to *Aleinu*![4] You could have *shoklt*[5] less today!

"It would be more appropriate for him to be a teacher instead of a merchant," the wagon driver further complained.

My father had actually lost himself in prayers a little, and he quickly said the *Aleinu*. He put on his thick coat and kissed us all, except for my mother. He was certainly embarrassed, or afraid to kiss my mother in the presence of the wagon driver with his whip in his hand.

"Be well! And children, in the name of God, I beg you, be good to your mother. You should not torture her about food. When I will come home in peace, there will be what to eat. Recite the *Shema*[6] before you go to sleep!"

And he told me to pray every day in the synagogue with the minyan and say a few verses of psalms every day. He gave the mezuza a kiss and went out of the house and into the wagon.

[Page 275]

The driver snapped his whip and ordered the horses: "Vyo!" The horses quickly ran with the wagon. We screamed out after them:

"Go in good health and come in good health!"

My mother and I remained standing on the threshold of the house and watched the wagon until it disappeared in the dark. My mother cried and wiped her eyes with her apron.

After eating our meagre supper, we children read the *Shema* with devotion and went to sleep. The entire night I did not close an eye. I looked out of the window in the sad, dark night and thought: we are sleeping in a house, in a warm bed, and my father is driving now through fields and forests. I strongly pitied him. It must be hard to be a father, I thought.

The three days that my father travelled were like three years to us. God helped, and my father came home in peace and brought back a barrel of kerosene. That, in those times, was a "treasure," and a treasure needs to be buried, hidden. We did that. We dug out a ditch near the stable and we dropped the barrel with kerosene in it. We covered it with boards and straw and animal dirt. It looked like a mountain of garbage. Nobody could have imagined that under that mountain of dirt a treasure was buried.

Our hearts were lighter after that task. Now we had to wait for the barrel to "grow" in value. For two weeks, we looked out of the window with joy, knowing what the secret mountain of garbage meant to us. My father went out to the marketplace every day and found out what the price was for the kerosene. Every day the price climbed higher. When my father saw that he could make enough profit, he was afraid to wait longer. So, he went to the marketplace and sold the barrel of kerosene to a man who also had the idea to risk everything, and then hide the barrel until it would grow more valuable.

[Page 276]

Now came the time to dig up the buried treasure. That also had to be done quietly. Nobody should hear and nobody should see. Late at night, when everything was sleeping and nobody moved, but the stars in the dark sky looked down, my father's two brothers-in-law helped with the work. These youths were needed for this task. My mother and I looked out through the window with beating hearts and shivered with fright. We saw the barrel of kerosene being lifted out of the ditch. Soon my father will get paid a large sum of money and we will be able to buy everything.

But our celebration ended. My father came into the house, and with a crying voice, told us that a tragedy happened — the entire barrel spilled out into the moist ditch. After so much fear and anxiety, everything ran out, including everyone's hopes. We all cried at the huge misfortune.

After this blow, my father tried his luck with other merchandise, but nothing worked. If it didn't run out, the price fell. One day, after all these lucky events, my father called to my mother and said to her:

"My dear Miryam, you should be informed that this kind of 'trading' where we tried to make some money is not the right way. You have a sign that the Creator punished us, and we lost money. Therefore, I have decided to trade in a kosher way and with merchandise which has no equal, merchandise that does not run out. And its price will never fall. I will sell learning because learning is the best merchandise!"

"And what do you think, my husband," my mother said to him, "you will have an income from it?"

"You talk like a silly Jewish woman. Income is from the Creator. He nourishes everyone. He will nourish us also."

And so my father went from speculator to teacher.

Translator's and editor's footnotes:

1. Boruch's father was Ben-Tzion Meren. For background on Boruch, see footnote 1 in his essay, "Episode," pp. 149–152. See Boruch's poem for his father, p. 255. – HS
2. As noted in other essays in this volume, Sloboda was a nickname for the Goldseker family, who came to Mlynov from Slobada. Here the nickname is used for Hirsh (Goldseker) Sloboda, Boruch's grandfather, who was the father of Boruch's mother, Miriam. It appears from this essay that Boruch's father, who was a Meren, was also distinguished by the "Slobada" nickname of his father-in-law, as if to say "Ben-Tzion, Hirsh Sloboda's [son-in-law]." – HS
3. Boruch was born in 1908. Since he was sixteen when this incident happened, it was probably 1924. – HS
4. The last prayer in the service. – HBF
5. Shook. Observant Jews shake or sway back and forth when they pray – HBF
6. The prayer that begins with "Hear O Israel." – HBF

[Page 277]

Chana Klepatch[1] – A Mlynov Tragedy

by Reuven Raberman[2]

Translated and edited by Howard I. Schwartz, PhD with Hanina Epstein

In the Mlynov tragedy, a link in the long chain would be missing, if the cry of the Klepatch family is not heard and that of their wonderful daughter — Chana.

The house — was one of those ones in which poverty and cold lie in wait under the beds and follow the movement of the babies who crawl on the cold floor and look for a piece of bread ... Chana, the eldest daughter, and second in line after [her brother] Motel, would implore her parents to cease for a while the "natural production" [i.e., having more children], but without success ... the father, a thin, tall man, was sick most of his life with different illnesses, while the mother had noble facial features and a nice figure — and this despite the special situation that visited her so often — taking care of so many babies.

The Daughter Chana

From the very beginning of her youth, the young girl experienced stormy life episodes, full of fury, in which were folded a family and personal tragedy unique in its kind. The surrounding villages, Smordva and Ostriiv,[3] the places where the father and mother came from, which were characterized by a tie to the land, to nature, and to darkness of night [i.e., no lights at night], bequeathed to her the wonderful mixture of ingenuity, personal initiative, a strong will with a full self-confidence.

Chana Klepatch, of blessed memory

[Page 278]

Many hopes hung on this whiz kid of Mlynov. How nice and refined was this young girl, with a peaceful disposition, smiling eyes, eyes that were never dull ... she reminded us of the good in our youth, she completely evoked amazement, aspiration, and confidence. While she was still in grade 3, they said that she was born for great things, a mind of a professor, with an analytical mind from birth, among the geniuses whom our parents thoroughly revere. Very quickly everyone recognized her sharp intelligence, her wit and rich imagination and all were amazed by her refreshing use of the Polish language and her store of folk sayings. She especially excelled in her appearances on the podium in public school. She was gifted by the theatrical muse and revealed a strong initiative in this area. In her lithe and flexible movements, she enchanted her listening audience and above all other amazing things, she impersonated the Polish insurrectionist heroine and emphasized the final verse in song, as if the following words were engraved on the tablet of her heart: "This is the insurrectionist leader – Emilia Plater!"[4]

During the Soviet Period [September 1939-June 1941]

The Klepatch family didn't secure the promised position among the families of the Soviet people [as promised in the Revolution]. The family preferred poverty, which had been its fate over the years, and it wasn't taken in by the delusion of Stalin's accomplishments. Their situation did not improve at all and with everyone they were strangled by the oppressive atmosphere of tyranny and insanity of "the Father of Nations."[5] Fate was very cruel to them in the year before the Nazi conquest, a time when the father of the family died, while the eldest son, Motel, was an accidental victim of an assassination attempt intended for a Russian officer and the same bullet that missed its target, killed [Motel] the guardian of the large family, who was serving as a coachman for a senior officer.

The army of the Nazi Ashmedai [prince of the demons][6] infused her with rage, contempt, and deep hatred for all the new humanistic concepts. Springtime feelings that characterized her over the years were transformed suddenly by a bellicose spirit, a vigorous and rebellious resistance, and extraordinary daring. She despised the silence born out of fear [of other members of the community] and didn't leave the Judenrat alone who, in her view, didn't act appropriately given the demands of the hour. Her large, penetrating, and sad eyes expressed sorrow, heart break, and the height of depression arrived about two months before the ghetto liquidation.

In the beginning with no choice, she took upon herself the difficult role as mother to the many children ... and when she was convinced that the "play" was coming to an end, being a very unusual master of intuition, she decided to suddenly throw off the heavy burden and to give daring expression to the manifestations of freedom, which beat inside of her and lit the fire of rebellion.

The Last Meeting

I will never forget our last meeting. At the conclusion of forced labor in Studyanka,[7] which was at the foot of the Kremenets mountains, I detoured into Mlynov to warn Chana, so that she should join us in the forest.

[Page 279]

"Yes," she said, "I heard much about your activities; the forest tugs at my heart, but how can I leave Mother and small children without supervision and a livelihood, especially when my father and my older brother are no longer living? — my forlorn mother will surely die from all her sorrow!" At first, I tried to convince her and point out the how matters would progress. I sensed the beat of her young and sensitive heart; her face paled like lime and tears glittered in her eyes. With difficulty she resisted the significant temptation and choked back the terrible pain that had accumulated during all the days of suffering. She stood standing upright, tears falling down her cheeks, she almost did not dare to lift her eyes towards me, fearing that she would burst forth in loud sobbing.

For a long moment we stood hugging this way, until finally she gathered strength, leaned against me and whispered in my ears, "We are seeing each other for the last time, my heart understands the evil, you go, my dear one, and may God be with your footsteps; I don't have the strength to abandon the little ones, nor is it simple to leave an unfortunate mother, but perhaps, perhaps at the last moment I will succeed in escaping." She was still standing petrified, when I waved to her with my hat and for a long time she looked at the abundant and promising forest towards which I was heading.

From the lips of Mlynov survivors, who met her in the last moments, I learned that, at the moment when the Ukrainian militia surrounded the ghetto, Chana tried her luck at escaping, but was caught in the barbed wire when the bullets of the murderers punctured her young heart.

May her memory be a blessing.

Shoshana (Reisel) Berger[8] on a River Ikva bridge

Translator's and editor's footnotes:

1.   Chana Klepatch (alternative spellings Klepacz) was one of seven children of Moshe Klepatch (1900–~1939/40) and Sara/Sorka (née Kaliner / also spelled Karliner) (1901–1942). Chana's father, Moshe, was a wagoner who was born in Smordva, the son of Yitzhak Leib Klepatch and Chana Yenta. Moshe's sister, Jessie (Chissa) Klepatch married Joseph Schuchman and joined him in Baltimore in 1921 with her four children. According to Joyce Jandorf, granddaughter of Jessie Klepatch, the youngest child of the Klepatch family in Mlynov, named Yisrael, was a hidden child with blond hair and blue eyes, who was later rescued after the war and later settled in Israel.

Chana Klepatch's mother, Sara/Sorka Kaliner is listed in Yad Vashem records as the daughter of Nakhman and Tzipora Kaliner from what is probably the village, Ostriiv, which was only 10 km from Mlynov and also close to Smordva, where her father was from. Sara Kaliner was a relative, and perhaps first cousin, of Toba Kaliner from Ostriiv, who married Moshe Holtzeker and whose son, Yaakov Holtzeker, contributed "My Hometown Mlynov," 226–228, to this volume and submitted some of the Yad Vashem records for the Klepatch family. Toba was the daughter of Reuven and Nehama Kaliner. Toba's sister, Machla (Kaliner/also spelled Kline in some records) married Avraham Gelman from Mlynov.

2.   Reuven Raberman was born in 1922 in Trovits (Targowica), Poland and was a survivor. His parents Barukh and Vitia (Kleiner) and a brother Mekhael (1914) perished. Reuven was a significant contributor to the Targovica Memorial book.

3.   The Hebrew is probably referring to Ostriiv, a village just 10 km west of Mlynov. Ostriiv is also mentioned as a village passed on the way to Trovits by Shmuel Mandelkern in "Yaakov-Yosi Goes to Israel," p. 210.

4.   Countess Emilia Plater (1806–1831), "the Lithuanian Joan of Arc," was a Polish Lithuanian noblewoman and revolutionary in the 1830 uprising against the Russia Empire. Her story inspired a number of works of art and literature.

5.   A term used by the Soviet propaganda to refer to Stalin.

6.   The mythic king of demons in Jewish demonology.

7.   Studyanka is 50 km (31 mi) south of Mlynov today and is on the way to the town of Kremenets which is 63 km south. Asher Teitelman in his story of survival recalls being taken to forced labor at Studyanka and his father Nahum Teitelman recalls this occurring in the winter of 1941 (pp. 40 and 321).

8.   Rosa Berger (1910–2004) was sister of contributor Aaron Harari. In Mlynov, her boyfriend was Boruch Meren, another contributor to this volume, and she helped Boruch get a certificate to make aliyah in 1937. Later in Mandate Palestine, she married Mlynov-born, Moshe Chizik (1909–1959). See the Berger family story on the Mlynov website.

[Page 280]

A Mlynover Page

The children of the Rav Gordon[1], of blessed memory
From left to right: Hershel, Moshe, Toybeshe

Eidel Liberman,[2] of blessed memory, in front of Rubinska Street

Translator's and editor's footnotes:

1.   Rav Gordon was rabbi in Mlynov, though politics prevented him from being elected rabbi of the Mlynov kehilla which included other towns, pp. 20. An account of Rav Gordon's death early in the Nazi occupation appears in several places in this volume (pp. 314, 352, 384). His daughter, Toybeshe, hid and survived and returned to Mlynov after the liberation (see p. 22). She eventually married and migrated to the United States. His two sons who survived were students in a yeshiva in Poland and with the Russian invasion in 1939 were evacuated to Japan and from there came to America.

2.   Eidel (alterative spelling Yidel or Idl) Liberman, son of Mordechai Liberman and Bracha (Gruber). Bracha was the daughter of Mordechai and Perel Gruber. Eidel's family perished including his siblings: Asher, Rivka, Miriam and Chaya. The fate of Yidel Liberman is mentioned in the essay by Yehudit (Mandelkern) Rudolf, p. 88, indicating he was accidentally swept up in a raid targeting 10–15 individuals suspected of being active in Polish political parties four to six weeks after the German occupation in June 1941. There are two other photos of "Y. Liberman," first name spelled with a yod, who may be the same person among a group of younger boys on pages 227 and 461.

[Page 281]

<u>Destruction and Annihilation</u>

[Page 283]

The Mlynov Community
at the Beginning of the Soviet Occupation

(September 17, 1939 – June 22, 1941).

Yosef Litvak,[1] Jerusalem

Translated and edited by Howard I. Schwartz, PhD with Hanina Epstein

The New Administration

On the first of February 1940, the military government in our area was replaced by a civil government. This was after a "referendum,"[2] which was held in the areas which had been annexed to the Soviet Union following the division of Poland between the Soviet Union and Germany. During that same referendum upwards of 99% of all the people eligible voted as usual in favor of the annexation.

All the important positions in the new civil administration, even in a small place like our small town, were offered to clerks who were imported especially from Ukraine, from the other side of the old boundary (the boundary between Poland and Russia before September 1, 1939).[3] Only the less desirable, essentially technical roles, were given to local clerks. In the [Communist] Party's local civil office, local men were not able to gain any kind of toehold.

Although theoretically one should not judge the policies of the regime based on what was done in a small town like Mlynov, it seems to me that anyone who happened to know the Soviet regime intimately will agree, because it is hard to believe that, in the installation of administration in the areas annexed to Russia, there was a room for accidental and atypical results, or that the matter was not carried out in alignment with the explicit policy and the clear and detailed guidance from the Center. Thus, in my opinion, one can also infer from the manifestation of policies and instructions which I witnessed in Mlynov, that they [those in the regime] were behind them.

The military government established only one other local entity: the village council (Mlynov had the status of a village). This council was in large measure a fictitious body for propaganda purposes only, and, also, in this area the council served as an implementation arm for the local military commander. The council ensured the full participation of all the town's inhabitants in the "referendum" on annexation. This village council was composed of a handful of local Jewish Communist members who were joined by one Ukrainian, a worker in the local flour mill, an ignoramus and boor, who never belonged to any political party and had no interest in politics.

When the military regime was changed to a civil government, apparently new orders were handed down from on high regarding the composition of the local government and selection of local men for the service of the State. A new village council was chosen and at its head stood the Ukrainian member mentioned earlier.

[Page 284]

The Jewish communists were all removed [from the council] on the pretext that they had been Zionists in the past. Moreover, they were disqualified from serving not only as representatives of the population but also in any government position whatsoever. (In other words, the new government completely overlooked the fact that already, during the last years before the Soviet conquest, these young people had ceased to be Zionists and had instead become Communist members, even suffering jail time for supporting Communism). It is possible, too, that another consideration being weighed was [the fact] that before the Soviet conquest there was not a Communist party in Poland recognized by Moscow, because it had dissolved earlier under the allegation that its ranks had been infiltrated by many provocateurs and, in fact, all earlier communists were suspected provocateurs, all the more so the young people mentioned earlier who had in truth once been Zionists and had family pedigrees that were not proletariat.[4]

To the new village council were appointed (i.e., "chosen unanimously"[5] at the suggestion of the government representative), 12 men, among whom was only one representative of the Jewish population, even though Jews comprised 50% of the population. The single Jewish representative was a Jewish woman — Dina Holtzeker[6] — who was chosen for the role, apparently because she had not been political in the past and because she had been formerly imprisoned, though her "stay" had been for criminal activity and not for Communism: She had grabbed a bank note [or bills] from the hands of a man — a Christian Czech – who had lent her money and she threw it into a stove right in front of him in his own home. She also lacked a proletarian pedigree and was a grocer. Before that, she had embezzled from a Jewish woman grocer, but that [woman] preferred to litigate before the Rav [following Jewish law] and not in front of gentile law courts. In any event, this woman had a bad reputation among all circles of the population, although it was difficult, of course, to establish if they chose her [for the council] because of her troubled mind, or as contempt and ridicule directed towards Jewish women in the population.[7]

The Economic Situation

The economic situation of the Jewish population was quite bad. As mentioned previously, the Jews of the small town were small shop owners, craftsmen, waggoners and butchers. Apart from one pharmacist, no one had independent businesses [since everything was nationalized], unless you include two kosher butchers[8] and four teachers and educators ("melamdim").

With the Soviet occupation, the source of Jewish livelihood dried up. All of the shops closed after their hurried, compulsory sale in only a matter of a few days. Only one "general store" continued to operate, which was established in the last years of the Polish government by Christian Poles as competition with Jewish commerce, with a sign "Christian Store" and the slogan: "What is ours is His."[9]

The sign changed, the store was reposted as state-owned and served from then on as the only place providing the population with all kinds of necessary commodities.

[Page 285]

Theoretically [it supplied goods] — because in fact, this store had only bread and meager portions of basic commodities. Most of the goods, if they arrived, were sold by vouchers, which were given to Soviet officials exclusively.

The Jewish tailors tried to organize a cooperative that operated in line with a government order. Since there was an obligation to work on the Sabbath, and even on Yom Kippur, many older tailors quit and remained unemployed. The other tradespeople also had no work since there was no demand and no concern [to retrain them]. The waggoners worked part time for different government authorities, but the amount of hauling was significantly reduced, and their wage was miniscule. About 20 young Jewish men and women obtained low-level clerical positions in the new offices. About 80% of the Jewish population remained without means of subsistence. It is unknown if the government had plans in the future for any kind of rehabilitation program for the benefit of the Jewish population, which had been deprived of their former livelihoods. In any case, during the 21 months of Soviet government until the Nazi occupation on the 22nd of June 1941, [the Soviet government] no efforts were made towards [their] "productivization." There was also no unskilled labor. Indeed, there was occasional seasonal work in agriculture in the nationalized farms like gathering beets, sugar, potatoes, but in these kinds of work the entire population was "drafted" with no exception, apart from the elderly, children, and infirmed, and there was no compensation for this compulsory labor since this work was theoretically "voluntary" to "save the crop."

In this situation, the Jews were sustained in part by the inventory of foods they were able to accumulate before the War, and from the barter of personal possessions with farmers in exchange for food. Some tried to engage in the black market, in other words, as a go-between in the business transactions mentioned earlier and in others, despite the great danger getting involved, but there was no other choice.

Therefore, to the extent possible to judge from the experience and example of one little town, although, as noted above, there is no reason to assume this small town was an exception — the Soviet government ignored the special situation of the Jewish population, that sprung from the unique economic and social structure that had crystalized over the course of generations. No efforts were made to constructively integrate them in society and in the Soviet economy. Moreover, the Jews were forced indirectly to continue non-productive occupations to subsist with one difference — that earlier, in capitalist Poland, the situation was at least tolerated by the regime, while in the new regime, this [non-productive] work was unlawful and brought on severe punishment in its wake. Furthermore — the former shopkeepers and their children, including those who had not reached maturity, were labelled as an asocial element and given special identity cards with the number 11 and other special symbols.

[Page 286]

With this kind of identity card, they were not able to go to live in the municipal seat, where it might be possible to learn a new profession, or acquire knowledge, so they could be transformed into a productive element.

The Jews were punished, therefore, for their lack of earlier productivity in the capitalist regime, as if this was their fault (according to the same logic they also had to punish the workers who were utilized in the capitalist regime) and the punishment was manifested as follows — the path to be transformed into productive member in the new regime was blocked — a situation that brought on still other punishments.

Community and Culture

Also, completely quiet and paralyzed was the communal and cultural life. The youth movement, charitable groups, and the official Community (kehilla) organization stopped functioning. The "cheders" closed and stopped teaching Torah and Hebrew. Only the synagogues were not harmed, in the meantime, but they emptied out anyway, because, apart from the elders who had nothing to lose, a person who held out hope of work did not want to taint himself with "clericalism" [i.e., as being religious] or as a "counter-revolutionary" for which going to the synagogue was understood to be a clear sign.

The "cultural" library was closed. All the books in it were destroyed, the majority of which were incidentally good literature and among them, the Yiddish sector, including even leftist and communist writers. In its place, a general cultural hall was opened, and assemblies for propaganda began, propagandistic films were screened, and dances took place every evening until midnight.

Apart from that, there were lessons for teaching the Stalinist Constitution,[10] but no profession-oriented courses, either for the youth or adults, nor courses to learn the official Russian and Ukrainian languages, knowledge of which was required to obtain clerical work of any kind. It is possible that here too, hidden considerations operated — since in any case the Ukrainians knew their own language and the Jews had no need to master it (the Jews, in fact, spoke broken Ukrainian but didn't know the rules of grammar nor how to write this language).

Translator's and editor's footnotes:

1. Yosef Litvak, born in 1917 in Kiev, to Motl-Meir Litvak and Mlynov-born Dvorah (Lamdan). Yosef fled East from Rovno where he was studying at the German invasion. Additional details about his life are documented in his earlier essay, "The Town of Mlynov," p. 53, footnote 1.

2. Unstated but implied is the assumption that the referendum was just a rubber stamp.

3. The Soviets didn't trust the local populations they had just occupied at the start of WWII and imported Ukrainian workers from the areas that had earlier been under Soviet rule.

4. Their disloyalty to the Soviet regime was anticipated because of nationalist aspirations in Zionism and as members of the bourgeoisie. These were the years of Stalin's reign and Soviet political repression. The years when socialist ideology and Zionism were viewed as compatible had long since vanished in the Soviet Russia.

5. Again, implying coerced votes as rubber stamps.

6. A Dina Holtzeker wife of Kalman is mentioned in the list of martyrs (p. 432). In the Holtzeker family tree documented by the Baltimore branch, there is a Kalman, son of Hirsch Holtzeker, one of the original five Holtzeker brothers in Mlynov. It is possible this Dina was his wife.

7. It also seems possible the Soviets anticipated that one who had been imprisoned by the previous government would be disgruntled and would be loyal to the new one.

8. The acronym "shochtim ve-bodkim" includes kosher slaughters as well as those who examine /supervise the related activities. In many cases, this was one and the same person, "the shochet."

9. Seeming to imply that "what is ours is Christ's" and implying "buy from your own kind." Slogans and signs such as this appeared during the state and Church supported anti-Jewish boycott and growing anti-Semitism in Poland between 1934–1939.

10. Referring to the 1936 Constitution of the Soviet Union.

[Page 287]

Part I

During the Shoah

Joint Testimony of: Yehudit (Mandelkern) Rudolf,[1] Fania (Mandelkern) Bernstein, David Bernstein[2]

Translated and edited by Howard I. Schwartz, PhD with Hanina Epstein

Life Under the Occupying German Government

As told by Yehudit [Mandelkern] Rudolf

Already on Sunday, June 22, 1941, with the outbreak of war between Russia and Germany, our little town, which had in it a Soviet airfield, was bombed. My mother was injured in her leg. During that same bombing, a number of people were killed, and several houses destroyed.

On Tuesday, June 24, 1941, in the afternoon, the Germans entered the town. Before their entrance there was a small dogfight. The Soviets fled town on Monday without putting up resistance. At 5 o'clock, on Tuesday afternoon, the first German soldiers entered our houses. My mother who was wounded, lay on the floor out of fear from the bombardment; my brother, Moshe, of blessed memory, was lying down pretending to be sick. The five or six soldiers who entered obscenely asked for pork. We responded that we were Jews and didn't have any pork. We offered them buttermilk. But when they heard we were Jews, they rudely shattered the pitcher and left the house.

A day or two after the occupation, they had already published a proclamation in writing, in Ukrainian and German, that Jewish men and women from age 14 and older were obligated to report to the market square for labor, equipped with work and cleaning tools. Whoever did not present themselves — would be shot. Immediately, the Ukrainian police was organized, its recognizable symbol was a blue-yellow ribbon on the left sleeve. The women were sent usually for cleaning work and the men — for digging and field work on estate of Count Chodkiewicz, who had disappeared already by 1939.[3]

A few days after the occupation, a group of young Jewish boys and girls were arrested for being Communist members in the past.[4] Chaia Kipergluz,[5] Rivkah Ber, Freidel Rivitz,[6] Yenta from the Mandelkern line[7] (my father's sister).

Some of the people — about 200 — who were sent to labor, were directed to the property of the Count Liudochowski in the village of Smordva; Jews from the nearby villages of Boremel and Dymidivka were also taken to that same estate. The head of the estate was Volksdeutscher[8] Grüner,[9] a cruel sadist who would wake the men up many times at night and command them to run. The running required running down steps. During the descent, he would whip the runners with an iron whip so that the men would fall down the stairs.

[Page 288]

A special treatment in the estate was enjoyed by the blacksmith Hersh-Ber (the name of the family I don't remember).[10] He received bread to satiate his hunger which he also shared with others. He also occasionally succeeded in getting medicines. He held a position there until the liquidation and was killed after that in the forest. When someone got sick, he would take the person on as an assistant, so to speak, and this is how he rescued him, because it was forbidden to be sick.

A month to six weeks after the occupation, the Germans sought out members of the Polish parties. They imprisoned 10–15 Polish men and accidentally incarcerated the Jewish young man, Yehuda son of Mordechai Liberman.[11] The Germans misled the families of the prisoners and even accepted packages that were intended for them [from the families], but it became known, that in fact, they murdered all of them immediately after the arrest.

One night, in the early days, the Germans entered the house of the Jewish shoemaker Shlomo Kreimer.[12] He had a beautiful daughter, Rachel – who, upon seeing them, escaped through the window. As revenge for this, the soldiers killed the two parents. Their son, Zalman, who was [laboring] in the village of Smordva, burst out crying when the rumor of his parents' murder reached him. A German soldier who noticed asked him the significance of his crying, and when the soldier heard the reason — shot him to death on the spot.

In the first period, until the erection of the ghetto, there was not yet a severe shortage of food. Most of the families had a stockpile of food. In addition, items still existed which could be bartered with farmers. Somehow each managed, even though bartering was forbidden. Despite the prohibition, the Jews were going to the homes of farmers and farmers were coming to the homes of Jews to barter.

Immediately after the occupation, the Jews were ordered to don a white ribbon with a blue Star of David (Magen David) on the sleeve. A number of months later, in the fall of 1941, they were ordered to switch the white ribbon with a yellow patch on the back and breast. This obligation fell on children 12 and older.

In the fall of 1941, the Judenrat and Jewish police were established. As the chairmen, they appointed six earlier shopkeepers, all friends: Mordechai Litvak,[13] Chaim Yitzhak Kipergluz[14] — formerly chairman of the community (kehilla); as secretary, they appointed Katzevman, formerly secretary of the community and Mordechai Liberman,[15] David the kosher slaughterer (shochet) (the family name I don't recall);[16] and Moshe son of Yaakov Holtzeker.[17] In the police were Zelig Zider,[18] Shlomo Schechman,[19] Peretz Tesler,[20] Tzvi Gering.[21] There were another two or three others whose names, I don't remember.

The area commissariat was in the town of Dubno. In the fall of 1941 (the exact date I don't remember) an order was promulgated to the entire district — to supply 3,000 Jews as construction workers to the town of Rovno to build barracks for the army. The Judenrat in Dubno did not want to send the heads of families and decided to take men from all the towns in the area. In the small towns, they didn't know about the goal of the operations.

[Page 289]

Usually, in each operation, there were Ukrainian police who surrounded the small town and the Judenrat communicated the order — to supply a specific number of men. The Judenrat prepared the lists. From Mlynov, they took at that time about 50 men. Men of the Ukrainian and Jewish police went house to house searching for the men on the lists. Some of the men fled to the fields and surrounding forests. In place of those who fled, whose names were on the list, they would take anyone they came across. The arrest of the men was accompanied by crying and wailing.

The men were in fact transferred to Rovno for work. For about two months, news of them was received. After they finished the work, all of them were murdered and not one returned. In order to deceive the youth who were working there, some of them were purposefully sent home for a vacation. These, obviously, confirmed the knowledge that the men were in fact working and were even receiving vacations.

About a week after this roundup, a Hungarian military unit came, whose task was to confiscate grains, legumes, and flour from the Jewish homes. Of course, they didn't strictly follow orders and instead took whatever was at hand. This is how the Jews lost their reserves of food. In spite of this, until the last moment, the majority of town's Jews did not experience real hunger, since they always succeeded in meeting their food needs through barter.

That same fall there were two other additional operations: a Gold Aktion and a Furniture Aktion. During the Gold Aktion the Jews were ordered to bring all their silver and gold implements, dollars and jewelry. They all got receipts for the items that were turned over. After the Gold Aktion came the Fur Aktion — at the end of the summer 1942. After this, Germans arrived with several hundred Ukrainian police and with wagons and confiscated whatever they found — bicycles, sewing machines and regular furniture. The operation stopped suddenly. A whistle was blown, and afterwards some furniture still remained in the spots they had been set when brought out [of the houses] but which they hadn't managed to load on wagons.

Among the first victims, already in the summer of 1941, was the Rav of the town — Rabbi Yehuda Gordon.[22] He was summoned from his home by the Germans and held a number of days in prison before he was brought out and killed. It was said in town that the Rav knew how to speak German well and therefore they interrogated and tortured him for several days. Afterwards, he was taken outside town and killed.

Before Pesach 5702 (April 1, 1942), the Judenrat received permission to bake matzah. The baking was done in two places and following all the regulations [for baking matzah according to Jewish law]. The Germans did not take an interest in the source of the flour.

In the late fall months of 1941, the Judenrat issued a proclamation indicating that anyone who had a work certificate would not be taken into the ghetto (there was already talk that a ghetto would be established) and would be considered a productive element. Fictitious weddings started between young women and men who were consistently engaged in different kinds of work, and in particular, artisans, including those who worked on farms, who were mentioned above. Afterwards, commerce in work certificates developed. There were different types of certificates. The "best" type were the "iron certificates" that were given to the dentists, goldsmiths, decorators, and all different kinds of artisans, that the Germans openly engaged for their own personal needs.

[Page 290]

An example of the commerce in certificates: Perel Mandelkern,[23] wife of Yitzhak Mandelkern[24] (living today in Israel), traveled to Dubno to get this kind of certificate for her sister-in-law. Coincidentally, there was a roundup [Aktion] in Dubno and she was swept up and murdered. In that same operation, 5,000 Jews were murdered in a plot of empty land where the Jews had been assembled. One of them Leib Vinokur[25] (who lives today in Israel) — took a plank from a fence, attacked one of the German guards, stunned him and was able to escape and hide. Afterwards, he was with us in the forest.

In Mlynov itself, it was difficult to get these certificates, but trade in them flourished in Dubno. Even before the establishment of the ghetto it was forbidden for Jews to travel from town to town, and the trip to Dubno was therefore unlawful; in other words, the Jews traveled with Ukrainian farmers, disguised [as farmers], and of course with the agreement of the farmers. Every trip like this, therefore, was life threatening. On one unlawful trip, Yaakov Nudler,[26] who traveled to purchase arms for the resistance organization, was grabbed and killed, as discussed later.

The Ghetto

In April 1942, the ghetto was set up. It was confined to two streets, Shkolna and Dubinska. Permission was given to Jews from the other streets to bring personal belongings with them. Those evacuated individuals entered the homes of residents of the two streets just mentioned. Most made personal arrangements [which houses to join] and for others, the Judenrat organized the operation. Due to overcrowding, sanitary conditions worsened. In our living quarters — of two rooms — our aunt also lived and the family of Grandmother with two grandchildren (The kids of Yenta[27] had been killed already at the beginning of the occupation). In general, the density reached 7–8 people per room. The ghetto was surrounded by a barbed wire fence and had two gates guarded by Ukrainian police. The Jewish police generally accompanied those who went out for work. Apart from those who left for work in groups, no one was permitted to leave the ghetto.

The general feeling was that one should do whatever possible to be outside the ghetto. Those who worked on agricultural farms were subjects of envy by the ghetto residents. My sister, Fania, worked in a German office for road work and had a work certificate. The German soldiers who were in charge of this office were Austrian and treated her fairly well. Every evening she returned to the ghetto. While at work, she connected with a Polish family by the name of Veitschork from whom she got food. She also initiated a discussion with them about hiding in the event of the ghetto liquidation. The head of this family was a sentry for the roads.

Immediately following the establishment of the ghetto, the feeling prevailed that this was the prelude to the general liquidation. A number of youth, among them my brother Moshe Mandelkern, the brothers Shlomo, Yaakov, and Yitzhak Nekunchinik,[28] the police[29] Zelig Zider, Tzvi Gering, Peretz Tesler and Shlomo Schechman; Rachel Liberman,[30] Rivka Liberman,[31] Liuba Chizik,[32] Hannah Veiner,[33] Zelig Pichniuk[34] and others, tried organizing resistance.

[Page 291]

At the head of the group was Avraham son of Ben-Tzion Holtzeker.[35] Shlomo Nekunchinik[36] who lived before the war in an isolated home outside of town, had connections with foresters who had weapons. One of the Polish foresters promised him to supply arms to the Jewish youth. The youth gathered money to purchase weapons and prepared kerosene to set fire to the ghetto when the liquidation was announced in order to create chaos and provide an opportunity to flee. The group secured two rifles, that were held by Avraham Holtzeker. It was agreed that if escape to the forest was successful, those fleeing would try to reach the forests of Polesia[37] and the groups of partisans, whose existence had already been initially rumored. The members of the group were assigned different roles. Members of the group would meet almost every evening but did not succeed in achieving much. The weapons were hidden in the "tent" which stood over the tomb of the Rabbi Aharon from Karlin from the Stolin dynasty.

Those who were on a farm in the village of Karolinka[38] prepared two bunkers in the forest which had work tools and blankets. These bunkers were intended to serve those who fled the ghetto at the time of its liquidation. The following made it: my brother, Moshe Mandelkern, Shmuel Gruber,[39] and Yitzhak Mandelkern.[40] It is worth noting that the underground group was comprised of young people from the various youth movements, which had previously been active in town: "The Guard," (Hashomer Hatzair), "The Young Pioneer" (HeHalutz Hatzair), and Betar — and a total unanimity prevailed among them. One fact stands out: proteges of the youth movements participated in the [underground] group apparently under the influence of the education that they received from the youth groups.

Further, in the late summer months of August / September 1942, rumors arrived about the ghetto exterminations in other small towns and cities. It was obvious that Mlynov's turn was approaching and the fate of death of the town's Jews had been decreed.

In September, it became known that the farmers in the area were ordered to prepare a large pit in the valley between the two towns of Mlynov and Mervits, that was called Kruzhuk, a distance of one kilometer from the town. The first victims that were thrown into the pit were the brothers Fishel and Shlomo, sons of Nahum Teitelman[41] (who lives in Israel). They left the ghetto without permission. Apparently, they wanted to go to some village to hide. They were grabbed in the evening hours and thrown into the pit.

Before the liquidation, all the Jews who worked outside the ghetto on the various farms were ordered back to the ghetto. Some returned willingly to be with their families, and some were brought by force by the Ukrainian police in a systematic fashion.

The Massacre

On the 8th of October 1942, the ghetto was surrounded by the Ukrainian police on German authority.

[Page 292]

With loudspeakers, they announced that it was forbidden to leave and periodically they brought groups of Jews and individuals, who were being returned to the ghetto from their places of work. Everyone understood this was the end. Men, women, and children went out to the streets. Panic and hysteria broke out. People prayed, cried, yelled, and huddled together with their families.

As it grew dark, the loudspeakers announce that everyone had to go into their houses, keep the lights off, and anyone who left a house would be shot on the spot. Now and then the sounds of isolated shooting could be heard and occasionally the rattle of a police motorbike in the ghetto.

Translator's and editor's footnotes:

1. The two female writers, Fania and Yehudit, are members of the Mandelkern family, children of Avraham Mandelkern (1890–1932) and Rivkah (Nudler) (1891–1942). Avraham and Rivkah had seven children. A photo of Rivkah and three daughters appears on page 472 of this volume. Rivkah perished as did two of her children, Moishe and Rosa, as recounted in these essays. The daughters, Faiga (Fania) Bernstein (1917–?) and Yehudit Rudolf (also known as Ram), survived and share their memories here. Their brothers Pesach (1911–1987), whose photo appears on page 227, Eliyahu (1921–2009), and Gedaliah (1915–2005) all made it to Israel at some point. It not known if or how this Mandelkern family was related to the family of Shmuel Mandelkern, who is also a contributor to this volume. The author, in fact, mentions Shmuel's brother Yitzhak Mandelkern below and does not identify him as a relative.
2. David Bernstein (alternative spelling Bernshteyn) married Fania Mandelkern during the course of the events recounted here.
3. The Count, a nobleman and a member of the bourgeoise, had fled ahead of the Soviet occupation in September 1939 knowing that the Communists would socialize all property and possibly imprison or kill him.
4. The Germans suspected Communist members of being loyal to the Soviet Union and thus a danger. See, however, the previous essay by Yosef Litvak which indicates that the Soviet occupying government also didn't trust the loyalty of the Jewish Polish Communists.
5. Chaia (1919–1942) was the daughter of Chaim Yitzhak Kipergluz (alternative spelling Kiperglaz) (1895–1942) and Sarah (1894–1942), the latter born in Trovits. Mention of this same incident in which Chaia was killed appears in Mendel and Sonia's essay, "Tragic Tales," p. 327. Chaia's father, Chaim Yitzkhak Kipergluz, was son of Yosef Kipergluz and Brakha (Gelman). Chaim is recalled as a friend interested in Zionism in around 1914 by Shmuel Mandelkern in his essay "Yaakov-Yosi goes to the Land of Israel" and elsewhere in this volume as president of the Kehilla (p. 90), as second head of the kehilla in "The Town of Mlynov" (p. 55), as the synagogue sexton in "Mlynov–A Kehilla for Mlynov," p. 21, and as a man known to give charity to the poor (p. 317). A photo of the Kipergluz house/store appears on page 151. Chaia's sister, Rachel Kipergluz

(married name Kleeman), is mentioned by Aaron Harari in "Youth Movement" (p. 69) as a participating in Zionist youth activities and making aliyah.

6. Freidl Rivitz was the daughter of Nute Rivitz and Chana Braker (who was born in Klevan). She was the sister of Bat Sheva Ben Eliyahu (née Rivitz), who contributed "The Home That Was Lost," 263-265 to this volume.

7. The Mlynov martyr list names a "Yenta Mandelkern" (p. 436) as daughter of Chaika and as sister of Isaac, possibly the Yenta referred to here.

8. A Nazi term meaning "German folk" and used to refer to ethnic Germans living outside of Germany.

9. See the *Encyclopedia of Camps and Ghettos*. Vol. II. Part B. Ed. by Martin Dean. Indiana University, 2021, p. 1429.

10. Probably Hersch-Ber Klaper (alternative spelling Klapir and Clipper). There was a family of blacksmiths in Mlynov by the surname Klaper. According to Yad Vashem records, two of the sons, Reuven and Mendel, were blacksmiths. One of the Klaper sons was named Tzvi (which means deer in Hebrew) and is the equivalent of Hersch in Yiddish. It seems plausible that the blacksmith mentioned here was this Hersch-Ber Klaper. A record of a "Sergeant Hersch-Ber Klaper, a blacksmith from Mlynov," lists him in the Polish armed forces as one who was taken captive and imprisoned in a camp for Jewish POWs. According to Yad Vashem records filled out by a cousin, Tzvi Klaper (1880–1942) was born in Mlynov in 1912 to Ben-Tzion and Charna (alternative Tsherna). The other children in the family included Abraham (1900–1942), Reuven (a blacksmith) (1908–1942), Mendel (a blacksmith) (1904–1942), and sisters, Chaia (1907–1942) and Hana (1911–1942).

11. Yehuda also known as Eidel or Idel, was son of Mordechai Liberman and Brakha (Gruber). His photo appears on pages 280 and 461 with additional notes there. According to Teitelman descendants, Bracha Gruber was daughter of Mordechai and Perel Gruber and sister of Rikel Gruber (see photo p. 477) with other footnotes there.

12. The beautifully made boots of Shlomo Kreimer, who was also lame, feature in the story told by Shmuel Mandelkern, "Self Defense in Mlynov," p. 137 with additional notes there about the family.

13. Father of Yosef Litvak, contributor of several essays to this volume including "The Mlynov Community at the Beginning of the Soviet Occupation."

14. See note 6.

15. See note 11 for details on the Liberman family.

16. It is unclear which shochet is intended. Names of shochets mentioned in the Memorial book include Pesach Gelman son of Itzi Gelman listed among the martyrs, a shochet named Moshe Gertnikh who was in Mlynov during the War, a shochet named Hanich (p. 317), and one named Sender Shoykhet (p. 99). Leizer Mohel was also a shochet who came to town in the 1920s as reported by the Mohel family story.

17. Moshe Holtzeker was the son of Yankel Holtzeker, one of the original five brothers to come to Mlynov. Moshe's son, was also Yankev (Yaakov) Holtzeker who contributed the essay, "My Hometown Mlynov," 226–227, which includes additional notes on the family.

18. A photo of the Zider families appears on page 463. Both Moshe (and his wife Freida) and Zalman Zider (and his wife Zelda) had sons named Zelig. A photo of Zalman Zider, son of Meir Hirsch Zider, appears below on p. 475.

19. Shlomo Schechman, son of Noach Moshe Schechman/Shuchman. Shlomo survived the war. See the essay about his father "Reb Noyekh-Moyshe," p. 246, and notes there. Shlomo's photos appear in the group of boys on pages 227, and 460 and later in life on page 478.

20. A photo of Peretz Tesler appears on page 478 along with his father Yaakov and grandfather Avraham. Peretz was also the brother of Liba (Tesler) Einstendig, whose survival story is told by David Sokolsky, *Monument: One Woman's Courageous Escape from the Holocaust*. According to Liba's account, Peretz was never part of the police. He was conscripted for labor in Rovno as described belo but managed to escape the murder of the other workers in November 1941. Since he was afraid to return directly to Mlynov, he made his way to a work farm in Smordva not far from Mlynov and managed to sneak into the Mlynov ghetto to be with his family. He had obtained an illegal gun from a member of the partisans who told him of two underground bunkers, which were located near the village of Karolinka. These same bunkers are discussed in this essay below.

21. According to the Yad Vashem record filled out by a cousin, Yehoshua (Gering) Geri, Tzvi (also Hershel) Gering (~1920—~1943) was born in Mlynov to Nekha Gering, who was the daughter of Yosel Shraga Kreitzer

the Cohen. Tzvi /Hershel was a soldier in the Polish armed forces and was killed in military services. Yehoshua indicates Gering relatives including his family lived in Rovno.

22. Here spelled Gordeen but more consistently in the volume he is called Rabbi Yehuda Gordon. See also, for example, p. 384 for an account of Rabbi Gordon's death.

23. A photo of Perel Mandelkern appears on page 478. According to a Yad Vashem record, she was born Perel Klotz (1912–1943) to Nakhman and Rakhel Leah in the Dubno region. Prior to WWII she lived in Mlynov. She died in 1943 in the Belzec Extermination Camp.

24. Yitzhak was brother of Shmuel Mandelkern, a contributor of "Self-Defense in Mlynov" to this volume. Since the author (who was a Mandelkern) doesn't identify Yitzhak as a relative, it is assumed that these two Mandelkern branches were not related.

25. "Leybush Vinokur" (alternative spelling Winokur) is mentioned as helping to rescue Batya Barber Blinder after the liberation in her essay a "Child in the Storm," p. 374. Possibly belonging to the Vinokur family identified in records submitted by a Luba Vinokur indicating her parents were Tzvi Vinokur (~1896– ~1942) and Reizel who were born in Dorohostai near Mlynov and who disappeared from the Dubno ghetto.

26. According to the list of martyrs, Yaakov Nudler was son of Khaikyl "Shnayder" Nudler, (the tailor) who owned the gramophone in the story told by Boruch Meren (pp. 199–201). Yaakov was the nephew of Aaron Nudler who is mentioned later in this story.

27. Yenta was described earlier in the essay as the sister of the author's father.

28. Alternate spellings include Nakonechnyuk, Nakonechnik Nakonechnik. The martyr list includes Shlomo, his wife Ester (who has a sister in Israel), Yaakov, Yitzhak and Rivkah. In the book recounting his survival story, Asher Teitelman reports meeting Shlomo Nekunchinik in the bunkers of the Smordva forest (p. 29) and indicates that Shlomo was shot when the Ukrainians discovered the bunkers and starting shooting (p. 34). The attack on the bunkers is described below.

29. See notes 18–21 above for background on these members of the Jewish police.

30. In the list of martyrs (p. 435), Rachel Liberman is daughter of Yehezkel Liberman and his wife Doba. She and her parents, perished. Her brother Herschel is listed at the time as living in Canada.

31. Rivka Liberman is the daughter of Mordechai and his wife Bracha (Gruber). She was the sister of Eidel (Yehuda) Liberman (see note 11). She perished with her siblings Asher, Eidel, Miriam and Chaya.

32. Luba (also Leah) is the daughter of Motel Chizik, who was a teacher in Mlynov. A photo of the Chizik family appears on page 457 with additional family details in footnote 8. Luba perished with her parents in Mlynov.

33. Likely referring to Hannah Veiner (alternative spelling Weiner, Viner) (born circa 1913), daughter of Beracha who is listed in the martyr list, p. 434. Hannah survived as did two of her siblings, Yehuda and Moshe, who left Mlynov at the German invasion along with Yechiel Sherman as described in his essay, pp 344–346. After the War, Hannah married Michael (Micha) Kilshtakov, who was from Mervits, according to descendants. She eventually migrated with her brother Yehuda to Tbilisi before making aliyah in 1962. The Veiners are cousins of Sunny Veiner a contributor to this volume, p. 251.

34. Zelig Pichniuk (alternative spellings: Pikhniuk, Pikhnyuk) (1920–1942) was born in Mlynov, a son of Yaakov (1892–1942) and Gitel (also called Evegenia Retzepter in the records) (1892–1942). He was a hairdresser. His photo in uniform appears on page 455. He was one of six children. He and his siblings Avraham (1922–1942), Rachel (1918–1942), Faiga (1920–1942) perished. His siblings Sonia (later Sofia Basina) and Bat Sheva were alive in Russia when the Memorial book was published. Sofia submitted Yad Vashem records for the family in Russian.

35. This "Avraham, son of Ben-Tzion Holtzeker," is probably the grandson of Moshe Holtzeker, one of the five original Holtzeker brothers who came to Mlynov. In the Baltimore Goldseker family tree, there is a "Benne" son of Moshe, who is likely a shortened form of "Ben-Tzion" mentioned here as father of Avraham. Based on the martyr list (p. 433), Ben-Tzion Holtzeker married Ester-Manya, daughter of Pesach Feldman from Boremel. Their son Pesach was killed in the Russian army and their children Avraham and Rivka perished with the ghetto.

36. See note 25.

37. Probably referring to Polesia, a marshy region lining the Pripyat River which extends into Volhynia.

38. On old maps, Karolinka appears just slightly northwest of Uzhynets' which is just 6 km east from Mlynov and then slightly north. It appears that the area has been incorporated into the Uzhynets' of today.

39. Shmuel Gruber and his brother Hanoch were sons of Israel Gruber and grandsons of Mordechai Gruber and Perel. Shmuel Gruber was married to Charna Goldseker (1898– ~1943), daughter of Shimon Goldseker. Their children were Shimon (1930–1942) and Yisrael (1934–1942). Shmuel and his brother Hanoch were first cousins of Rachel (Gruber) Teitelman and Sonia (Gruber) Teitelman who are contributors to this volume. Their fate is discussed further below.

40. See note 24.

41. See their father Nahum's poignant memories "In the Depths of Hell," pp. 314–324.

Part II

In the Valley of the Shadow of Death[1]

The Account of Fania (Mandelkern) Bernstein[2]

Translated and edited by Howard I. Schwartz, PhD with Hanina Epstein

Escape from the Town

Our house was by the gate of the ghetto. My mother begged me to leave the ghetto. We knew that my brother Moshe was in a bunker that he had prepared near the forest by the village Karolinka.[3] My sister Yehudit joined him a week before the ghetto was surrounded. My mother pressured me to try any way to leave — to bribe a policeman or by begging a policeman for permission to get out. She also prepared a bundle with all different kinds of necessities for me, and even remembered to include scissors, thread and needles and the like. I approached one Ukrainian policeman; his name was Shafortyuk. I pleaded and cried for him to let me go. I promised him clothing and gold. Initially he swore at me and threatened me with his weapon. I begged him many times, until he told me to come in the evening when it was dark. He told me to bring him all the things I had promised and leave it in a bush by the gate. He also told me that he would give me an opportunity to leave and would shoot his rifle in the air, in order to disguise my exit and cover it up. Initially we thought we would leave together with my sister Rosa and my mother. But in the end mother decided she would remain behind so she wouldn't weigh us down.

I approached the gate with just my sister. About 6.30 pm in the evening, I brought the policeman the bundle I had promised him. A watch, gold coins, and nice boots. At first, he refused to let my sister leave. But he didn't have time to argue with us, afraid he might not get his loot. He opened the gate giving us opportunity to leave, shot [his rifle] in the air, and also showed us how to proceed, so that we would not fall into the hands of police. Initially we crawled a long way so that we would not be discovered. We wanted to go first to the Polish family Veitschork whom I knew before this.[4] We walked all night long even though the distance was not far.[5] We got to the home of the Polish family. The woman of the household wouldn't receive us and even told us to go away or else she would turn us in. Apparently, she was afraid to hide us due to the close proximity to the town.

[Page 293]

We continued, therefore, to another Polish family where my sister Rosa had previously worked. The family name I no longer remember. In this home, we hid for an entire day. The woman of the household told us that that morning all the Jews had been taken from the ghetto and murdered in a pit that had been prepared earlier. She also consoled us but asked that we leave the home that night because she would not be able to hide us. We, therefore, went back on the road with the goal of reaching the bunker of my brother. To get there, it was necessary for us to again return past the town and by the farm of the Count where Germans were. We walked all night. We were frightened by every shadow. We rested in a Christian cemetery. Towards morning we reached the forest. We didn't know the way to the bunker, but we knew where the farmer lived who had helped my brother and with whom he stayed in constant contact. He was a Pole. We reached his house okay with the rising sun. But he refused to receive us out of fear. He maintained that they were looking for Jews and were shooting anyone who helped them.

We continued to the forest and met some Jews. Among them was Yechiel Sherman[6] (today in Haifa), Golda, daughter of Aharon Asher Khait [the tailor],[7] and her sister (both perished), and others I don't remember. We were happy to meet other Jews. We told them there was a bunker nearby, but they didn't know where it was. Thanks to the knowledge of the bunker, they attached themselves to us. We wandered around for several hours. We met Henich (Hanoch) Gruber.[8] I knew that he and his older brother Shmuel were among those who created the bunker with my brother. He surreptitiously told me that he couldn't reveal the location of the bunker while we were still together with the large group, because the place was too small. It was difficult for us to break free from the group. Finally, in the evening, we got away, first myself, and afterwards, my sister. Hanoch Gruber brought the two of us to the bunker.

The Killing in the Town

I will pause here and recount what I heard from Ezra Sherman,[9] who escaped from the truck that was carrying people to the killing ravine and also what I heard later directly from farmers — about how the massacre was carried out. The Germans loaded the people on a truck and brought them to the pit. A plank was suspended over the pit. People were ordered to strip and one by one get on the plank. Before they did so, they were ordered to hand over their belongings to the policemen. Opposite the plank stood a machine gun that shot those crossing the plank with constant bursts. In the ghetto itself, Germans and Ukrainians stayed behind and searched house to house for valuables and Jews in hiding.

On the day of the liquidation, about 900 persons were massacred and buried in the large pit. Another several hundred people, residents of the nearby town of Mervits, who had been absorbed into the Mlynov ghetto, were slaughtered also that same day. Afterwards, during the next few days, another sixty-six individuals were seized, who had been rounded up by the police, and were brought out, killed and buried in a mass grave in the courtyard of the large study hall in the middle of the ghetto. The day after the liquidation, thousands of Ukrainian farmers from the nearby villages flocked in and plundered those belongings that remained in the Jewish homes which the Germans hadn't wanted.

[Page 294]

In the Forests of Mlynov

When we got to the bunkers, I found my brother Moshe there, my sister Yehudit, and the Gruber family: Shmuel [Gruber], his wife Charna,[10] their two children, and Hanoch the brother of Shmuel, the one who had brought us. Yitzhak Mandelkern[11] was also there, one of his six children, Gershon, his brother Moshe and his sister-in-law Malka Milbaski. The meeting with the people in the bunker caused agitation. They hadn't believed it was possible to successfully flee from the ghetto. I told my brother and sister about the loss of our mother with all the people of the ghetto.

In the same area of the forest there was another bunker, where David, the son of Yaakov Holtzeker,[12] the brother of Menashe, was staying, and another 3–4 people whose names I no longer remember. The distance between the two bunkers was less than a ½ km. At night they would go out to the homes of Polish farmers in the villages of Zofiówka[13] and Lodvykuvkah[14] and to the houses of Czech farmers in the village of Novyny Chaska.[15] We still had a few valuables that we brought with us and in exchange for them we received bread and potatoes. In the bunkers we arranged cooking stoves and we would cook at night, so that the smoke would not give us away. Also during the day we covered up our footprints as much as possible. We kept in constant contact between the two bunkers.

In the beginning of December 1942, one day in the morning, Menashe Holtzeker[16] came to visit. He stayed with us for an hour. Suddenly we heard shooting nearby. We realized that the neighboring bunker had been discovered. My brother, Moshe, yelled immediately that we needed to flee. I was barefoot and fled this way despite the cold. We all fled and left all our things in the abandoned bunker. While still fleeing, we saw the Ukrainian police approaching our bunker after wiping out the neighboring one. We realized that we couldn't remain in that area, and we left in the direction of the forest near Smordva. The distance directly there was not more than 13–14 km, but we wandered around during the night doubling the distance. From the farmers, we heard that in this area Polish partisans had organized, and they welcomed Jews and some escaped Soviet prisoners into their unit.

At the head of this unit were the brother Yugilevych brothers.[17] They were farmers from a Polish village who were going to be sent for forced labor in Germany. They evaded the trip to Germany and in retaliation the Germans burned their houses and all their possessions. They themselves managed to escape and join the underground. The Germans gathered two hundred Polish men as a transport to Germany. The Yugilevych brothers and their men set an ambush for this convoy and succeeded in freeing it entirely from the hands of the German and Ukrainian escort. The first Jews who joined this unit were Moshe Kernitchuv, Simka Dvortchitz, Yitzhak Vaserman, Yaakov Buber and Yashkah Perlmuter, all five from Dubno.

[Page 295]

And a young man named Boris (Berel) and his brother Avraham, residents from Boremel, and others I don't remember. There also were about ten Soviet prisoners there who escaped captivity, most of them Georgians. The whole unit numbered about 30 people at that time, over time their numbers grew gradually.

The unit's presence in the forest was known to all the farmers in the area and they were afraid to encounter it. For that very reason we were drawn there. The unit set as its primary goal — to eliminate the heads of the Ukrainian villages in the area, which collaborated in operations with the Germans. They especially burned their houses and their possessions, thereby forcing them to be uprooted from their locations.

After a night of walking, we reached the forest by the village of Berehy where we rested during the day. We started looking for a fitting place to build a bunker. Along the way we equipped ourselves, from one farmer, with an axe and spade so that we could prepare ourselves a bunker. With great difficulty, we built a new bunker. One day we bumped into Jews who were also hiding in this area. These Jews didn't stay in direct contact with the partisan unit but, as noted, the very presence of the unit in the area turned it into a relatively secure refuge. Among those Jews were people from Mlynov: Meir Kwasgalter,[18] and his daughter Rachel (in Israel today), Aaron Nudler,[19] the son-in-law of Ben-tzion Polishuk, with a daughter and son, the brothers Shlomo, Yaakov and Yitzhak Nekunchinik,[20] the brothers Shlomo and Meir Schechman,[21] Hersch-Ber, the blacksmith mentioned earlier,[22] Golda and her sister from the Khait (tailor) family,[23] Natan Shiper,[24] Mendel Kwasgalter, and Avraham Drator from Dubno, with his sister Ema. A woman by the name of Kayla from the village Bokiima and a Jew by the name of Menusavsky from the village of Palcheh,[25] the family of Menusovitch, father, mother, with two children from Kozyn,[26] the Jew Butler from Dubno. There were other people whose names I don't remember. All of these people were scattered in many bunkers in the area, and each group tried to guard the secret location of its bunker. It is worth mentioning, that in the forest there was a well of pure water, that supplied water to the bunker inhabitants. According to farmers, this spring dried up in earlier years and only in this year did water begin gurgling …

For two months we felt relatively secure in the forest due to the "good" name of the partisan unit. Thanks to it, we received food from the farmers in the area who provided necessities, principally out of fear of partisan revenge, rather than willfully. Some semblance of life was created. Connections were made between couples; we would sing at night and hoped that we could hold our position until the end of the War and the victory over the Germans would arrive. The will to live was very strong — to continue to live in spite of it all.

One night when all the food was used up, I went out to obtain some food in exchange for the last ring that I still had with me. I went with my sister Rosa to the village of Klyn,[27] 6 km from our camp.

[Page 296]

It was rumored that evangelists lived in this village who didn't turn in Jews. We obtained a bottle of unrefined flax oil. It was a freezing night, and the way was very slippery. We walked very slowly but close to the bunker, no less, I slipped, and the bottle broke. I cried many hours from the heartache.

Hunted and Pursued

Over time, we split into small groups as much as possible to increase the possibility of escape in the event one of the bunkers would be discovered. Some of the people were based in section number 7 in the forest. I was in the group in section number 8. At the end of January 1943, a hunt was organized for the partisans and refugee families by the Ukrainian police under German command. Initially, section number 7 was attacked — which previously was considered the safest. The police advanced into the forest while firing. Eleven to twelve men, most from Dubno, were killed in that hunt. Also killed was [Itzhok], the son of Aharon Nudler, who was previously mentioned.[28] The bullet that killed the lad injured the hand of his little sister. Her father carried her on his back to a farmer's house by the name of Komarinitz, where the bullet was removed from the hand of the young girl. The farmer was an evangelist. By chance, there was a group of partisans remaining in that area who returned fire at the Ukrainians. The policemen withdrew from that area and moved to other areas.

After this pursuit, one group of the partisans decided to move to the forests of Polesia in the north to join with much larger groups of partisans. Another group stayed in place. Among the Jews who joined the partisans heading north — Devorjetz, Vaserman, and Avraham the brother of Boris.[29] The partisans decided that on their way north they would burn a large sawmill near Kremenets[30] that supplied the Germans with railroad ties.

One of the Yugilevych brothers had a son, a small boy, who was left in the care of a German woman who lived (among the residents) in a nearby village. He visited with her frequently and told her about the unit's trip north. The German woman informed the German authorities about it, which dispatched a large force to obstruct the path of the partisans. By the village Kamina Gorah,[31] the partisans were surrounded by about 25 German men. They held their position a full day in battle, and almost all were killed while bravely taking down many Germans. Avraham[32] and another partisan who was not Jewish managed to escape and ultimately reach the partisans in Polesia. Avraham returned with his unit to liberated Rovno in the beginning of 1944.

In hiding near the village of Semiga[33] was a family — two parents and a sister — of one of the young Jewish men [Aizia Wasserman][34] who had joined the group of the Yugilevych brothers in its trip north. The family hid with a Polish farmer. When the group arrived near the village Semiga, the young man went to visit his family. His desire to visit his family had been one of his motivations to join the group [heading north].

[Page 297]

The young man arrived at the farmer's house at night and asked if he could see his parents. The farmer told the young man that the members of his family fled that same day to the forest, from fear of the Germans who were known to be coming to the area, and indeed were grabbed and murdered by the Germans. The young man interrogated the farmer about the details of the event and also the fate of the family's belongings that they had with them. During the interrogation, he felt that the farmer was confused and hiding something. He thus started up with threats and punches. In the farmer's family was an old man — the farmer's father-in-law. The old man told the young Jewish man the truth about what happened. The Jewish family had many valuable things, and they were turning over some of them to the farmer in stages. The farmer decided to get rid of the Jews and dispossess them. He therefore told them that their presence with him was known to the neighbors. There was no other choice but to leave for the forest. He suggested they accompany him. He took work tools to dig a bunker and brought them to a specific place as if to fashion them a hiding place. There he killed them and buried them. The old man said that this contemptible, murderous deed does not give him rest and interrupts his sleep at night. Taking revenge for his family, the young man killed the farmer, his wife and his son. The old man, of course, he left alive. (This story is also included in the Memorial book for the community of Dubno.)[35]

One morning during the month of March 1943, early in the morning on a rainy day, our bunker was attacked suddenly by Ukrainians. In this bunker was only — me, my brother, and my two sisters. The Ukrainians yelled at us to come out or they would obliterate us with a hand grenade thrown into the bunker. Or, they assured us, if we came out of our own free will nothing bad would happen. The attackers were Ukrainians from the Bandera men,[36] who had also formed a nationalist underground that was both anti-Soviet and anti-German. They began to remove the roof of the bunker. We had no weapons. We hesitated to leave. Some were begging for their lives. My sister Rosa decided to go out first and she was shot on the spot. I went out and demanded to know why they had shot my sister. They claimed that they had shot into the air, and she had been wounded by accident. The exit from the bunker was such that only one person was able to leave at a time. When I came out, they told me to flee, and they would not do me harm. After me, my brother Moshe exited, and begged the attackers not to shoot him in exchange for which he promised to reveal buried valuables that he hid in a nearby place. They believed him and didn't hurt him. He didn't have any buried treasure, but he hoped that along the way to the treasure he would succeed in breaking away and fleeing. And indeed, he succeeded. We scattered in every direction and, only after the attackers left, did we gather together again. My brother, Moshe, found my sister Rosa severely injured. We brought her into the bunker. Since we didn't have a doctor or bandaging, she died after a day of great suffering. We buried her in a section of a cemetery where six other Jews were buried, some [who died] from wounds and some from weakness and illness.

Since then, our confidence was completely undermined. In the forest, the military sorties of the Banderites grew; [the Banderites were those] who desired at any cost to exterminate the remaining Jews — in part from hate and in part so that no witnesses of their crimes would remain, in light of the danger posed by the approach of the Soviets.

[Page 298]

Among the group of partisans who were pro-Soviet, a quarrel broke out. Some of them wanted to join the unit of the Bandera men, among them Georgians, Armenians, Khazars, and other minorities. The commander of the unit was against this — a Russian named Philip. The group as a whole gathered in the home of a White Russian[37] forester by the name of Ostap who, on the one hand provided hospitality to the partisans but, on the other hand, maintained a connection with the authorities and informed them about the movements of the partisans in the area. The partisan units were adding different people all the time, especially escaped prisoners. During one of the disputes, the leader Philip was murdered. Two weeks after the assassination, the forest was surround by Germans who arrived there following the snitching of the forester, Ostap. He informed the Germans about the partisans' place of encampment and the Jewish bunkers. On the other hand, he informed the partisans and the Jews about this hunt being prepared — in order to remove the suspicion that he was a snitch. All the Jews left the bunkers and tried to find hiding in the dense brush. The partisans did not leave their places, relying on their guards to successfully warn them of attacks.

When the Germans arrived, they detected the partisan guard and killed him. When the other partisans heard the shots, the men returned fire and retreated. Myself, my brother Moshe, my sister Yehudit and the Gruber family — hid near a spring in a place of dense undergrowth where there were no trails. We decided to remain there during the day and at night to return to the bunker. About 6 am in the morning, my brother told me to go up on the hill to see what was going on in the area. I saw two armed Germans approaching towards us. I immediately ran back to alert our people. Shmuel Gruber went up to check and to verify if indeed they were Germans coming. They saw him, shot him and wounded him. He fell and the Germans took him wounded with them to interrogate him. When we realized this, we all ran in single file in the opposite direction. Along the way we bumped into a group of Jews from a neighboring bunker. We told that them the Germans were on our trail, and they began to run with us. In this group were 8 people, among them my future husband David Berenstein. Along the way we saw the Germans from a distance but they didn't notice us.

When we returned to the bunkers in the evening, we learned from farmers in the area that the Germans captured Gruber alive and wounded, and that they discovered a bunker with 13 Jews, and also captured them alive and took them for the purposes of interrogation. Among these 13 Jews, was a Jew by the name of Fishbein, a refugee in Dubno from the center of Poland. With him was his wife, a young boy and his sister-in-law — the sister of his wife. He asked the Germans to relieve himself and succeeded in escaping. He reached us and told us what had happened to the group.

[Page 299]

From that point, our terror and feeling of danger mounted. We decided that we needed to change where we were staying. Yitzhak Mandelkern suggested returning to the forest around the village of Uzhynets' and Karolinka on the assumption that Jews had not been there for some time and that they would not search for us there. We knew already that the Russians were advancing, and we needed to hold on until their arrival. In any case, the news from the front gave us much encouragement in our fight to survive.

At that time, a group of escaped prisoners — comprised of minorities — united with a group of anti-Soviet partisans from the Bandera men. With the escaped prisoners was one local Jew, who had earlier joined them, and they included him thanks to his possession of weapons. His name was Yaakov Buber, a man from Dubno, who was previously mentioned. "His friends," who joined with the Banderites, treated him decently — and advised him to go to the Jews hiding nearby, since they knew that the Banderites would likely kill him. They left him with his weapon and added a single hand grenade. He therefore had a rifle, a pistol and grenade. He came to us and informed us of the danger to be expected from the Banderites. This event hurried our heading to the forests of Uzhynets'.

The transition to the Uzhynets' forest was not an easy operation. We needed to pass the village of Berehy, which was near where a large German force camped. We needed to pass there out of necessity due to the bridge there. There was also reason to assume that the bridge was guarded by the Germans. We thought therefore about fording the river. Not all of us knew how to swim. There were also children with us. We calculated and prepared, waiting for a dark night when it would be easier to cross.

282

Translator's and editor's footnotes:

1. An allusion to Psalm 23:4, "Though I walk through the valley of the shadow of death, I fear no harm, for You are with me."

2. Fania is the sister of the writer of the previous essay. See notes on the family there.

3. A small town identified on old maps slightly northwest of Uzhynets', just 6 km east and slightly north of Mlynov and appears to have been absorbed into that town today.

4. In the previous essay, Fania's sister explains that she had a work certificate to work in a German office and there connected with this family.

5. Apparently moving slowly and/or through difficult terrain to avoid detection.

6. Yechiel Sherman and his brother, Ezra, were sons of Moshe Sherman and Etel (Golisuk). Their maternal grandmother was Hanah Schuchman. Photos of the family and notes, pp. 462–463. Yechiel contributed the essay, "The Departure from Home," 344–346 to this volume.

7. Referring to two daughters of Aharon Asher Khait ("tailor") (alternative spellings Chait / Chayat). In the martyr list (p. 435), Aharon Asher Khait is listed as one of the Stolin Hasids with his wife Bat-Sheva, his daughter, Perel, her husband Yitzhak, [and other children] Golda, Batya, Faiga and their children. In the essay "In the Depths of Hell," (p. 318), Nahum Teitelman briefly mentions "Mr. Pesach-Aryeh Chayat [Tailor], and his son Aharon-Asher Berel Barben" as among the Stolin Hasids in the synagogue. Perel Khait (1916–1942) married Issak Lejbel from Boremel. A Yad-Vashem record filled out by Perel's brother-in-law, Abraham Lebell, indicates Perel (née Khait) was born in Mlynov in 1916 to Aharon Asher Khait and died in the woods near Smordva. She and her husband Issak had a three-year-old son named Pesach Aryeh.

8. On the background of Hanoch and Shmuel Gruber, see note 39 in the previous essay.

9. See note 6.

10. Charna Goldseker (1898–1942) was the daughter of Anna Fishman (1867–1914) and Shimon Goldseker (1867–1926), one of the five original Holtzeker brothers to come to Mlynov. Four of Charna's Goldseker siblings had already migrated to Baltimore (Ida Fishman Gresser, Eta (Goldseker) Fishman, Morris Goldseker and Samuel Goldseker) and one brother was living in Buenos Aires: Juan (Chuna) Golceker. Her sister, Eta, contributed "Jews from Baltimore," 495–496. Two of Charna's other married sisters also perished: Perel (Goldseker) Pressman and Baila (Goldseker) Kuliz/Collidge).

11. As noted in the previous essay, Yitzhak was a sibling of Shmuel Mandelkern, a contributor to this volume. In an essay dedicated to their brother Josef (p. 448), their parents are identified as Nechama and Menachem Mandelkern. In the list of martyrs, Nechama is listed with children, Perel and Moshe. The prior essay, p. 290, indicates that Yitzhak's wife, Perel, had gone to Dubno seeking a work certificate for her sister-in-law when she was unexpectedly rounded up with others and eventually killed.

12. David and Menashe were grandsons of Moshe Holtzeker, one of the five original brothers who came to Mlynov. Their parents were Yankel and Risia. The family photo appears, p. 245, and a photo of David is on page 247. Several of their siblings, Baila, Nachman and Tzipporah, were able to make aliyah. Asher Teitelman who was also in bunkers near Smordva indicates Menashe was with him when they later enlisted in the Soviet army in Rovno and then meets him again later in a hospital after they were both injured in different fighting units. Menashe was later killed in battle. See Asher's life story, *Happy is the Man*, page 37, on the Mlynov website.

13. Specific village not identified. The Hebrew seems to refer to Zofiówka, the Polish name for Trochenbrod, which seems unlikely since Trochenbrod was not a Polish village and because it was 85 km (52 mi) by road from Mlyniv quite a lengthy trip during the night.

14. Possibly Lukarivka which is just 11 km east from Uzhynets' today by road.

15. Probably what is today Novyny which is 13 km north of Uzhynets' today.

16. See note 12.

17. Following the spelling of the family name Yugilevych used in the Dubno Memorial Book in the essay, "The End of the Partisan, a Member of 'Betar,' Aizia Wassermann" which discusses the same partisans.

18. Meir Kwasgalter's photo, page 466, with his wife. He is mentioned by Shmuel Mandelkern as a participant in "Self-Defense in Mlynov." See note 75 there for Meir's background. His daughter, Rachel (Kwasgalter) Rabinowitch, survived and later filled out Yad Vashem records for the family.

19. Arke (Aaron) Nudler (1888–1948) and his daughter Elka (later Helen Fixler) survived the attack on the bunkers but his wife Masa Eata (Polishuk) and their youngest children, Itzhok and Feigale, were killed. Arke and Helen survived and made their way back to Mlynov after the War and then to the Pocking Displaced Persons

Camp. They both appear in the commemoration photo, p. 313. Arke died tragically in Pocking from routine hernia surgery which was required to immigrate. His two older sons, Morris and Harold Nudler, survived fighting in the Russian army. They eventually came to Canada and the US.

20. See previous essay, note 28 for family details.

21. Sons of Noach Moshe Schechman/Shuchman. Shlomo survived the war. See the essay about his father "Reb Noyekh-Moyshe," p. 246 and notes there. Shlomo's photos appear in the group of boys on pages 227, and 460 and later in life on page 478.

22. See previous essay page 288 and note 10.

23. See above note 7.

24. The occasion of Natan Shiper's death is mentioned in the book length story of Asher Teitelman, *Happy is the Man*, 33–35, who was also hiding in the bunkers near the Smordva forest. Asher recalls leaving the bunker with Natan Shiper for food. "One Sunday we walked up a road a distance of about 15 km. He was about 40 years old and was walking behind me. We got to one house. In the house were young Ukrainians. The situation did not appear optimal to us but they gave us food. When we left the house, they shot at us. Natan was wounded and died. I escaped to the forest. They pursued me. I hid in a pile of branches. I waited there until night fell. Then I got up and went to the bunker. I got there late at night." On the Yad Vashem record Asher filled out, he indicates that Natan died in 4/1943.

25. Perhaps Palche today, east of Lutzk.

26. 53 km south and slightly west of Mlynov.

27. Southwest of Smordva.

28. See note 19.

29. See the bottom of page 294 and top of 295 where some of these individuals were mentioned earlier as Jews from Dubno and Boremel who had joined the partisans.

30. The Kremenets north of Lutsk, not the one south of Mlynov.

31. Unidentified town. Not Kmienna Gora in south-western Poland, which is too far away.

32. Referring to the man named Avraham, brother of Boris, from Boremel mentioned on the top of 295.

33. The town Semiga is described by the Worldwide Association of Wolyn Jews as a train stop between Krements and Kamnitz where lumber was transferred and where some Jews lived. It is perhaps the town known today as Symyky between Lutsk and Kremenets.

34. Aizia Wasserman born in 1919 in Mizoch. A more detailed and somewhat different version of this story is recounted in "The End of the Partisan," in the Dubno Memorial book, where Aizia's life as a partisan is also discussed in more detail.

35. See note 34 for the reference.

36. The Bandera men or "Banderivtsi" refers to members of an assortment of right-wing organizations in Ukraine and the term comes from the name of Stepan Bandera (1909–1959) who was head of the Organization of Ukrainian Nationalists, which included the Union of the Ukrainian Fascists, known as the OUN-B. After June 22, 1941, the OUN-B declared an independent Ukrainian state and pledged loyalty to Hitler. The OUN-B death squads carried out pogroms and massacres with support from the Germans, many of which took place in Volhynia where Mlynov was located. In 1942, the OUN-B established the Ukrainian Insurgent Army (UPA). In 1943–1944, in order to prevent Polish efforts at re-establishing Poland's pre-war borders, UPA combat units carried out large-scale ethnic cleansing against Polish people, killing an estimated 100,000 Polish civilians in Volhynia and Eastern Galicia.

37. "White Russian" refers to ethnic Russians living in the area between Russia and Poland (today this includes Lithuania, Ukraine, Belarus, Latvia and Moldova). By the 1920s, the term was more commonly used for Russians who'd opposed the Bolshevik Revolution and fought against the Red Army.

Part III

Ceaseless Wandering[1]

From the pen of David Bernstein[2]

Translated and edited by Howard I. Schwartz, PhD with Hanina Epstein

One of the days at the end of May 1943 towards evening, we were in area 13 on a hill with Yaakov Buber, with my first cousin Beluma Bernstein (now in Russia) and with another young man by the name of Chuna, whose family named I don't remember (he lives today in Netanya). We went down to the spring to get water. When we descended the hill, we saw 6 armed men. We stopped, hid and they passed close by. We continued towards the spring. Along the way there were other bunkers of Jews. We decided to enter them and to warn them about the men we encountered. This was in section 9. During our conversations with a number of Jews, we heard Ukrainian voices. The Ukrainians had discovered a young Jew sleeping in a bunker and they were letting each other know. They got closer and it became apparent that the Ukrainians left him without harming him for the time being. We continued going to the bunker where, among others, was my present wife Fania. We approached and called for the people to come out. We spoke to them for a number of minutes and agreed that, upon returning from the spring, we would pass their way again.

[Page 300]

On the way to the spring, we had to cross a trail in the middle of a dense woods. We approached the trail and Buber suddenly decided that he felt grave danger and didn't want to continue. We didn't succeed in convincing him and we turned back with him. We approached instead a swamp nearby to get a bit of water even though it was dirty.

Along the way, we met a Jew from Dubno by the name of Butler. We asked him where he was going. He responded that he was going to the village Churtz[3] to a Polish acquaintance to ask for food. We got near the swamp and suddenly heard shooting from the direction that Butler had gone. We returned to the bunker where Fania was, to which we had promised to return. We stayed there outside the bunker convinced by a feeling of danger. We decided to leave that location the following day. Suddenly my cousin Bluma saw, from several hundred meters away, someone ducking down and aiming his rifle at us. We hid in the dense woods. We heard a thundering of men and shots at us from all around. We felt that we were being targeted by the attackers, so we wouldn't succeed in escaping; we also heard branches being broken by them. Next to me was Fania, Beluma and Chuna. I told them to wait until I tried crawling to find a way to escape. I suggested fleeing in fact in the direction from which the attackers were coming, on the assumption that they were actually heading towards our location, and we would thereby succeed in evading them. I told them to take off their boots so that they would not hear us, and I gave a signal at the moment that appeared to me best for bolting in the direction from which the attackers were coming. We heard much shooting. We thus didn't run in a straight line, but in a zigzag, to evade the bullets. In the meantime, it got completely dark. We ran for a long time without knowing how long we ran. We ran several hours, apparently a long distance, perhaps tens of kilometers, until we felt that we had completely left the forest and had become visible to those going by, if we encountered anyone. From a distance, we still heard grenades explosions and the fire of automatic weapons. We concluded that all those who had remained in the location from which we fled were tragically killed. In the meantime, hard rain started to fall.

Slaughter

Towards morning, we decided to return to see if despite everything someone remained alive. Fania's brother, Moshe, had been there, and her sister Yehudit, and she wanted to return whatever the cost. We thus returned slowly with extreme caution. Suddenly, we heard voices of our Jewish friends, seeking one another. The first one we found was Meyerson from Dubno wounded in the chest. He begged us to be shot to end his suffering. He died on his own after about a half-hour. Afterwards, we met all the other survivors, among them Yehudit, sister of my wife, Fania, who succeeded in sheltering in an abandoned house in the forest under a crate. She was 12 years old, small and thin, and thanks to this, succeeded in hiding under that very crate. David Holtzeker[4] explained that Moshe, the brother of Fania, was taken alive by the Ukrainians and they killed him. He also saw how they killed a man from Mlynov, Meir Schechman.[5] Among the others who died in that same attack there were:

[Page 301]

Shlomo Nekunchinik,[6] Charna Gruber [*née* Goldseker],[7] whose husband Shmuel was killed earlier; their two children, ages 5 and 7 survived with Hanoch Gruber – the brother of their father, and they perished after this.

One bunker further way, which was named for one of its builders, the Jew Teler from Dubno, was not discovered by the Ukrainians and its people remained alive. As an aside, this bunker really excelled in being well-camouflaged, and its people believed that it was impossible to discover. Those there were: Yitzhak Mandelkern and his small son Gershon, Avraham Dratver[8] (today in Holon [Israel]) and his sister Emma from Dubno (today in Kibbutz Maale Hahamisha [in Israel]), Malka Hamilbosky — sister-in-law of Yitzhak Mandelkern, and Teler mentioned earlier. A young woman of 17 years old was there who woke in the night screaming — because a man who was then with them — she saw him dead. She was stricken with hysteria, and it was hard to keep her quiet. The man, indeed, died afterwards that very night, in the incident described above, when he visited one of the bunkers (apparently an experience of telepathy).

We Went to a Different Forest

The following day, the group of the remaining survivors decided to leave the forest. We gathered 13 people[9] — Fania, Yehudit, Yitzhak Mandelkern, his son Gershon, Yaakov Buber, Chuna, Avraham Dratver, my sister, Emma, Malka Hamilbosky, Moshe — the brother of Yitzhak Mandelkern, Beluma — my cousin, Rachel Kwasgalter[10] and myself. Yitzhak Mandelkern led the way. We walked all night. We got to a small woods by Berehy towards morning. We stayed during the day in the woods and watched the movement of Germans in the area. At night we continued again and needed to cross the Ikva River. We saw a number of small dinghies and an isolated house. I suggested that the group hide in a cornfield. I approached the house, knocked on the window. The farmer fearfully opened the door. I was dressed in a German jacket and Spanish hat (which apparently had been lost by one of the volunteer Spanish soldiers who were with the Germans). I told the farmer that I was one of Bandera's[11] men. I also had a pistol which I pointed at him (the Banderites were pursuing Poles at that time). I told him that I was moving Polish prisoners. I demanded he give me a key to one of the locks on the dinghies. I also punched him to instill fear, and I warned him not to leave the house for an hour, or he would be shot. I waited until he went to sleep. He promised me not to leave his home until morning. I got a bundle of keys from him to all the dinghies there. We traveled in one dinghy via a couple of trips, 3 persons per time. The last one transported me. When we finished the crossing, I took the dinghy up on our shore without returning it to its previous place, so that the farmer would not be able to pursue us. The farmer also could not easily use the other dinghies since the keys remained in my possession. We continued on our way in the direction of the villages of Uzhynets' and Karolinka.[12] Along the way we got lost and walked a great deal further.

[Page 302]

We got to the area of these villages towards morning, though we wanted to reach the forest while it was still night. We hid during the day and felt too much movement around us. The following night we went to the village Karolinka which was populated by Czechs and therefore less dangerous to us. In that location, we dug a new bunker. At night we went out to the houses of Czech farmers. We appeared like Banderites and demanded food under threat of weapons.

One time, we took from one farmer: women's clothes, a small crucifix and identity documents for a young girl. I gave the documents to my cousin, Beluma, who didn't have the appearance of a typical Jew. She managed to get hired for work by a farmer and this also made it easier for us. Actual Banderite men came there but they didn't realize that she was Jewish.

The forest there was smaller and less dense, and we feared all the time that we might be discovered. We thought about perhaps moving north to the forests of Polesia and joining with the Soviet partisans there. During that same time, the Banderites distributed leaflets in the area, calling on Jews in hiding to come out of their hiding places and join them, since at this time they had already begun fighting against the Germans. This was a trap to eliminate in this way the last Jewish remnants. They caught one Jew from Dubno and convinced him that in fact they intended to help the Jews. This Jew believed them and revealed to the Banderites the hiding place of a Jewish family by the name of Sodovitzki — a man known from the community of Dubno. The murderers grabbed his wife and daughter and murdered them. Sodovitzki turned himself in after that and begged that they kill him. The Banderites killed him and the Jew who showed them the hiding place.

One time I was sick, covered with sores, and I needed a warm bath. I went with Fania to a Czech farmer to beg him for the opportunity to bathe in his home. We discovered that hiding with him were several Jews from Mlynov – Koppel Messinger[13] (now in the United States), Avraham Shek[14] and two other sisters from Dubno by the name of Hochberg. A Czech woman who was married to a Ukrainian came to the farmer's house. I realized that the woman was liable to snitch on us. Indeed, that same night Banderite men came to the threshing barn where the Jews were hiding. Avraham Shek was killed, Koppel Messinger and two Hochberg sisters managed to escape in the darkness.

Admist Czechs and Poles, Jews Are Saved

In the meantime, winter 1943–44 approached. We were able to arrange for Yehudit to attend to sheep, goats and geese with a Czech farmer by the name of Miller in the village Boyrica.[15] To avoid being discovered, we stayed in the bunker only at night; during the day we walked on paths that other people used, so that that our footsteps alone wouldn't stick out in the snow. We left various things in the bunker in order to check if someone had visited it during the day. One night we returned and were convinced that people had been there. We decided to leave again. Malka Hamilbosky, Dratver and his sister Emma, Yitzhak Mandelkern with his son Gershon — found a hiding place with a Czech farmer.

[Page 303]

Yaakov Buber met the two Hochberg sisters and made arrangements with another farmer. Moshe, the brother of Yitzhak Mandelkern, hid with a farmer, but was discovered after 3 days and killed by Banderites. Rachel Kwasgalter also found shelter with a different Czech farmer. Fania, Chuna and I did not find a hiding place.

We were aware of an abandoned Polish village, Pańska Dolina, whose residents left from fear of the Banderites and went to live in Lutzk. In the village there remained only a handful of young armed Poles, about 20 of them, to guard the property. They were fortified in four houses by the main thoroughfare. These Poles guarded their village with the acquiescence of the German authorities. We heard that a number of Jews were hiding in the abandoned houses (with the knowledge of the Poles who guarded the village). On the way to the village, we decided to check on the wellbeing of Yehudit, Fania's sister. We arrived at night to the farmer's yard and went in to sleep in his threshing barn. Early in the morning the farmer came out to work. Fania went out towards him and told him that she was the sister of Yehudit and asked about her. The farmer told Fania that two days earlier Yehudit was taken by Banderites. Fania began to scream and cry — why did he turn her over and not protect her? He softened up and asked her to go to the threshing barn, because in another 10 minutes Yehudit would appear. Indeed, Yehudit arrived and explained that in fact they had snitched on her, but the farmer sent a neighbor to the field to warn her and at night hid her well and decided to hide her to the end. He told the Banderites that she had fled to the forest.

Fania felt that Yehudit was withholding some secret from her. Finally, on the condition that the secret not be revealed, she explained that she was in a hiding place on the farmer's grounds with two other Jewish families. Brayer[16] and Brodman[17] — whom the farmer had hidden from the beginning of the eradication. This was revealed to Yehudit incidentally when the Banderites were looking for her; at that point the farmer hid her with these families. The families numbered 6 people, including a son who was 4. For their security, the members of the family wanted Yehudit to go with us, but since we didn't have a hiding place, we were not able to take her with us and we left her there. Thus, she stayed with this same farmer until the liberation.

When the Germans retreated, the Czechs left the village and, for the security of those hiding, put a covering of wood on top of them and scattered livestock manure on it. To the bad fortune of those concealed, German soldiers settled in with horses to the threshing barn where they were hiding. The men stood and with their backs supported the covering for 72 hours without it caving in! As to the fate of this family — the boy and his father died a short time after the liberation in the town of Rovno, the father from tuberculosis and the son from meningitis. The woman was pregnant when leaving the bunker and after the death of her husband married his brother, who had returned from Russia.

From the grounds of Miller, where Yehudit was hiding, we headed towards the village of Pańska Dolina, after hiding during the day with Miller.

[Page 304]

We went out on the way again at night and reached the village of Lebnovkah[18] — about an hour of walking from the grounds of Miller. It was a very cold night and a snowstorm occurred. Due to the storm, we were not able to continue walking. We felt that we were going to perish on the way, and it was imperative for us to find shelter. We approached a house, knocked on the window and presented ourselves as Jews. It is worth pointing out that the residents of this village were also Czech. The woman of the home opened the door and permitted us to enter and to warm ourselves. It is hard to describe how much we enjoyed the warmth that prevailed in the home. The woman bathed her children. We envied her and wondered — if we would ever be fortunate again to have a warm home where we could wash in warm water and soap? The woman of the home introduced herself, her name was Kunshk and she told us that her husband was on guard duty in the village. She gave us warm food and requested we hide after this in the threshing barn because if we were discovered in the house, the Germans would kill the entire family too; but if they discovered us in the threshing barn, we need to claim that we entered there without her knowledge and permission. Due to the storm, we remained in the threshing barn until morning. In the morning the woman told us, that in the village they were saying that the Germans were going to come to confiscate the pigs near the holidays, and therefore we needed to leave immediately. We therefore went back on the road, even though we didn't usually move about by day.

In order to reach Pańska Dolina, we needed to cross the Dubno-Rovno road that had a constant, active movement of German military men. Obviously, our appearances and clothes would easily give us away. We crawled towards the road. We hid in a ditch with the goal of crossing the road by exploiting a break between vehicles. One by one we crossed to the other side of the road and finally succeeded in reaching Pańska Dolina. Due to the intense cold, most of us had a urinary tract inflammation, causing suffering and pain, in addition to being inconvenient and uncomfortable.

Upon entering the village, a wagon passed with a Polish young man sitting in it whom Fania recognized as a friend from a class in primary school. He also recognized immediately that we were Jews and directed us behind the house where a woman from our town was hiding, Leah [Liza] Berger[19] (now in Uruguay). We entered this house and we found Leah inside. She told us that the farmers from that place were in Lutzk and returned occasionally in order to pick up grain and other necessities for sustenance. She was of the opinion that there was a chance that one of these families would turn over their house to us on the condition that we guard their property, since the Poles generally did this willingly, thereby increasing the chances their property would not be robbed by the Ukrainians.

The plan in fact came to pass. We were granted a house like this, and we also had enough food to be satiated from the stock of goods and from the farm. In addition to us, other people from our town who were hiding in the same village were: Rachel Kwasgalter,[20] Rachel Fisher,[21] Freida and Leon Kupferberg,[22] the Malar family (the parents and daughter) from Dubno and others. Together there were more than 50 Jews from the different small towns in the area.

* * *

[Page 305]

During that time, Polish partisans were organizing and training in the area who subsequently crossed the Bug River to join the organizations of Polish partisans on Polish land. As mentioned, the local Poles were armed and guarding the village from the Banderite gangs with the acquiescence of the German authorities. The Germans therefore trusted these Poles and did not organize visits to this village. The Poles, on the other hand, leveraged this situation to organize an underground against the Germans. This was reasonable against the backdrop of the situation at the front, since it was obvious to the Poles that the Germans were going to lose the war and that it would be good for them to improve their standing in the eyes of the Soviets, who would arrive in the future, by [becoming] anti-German underground fighters. The Polish units, therefore, were being exchanged. In addition — and also against the background of the general atmosphere — they all were patient with the Jews who were hiding with them and were assisted by them in different kinds of work. One time a new Polish force which numbered 120 men came to the village. The Polish groups also carried out punishment operations against Ukrainian villages that were earlier active against the Poles. With the Poles was a Jewish baker named Micael from Lutzk, who lives today in Israel. The Poles were looking for a doctor and weapons. There were rumors that in the village of Noviny Chiskia[23] a doctor was hiding by the name of Grintzveig from Dubno. They asked that one of us volunteer to go with them to find and to secure the trust[24] of the Jewish doctor and to add him to their unit. I volunteered to go with them. They gave me warm clothing and a weapon and we left at night for the operation. This was a group of about 60 men. The main mission of the operation was the seizing of weapons from the residents of the surrounding villages and taking the same opportunity to locate the Jewish doctor. We succeeded in seizing about 15 rifles, principally from Czech houses, but we didn't find the doctor. Afterwards, it became clear that he was hiding in another village. The Poles appeared in disguise, on their hats they put red military decorations and spoke Ukrainian and Russian, so that the local residents would think they were Soviet partisans. This disguise was necessary not just for the Ukrainians but also for the Germans, so that it would not become apparent that Poles — especially those in Pańska Dolina — were engaged in unlawful activities, a time at any rate when the operations of the Soviet partisans were already known.[25]

During the operation, the Poles stationed men for observation, concealed in different positions along the roads. Towards morning, a sleigh with two armed Ukrainians approached one of the guards in an observation post, and it became apparent that one of them was an officer from the Bandera gangs, who was returning from a consultation with the officers in the village of Dobryatyn.[26] The Polish guard ordered them to raise their hands. The Ukrainian officer thought, apparently, that there must be a misunderstanding and approached and brought out his pistol. The

Pole shot into the air. Upon hearing the shot, other Poles gathered and took the Ukrainian officer into captivity. He still thought they were Soviet partisans and he explained that in his gangs there were also Soviet partisans.

[Page 306]

I sat in the wagon next to the officer. We all traveled in the direction of Pańska Dolina. The whole way we spoke Ukrainian and Russian. Along the way we continued to interrogate him. He revealed that his name was Strodov and that he and his gang were fighting only Poles and Jews. He also gave up the location of his gang and its headquarters. When we got to Pańska Dolina, a Pole sat by me and said, "Now, it is okay to reveal," and he said to the Ukrainian — We are "Leechim"[27] from Dolina" ("Leechim" — a derogatory name for Poles by the Ukrainian nationalists). I added, "They are Leechim and I am a Yid, and now is your opportunity to live in the skin of the Jews who are being taken out to slaughter." The Poles beat him with heavy blows while giving a mocking rendition of the Ukrainian anthem.

In Pańska Dolina that same day, a group of men happened by, apparently senior officers from the headquarters of the Polish partisan movement in Lutzk. They organized a quick field justice for Strodov and took him away to be killed together with the coachman. According to what became known later, this Strodov had earlier been in the German police in Mlynov and the surrounding area and he was among the head of the death squads that liquidated Jewish ghettos in the area. After several days, a punishment brigade[28] went to a village in which the gang's headquarters was located, whose position Strodov had revealed. In this operation, the Poles succeeded in capturing and wiping out 6 additional Ukrainian officers.

After approximately two weeks, while the Polish force was still in the area, a group of Germans passed on the main road nearby — while the Poles were drilling in the field. The Germans noticed that these men were armed and thought, apparently, that they were Banderites preparing to attack the Poles in Pańska Dolina and opened fire on them.[29] The Poles returned fire but successfully escaped within 10 minutes. The fire was only to give cover for the escape. During the exchange of volleys, one Pole was mortally wounded. The Germans grabbed him, but he kept up his Ukrainian charade and his life left him without revealing the fact that they were Poles. He was brought to Mlynov and his heroic stance we learned about afterwards from the people of Mlynov. After this skirmish, the Poles left Pańska Dolina, but after a few days other Poles arrived in their place.

In the meantime, the front was drawing near. One day a Hungarian officer appeared and requested permission from the Poles for his retreating unit to pass by. These were Hungarians who fought on the side of the Germans but already during this time were trying to evade their duties and desert the front. This group was trying to reach the Hungarian border. In this unit was also a unit of conscripted Hungarian Jews, part of a Hungarian "labor army." The Poles permitted them to pass. The Hungarian Jews that came to the village were feeble from hunger and exhaustion. We gave them bread and tried to convince the Jews to remain with us, because here with us was a more secure place; for if they continued with the Hungarians, they were liable to fall together with them into Russian captivity.

[Page 307]

It is worth noting that only two Hungarian Jews remained with us, and they did indeed survive. The rest remained faithful to their Hungarian superiors and continued with them. It is not known what fate befell them.

Hardships After the Liberation

The Russians!

On the 5th of February 1944 in the evening, they knocked at our windows. We got up and opened the door. The men identified themselves as Russian scouts. They were 15 calvary riding on horses and among them was a sergeant major by the name of Falki. When he entered, he asked, "Who are you?" We responded that we were Jews. He got emotional; he turned to us in Yiddish and said that he had traveled over 1000 kilometers, and he not yet met Jewish survivors. He asked what we needed. The following morning a Russian unit entered. Falki came with them and with him was a Jewish captain named Boris Shalkubar and a Russian captain by the name of Volkov, and they brought the best stuff for us. Volkov had taken the Jewish boy Sherman[30] with him and attended to all his needs and cared for him like a father. Sherman accompanied Volkov all the way to Germany; there at the front Volkov was killed during one of the bombardments and Sherman reunited with his brother Yechiel,[31] who along with several other Jews was staying in Mlynov at the time (the two of them live today in Haifa).

When the front reached our area and the battles were raging, we found it necessary to advance behind the Russian lines, out of a fear of a temporary retreat, that can happen during a battle — and that the Germans would appear again, even if their days were numbered. We therefore headed to the town of Lutzk, where Jewish survivors had gathered from many different places — from bunkers in the forest and in the villages as well as Jews holding Aryan papers. We reached Lutzk the day of a Red Army holiday. That same day, the Germans started an offensive across the Styr River. We saw a strong movement [of troops]. It became obvious the Soviets were leaving the town, in other words, temporarily retreating. We asked the Soviet officers and soldiers for permission to join them, since we were Jews and must not fall into German hands a second time. They steadfastly refused us and did not permit us to go with them.

Therefore, we decided to go by ourselves — a group of 15 Jews — towards the city of Rovno.[32] We went on foot. The way was dangerous since there was a movement of a fighting army in the conditions of a front. We walked at night. It was a bitter cold night. In one village, we wanted to take a short rest. We entered the grounds where we saw Russian soldiers. A Russian captain came towards us with a pistol in his hand. We told him we were Jews who were heading in the direction of Rovno; we were cold, wanted to rest and were afraid to move at night because of the Ukrainian gangs. The officer said to us, "I don't care who you are; if I let you to enter, I will have to guard you and I will not be able to rest; therefore, get out of here, and if not, I will shoot you."

[Page 308]

We continued to walk and tried our luck at another house. We also entered a yard there. A soldier stood at his post. We repeated our story. He told us to wait there until he asked his commanding officer what to do with us. The soldier returned and called us inside. It became apparent that this time we had encountered a Jewish officer. He did not actually identify himself, but his eyes betrayed him. He commanded the owner of the house to spread straw for us for a night of rest. Towards morning, the officer came in and told us that for our own good it was advisable that we leave quickly and make progress towards Rovno. We went out to the main road. We tried to stop a military vehicle, but none stopped. The women with us decided to lie down on the road and thus force them to stop. We wanted to ride, not because we were tired of walking, but because we were afraid that if we went on foot, the Germans would overtake us. But even this tactic didn't help. Military men did indeed stop but berated the women and ordered them to depart.

We reached a junction where the road crossed railroad tracks; there was also a station there. A train passed and we tried to get on since it was moving slowly. I succeeded in getting on and dragged Yehudit in behind me. On this train, we successfully reached Rovno. This was a freight train, and no one took any interest in knowing who we were.

In Rovno

When we got to Rovno, we began wandering about the streets until we met Jews. It became obvious that survivors[33] were concentrated in two houses at the addresses 121 and 123, on a street called "May 3rd"[34] (the major street in Rovno was named during the Soviet government in 1940 in memory of Stalin). We were starving. In one of the houses, I found a slice of bread, which I brought to Yehudit.

In Rovno, a Soviet military authority was established. The authorities operated on the assumption, apparently, that the local population was comprised entirely of those who collaborated in German activities, and as usual this didn't bode well for the Jews. All the men ages 16 to 60 were stopped and expelled eastward to the rear. After this it became clear, that some of those expelled (among them also were some Jewish survivors who explained that they were Jews who had been in hiding during the German period, and that they were prepared now to fight against the Germans — to no avail) were brought to the front and served as a living screen in front of the Soviet fighting force. In other words, these unarmed men were sent to the front lines; when they were exposed to the Germans, they opened fire on them, thinking they were Soviet soldiers. In this way, the Soviet army exposed the German positions, and only then did the Soviets open fire in the direction of the Germans without concerning themselves at all about outcasts standing in the open fields — who were cut down by fire from both sides … Among them obviously were Jewish survivors, who were killed this way — after they survived the Germans in the Shoah. Among those killed in this way, I remember Yaakov Buber from Dubno and Leon Kupferberg, who were mentioned earlier, and many others whose names I no longer remember.

[Page 309]

I went by myself to "Voyenkomat"[35] (the enlistment office in Russian) and I thought, that if I volunteer on my own for the army, I will earn special treatment and not be sent with the gang of Bandera men for a role that I described earlier. I waited in line. When I entered, I told my story of survival; where and how I hid and that now I wanted to avenge the blood of my family members who were killed by the Germans. I had no documentation, obviously. The Russian officer asked me how I had remained alive. His reaction to my story was that if I had no documentation and I had remained alive — this was a sign that I also was one of the Bandera men and that I had collaborated in the German deeds, and I should thus go with the Bandera men for the roles that were assigned to them.

Fania meanwhile succeeded in arranging for work in a restaurant. Thanks to this we were saved from starvation. I was sick, malnourished, and covered with sores. I was only able to get medicine from the pharmacy if I brought a bit of fat and money. Fania worked only in exchange for food, and she would also sneak remnants of soup for me. She didn't receive payment and we had no source from which to obtain it. When Fania went to the pharmacy to obtain medicine she had nothing to pay with. With no choice, she decided to ask one of the officers for a few coins. When finally she mustered the wherewithal to make this request from an officer, he drove her out with contempt. She returned to me without medicine. In the meantime, the front had advanced to the Bug River and the German danger subsided completely. Since we hadn't managed to secure sustenance in Rovno, we decided to return to Mlynov, where at least Fania had a home.

In Mlynov

The gentiles who were living in Fania's house vacated two rooms for us; Fania and I settled in one and the second we turned over to other young Jewish women who had also survived. During that time, 25 survivors gathered together in Mlynov. We had been in Rovno for three months and we returned to Mlynov in May 1944. Gradually, civil life returned to its course. The Jewish men had special luck that the first lieutenant who worked in enlistment office (Voyenkomat) in Mlynov was a Soviet Jewish deputy officer, and it was he who protected us from the edict to send human fodder to the front. His name was Filko. During that period, we set up a memorial on the mass grave of martyrs from the Mlynov and communities. The impetus and initiator of the memorial was Berel Rabinovitch (today in Haifa). Later on, in preparation for the Nuremberg trials, Rabinovitch participated in a local committee to document the Nazi crimes.

In Mlynov, the local people already knew us and were not able to accuse us of collaborating in the operations of the Banderites or with the Germans. We received identity papers and in addition registered with the enlistment office (Voyenkomat).

[Page 310]

I felt a personal obligation to revenge the blood of my family members and my town Boremel. Not a single Jew returned to live in this town from the eight survivors in total! I was therefore afraid to return there. In the nearby town of Demydivka, a regional office of the NKVD[36] was established. I went there and proposed myself for a role exposing Nazi collaborators. I was appointed as a clerk in the department distributing identity papers.

The NKVD would go to a village, announce a curfew, and order the residents to present themselves to receive an identity card. Those who didn't appear could not get an identity card afterwards. When they presented themselves, I tried to identity the criminals whom I recognized from the period of the German rule. The suspects were detained. But to put them on trial I needed to find witnesses who were able to testify to their deeds. The murderers who didn't flee with the Germans relied on the fact that Jews hadn't remained alive, and that their neighbors and members of their people would not turn them over. Finding witnesses was not easy. The trials took place in Rovno before a military court. The witnesses it was possible to enlist were from a small number of Ukrainians who were Soviet supporters and who themselves suffered at the hands of the Germans and those who were dragged in by them.

Translator's and editor's footnotes:

1.   The title of the essay alludes to God's punishment of Cain for his brother's murder: "You shall become a ceaseless wanderer on earth." (Genesis 4:12).

2.   The previous essay (p. 298) recounts how Fania Mandelkern met her future husband David Bernstein (alternative spelling Berenstein, Bornstein/ Bernshteyn) as they fled from their bunkers which had been discovered.

3.   Identification uncertain, perhaps Church near Lutzk.

4.   Likely referring to David Holtzeker grandson of Ida and Moshe Holtzeker, one of the original five brothers to come to Mlynov. David's parents were Yankel Holtzeker and Risia. David and his brother Menashe were mentioned as being in the bunker in the earlier Part II of this testimony, p. 294 with additional notes.

5.   One of the sons of Noach Moshe Schechman and his wife Batya; brother of survivor, Shlomo Schechman. See p. 288 note 19 for additional notes.

6.   A photo of Shlomo appears on p. 467 with notes there, and in the earlier essay, p. 290.

7.   See earlier notes on Charna and her husband Shmuel p. 294, footnote 10.

8.   Possibly from the Dratver family from Dubno listed among martyrs in the Yad Vashem database.

9.   See Parts I and II of this testimony for earlier notes on the identity of these individuals.

10.   Rachel Kwasgalter survived, married fellow survivor Berel Rabinovitch and was living in Israel when this volume was published. See family photos on page 466. Her parents were Sheintzi (Gonik) and Meir Kwasgalter (1896–1942) who is also mentioned in the previous essay (p. 295). Her brother Chaim (1931–1942) also perished. Mendel Steinberg in this essay reports meeting Rachel Kwasgalter after the liberation (p. 368).

11.   On the background of the Banderites, see the notes on the previous essay, p. 297.

12. On old maps, Karolinka appears just slightly northwest of Uzhynets' which is just 6 km east (3.7 mi) from Mlynov and then slightly north. It appears to have been incorporated into contemporary Uzhynets'. The group is heading from the area west of Mlynov to the area east of Mlynov.

13. Koppel (Karl) Messinger (~ 1924–2008) was one of four sons of Eliezer and Malka, who both perished along with two of his brothers, David (Dov) and Chanoch, who are mentioned in the list of martyrs, p. 436. Family stories recall Koppel working in the forced labor camps and risking escape with some of the other young men. Koppel survived hiding in barns during the day and going out at night. He made his way to Israel in 1949, married, and had his first of two daughters. In 1960, his brother Victor sponsored Karl's family to come to the US and settle in Philadelphia where Victor and his family were living. Victor (Shmuel) Messinger was also born in Mlynov. He had been arrested by the Soviets after 1939 and deported to Siberia. He was drafted into the Soviet Army around 1942, fought against the Germans as a tank commander and was wounded. He made his way after the War to Philadelphia. The brothers reconnected in the 1950s by mail and were reunited in Philadelphia in the 1960s.

14. The list of Mlynov martyrs (p. 439) includes a Shek family (alternative spelling Shak): Mendel, Golda his wife, daughter of R. Moshe Nahman's, and children: Avraham, Devora, Freidil, and Beila. It seems likely Golda is daughter of Moshe Holtzeker, one of the five Holtzeker brothers to come to Mlynov. "R. Moshe Nahman's" (or R. Moshe Nachmanis) which is probably a shortened form of R. Moshe Nahmanis Holtzeker who is also the father of Rivkah (Holtzeker) Fisher (p. 437) and in the list of Goldseker martyrs (p. 432) as the father of Yehoshua Goldseker. See the discussion of the name "Moshe Nahman's" on p. 470 footnote 4.

15. Perhaps the nearby farming village of Bortnytsia, called Bortnica in Polish, 12 km south of Uzhynets', known as a site where Jews and Poles were massacred.

16. Yosef Brayer (or Braier), with a wife and two kids, were refugees from Sokoliki near Turka, Ukraine which is 315 km (196 mi) west of Mlynov. Like Mlynov, Turka was under Russian control from 1939–1941. When Germany attacked Russia in June 1941, some of the Jews from Sokoliki and Turka managed to flee East and were evacuated to the area around Mlynov. See the essay in this volume by Frida Kupferberg regarding the "Murder of the Sokoliki Refugees," 384–385.

17. Shmuel Brodman (1879–1942) and his wife Rozia (Frid) (1879–1942) were refugees from Sokoliki near Turka who had settled in Stomorhy which is just 6 km (3.7 mi) north of Mlynov. See also prior note.

18. Possibly Lebedyanka which is not far north of Bortnytsya where Yehudit may have been living with the farmer. Both are close to Mlynov and the group is heading north on their way to Pańska Dolina.

19. Liza Berger contributed the essay, "I Wandered Hungry and in Pain," 347–351. She was the daughter of Tuvia and Miriam Berger. She was one of three siblings. She and her brother Pinchas survived.

20. See note 10.

21. Rachel Fisher (alternative spelling Fischer) was one of nine siblings including Yafa Dayagi (=Sheindel Fisher) who contributed the essay, "Home and Youth Movement in Mlynov," pp. 247–250, which includes additional notes. Rachel survived and joined three sisters who had earlier made aliyah.

22. Freida Kupferberg survived and contributed the essay, "Murder of the Sokoliki Refugees," pp. 384–385, which describes the fate that befell the refugees from Sokoliki near Turka who were resettled in and around Mlynov.

23. Perhaps Novyna-Dobryatynska today which is not far south from where Pańska Dolina was.

24. Misspelled in Hebrew as "training" with an extra yod.

25. The Poles didn't want the Germans to realize they were fighting against them for fear of reprisals before the Russians reached the area.

26. A town only 8 km (5 mi) west of Mlynov.

27. Apparently, a derogatory term used by the Ukrainians as a description of Poles. Exact meaning not identified.

28. Possibly an allusion to the German, the Bewährungsbataillon / punishment battalions were "marching prisons" made up of convicts, felons, malingerers and thugs who were often assigned the toughest and most dangerous tasks. Here, the retribution unit was Ukrainian.

29. Ukrainians in the period of 1943 were involved in massacres of Poles and the implication here is that Germans wanted to prevent the attack, though according to historical sources Germans actively encouraged the ethnic conflict and hostilities.

30. Referring to the story of Ezra Sherman who survived and became a mascot for this Russian unit. See Ezra's interview posted on the Mlynov website.

31. Yechiel Sherman contributed the essay, "Departure from Home," 344–346.

32. Further east of Lutsk away from the offensive.

33. According to David Lee Preston, *The Sewer People of Lvov*, by the end of 1944 there were approximately 1,200 Jews in Rovno after the liberation; among them, the author.

34. It is unclear what holiday is being referred to.

35. Appears to be this Russian word for "enlistment office."

36. An abbreviation for People's Commissariat for Internal Affairs, later evolved into the KGB, carried out mass arrests, deportations and executions of German collaboratives and other prisoners held when the Soviet Union held Poland during WWII.

Part IV

Mlynov After the Liberation of the Soviet Army

Fania (Mandelkern) Bernstein

Translated and edited by Howard I. Schwartz, PhD with Hanina Epstein

Mlynov was liberated on February 6, 1944.[1] As mentioned above, we did not return to Mlynov right away with the liberation. We tried before this to get along in Rovno and only after we didn't succeed in this effort, and after we believed that the security conditions had also improved a bit in smaller places, we returned to Mlynov. There was another reason for this, since the authorities refused to permit us to live in Rovno, with the excuse that this was a district seat, and we weren't established residents and therefore we needed to return to the place we lived before the war. Of course, we were interested to see what remained of our home and possessions.

The returnees[2] to Mlynov were: myself, Yehudit my sister, David my husband, Berel Rabinovitch, Shlomo Schechman, the family of Nahum Teitelman (5 persons), Mendel Teitelman from Mervits and his wife, Sonia, and his sister Mamtze, Aharon Nudler and his daughter Lana,[3] Getzel (the family name I don't remember[4]) from Mervits, his brother Mendel and his sister Bunia, Hanoch Holtzeker (he fell afterwards in Kibbutz Negba in the War of Independence), Koppel Messinger, Yitzhak Mandelkern, and his son Gershon, Batia Grinberg from Mervits, Hannah Veiner, Tovyah Gardeen [i.e., Gordon] (the daughter of the Rabbi), Liza Zeburovitz from Lutzk, and also Freida Kupferberg, the family Goldreich (4 persons) – among the refugees [from Turka] who had been settled in Mlynov by the Soviets. And a number of additional people, who at the moment is hard for me to remember.

[Page 311]

In my parents' home, there were 10 rooms in two wings. During the German period, a number of families lived there. A portion of them apparently collaborated in German activities and they fled together with them. Two families continued to live in our house also after the liberation and were holding six rooms. Four rooms remained empty, and we settled into them — me and my sister Yehudit in one room; in the second room 5 single young women from those mentioned above; in the third room a Jewish family from Shchervitz[5] by the name of Grinsphun which included a widow, her sister, two daughters of the widow and a son who had been conscripted by the Soviets. It became apparent he was sick with tuberculosis, returned to his "home" and died about a month after he returned from the front. The fourth room served as a storeroom, kitchen, etc., for all the Jewish residents in the house.

One farmer brought me 100 kilograms of wheat saying that by doing so he was repaying a debt to my brother Moshe, of blessed memory. Little by little, we arranged different places of work. From the work itself, it was not possible to subsist. In addition, we therefore engaged a bit in the black-market for different necessities. The synagogue which had been empty during the German days was converted by the Soviets to a grain warehouse, even though most houses were empty and could have served this purpose.

Living conditions were very difficult. My sister Yehudit got sick with typhus, when I was absent for several days during my stay in the town of Demydivka. She was taken to a hospital room. The care there was very bad. Medicine was not available. Yehudit didn't believe that she would leave alive. So that I would know her final fate — she drew her palm by the bed on the wall and signed her name inside the palm of her hand. I found her in very bad shape. I got her much better food and cared for her personally. I also bribed her female doctor to permit me to care for my sister. In the neighboring village of Maslyanka,[6] a Polish military unit was stationed. I walked there to beg for medicine. To my good fortune, there were two Jewish doctors in that unit who took pity on me. They came with me to the hospital room and brought with them sulfa and other medicines. Thanks to their care, Yehudit survived and returned very slowly to full strength.

* * *

In the first months, the survivors who returned to Mlynov succeeded in freeing a number of Jewish children who remained in the hands of Christian families. One incident deserves special mention, because it aroused great tension between the Jews and the non-Jewish population. One of the displaced Jewish women, who was mother to a baby about one years old, around the time of the ghetto liquidation, left her daughter by the home of a Polish peasant family who lacked children. On the body of the baby, she stuck a note with the name of the girl and wrote on it that the girl had already been baptized as a Christian. The peasant couple brought the baby into their house and adopted her as a daughter. The mother hid in the forest and after the liberation, when she succeeded in getting work and settled into an apartment, she turned to the peasant family requesting that they return her daughter to her. They refused and the woman initiated a lawsuit. The justice of the peace ruled in favor of the Polish couple in the claim, since the Jewish mother didn't behave like a natural mother in "discarding" her daughter, and therefore was not fit for the girl to be returned to her. The Jewish woman appealed the ruling. The district court, by contrast, ruled that the girl should be returned to her Jewish mother noting that the mother had no choice but to "discard" her daughter with the goal of saving her in this way. It also ruled that the Jewish woman was liable to pay the Polish couple to cover the expenses of caring for the girl. The ruling aroused, as noted, tremendous tension. Thousands assembled at the court, but the outburst came to naught.

One of the survivors, Bunia [Steinberg] from Mervits, knew about a Jewish girl [Aviva[7]] whose family name was Feldman. Her parents, who perished, had placed her before their deaths with a Polish family. After the liberation, Bunia followed her for many weeks and succeeded one time in grabbing her and bringing her to the town [of Mlynov]. At first, the girl wanted to return to her adopted parents, but finally she relented and agreed to remain with the Jews. She is living today in one of the Kibbutzim in Israel or in the United States.[8]

Another young girl, Fisher,[9] whose parents lived before the war in the village of Mantyn,[10] also hid with a peasant family. The survivors bumped into her by accident when she came shopping in town with her "adopted parents." She was shocked when she met Jews. She was sure that there were no Jewish survivors, and that she was the only one in the world. But she hesitated at first to leave her adopted parents and she was convinced only after great efforts. Today she lives in [kibbutz] Kvutzat Kinneret, is married and a mother of children.

The young Liba,[11] daughter of Yaakov Tesler, hid with a peasant family pretending to be a Polish girl. The Germans sent her along with many sons and daughters of peasants to work in Germany alongside German farmers. After this, she was taken into Soviet captivity as a German woman. With great difficulty she succeeded — with the help of Soviet Jews — to prove she was a Jew and to free herself. She lives today in the United States.

* * *

Those eligible for conscription among the Jewish survivors were all drafted and sent to the front. By contrast, the survivors encountered a sympathetic attitude from the authorities in obtaining places of work (which in truth didn't sustain the person working but served to "justify" one's existence) and also in restoring living quarters and property. The requests to restore living quarters were negligible since the few survivors preferred to stay together and not be scattered among the gentiles. The state of security in the town itself was reassuring, but in the villages and on the roads outside town, the fear of the Banderite men was significant.

With their own money, the survivors erected a monument on the mass grave of the martyrs from the Mlynov community (kehilla).[12]

[Page 313]

The local authorities gave a license for this, and their representatives — including a squad of soldiers — participated in the unveiling ceremony. The ceremony was immortalized by a photographer (the photo is distributed among all the natives of the town who were in Israel).[13]

When the War ended and life no longer had the character of an emergency, the few survivors felt that they no longer had a place in the town and that they could not to continue a proper life among the ruins of the community. When the restraints of the War were removed, the local Ukrainian population also recovered which previously had feared vengeance from the Soviet authorities for its treachery and collaboration with the German activities. It became clear that the authorities had let go of the past to deal with the present and were not interested in being reminded of what was obliterated … The survivors were longing for a Jewish life and yearned to go to a much bigger Jewish community.

In December 1945, they left Mlynov and went to the town of Rovno, where several thousand Jews had already gathered. Later, when the possibility of repatriation to Poland was announced in the summer of 1946,[14] almost everyone returned to this country, some heading towards the Land of Israel and some to relatives in countries across the ocean.

*Commemoration for the martyrs of Mlynov-Mervits by the mass grave in Mlynov, after the liberation,[115]
in the presence of Shoah survivors [who are called out, if identified, in notes below]
Original photo courtesy of survivor Gerry Steinberg*

1. Nahum Teitelman
2. Mendel Teitelman, first cousin of Nahum #1
3. Mamtze Teitelman, sister of Mendel Teitelman #2, married Israel Genut in the displaced persons (DP) camp of Föhrenwald.
4. Yosef Teitelman, son of Nahum #1 and Rachel #8 and sister of Shifra #12
5. Arke (aka Aaron) Nudler, father of Yetka (aka Helen) #13
6. Mendel Steinberg, brother of Getzel #9, husband of Sheindel #7, father of Anshel #20
7. Sheindel (Grenspun) Steinberg, wife of Mendel #6, mother of Anshel #20
8. Rachel (Gruber) Teitelman, wife of Nahum #1, mother of Yosef #4 and Shifra #12
9. Getzel (aka George) Steinberg, husband of Pesia #14 and father of Zelig #16
10. Candlesticks of Pesia Steinberg #14
11. Ezra Sherman, young boy in Russian uniform who became mascot of Russian military unit
12. Shifra Teitelman, daughter of Nahum #1 and Rachel #8, sister of Yosef #4
13. Yetka Nudler (later Helen Nudler Fixler), daughter of Arke #5
14. Pesia (Wurtzel) (aka Paula) Steinberg, wife of Getzel #9, mother of Zelig #16
15. Bunia Steinberg, sister of Getzel #9 and Mendel #2, later married Yitzhak Upstein from Mervits
16. Zelig (aka Gerald) Steinberg, young son of Getzel #9 and Pesia #14
17. Aviva Feldman (later Meromi), young girl rescued from Polish family through the combined effort of Bunia #15 and her brother Getzel #9. Adopted as child of Getzel #9 and Pesia #14, a relative of Aviva, until Aviva was returned to an aunt in Israel.
18. Berel Rabinowitch, organizer of the event
19. Russian soldiers to protect the survivors during their commemoration

20. Anshel Steinberg, son of Mendel #6 and Sheindel #7

Translator's and editor's footnotes:

1.   The date appears to be in the Israeli format of dd/mm/yyyy. Appears to align with the Soviet offensive known as the Dnieper-Carpathian offensive from late December 1943 to early May 1944 which largely expelled Axis forces from Ukraine.

2.   Most of the names of survivors here have been mentioned in Parts 1-III of this testimony with notes. What follows is a list of names with reference page numbers to consult for photos and details.

o   Berel Rabinovitch, photo p. 466 and notes.

o   Shlomo Schechman, p. 288 fn. 19, photo p. 478, and pp. 227 and 460.

o   Nahum Teitelman, a contributor to this volume, pp. 314–324, wife Rachel (Gruber), a contributor to this volume (pp. 380–382), sons Asher (a contributor to this volume, pp. 38–42), Yosef, Shifra. See photo p. 482. See also the Teitelman story on the Mlynov website.

o   Mendel Teitelman and wife Sonia (Gruber) together contributed many essays to this volume. Photo page 325 and notes there.

o   Mamtze (Teitelman) Genut, sister of Mendel Teitelman. She married Israel Genut in the Displaced Persons Camp of Föhrenwald, photo p. 501.

o   Aharon Nudler and daughter, Yetka, here called Lana, (later Helen Fixler) mentioned in parts I-II of this testimony, and mentioned by Nahum Teitelman, page 343 with notes. See also the Nudler family story on the Mlynov website.

o   Getzel (George) Steinberg, his wife Pessia (Wurtzel), his son Zelig (later Gerald), his brother Mendel Steinberg, a contributor to this volume, pp. 358–369, and his sister Bunia (Steinberg) Upstein a contributor to this volume, pp. 387–402. Photos of Getzel's and Mendel's families appear on p. 505. They settled in the United States. See the book length account of Steinberg survival story on the Mlynov website.

o   Hanoch Holtzeker's photo on p. 455 with notes. He was a brother of David and Menashe Holtzeker who were mentioned in earlier parts of this testimony. After he survived, he made his way to Israel to join his sisters and died on May 5, 1948, in the battle for Negba. He is mentioned on page 256 and a photo of the family in Mlynov appears on p. 245 and of their home on p. 79.

o   Koppel (Karl) Messinger (~ 1924–2008) mentioned on page 302 with additional notes. His parents and two brothers perished. A third brother Shmuel (Victor) survived in the Russian army. Koppel went first to Israel and was later sponsored by his brother to bring his family to Philadelphia.

o   Yitzhak Mandelkern, brother of Shmuel Mandelkern, a contributor to this volume, is mentioned several times in Parts I-III of this testimony. He and his son Gershon survived and eventually made their way to Israel.

o   Batia Grinberg, possibly family of Noah Grinberg, whose photo is on p. 480 with notes about the family there. A photo of Fania Grinberg also appears on p. 463.

o   Hannah Veiner (1918–2002) (alternative spellings Weiner/Vainer) was daughter of Yitzhak and Beracha Veiner. She survived as did two of her siblings, Moshe (1917/1918–?) and Yehuda (1914–2007). Yehuda fled Mlynov when the Germans attacked in June 1942 along with other boys recounted in an essay by Yechiel Sherman in this volume, "Taking Leave of Home," pp. 344–346. Yehuda survived in Kazakhstan served in the Red or Polish army. After the War, Yehuda married Leah Likhter, a contributor to this volume, and Hannah married Micha Kilshtakov from Mervits, son of Ita and Yosef Kilshtakov. The two families moved from Dubno to Tbilisi and later to Israel.

o   Tovyah or Toybeshe Gordon, the daughter of Rabbi Gordon. Photo of Rav Gordon, p. 453. Photo of Tovyah and her two surviving brothers with notes p. 280. Tovyah survived in hiding and eventually married and migrated to the US.

o   Frida Kupferberg contributed, "Murder of the Sokoliki Refugees," pp. 384–385 with additional notes.

o   The Goldreich family appears in a photo on the bottom of page 463 and are listed as refugees from the area of Turka.

3. The name of Aaron's daughter was Yetka not Lana.
4. Getzel's family name was Steinberg.
5. Likely Shchurovychi, Ukraine, 65 km (40 mi) southwest of Mlynov.
6. About 3.6 km (2.2 mi) north and slightly west of Mlynov.
7. The young girl was Aviva Feldman. The planning and rescue was also supported by Bunia's brother, Getzel Steinberg. Bunia tells the moving story of Aviva's rescue in more detail in her essay, "Wandering During the Terrible Catastrophe," pp. 395ff with additional notes there. A more expansive version of this rescue story appears in the book length version of the family's survival as recounted by Bunia's daughter in *A Struggle To Survive*, now translated to English. Aviva ended up being informally adopted by the family of Bunia's brother, Getzel Steinberg, whose wife Pessia (Wurtzel) was also a relative of Aviva. Aviva appears in the photo on p. 505 with her adopted family in the Displaced Persons Camp of Pocking. At that time, Aviva's maternal aunt who made aliyah earlier learned of her survival and insisted on their reunification. In 1949, Bunia brought Aviva to Kibbutz Ein Harod where she grew up and became an artist who paints beautiful transparent horses through which one can see the countryside in the background, which reminds Aviva of her mother and lost childhood.
8. Aviva grew up with her aunt in Israel on Kibbutz Ein Harod.
9. Probably Rachel Fisher, sister of Yafa Dayagi (Sheindel Fisher), who contributed "Home and Youth Movement in Mlynov," 247–50 to this volume and describes their home in Mantyn.
10. Mantyn is just 6 km (3.6 mi) north of Mlynov today.
11. Liba Tesler was the sister of Peretz Tesler mentioned in earlier parts of this testimony. Liba's father Yaakov, photo p. 478, told her to flee the ghetto just days before its liquidation. The full account of her survival is told by David Sokolsky in *Monument: One Woman's Courageous Escape from the Holocaust* (2017). Liba appears in a group photo on page 469.
12. The "Mlynov Kehilla" refers to the communal organization that included a number of the other towns in the area as described in "Mlynov-A Kehilla for Mlynov and Its Surrounding Shtetlekh," page 16. Many of the residents of these towns were brought into the Mlynov ghetto when it was erected and were thus liquidated and buried in the pit dug between Mlynov and Mervits.
13. It seems the photo was distributed after the ceremony and retained by survivors. In this way, copies also made their way to the US.
14. The Soviet Union wanted Jews and Poles to be repatriated to Poland after the War and most survivors were happy to leave in any case.
15. "After the liberation" appears in the Yiddish which differs slightly from the Hebrew, which reads "in the presence of the Shoah survivors."

[Page 314]

_____

In the Depths of Hell

Nokhum Teitelman, Haifa[1]

Translated from the Yiddish by Hannah B. Fischthal, PhD
and from the Hebrew by Howard I. Schwartz PhD **with** Hanina Epstein

Edited by Howard I. Schwartz, PhD

"Lonely sits the town of Mlynov."[2] Tisha B'Av[3] was postponed to Sunday [on the Sabbath Parasha] Vaetchanan.[4]

Early on a nice morning, the 27th of Sivan 5701 [June 22, 1941], I shook off my sleep, got out of bed, and went out into the street. There was screaming, an uproar; we didn't know what was happening. The Russian landing field had been bombed, and we did not know who did it. The Russians were grabbing people out of their beds to make the repairs; my children were among them. We spoke in whispers. What could this be? We were a little mixed up, and we shivered. This went on until 4:00 p.m. when, suddenly, 18 German airplanes started bombing our shtetl Mlynov. All four sides were burning. It became dark; we wanted to run, but we did not know where. In addition, the children were still not back from work, and only God knew what had happened with them. People ran, but we waited, hoping our children would soon return. And so they did. Our children came running back, barely alive. My Asher was black, his face covered with dirt, because a bomb fell in the place where he labored. With him, in that place, was Shaye the psalm-chanter's son-in-law. A rock tore off one of his hands, and he was saved by a miracle.

We locked up our house with all our possessions inside, and we left for Mervits. We came to my brother-in-law Mendel.[5] The airplanes also targeted Mervits. They flew over the roofs. We went to a village about 3 kilometers away, and we lay there until Tuesday. Then we returned to Mlynov. We entered our house, and we rationed the bread.

Early Wednesday the Germans invaded, and they shot Russians. We left again, going in the same direction, and we stayed there until Friday. We started to ride and walk home. We were a few families, 40 people in all.

[Page 315]

A few had horses and carts carrying whatever they had taken with them.

Riding through Nowiny Dobratinsky,[6] we were stopped and assumed to be spies. We were ordered to stand up to get shot. When we were ready for that, an officer came and asked if any of us could speak Czech. My Rokhl[7] responded right away, and so did her sister Khayke. They threw themselves at the officer's feet, and they told him everything, that we were from Mlynov, and we were going home. He freed us right away; he told us to go. We went straight back to Mervits-Mlynov.

On the way we saw how Christians were carrying off Jewish possessions. We even recognized our own things, but we kept silent until we came to our house. When we went inside, it was worse. Everything was broken. We had been robbed, and the house was full of feathers because the thieves shook the feathers out of the pillowcases, and they packed everything that was in the cupboard in them. The store that had been full of grain and some flour was cleaned out. We were left with the four walls.

But that was not enough. Soon several Germans marched into our house. They asked what we were doing there, and who we were. At first they said they were searching for weapons, but they meant something else. They started to bother Shifrele,[8] even though she was still a child. We bought off the villains. We then left our home to go to Yoysef Zelig's, Khayim Berger's son-in-law. We observed Shabbes Parashat Chukat[9] there. It was the third of Tamuz [June 28, 1941].[10]

We returned to our house on Sunday, because that Shabbes the Germans had invaded Rivne, and the front had already moved up. They began to demand forced labor. We registered with a Jakubowski from Mlynov. We did not know him. People said that he was a German spy disguised as a Pole. We worked at various jobs, and we got used to it. Someone who was soft-hearted brought us a little flour from what had been stolen from us. For example, we had a neighbor Ratjewski across from us. He had made off with several meters of flour; he brought me back, out of pity, a few kilos of my own flour.

[Page 316]

It was similar with other Christian neighbors up until that tragic Shabbes Parshat Balak,[11] when the killings started.

Shloyme Shister had been captured. He was lame. He was taken to Yoysef Gelberg's mill where he was shot without an explanation.

The Black Sabbath, Parasha Balak,[12] the 17th of Tammuz 5701 [July 12, 1941]

I got up in the morning and saw the gifted Rav, Mr. Yehuda son of Mordechai Gordon, righteous man of blessed memory, passing my house, and walking towards Mervits, so as not to profane the Sabbath. I thought, "perhaps I too should try to leave town," and I walked straight to my brother-in-law, Yaakov Schichman, z"l.[13] He was living at the end of town and suddenly, when I was already there, I heard shooting, and I went outside with my brother-in-law and we hid among the grain in the field. The grain was already reasonably tall, and that same Shabbat the bitter enemy entered the synagogue of the Trisk Hasidim in Mervits and killed Motel Tesler;[14] He was already close to one hundred [years old]. [They murdered] him and another poor man. Near evening I returned home, and I met older men along the way, among them was my uncle, R. Chaim Meir,[15] which the bitter enemy had reduced to younger men by removing their signature beards … I entered home safely, with great trepidation, because they had already told me what had happened to them that same Shabbat.

The following morning, I got up and took the scissors and cut my own beard and went with all the others to their respective work. By the time I returned in the evening from work, we had already heard about eighteen dead, and among them, the gifted and holy Rav Yehudah Gordon, and thus fulfilled in us [the Scriptural verse]: "you shall be in terror, night and day, with no assurance of survival" (Deuteronomy 28:66).

"For These Things Do I Weep" (Lamentations 1:16) – 18th of Tammuz (5724) [Sunday, June 28, 1964][16]

Sunday of Pinchas,[17] the 18th of Tammuz,[18] 5701 [Sunday, July 13, 1941], the day the first martyrs of Mlynov fell at the hands of the Nazis, may the latter names be blotted out. There are images, which are engraved in your memory, and despite the changing of seasons and the passage of time, still stand living and exist before you.

Mlynov sinks into the depths of oblivion, she was and is no longer. In her were rabbis, Hasidim, from the branches of Trisk, Karlin, Stolin, Olyk; merchants, laborers, Zionists, scholars, tailors, shoe makers. They were simple Jews, full of good deeds (mitzvot) like pomegranates, but they are no more. Together with the whole of Polish and European Jewry, they went heavenward, murdered and strangled by the Nazis, may their names be blotted out, and they sanctified the Name of Heaven and name of the People with their blood.

Mlynov was a small and young town, mostly Jews from Ukraine, near the town of Dubno.

[Page 317]

The town merited great recognition, when in the year 5632 (1881–1882) a holy and righteous man (tzaddik) came there, a paragon of the generation, our teacher and rabbi, Aharon Karlin,[19] who wrote *Bet Aharon* (Aaron's House), grandson of the saintly and holy Aharon HaGadol, and after a few days passed away on the 15th of Sivan and ascended on high. The local Hasidim built him a memorial on his grave there, and annually on his memorial day, thousands upon thousands of men came, and this is how events continued until the Second World War, and I, the writer, after the War merited in 5704 [Sept. 1943–Sept. 1944] and 5705 [Sept. 1944–Sept. 1945] to prostrate myself on his grave and light candles in the memorial,[20] the building was already broken and destroyed.

The people of the town, Mlynov, were Jews who respected heaven, happy with their lot, and satisfied with little. These Jews enjoyed laboring with their hands, and after a back-breaking day of work would go into the synagogue to study Torah. Some learned Gemara,[21] some learned Chumash and Rashi,[22] and some recited Tehillim [Psalms]. Nuta Dov Berger[23] stood beside the pulpit and studied the holy Zohar,[24] R. Moshe Arelas[25] studied Midrash on Sabbath afternoons, and by his side sat Neta Malar and Chaim Malar and Neta Sosish, with all the artisans and blacksmiths, and R. Yehuda Leib[26] studied Ohr Hachaim Hakadosh [The Light of Life][27] with the men, as did I. I remember that when Rav Nahman Wulach[28] would stand by the pulpit with his book of Tehilim [palms], and the voices broke through outside, and R. Avraham Moshe-Aharon would sit at the east [wall] with his tallit and tefillin,[29] and R. Mordechai Meir Shrentzel[30] was the gabbai [sexton] in the large synagogue, and last but not least, R. Chanoch Hanich, the kosher slaughterer (shochet), when he began to pray the additional service (musaf), during the Days of Awe, and began to sing the Hineni[31] prayer, "Here I am, impoverished in deeds and merit" — the walls of the study house were trembling from all the people praying.

Decades passed since then, but this town, with its exemplary people, is still standing before my eyes: When R. Hanich went on the eve of the holy Shabbat to the study hall with his long clothing and white socks, a tall conical hat made with the acronym SMVT, that stands for "turn away from evil and do good" (Sur Mera Veaseh Tov) and he would pass by the shops and call out: "Shabbat, Shabbat" — then all the inattentive[32] persons who were still in the stores, shook from fear, and quickly and immediately all of us closed our stores. And most all of them fulfilled the commandment of charity (tzedakah) and acts of lovingkindness, and when they needed charity, they already knew the places of Shlomo Zeltikis and woman Rachel Shivis,[33] and others. In the latter days, [it was] Tzvi Falik, Chaim Yitzhak Kipergluz, and no one told another, "I'm sorry there is not enough room,"[34] because the hands were open for charity, healing, and deeds of lovingkindness. And where are the righteous women of our town, Mlynov? Shaindel, Bluma, Dvora Shrentzel, Mima Eta, Meril the shochet-ke,[35] Batia the shochet-ke, Ronya-Rivka Moshe Leibe's [daughter],[36] Eta Garshynes, [37] and among them my mother, and others. I remember that when all of them walked from the shul, they decided that they needed to travel to Trisk, then all of them unanimously said "we will do and we will listen";[38] on Sunday they hired Yosef Garshynes, and they traveled, and among them my mother, may her memory be a blessing.

[Page 318]

The review is too short to write about each woman, I will suffice with a few words, and I am not adept with language to describe the Stolin Hasids, R. Yitzchak Leib the mashgiach,[39] Avraham Kholis,[40] Yaakov Shimon Rosenfeld, R. Tzadok Shulman,[41] R. Pesach-Aryeh Chayat [Tailor], and his son Aharon-Asher Berel Barben, R. Yitzchak Staroste[42] and his son Aaron, Shmuel, Asher, Avrumke,[43] Aidah, and so on and so forth. When they began to pray, all my bones shall say…[44]

In Hell

We got used to it. Early in the morning we ran to the main plaza, and we waited to be taken to various jobs. Soon Germans came for laborers, and they divided us up. One village needed 50 Jews, another needed 100, and so on, until the plaza was emptied. The Christians stood at a distance and laughed. A few even taunted the Jewish merchants.

A Christian came over to me and teased, "How expensive is wheat?"

Because aristocrats had many fields around Mlynov, the Jews were distributed for fieldwork at harvest time. Some were sent to Arshychyn-Smordva, Berega, Bokiima also to Mlynov, and we became land-workers: cutting, tying, threshing, and cleaning. We were fine with the work, as long as we had our lives.

One evening, having come back tired from work, unable to straighten up from having tied up wheat, a German burst in the door and ordered: "Come!"

I had to go. To where I did not know. My wife and children were crying, certain that I would be shot, because that was nothing new. The German who took me also took Yoysef Wurtzel, Khayim Berger's son-in-law, and Nosi [Natan] Shiper, the son of Yitskhok Ulinik. We marched in threes. We were taken through the town to the house of attorney Revtshinski. There they started to ask us what our occupations were, and many more questions until late at night. Back home they had no doubts that we had been murdered, because practically every day several people were taken to the Nantyn Forest, and they were shot.

After sitting there several hours, I was the first one to be called in. The result: I had until tomorrow 12:00 to deliver 120 cakes of good soap; if not, I would be shot. Nosi: [the obligation of] two kilos of tea. Yoysef Wurtzel: 3,000 cigarettes. And we were escorted home since we were not permitted in the streets after 6:00 pm.

When I knocked on the door of the house, those inside thought I had come from the other world.

[Page 319]

At night nothing could be done. In the morning, the three wives got together and went through the town to collect the soap, cigarettes, and tea. We put together the products with great effort, because everything had been plundered earlier. For us it was life or death. And God caused the Nazis, may their names be blotted out, to be satisfied with the [effort] of the people. The Germans accepted the goods and ordered us to go home. They took other people right after us: Avraham Gelman, Yankev Golzeker, and Yoysef Gelberg.[45] All curses and calamities came true.–[The life you face shall be precarious;] "you shall be in terror, night and day, with no assurance of survival." (Deuteronomy 28:66)

* * *

So we worked until the harvest was done. On [the fast day of] Tisha B'Av,[46] I was working together with more Jews. For show, we each brought along a bottle of water with a piece of bread, but we did not eat or drink [because of the fast]. We kept spilling out a little water, so that the Germans would think that we were drinking it. We only worried what we would do if work would let out.

Soon after the holiday, around the month of Cheshvan,[47] I searched for work with Christians, because many rich, elderly Christians were permitted to take Jewish workers, since the young people were serving in the war. They were allowed to take a few Jews for hard labor, provided the Jews would not be in the town. I needed the earnings of a piece of bread, because we had to sell what was left for a couple of kilos of flour after "hail and locusts" destroyed everything. Searched and found: I connected with a very well-known Czech, Pani Nokhum, an old man who was alone. He had permission from the authority to take a Jew for labor. I worked for him. He was very happy with me, and I also was happy with him in that time of doom and gloom. It was not that very far; it was 8 kilometers from Mlynov. Friday after lunch I used to walk home, and early Sunday morning I would walk back to him. It was already known that I work for Guladkin. And so the time went, until the 1st of January 1942, when Mlynov was organized. Everyone had to work for the Germans; just a few worked for Christians with permission from the Germans.

[Page 320]

The beginning of January 1942, the Germans started to search for repositories of grain. There was an order that 4-5 meters of grain from every hectare had to be given over for Germany, may its name be blotted out. In addition, effective laborers were needed. Because I had been a grain merchant, and because I had a little "Protection," my uncle Mati Liberman z"l added me onto the list of the workers at the grain outlet, and I started to work back in the town at the repositories. People were simply jealous of me. The director was a Ukrainian, a big hooligan, an anti-Semite. He was called Flint, but to me he was one of the best. When he felt like it, he sent for the police very early, and whoever came to his office to register was beaten by the police without a reason. Except for me.

He became a good comrade to me. He found out that I was the best worker and also a specialist. He gave me the key to the repositories, and also the receipts from the grain, so that I became an assistant to him. I used to stand alone [without supervision] by the scale intaking the grain, and also at distributing the grain. The day on which the grain had to be given out was a day of reckoning. 10 trucks, sometimes more, used to come for the grain. So an order was given that all trucks had to be loaded in 2-3 hours; if not, the workers would be shot. One can imagine what kind of rush it became. It was hardly possible to gather everything into sacks, tie or sew them up, weigh them, and load them onto the trucks in time. The sweating laborers were filled with terror that they would take too long and be shot.

And so it was the entire time. Before Shavuos, when the German Kommandant Schneider left for a month's furlough to Germany, the Ukrainian Commander Navosad and community official Sovitski created the ghetto. The second day of Shavuos,[48] all Jews from Mlynov, Mervits, and from the surrounding villages had to leave their houses and move into the inner street. 5–6 large families, and more smaller families, were put in one house. We were fenced in with thick barbed wire. Standing at the gates were Ukrainian soldiers.

[Page 321]

Nobody could go in or out unless going to and from work, accompanied by guards.

10 days in Sivan,[49] trucks from Dubno came to take grain from the repositories. A German, standing by the scale, said to me that he would not wish to be in Dubno the next day. That same night the first *Akcja* [*Aktion*][50] in Dubno took place. Among the victims were several from Mlynov: Yitzhak Mandelkern's wife, [51] Mrs. Bershtivke, and another person. That day they had gone to Dubno to settle something, with permission from the Mlynov Committee. They remained there among other martyrs.

* * *

This history happened in the middle of August 1942. They took workers from surrounding villages to Studynke,[52] including my Asher. He had returned from Rivne barely alive. The next day he was caught and taken to Studynke. Coming from work at night, I saw two women and several girls in the yard of Hirsh Slobodar[53] (I lived there in the ghetto).

I asked: "Who are you and where are you going?"

They answered me that they were from Ostrozhets, and they were going to Studynke. And as it was already late, they want to stay overnight; the Christians didn't want to drive at night. We were tired, and we were not permitted to use any candles. Full of fear and terror, we fell asleep. The girls also went to sleep in Ayzshe Goldseker's attic.

12:00 midnight I get up from sleep, as though somebody would have woken me and asked, "Why are you sleeping?"

I went outside. Darkness. I slipped out quietly. I heard crying and begging, "Leave me alone."

I listened and I heard that the crying was coming from the attic where the girls were sleeping. I figured that the Christians wanted to rape a few of the girls. I started to scream to the Christians that I will go to the military and report them. It became quieter, so I went back very quietly and lay down. I believe I was informed in my sleep to save a Jewish soul. The thought did not allow me to rest. I went out again, and I heard more cries and pleadings.

[Page 322]

So I woke up Rokhl and the rest of the people in the house, and I told them what was happening here. They did not want to leave the house, but I tore out, ran to the gate, and started to scream more. Several soldiers jumped out and started to beat me. Rokhl came over and held me back because I had already fallen like a dead man. Then they started to hit her; both of us were practically killed. They left. It burned their hearts that I had interrupted them. Just then the people in the house came out, and they started to save us, and there was a commotion in the ghetto. They saved us with water. In the morning Dr. Rozental came with a nurse, Esther Vaytser. Dr. Rozental said that Rokhl was in a greater danger than I because they put holes in her head in several places. A few days later, it turned out that I was in greater danger, because my lungs had been punched in. Only God helped us both to recover. It took several weeks. Maybe I earned the privilege because I had saved a Jewish soul, "whoever saves a single life in Israel, it is as if he save the whole world."[54]

On a Bitter Day

On the 20th of Tishrei 5703 (Thursday October 1, 1942), on a bitter day, two of my sons were killed, Efraim-Fishel and Shlomo-Bentzion. On Thursday, the 4th day of the Intermediate days of Sukkot,[55] the eve of Hoshana Rabbah, as was the custom in the morning, we all went to work, each to his own place, and I to my place of work. I took the keys to the storeroom and entered the storeroom and had already begun to work, when suddenly they came with Job's news [terrible news], that they are preparing too quickly the graves for us and today-tomorrow they will accomplish it. We already expected the tragic day, because in all the surrounding areas they had already finished with the Jews. All of us that worked there knew already. We looked at each other with sorrowful eyes. Everything fell from our hands. In addition, we were forbidden to show sorrowful faces.

And so we arranged with a Pole to hide our children. I got out of the storehouse and ran into the ghetto, because I had a card that gave me permission to go in and out of the ghetto. I wanted to give the good news to Rokhl. I did not have much time, because I had to run back.

[Page 323]

Actually, my children Fishl and Shloyme came right into the house. We asked them if they wanted to run out of the ghetto themselves and go straight to the Pole Zarembah, and they said "Yes." So I led them out of the ghetto. They went on a side path. After they had gone a short distance, they were captured and shot on the spot.

Soon there was a commotion in the ghetto. People heard that Nokhum's children were shot; the bitter news reached me. My sister Yente wanted to quiet me down, so she told me that she was just informed that my children went straight to Zarembah, and it was not true that they had been shot. So I was mixed up. I went to the director, who was good to me, and I begged him to give me a certificate authorizing me to go to the village magistrate with a letter about prices, and with that letter I went freely. I had been stopped several times; each time I showed the letter, and I was let through. When I got there: the children were no longer, and I, where should I go?[56]

I came back in great pain. Asher was already home from work. I sent him with the same letter — maybe he could save himself; there was nothing to lose. And so it was; he took the letter and he was allowed through, and he arrived at Zarembah's in peace.

The next day was Hoshana Rabbah. I thought, what more is to be done? We heard very early that one girl from the 12 who used to work for Gorlinski in the yard got sick; so we sent [my daughter] Shifre in her place. We told her that going to Gorlinski, she should turn and head straight to Zarembah's, where Asher was. We also sent [my son] Yosele away with a Christian whom I had given a nice quantity of merchandise. Now I remained with Rokhl. What should we do next? I wanted to send Rokhl away, and I would stay here in the ghetto together with all the Jews. I had a plan: A Christian from home was at the storehouse. I promised him that I will write an order for him to receive several meters of grain. I had the papers on me. For that, he should take Rokhl out of the ghetto. Naturally, she had to disguise herself as a Christian.

[Page 324]

And so it was. My wife Rokhl agreed but on one condition, that I should also come to Zarembah's, and if not, she would come back with the children. But how could I come since everybody knew me? All this was going on early in the morning of Hoshana Rabbah, because just on that day I was in the storage area of the synagogue (the Germans used it for a warehouse), and one side of the synagogue was in the ghetto, and the other side was outside the ghetto–so I could accomplish all these difficult things.

Now I remained alone in the ghetto. Rokhl with Asher and Shifre with Yoysef were in the village of Pańska Dolina.[57] And my children, z"l, my sons, my treasures Efraim-Fishel and Shlome-Bentzion, were lying covered with a little dirt from the Nazis and Ukrainians, may their names be blotted out. It was already 12:00 noon. I closed the storehouse, and I gave the key to the director. I went for an hour to the house in the ghetto where I lived with Fishl-Kritser. His wife wanted to give me something to eat, and I did not want to take it. I sat down and thought about what I should do. If I would go there, I knew that I would certainly be killed; if I did not go there, I was afraid that Rokhl and the children will come back. I could not decide what to do, until a decision came to me, that I should go to the storehouse for the key. I will ask him again to give me a certificate to go to the village magistrate about prices. I will tell him that I am again going to search for my children. And I went and stood in front of him.

He said to me: "Take the key and go."

I kept standing.

He asked me: "Why are you standing?"

I explained that I wanted a certificate, because I was told that my children are in Dolina.

He said to me, "Do not talk nonsense. Your children were shot."

He even knew where they were buried.

Seeing that I had no choice, I said to him:

"Listen, Sir, you want me to stay alive? Then give me a mission to go there, because I see that the end is coming." He thought and thought and said, "For you, I will do this." And he gave me a letter for the head of the village with a stamp, indicating I was going on his behalf, and allowing me to come and go without harm. I went with no incident, and we [the members of the family] met there together, already it was the eve of Shemini Atzeret.

Translator's and editor's footnotes:

1. Nahum Teitelman (1890–1976) and his wife who was also his first cousin, Rachel (Gruber) (1894–1980) lived in Mlynov where they had six children. Rachel's sister was Sonia (Gruber) who had married Mendel Teitelman, both significant contributors to this volume. Nahum was a middleman for a robust grain business that bought grain from local farmers in the area and sold the grain to distributors in other larger towns. Their large home was combined with their business and included storage granaries and a store where local farmers could buy goods when they came to sell their produce. Nahum and Rachel's two sons, Efraim-Fishel and Shlomo-Bentzion, were among the first Mlynov persons thrown into the mass grave in a story that Nahum recounts here. The amazing story of survival by several Teitelmans is told in a firsthand book-length account by their son Asher, who is also another contributor to this volume. – HS

2. Lonely sits the town of Mlynov … Compare to Lamentations 1.1: Alas! Lonely sits the city Once great with people! She that was great among nations Is become like a widow; The princess among states Is become a thrall." Here Nahum evokes the poetic lament over the destruction of the first Temple in Jerusalem to describe the destruction of Mlynov. Throughout this essay Nahum remembers the events that took place in 1941–1944 based on their associations with the Torah Portion (parasha) that was read each week on the Sabbath. – HS

3. Tisha B'Av, literally "9th of Av," is an annual fast day commemorating the destruction of the Temples in Jerusalem. It falls on the 9th day of Jewish calendar month Av unless, as is the case here, that day happens to be a Sabbath. Since Sabbath joy takes precedence over sadness and mourning, the fast is postponed to the next day. – HS

4. The particular Sabbath which fell on the 9th of Av was when the Torah Portion Vaetchanan (Deuteronomy 3:23–7:11) was read in synagogue. – HS

5. Referring to Mendel Teitelman, a cousin of Nahum. Mendel and Nahum's wives were sisters. – HS

6. Probably Novyna-Dobryatyns'ka, 7.2 km (4.4 mi) from Mlyniv today. – HS

7. His wife, Rachel (Gruber) Teitelman. – HS

8. His daughter Shifra (Teitelman) Grossman (1928–). – HS

9. The Parsha is the weekly Torah reading; Nahum remembers when events took place based on the Parsha that was being read that Sabbat. Parsha *Chukat* [Statute], Numbers 19:1-22:1. –HBF and HS.

10. Seven days since the Germans launched their attack on the Russian-occupied Poland. – HBF

11. Parsha Balak, Numbers 22:2-25:9. – HBF

12. See previous note. The reading on this Sabbath involves Balak, the Moab King, asking Balaam to come curse the Israelites who have been winning battles. Balaam's ass sees an angel blocking the path and Balaam realizing his folly finally blesses the children of Israel. – HS

13. Yaakov Schichman had married Chaika (Gruber), the sister of Nakhum's wife, Rachel. – HS

14. See photo of Motel Tesler, p. 473. He was a member of the Grenspun family. "Tesler" meaning "carpenter" was a nickname. – HS

15. Chaim Meir Teitelman was the brother of Nahum's father, Efraim-Fischel. – HS

16. Nahum appears to be thinking back from 1964 to the same day in 1941. – HS

17. Torah reading Pinchas (Numbers 25:10-30:1). – HS

18. The 17th of Tammuz is a fast day that starts three weeks of mourning leading up to the fast of Tisha B'Av. – HS

19. Aaron Ben Asher of Karlin (June 6, 1802–June 23, 1872), known as Rabbi Aaron II of Karlin. His writing, Bet Aharon, contains his kabbalistic and exegetical reflections on the 5 Books of Moses. He was the grandson of the dynasty founder, Aaron ben Jacob Perlov of Karlin (1736–1772), who was known as Aharon HaGadol. – HS

20.   The Hebrew term used here and elsewhere is "aron" meaning, "ark" or "cupboard," and may allude to the aron hakodesh, the ark of the Covenant. – HS

21.   Gemara is the Aramaic legal commentary on the Mishnah, the foundational rabbinic code of law. – HS

22.   Rashi is a well-known commentator on the plain meaning of the Five Books of Moses. – HS

23.   Nuta-Ber Berger is father of Wolf Berger and the grandfather of Aaron (Berger) Harari, a contributor to this volume. – HS

24.   The Zohar is the primary text of Jewish mystical tradition of Kabbalah and contains an allegorical interpretation of the Torah. – HS

25.   Refers to Moshe, son of Aaron Hirsch. Moshe is the brother of Daniel Hirsch whose ghost came to Mlynov in the story told in the essay in this volume by Shirley Jacobs, "A True Event in Mlynov from 96 Years Ago," 196–198. – HS

26.   Likely Yehuda Leib Lamdan, father of Yitzhak Lamdan. – HS

27.   The nickname for Chaim ibn Attar, a Talmudist and Kabbalist, who wrote commentary on the Torah by this same name. – HS

28.   The father of Yankel Wulach who became Jacob Wallace in Chicago. Jacob migrated to Chicago with some of the Berger family. Two of Jacob's sons, Morris and Isadore, migrated to Chicago and were among the boys from Mlynov who migrated to the US via Buenos Aires, as documented on the Mlynov website. – HS

29.   With prayer shawl and phylacteries. – HS

30.   The grandfather of Lipa Halperin from whom he learned the fable about how the Ikva River got its name. See the story in Lipa's essay, "The Mill," pp. 13–15. – HS

31.   The Hineni is the introductory prayer for the Musaf service on Rosh Hashanah and Yom Kippur in which the leader of the congregation asks for the ability to pray. – HS

32.   The term here is "uncircumcised ones" and may refer either to those who are not Jewish or to those who are not paying attention. Since the context seems to imply that they were ignoring the Sabbath, it is translated as "inattentive ones." – HS

33.   The text seems to imply that the places of these two were known to always give charity. – HS

34.   A possible allusion to Pirkei Avot 5:5 on the 10 wonders wrought for those in Jerusalem including that "no man said to his fellow: the place is too congested for me to lodge overnight in Jerusalem." – HS

35.   Seems to be the names of the wives of the two shochet's in town. – HS

36.   Possibly Rikva Demb, daughter of Moshe Leib Gruber. – HS

37.   Possibly Gershon's Eta, referring to Eta Schuchman, daughter of Gershon.

38.   Quoting Exodus 24:7 when Moses read the record of the covenant before the people, they said, "we will do all that the Lord has spoken." In later rabbinic interpretations, this verse indicates true faithfulness, since the people say they will act before they ask to hear. Nahum seems to be implying here that the women of town were faithful and proactive. – HS

39.   A mashgiach is a person who supervises the kosher status of food or an establishment. It is possible this Yitzchak Leib is the one referred to sometimes as the "shochet Itzi." – HS

40.   Mentioned in the essay by Moshe Fishman as the person who tended the eternal light in the rebbe's memorial, "Mlynov in the Past," pp. 60–61. – HS

41.   Tsodik is the great-grandfather of Howard I. Schwartz, the editor of this volume. Tsodik Shulman married Pearl Malka Demb. Most of the Shulman family migrated to Baltimore in 1921. – HS

42.   Yitskhok or Icik Ferteybaum, the grandfather of Sylvia Barditch-Goldberg, remembered as "Staroste," whom she writes about in her essay, "Stoliner Hasidism in Mlynov," pp. 80–81. – HS

43.   A photo of Avrumke by Aaron Harari from his 1937–38 visit appears in the essay, "Small Shtetls, Large Families," p. 258 of this volume and is labelled a typical character in Mlynov. – HS

44.   Quoting Psalm 35:10. The full verse reads, "All my bones shall say, 'Lord, who is like You? You save the poor from one stronger than he, the poor and needy from his despoiler.'" The entire psalm talks about the angel of the Lord saving those who are attacked and call out to the Lord. – HS

45.   Yosef Gelberg was the wealthy owner of the mill in town. There was more than one Yankev Goldseker in Mlynov. This one may refer to the son of Moishe Holtzeker, one of the original five brothers to come to Mlynov. A photo of his large family photo appears on p. 245 of this volume. It probably does not refer to the Yankev Golzeker who contributed to this volume (pp. 226–228) since he was fighting with the Russian army. – HS

46. A fast day, traditionally the saddest day of mourning for Jerusalem in the Jewish calendar. – HBF

47. October-November in the Gregorian calendar. – HBF

48. The first day of Shavuot began the eve of Thursday, 21 May 1942. – HS

49. May-June on the Gregorian calendar. – HS

50. German military or police operation involving mass assembly, deportation and killing; directed by the Nazis against Jews. – HS

51. Perel Mandelkern, wife of Yitzhak, discussed above p. 290. – HS

52. Probably Studinka today. – HS

53. Nickname for Hirsch Goldseker, grandfather of Boruch Meren, whom Boruch writes about in this volume in "An Event in the Shtetl," p. 188. – HS

54. A paraphrase of Mishnah Sanhedrin 4:5. – HS

55. The days between the festival days that begin and end the Festival of Tabernacles. – HS

56. Possibly an allusion to Genesis 37:30 where Rueben comes back to the pit to find his brother Jacob missing. – HS

57. Pańska Dolina was a stronghold of partisan resistance during the German occupation. – HS

[Page 325]

Tragic Tales

by Mendel and Sonia Teitelman[1], Haifa

Translated from the Yiddish by Hannah B. Fischthal, PhD and from the Hebrew by Howard I. Schwartz PhD with Hanina Epstein

Edited by Howard I. Schwartz, PhD

The First 10 Murdered by the State[2]

Our first 10 slaughtered were eight young people z"l from Mlynov and Mervits, plus two old Jews z"l who were killed the day before them on Shabbes afternoon, 17 Tamuz 5701,[3] in the Trisk synagogue in Mervits. One of them was Reb Motl Grinshpan,[4] called Motl Tesler,[5] over 90 years old, and the *shammes* [sexton] in the Trisk synagogue. He lived there and he was shot there.

*[This photo without a caption in the original volume is of
Mendel and Sonia Teitelman]*

The second old man was killed with him in the same place. He was dumb and poor; nobody ever knew from where he came or to whom he belonged, but he would stay in Mervits longer than in all other surrounding shtetls. After wandering around Mlynov, Trovits, and Demydivka, he would return to Mervits at the end of the week and stay overnight.

[Page 326]

His place was always next to the stove in the men's synagogue. Motl, on the other hand, used to sleep and live[6] in the women's synagogue, also next to the stove.

On that perilous day, 17 Tamuz, Shabbes, about noon, when they were both sitting in the synagogue, not a single creature in the shtetl felt cheerful, even though in the early morning hours we still prayed with a minyan, and I still said Kaddish for my mother, may she rest in peace. The Mlynov Rabbi z"l had a premonition to not be in Mlynov, although up to then nothing had happened.[7] He came running in the early morning to Mervits and prayed together with us. After praying, he left for Stomorhy[8] to the fleeing Jews there, and he remained with the Keler family, z"l, thinking that when the situation would stabilize a little, he would return home. During the same early-morning hours, the Mervits village magistrate ordered people to clean up the remains of things abandoned in houses that had been populated with Russian tractor drivers. About 10 of us willingly registered for this work. We had a bad premonition after a few people from Mlynov related that the army with angry Germans, may their names be blotted out, had returned from Dubno that morning. At work, we heard rifles shooting, but we were used to that, because every day we heard rifles shooting here at fish in the river, Mervits, and at Stomorhy Jews.

The first were the two old Jews, Reb Motl Shammes [the Sexton] and the deaf pauper. Everyone in the entire shtetl, without exception, ran out to the fields at the first shots and hid among the tall ears of corn, which were still standing in the field. Not one happy creature remained in the shtetl. As elderly and deaf and dumb people did not orient themselves so quickly as to what was going on, the two victims remained sitting in their places, eating the tiny portion of *tsholent*[9] that they had prepared the day before. And when the murderers, may their names be blotted out, opened the door and saw them, they shot them both on the spot, leaving them in pools of blood. Then they left to search for more victims.

[Page 327]

We first learned about their deaths in the evening when we all, very frightened, returned home. The meaningless death of the two old, poor, innocent people, the first victims, spread terrible fear and great pain throughout the shtetl. All realized that the murderers' goal was to kill people who were in no way guilty of anything, and nobody had to account for the murders.

* * *

Sunday, the 18th of Tammuz 5701 [July 13, 1941],[10] we were ordered to gather in Mlynov in the middle of the marketplace. Accompanied with beatings and curses, we were led from there to the Mlynov airfield, not far from the Count's palace. We fixed damages caused by bombs, and at the same time, we helped to shlep assorted means of war out of the mud. We were beaten and abused at work, but who reacted to such things?

2:00 p.m. a murderer came over, dressed only in a bathrobe, holding a revolver in his hand, shooting the entire time in the air, and said that whoever could speak German should report to him. Shloyme Marer z"l reported to him (he died two weeks later, when a bandit led him, Khaye Kipergluz z"l,[11] and a few others to the gelding place, and without any reason killed them there). The murdering German told him to announce that those who worked at the heavy chests should go with him. The eight young people went in front. They were accompanied by a few others whom he had picked out to stand a little farther away. He ordered the eight young men to stand up to be shot. He killed them all with his own unkosher hands. Afterwards, he called the next group. In the beginning, everyone had to dig his or her own grave, and to cover up graves next to them until their strength gave way before being shot. Those who were accompanying the victims finished everything. When they returned, they were unable to speak until nighttime; they had simply lost their language skills.

The mourning spread to everyone in the environment, even affecting a large number of our murderous neighbors, who at that time were not used to such things. The families who had young children, husbands, sons, and fathers of young infants torn from them, lamented the most. Their cries went up to the sky.

[Page 328]

A stone could have melted from their tears and hysterical screams. Even a few Christians were astonished. It moved a few of them to respond that the edict had to be a mistake. If a tractor ran over a field-telephone-wire and tore it, so the suspicion fell on the Jews who worked in that area. Another person had a different explanation. We saw that it made an impression on the Christians mostly because that was still the beginning. Mass murders were still new. Later, of course, they became a routine habit; nobody paid any attention to such slaughters.

Before I will publish the names, I want to note that on that same day, several bandits were brought by Zalevsky[12] to Stomorhy, who at the same time killed a larger number of the Jews there. Among them was the Mlynov Rabbi, Rabbi Gordon, z"l, and a Jew from Mervits, Zelig Moravitsky, z"l, a barber. They had hidden there waiting for the rage to pass, and they were killed together with those who had received them.

And these are the names of our first 10 murdered by the state:

1. Reb Motl Grinshpan, z"l
2. A dumb pauper, without a name, z"l
3. Reb Dov Ber Moyshe Litsman, z"l
4. His sister-in-law's sister-in-law Pesi, z"l
5. His brother-in-law Borukh Likhter from Mervits, z"l
6. Reb Moyshe son of Peysakh Kugul, z"l
7. Reb Moyshe son of Shaye Fishman, z"l
8. Reb Borukh son of Fayvish Likhter, z"l
9. Reb Moyshe son of families Ezris Kulish, z"l
10. Reb Moyshe son of Khanina Upstein, z"l.[13]

These were the first ten victims who were murdered when we still thought that things would not be that horrible; we have not forgotten them in the general catastrophe.

Enemies and Murderers Around Us

More victims were killed all the time.

[Page 329]

Here the lame shoemaker, z"l; here Chaia, z"l, the daughter of Chaim Yitzhak Kipergluz, z"l;[14] and others. By the way, in Dubno-Lutsk-Rivne, mass slaughters had already taken place. And regarding beatings and tortures, it is unnecessary and difficult to describe them. On a nice Friday morning (before Tisha B'Av 1941)[15] the bandits, as demanded by the Ukrainian population, drove into Trovits and Ostrozhets with tanks and trunks, and captured practically all the young men not far from their shtetls, and simply shot them. At that time my brother Nakhman, z"l, and my sister Esther z"l[16] were in Ostrozhets.

And so enemy ranks came into every Jewish community — Rivne, Dubno, Lutsk, and Klevan. The Jewish ear did not reach further. Moving was fraught with danger to our lives, both because of the local population and because of the German criminals, may their names be blotted out.

In the first weeks also came about the events of the refugees from Turka who were in Stomorhy. Tragically, they were denounced by a Christian and murdered. Murdered with them were the Rabbi of Mlynov, Gordon, z"l, Mendl Lumer, z"l, Muravitsky the barber, z"l, and the people from Turka whose names I do not remember, unfortunately, except for a few, such as the Koler family, z"l, the Zinger family, and two young couples from their group. Also at the same time my brother-in-law Ben-Tzion,[17] son of Yoysef Gruber, z"l, was killed in Lutsk, where about 2,000 Jewish youths had been murdered. His wife Gitl with her child Yehudis, z"l came running to us in Mervits, thinking that there it was more protected. They also perished in the general murders of the Mlynov ghetto.

It is difficult, very difficult, quite impossible, to bring out every rotten thing on paper. Between one slaughter and the next there were supposed signs that the situation was improving, and we wanted to think — maybe? Maybe this will have been enough? So little by little, about 9–10 months passed, and in that time, in addition to murder, plunder, and deathly fear, the Jewish people were emptied of their gold, jewelry, butter, and everything of value which we had been using the whole time as exchanges for bread. And the mark of Cain,[18] meaning the yellow badge worn in the front and in the back, warned others from far away of every Jew who was seen wearing even clean clothes, not to even think about wearing a fur coat, because that was simply life-endangering.

[Page 330]

A "Useful Worker"

I was lucky. As a former owner of a mill, I was grouped with the six families who were employed in Yisroel Vortsel's mill. There I succeeded in being a "useful worker" as was Srolik Wurtzel [Vortsel] z"l, his brother Mayer z"l, his brother-in-law Fishl z"l, and his cousin Yoysef Feldman z"l from Berestechko. Gershon Upstein z"l was a useful carpenter, and Borukh Lokrits z"l was a useful blacksmith. And we all, with all kinds of tricks, kept our families in Mervits supposedly for work, even in the time of the closed ghetto. There were plenty of death scares in the mill. We had the burden of supplying the population with bread, as far as we only could, and that was fraught with danger to our lives. And still God protected us, and we succeeded, as much as possible, to feed the ghetto with bread. And even though enemy ranks came from many places, wherever there were Jews, there was still a spark of hope not yet extinguished — maybe? Maybe? Maybe God will actually perform a miracle? Because without miracles there was not a single prospect for rescue.

We could see the strong, healthy, bloody beasts who penetrated further and further into the deep woods, and only news of their victories came from the front. Unseen, far from the front, the Germans were already dividing the plundered goods. For example, the Mlynov estate with all its goods was given to a retired German, an old dog, a huge villain. He managed the plundered goods with the palace, having the full assurance that it was his to keep forever, as an acknowledgement for his excellence in the military.

The Jewish population, with its committee at the head, was deadly frightened of him. There were no shootings, because he used up all the labor energy for himself, but the murderous beatings, which the old dog himself gave for every inexactness, were merciless. I do not remember his filthy name.

[Page 331]

The only people with whom he had decent relations were the dentist Berman and his wife, z"l, and someone called Shnayder. We protected ourselves a little with all kinds of bribes.

The local Christian population believed that while Shnayder was in Mlynov, nothing terrible would happen (even that very pleasure they also did not allow us). Maybe there was a small kernel of truth to it, because when Shnayder left Mlynov for a time, the evil edicts worsened. And during the wholesale slaughter he was gone.

Ghetto, Evil Decrees, and Sacrifice

The mixed situation held on until just before Shavuos in May 1942. Then an order suddenly came that the Jews from Mervits and from the surrounding area, meaning from the villages, should all move to Mlynov. Starting in Shul Street[19] until Kisil Yoel's, and until the synagogue near the puddle, the area was fenced off with a heavy barbed wire and isolated from the general population. Only two gates would allow Jews to be taken out for labor. A decent pen cannot in any way describe how the Jews from all the other Mlynov houses had to press themselves together like herrings in houses that had been already emptied of furniture, bedding, and household things; this tragedy I cannot describe in any way. I was also present where my sick brother Yankev-Yoysef, z"l, with his family, and my old uncle Khayim-Mayer z"l,[20] with his children and families, and my uncle Yankev Gruber, z"l, with his wife, and more people, were forced into the ghetto. Nobody in the world could picture such things.

In front of our eyes, we could see the beautiful days of May in Europe, with their full beauty, where both nature and humanity live and laugh. From the big light our darkness increased.

In the ghetto, the decrees became harsher. The news coming from every neighborhood was bad. And just like the Mlynov kehilla was united with all the surrounding shtetlekh, so it was with the ghettos.

[Page 332]

In all the shtetls like Ostrozhets, Trovits, Demydivka and Boremel, ghettos were made on the same days for the Jews. Terrible news from one ghetto to the next came very often. For example, in Boremel, a German dog, may his name be blotted out, demanded something. As it was not quickly enough performed, he took out the leading Jews to the end of the shtetl, and he shot each one with his filthy hands. Among them was my friend Noyakh Grinberg z"l. I do not remember the names of the other martyrs. We heard terrible news all the time.

The horrific situation lasted four months. And this time Motl Litvak z"l,[21] Chaim Yitzhak Kipergluz z"l,[22] Moyshe Zider's[23] two sons, and others, would steal out almost every day and go to the mill in Mervits at night, and talk about ways out, which was useless. During the four awful months in the closed ghetto, the edicts got worse every day. It is not possible to paint that picture, not even by someone with the greatest strength, knowing that the end would be–extermination. Rosh Hashona 5703[24] approached. We could see our sentence in front of our eyes. The days from Rosh Hashona until Sukkos went by quickly. The ghetto was totally sealed. For what purpose?

On the last Shabbes, I think Shabbes during Sukkos, people gathered in the synagogue. Women and children came to the last prayer. I did not have the privilege of attending. It was enough for me to hear about it from the Christians, who were supposedly not as murderously purposed towards Jews. From the closed ghetto, on the last night, half the people ran out, loaded up with axes and with pieces of iron in their hands, ready for everything, and ran wherever their eyes carried them. Practically all of them, not being fit for the fields or forests, with the rains and cold, with small children and old people, fending off persecution and murder from local enemies–practically all perished, with very few exceptions, like Kopl Messinger, Ezra Sherman,[25] and a few more, in the Smordva forest.

I alone succeeded the first days of the sealed ghetto to remain outside, with a friendly Pole (Marian Baretsky) in Mervits.

[Page 333]

My wife Sonia, knowing that I was there, came running through the fields to me. Also others, from the few who survived, succeeded through various ways to get out at the last minute.

My brother-in-law Nokhum's two sons, Fishl and Shloyme, z"l, were the first victims who were caught running away. Local Christians beat them to death with sticks. Several days later, on a Friday morning, the martyrs in the ghetto were murdered.[26]

28 Tishrei 5703. [October 9, 1942]

Regarding how the people hidden in mouse holes felt, I would only wish, that the Germans and all the enemies of the Jews would feel that way. The main question standing before us survivors was if we still had a taste to continue living? The thought started to plague us: for what? And with whom?

I understand that more than one of the future generations will judge our behavior, and our treatment of the old and weak, and they would ask: "What happened to them?!" Why did they not want to understand, that even to die it is better as heroes and not like cowards? Where was their organized strength? And why did it not work?"

Future generations will also bring proof in writing of the heroic struggles of the partisans in various occupied enemy areas. So why were we not organized? What was standing in the way?

But the first answer to that horrible question is that all the tragedies did not happen at one time. Between one tragedy and another, there were breaks, with signs of ending, with a suspicion, maybe for good, maybe that would be the last of the evil acts? The extermination work was so refined and organized, that what was happening on the fronts did not interrupt the plan. Additionally, local bandits robbed the Jews before the civil thieves.

[Page 334]

Furthermore, partisans began to organize quite later, when all Jews from all nations had better chances to defend themselves. In addition, they were not few, like us in the shtetls, but rather hundreds of villages that had hidden weapons from earlier, that had been tied to the fields and forests for generations. That was unlike the larger part of the Jewish population, which had in its life never been in a forest. Still their resistance came about much later after the Jewish extermination, and after the merciless extermination of the millions of Russian prisoners, in whom the partisans saw brothers of their blood and flesh. Slowly, slowly, first they fought the Ukrainian bandit militia, afterwards village after village. Take, for example, what happened in Malyn! Men and women, young and old, all were burned together with their houses. And more, many more such nice deeds. The resistance then grew. And at the end: about a half of the population of Jews ran out of the ghetto that last night, and what kind of end did the local population make of them?! Did a large part of the Jewish population fare better in the mass graves instead of strict burials?

Where Do We Hide?

And now, after the slaughter: where do we hide today? Yesterday we succeeded in hiding in a haystack at a Pole's. We were three souls: my sister Mamtzi,[27] who knew where we were, stole over to us one evening. Sitting like this Shabbes, 29 Tishrei 5703 [October 10, 1942],[28] in a little forest with the taste of life, not eating until nighttime, we noticed a shine from a farmer's hutch and heard barking from a dog who detected us with his dog sense.

[Page 335]

A 12 year-old son of the farmer came over to us and quieted the dog so it would not bark. He understood that we could only be Jews. And with his first words he told us to wait and hide among the trees, because a Ukrainian was visiting in his house. His parents were Polish and their name was Bogdan. We saw him as an angel from heaven. One thing surprised us—who are they? We know the area with its poor farmers so well, like Kozlavsky, Petrovsky, Baranovsky, and others—and who is this Bogdan? None other than an angel from heaven. After a little while passed, Bogdan's boy Zigmund came back to us to announce that the Ukrainian guest left, and we could come in in peace. At the entrance we immediately recognized the farmer and his wife. When he saw us, he crossed himself several times, and swore he would risk his life to save us.

Hungry, we ate hot, cooked potatoes with the skins that had been prepared for the one pig, and we ate them with cooked mushrooms. Unfortunately, Bogdan did not own anything better, like bread. Never in our lives had we eaten anything so delicious. His gifts to us grew when he brought straw inside and told us to rest. At dawn we would go out to his poor barn, dig ourselves in and cover ourselves with the few sheaves. Our contentment had no measure, and we saw godliness in him, as though he were sent from heaven, because a person with such an open heart, at that time, was a rarity.

The sweetness of our sleep on the straw after our rich supper, and the miracle we experienced, is very difficult to write about.

[Page 336]

More difficult is describing our gratitude when Bogdan proposed afterwards that we remain in his extremely poor, half-open stable. He wanted to dig a storage space for us underneath the pig pen; that would be well disguised and protected from suspicious strangers. Our joy was very large.

A few days went by which seemed like years. The farmer brought us very sad news about Jewish survivors who had been discovered by Ukrainians after the general slaughter, and how they were subsequently murdered. What will be our end? In the meantime, we started to sense the smell[29] of other remaining Jews in the area. Among them, my brother-in-law Yankev Shekhman,[30] his wife Khayke and their children: Perl, Avraham, Shimeon, Yoysef, Asher, Ezriel; my brother-in-law Note [Gruber][31] with his wife Maryem [Sherman] and child Shifre; the others remained in the ghetto; Zelig Shekhman and Basye and another sister; Yitskhok Eshes and his wife Khotsl with their son and daughter, and an entire family Koretky from Trovits. In addition, we received word that there was a large group of Jews in the Smordva Forest. Meanwhile, we heard the good news about the large defeat in Stalingrad. Because of suspicions about the Ukrainians, the Germans called together the Ukrainian military on a very good morning, supposedly for exercises, and shot them like dogs. That brought us much satisfaction. All of this gave us even more courage and hope — maybe maybe? Maybe God will still help, at least the remnants?

Our good caretaker, our Bogdan, comforted us every time with hope, saying that we will survive our enemies. His words were like a bandage on our wounds. Passover 1943 we had bad news about another group of Jews who were discovered; their own protectors had turned them in: Srolik Zelig's with his wife and children, Note Raykhman and family, my brother-in-law Yankev Shekhman with his family, my brother-in-law Note [Gruber] and wife and child, Yoysef Neli and Motl Feldman from Brestetsky, Zelig Shekhman and his two sisters, Yitskhok Eshes and family, the family Korotke from Trovits, a family from Lutsk, and many more.

[Page 337]

And that brought us despair and the constant thought–and when will it happen to us?

Battles between Poles and Ukrainians

On the first night of Passover there was a sudden, heated struggle between the local Ukrainians and Poles. The Ukrainian bandits, who did not have a smaller share in our tragedy than the German murderers, may their names be blotted out, and many times they even had a larger share, had old accounts with the Poles from the time Poland was the ruling country. As they sensed the retreat of the Germans, they started to prepare a three-pronged battle against the Jews-Poles-Germans. And even though our stay at the Bodgan's was dangerous because of the Ukrainians, sometimes people benefit when two enemies argue. And so it happened with us. The spring came with hope. Many Polish houses in the area were burned down; that drew out Polish sympathy to the oppressed. Opposition started to be heard from the Poles who had not been burned out, who had among themselves many former Polish officers, learned in weaponry. At the head stood the Kozlovsky brothers, the Tsibulsky brothers, and others. And with weapons in their hands, they turned against their attackers. That gave us chances to move around them more freely. The Ukrainians attacked often, but the Poles heroically pushed them out, with losses on the Ukrainian side. So the entire summer of 1943 stretched until Fall. In the meantime, Jews with weapons came to us: those were the cousins Sady, one is in Tel-Yoysef today, and Leybush Vinokur.

Depending a little on them with their weapons, we left for the forest. Because of the frequent attacks by Ukrainians, the Bogdan family came to our shelter more than once for the night–waiting for the rage to pass.

[Page 338]

Shloyme Moliner from Dubno with his wife, son, and daughter joined us in the forest, as did Yudl Shikhman with his two daughters, and Moyshe Neyter. In addition to my wife Sonye and sister Mamtze and me; my niece Sore Shikhman[32] z"l with frozen feet; Basye, Nakhman Goldseker's wife, and her daughter Shoshana, four years old; Razi with her child Temy, four years old; Yudl Shikhman with his two daughters; Feyge Mandelkern with her husband, Bernstein from Boremel; and the Raverman brothers from Trovits, today in Haifa; Yoyne Veyner, today a policeman in Haifa; and another two younger boys from Trovits, were in the forest together.

We started to sense steps towards salvation. At times a small group of partisans would get lost and come to us, and they told us about massive German losses on the fronts. We started to be aware of signs of deliverance.

Our Christian Angel

I have here the privilege of talking about our dear Bogdan, who kept us together. All Jews, without exception, who wandered in that part of the woods, meaning Novyna-Dobryatyns'ka at the Pańska Dolina, had only one address: Bogdan. A secure trustworthy man. When we needed to dig shelters, and for everyone separately so that not all would be discovered together, I was the digger. Where to get a shovel, a saw, a spade? At Bogdan's. And to know exactly where to make the shelter, so that it would not, heaven forbid, be close to a Ukrainian community, whom do we ask? Bogdan. And for provisions, if we wanted to go to a secure farmer in the area at night to get food, and we don't know our way through the forest paths, we took Bogdan with us. He never refused. He did all that not for riches, but because of his kind character and his goodness.

I want to add, that in the course of that time many unfortunate events occurred, and always, Bogdan's help was the first and the most useful.

Salvation

On a certain early Shabbes morning at the end of February 1944, when we finished breakfast, we saw how both daughters of Yudl Shikhman, who had spent the night in abandoned Polish houses, came running to us in the forest, and fearfully told us that an army of Hungarian troops with German leaders hurried by the main road going to Styr and Trovits![33]

[Page 339]

A puzzle. Is that a retreat? Maybe! Rokhle Kwasgalter, who was with a Czech posing as an Aryan, and who knew about us, had permission to come this Shabbes during daylight to Bogdan, also with the same news. It was unbelievable. We were still sleeping in the forest in our shelter. We started to hear more and more such reports until the afternoon. Our joyous assembly was in Bogdan's hutch. Moyshe Neyter came in and announced that the Germans will no longer be here as rulers! **We were in a dream**. It was unbelievable. We heard distant shootings from artillery, and various flyers who gave the impression of spring birds, and still we did not want to believe it. Three days later, a soldier from the regular Russian army also came to Bogdan's house, and he openly and clearly announced that the Russian army is already headed towards Lutsk.

We made a blessing on the first night that we slept in a house above the ground and not under the ground.

* * *

Soon Getzel, Pesia and Bunia Steinberg[34] with their children; Mendel and Sheindel Steinberg with their child, Liza Berger;[35] the Goldreich family and their child; and the Kupfenberg brothers and sister, soon appeared. We all greeted each other with bloody tears and joy and mourning. We had a premonition that someone from our family will come out of hiding. And so it happened with the sudden arrival, into Bogdan's hut, of Nokhum, Rokhl, Asher, Shifra and Yoysef. In truth, they crawled, not walked, because the last few days of the liberation they were simply in great danger, and because of that, they had to lie in storage a long time, and had to eat and drink and press tightly together in a small ditch.

[Page 340]

It took them a long time until their legs healed, and even now they still feel pain from those days. And then we met Yitskhok Kozak[36] with his surviving family. Also Eli Vaytser's wife and sister, and a few others. We all decided to get to Rivne.

Rivne

There could not be any talk of turning back to Mlynov. Mlynov was then very thickly occupied with the military and was always being bombarded by the Nazi beast, which was still throwing itself in convulsions. So, therefore, we came to the decision of Rivne. The motives: further from the front, a larger city. In addition, we wanted to escape the very serious danger of the Ukrainian bandits, who even after liberation, more than once, murdered surviving Jews. We understood that in Rivne this danger was smaller.

Getting over to Rivne just with our skinny bones was not difficult, because we absolutely owned no baggage. And so we made it. We arrived in Rivne, met with other survivors like us from Varkovychi, Ozeriany, Klevan, and so on. We hugged each other, and we screamed at what became of us. We cried ourselves out. Then we started to look around at where we were in the world.

And fresh troubles began. There were troubles about mobilization, straight into the fire; there were troubles from heavy bombardments; there were less important troubles of hunger and cold. The last had absolutely no importance with us. I personally, like many others, was exhausted, and I limped on one leg, an inheritance from the forest. I was overgrown like an animal; I made the impression of a Jew in old age. So I aimed to work in Gam's mill in Rivne. And that protected me a little from being drafted and a little from hunger. As much as I could, I shared my piece of bread with another person. So, for example, Moyshe Goldseker's son came to me (Misha with the beard).[37] He had been mobilized to work in the mill. He was hungry and thirsty, so I provided him with a couple of rolls, and so on.

But what does one do about the bombing? A very serious problem, which doesn't allow for rest during the day or night.

[Page 341]

I was accidently made aware, on a certain day, that my sister Mirel's z"l two children were found living in Staryi Chortoryisk near Kovel. I immediately sent an old Jew, with quite a white beard to bring them to me. He agreed to do it on one condition, that I should take a third child. Not thinking, I agreed. Said and done. The Jew brought three children the next day: Motel, Lyuba, and Perele.[38] Being reunited with the children was indescribable for my wife Sonia and me. But that same night, the bombing from hundreds of airplanes was so strong, that we meanwhile did not talk about our lives, but strongly regretted that we had brought the children to such danger. And this time God helped; we were saved from that terrible night also.

To Mlynov!

At dawn in May 1944, we headed to Mlynov, being sure, that as the front was already past Lemberg, they will probably not bomb such small points as Mlynov. We arrived in Mlynov. The excitement was quiet. We met there Berel Rabinovitch, Shlomo Schechman,[39] Toybhse the Rebbe's [daughter]. Shaulik Halpern,[40] who was with her in hiding, was drafted at liberation. My wife Sonia and I brought with us her sister Mamtze and the three children. Nokhum, Rokhl, Yoysef, and Shifre. Asher had already been mobilized. We also met there Hannah Veiner; Yitskhok Mandelkern with his child; Yente-Leye Likhter; Chaya Fisher, today in Kinneret; Feyge and Itke Mandelkern; Leybush Vinokur; and my sister-in-law's daughter, Sore z"l; as also Ezra Sherman, the Goldreich family, and a few numbered Jews from the area.

Slowly the nightmare of the long night started to lessen, which so fatally ended for all of us Jews. We could not look around for who was missing, but we could only see who was still there. Hard! Very hard going around to the cemeteries, and all of your dear ones are dead, and they will never be here again.

[Page 342]

And the thought is plaguing, if it was appropriate to protect our bones? And maybe flesh will grow on them again? But life is stronger than everything. The Jewish people never suffered such a large catastrophe in its bloody history. We had serious thoughts. And with them we started to think about our Return to Zion.

What we did in Mlynov over the next 15 months after liberation is less important. We put up a monument for our martyrs; God knows if it is still standing there today. Coming to Mlynov from Rivne, with my brother-in-law Nokhum and Itke Mandelkern, we cleaned up a little the practically broken *ohel*[41] on the Mlynov cemetery, and observed a yahrzeit like in the past. The notes were still around the *ohel* which Jews from Mlynov, and from far, wrote. With hot tears the requests had been thrown on the Karliner holy man's grave. Regarding tombstones, there were practically none left in the cemetery–all were torn out, and spread for sidewalks all throughout Mlynov, wherever they were needed. It made the impression of an act of vengeance to those long dead. To return the monuments to the cemetery was physically impossible for us. Also, the ruling power did not have a need for it. The only monument not ripped out was Yoysef Berger's, may he rest in peace. And we, even though very weak, put it back in its place. How is it today?

In Mervits practically everything remained in the cemetery as it was, practically untouched.

Walking over the streets in Mlynov in that time, when many, many of our dearest dead were like thorns in my eyes, at least I had a little satisfaction. It is still fresh in my memory. The first Shevuos holiday after our return to Mlynov from Rivne, with Nokhum's over-exertions, we used more than our strength to clean out the women's synagogue a little, so that we could remember the souls.

[Page 343]

It is not easy to portray the hysterical picture of the few people, and the bloody tears they poured out in the Women's synagogue that first Shevuos since we were freed. The tears surely poured together with those tears of the former kehilla in the ghetto, on the last Shabbes during Sukkos, barely two years ago, chanting then the last prayers of an entire condemned people in that same house of worship.

We had to proceed with daily business. The broken, walled-up large synagogue we transformed into a storehouse for grain. It would be easier for survivors to gather there instead of allowing it to be slowly town down for bricks, which the population needed then because of the ruins from the war.

* * *

I believe, according to the letters which I often receive from a Mervits farmer, that the synagogue is still standing. Regarding the remaining houses, the best and walled houses were still in order. Good houses were turned into institutions. For example, Shimon Schechman's house became a NKVD. Meir Kwasgalter's house became an office for mobilization. Deaf people lived in the Rabbi's house. Getzel Steinberg's house had his family; in Moyshe Zider's house was Mendel Steinberg and family. Nokhum and family in his house. In Arke's [Nudler], may he rest in peace, with his daughter [Yetka Nudler];[42] in his house, Shlomo Schechman. Berel Rabinovitch was with them in their house.

There was no way I could live in Mervits. I thought that in Mervits I would continue to see the terrible pictures always in front of my eyes. Therefore, we cleaned up a room in the ruins of Yankev Tesler's[43] z"l house and I lived there with my family.

We knew well, both from the stories of local Christians and from the unearthing which the authorities did then for its own purposes, that practically every Jewish house was a cemetery. And so we went around day and night on a large cemetery. To memorialize everybody with monuments was not possible.

Are there any comforts in life for such a tragedy?

Translator's and editor's footnotes:

1. For the background of Mendel and Sonia, see bios on the Mlynov website. – HS
2. The allusion is to 10 Jewish learned martyrs tortured to death on orders from Roman Emperor Hadrian in 135. – HBF
3. 12 July 1941. – HBF
4. A photo of Motel Tesler and his son Benjamin's family appears in this Memorial volume, p. 473. In Yad Vashem records the family surname is spelled Grinshpan. – HS
5. "Tesler" means carpenter. – HBF
6. As noted above, he lived there because he was the sexton of the synagogue. – HS
7. See also Nahum Teitelman's account of seeing Rav Gordon headed to Mervits, p. 316 of this volume. – HS
8. A hamlet called "Stomorhy," 6.3 km north of Mlynov. An alternative name is Stomorgi. – HS
9. Meal eaten during Shabbes, prepared the night before – HBF
10. 13 July 1941. – HBF
11. The Kipergluz family appears in the list of martyrs. The surname appears as Kiperglaz and Kipergluz in Yad Vashem records. Chaia (1919–1942) was daughter of Chaim Yitzhak Kipergluz (1895–1942) and Sarah (1894–1942), who was from Trovits. Chaia also had a brother Yosele. Her father, Chaim, was the son of Yosef Kipergluz and Brakha (Gelman). Her sister, Rachel (later Rachel Kleeman) made aliyah. – HS
12. Possibly Erich von dem Bach-Zelewski, a high-ranking SS commander of Nazi Germany, who was responsible for the *Bandenkampfverbände* (bandit fighting formations) which rounded up and killed Jews in a number of areas including eastern Poland. – HS
13. Probably the man remembered as Eli Moshe Upstein, father of Leazar Upstein. See mention of Leazar son of Eli Moshe Upstein buying an ark in the essay in this volume by Sonia and Mendel Teitelman, "Joys and Sorrows in Mervits," 167–180. See footnote 14. – HS
14. See note 11. – HS
15. August 2-3, 1941. On this date, Heinrich Himmler received approval for the "final solution." – HBF
16. Mendel is referring to his siblings, Nahman Teitelman, and Ester (Teitelman) Gruber. – HS

17. Ben-Tzion Gruber was the brother of Mendel's wife, Sonia. – HS

18. The mark of Cain refers to the mark that God gave Cain after his murder of his brother Abel in Genesis 4:11–16. The mark was a sign of God's protection of Cain from anyone killing him. – HS

19. In Hebrew referred to as Synagogue Street and appears to be the same street called "Shkolna." – HS

20. Chaim Meir was the brother of Mendel's father, Abraham. – HS

21. Father of Yosef Litvak, one of the individuals on the Book Committee for this volume and contributor of several essays with notes to this volume. – HS

22. The father of Chaia Kipergluz. See note 11 above. – HS

23. In the list of martyrs, Moyshe Zider has two sons: Avraham and Zelig. Moyshe's wife was Frida. – HS

24. 1942. – HBF

25. Listen to Ezra Sherman speak about his experience of survival, on the Mlynov Website. – HS

26. October 9, 1942. – HS

27. Also spelled "Mamtze" (Teitelman), she survived and later married Israel Genut. – HS

28. October 10, 1942. – HBF

29. It is not clear if this was meant literally or figuratively, as in "sense the presence of." – HS

30. Sonia's sister, Chaika (Gruber), married Yaakov Shichman (variations Shekhman/Schechman). – HS

31. Note Gruber was the brother of Sonia Teitelman. – HS

32. Sore (Shichman) later, Sara Vinokur, was daughter of Sonia's sister, Chaika (Gruber) and Yaakov Shichman mentioned earlier. She survived when her family was discovered. See the account in Asher Teitelman's memoir. –HS

33. Torhovytsia, today. – HS

34. For the moving Steinberg survival story, see *A Struggle To Survive* on the Mlynov website. – HS

35. Liza Berger was the daughter of Tuvia and Miriam Berger, and a contributor to this volume. Her parents and sister perished in the Shoah. Her brother Pinchas survived in Siberia with the Russian military and later made his way to Israel. Liza and her husband later made their way to Brazil. See the Berger Family story on the Mlynov website. – HS

36. See the essay contributed by Itcik Kozak later in this volume. – HS

37. See the reference to "Moshe with the beard" in Samuel Mandelkern's essay in this volume, "Self-Defense in Mlynov," p. 120. Moshe was one of the elders approached with the idea of self-defense. – HS

38. Mendel's sister, Mirel (Teitelman) was married to Yehuda Schwartz. Their two children were Motel (Max) and Liba. – HS

39. Shlomo Schechman was one of five children of Moshe and Feige Schechman. His father, Moshe, was a brother of Joseph Schuchman. After surviving, Shlomo subsequently married Liza Zabirowciwz and they had two children, Morris and Reuben. Morris was born in a train on the way to Föhrenwald. The family eventually settled in Baltimore. – HS

40. Shaulik (Saul) Halpern was grandson of Lipa Halperin and Pessia (Hirsch). He was conscripted and survived in the Red Army. In the displaced person camp, Pocking, he married Leah Fijalkow. They married in 1946 and had a daughter, Arlene (Halpern) Leder there. The family subsequently migrated to Toronto. See the Hirsch family story on the Mlynov website. – HS

41. Monument tombstone for a Rebbe, in this case, for Rebbe Aharon II of Karlin. – HBF

42. Yetka Nudler (later Helen Fixler) survived with her father in the Smordva forest. Her siblings and mother were killed during one of the raids of the Smordva forest. Her two brothers survived in the Russian army. See the Nudler Family story on the Mlynov website. – HS

43. Yankev (Jacob) Tesler was the father of Liba Tesler. On her survival story, see David, Sokolsky, *Monument: One Woman's Courageous Escape from the Holocaust*. – HS

[Page 344]

Taking Leave of Home

by Yechiel Sherman[1], Haifa

Translated and edited by Howard I. Schwartz, PhD with Hanina Epstein

June 22, 1941. It is 4 am in the morning. I had just begun to dress to head to work. Suddenly I heard a loud, strange noise. It was like the houses were moving from their foundations. I went outside quickly but didn't see a thing. I began walking towards the town center. By the home of Rabinovitz, I already saw several Jews standing and saying that they had bombed airfield on the other side of the Ikva River.

Already by 9 o'clock that same day, talk began about the war that the Germans declared against Russia. Many people were standing and talking about this disaster, even though they couldn't relate any details. But already by 2 o'clock in the afternoon, when I walked in the direction of the general store, which at that time was opposite the house of Aba Grinshpun,[2] I heard and suddenly saw suddenly aircraft approaching from the direction of Dubno and beginning to drop bombs on the airfield and afterwards also on Mlynov itself.[3]

Already, by this time, some people had been killed and the panic had broken out. Tremendous fear pervaded everyone. They began to run from the town in every possible direction. I and my family, my sister Sheindel, my brothers Yosef and Ezra and also grandmother, Hannah, and aunt Tzvia fled to the village of Sloboda.[4] There we had an acquaintance, a gentile, Arsim the tall one.

We entered his hayloft and stayed there. Other people and families from Mlynov gathered there. That same night they all stayed with Arsim. The following day, we began to analyze the situation, but in the morning, we still lacked information that could help us with this. We observed only that the [Russian] military quickly made an escape in the direction of Russia. What to do? I was then 18 — and it was my opinion that there was no compelling reason to remain here and wait for the Germans to arrive. A clear and decisive sign to me was [the fact that] that same Arsim — with whom we stayed the night and in whose shade we spent time — already in the morning drank vodka to the wellbeing of Germans and the life of Ukrainian independence. We grasped that our end would be bitter.

That same day, the 23rd of June 1941, I bumped into Pinhas Klaper,[5] Moshe and Yehuda Veiner[6], Gertnich Koftziav[7] — and we decided to flee at night towards the Russian border. I alone went back again to Mlynov to convince a few young men to flee together with us, but I was not successful. Among others I met was Icek Kozak[8] and asked him to permit his son Ruben to go with us — but he refused. I returned to Sloboda. Along the way, I met Yehezkiel Liberman,[9] who lived along the road to Sloboda, and he asked me, "Yechiel, where are you going?"

[Page 345]

I told him that I and a few other friends were fleeing to Russia. He started persuading me not to flee: The way was full of danger, and we were liable to be killed. I didn't heed him, and I continued to the village of Sloboda. I recounted what had been done in Mlynov and people's opinion about our fleeing — Only members of my family, among them my father Moshe Sherman, favored my fleeing.

It was Monday, the 23rd of June. We gathered again. I, Yechiel Sherman, Yehuda Veiner and his brother, the teacher Bershetyuvka, Pinhas Klaper, Koftzia Gertnich — we got on bikes and began to flee in the direction of Russia. Obviously, we lost track of another along the way ... Only Moshe Veiner and I persisted fleeing together until we reached the border.

Home of Dr. Wissotzky [Vislotsky] in Mlynov

Only then did the troubles begin and also ... the longings for brothers and sisters whom we left behind. Each day we heard the news, in which the Germans were advancing and destroying everything, killing Jews. In all honesty, we didn't believe it, but indeed this reality came to pass.

While I stayed in Russia much happened to me. Innumerable experiences.

[Page 346]

Until March 1942, I was in a collective farm (Kolkhoz), after that in the Red Army and on the front until the end of the War, which ended for me when I was already in Germany near the Elbe River when meeting the American army on May 10th, 1945.

* * *

On March 1944, while I was advancing with the Red Army towards Germany, I was very close to my town Mlynov, and I decided to get home whatever the cost. After three days of travel, I reached the entrance to the Mlynov forest. Even as I entered the town, I witnessed the great destruction the Germans brought about. I first entered the cemetery and saw that they had demolished it all. I looked for the gravestone of my mother, who had died already by 1938, whose burial location I knew — but I was not able to find anything; The Germans had taken the tombstones for paving sidewalks.

I started to enter the town, along the way I stopped by each house, and thinking perhaps I'll find someone at home — but I found not a soul ... until I came to one Pole, a carpenter named Dimar; he had been living near Moshe Shakrov[10], the shoemaker. He didn't recognize me since I was in military uniform. He began to tell me the names of those who remained alive. All of them, I found at the home of the town's rabbi [Rav Gordon[11]]. I found Tobeyshe [the rabbi's daughter], Getzel [Steinberg] and his brother [Mendel] from Mervits.[12] And also Berel Rabinovitch and Shlomo Schechman; the other survivors already left for Rovno.

They told me about the great destruction perpetrated by the murderers. Nothing remained for me to do in Mlynov — and the next morning I got up and returned to my unit. After a while, I got a letter from Mlynov that my brother Ezra was alive. But I was already far away from the town. Ezra had hidden with a gentile and by a great miracle he remained alive. At the time of the liberation, he entered the Red Army[13] and advanced with it. We were not able to meet until the end of the War; but once we met, we have not been separated again to this very day.

* * *

Let all their wrongdoing come before You,
And deal with them, as You have dealt with me

(Lamentations 1:22)

Translator's and editor's footnotes:

1.   Yechiel Sherman was one of the eight individuals on the Book Committee for this original volume. He was the son of Moshe Sherman and Etel (Golisuk) Sherman and was the namesake of his paternal grandfather. His mother, Etel, was the daughter of Hannah (Schuchman). His parents and grandmother's photo appears on page 462 with additional notes.

2.   Aba Grinsphan (alt. spellings Grenspun, Grinsphan and Greenspun) is listed as one of the martyrs in Mlynov, p. 434, with his wife Pesia, Moshe and Yaakov.

3.   See the other accounts of this early bombing and its aftermath by Asher Teitelman, pp. 38–41 and Fania Mandelkern Bernstein, pp. 287–288.

4.   A small village outside of Mlynov on old maps, probably incorporated into today's town Uzhynets'. The Holtzekers in town were nicknamed "Sloboda" because they had lived there before coming to Mlynov which is where Moshe Fishman met them originally. See Moshe Fishman's comments, p. 60, and that of Mendel and Sonia Teitelman, p. 256.

5.   Alt. spellings Klaper / Klapir. See his photo with young men on page 461 with notes there.

6.   Moshe and Yehuda Veiner (alt. spellings Weiner, Vainer, Veyner) were sons of Beracha and Yitzhak Veiner and both survived as did their sister Hannah. After the War, Yehuda later married Leah Likhter who contributed "In Fear and Pain," pp. 382–383, with additional notes there.

7.   "Koiftze" or "Kuftzia" Gertnich refers to the young man named Yosef Gertnich Ganon who survived and contributed the essay, "Memories of Home," pp. 261–262, which briefly refers to this same period of time. He appears in the photo on page 458, one of the sons of Moshe Gertnich and his wife Sorke (Shrentzel). In Israel,

he took the surname Ganon. He was first cousin to Lipa Halperin (their mothers were sisters) who contributed several essays to this volume.

    8.   Icek Kozak survived with his whole family. See his contributed essay, "What My Family Endured," pp. 354–357 with additional notes.

    9.   Yehezkiel Liberman and his family appears in a photo on page 468 with notes.

    10.   Moshe Shakrov (alt. spellings Shekrev, Shakrav) appears in the list of Mlynov martyrs, p. 439, with his wife and children, Yechiel, Devorah, Rivkah. A son Eliyahu is at the time in America.

    11.   Rabbi Gordon's home.

    12.   See the background for these individuals in the account of the survivors in Fania (Mandelkern) Bernstein's essay, "Mlynov After the Liberation of the Soviet Army," pp. 310–313.

    13.   He was taken in as a mascot by a Russian officer.

[Page 347]

I Wandered Hungry and in Pain

Liza Berger, Brazil[1]

Translated from the Yiddish by Hannah B. Fischthal, PhD

Edited by Howard I. Schwartz, PhD

My agony started when the bandits first came into the shtetl. They caught people for labor. The Judenrat supplied the workers..We were about 50 girls, women, men, and children. Girls were chosen to wash the vehicles in the river.

20 trucks were brought in, and we girls stood in the river up to our belts and washed the vehicles, from 10:00 a.m. until 6:00 p.m. It was September 1941, and it was very cold, freezing. When we were told to go home, we each received three blows from their guns — that was our pay.

When we got home, we had nothing to eat; the farmers had not brought anything into the shtetl that day.

* * *

We young people got together and agreed that we need to accomplish something and not be so naïve. We decided to escape into the forest. We left near Mantyn.[2] The boys found a barn. They remained there while we girls searched for bread. When we came back, we found the boys naked and dead. Our aimless, lifeless wandering began then. No Christian we approached wanted to give us a piece of bread, and we did not have where to rest our heads.

The other girls separated from me, and I remained alone in the forest. I was in Pańska Dolina[3] at night, and I tried to go into a Christian's barn. He saw me and drove me out of there. That was midnight. The snow was a meter high. It was in November. I was only in a pair of shorts, without shoes and without a dress, because a few Ukrainians had caught me earlier and demanded money.

[Page 348]

I gave them all my clothes.

Like that, I would search for something to eat at night. I used to grab and devour like a wild animal. Sometimes a farmer threw out a couple of dirty potatoes. Many nights I was too late, and I had to go back into the forest with nothing. On the way I saw the Angel of Death, cold and hunger, in front of my eyes.

One time I snuck into a barn very late at night. I suffered from extreme hunger and cold. I fell asleep there. I dreamed that my mother was coming to give me a piece of bread. I got up. It was only a dream. My soul felt a premonition that in this barn a person can starve. A farmer came out with a little cup of cold potatoes. When he came into the barn, he found me bellowing. When I saw him, I wildly grabbed the cup and almost bit him. When I finished the small amount of food, I felt a little quieter.

* * *

December 25th. The Christians went to church until midnight. I was very weak. I had not eaten again for five days, so I thought, let it already be what it will be. I can no longer endure it. I went to search for bread, hoping maybe someone will have pity on me. I knocked on the door of a Pole.

Immediately I heard from inside: "A Jew is there!"

I was practically naked. My feet were wrapped in rags. When the Christian woman opened the door, she saw a living corpse. She got scared, and she threw over a piece of bread and a piece of onion and started to scream out to her family, "You see how a woman became crazy"!

I was happy with the little piece of bread. Then again, another five days without food. I was in the forest. I went again to search for something. From a distance I saw a house, and I started to walk there. The way was as long as the Jewish exile. I could not reach the end. It was 3:00 a.m. and it was freezing, about 30 degrees. The sky was full of stars and the moon was full. When I came out of the forest, I saw that someone was following me.

[Page 349]

So, I started to run. He ran after me. So, I lay down under a hill. Then I realized that I had been chased by my own shadow. It was very difficult then to pick myself up and go further, and if it were not for the power to live and survive, it would have been very easy to remain there forever.

* * *

One time I went to a Pole in the village of Pańska Dolina, a rich village. When I got to the door, they immediately recognized me, "Liza Berger!" They took me into a corner of the kitchen, so that I could not be seen from outside, and so that I would not dirty their house with my lice. They gave me a piece of bread with a glass of milk. The oldest daughter kept pouring me more milk, but she did not add any bread. However, when the daughter went out of the kitchen for a minute and I noticed from a distance a couple of raw potatoes and seven carrots, I swallowed them up in one minute!

* * *

One evening a Pole called me into his house and gave me a little food. I stood like a dog and ate it up. Suddenly a division of Germans came into the village; they were searching for Jews. The Pole tore the food out of my hands and chased me out. My life was at risk.

I said to the Christian, "If I will go out, I will be shot — so it would be better for me to sit at the table with you, and everything will look okay."

They consulted each other, and an older woman had a suggestion: they should put me in bed and bind up my head and say a child is sick. And so it was. I was put into bed. The German bandits came into the house and searched for Jews. They went into the barn, into the stalls, and searched. Then they left with "*Wiedersehen.*"

* * *

One time I came out of the forest and went to a woman who was well off near Mlynov. I knew her for a long time. She was a widow, and I had an account with her. I thought she would let me stay in her stable. An entire night I was lost and could not recognize the village. It was almost 6:00 a.m. when I came to her.

Her reception was cold. She asked me how I dared to come to her, when there were so many Germans around.

[Page 350]

She quickly led me out and told me to sit down; she will go and make me something to eat. She made me a warm cup of milk and led me to an unfinished house nearby. On the ground she gave me the milk and a large piece of bread. And she told me she will go to another village to get me something to wear.

But when she went out of the house, I heard her say to her mother that she was going to the village magistrate. And I did not like that. So, I stood alerted, and through the cracks of the unfinished wall I saw her leading the magistrate in order to hand me over to the Germans.

The house was near a river. I jumped out of the window into the river, into reeds.

The Christian came into the house and started to scream, "Liza, where are you? I want to give you something to eat."

I heard all that while lying in the river. She asked her mother, "Why did you let her go?"

And to the magistrate, "You will certainly think that I fooled you."

I heard all of that. I lay in the water, cold and wet until the evening. At night, birds with long and sharp beaks pecked me.

Almost dawn, when the hens crowed the third time, I came out of the water and started to run as much as I could. After running a long distance, I came to another shtetl with cows. I became warm and the lice sucked my last bit of blood.

But that did not last long. The owner came and drove me out with wires, so I ran further. To where? Barefoot, scantily clothed, and additionally in the middle of the day. I was half dead when I got to the forest.

Even more bitter times started. No Christians let me cross their thresholds. The snow was very deep. One time I left the forest and let myself go to a village, to a Pole. I was starving. That was a Sunday. I figured that Sunday the villains would not come, but my reasoning was wrong.

[Page 351]

The Germans actually came on Sunday to catch Poles and send them to forced labor in Germany. I was also caught, and we were transferred to Dubno to the train station.

Translator's and editor's footnotes:

1.   Liza Berger was the daughter of Tuvia and Miriam Berger. She was one of three siblings. She and her brother Pinchas survived. Her sister, Raisel, and her parents perished in the Shoah. Liza's father, Tuvia, was a brother of Wolf Berger and Faivel Berger, and Liza was thus a first cousin of Aaron Harari one of the major contributors to this volume. Read more about Liza's story and the Berger family story on the Mlynov website.

2.   Mantyn is 5.8 km (3.4 mi) north of Mlynov by road and even closer as the crow flies.

3.   Pańska Dolina no longer exists but was between Mlynov and Lutsk. It was a stronghold of Polish resistance. Other Mlynov refugees such as Sonia and Mendel Teitelman also hid in Pańska Dolina.

Regrets

by Aleph Katz[1]

Translated from the Yiddish by Hannah B. Fischthal, PhD

Edited by Howard I. Schwartz, PhD

Why is it exactly like this?

An eternal "oy" flickers in the question,
Like the wick in the candle of a mourner.

He cries and he demands, like the writing on a wall—
As it argues and demands with its stone writing
The short summary of an epitaph.

He cries only because of himself, from regrets,
Even if no ear hears him;
He tears it out of his heart and he speaks
Like songs from a bird, like a poet sings.

There is no power that can contain him,
Not allow him to speak—the "oy" banished
Through years of pain since the beginning of time—
Because pain becomes renewed with its initial sharpness
In everyone separately who suffers a loss.

Editor's Footnote:

1.   Originally born Moshe Katz in 1898 in Mlynov, "Aleph" as he came to be known as a Yiddish poet, came to the US in 1913 with his mother and two siblings. His mother was called "Henia Arelas," Anna the daughter of Aaron [Hirsch], and one of several Hirsch siblings to come to America. Aleph's father was Chaim

Yeruchem Katz. You can read more about Aleph's background, pp. 489–490. Aleph's photo appears on p. 490 and his mother, Henia Arelas on p. 500 of this volume. See also the Hirsch family story on the Mlynov website. – HS

[Page 352]

Holocaust

by Shaulik Halpern, Toronto, Canada[1]

Translated by Hannah B. Fischthal, PhD

Edited by Howard I. Schwartz, PhD

The 22nd of June 1941, the Nazi murderers trespassed over cursed Polish earth and, like lightning, conquered Poland in hours.[2] They immediately started to murder the Jews, and Jewish blood was pouring.

Screams of woe were soon heard from Jewish homes. The Nazis ran around like devils, like wild bloodthirsty beasts, from house to house. Battered mercilessly, murdered without an explanation. "*Jude Schwein,*" and "*Jude, heraus!*" [Jew pig; Jew, get out!] were all that was heard. Mothers pulled their hair out of their heads. People ran wherever they could. Children were torn from their mothers, and mothers from children.

The Ukrainian murderers helped them with their nauseating work. Shooting was heard from one corner of the town to the other. Already in the first days, in their horrible manner, they shot our rabbi, Rabbi Yehuda Leyb Gordon, who had earlier been tortured in a village near Mervits. They also shot 10 young children on the landing field, accusing them of espionage.

We lived in fear. No eating and no drinking. Like for Pharoah, we labored hard. The 10th of July 1941, the shtetl was fenced in with barbed wire. The Jews were driven from the surrounding area to Mlynov. The ghetto had been created. The Ukrainian police guarded us day and night. The number of illnesses multiplied; people died of hunger, need, and fear. Bodies were swollen from hunger.

Every day new orders came from the murderers: today, supply gold; tomorrow, silver, clothes, furs. Every day we survived the difficult burden.

And all at once, the 10th of October 1942[3], we heard that graves were being dug between the mountains to bury the slaughtered, innocent Jewish population.

[Page 353]

The ghetto was well surrounded by the Ukrainian murdering police and with SS people. People searched for ways to tear out of the enclosure — but it was too late!

Early in the morning, trucks full of SS came into the shtetl. Women and men, old and children, were flung out of the houses and brought to the graves. Undressed, naked, they were positioned in rows near the graves, and mercilessly shot and thrown into them. The heartbreaking scenes are indescribable; many children were simply buried alive.

This was how Mlynov-Mervits was liquidated, wiped off the earth; that is how our parents, brothers and sisters became martyrs; that is how our dearest ones were torn away from the world. We will never forget them!

* * *

Some were able to save themselves and run into villages and forests, but they were very few. I also was among the lucky ones. Together with Toybeshe Gordon, we were able to hide by good Czechs who saved us; we will never forget them.

We will also remember, to their shame, the Ukrainian murderers who, with their dirty hands, helped the devil to kill our dear ones. We must remember how after their nauseating tasks, they ran into the emptied ghetto and robbed everything that was remaining. They danced for joy.

Translator's and editor's footnotes:

1.   Shaulik (Saul) Halpern was born in Mlynov in 1912 to Yosef Halperin and Cipa Rywiec (possibly a variation on Rivitz). He was one of six children. His paternal grandparents were Lipa Halperin and Pessia (Hirsch) making Saul a first cousin of Lipa Halperin, another contributor to this volume. Apart from Saul's brother, Benjamin, who went to Russia and survived, all of Saul's siblings perished. Saul is in the photo of the Zionist Youth on page 73, in the backrow, third from left. See the Mlynov website for the Hirsch family story. – HS

2.   The date of the German invasion of Poland was 1 September 1939; 22 June 1941 was the date the Germans first attacked the Soviet Union, including Ukraine – HBF.

3.   Other contributors to this volume indicate that the liquidation occurred on October 8th or 9th, 1942.

[Page 354]

What My Family Endured

by Icek Kozak[1], Philadelphia

Translated from the Yiddish by Hannah B. Fischthal, PhD

Edited by Howard I. Schwartz, PhD

As soon as the Germans came in, they took us, a group of old and young Jews, to work on the military airfield. Several murderers went over to the people who were working, and they chose the best-looking boys. My children and I were standing a little further away and we saw how the murderers shlepped 10 boys down into the old trenches which were there from the First World War. The boys were killed there;[2] Shloyme Sherman[3] (he was the eleventh) covered them with dirt. Afterwards he came back.

Shloyme did not have to be asked about the boys; his face told us everything. I will never in my life forget that day. The mothers in the shtetl looked for their children to come home before night, but they were already dead.

* * *

The next day, several Jews and I left to work for Uzhynets', [4] on the bulwark, and we worked there a long time. In the beginning we would go home every night to sleep, until something happened.

My children and I came home tired from work. We sat on a bench in the yard to rest up a bit. Two Ukrainian murderers came over to us and told us to take two shovels and go with them. My younger son Moyshe and I went with them. On the way, they picked up Moyshe Shnayder and Avrohom Koval, and led all four of us to the S.S. From there we were taken underneath Yosl-Mayer's mill,[5] and the murderer told us to dig a grave for us four. We saw black in front of our eyes. Many Germans were standing around us.

[Page 355]

All of a sudden, we heard a shot. Another murderer called us away, and we saw a dead Russian. We buried him. The grave was too large for one person, and the killers started to look at us. In the end, they told us to go home. We were afraid because it was nighttime. My Moyshe, barefoot, stepped on a broken beer bottle and his foot was badly injured. The blood poured out.

The next day we went to work on the bulwark. Moyshe went also, even though his foot was swollen. He was afraid to remain home. From that day on, we did not return home at night. We spent our nights at the bulwark.

* * *

The summer passed and outside it became cool. The Judenrat sent for me and said that the Germans needed a driver, so they confirmed that I would do it. I drove the Germans wherever they needed to go. When these Germans left, they turned me over, together with the horses, to the Sovitsky, the Russian official of the community. The official gave me a paper so that the Ukrainian police would not trouble me.

After Passover 1942,[6] in the afternoon, they started to catch Jews. My Reuven and I hid in the small attic, and my Moyshe was with a Christian for whom he worked. They searched for but did not find us, so they took [my wife] Chava with the two girls. In the morning, I went to Mervits to Sovitsky and took the garbage out of his stable. Two policemen came over, one a Ukrainian and one a Jew, Yosl Kanamins from Mervits, today in America.

The Ukrainian policeman did not want to take me and said to the Jewish one that I was not a Jew, but the Jewish one said: "Take him; he is a Jew."

We were taken to Dubno and concentrated in a synagogue. Suddenly, many Ukrainian policemen came over and called out for us to leave the synagogue. I went into the *shammes's*[7] little room, and I hid in a small closet.

[Page 356]

It was hard even for a child to hide there. When the people were taken to the train, I jumped over the barbed wires of the Dubno ghetto, and I went home. The mothers and women asked me how I had saved myself, so I told them that it was because of Sovitsky's paper.

* * *

I continued to drive Germans with horses and wagons. My Reuven worked in Kozyn,[8] and Moyshe was in Studyanka near Kremenets.[9] The German whom I drove around thought I was a Russian. He assigned non-Jews to work in Germany.

One time I was with my German at a Czech's in Novyny.[10] When I needed to give the horses a drink it was raining, so I put on my jacket. I forgot that my two yellow patches were sewed on it, and the German saw this through his window. He called me in and asked about it, so I answered in Ukrainian that the day before I had killed a Jew, and I had taken his jacket. The Czech translated my words into German, and my excuse was accepted.

* * *

Now my real troubles began. All the Jews were in the ghetto while I drove around with my German. Every day I would come home and tell all the latest sad news: here the shtetl was destroyed, and there another shtetl was liquidated. I used to go to Christians that I knew, and I begged them to allow me to hide there. They answered that maybe they would accept my sons and me, but Chava and the girls, no way.

Then I received a promise from a Ukrainian with the name Anapry Tsereshok, who lived in Mervits. With great effort and step by step, I little by little brought over my entire family with my wagon, for which I had the certificate. I would lay each of them one by one in the wagon and pile hay on top. This way we all got together at Anapry's, the Ukrainian's. Meanwhile graves for the little Jewish children were prepared. That was Thursday, the 1st of October 1942.

[Page 357]

At Anapry's, we hid in his earthen hut, but we did not receive any food; Anapry himself didn't have any to spare. He was a poor Christian. We used to sneak out at night and go on the fields, but not near Mervits. We especially went a couple of kilometers further, so that we would not be recognized. Once we found two rotten onions, so we ate them up at once. That did us harm and we got sick from them.

* * *

We were with this Ukrainian until the 14th of January 1944. The local Ukrainians had learned about us. Remaining there longer with Anapry was very dangerous. Anapry and his wife came over and warned us to run away. The weather was then extremely cold, and the snow was very deep. We had nothing to wear. Whatever we used to have, we had sold for a piece of bread. We left and entered a dirt hut that belonged to a Pole. All the Poles had left the area, fearful of the Ukrainians. They would come during the day to feed their animals, but at night they slept in Mlynov.

When the Pole and his wife came in the morning and saw us in their home, the man said nothing. He cooked a few little potatoes for us, and he warned us that "At night we could have Ukrainian guests" when they would come to burn the Polish villages. We had no choice; we had no place else to go.

The Soviets entered and freed us on the 9th of February.

* * *

[The great day of the Lord is approaching],
...That day shall be a day of wrath,
A day of trouble and distress,

A day of calamity and desolation,
A day of darkness and gloom
A day of densest clouds.

(Zephania 1:15)

Translator's and editor's footnotes:

1. Icek Kozak (1899–1994) married Chava Bichman (also spelled "Bickmouiu") (1903–1991). They had four children: Rubin (1922– ~2016), Morris (Moshe) (1924–2012), Jean Litz (Genia / Genendal Vidravnik) (1928–1998) and Karen Lowenthal (Kreina Kozak) (1931–). Family indicates there was also a son Kalman who died around the age of 10 before the Shoah when he was beat up after school by gentile boys and had a brain bleed. A photo of the family appears on p. 506 and a photo of Rubin on p. 467. After their liberation they made their way to the Föhrenwald displaced persons camp. They arrived in New York on April 1, 1947, and headed to Icek's brother, Jack Kossack who had come to the US before WWI and settled in Philadelphia. – HS
2. This took place on July 13, 1941 as reported by Nahum Teitelman, p. 314, and by Mendel and Sonia Teitelman, p. 325, separately in this volume. – HS
3. Shlomo Sherman was a son of Yechiel and Leah Sherman and a sibling of Moshe Sherman, the father of Ezra and Yechiel Sherman, both survivors. The younger Yechiel Sherman is a contributor to this volume and survived the War in the Red Army. Ezra hid in the attic of a shed on the day of the ghetto liquidation and survived wandering in the countryside until the end of the War. – HS
4. A close village just 5 km (3 mi) outside of Mlynov to the east and slightly north. – HS
5. Yossel Gelberg was the owner of the mill and was son of Pinhas Meyer Gelberg. – HS
6. Passover began April 1, 1942. – HS
7. A synagogue official. – HBF
8. Kozyn is 53 km (32 mi) south of Mlynov and southeast of Dubno. – HS
9. Kremenets is 63 km (39 mi) south of Mlynov. Probably referring to Studyanka which is just off the road to Kremenets and 53 km south. Nahum Teitelman also reports in this volume that his son Asher was taken to Studyanka to work. – HS
10. A village close to Mlynov, just 14 km (8.6 mi) northeast. – HS

[Page 358]

The Terror Of Annihilation

by Mendel (Anshel's) Steinberg[1]

Translated from the Yiddish by Hannah B. Fischthal, PhD

Edited by Howard I. Schwartz, PhD

October 1942. I was then working in the so-called M.T.S.[2] We were 13 Jews, among us the Rav of Mervits, Shmuel-Ber Katz. From the Judenrat, of which a few members were then in Dubno, I learned that by the 10th of October our entire neighborhood needed to be *Judenrein*. By that date, all the Jews had to be slaughtered.

So I went to a Christian whose name was Andrey Kravets[3], and I promised him riches if he would hide my wife, child, and myself. I used to deal with this Christian, and he knew that I was one of the richest people in the shtetl. He agreed. So I went back to the M.T.S. and begged the director to send a horse and wagon into the Mlynov ghetto to bring over my wife (Sheindel–Benyomin's [daughter]).[4] My son Anshel had stolen out of the ghetto earlier and had come to me.

One of my cousins, Memtsi Note's, also worked with me. I asked her to travel to my wife and bring her back. I gave her a letter to take along to my wife, that she should take out all the expensive things that were hidden in the old sofa, as much as she was able. The horse and wagon would wait for her, and she should slip out of the ghetto. My wife, however, got very frightened. She came to me only with two large breads. Our entire fortune remained in the ghetto.

But I myself had a nice quantity of gold five-ruble coins plus $200. It was *Shemini Atseres*.[5] I left my job and said:

"Children, run wherever you can; today or tomorrow everyone will be exterminated!"

We kissed each other and cried, and we left. We went into a dirt hut that was standing in the middle of the field, and we waited until it was very dark. Then we left through the fields to Andrey Kravets, who a had prepared a place for us in a dirt hut that was standing in the middle of the field.

[Page 359]

After two days Andrey came to us and demanded that we leave. He was afraid he would be shot together with the Jews. No talking helped. So I left for where my brother Getzel was hidden; I knew the place. My brother advised me to go to Alexey Novartsky. So, I went to that Christian. Coincidentally, Srolik Zelig's with his wife Ite and his two girls came to Alexey at the same time. He got very frightened, and I had to leave. A few months later those Jews were killed there.

I was thinking of a Christian, Martin Gabovsky, who lived in Pańska Dolina.[6] But I went instead to another Christian, Soldatuk. I used to do a lot of business with him, and we were very friendly. When I came to him, he was in a dirt hut, and he was grinding. It was late at night, and I did not know what to do — go inside to see him? He had five Christians with him, all of them *Banderovtses*[7] who searched for Jews to murder. I risked my life, and I went inside to see him. Maybe really this is how we will be saved? Here the Christians maybe will not kill me? I turned to him and said that my life was in his hands. The oldest Christian, Andrey, was with him; he is located now in Czechoslovakia, and I still write to him up to this day. At first they were frightened, but afterwards Soldatuk said that he had to get advice from his wife, and he went to ask her. He came back with the news that such a good Jew as I am needs to be saved. So I left to get my wife and child and we went into a little stall where he used to store wood.

The next day I told him of the fortune that I left in the ghetto in the house of Moyshe the tailor. Moyshe[8] was my wife's uncle. The Christian knew him too. He told me that he will go to Mlynov. So I gave him a letter to Moyshe, he should take the things out of the sofa, and my wife's brother, Yosel Grinshpan,[9] should smuggle it out of the ghetto. I also begged for Zelig, one of Moyshe's children, an engineer, to come join us, so that we could be together. The Christian agreed. The outcome was, however, different. Moyshe was not home. He was working.

[Page 360]

And his wife wrote a note that she was afraid to send the things out. She would not send Zelig[10] — what will happen to everyone, will also happen to him. The end was, that after the general slaughter, all four of them were shot: Moyshe, his wife, and the two children.

I told the Christian, that if he had brought me nothing from Mlynov, I had nothing. However, he need not worry, because my brothers were hidden close by, and they had many gold five-ruble pieces and dollars, and I would be able to take cash from them. I did not want to tell him about my own money and gold that I had with me, because I was afraid. There were many instances where Christians robbed the money and murdered the Jew. He was content. The next day I told him that my wife had a dream about her grandfather, a Jew over 90, who was the first victim in Mervits.[11] The Christian knew him well.

"Her grandfather told her, in the dream, that she should not leave this place where she is now. She should not leave, because it is the only place where we can remain alive. Nothing bad will happen to the family supporting us."

I told him that. If he would ever want to drive us away, I would use the dream.

Friday, 29 Tishrei [Oct. 10, 1942], Soldatuk was in Mlynov where he heard that all the Jews in the ghetto had been exterminated.[12] If anyone would find a hidden Jew, both the hider and the Jew would be killed. He came to us at night when we were lying down, and he told us to get out. My wife started to cry. How can she leave from there after such a dream?!… However, not a single thing helped — we must go! I went to all the Christians that I knew, with whom I had had business dealings, but nobody wanted to let me in.

I went back through the fields to my wife and child hiding at Soldatuk's. I saw on the field a little ditch. That was a potato field. On that place grew a few willow trees. I took long pieces of wood, and I put them on the ditch. On top of the wood, I put potatoes and plants so nobody could tell that it was a trench.

[Page 361]

I took my wife and child away from the Christian, and we went into the ditch on his field. It was very small; we could only sit in it, not lie down. We were there three days and Soldatuk did not know it. He thought that we went to someone else. We had left all our things in his hut; we only took my *tallis* and *tefillin* and something to eat.

On the third day, he noticed the ditch. He came over, pushed aside the potatoes, bent down a little and asked me, why I did not leave his property. So I answered him that my wife did not want to leave because of the dream with her grandfather.

"I arranged another place with Safke Krave." He was a rich Christian. "But when I came to get my wife, she did not want to go."

Meanwhile, Soldatuk liked this new "place to live," and he told me that he will bring me something to eat. I informed him that I had been at my brother's hiding place and took from him 100 rubles in gold, which I immediately gave him.

That same night, the Christian came again and brought us food. He said that when his wife heard how we were lying in the ditch she wept, and they decided to make us a hiding place in his carriage shed where he kept his machines. I went right over and spent the entire night digging the new ditch; it was large, and all three of us could lie down. On top of the ditch, we put machines, ploughshares, and other things, and nobody could tell. The entrance hole we made on the other side of the wall, where the horses were. We stayed there. Every time, when Soldatuk heard that Jews were being caught, he would chase us from the place. Then I would say that I was going to my brother to get money to give him, and thereby shut his mouth. When I would go out, I used to go to a Pole that I knew, Fartun Zikofsky, and there I would hear all the news about what Jews were caught, about the front, and so on. Once he told me that the day before he had seen Nokhum Teitelman (now found in Israel). He knew where he was located, but he would not tell me. The decent Poles would act that way — they would not tell. I went back "home" through the fields.

[Page 362]

* * *

Soldatuk came to me after Passover[13] and told me categorically that we had to leave. I already wrote that I always used to give him gold five-ruble pieces, which I supposedly got from my brother. But now he was concerned about something else:

"The Poles," he said, "attack the Ukrainians, and they set fires and murder."

He was afraid that they will find out that he is keeping Jews. I responded that my wife was now sick and as soon as she would be better, we would go to my brother or to the rich Christian Safke Kravets. He waited a week. After that he came again and threatened that if I do not leave his place, he will have to do something. But where do we go? I thought, that as long as I could, I will delay him, because it was already all the same to me. If we would go, we would meet death, and if we would stay, he would turn us over to the Gestapo. Every day, therefore, was a gift.

At night I went out and told him that I was going to the new place, but in the morning, I returned to the ditch. He was upset–why were we not going away? So I made up a new story, that I went to Safke Kravets, arranged the place and came to take my wife, but my wife refused to go because of her dream, that only here would she survive; if she would leave, she would be killed. He could see a sign that the dream was correct: she dreamed that nothing would happen to the Christian protecting them, and that was true. From all the families, men were taken for work to Dibrova, and only he was not bothered.

"And secondly," I said, "she is sick, so how can she leave?"

Again, we had another few days. Every day he used to come and ask how my wife was; he waited every day for her to die already. I also learned he had a plan to kill her; after all, she was dying anyway. Meanwhile, I was able to drag out the time.

Then the village was burned down. A large Christian came into the barn and drove out all the animals because the entire village was burning, and the fire already had reached our neighbor. Afterwards he closed the door from the outside with an iron stake. The surrounding houses were on fire.

[Page 363]

The smoke odor was inside, and we were locked in! We did not have a single thing with which to break down the door. We started to scream and say goodbye. But God here performed a miracle–our boss's house did not catch fire! When he came again, I explained to him that it was more proof that the dream was correct. Then I begged him to permit me to dig out a ditch in his field, and he gave me permission.

* * *

Saturday night I went out to his potato field and dug a ditch. I covered it with wood. On top of the wood, potatoes were growing in the dirt; from outside nothing could be noticed. The ditch was quite large. All three of us could lie down comfortably. But we were missing something to eat and drink, because everyone in the entire village had escaped into the shtetls and very few people remained.

And after a miracle, another big one: The next morning, Sunday, after I had brought my wife and child into the ditch, the Christian's entire house was burned down, including the place where we had been hidden. Our things which we had not taken out when we left were burned up. The owner was not home — he had left earlier for the shtetl Trovits. After the fire, he came back. He searched for our burned bones, and as he did not find them, he went to search in his field. There he noticed something, because the potatoes on the ditch had not yet been gathered.

He started to scream: "Pan Ansheluk, Pan Ansheluk!"

That is what he called me. I recognized his voice, picked up a kind of box and called him over. He came to the hole and explained how he searched for our burned bones. I begged him to bring us something to eat, and mainly a little water for my child. He promised me he would fill up a pitcher of water and leave it in his walled cellar and that I should go get it at night.

At night I went to get the water. Meanwhile, on the way, Ukrainian Christians lay in wait for the Poles. The Christians grabbed me.

[Page 364]

I knew two of them and their fathers. I had dealt with them for many years. They beat me up so badly that they assumed they killed me; and then they left me lying on the ground. My wife in the ditch heard me scream a kilometer away. My screams were also heard by the Pole Zikovsky, to whom I used to go. He heard my last groans.

I lay like that a long time and roused myself a little. With all my strength I got up and started to think where I was. Afterwards I slowly crawled and barely shlepped myself into the ditch. I met my wife and child dressed — they wanted to give themselves up to the Gestapo; they thought I was already dead. We all went back into the ditch. I lay wounded and beaten and did not even have anything with which to tie up my wounds.

Monday at dawn my wife heard the owner's voice: "Mendelekha, Mendelekha!"–not "Ansheluk." She opened the hole and called the owner. Seeing me, he crossed himself. He thought I was already dead.

He screamed at me: "Get away from here already; you did not tell me that there are Jews around here with weapons!" I started to cry that I didn't know anything, not about Jews and not about weapons.

So he told me this story: yesterday two Christians came to him, Pavlo and Volotke, and they told him that in his field they caught and killed Mendel Ansheloyks. And when they told their commander, he got angry because they didn't bring him in alive, because if he is here, there are more Jews to find. I would have had to tell, because they cut pieces out of you, and you must tell. The commander ordered them to bury the Jew, because if the Gestapo would find out that he was not caught alive, they would scream. The Christians went out to find the body, but people started to shoot, and who then would shoot if not Jews? They did not find the dead body; probably the Jews buried him.

I explained that the shooters were Poles who had heard my screams.

[Page 365]

"The evidence that there were no Jews who buried me — is that I am still alive!"

The Christian again ordered us to go because the others will find us. I answered that we will not leave, and we will be careful. He asserted he will not come here anymore because he was afraid. That actually was his last visit, because the Poles killed him. That was the night before Yom Kippur.[14]

* * *

A short time later. At night I left the ditch and went to Andrey Kravets to learn about the war, and to beg him for something to eat; my child was pleading for a piece of bread. I went to the window and knocked. Andrey saw me and let me into his house. Everyone in his house stood up and cried looking at me. In his house was his son-in-law from the village Pidhaitsi.[15] He was a commander of *banderovtses* searching for Jews, so I got very frightened. They noticed my fears, and he assured me that he will not do me any harm. Andrey said that he will cut my hair and shave me. I was afraid he might cut my throat with his razor-knife, but I had no choice. He cut my hair, gave me a good meal and a nice package of food. I made up a story that I was staying at the house of a Pole who was not home. I quietly returned to the ditch. Imagine the joy when my household members saw a bread and something more to eat!

But from then on, I was afraid to go out, and for a while I only went out to take some greens, apples, and more fruits which were growing in the surrounding orchards. However, as I wanted to know what was going on in the world, I went again at night to the same Christian, to Kravets. When I came over to his orchard, he recognized me and said that nobody was in his house because they were afraid; the family was in Dobryatyn. He went into his house and brought me a bread with a piece of butter and said that a Christian, Petro Ivan, was in his house and would also give me something to eat. So I left the bread and butter and went inside to see Petro. Petro was happy to give me something to eat, but he told me to leave right away.

[Page 366]

I went back to the tailor to take the bread and butter. He told me that he was going away now, and that no longer was there any bread and butter.

I immediately understood that something had happened. Nearby, there was a wheat field that had not been cut yet. I went there and started to run, but someone was shooting bullets at me! I ran on the side of the Polish colony where they were afraid to run after me. I waited the entire night in the Polish colony, and before daybreak, slowly, hunched over, I went back to my ditch. My wife and child thought that I was already murdered. From then on, I did not go anywhere — if God had shown me a miracle and I was not killed, I would not go anywhere anymore!

Winter was approaching. What will we do without food?! The entire colony had been burned down. I went into a few burned houses and found a piece of iron and burned pots, and I brought them into the ditch. I picked potatoes and onions in the field and at night, in the dark, I would cook. I had 14 matches altogether. I used to pray to God when I had to make fire that the first match would light. If the first match would, unluckily, not catch fire, we all cried as though someone had died. Without matches we would starve because nobody was in the vicinity.

* * *

Another few weeks passed. During a snowstorm, I went out of the ditch to carry out the slops and take in a little snow for water. Being outside I heard a commotion on the highway. From a distance, I heard soldiers marching. I heard talk, but in which language I did not know. As it turned out, it was not German. That night we did not sleep. I stuck my head out of the ditch a little bit. Day was approaching. Meanwhile I saw that two riders on horses were getting close to the direction of our ditch, so I covered up the ditch and listened — they were speaking Russian!

[Page 367]

With great surprise I screamed out "*tovarishtshi*[16] (friends)!" and I stuck out my head. They got scared and aimed their rifles at me.

I screamed to them: "Don't shoot, I am a Jew. My wife and child are here with me!"

They told me to raise my arms. They got down from their horses, went over to the ditch, and saw my wife and child. They asked how long we had been lying in the ditch. I told them that we had been lying like that for nine months. They began to cry.

They asked, "Why are you still lying there? We have been here already for eight days! Go to our headquarters and they will help you. We have to leave now."

They pointed the direction. Crying, they went away from the ditch.

I alone came out of the trench. First, I went to the place where my brother Getzel had been hidden. That he was murdered I knew — Andrey Kravits had told me. Getzel had been in a dirt hut near Dobryatyn, and he was killed there. I also knew that my brother, before he died, knew about my "death," because when the two Christians killed me, the Pole Fartun heard my last screams. He told Sharek's Christian, with whom my brother was staying; my brother had learned of it from him.

So I went to that Christian. But everything had been burned down, and nobody was there. I decided to go to the headquarters; maybe I would learn something helpful. On the way I met a Pole that I knew. We used to call him "Yarmashke the drunk." He saw me and said, "Good morning, Pania Mashka." He thought that I was Moyshe the shoemaker, because now I had a beard like him. The entire time I had no mirror and therefore did not know what I looked like. Yarmashke told me that there are Jews in Pańska Dolina at a Pole's.

When I arrived at headquarters, I was suspected of espionage. They even examined my beard to see if it were not glued on. I started to tell them everything that happened to me. Hundreds of soldiers surrounded me and listened to my stories.

[Page 368]

I looked like a wild person. A captain approached. He sent away the soldiers and asked me himself what happened. I told him everything, and he cried. He gave me something to eat and told me to bring my wife and children. However, I left for Pańska Dolina to search for Jews.

I came to a certain house and saw three girls whom I knew well; we had grown up together. They were Rokhele Kwasgalter,[17] Liza Berger,[18] and Frida, Zshanka Goldreich's sister.[19]

Through the window I heard, "There's a Jew coming to us."

I was very surprised — why are they not using my name, Mendel Anshel's [son]? I went inside and they asked me, "Uncle, who are you?"

I answered: "Liza, you don't recognize me?! Rokhele, Frida — you don't recognize me?!"

I began to cry and say that I am Mendel Anshel's [son]. They all started to weep, and they soon asked me if Sheindel was alive. I told them everything. They gave me a bread. They had baked bread. They also told me, that at Mesarke[20] in the forest — as far as they knew — Baske Sues and Reuven Goldreich were there with Zshanke and the children. I got right up and left to go to them.

When I got there — again the same question: "Uncle, who are you?..."

From them I learned that my brother Getzel, with Pesia and the child [Zelig], were alive; also my sister Bunia was alive. They told me that they were with a Pole. It became late and they told me to bring Sheindel and our child. I knew that they will soon think it over, so I left to get them. When I got to the ditch, it was already dark. I came in and told everything that I saw and heard.

My child saw the bread, so he immediately put it under his lice-ridden shirt and said, "Nobody will eat from it," only he himself.

We lay at night in the trench. That night there was a big snowstorm; there had been none like it yet that winter. We got out of the ditch and started to walk, but my wife fell down and could not go. My child could not walk at all, so I carried him a little, and put him down, then I carried my wife a little and put her down.

[Page 369]

And so I suffered until I came to a road; soldiers riding by had pity on us, and they took us up to Mesarke. There were Jews from the shtetl there. When we arrived, it was evening — that was the Friday before the new month, Shevat 1944 [January 25-26, 1944].[21] The first Friday in the new world!

Imagine the meeting with Baske Shues and the Goldreichs! After 18 months with my wife and child in one ditch! The next day, Shabbes, at dawn, I left for the place where my brother was, with another two families: Nokhum and Mendel Teitelman's. I came in and said, "Gut-shabbes."

They asked me right away: "Who are you, Uncle?"

My brother and my sister were not in the house then. I again cried and could not speak; I could not say a word. I only wept.

"Uncle, why are you crying?"

They did not know who was crying. My brother came into the house and saw someone who did not speak but only cried. He also did not recognize me!

He asked them, "Maybe he is dumb?"

They answered: "When he came in, he said, 'Gut-Shabbes.'"

My brother started to talk to me: "Do not cry, Uncle, we also lost our families, and we are not crying."

And he still did not recognize me.

He talked a long time until I came to myself and shouted out: "My brother, you do not recognize me?!"

There was screaming.

"Mendel, they didn't kill you!"

And he told me how Sharek's Christian informed him about my death. He told me how our mother and our two brothers, Hershl and Yankel, were killed. I had not known this, because I had been the first in the family to leave the ghetto.

We were together in this place for a week. After that we all went to Tsheshke Novene's[22] where we met my wife's brother, Yosel,[23] and Berel Rabinovitch, and also Shlomo Noach Moshe's (son),[24] Shaulik Halpern,[25] and Toybeshe the Rabbi's [daughter].[26] From there we went to Rivne.

Translator's and editor's footnotes:

1. Mendel Steinberg (1909–1998) was one of three Steinberg siblings from Mervits who survived the Shoah. A photo of Mendel, his wife Sheindel, and their daughter Susie in Cleveland appears on p. 505 of this volume. See the Steinberg Family story on the Mlynov website and a link there to a book length account of the family's story. – HS
2. *mashinno-traktornaya stantsiya* [machine tractor stations]. Soviet Union-owned institution that rented heavy agricultural machinery to collective farms. – HBF
3. Tailor. – HBF
4. Sheindel Grenspun was daughter of Benjamin Grenspun (also spelled "Grinshpan" and "Greenspun") and Sura (Tepler). A photo of Benjamin and his wife and children, and his father "Motel Tesler," appears on page 473 of the Memorial volume. The family appears in the martyr list for Mervits, p. 441. – HS
5. The Jewish holiday of Shemini Atzeret, which falls at the end of Sukkot, began that year the evening of the 22nd of Tishrei, 5703 (October 2, 1942). – HS
6. A village near Mlynov that no longer exists which was one of several points of Polish defense against the far-right Ukrainian ultranationalist Ukrainian People's Revolutionary Army (OUN-UPA). Residents there assisted Jews and Poles who escaped. Other Mlynov and Mervits refugees who mention being in Pańska Dolina were Mendel and Sonia Teitelman, Nahum and Rachel Teitelman, and Liza Berger. – HS
7. Banderites in English. Various right wing groups part of Union of Ukrainian Fascists OUN-B who committed atrocities against the Poles and Jews during WWII. – HS
8. Sheindel's uncle, Moshe Grinshpan (also "Grenspun"). A Moshe Grinshpan appears in a photo in this volume, page 203 which includes other Grinshpans: Meyer, Yitzhak and Bat-Sheva. – HS
9. Also spelled Grenspun and refers to Joe Greenspun who survived and moved to Cleveland. – HS
10. Appears to be the name of Moshe's other son. – HS
11. Referring to "Motel Tesler Grenspun" the grandfather of his wife, who appears in the photo on page 473 of this volume. "Motel Tesler" is identified as the nickname of Motel Grinshpan in the essay by Mendel and Sonia Teitelman, "Tragic Tales," 324. They write that "Reb Motl Grinshpan, called Motl Tesler, was over 90 years old" when recalling the first deaths in Mervits. Nahum Teitelman, "In the Depths of Hell," p. 314, also gives an account about what happened on July 12, 1941 (just weeks after the Germans occupied Mlynov) and recalls "the bitter enemy entered the synagogue of the Trisk Hasidim in Mervits and killed Motel Tesler; He was already close to one hundred [years old]. [They murdered] him and another poor man." – HS
12. By other accounts the liquidation of the ghetto happened on October 8th or 9th, 1942. It is unclear if Mendel is misremembering or whether Soldatuk was misinformed or just heard that the liquidation was coming. – HS
13. Passover began April 1, 1943. – HS
14. It is no longer clear which year Mendel is talking about. Yom Kippur began in 1943 on October Fri, Oct 8. – HS
15. Probably Pidhaitsi not far from Lutsk. – HS
16. Comrades. – HBF
17. Rachel (Kwasgalter) Rabinovitch survived. Based on records she filled out in Yad Vashem, in the Mlynov liquidation she lost her father Mendel (1896–1942), mother Sheina (1900–1942) who was born in

Rovno, her brother Chaim Monik (1931–1942) who was born in Rovno. The parents of her father Mendel Kwasgalter are listed as Faivel and Leah (maiden name unknown). – HS

18.　See Liza Berger's story, "I Wandered Hungry and in Pain,"346–351, this volume.

19.　Possibly related to David Goldreich (or Goldraykh) who may have been a survivor from Mervits, as reported by Gerald Steinberg. – HS

20.　The place has not been identified on contemporary maps but is assumed to be close to Pańska Dolina, where Mendel met the other survivors. – HS

21.　January 25-26, 1944. The Friday before would have been January 21, 1944. – HBF

22.　Probably referring to the home of the farmer named Totchkah who lived in a village near Pańska Dolina who is mentioned numerous times in the book length narrative of Asher Teitelman as assisting the survival of Teitelman family members and as coordinating communication between the Teitelmans when they were scattered in different hiding locations. – HS

23.　Sheindel's brother Yosel (Joe) Greenspun. – HS

24.　Shlomo (Solomon) Schechman, son of Noach Moshe Schechman. – HS

25.　Saul Halpern, a descendant of the Halperin and Hirsch families. – HS

26.　The daughter of Rabbi Gordon, who is in photo on page 280 this volume. – HS

[Page 370]

Where Do We Go?

by Miriam Barber (Blinder)[1]

Translated from the Yiddish by Hannah B. Fischthal, PhD

Edited by Howard I. Schwartz, PhD

We had a decent life in Mlynov. My father was a tailor and had a good clientele. My mother managed the household. I had just turned 13 when the German-Russian War broke out.

***

June 1941. As soon as the Germans entered the shtetl, a succession of big troubles began, which increased from day to day. Beatings, cutting off beards, and other terror tactics were a daily occurrence.

In our house our big troubles started earlier than everywhere else, because my father had been taken right away. Unfortunately, he did not return. My mother had to become the breadwinner for the whole family. The bread rations were then 90 grams of bread a day,[2] and even children had to go to work.

I, therefore, looked for a way to help the family with some food. I went to work for a farmer with the name Grabavetski. The work was difficult, but I was glad because the farmer helped me to feed my house somewhat. When I used to bring home the little bit of food, it was a holiday in the house. My mother always waited for me and used to always go to the ghetto fence to be able to see me from a distance.

* * *

But death was getting closer. I remember the last day before the ghetto was hermetically sealed. My mother warmly gathered all of us children and kissed us; the source of her tears had already dried up. That was the last time I saw her.

And now I started a series of hiding. I began to wander, in the nights, from place to place. During the day it was impossible to walk around without having a job.

[Page 371]

And so I went to a forest, and I met seven Jews there who were hiding in a sod hut. They allowed me to stay with them.

Winter. Snows and rains. The clothes on our bodies were filthy and soon were completely torn — but not a thing affected our health. Nights we went out to more or less secure houses begging for something to eat. Thanks to our neighborhood having a Czech population that generally was tolerant of us, we were successful in getting a little food from time to time. We asked several of the better Czech families, who lived deep in the forest—Frankov, Tikhov, Halatke,[3] and so on — and they sustained our souls.

One day we were attacked by a group of *banderovtses*;[4] they discovered us through our footsteps left in the snow. They came to our ditch searching for good things. When they found nothing, they told everyone, except for me, to get back into the ditch.

One of them asked me, "Say, do you want to live?"

My answer was: "I am still a child and I have not yet benefitted from life. You surely have children — do you not want your children to live?"

My words, evidently, worked and they let me go. They gave me a few good wishes and led me out of the forest (they did not know that I knew the way well), and they even warned me to not go to the Ukrainian side, only the Czech, because the Ukrainians would kill me.

I left, but where to go now? …

Meanwhile it was getting dark. I moved towards a house and recognized that a Czech family called Shirts lived there. We used to often receive a piece of bread from them. They had a girl Kzshysya, and she recognized me. She called her mother over and I told her everything that had happened to us. She was surprised that the *banderovtses* left me alive; she simply couldn't believe that such a thing could happen. She told me to go into the barn and bury myself with straw. She brought me warm food. She did this a couple of days, until a worker, a stranger, discovered me.

[Page 372]

Then I had to abandon the place, in order not to betray my good people.

I left again. But where does one go farther? With great sorrow, I decided to go back to Mlynov. By then everything was all the same to me. I went at night and arrived in peace. My steps led me to the family Grabavetski, for whom I still worked when I was in the ghetto. And here again I had difficulties — if the maid would see me, they would not let me in, being afraid of her. So I went up to the hay in the attic; I knew all the little corners there. In the morning, when the server came to get hay, he discovered me and reported me to the owners. Quietly, they took me away and locked me in a room and gave me a meal. But after two weeks, they told me I had to go, because the servants had discovered me again. So I had to go again — but to where? . . .

Not having any other choice, I went once more to the good woman Shirts. I arrived there in the evening, and I saw her immediately. Crying, I explained to her that if she would not let me in, I would end my life. That moved her. She promised to support me. She brought me warm food, made me a warm bath, and gave me clean clothes. I remained with her again.

A little later I suddenly saw a strange woman bringing me food. I was very frightened, but the woman calmed me down, and she told me that she was taking me to her own place, and that I would be able to go about freely. From great joy I cried and kissed her. She said she would wash all my clothes, so as not to bring any diseases into her poor house. She also told me that she was a Ukrainian who married a Czech.

We made up that I should first go to the Grabavetskis in Mlynov and bring over my clean clothes. The woman succeeded in convincing Shirts's son to take me to Mlynov; that was at night. I arrived in a big frost and the door of the stable was locked … I was afraid to go into the house — maybe a stranger was sitting there? So I went into the pigpen; it was warm there. I thought that in the night somebody would come in, and I would be able to speak with him.

[Page 373]

I managed a little straw but I could not sleep. It was very cold. So I decided to wake up the boys — I knew where they slept. They told me where to sleep on the ground. The next day they hid me again. I was there two weeks.

I took a few clothes and went to Mrs. Shirts. She immediately took me into the basement until nighttime. Then my future caregiver took me in with love. Her name was Tikhi. Her husband and children loved me too, and despite their poverty, they took care of all my needs. I felt happy there. I used to work for Shirts and give them my earnings.

Until — the Russian army liberated the neighborhood. Then I was really free. I left for Dubno, where I found an aunt with a six-year-old child who had been saved.[5] I was in Dubno a short time and met my good, future husband there. With him I arrived in our country.

Drawing water. The water carrier.

Translator's and editor's footnotes:

1.   Miriam (Blinder) Barber was the only one of her immediate family to survive. Her parents both born in Mlynov were Berl Blinder (~1902–1942), a tailor, and her mother Gitel (Hachman/Hechman) (~1907–1942) a seamstress. Records Miriam filled out in the Yad Vashem database list her siblings as Yeshayahu (1922–1942) and Efraim (1933–1942). The martyr list in this volume indicates other siblings: Devora, Riva and Eta. The family lived in Mlynov on Shkolna Street.

It appears that Miriam is the young girl of thirteen who was retrieved after the liberation from a farm by her aunt Rochel Hachman who had also survived with her young daughter Tama (Hachman) Fineberg. In her   Shoah   Foundation   interview   Tape   3   (3:30) https://vhaonline.usc.edu/viewingPage?testimonyID=18614, Tama Fineberg speaks about the moving rescue of her cousin "Mala." Mala lived with them for a while before meeting a young man who had served in the Russian army and lost a leg. The couple made aliyah. Mala's mother, Gitel (Hachman/Hechman) Blinder was the sister of Tama's father, Leib Hachman. – HS

2.   Roughly the equivalent of two slices. – HBF

3.   Possibly the same Czech family mentioned as the "Holatko" family by Asher Teitelman in his family's survival account pp. 33ff. The Holatko family played a critical role in their survival. Joseph and Anna Holatko were later recognized as among the righteous in a Yad Vashem commemoration. – HS

4.   Banderivtsi or Banderites, followers of Stepan Bandera, and members of the right-wing fascist Ukrainian organization OUN-B. They formed death squads, carried out pogroms and hunted Jews for money. – HS

5.   See note 1. – HS

[Page 374]

A Child in the Storm

by Basye Kaptshik[1] (Blinder), Haifa

Translated from by Hannah B. Fischthal, PhD

Edited by Howard I. Schwartz, PhD

To be among the living is a natural thing, but to be among the dead, nobody heard of it. I was someone who remained alive by being among the dead. As frightening as this seems, it is a fact that I was saved by hiding for a while among the tombstones. I was with my older sister Khaye, then a child of 10; an old woman from Mervits, Freyde Teitelman; and her three grandchildren Rikil, Mordkhe and Maye, may their memories be blessed. We ran away from a hiding spot in the ghetto a day after the general slaughter. We were driven away from every Christian house. Not having where to hide ourselves from the eyes of the murderers, Freyde Teitelman, may she rest in peace, led us to the former trenches that were dug for the First World War in the cemetery at Mervits. We were there a few days (weeks?). Every evening Freyde sent us out to beg for a piece of bread and a little water, and that is how we were nourished.

According to older people, the children of townspeople tell me, Freyde used to pray every day, all day, in the ghetto, begging God, with hot tears, that she be buried as a Jew in the Jewish cemetery. That was her goal. As an old woman, she sensed that she would not be able to wander around in these circumstances for long, but she saved three grandchildren and my sister and me. We all were hidden well. The evening after the slaughter, late at night, she gathered the surviving children, I among them, and led us straight towards the Mervits cemetery. Wherever we had tried to beg for help, we were refused. We had even been threatened to be handed over to the hands of the murderers. So there was no choice. We had to run further so that daylight would not expose us. Freyde took us to the trenches, and that is where we were, with Freyde in charge and supervising us.

[Page 375]

From Danger to Danger

Every evening we would beg for a little food from the better Christians in the area. One night, when I returned with a little food I obtained from begging, I did not find them there anymore. As it was still in the early evening, I went to the Christian family who had always lived as keepers of the monuments to ask about my people. I was answered that they were no longer alive — a murderer shot them. They advised me to run away from there, because it appeared that one of the neighbors had betrayed them. How I, as a seven-year-old child, reacted to all this misery, I do not remember anymore. One thing my childish wisdom did tell me was that I could no longer live among the dead in their graves, and I had to protect myself from evil eyes.

That same evening, I went to wherever my eyes led me. I went to Mervits into a house neighboring Mendel Teitelman. The Christians saw and laughed at me.

"There is a sight, a small żyd (Jew)!"
At that same moment I noticed one of the sons of the house laughing. I, even though a child, feared treachery. In a few minutes I was out of their house. I entered the nearby empty and abandoned Jewish house of my Uncle Shaye. I heard the Christians searching for me.

They kept asking: "Where did that small soul suddenly go?"

A woman said she would bring in a so-called "specialist" who could very easily shoot a Jew, because she claimed she was not capable of killing such a little one. In that heated moment, I got out.

I still do not understand what kind of secret strength protected me in various situations from murdering hands. How did I, so young, understand that I needed to run from that place? And so I went in the direction of Lutsk, not knowing where I was going. I accidently met, wandering near a forest, my cousin Moyshe Neyter[2], older than I, a boy 17 years old. He took me into the forest where he himself was hiding in a fox hole.

[Page 376]

I thought I had found an angel to help me. But my cousin Moyshe started to realize how much more difficult his ability to survive was with me around. I had no clothes or shoes. My childish feet were wrapped in rags, extremely filthy. I also had a skin disease. I understood that I was not allowed to cry. That would not give him any problems, but he had bigger worries about food and clothing.

After a little while, he naturally started to feel I was a burden. He had an idea to get me out of his place. He explained to me, as far as I can remember, that I was sick, and that I had no clothes or shoes. Here my life was very dangerous. Therefore, he said he decided to send me away. As a little girl I would be in less danger.

He led me out of our hiding place, took me to a house, and he told me, "Go inside the house. I was promised that you would be kept inside."

I have never suspected any bad motives on his part. It is possible that he saw I would not last long.

"No choice," he thought, "Maybe someone will take pity on a child."
I entered the house with Moyshe's promise.

I said, "Moyshe told me that you will take me in."

They were simply amazed. What Moyshe? Who Moyshe? Their murderous hearts had no pity for me, and they quickly drove me out.

I tried my luck and went into another house, where I found an older woman with a young man, maybe a relative of hers. The man quickly glanced at me, and he did not need to spend a long time asking questions. He immediately recognized my Jewishness. He demanded I go out of the house with him. With curses and insults he was ready to take me to have me killed. The older Christian woman started to beg the murderer not to bring any child into her house, and he agreed with her.

[Page 377]

He gave me a strong kick which booted me out of the house. With hasty steps, I went further, passing the couple of houses in the village of Krasnaya Gora[3]. Not knowing the way, I ended up in a large creek. I became very wet, very exhausted, very hungry, and soaked through and through. I came into a neighboring village.

My Savior Angel

Depressed and despairing, I started to go wherever my eyes led me. I did not know where and in what kind of village I was. I marched helplessly during the day, where the Jewish remnant was not permitted to show itself. In the early evening I went to a poor hut. As if testing it out, I begged for a piece of bread. With my childish understanding, I observed what kind of house it was, and I usually tried to gage what kind of reception I would have. I found in the house only a middle-aged woman. With a sorrowful but motherly hand, she immediately gave me a piece of bread, and she invited me to share her poor supper with her. I accepted gratefully. Without my asking, she proposed that I sleep with her. I remained there overnight. I had felt in her a motherly attitude towards me. Immediately that same day, she washed my wounds with warm water, and she washed out my few poor, filthy, half-torn clothes. And she did that several times until she had cleaned up my dirt and uncleanliness. With a primitive, old-womanish cream, she healed the skin disease I had picked up when I stayed in the forest.

I felt her motherly hand everywhere. With her good heart, she adopted me as a daughter, and worried about me like she would for her own child. Certainly a few evil neighbors looked at this with critical eyes, and I do not know what stopped them from handing me over to the government to do to me what was done to all the other Jews.

[Page 378]

A kind of secret power watched over me and protected me from all the evil. My adoptive mother showed me devotion and protection. She gave me the impression that she would do anything to save me.

My life normalized, so that I almost forgot that this was not the home into which I was born. I had early on taken over a part of the responsibility of my poor bread-giver's tasks. I helped, meaning I fed her cow and her poor single pig, travelled with her into the forest to bring in wood for cooking and warming our poor hut. I grew to be a part of her family. She immediately changed my name to "Vira"[4], and I became "Virni"[5] to her, devoted to her and to everything around her. Because of her care and dedication to me, I began to forget my roots, and with my childish mentality I did not hope for anything better.

Liberation and its Problems

This life stretched out until the hooligan power aborted, quickly abandoned the territory, and retreated, which was in the beginning of 1944. And even though I had so connected with my protector, and could not think of anything better, something in my childish mind reacted to our total liberation. I wondered if I would find someone alive from my family, and then all of us together could thank my protector for her good deed.

To my great disappointment, I did not find anyone from my family still alive. With my visits to Mlynov, I was discovered by Jews who had miraculously survived.

A secret hand attracted me back to my source and roots, but my childish mind started to gnaw at returning to my savior. When Leybush Vinokur came and ordered, like an official leader, that my protector must free me, and he took me, I really experienced terrible moments of conscience. I was grateful to and had bonded with my protector. I suffered on two levels: on one hand, I was attracted back to my own people, and on the other hand, it was hard for me to separate from my faithful savior, who, like a mother, protected me from harm. I was bound to her with all the threads of my soul.

[Page 379]

When I had been in Mlynov several days, more than once I expressed myself and cried, "I want to go back to my aunt."

Several times I was brought back on the way, when, longing for my savior, I had started to run to her village.

In Mlynov itself there were a few Jewish souls, and in every house, there was an addition of a found Jewish soul. So, for example, three children of Mendel Teitelman were found; by Mendel Steinberg there were a few children and parents. Also at his brother Getzel's there were children. The Goldreich family took me. Even though they had their own two small children, they took me in and gave me a loving home until I came to Israel and became independent. I will never forget the care they gave me.

My savior, whose name was Vladimirets, from the village Boyarka[6] near Mlynov, with her family, also became attached to me. When I was in Mlynov, she would come to visit me because she missed me. I admit that I grew to love the family Vladimirets. I will never forget them my whole life. It must be said that their help to me, what they gave me, can never be repaid; there is no amount of payment for such aid.

From my own family I have nobody in the world. The villainous hands, in my earliest youth, took away my father Yitskhok Blinder, may he rest in peace, and my mother Pini, and my grandmother, and my aunt Roza[7], already a widow due to the murderers of her husband Zelig Muravitsky, one of the first victims; and her baby born afterwards in the ghetto, Yankev Zelig. And my Uncle Shimeon[8] and wife and children, and many many more of my family, whose names I unfortunately do not remember. I strove to go to our land, and I built a nest there for my husband Gad Kuptsik and myself, with our little son Yigal and our little daughter Einat, surrounded by my friends from our Mervits, and by my special friends, the Goldreich family.

Translator's and editor's footnotes:

1.   The author is listed as Batia (Blinder) Kopchak (and Kopciak) in the Yad Vashem records she filled out about her family. Batia was the daughter of Yitzhak Blinder, mentioned below in this essay, and Penina (Neiter) who was born in Muravica (Mervits) in 1913. Batia had an older sister, Khaye, mentioned in this essay. It seems probable that Batia was the first cousin of Miriam (Blinder) Barber who wrote the previous essay in this volume and that their fathers, Yitzhak and Berel Blinder, were brothers. Batia's mother, Pnina, was daughter of Yaakov (Jaakow) and Yakhed (Jachid) Neiter. They also had a son, Shimon, and a daughter Roza. Shimon Neiter was born in 1907 in Muravica (Mervits) and married a woman named Golda and had three children. Roza (1917–1942) married Zelig Muravitsky and they had a son Yankel. All of this family died in the ghetto liquidation except Batia. – HS
2.   Related through her mother, Pnina (Neiter). There is a mention of a Moshe Neiter in the list of martyrs, p. 436, who was in Russia but the reference is cryptic and not clear. – HS
3.   Probably a village between Mlynov and Lutsk but no longer identified on maps. – HS
4.   Ukrainian, "faith." – HBF
5.   Ukrainian, "faithful." – HBF
6.   Perhaps Boyarka 48 km (29 m) east and north of Mlynov. – HS
7.   Her mother's sister, Roza (Neiter) Muravitsky (1917–1942) married Zelig Muravitsky and they had a son Zelig. – HS
8.   Her mother's brother, Shimon Neiter who married Golda and had three children. – HS

[Page 380]

In Those Times

Rokhl Teitelman, Haifa[1]

Translated from the Yiddish by Hannah B. Fischthal, PhD

Edited by Howard I. Schwartz, PhD

Even though my head is not working too well, I want to describe a few memories of what we, and mostly I myself, survived. One night a German policeman came in and took my son Asher[2] out of bed. The Germans did not even allow us to go along to see where they were going. When it became daylight, we went out into the street, and we heard that many young people had been taken, but to where — nobody knew. It took a longer time until we learned that they were in Rivne at forced labor for the Germans.

Sometime later I learned that Yankev Goltseker z"l[3] went to Rivne, and after a couple of days he brought home his son Dovid; but his son-in-law was still there. I went to him and begged him to tell me the secret as to how he managed it, but without success. However, he promised me that if he would succeed in getting his son-in-law out, then he would tell me everything.

And so he did. The following week he brought his son-in-law home. He also gave me a note from Asher saying that we should save him if possible. I started to research possible ways to travel to Rivne. It took several days until I was able to get a Christian driver, but he could only go on Shabbes. Understandably, this was a very big problem for me and for my sister Chaika — her son was there too.[4] So I ran to Mervits to Uncle Khayim-Mayer z"l for advice.[5] He affirmed that to save a person one could travel even on Shabbes. Yankev Goltseker explained everything to me, told me with whom I needed to meet, and how to handle everything.

[Page 381]

Going to Rivne was extremely dangerous. We met Avraham-Chaika's [son][6] who had been freed because he was very sick. But as to my son Asher — there were no excuses to free him because, very unfortunately, he was completely healthy. I additionally wanted to do a good deed by rescuing Lipe Halperin,[7] who was there too. His family begged me to do whatever I could for him, and I told them I would do whatever was possible. I could free them only via a Jewish woman who lived with the German Commander. I had her address, and I had to arrange everything through her.[8]

When I found her, she informed me that I needed a red ticket from Dr. Tsaytlin, an older person. I had enough money for everything, but, sadly, I could not accomplish anything with money. The doctor said that money is worthless when a person faces death every minute, and he lived under circumstances that were worse than anything faced by the poorest pauper in our town. So I started to beg him and I explained that by saving a young child from death, he will also be saved from death. I told him that to accomplish everything, we needed a mediator. I reminded him that when I had been very sick, really very, very sick, Sheyntse Maizlish led me to him, because she was his patient, and he saved me. He was, thus, the intermediator, and I wanted him to be our good facilitator now too, by giving Asher a red ticket. I do not remember how much money was involved.

With tears in his eyes, he gave me the ticket, and I took it to the woman. That was Monday. She told me that everything would be done the next day. That cost thousands, but I had enough money. Tuesday I again went to the doctor and begged him to give me a ticket for Lipe. I explained that his mother was a widow, and he supported the family. He gave me the ticket, and I went again to the woman. She had to wait for Wednesday.

I was staying then at Khayim Nakanyetshkin's daughter's place. I was in danger the entire time.

[Page 382]

Every day people said there would be an *akcje*[9] that night against the remaining Jews. I barely survived Wednesday. I took out the two tickets to free Asher and Lipe, and I gave Lipe his ticket and Asher his. I was ready to go home, but Asher lost his ticket! Lipe went home, and I remained with nothing! So I ran again to the woman and told her she must go to the same office so I could get another ticket for freedom. But as it was already late, and there was nobody to write it up, I had to wait until the next day. Meanwhile I reported the loss to the police, hoping maybe somebody would appear with that ticket. And actually, Thursday, I did receive that same ticket. A Jew had found it and he had brought it to the office.

This is how we, meaning Asher and I, were saved from our deaths for the first time. That same night all those who had been with Asher were murdered. Among them were many from Mlynov. Unfortunately, Lipe was murdered later.

Translator's and editor's footnotes:

1. Rachel Teitelman was born Rachel Gruber, daughter of Yosef Gruber and Shifra (Teitelman). She married her first cousin, Nahum Teitelman, who is also a contributor to this volume. See more on the background of the Teitelman family on the Mlynov website. – HS
2. Asher Teitelman is one of the other contributors to this volume. – HS
3. Refers to Yankel Holtzeker son of Moishe Goldseker, one of the five original Goldseker brothers to come to Mlynov. Yankel married Risia (or Ritzia) and they had 12 children, one of whom is the Dovid mentioned here. A photo of the large family appears on p. 245 and of their home on p. 79. Most of the family did not survive. Two daughters and a son made aliyah before the War. Tzipporah Sulovsky-Holtzeker (1910–1986), the second oldest, made aliyah in 1933. Her sister, Baila (Holtzeker) Wildikan (1914–1990) followed in 1941. They were joined by a brother, Nahman, whose story is not known. A young brother Hanoch was nine when the War broke out and during the German occupation fled to the forest with his brothers. He survived and joined his sisters after the War in Kibbutz Negba. He was tragically killed on May 25, 1948 in the Negev by an Egyptian shell. The names of the children in the list of martyrs (p. 432) are: David, Abraham, Menanshe, Khona, Mindl, Batia, Libe and Hanoch. – HS
4. Rachel's sister, Chaika (Gruber) married Yankel Shichman. They had four sons. It becomes clear in the narrative that her son Avraham was the one in slave labor in Rivne. – HS
5. Referring to Chaim Meir Teitelman, her mother's brother. – HS
6. Referring to her sister, Chaika's son, Avraham. – HS
7. Probably refers to Lipa Halpern, son of Yosel and Tzipa (Riwiec), and the brother of survivor Shaul Halpern. The Lipa Halperin who survived and contributed to this volume was a first cousin who had left Mlynov and made aliyah in 1937. – HS
8. Asher Teitelman in his memoire indicates he was the one who coordinated the escape. – HS
9. (Pol.) Murderous campaign. – HBF

[Page 382]

In Fear and Pain

by Leye Veyner-Likhter[1] ,Haifa

Translated from the Yiddish by Hannah B. Fischthal, PhD

Edited by Howard I. Schwartz, PhD

When the Germans took over our shtetl Mervits, my brother was in the Soviet army. Yet, he managed to come home to his wife the next day; he had succeeded in running away from captivity. They were expecting a baby. However, their joy did not last long.

Hard times started. Besides being subjected to forced labor, people were murdered for no reason. Every day there were tragedies. The enraged, drunken Ukrainians and Germans used to go around at night with revolvers in their hands and they would rob houses.

[Page 383]

* * *

We were forced into the Mlyniv ghetto. It was very crowded. We were all enveloped in the fear that someone would shoot us any minute. Every night someone would be on watch to learn when the S.S. was coming.

29 November 1940,[2] at dawn, we heard the Germans scream, "Lauz!"[3] Then we knew that they were coming to get us. When they entered my house, I hid behind the door. I wanted them to shoot me in the back. I had heard them take out the dearest person I had in the world, my mother. They also removed the other people. It is hard to describe those terrible minutes.

I came out of hiding at night. The tall gates of the ghetto were open, and I left for the fields. As the grain had already been cut, I hid among the potatoes. I do not know how many days I was lying there, but hunger and cold drove me into the villages, of course only at night.

I made myself dumb so that my language would not betray me. I went from place to place. It was very dangerous because German and Ukrainian policemen were around. When I came to the Czech village of Malyn,[4] I went to the hospital since they needed workers. I started to weep when I saw the doctor because I felt I could trust him. The doctor asked me, in Polish, if I were pregnant. I answered him that my problem was even worse — I am a Jew. He advised me to get away from that neighborhood. Actually, the next day, after I left the village, the Germans burnt down the town completely. Not a single person had been allowed out. This was revenge because a German had been killed earlier near that village.[5]

I worked as a Christian in various places. When the war ended, I could not travel to our shtetl to witness the destruction. My family and I arrived in Israel via Georgia [in the Soviet Union]

Translator's and editor's footnotes:

1.   Leah Likhter was born in Mervits probably around 1917–1920. In this essay, she describes how her family was taken into the Mlynov ghetto and gives a brief account of how she managed to hide and escape while her mother was taken away. She mentions only the existence of brother and a mother in this essay, perhaps the Ida Likhter and her son Boruch listed in the Mervits martyr list (p. 442). After surviving the War, Leah met and married Mlynov-born Yehuda Veiner (alternative spellings Weiner/ Veyner/ Vainer) in Dubno. Yehuda Veiner was the son of Yitzhak Veiner (mother's name unknown). He had left town with other Beitar members shortly after Germans had started their invasion the week of June 22, 1941, a story also recounted by Yechiel Sherman (pp. 344-246). Yehuda tried but failed to get his family to leave with him. As a young refugee, Yehuda wandered around Russia eventually staying somewhere in Kazakhstan until after the War when he returned to Dubno and met and married Leah. Yehuda's two younger siblings Hannah Veiner (born ~1913/1913) and Moshe Veiner (born ~1915) also survived.
After the War, Yehuda and Leah remained in Dubno and in 1947 had a son Yitzhak (Vasha) Vainer and a second son, Baruch in about 1950. Around 1962, they moved to Tbilisi, Georgia and then managed to make aliyah in 1967. In Israel, they stayed initially with the family of Sunny Veiner, a cousin and contributor to this volume (p. 251). In the army in Israel, Yitzhak eventually adopted the surname Einav. – HS
2.   The writer appears to be misremembering the date or a mistake was made. The Germans didn't enter Mlynov until the week of June 22, 1941, when they invaded the Russian occupied parts of Poland. The ghetto liquidation was recalled by others as occurring on October 8th or 9th, 1942 which was the 28th or 29th of Tishrei 5703. Perhaps the writer or editors converted the Hebrew date to the wrong date on the Gregorian calendar. – HS
3.   [Louse]. The Germans always screamed "Raus!" [out!]. – HBF
4.   Malyn is due north of Mlynov today and 28 km (17 mi) via indirect roads. – HS
5.   The author is describing the massacre at Malyn which took place, July 13, 1943. The adult Jewish population had already been shot and the children buried alive in 1941. – HBF

[Page 384]

Murder of the Sokoliki Refugees

by Frida Kupferberg[1] ,Haifa

Translated from the Yiddish by Hannah B. Fischthal, PhD

Edited by Howard I. Schwartz, PhD

Here is a short report of the terrible suffering and the murder of the Jewish farmers who came from the village Sokoliki near Turka.[2] They were killed in the villages around Mlynov as well as in the Mlynov ghetto.

Jewish farmers lived in the villages of Stomorhy[3] and Hintsharekhe[4] near Mlynov. In April 1940 they were deported by the Soviets from their hometown Sokoliki near Turka to the Mlynov region where other farmers had been taken.

Instructed by the Pole Zalewski,[5] the Germans entered Stomorhy from Dubno three weeks after the outbreak of the German-Russian war; that was Sunday, the 13th of July 1941, the 17th of Tammuz, a fast day for Jews.[6] It was a double day of sorrow because the Germans had taken over. They attacked a Jewish house where two families were living. With screams and violence, the Germans forced everybody out into the garden, and then they shot the Jews one by one. The last one shot was Moyshe Fayler's young, very pregnant wife. Moyshe Fayler with his wife and mother; Ester and Shmuel Zinger, Royze Zinger, Leyb Fram, and another boy were murdered.

After that the Gestapo ran into the house of Volf Keler. Volf Keler[7] was a learned Jew who sat and studied Gemara. His four sons followed the same path as their father. The Gestapo forced Volf Keler, his four sons, Moyshe Gelmakher, Mudil Frab, as well as Mlynov Rabbi Gordon, who had spent Shabbes with Volf Keler, to the house where those who had been killed were lying. Relatives and neighbors were ordered to put the bodies in a wagon and take them to a ditch. Afterwards they followed the corpses in the wagon up until the heaps of excrement before Mervits.

[Page 385]

There had been an open ditch in that place for a long time. The Jews were ordered to dump the murdered bodies into that ditch. Afterwards the Germans also shot the Mlynov Rabbi, and he fell into the ditch. The Gestapo took Volf Keler with his four sons Berish, Moyshe, Hirsh, and Shimeon, and another two victims, Moyshe Gelmakher and Moydl Frab, to Dubno. They were thrown into prison, where they were all killed. The rest of the Stomorhy Jews were beaten and forced by another division to Mlynov, where they were distributed for various labor assignments. The horrible events of the 13th of July remained in my soul. A year later, the rest of the Jews from Stomorhy and Hintsharekhe were murdered in the Mlynov ghetto.

* * *

I want to report here a second instance, which happened at that time in the village Hantsharekhe near Mlynov to the family Gelobter, consisting of a father, a mother, and two frightened little sons. Shortly after the Germans took over, the Gestapo went to the Gelobters. They led the two boys into the garden, told them to dig a grave, positioned them in front of the grave, and shot them. The bodies fell in. In the evening, when their father went to pour dirt in the grave, he heard the voice of a son: "Father, I am still alive!"

He pulled his son Yoysef out of the ditch. The boy was wounded very badly. His father took him to the hospital in Dubno, where he had a bullet removed from his throat; he still had a bullet stuck in his back. Yoysef Gelobter lived for more than a year after that. I saw him in the Mlynov ghetto, where he was killed together with his parents.

I want to mention here, that among the surviving Jews, Shloyme Breyer, with a child of six years, died from tuberculosis four months after the liberation. Father and son had gotten sick in their bunker where they were hiding. And Leon Kupferberg also survived to be liberated. He was recruited by the Soviets, and he fell as a hero in Libave,[8] Latvia, the 23rd of January 1945.

Translator's and editor's footnotes:

1. There were a number of Kupferbergs from Turka and the nearby town of Sokoliki who died in the hamlet of Stomorhy and/or in the Mlynov ghetto. Several Kupferbergs are included in the list of martyrs from Sokoliki in this volume, p. 445. Yad Vashem records indicate Yitzhak (Icik) Kupferberg (1886–1942) married Tzvia (Trieber) and were brought to Stomorhy or Mlynov during the War where they were killed. Another Kupferberg family from Turka in the area was Yoel and Sara (1912–1942) with two children, one age 7, and Dzunia age 4. It is unknown how the author is related to these families. – HS
2. Sokoliki is currently in Poland close to the Ukrainian border and close to Turka, Ukraine. Alternative names for Turka are Turka al nehar Stry [Hebrew], Turka and Stryjem. On current maps, it is 315 km (196 mi)

to Mlynov. Like Mlynov, Turka was under Russian control from 1939–1941. When Germany attacked Russia in June 1941, some of the Jews from Sokoliki and Turka managed to flee and/or were evacuated east. – HS

3.   A town 6.2 km north of Mlynov on the road to Lutsk. Alternate name: Stomorgi. – HS

4.   Possibly Arshychyn which is 4.3 km south from Mlynov. – HS

5.   Erich von dem Bach-Zalewski, high-ranking SS commander. Among his other crimes leading to the murder of millions, he oversaw the extermination of Jews in Belarus from July-September 1941. – HS

6.   See Mendel and Sonia Teitelman's account, pp. 326–328, of similar events in Stomorhy as well as Nachum Teitelman's account of the same day, p. 316. – HS

7.   Mendel and Sonia's account also mentions the Keler family. – HS

8.   Today Liepāja, Latvia. – HBF

[Page 386]

During the Shoah

by Gedalia Lahav[1] , [Kibbutz] Mizra

Translated and edited by Howard I. Schwartz, PhD with Hanina Epstein

It was the beginning of December 1942, when that I fled from my town Aleksandriya, [Russia] near Rivne and came to Dubno. Volyn was at that time "cleansed" of Jews, and displayed on the town buildings were placards with shining white letters: "Whoever finds a Jew must bring him [or her] to the police and will receive a reward["]; the reward – sugar, schnapps so forth. Horror overcame me. Indeed, in my pocket was a forged identity document — but even so, what should I do and where should I turn? I was aware that in Mlynov there a large estate that needed workers. So I traveled to Mlynov and obtained work there and stayed working until the liberation of the city. Already by the time I got there, not a single Jew remined. Through contact with the population, I became aware that all of them had been shot and thrown in pits which were outside the town (by the slaughterhouse). Truly, after some time, I saw the place with my own eyes. Two mounds of dirt 2–3 meters high covered the pits. What could I do but secretly shed tears, lest someone see me?

During the month of January 1943, when I was sitting by a barber (opposite the Catholic Church) I saw an image that made all of me shake. I saw myself [in the barber's mirror] white as lime and I made a gargantuan effort not to arouse any suspicions that I was a Jew. I saw a family of Jews being transported by armed Ukrainian police. The barber let loose with the words, "Hell, these Jews are like ants. The more you eliminate them, the more they spring forth from the cracks." I didn't respond; I sat in silence. That same winter I also heard that in one village (the name is gone from my memory) they discovered 7 more Jews and their fate was like the rest of the Jews.

I personally did not come across any Jew. Most of the Jewish homes stood on their foundation and only a few were destroyed. The homes were occupied, especially by poor Poles and survivors, who fled for fear of their annihilation by the Ukrainian gangs.

* * *

Do not forget. Breath in our death. Remember to live with the knowledge of the martyrdom

(Avraham Sutzkever)[2]

Translator's and editor's footnotes:

   1.   Gedalyia Lahav (1919–1995) was born originally with the surname Schleifstein in Aleksandriya, Russia, now Oleksandriia, Ukraine. He made aliyah in 1947 but was retained in Cypress by the British before finally reaching Israel in 1949. Lahav published a book about his experiences.
   2.   One of the most important Yiddish poets of the second half of the 20th century (1913–2010), Sutzkever has been called "the greatest poet of the Holocaust." During the Shoah, he led the Paper Brigade, rescuing a large number of cultural items from destruction. He wrote poetry that was rescued and later left a deep impression on the public. He survived and later in 1947 made aliyah to the Land of Israel.

[Page 387]

Wandering During the Terrible Catastrophe
(Excerpt from witness testimony in Yad-Vashem)

by Bunia Epstein,[1] Haifa

Translated from the Yiddish by Hannah B. Fischthal, PhD

Edited by Howard I. Schwartz, PhD

In the Mlynov Ghetto

I had been home the entire winter. After Passover I saw that the times were bad. Jews had to foresee the future and make plans to save themselves.

Every year we used to have business dealings with a nobleman, Vasko Poholuk Nikolayev. My brothers Yukal and Hershl and I went to him now and established ourselves as field laborers. More Jews were there in addition to us.

The first or second day of Shavuot (I don't remember which), we were ordered to go straight to the ghetto in Mlynov.[2]

(*Interviewer: "How many Jews were in Mervits?"*

"I don't remember exactly. It was a small shtetl. There were about 100 families. Mlynov was a larger shtetl with more Jewish families.")

We were forced into the ghetto. Our family — my mother, two brothers and I — were housed together with the Judenrat; we in one room and the Judenrat in the second room. When first entering the ghetto, the Germans robbed the Jews of whatever they had: potatoes, flour, oil, clothes. They tried to rob us too, but I resisted them and did not allow it. These were Hungarian soldiers; they did not take anything from us.

My mother remained in the ghetto while my two brothers and I continued to work outside of the ghetto for the nobleman Vasko Poholuk. Shabbes I would come home to my mother. One time I felt like seeing my mother in the middle of the week, so I came home. My two brothers remained working in the village of Pobredov [today Pereveediv].[3]

* * *

[Page 388]

The Judenrat had bribed the Ukrainians to inform them when the slaughter will take place. That was Rosh Chodesh Elul.[4] Trials were made to see where the Jews would run. In the middle of the night, 12:00 midnight– 1:00 a.m., the Ukrainians came and reported to the Judenrat that the entire shtetl would be massacred that night, and whoever wanted could flee. The gates would be open.

I took my mother and we fled. My grandmother lived at the edge of the ghetto, right at the fence that was very high. She used to have a very large orchard. A whole night we were lying hidden among the trees. We planned that if we would hear something, we would jump over the fence and run away. At the end: daylight came, and nothing had happened. The Jews returned to their residences in the ghetto. As stated, the Christians wanted to see where the Jews would run. They made fun of the Jews.

I continued to work in Pereveediv. The first day of Rosh Hashana I worked; it was a Shabbes.[5] As the next day was the Christian Sunday, I was sent home. I went home for Yom Kippur.[6] I also came home the second day of Sukkot.[7] That was the last Sukkot that I was together with my mother and brothers. GRAVES WERE BEING DUG …

After Sukkot I left for work and my mother remained alone. That was on the second day of Chol HaMoed Sukkot.[8] While I was laboring in the field, my heart was embittered, wounded. I took a look — my mother had come! She was very frightened.

"Mama, why did you come?" I asked her.

"My child," she said, "they are already digging our graves…"

She had taken nothing with her. She made leaven to be able to bake, because this was the eve of Hoshana Rabbah.[9] She had left it and ran away. People are foolish; while they live, they want to eat.

I asked her: "Mama, why did you not bring anything with you?"

I got up and went to the ghetto before evening. I did not go straight to the ghetto. First, I went to Mervits; I slept in a Christian's house.

[Page 389]

In the morning I went to the Mlynov ghetto. I came into our room, and I started to bake. As I was baking, I was told that that people had already been murdered. Whoever had tried running out of the ghetto had been killed on the spot. Among the murdered were the Teitelman's two boys.[10]

Women asked me why I came back into the ghetto now, when the whole time I was out of it. I answered that it was probably fated that I should be slaughtered together with all the Jews. I continued to bake, but I was very nervous. Whatever food there was in the room, I put into the oven and baked.

I got out of the ghetto. I saw and heard a loud commotion. The people were petrified; they complained and cried. Khatskl Liber came to me and said:

"Bunia, you have a permit. Take it and go. Pretend you don't know anything."

I understood what he meant very well. In any case, I was sentenced to death. Why did I need to die together with everyone, to stand in a row and wait to be shot? I thought I would go to the gate so I would be shot right away and save myself from having to see how they shoot others. I packed up two bags of food. I put on a yellow sweater with two patches (I put on a yellow sweater so that the two yellow patches would not be visible) and a scarf on my head. I put my shoes over my shoulders. I went out of the ghetto like that. The Germans and Ukrainians were standing around and did not recognize me. They thought I was a Christian.

And that is how I got out of the ghetto. When I came to the bridge behind Mlynov, a Pole came and took me into his wagon. He asked me where I needed to go. I answered that I needed to get to Pereveediv. He told me that I should ride with him to Smordva because all the Jews were being shot there [in Pereveediv]. The graves were being dug. But my mother was in Pereveediv, and I had arranged places in which to hide, so I did not want to ride with him to Smordva. He took me to Pereveediv.

[Page 390]

When I arrived, I met with my mother and two of my brothers. We waited until nighttime. We had arranged to stay with a Christian in Dobryatyn. My older brother Hershl remained with a Christian in Pereveediv (naturally, he paid the Christian). My mother remained there too because she could not swim; to get to Dobryatyn one had to swim across a river. We said goodbye, and Yukal and I swam across the river at night.

We Search for Hiding Places Among Christians

The Christians cried over our great catastrophe.

We put our clothes on our heads and swam across the river. Coming out of the water, we got dressed and went to the Christian who had agreed to give us a place to stay. He had prepared a place for us in a haystack. We both crawled into it and slept there that night.

Before dawn, my brother Yukal got up and went to Pereveediv to bring my mother. That was the first day of Simchat Torah.[11] Yukal took her at night. They needed to go around a stretch of 15 km from Pereveediv.[12]

Yukal and my mother arrived in Dobryatyn [on] Simchat Torah at night. The next day, the Christians announced to us that we must leave. They didn't have room and they were afraid. My mother, during these couple of days, became half a corpse. When she arrived, I came out of the underground hideout. I looked at her and she at me, but she could not speak a word. After the Christians told us that they do not have a place for us, my brother Yukal took my mother back to Pereveediv, where she had been earlier. My brother Getzel with his wife Pesia and their four-year-old child were in another burrow in the village of Dobryatyn.

At night we went to look for another place. My brother found one with Ritsawjuk,[13] a very good gentile and a rich one. He took us in. However, he did not know about me. He only knew about three people hiding.

[Page 391]

He took us into his earthen hut. That is where we lay down. I was covered with straw, so that when the food was brought up, I would not be seen.

(*Interviewer: "What was the name of the village?"*

"Pańska Dolina.")[14]

The Christian kept us several days, up until the slaughter. Friday would be the slaughter. All the Christians traveled to Mlynov to see how the Jews were being killed. It was a big holiday for them.

Wednesday night my brother Yukal came and spent the night with us. We begged him to stay. He did not want to because he already had a place to hide. His place was at Votka Pahaluk's, where there were another 20 Jews.

As stated, Friday [Oct. 9, 1942] was the massacre of the Jews in two shtetls, Mervits and Mlynov, and the gentiles went to see the wonderful festival. Ivan, the son-in-law of our Christian Ritsawjuk[15] also went (his family I do not remember). While traveling, he saw how my brother Hershl, who had been hidden in a cellar, was being led to the slaughter. My brother said hello to him. When Ivan came home, he told us about it. He himself was a very fine person.

Saturday morning people came to the house, and they all started laughing about how the Jews had been shot: [they were saying] this one was lying with his legs up, and that one with the legs down. We were silently listening to what the Christians were saying. We were not permitted to cry or sigh, because we ourselves had been sentenced to death.

Saturday afternoon, Ritsawjuk's daughter came up to us and told us that they can no longer keep us. We must go, because in the village an official held a speech that whoever was hiding Jews would get shot together with the Jews.

Further wandering

We had no choice. My brother Getzel picked the baby[16] up in his arms and we left. It was raining. We kept walking. Getzel begged many Christians to let us in, but not one agreed. It was almost dawn. Seeing that we had no other option, my sister-in-law, the baby, and I went to another Christian's dirt hut.

[Page 392]

Getzel went further to a village searching for a place for us.

After wandering the entire night, we were exhausted. It was pouring. We fell asleep in the hut. 15 Jews were hiding at this Christian's place. Among them were my sister-in-law Pesia's brother Srolik Wurtzel [Vortsel],[17] his wife Ite, and their three children — Pete (the oldest), Leye, and Zelik. The other family was Ite's sister Frida with her fiancé Peysakh Litsman; there was Note Raykhman[18] with his daughter Brokhe and son Mordkhe, and the oldest daughter Memtsi.

We did not see each other. We spent the night and the entire day in the hut. At night my brother came and said he found a place. We took the baby and started to go further. We came into the village, which was not far from Dobryatyn. The Christian houseowner there was named Dymytry. He made a burrow for us in the haystack where even a single person could not enter, and yet we four people squeezed in. We were lying all crowded together. Anyway, we older people knew that we needed to suffer, but the baby wanted to eat. He wanted to see how the birds fly, so he started to cry. When he was crying the Christian came in and said my brother and his family must leave, but he wanted to keep me.

My brother had no choice. If he was told to go, he had to go. So he, his wife, and the baby left. I remained.

The Christian took me to the attic where the pigs were. I had a fur coat with me, so I was lying wrapped up in the fur coat. My job consisted of crying. I cried by day and by night. The Christian woman used to come several times to give me something to eat. She did not come up; she used to throw the food up.

I was there two weeks. I had the appearance of a dead person, half a corpse. Sunday the Christian woman came upstairs and told me to leave because a speech was held in Dobryatyn that if a Jew would be found, the Christian would be burned together with the Jew.

[Page 393]

Therefore, the family was frightened. I was not familiar with the villages, and I did not know where to go. I begged them to give me at least one more day, as though my heart had a premonition …

The nephew of the Christian where there were 15 Jews hiding proposed to take me, but only on the condition that I live with him. My brother Getzel agreed. But I said that it would be better for me to be struck dead than to live with a Christian.

That Sunday night when Dmytry told me to go, I heard that the Christian was there. I was alone in the attic, so I became very frightened that he would come up to me. I could not scream, and in his arms I am [completely powerless] — so he could do whatever he wanted with me. I remained lying in terror. I do not know if I was sleeping, or if I had fainted. I heard someone screaming "Bunia!" I thought that the Christian was calling me. I awoke, either from sleep or from a faint, and I saw my brother Getzel standing in front of me. I started to cry. My brother told me to come with him because he had found a place for everyone.

My brother went to the previous place at Ritsawjuk, where he was with his wife and child. Afterwards he found a place in Pańska Dolina with the Pole Poljak Sharek, whom he paid very well. We went back to Ritsawjuk to get his wife and child. Together we went to Sharek.

We arrived at Sharek's on Rosh Chodesh Kislev.[19] It was already terribly cold. Sharek had made a place for us, also in a haystack. This place was large. We were freezing cold. We were immediately given a tea kettle with tea, and we warmed up.

The second night my brother and I left for *Kutsys*[20] where we had taken our things out. We brought bedding — padded blankets and pillows. We were lying in the haystack under our bedding. But it was still freezing. We held a bottle of water for the child under the covers; it froze. Then Sharek said he would make an underground hideout for us.

[Page 394]

At night my brother Getzel and Sharek's boys made a hideout for us. Where was it? In the stall where the animals were kept. They dug a ditch which they covered with boards topped with hay and then dirt. The animals were standing on that. The entrance was through the trough where the animals were fed. It was very good there for us. They fed us very well. They were very good people, and they were very sympathetic to us. The woman of the house, Sharek's wife, said that we were sitting all the time in a ditch without air, so therefore we needed to eat well. Twice a day she gave us meat, pork, milk, and cream — the best food. But we paid them well. I had taken practically my entire fortune to Voske Pahaluk; I had also given a little to other Christians.

Terrible News

As stated, we had it good. The food was very good. But what came of it? We mourned a great deal. We had heard Yukal was murdered with another 20 Jews. We were even told that the Ukrainian Commander of Mlynov undressed Yukal. Yukal had been wearing a pair of officer's boots. He had gold with him. The commander took everything away from him and then shot him.

One night my brother Getzel said that he was going to another Christian to get a few things. His wife Pesia went with him. I remained with the child. By nighttime, Getzel and Pesia had not come back. I lay and cried and prayed to God that the parents should return to their baby. They returned just before dawn, but they gave me a bitter report.

When they came to the Christian, they received very bad news. 15 Jews had been killed, about whom I already spoke. Srolik Wurtzel [Vortsel][21] with his wife Ite were murdered on the spot with their three children. Note Raykhman started to run, so they shot and wounded him. His son Mordkhe carried him on his back. The Ukrainians took Memtsi to headquarters, where she was kept for three days and then shot.

[Page 395]

All of them were taken to Mlynov, where they are buried.

After eight days we heard more grim news about Yosel Feldman,[22] his wife Anila, his daughter Aviva, 2 ½, and his brother Motl who had run away from the slaughter. Understandably, the child caused difficulties. She wanted to run around on the street, and she wanted to eat, so she cried. They were afraid that they would be killed because of her. So they paid a lot of money to the Pole Zarembo[23] to take the child to Kivrets [Kivertsi],[24] where he had family. Afterwards Zarembo ordered them to leave because someone came to search for Jews. They were not found. The three people left and went near Dobryatyn to a Christian woman, a widow, who took them in. They paid her a lot of money. She took them to a box-like annex behind the oven. She said that she would make an underground hideout for them. Days went by and the woman did not make a hideout. They started to ask her why. She answered that she would do it that day.

She brought them food that consisted of a barley cereal.[25] She went away. That was at night. It did not take long until Ukrainians and police came. They hacked down the door, threw it down in the middle of the room, took a sheaf of straw, and lit it. They went to our spot behind the oven and told the Jews to climb up. The room was already besieged with Ukrainian police. The Feldmans did not want to come up. Yosel jumped out of the window; they immediately split his head open. His wife, Anila, and Motl were brought up. It turned out that Ivan, Ritsowjuk's son-in-law, was ordered to take them to Mlynov.

On the way Anila took out a kerchief and wound it around Yosel's head because it was bleeding heavily (Ivan told us later). Ivan knew the child was not with them, and he knew where she was. He was smart, not an anti-Semite.

Through gestures, he understood what Anila expressed. She had taken out a photograph and a kerchief and gave it to him, as if to say: if the war will end, give it to my child as a remembrance. They were shot in Mlynov.

[Page 396]

They were buried with their Wurtzel [Vortsel] family (from the 15 Jews).

* * *

We, in the ditch, lived only with dreams. What we dreamed at night we related in the morning. One time the Mervits Rabbi came to me holding a Torah in my dream. The Torah had golden letters.

The Rabbi screamed out loud: "Bunia, pick a letter, I will make a promise." (*Interviewer: "What was the name of the Rabbi?" --"Don't remember."*)

In the morning I narrated my dream to my brother and sister-in-law.

I added: "Master of the universe, I do not know if I will remain alive. But, if I will survive, I vow to save the child of Yosel Feldman, so that she should not remain among Christians."

Polish-Ukrainian Quarrels

We stayed at Sharek's for nine months. After that very bad times started for us. The Ukrainians and the Poles started to burn each other's property, so the Poles from Pańska Dolina left for Lutsk. We remained in the ditch, not having where else to go. Sharek and his Christians remained also.

Every evening my brother Getzel would go up to the attic as a look-out, because if someone would set fire to Sharek's house we would have to run to save ourselves.

One night after Shavuot, Getzel came running and screaming: "Children, we are burning! Give me the baby!"

We were sleeping. We grabbed the naked child and gave it to my brother. My sister-in-law was sick just then and could not move. Her back was hurting her; she suffered from lumbago.[26] I was young then. I packed up my bag and climbed down. I saw Sharek's house was already burning.

I ran to the hideout and started to scream: "Pesy, come quickly, we are on fire!"

With all my strength, I shlepped my sister-in-law out of the ditch. We could not walk. With great difficulties we crawled out of the burning house. There was shooting too.

[Page 397]

Had they known that we were Jews, they would certainly have shot us, but they did not know. We crept over to the fields. The evening was horrific. The entire village was burning. We were lying hidden in the field together with Sharek and his boys. My sister-in-law was crying pitifully because she did not know where her husband, my brother, was, nor the child. She said she did not want to live, because she did not have her husband and child.

We looked: someone was walking [towards us]. Vladek (one of Sharek's boys) wanted to shoot. My sister-in-law said: "Maybe it is Getzel?" And it was Getzel with the baby. What the child looked like is indescribable. My brother was half dead from fright.

We did not have anywhere to stay. At night we left for the fields because we could not stay here longer. We were lying in the grains eight days. During the day it was burning hot and at night it was cold. It also used to rain. We ate grain from the fields. We drank the green, stinking water from the puddles that were full of frogs.

Further Events

We realized that we could not take it anymore. I remained in a faint.

I said, "What will be, will be. Let them kill me."

We picked ourselves up and crawled to a Christian's attic. The Ukrainians had left. We were lying in the attic. Before dawn I would gather green cherries and come back. We used to eat them and drink from a pitcher of water. Meanwhile the Christians returned home, including the person in whose attic we were lying. He made a ditch for us and continued to hide us.

* * *

In the winter of 1943 (I don't remember the month), after the big frosts, it started to get bad for the Ukrainians. There was a raid in Dobryatyn. The Christians made larger hideouts. The entrance and exit were on the field. They were lying in the same ditches as we were.

[Page 398]

Ivan's wife came down to lie with us in the ditch. The Germans had taken Ivan. Underneath, in the ditch, we did not know what was going on above ground. All of a sudden, we heard axing. We thought that our hideout was being axed. It turned out that the Germans had caught chickens and they chopped off their heads in the trough. We thought that they had found our ditch and were searching for us. My brother Getzel had already said goodbye to us, and he said that he wanted to be shot before his child. A while passed and thank God, the ditch was not discovered. It was already night-time. The Germans left the houseowner alone. He came down to us and informed us that we had to leave, because he did not want to keep us any longer.

"I held you for six months; I am afraid to hide you more. If the hiding place would be opened and they would find you together with my wife, she would be shot with you."

What do we do now? The snow is high, we are barefoot, we have no warm clothes. We picked ourselves up in the night and went further. That was already the end of 1943. My brother led me to a Christian who was the German secretary. The German wanted to save himself. The end of the Germans was coming. They suffered losses on all sides. So this Christian thought that he would be able to save himself through me. He kept me behind the oven. He gave me very good food.

Getzel with his wife and child went to another Christian also called Ivan.

I want to add, that before I separated from my brother Getzel, we went one night to beg food from another Christian, because we had very little to eat when we were staying together. We knew that we could go to this person because he was a Communist. When we came into his place, he ordered us to hide, because somebody was there.

He led us out to the earthen hut. At the hut somebody came over; Getzel recognized him. He was a Russian soldier with whom Getzel had worked for the Russians. Now the soldier was a partisan.

[Page 399]

When he saw us, he started to kiss Getzel. Getzel was very overgrown with hair. The partisan gave him a razor knife and Getzel shaved himself and fixed himself up a little. The partisan also brought us food — pork, bread, radishes. He sat with us an entire day and told news, what was going on at the front.

Getzel announced: "I do not know if we will survive. But you will surely live, so I want one thing from you. You need to know that Voske Pahaluk killed 22 Jews; among them was my brother Yukal. I want you to take revenge on him."

The partisan promised and wrote it down. There was another Christian in whom we needed to take revenge. It did not take long. The next day, we heard that unknown people came to Voske Pahaluk at night. They captured and took him, nobody knew where. They also took Tsanyuk and a third Christian whose name I do not remember.

As said, I was with one Christian and Getzel was with another. We were not far from each other, about 5 km from Mervits. The Christian took very good care of me; gave me the best things to eat. My work consisted of sitting behind the oven, crying, and plucking feathers for the woman.

One time there was a raid on *Kutsys*. The German secretary took me down into the hideout (all the Christians already had hideouts); he himself was not afraid as he was the Secretary. But if someone would find a Jew with him, he would be shot. I lay in that ditch an entire day; I was buried alive. I thought: why do I need to suffer more? I wanted to end my life, but I had nothing to kill myself with. I tore my hair from my head; I bit myself.

He came back at night to take me out. He crossed himself a few times and asked me what happened to me. He put me back behind the oven and I continued to live. I sat alone, cried, and moaned. Up until now I had been sitting with my brother and sister-in-law.

[Page 400]

* * *

I decided out of my own free will to go away. What will be will be! I will go to my brother. One night I got up, wrapped my feet in rags. The snow was high. I went to my brother, and we again sat together. The fronts were not far away. We heard shooting already. My brother would climb out of the ditch and go up in the attic to hear the shooting and how revenge was being taken.

I no longer had the patience to sit in the ditch. We heard the front was near Rivne.

I got up and said, "What will be, will be. I am going back to my shtetl Mervits."

I knew a Christian, Anapry (I do not remember his family) who lived near us, a Ukrainian, a very fine person. He had hidden six people, an entire family (located in America now) — Icek Kozak,[27] his wife and four children, two sons and two daughters. They were from Mlynov. That Christian was our best, good friend. He had told me that he wanted to hide us, my mother, me, and the children. But I was afraid of his son Alexey harming us.

I left to go to Anapry. It was winter; there was a lot of snow. On the way I saw German tanks. They did not recognize me. Before daylight I arrived in Mervits. A neighbor, a Jew hunter, saw me and recognized me. I went to Anaory's. It did not take long until the Jew hunter came in to search for me. He said he had seen me, and he asked where I was. I sat in another room. Anapry's wife responded that she knew nothing; she had not seen me.

I hid under the bed for two days. The Christians did not know what to do with me. They gave me food and drink. The front kept getting closer. On the third day, the woman came to tell me that the Russian partisans had come. The partisans asked if there were any hidden Germans. They found me sitting, so they asked who I was.

[Page 401]

I answered, "I am a poor Jewish child."

They were very happy with me and begged me to tell them how I had been hidden. I told them.

The next day the Russians came. The front was in Mervits in January 1944. Russian headquarters had been established in Anopri's house. From headquarters I was asked who I was. I answered that I was a Jewish child. There was a Russian Jew there. When he saw me, he was as happy as when a father finds his only child. The first thing he did was to bring me clothes and a pair of shoes.

Problems after Liberation

A few weeks passed. The war had ended for us.

Now we had to think about ourselves, about getting food, about earning money. It was after Shavuot. I remembered my vow; I needed to get Yosel's child who was in Kivertsi[28] near Lutsk. But I did not know exactly where that was.

In Mervits I had a very good neighbor, a Polish woman, who knew where the girl was. She said she would travel with me. She loaned me a dress and a pair of shoes, and we left for Kivertsi.

The Polish woman showed me where the child was. Her name was Aviva. She used to know me very well, when she was two and a half, when she used to come into our home. But now, when I came to get her, she was five.

I came into the house and asked about her. The Christian woman called her in.

I asked her, "Aviva, do you remember me?"

"My name is not Aviva, but Vishya."

She did not recognize me. I had with me as proof her little coat that her mother had bought her, a very pretty little coat. My brother had seen it in another Christian's house, and he took it. I showed it to her.

She recognized it and screamed out: "Oy, my coat!"

[Page 402]

She ran over to me. I hugged her and started to weep. The Polish woman cried, looking at me. After that I told the woman why I had come. As I am the girl's family, I came to get her. The woman responded that if the mother would come for the child, she would give her up. But as I was a stranger, she would not give her to me. However, if I wanted to give her 500 gold five-ruble coins, she would give me the child.

"But where can I get that?" I asked. "I myself have nothing to wear. If you do not believe me, ask my neighbor. Even the dress I am wearing is not mine."

She made a gesture to the little girl who then called me "*parszywa żydówka*"[29] and spat at me.

* * *

After extreme difficulties and obstacles, I managed to save the child and I brought her to Israel.[30]

Translator's and editor's footnotes:

1. Bunia Epstein (1912–1995) was born Bunia Steinberg in Mervits to Asher Anshel Steinberg and Chana (Lerner). She and her two siblings Getzel (George) Steinberg and Mendel Steinberg survived. Mendel is also a contributor to this volume. After her liberation, Bunia married Yitzchak Upstein from Mlynov. The couple migrated to Palestine and the family name became Epstein in Israel. The Steinberg survival story is narrated by Bunia's daughter, Shoshana Baruch, in a book length narrative, published in translation on the Mlynov website. Her son, Charles (Hanina) Epstein, is one of the Hebrew translators of this volume. – HS
2. The author is remembering the order for Mervits residents to move into the Mlynov ghetto on May 22nd or 23rd, 1942. – HS
3. Pereveediv today, 7 km (4 mi) from Mlynov, on the road past Berehy and at the turn off to Smordva. Hereafter the contemporary name Pereveediv is used. – HS
4. New month of Elul, August 13, 1942. – HS
5. The first day of Rosh Hashanah fell on Saturday, Sept. 12, 1942. – HBF
6. Erev Yom Kippur was Sunday, Sept. 20, 1942. – HBF
7. Sept. 27, 1942. – HBF
8. Sept. 29, 1942. – HBF
9. The eve of Hoshana Rabbah was Oct. 1, 1942. – HBF
10. Referring to Nahum and Rachel Teitelman's two sons, Efraim Fishel and Shlomo Benzion. See Nahum's account, p. 322. – HBF
11. Oct. 4, 1942. – HBF
12. Since their mother could not swim across the Ikva the way her children had, they had to circumambulate via the roads which was more dangerous, and which made the distance much longer. – HS
13. Spelled "Ritzvuyuk" in the translation of the book length version of the story cited earlier. – HS
14. Pańska Dolina was an area of Polish resistance between Mlynov and Lutsk that longer exists. – HBF
15. Also spelled Ritzvuyuk in the book length narrative. – HS
16. Referring to Getzel's son Zelig (later Gerry Steinberg). – HS
17. Also spelled Wurtzel. Getzel's wife, Pesia and her brother, Srulik Wurtzel, were children of Zelig Ulinik Wurtzel and Sooreh (Gruber). – HS
18. Also spelled Raikhman, the family is listed as martyrs from Mervits p. 443. Nute Raikhman, his wife Faiga, his sons Moshe and Mordechai, and their children, Mamtzi and Beracha, Yosef, and Yozyf and the family. – HS
19. Nov. 10, 1942. – HBF
20. This place has not been identified. – HS
21. Pesia's brother and family. The family name is also spelled Wurtzel. – HS

22.   The book length account indicates that Pesia, Getzel's wife, was related to Yosel Feldman via the Gruber family line. Pesia was the daughter of Zelig Wurtzel and Sura (Gruber). Sura's sister, Rachel (Gruber) Feldman was the mother of Yosel Feldman. In the ghetto, Bunia befriended Yosel's wife Anila (Neli). – HS

23.   Possibly the same Polish family that helped save the Teitelmans in Pańska Dolina referred to as the Zarembah family in their account. – HS

24.   Assumed to be the town called Kivertsi today which is 48 km from Mlynov and just 16 km northeast of Lutsk. – HS

25.   Following the Hebrew translation of the Yiddish. – HS

26.   Drawing on the book length account here. – HS

27.   See essay by Icek Kozak, "What My Family Endured," pp. 354–358. – HS

28.   Kivertsi 16 km northeast of Lutsk. – HS

29.   [Pol] Lousy Jewess. – HBF

30.   The detailed rescue of Aviva Feldman is told as part of the longer Steinberg family story, published on the Mlynov website. – HS

[Page 405]

In Memory and Mourning

In Memory and Mourning

by Sonia and Mendel Teitelman

Translated from the Yiddish by Hannah B. Fischthal, PhD

Edited by Howard I. Schwartz, PhD

I am tough. A few others and I had the luck, through a miracle from our Supervisor, to remain alive. Therefore, the holy duty of collecting and inscribing the great spiritual worthiness of our martyrs, who were killed so tragically, is incumbent on us. The nicest traditions of our people were erased with their deaths. As stated, this needs to be done by those who miraculously survived while they still live.

The destroyed beautiful lives should be portrayed with all their colors, and they should be written with golden pens as a guide to our future generations. May the coming generations take them as an example for their own lives. We have nothing to be embarrassed about the poor lives of our martyrs because they were poor in material goods but quite rich in spiritual and in moral values.

In Yad-Vashem

by N.D. Korman

Translated from the Yiddish by Hannah B. Fischthal, PhD

Edited by Howard I. Schwartz, PhD

The eternal light burns
It flickers in my heart—
The fire flames here
It burns our bodies.
From yesterday's past,
Dark, black—
Memory, do not erase!
Make notes, write it down!
Write it down here for generations
That will come
To cry, to lament,
The eternal Jew.
And maybe someone will
Say Kaddish here?
And maybe someone will
Write a poem. . .

[Page 406]

Yad Vashem[1]

by Yochanan Viner,[2] Kiryat Hayim

Translated and edited by Howard I. Schwartz, PhD with Hanina Epstein

I, Yochanan Viner, come to recall the memory of my loved ones: my parents, my father Mendel and my mother Baila Viner and my brother who was born on the eve of the Holocaust and was called Chaim [Life], and the beloved brothers of my father and my mother, who have no one to recite Yizkor.[3]

As a survivor of a town of Jews, I am joining in the memorialization of Jews from the towns of Mlynov-Mervits and the surroundings in the Volyn region in Poland and am participating in the publication of a Memorial book to our beloved ones who were killed in the Shoah, which took place in Europe in this century. These lines here are a memorial candle[4] to the souls of my parents, my brother, and all my beloved ones, and this perpetual memory written in this Memorial book will be an eternal witness to the future.

* * *

Adults say that the past is not forgotten and perhaps because we lost such an important part of our lives, the entirety of childhood and pleasant youthful lives, and because that childhood was so cruel and bitter, filled with blood and tears, we remember it, even though we so much want to forget it all.

It was a village. Jews lived there and raised families. There, my father also lived. He was born to a home of believers, whose hope always was for good and who believed in good. They all dreamed of becoming old in that place, to see children and grandchildren and die in old age in peace. But fate decreed otherwise, and the War broke out.

Its goal was the final solution of the Jews. The evil didn't distinguish between people. One night all of them were chased and in the morning, everyone was assembled, with only a small bag, in the same area of confinement. Exhausted from being hunted, fearful of coming day. Pressed together, withdrawn into themselves and full of thoughts about what the day will bring and what will now be. The mother continues to fret over her small children, the father prays with all his heart for good. Everything is as usual, all like it always was. The blade goes up and up and the belt tightens around the neck and there is no savior and no rescuer, and none to encourage: "Be strong, Jews!" and "Shema-Yisrael" helps a bit and intensifies uncertainty about redemption. All go, row by row, to the place of annihilation. Only my father remained,[5] an ember from that Jewish family that was lost inside kilns of fire. And we were born to be a rock of redemption, so as not to forget. To teach the generation after generation about the history of the six million.

[Page 407]

A branch was severed from a large tree of the people. And with that branch fathers and mothers were lost.

Today, we come to memorialize. Always remembering at a special time, and in a dream, and some moment during the day. It is not possible to forget the entire past. It lives in us, and we are children of the Shoah. It was our fate to be content building the homeland. And today, after years, we are obliged to take an oath to continue to remember and not forget. But to live. To live on the condition that every stone and home built, that every tree and flower planted, will thereby cry out and lift up the memories of our loved ones.

Bailah Viner[6]
Daughter of Yohanan Viner, son of Mendel and Bailah.

Translator's and editor's footnotes:

1.   Yad Vashem (meaning "a memorial and a name") is the name of Israel's official memorial to the victims of the Holocaust. It was established in 1953. This reflection may have been written for a visit to the memorial around the time this Memorial book was published. His daughter, Bailah, signed her name at the end of this reflection suggesting she transcribed these words from what her father said.

2.   Yochanan Viner (born around 1928–1932) was a child survivor. He was born to Mendel and Bailah Viner. In an interview he gave for the Zekelman Holocaust Center in Michigan, he recounts how his mother helped him escape from the ghetto. She watched and learned the routine of the Ukrainian guards every night until she knew when he could slip from the house without being caught. One night she opened the door and told him it was time to leave. He was about 10 years old and survived alone in the forests and begged for food at the home of Czech farmers. After surviving the War, he eventually was helped by the Jewish Brigade to get to Palestine. There he eventually settled in Kibbutz Beit HaArava and later Kibbutz Alonim.

3.   Yizkor is the memorial prayer said to commemorate the death of a beloved one.

4.   A candle is traditionally lit on the anniversary (yahrzeit) of a family member's death.

5.   It seems that the daughter Bailah is speaking here rather than narrating her father's voice.

6.   It appears that Bailah, Yohanan's daughter transcribed this reflection, though in the second half she may be speaking in her own voice.

Now

by Yitzhak Lamdan,[1] Holon, Israel

Translated and edited by Howard I. Schwartz, PhD with Hanina Epstein

How many nights, my people, heavy of heart and lacking sleep
I tortured my soul with books of your accounts![2]
Angry and wounded, like a dried out field of shrubs,
between the pages of "debt," a dry path, whose flank is a path in sorrow
And the columns of "credit," which are turning green, like a shepherd who is silent and planning,
Love and hate both together – –

Now I close the books. I won't request an accounting.
Time for your heart to contribute working the uncivilized desert.
And every gentile dog, sinks its teeth in your flesh
And in their gnawing, your flowering[3] will bring forth every swine from the forest of peoples.
And all clouds of man will pass over your head and drop hail of hate
At a time like this, my people, again there is nothing in my heart for you,
But only love!

Translator's and editor's footnotes:

1. Yizkhak Lamdan (1899–1954) famous author of the poem Masada. See his profile below (pp. 487–88) and his earlier poems in this volume with notes there about his life. The date of this poem is not known.

2. The poem appears metaphoric and can sustain several meanings. It appears to use a financial accounting metaphor for a moral one. The columns of a ledger showing credit and debt serve as an analogy for the gains and losses of transforming the desert land into greenery, and for a moral accounting, as the poet's people experience and can expect the pain and hate of other peoples. The date of this poem is not known.

3. Possibly pun on "skin rash" and "flowering."

[Page 408]

My Lamentations

by Yaakov Mohel,[1] Holon, Israel

Translated from the Yiddish by Hannah B. Fischthal, PhD

Edited by Howard I. Schwartz, PhD

On the yahrzeit of your death, I light a memorial candle in your holy memory. I am looking at the flickering little flame of the candle, and heavy, sad thoughts painfully and deeply press upon my heart.

I see in the flickering flame a distant reflection of your last days and hours spent in tragic, horrible expectation of what had to come, the unalterable end. You all stand in front of my eyes like you stood in the cellar room where you had hoped to find a hiding place, already sentenced, having just a weak spark of hope. You were bursting from hunger, with eyes full of fear and terror, weak, alone, abandoned by everyone, even by God, in whom you had believed all these years, as well as by "civilized" humanity.

I see how the murderer marched into your house; I hear his teasing laughter when he shlepped you out of the ditch; I see how he forced you to undress naked. I hear your last parting words mixed with pleadings and crying; they torture my ears. I see your last convulsions; I hear your last dying breaths. I also hear the big scream for revenge, which tears up all the heavens, screams and demands, screams and orders:

"Do not forget! Never forget!"

Mama, can you be forgotten?! Our last goodbye and your words, "Go, but we will never see each other again," ring in my ears like a large act of guilt. I would have needed to carry you out of the fire with my hands! Mama, why was there no miracle?! Had you not deserved to be saved through a miracle? Had you not devoted your entire life to helping people? Were you not the symbol of the highest human ethics and morality? I see you now in your last gruesome moments, how you spread out your motherly hands and you wanted, in your deep despair, to prevent your children from the hateful voices. You, the eternal mother, whose devotion had no limits, whose feelings of sympathy surpassed all acceptable human norms.

Mama, I see you so often in different forms, but I always see you astonished and wondering. I know: you could neither grasp nor understand the terrible sentence that was carried through onto you and your people. The question "Why?" may have hurt more than the bullet in your heart.

Father, I see you now during the interval that divided your death from the deaths of your wife and children. You went to search for a little piece of bread for them; when you returned, they were already dead. I see you bent into tenths, broken, near the corpses of your family, not even having the possibility of bringing them to the cemetery. I see you as hunted like an animal by the wild bands, lost, resigned.

And whenever I think of your last days, a hard ball rolls in my throat, and I do not want to cry, but rather scream in suffocating pain. Father, where are your tallis and tefillin? Where is your *kittle*[2] in which you hid your tears and prayers year in and year out in the fearful days of law and forgiveness?[3] Is this the reward for your learning?! Or is this the payment for your days and nights spent in following God?! Is this the compensation for your whole life that was brought as a sacrifice for higher human ideals, for human justice, and for Godly beauty?!

Father, I bow my head deeply in front of your unknown grave and wring my hands in deep sorrow. Filthy people despoiled and gassed your tallis and *kittle,* the same ones who raised the axe above your head. They shamed and made fun of your holy things while you are lying in a cold and strange earth. You are still waiting for someone to combat your injustice. The injustice is so huge that it screams out at the heavens, but nobody can compensate for it, nobody can alleviate it. The same holds for the injustice against your people.

I recite your name with holy shivers, and I swear to never forget your martyrdom. Your memory will remain in our hearts forever. Like a beacon in a lighthouse, your beautiful virtues will serve as an example for the coming generations. Your name will be written with burning letters in the pantheon of the holy martyrs who were sacrificed for *kiddush hashem,* sanctification of the Name.

Written on the fifth yahrzeit

Translator's and editor's footnotes:

1. Yaakov Mohel was one of seven children of Rabbi Leizer Mohel (1872–1942) and Hanna Beila (Kaszkiet) (1882–1942). The Mohel family came to Mlynov from Boremel in 1924–1925 when Rabbi Eliezer, a shochet and mohel, was hired for a position in town. The two parents and three sisters, Batya (1906–1942), Bouzke'leh (1926–1942), and Yenteleh (1930–1942) perished in the Shoah. Four children, Yaakov (1911–1974), Yehuda (1908–1989), Chaika (Chaya) (1916–1985) and Devorah (1914–1987) survived the war. The essay that follows this one describes what happened to the family left in Mlynov. Yehuda's amazing life journey and survival story is documented in detail by his son Dani Tracz (Issachar Mohel), *Riva and Yehuda: Life Story of Trancman, Mohel, Tracz and Ben-Eliezer Families,* 2015). – HS

2. A religious man wears this white linen robe in the synagogue on holidays, at his wedding, and when he is buried. – HBF

3. The 10 Days of Awe between Rosh Hashana and Yom Kippur. – HBF

[Page 410]

A Murdered Family

by Y. Mohel[1]

Translated from the Yiddish by Hannah B. Fischthal, PhD

Edited by Howard I. Schwartz, PhD

Wandering in Uzbekistan, several months after our areas were liberated from the Hitler troops, we received a letter from Sore Neyter,[2] a girl from Mervits. It shook us up and greatly astonished us. To our great regret, it got lost, but every word of hers was engraved in my mind, and I surely will not be falsifying anything when I will present it now.

"The terrible deprivations, pain, and troubles that we withstood from the Germans and Ukrainians since they came into Mlynov is indescribable. But I want only to describe how your family was killed; I was a witness to it. A while earlier we young Jewish girls were taken to perform heavy labor in the fields of the Smordva Count.[3] We were driven in the fall and winter, barely dressed, while it was still dark out. Going past the Ikva river, many girls were forced to go into the ice-cold water, and they made fun of us. The work was very difficult. They lashed us with whips if we needed to catch our breaths.

"I worked in a group with your sister Bouzke'leh. I remember how your Bouzke'leh had saved something from the 100 grams[4] of bread that each one of us received for 12-13 hours of punishing work, and she carried it home for her sisters and parents who did not even receive the 100 grams. I remember how we got together a few times at night, hidden from strange eyes, when Bouzke'leh used to read her poems that she had composed. It is hard to understand from where she took so much strength and courage, in such inhumane circumstances, to write poetry. Her poems were bitter, full of hatred and abhorrence of the German executioners and their Ukrainian assistants.

[Page 411]

"So stretched the weeks and months like heavy lead until we approached the final liquidation of the remaining few Jews. Everyone searched for possibilities to hide, but there were no prospects. Your father made a hiding place in the kitchen. He cut out two boards from the floor and fitted them back perfectly so they would not be visible; and he put his entire family underneath. He also invited me to go into that underground basement, but I didn't like the hiding place. I decided to hide in the top of the chimney; I put a board between the bricks and let myself down.

Mohel house

[from left to right] Rivke, [in the window] Rizl, Seril, Dvoyre [Mohel], Khayke [Mohel], Reyzl, Batya [Mohel]
(original photo courtesy of Dani Tracz)[5]

[Page 412]

"And so I stayed in the chimney about three days and three nights without food and drinks, with one shirt. It was October. Cold winds blew; it rained. I often lost consciousness from suffering; I felt that I was almost at the end. But on the third day I awoke from my unconscious position when I heard the murderers tearing into your apartment. They searched everywhere, including the kitchen, and I heard how they discovered the hiding place! I heard how they shlepped everyone out one by one, then lined them up at the wall and murdered them. The words that Bouzke'leh told them still ring in my ears:

"'You can kill us, but my brothers will take revenge on you! Our innocent blood that you shed will not protect you. Your end is very near!'

"At these words a salvo was heard, and it became terribly quiet. I do not know with what strength I lasted until the evening. I got out of the chimney and, thanks to the darkness of the night which additionally was cold and rainy,

I succeeded in getting out to the fields. And like a driven animal I ran around over the fields and forests until I survived the liberation."

* * *

That is the short summary of the death of a family. My father, may he rest in peace, was not there when his family was shot. He had gone out somewhere searching for food; when he came back, everyone was dead. He ran around like a crazy person until the next day. Then the Germans murdered him not far from the slaughterhouse where he had worked for so many years.

And so came the bitter end of Reb Leyzer the kosher slaughterer from Mlynov, his wife Khana-Leye, daughter Basye, daughter Brukhe (Bouzke'leh), and the small 10-year-old Yenteleh.

Translator's and editor's footnotes:

1. The is a letter written in 1944 by Yaakov Mohel to his brother Yehuda Mohel in 1944 about the fate of their family. See the previous essay for background on the Mohel family. – HS
2. It is not clear how this Sore or Sarah Neyter (or Neiter) was related to the Neiter families listed among the Mervits martyrs or to other Neiter descendants who survived. Batia (Blinder) Kopchak who contributed an essay to this volume, for example, was daughter of Pnina (Neiter) who married Yitzhak Blinder. – HS
3. See Liza Berger's essay "I Wandered Hungry and in Pain," p. 347, which describes the same situation. – HS
4. 100 g. = 3.5 oz. – HBF
5. The courtyard of the Mohel house. The Mohel sisters are Batya (on the right), Khayke (Chaya) (standing center), Dvorah (to her right). In the window sits another Batya who married Yitzhak Mohel. – HS

[Page 413]

The Litvak Home

by Yosef Litvak,[1] Jerusalem

Translated and edited by Howard I. Schwartz, PhD with Hanina Epstein

My father, R. Mordechai Meir, son of Yaakov-Zelig, and Chana Litvak,
My mother Rivkah-Devora,[2] daughter of Yehudah Arieh and Liba Lamdan,
may their memory be blessed.

My father, of blessed memory, was born in the town of Slishtch-Zuta[3] in the year 5641 (1881). The years of his childhood and youth he spent in the town of Brisk (Brest-Litovsk) [now Belarus], where his father, my grandfather, was head cantor in the great synagogue during the tenure of Rav Gaon Chaim Soloveitchik[4] as the rabbi of the town. He studied holy subjects in cheder, and for a few years with a private teacher studying the Russian language and the principles of accounting. At the age of 18, he left his parents' home for an independent life in Kiev. On his own initiative, he learned accounting management and civil engineering and in a short time reached the level of supervisor in one of the large Jewish contractors in Tzarist Russia.

In addition to his professional education, he studied and read voluminously and acquired an extensive Jewish and general education and expertise in Hebrew literature, Yiddish and Russian. Likewise, during his entire life he was interested in and had a great love and knowledge of music, whose foundations he learned from his father. In 1912, he married my mother. After hardships and much wandering during the civil war in Russia and the pogroms against Jews in Ukraine, he settled with his family in the small town of Mlynov in 1922.

Despite being very preoccupied and busy with difficulties of making a living, which was obtained with great difficulty, he expressed interest in many activities of public need and in particular in the arena of Zionist activities. In the first years after the First World War, he organized and led welfare activities in the town on behalf of the American government assistance fund and on behalf of the Joint [The American Joint Distribution Committee]. He set up a kitchen to feed children and distribute necessities and he led the committee to help orphans. After this, he set up and managed, with no renumeration, "a charity fund" to help shop owners and artisans. Similarly, he set up a bank for the same purpose, that lasted only a few years. In the arena of Zionist activities, he led the local Eretz Yisrael [Zionist] office which organized the aliyah of the first pioneers during the years 1923–1926. He served as permanent chairman of the nomination committee for the Zionist Congress, [and] he was one of the principal active members in all the Zionist work: the distribution of shekalim,[5] cultural funds, etc.

For several years, his home served as a center and meeting place for the active Zionist members in that location.

[Page 414]

In the beginning of the Soviet occupation, he was imprisoned following the local Yevsk[6] snitching. He was freed after a few days thanks to a Soviet military prosecutor, a Jew with a warm heart, but he continued to be under the watch of the secret police during the entirety of the Soviet government.[7]

During the Nazi occupation he was appointed secretary of the Judenrat in the ghetto. He performed this coerced, wretched role with integrity, with honor and decency. He was beaten several times in a cruel fashion by the Nazi in charge for refusing to fulfill his extortive demands. He died a holy death — with my mother, of blessed memory — by the hands of the murderers from Ukrainian police, when they attempted to flee from the ghetto a few days before the general slaughter of the community, at the end of Tirshri 5703 (beginning of October 1942) and the place of their burial is not known. May their memory be a blessing. May their souls be bound in the bond of life.

* * *

My mother, of blessed memory, was born in the town of Mlynov in the year 5649 (1889). She didn't study during her lifetime in any kind of girl's religious high school but still she mastered several languages and read a great deal. She was faithful to the tradition of her father's home and combined it with a progressive outlook. She had an exemplary character as a Jewish mother, sharing the burden of the household income and dedicating the best of her efforts to effectively care for her children and educating them for an ethical life and to be faithful Jews, with their whole soul and might. She excelled in diligence and kindheartedness and employed her ethical character as an example to her children and everyone who knew her. She died a holy death together with her husband. May her memory be a blessing. May her soul be bound in the bond of life.

Translator's and editor's footnotes:

1. Yosef Litvak contributed two essays to this volume including "My Hometown Mlynov," pp. 53-59, with additional notes about his family and background. Yosef was born in Kiev in 1917. Yosef was away studying at a teacher's college in Rovno when the Nazis invaded. He fled east and survived in Russia and

eventually made his way to Palestine. His parents were both killed in the liquidation of the Mlynov ghetto. His parents' photo appears on page 454.

    2.   Rivkah-Devora was the sister of the poet, Yitzhak Lamdan.

    3.   The town was called Selishche Mala in the Russian empire and Male Sedliszcze after WWII. It was 22 miles NE of Rivne and 9 miles ESE of Kostopil. It does not appear that there is any settlement there currently.

    4.   Also known as Reb Chaim Brisker (1853–1918), Soloveitchik was considered the founder of the "Brisker method," a method of highly exacting and analytical Talmudical study.

    5.   See also Litvak's similar discussion in "My Hometown Mlynov," p. 53. The Zionist shekel was the name of the certificate of membership in the Zionist Organization given to every Jew who paid annual membership dues. The name comes from the unit of weight and currency used in the First Temple period. Purchasing the Zionist shekel expressed identification with Zionism and its goals. The revenue from the sale of the shekalim (plural of shekel) was used for Zionist activities. The number of delegates that each country sent to the Congress was determined based on the number of shekalim sold in that country.

    6.   The Yevsektsiya was the Jewish section of the Soviet Communist Party originally founded with Lenin's approval to bring the communist revolution to the Jewish masses. They regarded Jewish Zionist organizations as counter-revolutionary.

    7.   Litvak contributed a longer essay on this period, "The Mlynov Community at the Beginning of the Soviet Occupation," pp. 283–286.

[Page 415]

A Memorial Candle [for Chaia Kipergluz]

by Y. L.[1] [Yosef Litvak]

Translated and edited by Howard I. Schwartz, PhD with Hanina Epstein

For Chaia Kipergluz,[2] daughter of Mr. Chaim Yitzhak and Sara Kipergluz

Chaia, of blessed memory, was born in Mlynov in 1919. She excelled in her childhood in intelligence and natural talent in many different ways and with much charm. She finished Polish elementary school in 1932. Due to the absence of a high school in the town where she lived, she did not continue with formal studies. [Still,] she expanded her reading in high quality scientific[3] literature in Polish, Yiddish and Hebrew. She stood out among her peers and her manners were pleasant.

From the age of 9, she was a protégé of the youth movement "The Young Guard" (Hashomer Hatzair). She was visibly involved in many activities in the movement in all the different areas and filled responsible roles until the breakup of the movement with the Soviet invasion in September 1939. Among other things, she exhibited a natural talent for dramatic plays and narration and filled a central role in all plays and celebrations in the movement over the years.

*[Page 415]*She yearned and strove to make aliyah to the Land [of Israel]. Her leaving for a training kibbutz was held up by a family tragedy when her only brother, who was 10 years old, drowned in the river, in the summer of 1938. Her older sister made aliyah before this, and Chaia was not able to leave her parents alone in their heavy grief.

With the Soviet occupation, she experienced great personal suffering and difficult persecutions along with all the past members of the Zionist organizations at the hands of the Soviet secret police following snitching by the local Yevsektsiya [the Jewish section of the Communist party]. Despite the persecutions, she succeeded in obtaining a job and quickly climbed the ranks.

In the early days after the Nazi invasion towards the end of July 1941 she was arrested together with about 20 other Jewish youth – the best of the local Jewish youth – for being "Communists."[4] All the members of the group were taken out to be killed about 3 days after their arrest following severe beatings by their Nazi torturers and their collaborators from the Ukrainian police men.

May her memory be a blessing and may her soul be bound up in bond of life.

A modest memorial to her memory from a friend from her youth.

Translator's and editor's footnotes:

1. "Y. L." is assumed to be Yosef Litvak, who wrote the preceding reflection and who also submitted the records for the Kipergluz family to Yad Vashem where he listed himself as a friend of the family.
2. Chaia Kipergluz (1919–1942) (alt. spelling Kiperglaz) was one of the young people arrested and killed for supposedly being a Communist shortly after the Nazi occupation. Her father Chaim Yitzhak (1895–1942) was the son of Brakha (Gelman) and Yosef Kipergluz. He is mentioned several times in this volume: as a friend of Shmuel Mandelkern in the prank about Yaakov-Yosi, p. 216–217, as president of the Kehilla (p. 90), as second head of the Kehilla in "The Town of Mlynov" (p. 55), as the synagogue sexton in "Mlynov–A Kehilla for Mlynov," (p. 21), and as a man known to give charity (p. 317). During the Nazi occupation, he was forced to be a member of the Judenrat. A photo of the Kipergluz house/store is on page 151. Chaia's mother, Sarah, was from the town of Trovits. A sister Rachel Kipergluz (married name Kleeman) is mentioned as having made aliyah in an earlier essay (p. 69). She had a brother Yosele, who died in a manner described in this story.
3. "Scientific" here might have a broader meaning and refer to various books of secular studies.
4. See Litvak's discussion in "The Mlynov Community at the Beginning of the Soviet Occupation," p. 284.

The Sherman-Golisuk Families

by Yechiel Sherman[1]

Translated and edited by Howard I. Schwartz, PhD with Hanina Epstein

Two brothers, Yechiel and Ezra, survived from two large families: Sherman and Golisuk (Mother's side). In the family of Father, there were four brothers: Shlomo, Ben-tzion, Feivel and Moshe (my father); and two sisters; Sarah-Bracha and Miriam — and all the children. On Mother's side: the grandmother Hannah Golisuk [née Shuchman], Yosef Mutia, Shmuel, Pesiah, Byka, Tzvia and Etel (my mother) — and all the children.

All of them were murdered by the debased (tameh) bitter enemy.

May their memories be a blessing.

Translator's and editor's footnotes:

    1.   See Yechiel's other essay, "Taking Leave of Home," pp. 344–345, with additional notes about him and his brother. See family photos on page 462.

[page 416]

My Ester and Nakhman z"l

by Mendel Teitelman[1]

Translated from the Yiddish by Hannah B. Fischthal, PhD

Edited by Howard I. Schwartz, PhD

When I remember my brother Nakhman z"l and my sister Ester z"l,[2] my heart melts from pain and stress. I cannot forget them even more than I cannot ever forget my brothers Yankev-Yoysef[3] and Shaye z"l,[4] and my sister Mirel,[5] with all their families, and all of my relatives and friends. I do not know why; I cannot express it with words, but I feel them much more in my heart. The reason for it is possibly because they were among the first victims in our shtetls.

My brother Nakhman, as is known, lived in Trovits.[6] He had a reputation there as a buyer who was sharp and wise. He was also materially well situated. The truth is that nothing good was missing in his childhood, as we all grew up in a rich household.

Right after WWI he married Khane Goldman z"l from Lutsk. He suffered terribly when his wife died in childbirth; that broke him physically and spiritually. We did not believe that he would ever again get back on his feet. And when, in great despair, he wanted to go out into the world and emigrate to Argentina, I was the first to persuade him away from taking that step. I did not have any intentions; it was simply hard for me to part with him. I never envisioned anything bad coming. The end of his tragic experience was that he did get back on his feet. He married Shayndl Ackerman[7] from Trovits, revived, and was active in all cultural areas of Trovits. At the same time, he was a Zionist advisor until the start of the war. With the arrival of the Soviets in our neighborhood on 17 September 1939, like everywhere then, all advisors had to put aside their businesses and erase their tracks.

[Page 417]

He, like his friends, started slowly to adjust to the new situation, although with great difficulties because formerly he had been a wealthy businessman. We are not talking about the degradation, as it did not matter if one could sit in peace.

The black clouds of the world-murderers came, with the help of the local Christian neighbors, on Friday, the 8 of Av 5701 [August 1, 1941].[8] With tanks and machine-guns, they surrounded all of Trovits. They took most of the Jewish men not far from the shtetl, and then shot them all. That black Friday, which orphaned practically the entire shtetl, did not omit my brother Nakhman; having done nothing wrong, he was also murdered that day with the others. When, a few days later, I learned about that great tragedy, I mourned with my family double. It especially pained me that I was not a factor in aiding his desire to go out into the world. To write about this with all the details, after 25 years, is not easy, but the pain in my heart is still fresh.

The same happened with my sister Ester. The same Friday of the Trovits catastrophe was also the Ostrozhets catastrophe. That same Friday, they also made a death pogrom on practically all the Jewish men there. My brother-in-law Meir Graber z"l hid himself well, but my sister Ester was sure that nothing bad would happen to her since she was a woman, and they had not killed women yet.

And so you were, my dear brother and sister, among the first victims torn away from us forever, for no reason. We could not sit shiva,[9] tear our clothes in mourning, or even say *kaddish* over your young deaths. You, my dear brother, left a wife and a family. And you, my dear sister, left a husband and three dear children who were extremely beautiful and wise. Your bright figure stands in front of my eyes.

Translator's and editor's footnotes:

1. Mendel and his wife Sonia (Gruber) were the most prolific contributors to this Memorial volume and tell their own story in "Tragic Tales," in this volume. Mendel was born in Mervits, the son of Abraham Teitelman (1850–1922) and Rivka (Halperin), and one of nine siblings, most of whom died in the Shoah. His year of birth is given variously as 1893 and 1900. Mendel and Sonia's story is told in greater background on the Mlynov website. – HS

2. According to Yad Vashem records filled out by Asher Teitelman, Mendel's sister Ester Teitelman married a man named Meir Graber and had three children. – HS

3. Yankev-Yosef (1896–1942). – HS

4. "Shaye" is a form of the name "Yehoshua" one of the brothers listed in Teitelman family trees. – HS

5. Mirel Teitelman (1908–1942) married Yehuda Zev Schwartz. Two of their children, Liba (or Libby) and Max, survived. – HS

6. Today, Torhovytsia, Ukraine. Also known as Targowica. – HBF

7. In an earlier essay "Mlynov–A Kehilla," p. 19, Mendel mentions that the rabbi of the entire Mlynov community (kehilla) was a Rav Ackerman from Trovits. Shmuel Mandelkern also mentions (p. 211) visiting with an Ackerman family in Trovits when he was fund raising to send Yosi-Yaakov to the Land of Israel. It is unknown whether these Ackerman families are related. – HS

8. August 1, 1941. – HBF

9. Sitting shiva describes the observance of Jewish mourning practices following the death of a family member. Kaddish refers to the prayer of sanctification said when a parent or other close family members dies. – H

[Page 418]

In Memory

by Rachel Givon (Shapovnik)[1] [Kibbutz] Givat Brenner

Translated and edited by Howard I. Schwartz, PhD with Hanina Epstein

When I left my parents and my brother Levi and Mlynov, I knew that I was leaving my parents while they were suffering ... and in an extremely hard financial situation. All sorts of thoughts were running around in my head, and nothing was clear or certain. I didn't know if I would be able to help my family or whether I would see them again.

Only one thing was clear to me. I was leaving and making aliyah to the Land [of Israel], to a kibbutz and fulfilment. The idea and the way, which the [youth] movement instilled, was being realized, and in my heart there was hope, great hope, that my brother Levi would soon be able to make aliya to the Land and together we would be able to help [our] parents.

* * *

I remember how you promised me, that you would do everything in your power to make aliyah to the Land [of Israel] and together we would also be able to bring our parents. We had great hopes together, my brother. How I wanted to see you my brother ...

But it was only an accident that separated us — and only I was saved.

* * *

I also remember Batya Mohel[2] at the time I left her. [She was] the first one who came to our house to assist and encourage. I totally loved talking with her, because Batya had an understanding and personal relationship to every one of us, and whoever was in close to her knew her personable nature.

Translator's and editor's footnotes:

1. Rachel Givon (born Rachel Shapovnik) appears in Zionist youth group photos on pages 8 and 460. Her son appears as one of the fallen soldiers in Israel, p. 455. The rest of her family perished in the ghetto liquidation. Her father was Abisch Schapovnik (1882–1942) and her mother Chaia (Fridman). In this essay, and in Yad Vashem records, a brother Levi is mentioned who was born in about 1911. The Mlynov martyr list, p. 439, also includes a brother Moshe (born in about 1926 according to Yad Vashem records) and a sister Brakha. For unknown reasons, Brakha does not appear in Yad Vashem records.
2. Batya Mohel was a sister of Yaakov Mohel who contributed "A Murdered Family," p. 410–412, with additional notes there about the family.

My Family

by Chaya Moses-Fisher[1] Kvutzat Kinneret

Translated and edited by Howard I. Schwartz, PhD with Hanina Epstein

I am Chaya Moses, daughter of Meir and Toibeh Fisher

I made aliyah to the Land [of Israel] in 1946 and lived in Kvutzat Kineret. I am one of the survivors of the terrible Shoah. I don't know how the miracle happened — in those days there were many Jews who were much more experienced; but they did not escape the claws of the German murderer and their Ukrainian collaborators.

At that time, I was a 14-year-old girl.

[Page 419]

We were a large family with children, and each child found his [and her] place on the learning bench, in the morning in the Polish school, and in the afternoon with Esther the teacher (the "melamedke") [the smart woman], which is what they called her in the town. She taught us Hebrew. Our home had a general educational atmosphere.

Our father, peace be with him, was the source of this atmosphere. My mother passed away when I was still a small girl and my mother's sister, my aunt Devorah, raised us and also her own children. My father was a progressive man loved by all people. He had an amazing character, always ready to help another, always a smile on his face with a cigarette in his mouth.

A refrain we heard all the time from Father was: "When my kids grow up, I will not send them one by one to the Land of Israel — we will make aliyah as a whole family." And other sayings of Father stick in my memory from the day I left home during the Shoah. "If you stay alive, remember that you came from a Jewish home."

* * *

When I was captured by the Ukrainian police, they questioned me up and down about whether I was a Jewish girl. This was a very difficult interrogation. There was one Ukrainian policeman there, who once worked in our flour mill ... He suggested to his policeman friends that he should interrogate me by himself and if he came to the conclusion that I was a Jewish girl — he would shoot me with his own hands. When I entered to a special room with him, he turned to me and said, "Hold your position (in other words, that you are a Christian). They don't have any proof. But don't return to your previous place, because they will come there to interrogate; leave that place ..."

That same "righteous man" wiped out the Wurtzel family[2] even though he also worked with them.

And these are the names of my beloved ones who were murdered by the Nazis murderers and Ukrainians. Meir, my father; Devorah my aunt; Shmuel, Tzvi,[3] Fruma, Shlomo, Moshe, Chanoch, Efraim. I was fortunate to make aliyah and to create a family. We have two sons and a daughter. They should read and know what Amalek did to us.

Translator's and editor's footnotes:

1. Chaya Fisher was the daughter of Meir and Tobe Fisher. The names of her siblings who perished are given below in this essay. Her father Meir was the brother of Shimon Fisher, the father of contributors: Yaffa Dayagi (Sheindel Fisher) "Home and Youth Movement in Mlynov," pp. 247–250, Bella/Baila Halevi Fisher, p. 422 and Miriam Fisher p. 423 whose short essays follow.

2. There was a large Wurtzel (alt. spelling Vortsel) family in Mervits, descendants of Doovid and Meerel Wurtzel, the patriarch and matriarch of this family. The reference here probably refers to the descendants of their son Zelig Ulinik Wurtzel who married Sooreh Gruber. Of their seven children, only their daughter Pessia (Wurtzel) Steinberg survived with her husband Getzel and son Zelig. A photo of several of her brothers who perished appears on page 475. The other two children of Doovid and Meerel Wurtzel each had large families. Their daughter Sorke Wurtzel married Isaac Flaisher / Fleisher and they migrated to Philadelphia where they settled and had family. Doovid and Meerel's daughter, Ronya Leah Wurtzel, married Yankel Volf Katz. Five of their nine children emigrated to the US and Canada: Louis Katz, David Katz, Maurice Katz and Bessie (Katz) Schnider settled in Saskatchewan, Canada. Their daughter Bella (Katz) Cohen settled in the suburbs of Boston Massachusetts.

3. Appears as "Herschel," which is the equivalent of the Hebrew Tzvi, in the list of Mlynov martyrs.

[Page 420]

To the Memory of My Beloved Ones – My Parents, My Brother and My Sisters

by Baila Holtzeker,[1] [Kibbutz Negba]

Translated and edited by Howard I. Schwartz, PhD with Hanina Epstein

It was September 1939. The evening of Rosh Hashanah. All the Jews were getting ready to go to the synagogue — when they came to tell us to leave town. That day complete bedlam ruled. We fled to the villages without taking anything at all, and after a number of days we returned, because the Russians[2] entered the town which was quickly converted to a place of shelter for several hundred. On the streets of the town one could hear, in addition to Yiddish, — Polish, Russian, and so forth. It was possible to recognize the [origin] of refugees through their exchange of words. From all ends of the land came many Jews, young and old, religiously observant and secular. The common goal was to continue living. The Jews who came to Mlynov regarded it as a temporary shelter until the fury would subside. People who lost their land from under their feet and lost a sense of self-confidence were transformed into refugees not only in the eyes of others, but in their own eyes …

* * *

A few memories and youthful experiences bound up in this town, in which the best years of our youth were spent. We will remember all the Jews of the town burdened with suffering, working people, who struggled all the days of the week, who fought hard for their living to enjoy the coming Sabbath with serenity and love. We will remember the scenery of our town, its forests, the wide market, the narrow alleys, which we strolled on long nights from one end to the other; We will remember the effervescent youth. But the heart does not give us peace or rest, when all that is precious is remembered. Parents, brothers, sisters, grandfather, uncles, aunts, and cousins.

Father and Mother were good hearted and sentimental. They were calm, serene, and loving towards their children. I remember when the Soviets were still in our town, they entered our house and demanded the keys to our store. With trembling hands, father gave them everything. When they left, Father was sad and worried and said "How can I support my 12 children?" And he added, "It is good that Tzipporah[3] is in the Land of Israel."

On that day, trouble and suffering began. Immediately, they conscripted Nahman[4] and Avraham to the Red Army. My eldest brother, David, began looking for work and he worked as a clerk; my sister Miriam also worked as a clerk. In the identity papers of Father, they wrote the number 11[5] — if only they sent him to Siberia, perhaps one of them would have remained alive. But Father paid a great deal of money and remained in Mlynov and was buried in Mlynov. To me he said, "You have an opportunity to flee, do it; what depends on me, I will try [to do])."

[Page 421]

I caused my parents, brothers and sisters no small amount of grief. More than once I attempted to flee via the window in the middle of the night when it was snowing, because I was not a citizen.[6] The day I received notification to come to Rovno, to pick up my authorization to make aliyah, father went with me. A full day I was in examination and father wandered around outside. It is not possible to forget the love and devotion of parents.

We were 12 children. The parents, my adult sister, Tevel, and her husband Baruch, and their children Soma, Miriam, Batya, Liubaleh — were buried together in the mass grave in Mlynov. My brothers Avraham and Menashe[7] fell in the Red Army. My brother Chuna — his school friend killed him because he liked my brother's boots. My older brother David was killed in the forests,[8] and my younger brother Henochal [Hanoch][9] passed through the seven gates of Hell. More than once he struggled with the master of death and prevailed, [and experienced] wandering, refugee camps, Cyprus.[10] He was killed in [Kibbutz] Negba on the 16th of year 5708, May 25, 1948 [just days after Israel declared Independence on May 14 1948].

And though his experiences were deeply unbearable [before his death], he was not heartbroken; he was tough in body [with the will] to continue to live and create.

* * *

And these are words of Menachem K., who eulogized Hanoch, my brother who was killed in Negba:

Who in essence was Hanoch, did we know him as he should be known? How did we relate to him? Hanoch, Hanoch, only recently you arrived. In Negba, you joined us, and became beloved to us. You made friends, good friends. You wanted to erase completely your past; to forget the forests of Ukraine, the hiding places among the Christians, the [displaced persons] camps on impure German lands. To forget Cyprus, the boredom and the atrophy of captivity. To start a new life with us, among us. To go with head held high. To work in a carpentry shop which you adored. To learn all that you missed during the War years. You were happy that you were close to your sisters, together with them in one kibbutz. How enthusiastic you were traveling to the Negev to establish a new outpost. And in Nir Am, when we built a hospital, you loved the work, doing all of it, even that which you didn't know. You did the right thing, Hanoch. You were a talented young man, with a strong will. You wanted to learn much in a short time with your efforts. You also learned to play the flute. Playing music was your passion. And how you could dance! You put all the boys to shame. You were comfortable joking around, and you were also happy and cheerful. How can I forget you, beloved Hanoch! I am your longest-term acquaintance. From Germany, when we got involved in our [youth group] movement activities until your last days — I was full of admiration for you. A few times I saw despair and feelings of inferiority mix confusingly together inside you. But the cloak of despair dissolved quickly at the first happy word. This, Hanoch, is how you appear in my memory, my precious Hanoch! Will I no longer be able to glue boards together with you, play volleyball, sing, and horse around? Must I really believe that the shell injured you, as your hand pressed the Bren [light machine gun] – Is it true [you are gone]?

Translator's and editor's footnotes:

1.   Information about Baila and her siblings was provided by her granddaughter, Lior Wildikan. Baila (Holtzeker) Wildikan / Vildikan (alt. spellings Holzeker, Goldseker) (1914–1990) was the daughter of Yaakov Holtzeker and his wife Risia. Baila's grandfather was Moshe Holtzeker, one of the five original Holtzeker brothers to arrive in Mlynov. Yaakov and Risia had twelve children and a photo of the family appears on page 245. Baila's older sister Tzipporah (1910–1986) made aliyah in 1933. Baila was also involved in the Zionist Youth Group Hashomer Hatzair and went for her training (hachsharah) in Czestochowa. For a variety of reasons including the outbreak of War, she was prevented from making aliyah. In 1941, she made the dangerous journey from Moscow to Odessa on the Black Sea and then took a rickety boat to Turkey. She continued by land to Syria and Lebanon until she finally made her way into the Land of Israel. She joined her sister, Tzipporah, in the new Kibbutz Negba. There she married and had two children, Sare and Hanoch, the latter named for her brother who is commemorated below.

2.   They fled when Germany attacked Poland afraid that the Germans would reach Mlynov. But Mlynov was in the section of Poland allocated to Russia under the non-aggression treaty that Russia and Germany had concluded before the start of the war. A similar story is told by Asher Teitelman in the book length account of his life on the Mlynov website.

3.   Tzipporah (1910-1986) was the second eldest child in the family. She made aliyah in 1933. Her group went first to Rishon LeTzion and then Givat Keren Kayemet where she worked in orchards and fruit packing. She later moved to Kibbutz Negba. Tzipporah and her longtime boyfriend Meir never had children.

4.   Nahman Holtzeker made it to Palestine or Israel at some point and took the name Krul Levi. His daughter Chaia David (earlier surnames: Levi / Holtzeker) contributed records to the Yad Vashem database.

5.   The number 11 identified a person as an asocial or nonproductive element of society, according to the earlier essay by Yosef Litvak, who discusses the beginning of the Soviet Occupation, p. 285.

6.   Perhaps Baila had not been given identity papers because she was involved in the Zionist youth group and was seen as a Communist, as described in the essay by Yosef Litvak about the Soviet occupation, pp. 284.

7.   In the testimony by Fania (Mandelkern) Bernstein, "In the Valley of the Shadow of Death," p. 291, Menashe is recalled visiting bunkers, and Avraham is recalled securing rifles before the liquidation.

8.   The two testimonies by Fania (Mandelkern) and David Bernstein mentions David in the bunkers, pp. 294, 300.

9.   See a photo of Hanoch (1930–1948) p. 455 and mention of Hanoch being among the returnees to Mlynov, p. 310.

10.   In his attempt to reach Palestine, he was taken to the British internment camps in Cyprus. As indicated in the commemoration that follows by Yosef Tomer, Hanoch serendipitously ended up traveling on the same ship of illegal immigrants with the Teitelman family and was with them when they were turned away from landing in Palestine and forced to Cyprus.

[Page 422]

In Memory

Bella Halevi[1] (from the Fisher line), Tel Yosef

Translated and edited by Howard I. Schwartz, PhD with Hanina Epstein

When I close my eyes, I see all of them: My dear parents, my brother and my sisters, my uncles and aunts and cousins, good neighbors, and the entire town. They all are standing alive before me ...

It is February 2, 1936, when I made aliyah to the Land [of Israel]. I departed with great hope that I would be fortunate to see them in the Land, but they were not able to come to us and live in the State of Israel.

Seven am in the morning. Heavy snow descends. I left Mlynov in a wagon towards Dubno to the train station. It is hard to describe how crowded it was with people on all sides offering farewell blessings.

My father and Binyamin came with me, of blessed memory. Mother and the other children stayed in the doorway of the house without uttering a sound. Only grandmother said, "I envy you; you are young and going to the Land of Israel. Is it possible I too will be fortunate to see the Holy Land?"

I will list those were not so fortunate: My dear father Shimon Fisher, my mother Tova; my brother[s] Tzvi,[2] Binyamin and Shmuel; my sisters Ester and Breindela, and grandmother from my mother's side, Pesia Giz.[3]

I recall the Gertnich family, who were cousins.[4] Yeshayahu[5] and Perel and their children: Moshe, Rachel, Faiga, Miriam and Yaakov. And also, the brother of Yeshayahu: Yitzhak. Their children, Moshe, Hershel and Miriam.

I recall Faiga Margulis with Chaim Neinstein.[6] Faiga was exceptionally talented in theatrical plays and music.

We will not forget them forever.

Translator's and editor's footnotes:

1. The daughter of Shimon Fisher and Toba (Guz). She was a sister of contributor Miriam Fisher (see next reflection) and Yafa Dayagi (Sheindel Fisher) who contributed the essay on "Home and the Youth Movement," p. 247–250 with additional notes on the family there.
2. Also called Herschel in some records, the equivalent Yiddish name.
3. Also called Pesia "Goz" or "Guz" in Yad Vashem records. She was born in Mervits in 1873 to Shmuel and Sheindel. Her husband was Asher and her maiden name was Fridman.
4. Alternative spelling Gertnikh. The Hebrew term "keruv" used here can mean "relatives" or "friends." But in the next short reflection by this writer's sister, the Gertnich family is identified as relatives on their mother's side. This probably explains why a photo of the Gertnich cousins is placed on page 248 in the middle of the essay written by their other sister, Yafa Dayagi (Sheindel Fisher). Another photo of the Gernich family appears on page 458.
5. Yeshayahu Gertnich (b. 1878) and Yitzhak Gernich (b. 1883) were sons of Mordekhai Gertnich. In Yad Vashem records, Yeshayahu is called a rabbi and Yitzhak's son is described as a schohet in Demydivka.

6.   Chaim Neinstein appears with his wife in the photo on page 457 with additional notes. According to Yad Vashem records, Chaim's wife was Reizl Margulis.

On the Altar of Our Birthplace

Yosef [Teitelman] Tomer,[1] Ramat Gan

Translated and edited by Howard I. Schwartz, PhD with Hanina Epstein

Hanoch[2] son of Yaakov and Risia Holtzeker, was one of the youngest of Shoah survivors in Mlynov. The youngest son of one of the large families with many children in the town.

After the liberation from the yoke of the Nazis, the remnants of survivors began to gather in Mlynov and he was among them. Being alone, he took shelter in the company of our family during the time we stayed in Mlynov.

Our paths diverged when we left Mlynov on the way to the Land [of Israel]. Hanoch stayed with a group of children [going] to Poland and Germany while our path was via the refugee camps in Austria. After the vicissitudes of the long journey, we met again serendipitously and this time on a boat of illegal immigrants on our way to the Land [of Israel]. Hanoch was happy in being fortunate finally to realize his dream, to join the remnants of his family, his sisters, in Kibbutz Negba.

Indeed, Hanoch was able to reach his sisters before the outbreak of the War of Liberation [i.e., Israel's War of Independence] but the happiness did not last long. He participated in the defense of Negba, a heroic position in the War of Liberation, and there he fell. May his memory be a blessing.

Translator's and editor's footnotes:

1.   Yosef (Teitelman) Tomer was the son of Nahum and Rachel Teitelman, both contributors to this volume. He survived with his siblings Shifra and Asher, who is also a contributor. See their essays for additional notes on the Teitelman's survival story.
2.   Hanoch was the brother of Baila Holtzeker who commemorated Hanoch's story on the previous page.

[Page 423]

To the Memory of a Family

Miriam Fisher,[1] Haifa

Translated and edited by Howard I. Schwartz, PhD with Hanina Epstein

In 1936, I made aliyah to the Land [of Israel]. I left my beloved family — father, mother, grandmother, brothers and sisters. I left all my cousins and acquaintances. I will never forget the separation from my parents and the other members of the family; the dream and hope were that, after a time, we would be able to bring the family [to the Land of Israel] and all of us would be together.

I held onto this dream for three years until the outbreak of the War. In the beginning there was some consolation that our area had not fallen into German hands, but as is known, in 1941, all was cut off, the German murderers conquered our area among others. We knew that significant troubles were afflicting our Jewish brethren, but it never occurred to us that they would kill them all. We regretfully deluded ourselves. We were under illusions until the end of the War, when the horrible truth became known to us.

[Page 424]

In our home, there were twelve people — only my sister Rachel remained alive. Tremendous pain accompanies us in our lives and our lips cannot adequately express our feelings.

I commemorate the names of our beloved ones who died at the hands of the Nazi murders with the help of the Ukrainians.

Father – Shimon; Mother – Teuvah; Grandmother – Pesia; My brother – Tzvi; his wife Rikvah, from the Goldseker family, two small girls, Chisha and Freida; my brother – Binyamin; my brother – Shmuel; my sister – Ester; my sister – Breindelah;

After the liberation I began searching for my sister Rachel, who remained alive. She was already far from Mlynov and I meanwhile had moved from the place I was living. Until finally I received a letter from her.

* * *

Father loved agriculture, and in particular caring for fruit trees. Where we lived, he would plant seedlings and successfully nurture them. During my first years in the Land, I was in an agricultural farm with many fruit trees. It was a dream of mine that my father would come to the Land and be able to dedicate himself to fruit trees. But we didn't succeed in bringing them. They did not realize what we did: to see the fall of the Germans and the establishment of the State of Israel.

* * *

I will remember my uncle Meir, my father's brother, with his family. One daughter remained living, today in Kevutsah Kineret.[2] My father's sister, my aunt Silvi, was murdered at the German hands. Her husband died fighting in the WWI. Her only son remained alive, joined the Russian army, and is now in the Land [of Israel] in Kefar Hasidim.

There was a family of cousins on my mother's side, the Gertnich family,[3] none of whom remained alive.

The mother Perel; the daughters: Rachel, married with children; Faiga with her family; Maikah was also apparently married, the sons Moshe with his family; Yaakov. The father died before the War.

Translator's and editor's footnotes:

1. Miriam Fisher's tribute follows that of her sister, Bella HaLevi. See additional notes about the family on the preceding page.

2. Meir's daughter, Chaya Moses-Fisher contributed the tribute, "My Family," pp. 418–419.
3. See notes on page 422 about the Gertnich family.

[Page 425]

In Memory of the Minyan of Jews in Peremilowka [Peremylivka][1]

Tova Wahrman [Grinshpun],[2] Ramat Gan

Translated and edited by Howard I. Schwartz, PhD with Hanina Epstein

Near Mlynov was a village called Peremilowka [today, Peremylivka] — the village of my birthplace and where I lived – and which had a minyan of [ten] Jews and no more. Even though it was about 15 km [9 mi] from Mlynov to our village, there prevailed — among the minyan of its Jews who lived among the gentiles — a very vibrant Jewish life. A handful of children from two families,[3] who dwelled in the village, studied in school in the nearby Mlynov, and this minyan which included all the Jews of the village, was tied in all its "arteries" to the Jews of Mlynov. Among this small group of Jews, the family Grinsphun[4] stood out in warm comforting hospitality for all Jews who happened to be visiting in the village. Especially acquaintances and many relatives of the family came to stay as guests under the roof of this family during the summer days. To this day, I am reminded of many different people who are located today all over Israel and the blessed and nice days and nights that they spent with this family in the heart of nature by the village and the warm and maternal atmosphere. It is worth noting, in particular, that during festivals and special Jewish occasions, Jews from nearby villages would gather in the house of R. Yoel-Leib Grinsphun and his wife Rachel, of blessed memory, to pray and pour out their hearts before the Creator of the World. The Torah reader was the homeowner himself and he would take care of inviting the prayer leader from nearby Mlynov who would go before the [Torah] ark. Especially, the prayer leader R. Eliezer Mohel,[5] of blessed memory, is remembered positively — a reverent Jew who avoided sin and was also a sage who was knowledgeable in Torah. From time to time, Jewish beggars appeared in the village, among them entire families from the nearby district. Most of them visited the home of the Grinsphun family, who received them with open arms, fed them until they were satiated, and even filled their sack with provisions for the way and clothes and even donations of money were not withheld.

* * *

There are many memories of the village and our home from those distant days, but buried deep in my memory is a terrible and very shocking incident which occurred on the eve of Yom Kippur — during the prayer "Kol Nidre"[6] in our home — with the outbreak of the War between Poland and Germany in the year 1939.

It was a stormy fall night; an angry rain fell intermittently. Suddenly — when all were absorbed in the holy prayer on the holy day — a large, blinding light shone through the window. For a moment I imagined that the whole area was going up in flames of fire. And suddenly against the background of this sea of flames, were outlines of hunched figures wet from the rain.

[Page 426]

They arrived quickly and drew close to the house. The prayer "Kol Nidre" stopped, and the eyes of all the people praying turned towards the arrivals — Jews from Mlynov, Dubno and other nearby towns.

Terrifying news was on the mouth of these Jews. "The German Nazis set fire to the village Boskovitz,[7] a village that is 7 km [4 mi] from our village. Bedlam and fear prevailed among all the people praying at the sight of the terrified Jews and, upon hearing the news on their lips, most broke out in bitter crying. But the homeowner, R. Yoel-Leib, didn't lose his wits and tried to calm the uproar. His voice reverberated loudly: "Quiet down Jews, continue praying – and the Holy One, via the merit of Yom Kippur, will save us from the hands of the murderers." And truly, the words of R. Leib came from the depths of his heart, calmed the atmosphere and the prayer continued until the end.

At the end of the prayer, the daughters of the homeowner, Rivka, of blessed memory, and the youngest of the daughters, Gitla, may she live a long life, prepared the home to absorb the broken refugees. There were many rooms in the house and every family was limited to a particular room and individuals found a spot in the attic of the threshing floor, a storage place for fodder. They spread sheets and bedding — and everyone slept from much exhaustion.

At the break of dawn, quiet prevailed in this area and it became clear that the number of refugees who arrived was greater than thirty souls. But anxiety consumed the heart of the refugees and members of the household — the Germans are liable to reach our house and God forbid they wipe out all of us. But the homeowner, R. Yoel-Leib, again calmed down the refugees and called for those gathered to exercise self-control and believe that God would protect us from all evil. Most of the refugees stayed in my parents' home for more than two weeks. The firstborn son, and also Avraham and Rivkah Mohel packed their bundles and headed towards the Russian border; Batya Matz traveled to Zurnov,[8] a village that was about 20 km from Peremylivka. My sister, Bat Sheva, of blessed memory lived there. Other young people left our house and returned to their homes and the elderly remained in our house until the fury passed.

After a number of days, we heard from a distance of several kilometers a clatter of tanks of the Red Army — and immediately the rumors spread that the Russians had reached our village. The Polish and Ukrainian neighbors, infamous anti-Semites, were perplexed at the sight of the Russian soldiers, who were generally hated by them. These neighbors began to flow to my father, who was very popular with them, in spite of his Judaism, to ask their questions "Have the Russians come to destroy us or to save us?"– – –

Let this be a candle of tribute to the very small community of only a few Jews among the other millions of Polish Jews, who once were but are no longer. – – –

Translator's and editor's footnotes:

1. Likely Peremylivka, Ukraine today which is consistent with the distance from Mlynov described in this essay. The town is east and slightly north of Mlynov on current maps.
2. The spelling of the author's married name in English is uncertain. Tova Wharman (alt. spelling Varman, Warman) was born Tova Grinshpan [alt. spellings Grenspun and Greenspun]. Her father, Yoel-Lieb Grinsphan, described in this essay, is listed among the martyrs (p. 446) of Peremylivka. Her mother, Rachel, died before the war. Her siblings Yitzhak and Bat-Sheva, who both perished, are in the photo of the young people by the Count's waterfall on page 203. In addition to Tova in Israel, a son was living in Israel, another son Micael was in France, and a daughter Mania in Canada.
3. The family of this writer, the Grinsphans, and the Burshtein family.
4. The writer's family described in previous note.

5.   Eliezer Mohel was a shochet who came to Mlynov in the 1920s. A photo of Mohel children and their home is on p. 411 with an essay by his son Yitzhak Mohel with additional notes.

6.   Kol Nidrei ("All Vows") is an emotional declaration that ushers in the Day of Atonement by declaring all vows taken in the future to be void and asking for the sins of the congregation to be forgiven.

7.   Uncertain. Perhaps Bohushivka or an odd spelling of Varkovychi.

8.   Perhaps Zhorniv or Zhornyshche, both about the appropriate distance.

[Page 427]

A Ballad of a Tree

by Dvora Mohel-Yarnitsky,[1] Natanya [Israel]

Translated from the Yiddish by Hannah B. Fischthal, PhD

Edited by Howard I. Schwartz, PhD

On the right—our community,
On the left—Yosel Meir's[2] mill
Rising on green lawns,
Full of yellow flowers.

Reaching until the monument on a mountain
Is the highway made of large, pointy stones;
That is the Mlynov-Mervits road—
Every one of us remembers it.

And after that a straight road.
On the right—standing even now in front of my eyes—
The old tree, with two large branches
Like arms stretched out to the sky. . .

Children, we heard a legend about the tree,
That an important holy man was killed there,
And before his death he stretched out his arms to the sky—
And he was buried on that very place.

And we were told: a miracle happened—
A tree grew, the holy man not forgotten.[3]
Childishly naive, I believed this completely,
And it never troubled me to look at the tree.

Waking up in my memory are
Carefree, happy, summer days

From those times, from my childhood years,
In the shadow of the old tree on Mervits Way

When I went into the fields with my girlfriends,
(Feygele Grinberg,[4] z"l, beloved of many)
Radiant, happy among golden ears of corn—
Picking blue flowers and red poppies,

[Page 428]

And when we became tired and sweaty,
We found rest in its shadow.
Sometimes we were also protected from sudden rain
Under branches of our old friend, the tree.

***

On the road from Mlynov-Mervits
Graves were dug
Opposite our old friend, the tree.
Parents and brothers buried alive.

And you, old tree, what can you tell
Of that black day now distant?
Although you did not stand indifferently-cold
When murderers without hearts murdered. . .

You, sole witness, heard all, saw
How the unhappy ones were led to their deaths;
You heard their lamenting screams of woe
And you saw their blood—redder than red.

You saw the last struggles
Of life, bleeding--young, full of love,
To quickly aged, gray, old people,
Of mothers and fathers, broken, tired.

Did you break your branch arms
In great pain? -- --
Did your yellow-green leaf-eyes burn
Or look with cataracts on their deaths? . . .

Did your friend-storm
Carry into all the corners of the world their "Shema Yisroel"--
East, west, north, south—
And stop somewhere?

[Page 429]

Did the golden fields, wheat and corn,
Swallow their wild grief
In those distant days during Tishrei,
On both sides of the Mlynov-Mervits way?

* * *

Old friend of my youth, see,
I cannot even go to their grave,
Nor pour out my grief and pain
Nor bring their flowers on stone.

May then birds on your branches say kaddish[5]
And be guardians over the holy place.
May autumn winds carry your golden leaves
To cover the mass grave of murdered Mlynov-Mervits.

During field work next to [the home of] Chotka Bialkosky[6]

Translator's and editor's footnotes:

1.   Dvora (1914–1987) was one of the Mohel children who escaped in 1941 when the Germans attacked the Russian held parts of Ukraine. She appears in the photo in this volume on p. 411 sitting in front of the Mohel home and is in the photo of Hashomer Hatzair on page 73. For further background on the Mohel family, see the notes on "My Lamentation," pp. 408–409, and the essay "A Murdered Family," pp. 410-412, by her brother, Yitzhak Mohel. Dvora's escape is also in the book length story of her brother Yehuda Mohel's life. Yehuda who was with his wife in Demydivka fled east with a wagon he had procured and met up with his brother Yitzhak, sisters Chaika and Dvorah in Dubno. They piled into the wagon and all fled east. – HS

2.   "Yosel Meir's" refers to Yosel Gelberg son of Meir, who was the owner of the mill. – HS

3.   Alluding to "The Tree That Resembled a Menorah," p. 31, that grew on the spot where the Karliner rabbi, Rabbi Aaron II of Karlin died between Mlynov and Mervits. – HS

4.   Perhaps a younger relative of Faiga Rakhel Grinberg who was born in Mlynov. Yad Vashem records submitted by a son, Shlomo, indicate Faiga Rakhel Grinberg's family name was Ingerman and her father's name was David. Faige Rakhel married Moshe Grinberg who was from Demydivka and she lived there with him during the war. They had four children. She was 60 when she died in 1942 in Demydivka suggesting she had been born in 1882, thus apparently too old to be a friend of Dvorah Mohel. – HS

5.   Kaddish refers to the prayer of sanctification said when a parent or other close family members dies. – HS

6.   Zelig (Gerry) Steinberg, who was born in Mervits, recalls his parents telling him this was a photo of workers on a gentile farm near Mlynov and some of the workers were Jewish. The gentile named Bialkosky is also mentioned in the essay by Sore Shichman-Vinokur, "Nazi Crimes in the Volyn Neighborhood," p. 449 in whose home she secured a position as a maid and who helped her entire family escape the ghetto.

The man kneeling on the left is Fishel Kleinberg, a brother-in-law of Gerry's mother, Pesia (Wurtzel / Vortzel) Steinberg. Standing next to Fishel is his daughter, name unknown. Records submitted to Yad Vashem by Mendel Teitelman, another contributor to this volume, indicates that Fishel was born in Berestechko, Poland in 1895 to Azriel and Leah Kleinberg and was a flourmill owner and married to Gitel (Wurtzel)

According to a family tree documented by Naomi Tomer in the Teitelman family, Fishel's mother's maiden name was Leah Gruber and she was one of the daughters of Mordechai Gruber. That would make Fishel and Gitel, first cousins (their mothers Leah and Sooreh were sisters. According to the same family tree, Fishel was one of eight Kleinberg children: Ester, Moshe, Sarah, Etel, Rahel, Eta, Freida, and Fishel and all perished. – HS

[Page 431]

List of Mlynov Martyrs

Translated and edited by Howard I. Schwartz, PhD

Note to the Reader: Page numbers in these tables refer to original book page numbers

		Editor's notes
GORDON	The Rav Gordon Rabbi Yehuda, Chantzia, the rabbi's wife. [Children] Beracha, Chaya, Devorah (Hershel, Moshe and Tova are in the United States).	See photo of Rav Gordon, p. 453, his surviving children, p. 280. On his being an early victim, p. 289, 315 and 384. On his candidacy for chief rabbi, p. 18.
ALEF א		
EISENBERG	Abraham, Chaya Sarah his wife.	
EINGBER	David, Rachel his wife; their children: Bayta and Nehumkeh	alt. spelling Inberg
ISKIEWICZ	Eliezer, Feiga his wife; children: Shlomo (disappeared after the Battle of Stalingrad), Sheindel, Raizel (their son Moshe survived and is Israel)	alt. spelling Isakovich, photos 464, 477, essay by son Moshe p. 88

ISKIEWICZ	Nute and his daughter Zlata, perished in Lutzk (the daughter Sarah is in Israel, the son Avigdor is in Canada).	alt. spelling Isakovich, family photo 465
EPSTEIN	Micael, Belumah his wife and his family.	

BET ב

BREVDA	Yaakov, born in Baranowicze (Baranovichi), Leah his wife from the line of Manis Zutelman; children: Sonny, Yonah, Reuven.	
BLINDER	Berel, Gitel [née Hachman / Hochman], Yeshayahu, Devorah, Ribah, Eta, Efraim (fortunate to have a daughter in Israel-Miriam)	Daughter Miriam Barber Blinder contributed essay, p. 370.
BARTNIK	Yitzhak, Bat-Sheva his wife; [children] David and Sarah.	
BERGER	Tuvia, Miriam his wife, Raisel (fortunate that their son Pinchas is in Israel and their daughter Liza is in Brazil).	Liza's essay, p. 347.
BERGER	Tzvi, his wife Chaya; daughter Bailah; son Nuta Bir, son Yosef.	
BERGER	Shraga (Faivel), Matil [nee Shulman] his wife, Batia their daughter.	See photos p. 75 and 76 and essay there.
BERGER	Zeev son of R. Nuta-Bir, Golda his wife, Chana their daughter. They were fortunate that their son Aharon [Harari] and daughter Shoshana [Rosa Chizik] are living in Israel; Yisrael [Sol], Kalman [Karl] are in the United States and Shaul in Russia.	See photo p. 76 and essay there.
BERGER	Chaim	See photo of his daughter, 479, host of Zionist leader, p. 69
BERMAN	Meir, Etil his wife and their son Avraham (dentist)	
BLINDER	David, his wife Brendl	
BURSHTEIN	Shmuel, Leah-ke [née Braker] his wife from the village Peremilowka (today Peremylivka)	alt. spelling Bursztejn, Burshtein Bursztejn); see essay p. 425 on Jews from Peremylivka
BRONSHTEIN	Beracha, daughter of R' Moshe Aharon.	

BRENER	Pesach, Sarah his wife, Hersh-Ber, Yukal, Menachem, Malkah.
BER	Tzvi, Sarah his wife; Nisel, Devorah, Batya.
BER	Shmuel, his wife Chaya.

[Page 432]

Editor's notes

GIMEL ג

GOLISUK	Hannah [née Schuchman] widow, daughter Tzvia, son Shmuel, Yosef, Mutia, Buka, Pesiah.	See photo p. 462 and essay of grandson, Yechiel Sherman, p. 415.
GOLDSEKER	Chatzil from Boremel.	alt. spelling Holtzeker;
GOLDSEKER	Yaakov; Risia his wife; David, Avraham, Menashe, Chana, Mindel, Batya, Liba, Hanoch (their son Nahman and their daughter Baila and Tzipporah are in Israel).	alt. spelling Holtzeker; See family photo p. 225, and essay by daughter Baila, p. 420
GOLDSEKER	Risel daughter of R. Yoel, widow of Pinhas Holtzeker; Tovah her dauhgter, Avraham her son.	alt. spelling Holtzeker; husband Pinhas was probably son of Moshe Holtzeker. It is possible she was a first cousin, daughter of Yoel Holtzeker, one of the five original brothers who arrived in Mlynov.
GOLDSEKER	Kalman, Dinah his wife.	alt. spelling Holtzeker; Kalman was son of Hirsch Holtzeker, the eldest of the five Holtzeker brothers to come to Mlynov. See mention of Dina Holtzeker on page 284.
GOLDSEKER	Yaakov son of R. Hirsch [Holtzeker], Rachel his wife; [children]: Avraham, Batia, and Tzviya.	alt. spelling Holtzeker; son of Hirsch Holtzeker, the eldest of the five Holtzeker brothers to come to Mlynov. See prank on Hirsch's home and daughters on page 134.
GOLDSEKER	Avraham son of Aisik [and Perel daughter of Itzi Shochet], his [Avraham's] wife	alt. spelling Holtzeker; Avraham's father, Aisik, is also the son of Hirsch Holtzeker. A photo of Avraham's brother, Aba, appears p. 479 with additional notes.
GOLDSEKER	Yona-Reuven, his wife.	alt. spelling Holtzeker; Yona-Reuven was grandon of Yankel Holtzeker, one of the

		original five brothers to come to Mlynov, and son of Moshe Holtzeker. He was brother of contributor Yankel Goldseker, p. 226
GOLDSEKER	Moshe, son of R. Yoel [Holtzeker], Liubah his wife; from Greater Dubno; daughter Batya, sister Chaya, Mordechai (the son Yoel is in Russia).	alt. spelling Holtzeker; his father Yoel Holtzeker was the youngest of the five brothers who came to Mlynov. See photo on page 472
GOLDSEKER	Yehoshua son of R. Moshe Nahman's, Sima his wife, Avraham, Batya, Nahman from the line of Yosef Gelberg (Pinhas his son lives in Russia).	alt. spelling Holtzeker; Yehoshua, called "Yeshea" in the Baltimore Goldseker tree, was son of Moshe Holtzeker, one of the original five brothers to come to Mlynov. HIs photo with two of his children appears on page 472 and a photo of his sister Rivkah Fisher, daughter of Moshe Nahman's, p. 470, with notes there on possible meaning of "Moshe Nahman's." See also Golda Shek below who is also daughter of "Moshe Nahman's"
GOLDSEKER	Nahum, Henia his wife daughter of R. Nahman from Dobryatyn; Nahman, Yaakov, Avraham, Feiga, Pinya (Rafael their son is in America [=Ralph Golz]).	alt. spelling Holtzeker; Nahum was son of Moshe Holtzeker, second eldest of the original five brothers who came to Mlynov.
GOLDSEKER	Ben-Tzion, Ester-Mania his wife from the line of Pesach Feldman from Boremel; Pesach was killed in the Russian military. Avraham, Rivkah.	alt. spelling Holtzeker; Ben-Tzion (called Bene in the Baltimore Goldseker tree) was also son of Moshe Holtzeker, one of the original five brothers. The son Avraham helped lead resistance in the ghetto, p. 291.
GOLDSEKER	Aisik (Yitzhak), Perel his wife daughter of R. Itzi Shohet, of blessed memory; Aba their son.	alt. spelling Holtzeker; Aisik is the son of Hirsch Holtzeker. Perel's father, R. Itzi Shohet is listed as a father of Pesach Gelman and that may be the family name. Their son Aba's photo, p. 479.
GOLDSEKER	Moshe Goldseker, son of R. Yaakov [Holtzeker], Tova [Kaliner or Kline] his wife from the line of R. Reuven Ostriyever [=Ostrog]; Yona Reuven, Chaya Baila, Rivkah, Genendel, Pesia (they are forunate their sons Avraham and Yaakov are living in Israel].	This Moshe is son of Yankel/Yaakov Holtzeker, one of the original five Holtzeker brothers who came to Mlynov. Moshe's son, also Yaakov, is a contributor to this volume, p. 226.
GOLDSEKER	Yehoshua son of Yaakov [Holtzeker], Tova his wife; Avraham, Rivkah, and	Yehoshua (also known in Baltimore as Yeshea) is brother of Moshe in previous entry and son of Yankel/Yaakov, one of

	Beracha. (They are fortunate their daughter Pesie is living in Israel).	the original five brothers to come to Mlynov. His wife Tova was born in Berestechko.
GOLDSEKER	R. Moshe Nahman's (or Nahmanis).	Identified as Moshe, one the five original Holtzeker brothers who came to Mlynov. Father of Yehoshua further above; See noteson page 470 note 4 on possible meaning of Nahman's.

[Page 433]

		Editor's notes
GITELMAN	Moshe, his wife Sal, Yehudit, their daughter.	
GELBERG	Yitzhak, Chava his wife from the line of Koshuk from Mizoch; their children Meir, Tovah.	
GELBERG	Gershon, Beilah his wife, from the line of R. Moshe Nahman's Holtzeker; Yitzhak, Pinchas, Avraham, Ester	Gershon was a son of Yossel / Yosef Gelberg, the owner of the mill, listed next.
GELBERG	Yosef, Sara Devorah his wife, her sister Leah, their grandson Meir (a stem of this family is in Israel: grandson of Yitzhak ben Avraham.	Yosef/Yossel was owner of the mill in town and one of the community leaders, as discussed on pages 53-59, and His grandson Yitzhak Gelberg survived. See the Gelberg family story.
GELMAN	Avraham, Machla [nee Kline/Kaliner] his wife, daughter of R. Reuven, of blessed memory, from Ostryiiv [probably Oztriiv].	According to Yad Vashem records submitted by this volume contributor, Bat Sheva Ben Eliyahu, who identifies herself as a cousin, Avraham was son of Micael and Batia Gelman. Four of their daughters also perished. Avraham's wife, Machla (born Kline/Kaliner), was a sister Toba (Gelman) Holtzeker, mother of Yaakov Holtzeker, who contributed to this volume, p. 226.
GELMAN	R. Pesach, shochet, and scribe of Torah scrolls and mezuzahs, son of R. Itzi the shochet, of blessed memory.	Unknown if related to the Pesach Gelman from Mervits who died before WWII and is in family photo on p. 473 with son Eliyahu Gelman, who contributed essay on p. 253.
GALPERIN	Yisrael, Rivkah his wife, daughter of R. Mordechai Meir Shretzel; Chaika, Elka,	alt. spelling Halperin; Yisrael was son of Lipa Halperin and Pessia (née Hirsch) Their son Lipa contributed several essays

	Batya, Avraham (their son Lipa passed away in Israel).	to this volume. Photos of Lipa, his mother Rivkah, and grandfather Modechai Meir appear on page 458 of this volume. Some of Lipa's other sibligns appear in the photo on 248.
GALPERIN	Tziupah, widow of Yosef Halperin; Dov her son-in-law, Hadi his wife. Rosi (Benyamin is in Russia, Shaul is in the United States).	alt. spelling Halperin; Yosef/Yosel Halperin was a brother of Yisrael (previous entry). Shaul / Saul Halpern survived the Shoah and migrated to Canada.
GELER	Asher, Rachel his wife, his daughter Machla, his daughter Ester.	
GELER	Moshe, Chaya his wife.	
GELER	Moshe, his wife Rusya, his son Zeev, his daughter Machla.	
GELER RABINOVITZ	Mania, Gitel Geler Rabinovit[ch] (their brother Berel Rabinovitch in Israel)	alt. spelling Rabinovitch. Berel Rabinovitch, who survived the Shoah, appears in the photo on page 467 and is described as the initiator of the commemoration by survivors, p. 309, and appears in the photo of that ceremony, p. 313.
GELER RABINOVITZ	Chaim, Devorah [Berger] his wife; Shlomo a son Tzisl a daughter.	alt. spelling Rabinovitch; A photo of Chaim is on page 478. His wife Devorah was daughter of Yosef and Malka Berger.
GANTZMAN	R. David, shochet and inspector, Malkah his wife; Yaakov, and Mani.	
GRUBER	Tova and her son Hanich and her daughter-in-law, Frieda	Tova was married to Yisrael Gruber who was son of Mordechai Gruber and his wife Perel. Hanich (also Hanoch) and his brother, Shmuel, was in the bunkers outside Mlynov as described on pages 293–294.
GRUBER	Shmuel, Charna [Goldseker] his wife and the children, Shimon and Yisrael	Shmuel and Chara in photo p. 471. Shmuel Gruber was son of Yisrael Gruber and Tova. His wife Charna (Goldseker) was daughter of Shimon Goldseker. They were in the bunkers as described in the tetimonies on pp. 291, 294, 298, 301
GERTNIKH	Moshe son of R. Yitzhak (shochet in Dymidivka) and his wife.	alt. spelling Gertnich. Son of Yitzhak below.

GERTNIKH	Moshe, son of R. Mordechai Shmuel, of blessed memory, Sarah his wife daughter of R . Mordechai-Meir Shrentzel, of blessed memory; Shmuel [and] Faiga (their son Kuftzia is in Israel)	alt. spelling Gertnich. A photo of the family p. 458. "Kuftzia" refers to Yosef (Gernich) Ganon who contributed to this volume, p. 261.
GERTNIKH	Yitzhak (Yitzhak they called glazier), Tehila, his wife native of Trovits, their son Moshe, shochet and examiner in Demydivka, and Tzvi.	alt. spelling Gertnich; Brother of previous Moshe and Yeshayahu below.
GERTNIKH	Yeshayahu, son of R Mordechai Shmuel, of blessed memory, Peril his wife; Moshe their son and his family perished in Trochenbrod; Rachel perished in Mizoch (Nimrober); Feiga, Meikah.	alt. spelling Gertnich; Brother of Yitzhak and Moshe above.

[Page 434]

		Editor's notes
GRINTZVEIG	Zisia, Rivka [Schwartz] his wife.	Rivka was a niece of the Schwartz brothers who came to Baltimore. Her parents name are unknown.
GRINIG	Naaca, daughter of R. Yosel Shraga Kreitzer, the Cohen; Tzvi.	
GRIN	Avraham, Kutzka Rachel his wife, daughter of R. Moshe Melamed and their family.	See family photos, p. 465 with additional notes.
GRIN	Devorah, wife of R. Leib Grin; their children: Hershel, Leibish	See family photos, p. 465 with additional notes.
GRIN	Ben-Tzion, Zalta his wife, son Arieh and his family.	See family photos, p. 465 with additional notes.
GRINSPHAN	Aba, Pesia his wife; Moshe and Yaakov.	alt. spelling Grinsphun, Grenspun, Greenspun.
GRINSPHAN	Ben-Tzion, Dina his wife; Eliezer, Binyamin, Moshe, Miriam.	alt. spelling Grinsphun, Grenspun, Greenspun. This Binyamin or the one listed in Mervits list of martyrs is in the family photo on page 473
GRINSPHAN	Yaakov, Mishkah his wife, and her family.	alt. spelling Grinsphun, Grenspun, Greenspun.
GRINSPHAN	Gisiah, wideo of R Moshe from Mervits, daughter Nechmakah.	alt. spelling Grinsphun, Grenspun, Greenspun.

DALET ד

no entries

HE ה

HOFSHTEIN	Pesakh.	
HESHIS	Yitzhak, Chatzil his wife; Penina, Eliyahu.	
HELMAN	Liba and her family; daughter Manis Zutelman.	There was a Zutelman family living in Mervits. Two of them came to Baltimore: Paul Zutelman became Paul Shulman. His brother became Frank Settleman. They appear in a photo on page 203.
HERBSMAN	Hershel son of R. Moshe Melamed, Sara his wife; Beilah, Liba, Yosil, Yisrael.	Brother of Kurtza, wife of Avraham Grin above.

VAV ו

WULACH	Moshe, son of Natan HaCohen and his wife; Lohakah their mother, Tzvia, Menunah.	alt. spelling Vulach; Brother Jacob Wallace who migrated to Chicago.
WULACH	David, son of Natan HaCohen and his wife.	alt. spelling Vulach; Brother of Jacob Wallace who migrated to Chicago.
VEIZER	Elka, Eta their daughter, Nekhama their daughter. (Their daughter Polyah and son Eliyahu are in Israel).	alt. spelling Veiter, Weitzer.
VEINSHTOK	Zinia [Zina, Zanvil], Roza his wife; the mother Sonia, wife of R. Moshe Apoteker from Mlinov (their daughter Dina [Klingbeil] is in Israel)	alt. spelling Wajnsztok, Vinshtok; A David Apithoker appears in the photo on page 203.
VINOKUR	Baila from the line of Slivka Morkovitch, widow most of her years, no children; wiped out in town and by Dubna.	
VEINER	Abrahamkeh from the Stolin Hasids; he was single.	Mentioned as a unique character and teacher, p. 265. His photo is on page 256.
VEINER	Asher (who is called Kreimer [lame]) Batya his wife	

| VEINER | Beracha, wife of R. Itzi, Chana Brendel's [mother?] (son and daughter Hannah and Yehuda and their families made aliyah from Russia to Israel). | alt. spelling Weiner. |
| VEINER | Yaakov (from the town of Uzhynets', Breindl his wife; Avraham and Feiga (their son Sunny in Israel) | alt. spelling Weiner; Feiga's photo 480, Sunny's contribution 251 and notes there. |

[Page 435]

		Editor's notes
WEISFELD	Khana (nee Gruber), their children Eliyahu and Perel (their son Meir is in the United States)	alt. spelling Veisfeld; Khana Gruber was daughter of Mordechai and Perel Gruber.
WURTZEL	Yosef son of R. Zelig Ulynik from Mervits, Rachel his wife daughter of R. Chaim Berger; Mordechai, Zelig, Gedaliah, Yaakov.	alt. spelling Vortzel; Photo on page 474.

ZAYIN ז

ZAZULI	Eliyahu, his wife and his family.	
ZEID	Yaakov and his wife.	
ZIDER	Zalman, his wife Zaldah, their sons Zelig and Avraham-Aharon.	Photo of family p. 463. Zelig assigned to Jewish police, p. 288
ZIDER	Moshe, Freida his wife (from Mervits), Avraham, Zelig their sons.	Photo of family p. 463. Zelig assigned to Jewish police, p. 288

CHET ח

KHEIM	Yudel and his wife.	alt. spelling Chaim.
[KHAIT]	Aharon Asher from the Stolin Hasids, Bat-Sheva his wife, Perel, her husband Yitzhak [Lejbel], Golda, Batya, Faiga and their children.	alt. spelling Chayat; Briefly mentioned among Stolin Hasids in synagogue p. 313.
KHINKES	Tzvi-Zeev, Ester his wife (the midwife) from Trovits their son Shaul, lived in Boremel.	
HACHMAN	Leib, his wife [Rochel] and his family.	alt. spelling Hochman, Hechman;

The daughter, Tama (Hachman) Fineberg, the youngest of six children, survived and gave testimony for the Shoah Foundation. She was first cousin of Miriam Barber (née Blinder) who contributed the essay on page 370.

TET ט

TEITELBAUM	Binyamin, Rivkah his wife from the Khinkes line; Yitzhak their son and Silka their daughter.	alt. spelling Tatelbaum, Teitelbaum, Ferteybaum; Binyamin was an uncle (the mother's brother) of Sylvia Barditch-Goldberg, a contributor to this volume. Binyamin's father was the Stolin Hasid called Yitskhok Staroste, described by Sylvia p. 80. Binyamin is mentioned in Sylvia's essay, "Visiting My Grandparents," p. 266. Another brother Harry (Usher) Teitelbaum came to Baltimore in 1911. Photo 498.
TEITELBAUM	Yosef, Hudel [Edel Halperin] his wife; Chaim their son, Silka their daughter (their son Zeev is in Israel)	
TEITELMAN	Fishel and Shlomo (two sons of Nahum and Rachel Teitelman, who live in Israel).	Photo page 479, story page 322.
TEITELMAN	R. Anshel from the Trisk Hasids; Zelda [Paken] his wife; Asher their son (their son Moshe [Tamari] the writer lives in Israel)	Anshel was brother of Nahum Teitelman, contributor to this volume. Photo of family on p. 468. Anshel's son, Moshe Tamari contributed essays, p. 30 and 32.
TILIMZEIGER	Ezra, Chana his wife; Chaim.	
TILIMZEIGER	Yeshayhu and his wife	A son of Ezra and Chana.
TESLER	Yitzhak, son of Yaakov, his wife; their sister Belimah	Brother of survivor Liba Tesler. Photos on page 478.
TESLER	Yaakov, Belumah his wife; Peretz, Hinda, and Yitzhak.	Father of Yitzhak and Liba. See prior note.

YOD י

YENUBAR	Moshe and his wife Reiziah.

406

YITZHAK	son-in-law of R. Moshe Nahman's, Tsvia [Holtzeker] his wife.	Yitzhak is likely a first name. Moshe Nahman's is believed to be Moshe Holtzeker, one of the five Holtzeker brothers who came to Mlinov.

KAF כ

KATZ	Avraham, his wife Pesia, daughter of Chuna-Gershon, and their son Yaakov.	I think she is daughter of Chuna Gershon because there is no semicolon after her name.
KATZ	Zanvil, Beracha his wife; their sons: Tzvi, Arieh, Moshe, Avraham and their wives.	Photo of family p. 476. Daughter Bayta survived with husband Yitzhak Mohel. Batya is in window in Mohel house photo, p. 411.
KATZ	Shmuel.	

LAMED ל

LIBERMAN	Aisik, Etil [Nekunchinik] his wife, and their son Rafael.	
LIBERMAN	Yehezkiel, Doba his wife; Rachel their daughter (their son Herschel in Canada)	

[Page 436]

		Editor's notes
LIBERMAN	Mordechai, Beracha [Gruber] his wife; Asher, Eidel, Rivkah, Miriam, Chaya.	
LITVAK	Mordechai [Motel], his wife [Devora] Riba, daughter of R. Yehuda Leib Lamdan, of blessed memory, (this son Yosef and daughter Pepe [Penina] in Israel)	Photos on page 454. Son Yosef contributed several essays, pp. 53, 283, 413.
LOMAR	Mendel	
LERNER	Perel	Perhaps related to family of Joseph Lerner who migrated to Baltimore.

MEM מ

MEIRZON	Aba, Pesia his wife, and their daughter.	alt. spelling Meyerson Meierzon; Pesia (Grin) Meirzon in photo on page 464.
MORER	Shlomo, Buzia his wife from the line of Zacryhu	alt. spelling
MOHEL	R. Eliezer, local kosher slaughterer and examiner, Chana-Leah his wife (from the line of Kaszkiet from Lutsk), Batya, Buziah, Yenta (their children Yudel, Yaakov, Devora and Chaya are in Israel)	alt. spelling Mojel, Moyel; A photo of the Mohel home and daughters on p. 410 with essay by son Yitzhak Mohel, 408 and 410, and essay by daughter, Dvora, p. 427.
MUCHNIK	Shmuel and his wife.	
MANDELKERN	Rivkah, Moshe Mendelkern, Shoshana Mandelkern (their children Pesach, Eliyahu, Feiga and Yehudit, are in Israel).	alt. spelling Mandelkoren; A photo of Rivka and daughters p. 472. See survival testimony of daughters Yehudit and Fania, 287–314.
MANDELKERN	Chaika, Yenta and Aisik.	
MANDELKERN	Nechama, Perel and Moshe (their children Shmuel and Yitzhak are in Israel, Yosef died in Israel; Perel also has a son in Israel, Gershon).	alt. spelling Mandelkoren; Son Shmuel contributed essays, 116 and 208. Photo of Yosef, p. 448–449
MESSINGER	Eliezer, Malka his wife; David and Chanoch (the sons Shmuel [Victor] and Koppel [Karl] in the United States).	Koppel is mentioned on pages 303 and 331.
MEREN	Ben-Tzion (local prayer leader), Miriam [Holtzeker] his wife, Seril their daughter (their son Baruch-Yitzhak is in America).	A photo of family on p. 456. Son Baruch contributed several essays including a profile of his father, 255. His mother, Miriam, was daughter of Hirsch Holtzeker, the eldest of five Holtzeker brothers who came to Mlynov.

NUN נ

NUDEL	Pesach, his wife Zimel; daughter Sarah and her family; daughter Freida.	
NUDLER	Khaykl (Khakly they call schneider [tailor]), Bat-Sheva his wife; Avraham, Yaakov, Elka, and Feiga.	A story about Khaykl's gramophone on p. 199. Khaykl's father's name is Shloyme and thus appears to be the brother of Aaron Nudler, father of survivors Helen (Nudler) Fixler and her

		brothers, Harold and Morris who were in the Red Army.
NUDLER	Matityahu, Chaika his wife from the Mandelkern line and their family, Mendel, Feiga.	
NEYTER	Sarah (Moshe and his wife live in Russia); Chaim his brother-in-law and his wife.	alt. spelling Neiter. Moshe Neyter met in woods by cousin, p. 374. Sarah wrote to Yitzhak Mohel on fate of his family, p. 410.
NEPOMISHCHI	Yaakov, Malka his wife, daughter of R. [Efraim] Fischel Teitelman; Asher the son, Chaya the daughter.	alt. spelling Neformnishi; Malka was a sister of Nahum Teitelman, a contributor to this volume.
NEKUNCHINIK	Gershon, Hashkah-Nehama his wife; Rafael their son, Golda and Chaya.	alt. spelling Nakonechnyuk, Nakonechnik Nakonechnik; See pages 290, 300, photo p. 467
NEKUNCHINIK	Shlomo, Ester his wife (from Trovits, her sister is in Israel); Yaakov, Yitzchak, Rivkah	alt. spelling Nakonechnyuk, Nakonechnik Nakonechnik; Shlomo's photo, p. 467, mentioned as head of the youth organizing resistance to Nazis, p. 290.

[Page 437]

		Editor's notes
SAMECH ס		
SEGEL	Mekhael, Khasia his wife.	
AYIN ע		
EPEL	Yitzhak, Henia his wife.	alt. spelling Apil
PE פ		
POLISHUK	Ben-Tzion and his wife.	alt. spelling Polashuk; Father of Masha Eatta Polishuk who married Aaron Nudler. Grandchildren Helen (Nudler) Fixler, Harold and Morris Nudler survived and settled in Canada and Oakland. Son Pesach (Ellis) migrated to Baltimore.

PICHNIUK	Chaim, his wife Rivka	alt. spelling Pikhniuk Pikhnyuk; Chaim was son of Yaakov and Gitel below.
PICHNIUK	Yaakov Yukel, Gitel, Zelig, Avraham, Rachel, Faiga (Sonia and Bat Sheva in Russia).	alt. spelling Pikhniuk Pikhnyuk; Yaakov is listed as a hair dresser in Yad Vashem records. Gitel's family name was Retzepter. Zelig in photo in uniform, p. 455, is also listed as one of the youth organizing resistance, p. 290.
PICHNIUK	Pesia	alt. spelling Pikhniuk Pikhnyuk; Pesia was mother of Yaakov.
FISHMAN	Tzvi	
FISHMAN	David and his wife.	David Fishman was the brother of contributor, Moshe Fishman, p. 60.
FISHMAN	Kalman, Chaya his wife, their sons, Pesach, David, Shimon, Asher Yosel	Kalman was the son of David Fishman.
FISHER	Meir, his wife Tovah; Shmuel, Herschel, Fruma, Moshe, Shlomo, Ephraim, Hanoch. (daughter Chaya is in Israel on Kibbutz Kinneret.	alt. spelling, Fischer. Meir is brother of Shimon below. Daughter Chaya Moses-Fisher contributed essay on her family, p. 418.
FISHER	Tzvi, son of Shimon from the village Mantyn; Rivkah his wife, from the line of Moshe Nahmanis Holtzeker.	alt. spelling, Fischer. Photo on page 470. Tzvi was the brother of contributors, Yafa Dayagi, p. 247, Bella HaLevi (Fisher), p. 422 and Miriam Fisher, p. 423. Rikvah's father Moshe Nahmanis is believed to be Moshe Holtzeker, one of the five Holtzeker brothers who came to Mlynov.
FISHER	Shimon, from Mantyn, Tobiah [Tova Guz] his wife; Binyamin, Ester, Shmuel, Breindl, Tzvi and the grandmother Pesia Guz (the sisters Miriam, Baila, Sheindel, and Rachel are in Israel).	Shimon and Toba were parents of contributors, Yafa Dayagi, p. 247, Bella HaLevi (Fisher), p. 422 and Miriam Fisher, p. 423. Photo on page. 470
FELTZHANDLER	Chaim Moshe, his wife Freida.	
FRIDMAN	Nahum, son of R. Yosil Shichnas from Mervits (the educator of most of the children of Mlynov, Mervits and Lutzk in Torah and haskalah (enlightenment), Pesia his wife, Yosef and Yisrael.	alt. spelling Friedman, Freedman; Possible photo of "Israel Freedman" p. 481

| PREZIMENT | Yaakov, Chana-Gitel [Gelberg/Goldberg] his wife; Leibish and their daughters. | Photo of family p. 473. Chana was daughter of Labish Gelberg and Eta Leah (Schuchman). |

TZADIK צ

| TZWIK | Eta Mendel Brendel | |
| CHIZIK | Mordechai the great tacher who instilled Torah in the youth of our town, Rut his wife, Liuba his daughter. The son Meir is in a Kibbutz. Moshe, of blessed memory, is also in a kibbutz. | alt. spelling Tzizik; A photo of the family appears on p. 457. Liuba helped organize resistance, p. 290. Moshe married Mlynov born Rosa Berger in Palestine and later died from a poisonous snake bite. |

QOF ק

| KULISZ | Peisach, Baila his wife from the Holtzeker line; Yenti his sister, Chana the mother. Beracha Kulisz-Feinbilt was eliminated in Vurkovitz with her husband Yankel, their son Ben-Tzion, their daughters, Golda, Henia, Moshe and Shimon. | alt. spelling Kulish, Collidge; Photo of Baila and her family p. 471. Baila was daughter of Shimon Goldseker, one of the five Holtzeker brothers to come to Mlynov. Several of her siblings migrated to Baltimore before and after WWI including contributor Eta (Goldseker) Fishman, p. 495. |

[Page 438]

		Editor's notes
KWASGALTER	Meir, Sheintzi [Gonik], his wife, Chaim["Monik"] their son. They were fortunate their daughter Rachel Rabinovitz is in Israel)	Photo of Meir and Shentzi, p. 466. Meir was son of Faivel and Leah and was a pharmacist. On Meir as reservist in self-defense, post WWI, p. 131, Meir and Rachel in the bunkers, p. 294 and Rachel wandering, 367.
KWASGALTER	Menachem Mendel son of R. Yankil, Babtzia his wife, Zalta (Grin), Chaim.	Menachem Mendel was son of Yaakov and Rivkah, next. Photo of daughter Zlata, p. 465.
KWASGALTER	Yaakov, his wife Rivkah.	
KOLTUN	Arieh, his wife and his family.	

KOLTUN	Moshe, his wife Bat-Sheva from the Klaper family line, their sons Leibish, Avraham, Batya, Baurch.	
KUGAL	Pesach, Feiga his wife and their son Moshe.	alt. spelling Kugal, Kogul.
KUGAL	Baruch, Sara his wife.	alt. spelling Kugal, Kogul; See photo 481.
KEVITSKI	Yaakov, his wife Gitel.	
KIPERGLUZ	Chaim Yitzhak, Sarah his wife from the line of Marnitz from Trovits; Chaia their daughter, Yoseleh, their son, Beracha the mother (they were fortune their daughter Rachel Kleinman /Kleeman is in Israel).	alt. spelling Kiperglaz; Chaim Yitzhak was the son of Yosel Kipergluz and Brakha (Gelman). He is mentioned working on a Zionist scheme with Shmuel Mandelkern, p. 216, as a president of the community (p. 90), as synagogue sexton (p. 21), and later part of the Judenrat, p. 288. Rachel made aliya, p. 74, Daughter Chaia was arrested as a suspected Community after the Nazi occupation (287). A tribute to Chaia, p. 414.
KLEPATCH	Moshe Yosef son of Rabi Yitzhak Leib from Smordva, of blessed memory, Sorke [Kaliner] his wife; Gitel, Reuven, Chana, Yitzhak Leib, Batya, Mutel.	Tribute to and photo of Chana Klepatch, p. 277.
KLAPER	Reuven, his wife Sarah.	Reuven was son of Ben-Tzion and Tsherna.
KLAPER	Mendel and his wife.	Mendel was son of Ben-Tzion and Tsherna and a blacksmith.
KLAPER	Avraham and his wife; Mendel and Reuven; Tsherna the mother	Avraham's mother Tsherna had married Ben-Tzion Klaper. Avraham married Khaia Shteinkroin.
KRITZER	Yerachmiel, Doba his wife [sic]from the Mandelkern line; Yosef, Shimon, Tova.	
KRITZER	Avraham, Chaya his wife, Eta, Yosef.	
KRITZER	Fishel, Beracha his wife; Tova, Freida, Sharga, Rivka.	
KREIMER	Shlomo (Shlomo, the lame shoemaker) Teltzi his wife; Yaakov, Rachel, Aharon, Shmuel.	Shmuel Mandelkern takes shelter in Shlomo's shoemaking shop for protection, p. 138.

RESH ר

RIVITZ	Avraham and Rivkah [Klaper] his wife; Bat-Sheva, Rachtzi, Yaakov.	alt. spelling Ribitz, Ribic, Riwic; Avraham is son of Chana and Nute below.
RIVITZ	Chana [nee Braker], widow of R. Nute Rivitz; Freidel the daughter (the daughter Bat-Sheva is in Israel).	alt. spelling Ribitz, Ribic, Riwic; Photo of family, p. 70. The daughter Bat-Sheva contributed essay p. 253. Mother Chana was from Klevan.
RIVITZ	Yitzhak and his wife Basia [Gonik]; Roni and Nute.	alt. spelling Ribitz, Ribic, Riwic; A son of Nute. Basia was born in Luck.
RIVITZ	Mutil and Devora [Kuperman] his wife from Berestechko; Pesie, Naami, Zalteka, Nute.	alt. spelling Ribitz, Ribic, Riwic; Mutil also called Mordechai was a son of Chana and Nute.
REIS	Yosef, Brakha his wife, Henia.	alt. spelling Rajs, Reiz; Contributor Bat-Sheva, p. 253, identifies family as relatives in Yad Vashem records.
REIS	Tzvi, his wife and their son.	alt. spelling Rajs, Reiz.Tzvi also called Hershel was a son of Yosef and Brakha. Contributor Bat-Sheva, p. 253, identifies family as relatives in Yad Vashem records. Perhaps young man called "Rayz" (same spelling) in photo on p. 227 is son or father.

[Page 439]

		Editor's notes

SHIN ש

| SHAPOVNIK | Abisch, Chaia [Fridman] his wife; their sons Levi and Moshe, and their daughter Berakha (their daughter Rachel is in Israel). | alt. spelling Schapownik; Abisch is described as beggar in humorous story about his horse and self-defense after WWI, p. 132. Daughter Rachel Shapovnik wrote tribute, p. 418, and appears in Zionist Youth group photo, p. 71, 8, 460. She changed her name to Givol in Israel. Her son was killed in combat in Israel, p. 453. |
| SHEFER | Mordechai, Malka his wife, from the Aisik Holtzeker line. | alt. spelling Shafir; Malka's grandfather was Hirsch Holtzeker, one of the five Holtzeker brothers to come to Mlynov. Her mother was Perel "Shochet" |

		daughter of Itzi (and possibly from the Gelman family line). Her brother Aba appears in photo, p. 479 bottom row, with additional notes.
SHEFER	Zecharia, his wife Golda; Chanoch and Yitzhak.	alt. spelling Shafir.
SHULMAN	Shlomo, Chantzi his wife, daughter of R. Yehuda Leib Lamdan, of blessed memory.	Chantzi was sister of the poet Yitzhak Lamdan and Devorah Litvak. Shlomo possibly a relative of Tzodik Shulman who migrated to Baltimore.
SCHWARTZ	Beinish, Faiga his wife from the line of R. Yitzchak Rabinovitch; Sheintzi his mother, their daughter Nusia.	alt. spelling Svartz; A photo of Beinish on p. 478 with notes. A nephew of the Schwartz brothers who came to Baltimore. Beinish is likely the brother of Rivkah (Schwartz) Grintzveig listed earlier.
SCHEINBOIM	Yehoshua, Elka his wife from the Rabinovitz line.	
SHIPER	Yaakov, Reizel his wife and his family.	alt. spelling Shafir.
SHIPER	Natan, son of R. Itzi Ulinik, Gitel his wife, daughter of R. Shlomo Zalman, of blessed memory, from Mervits.	Itzi Ulinik was wagon driver for Sylvia Barditch's trip to Mlynov, p. 266. Natan was in bunkers with others, p. 294 with additional notes. Asher Teitelman in book length account, *Happy is the Man*, reports Natan was killed when they left the bunkers looking for food, pp. 33-35.
SCHECHMAN	Batya, widow of R. Noach Moshe Schechman; Meir and Mordecia.	alt. spelling Schuchman, Shakhman; (Not to be confused with Shichman family from Mervits.) Batya recalled by descendants as "Feiga." Tribute to Noach Moshe on page 246. Noach Moshe was son of Gershon Schuchman and Shaindel Bluma. His siblings included Eta Leah (Schuchman) Goldberg, Joseph Schuchman, and Hanah (Schuchman) Golisuk. Son Shlomo survived and settled in Baltimore.
SCHECHMAN	Aharon Shmuel, Pesia his wife; Leah, Belumah.	Son of Batya (Feiga) and Noach Moshe.
SCHECHMAN	Shimon, Pesia his wife; Sarah their daughter.	Son of Batya (Feiga) and Noach Moshe.

SCHECHMAN	Yitzhak, Pesia his wife; their daughter Sheindel.	Son of Batya (Feiga) and Noach Moshe.
SCHECHMAN	Ben-Tzion (the carpenter) Tuviah his wife; Yaakov.	Son of Batya (Feiga) and Noach Moshe.
SHLAYEN	Yaakov, Sarah his wife; Moshe, Henia.	
SHNEIDER	Ben-Tzion and Shoshana his wife.	
SHNEIDMAN	Aharon Yitzhak, Sarake his wife; Zalman, Chaya, Ester, Leib, Taamah, Ana.	
SHKOLNIK	Chaim, Liba his wife from the line of R. Yoel Holtzeker Avraham; Chasia, Eliyahu, Batya.	Liba is daughter of Yoel Holtzeker, youngest of the five Holtzeker brothers to come to Mlynov. It is unclear why the name "Avraham" appears after Holtzeker unless he is one of the sons and punctuation is incorrect.
SHEK	Mendel, Golda his wife from the line of Moshe Nahmanis [Holtzeker]; Yehiel, Devora, Rivka, (Eliyahu in America)	Golda's father, Moshe Nahmanis, is believed to be Moshe Holtzeker one of the five brothers who came to Mlynov. See notes under Holtzeker. Son Avraham Shek p. 302 was mentioned with a Czech farmer in testimony, p. 302.
SHIKREV	Moshe and his wife; Yechiel, Devorah, Rivkah (Eliyahu in America).	alt. spelling Shakrov, Shekrev; Yechiel Sherman mentions him as a shoemaker when he returns to Mlynov for the last time, p. 345.
SHTEINSHNEID	David from the line of Moshe Gontchear. And his family (their daughter Pola [Grinstein] is in Israel).	alt. spelling Shteynshnayd; Pola Grinstein was living in Los Angeles when she submitted records to Yad Vashem about her mother Tzirla or Gizla.
SCHREIBER	Binyamin, Hinda his wife; Yitzhak, Soni.	
SHERMAN	Moshe, his wife Etil [Golisuk]; Sheindel, Yosef (they were fortunate their sons Yechiel and Ezra are in Israel).	Photos of Moshe and Etel p. 462 with notes. Son Yechiel contributed essays, pp. 344 and 415.

[Page 441]

List of Mervits (Muravica) Martyrs

Translated and edited by Howard I. Schwartz, PhD

		Editor's notes
ALEF א		
UPSTEIN	Eliezer and his wife Sheindel.	alt. spelling Opshteyn, Ephsteyn Epstein; Parents of Hanina Upstein, listed next. Eliezer, also called Leazar, was son of Eli Moshe. Leazar dedicated the ark in the synagogue, p. 176. Mentioned as one of the large families in Mervits, p. 256.
UPSTEIN	Hanina, his wife Raizel [Kugel] and the family.	alt. spelling Ephsteyn, Epstein; Hanina was son of Eliezer and Sheindel. He married Raizel Kugel, daughter of Abisch and Mali Kugal. They had five children. Their son, Yitzhak, was conscripted and survived WWII in Siberia. After the War, he returned, found the rest of his family had perished. He subsequently married Mlynov survivor, Bunia Steinberg, who contributed an essay p. 387. Their son, Charles (Hanina) Epstein, is the Hebrew co-translator of this volume.
EIZEN	Feibish, his wife Chaia-Leah and their children.	
AVRAHAM	[last name unknown] son-in-law of Yenta Shikhman, his wife Rachel and their children.	See below for Yenta (Teitelman) Shichman. This son-in-law named Avraham is assumed to be the husband of her daughter Sheindl.
EPSHTEIN	Sima, her son Yitzhak, Mikhel and Yisrael, her daughter and family (the son Nechemiah)	alt. spelling Epstein, Opshteyn and Upstein.
EPSHTEIN	Hirsch, his wife Belumah, his son Yaakov, his son …	alt. spelling Epstein, Opshteyn and Upstein.

EPSHTEIN	Gershon, his wife Shifra.	alt. spelling Epstein, Opshteyn and Upstein; A Gershon Epshtein / Upstein appears in the photo on page 474 with two sisters with additional notes.
EPSHTEIN	Gershon (son Pesach), his wife Buni and his son.	alt. spelling Epstein, Opshteyn and Upstein. A Gershon Epshtein / Upstein appears in the photo on page 474 with two sisters with additional notes.

BET בּ

BERESTETZKI	Natan from Pian [perhaps Pyannye, Ukraine], his wife and her family.	
BLINDER	Yitzhak, his wife Pinia [Penina Neiter], her mother with her son-in-law Zelig Muravitsky.	Their daughter Bata Kapshik Blinder contributed A Child in the Storm, pp. 374–379 with additional notes there.

GIMEL ג

GRENSPUN	Motel [called Motel Tesler]	alt. spellings Gruenszpan, Grinshpun, Greenspun, Grenspun; Referred to as "Motel Tesler," he was married to Risha. He appears in a photo in old age with his sons family p. 473 with additional notes. Motel Tesler is remembered, p. 316, as the first to be killed by the Nazis on in the synagogue, on July 12, 1941. Granddaughter Sheindel (Grenspun) Steinberg was a survivor and married to contributor Mendel Steinberg, pp. 358–369.
GOLDENBERG	Zelig, his wife Chaia, their son and their daughter.	
GELMAN	Raizi, her daughter [Yente], her son-in-law Binyamin [Fleisher] and his wife Ester [Raizi's other daughter], and her family [with their three children: Lea, Perl and Hershel.]	A photo of the family on page 473 with additional notes. Raizi was married to Pesach Gelman who passed away before the Shoah. Their son Eliyahu, who made aliyah in 1938, describes his family in his contribution to this volume, p. 259.
GRENSPUN	Benyomin, his sons and daughters.	alt. spellings Gruenszpan, Grinshpun, Greenspun, Grenspun; A photo of the family on top of p. 473 with notes. Benyomin was son of "Motel Tesler"

		and Risha, and is listed in Yad Vashem records as an artist. This is the family of survivor Sheindel (Grenspun) who married Mendel Steinberg. Her mother is remembered as Sara Tepler from Trochenbrod.
GRUBER	Ben-Tzion, his wife Gitel [née Margulis], and their daughter Yehudit.	Photo of family on p. 457 with additional notes. Ben-Tzion was son of Yosef Moshe Gruber and Shifra (Teitelman), and brother of Sonia and Rachel Teitelman. A tribute to Ben-Tzion appears on page 241.
GELER	Yehuda-Leib, his wife and the family.	
GRUBER	Nute, his wife Miriam [Sherman], his son Yechiel, his daughter Shifra, his daughter…	Nute was grandson of Mordechai and Perel Gruber. His parents were Yosef Moshe Gruber and Shifra [Teitelman] and he was the brother of Sonia (Gruber) Teitelman and Rachel (Gruber) Teitelman, contributors to this volume.
GRUBER	Yaakov, his wife Wali (Shkrinikov]	Son of Mordechai and Perel Gruber and brother of Yosef Moshe Gruber.
GRENSPUN	Berel, his wife and the family.	
GRUBER	Meir, his wife Ester and the family.	

[Page 442]

		Editor's notes
VAV ℩		
WURTZEL	Meir, his wife Rachel and the family.	alt. spelling Vortsel; Meir was son of Zelig Ulinik Wurtzel and Sooreh Gruber. His paternal grandparents were Doovid and Meerel Wurtzel. His maternal grandparents were Mordechai and Perel Gruber. His sister was survivor Pessia (Wurtzel) who married Getzel Steinberg. A photo of his brothers, p. 475.
WURTZEL	Israel, his wife Eta, his daughters Perel and Leah, son Azriel	alt. spelling Vortsel; Israel or "Srulik" Wurtzel was brother of Meir (previous). His photo on p. 475.

| VINER | Shia, his wife and his son, his brother Mendel and his family. | Shia (Yeshayahu) and his brother Mendel were sons of Yohanan and Khaia Viner. Mendel was married to Bilha (Kaliner) and their son Yohanan was a child survivor. His mother sent him out of the ghetto and he survived in the forests as told in an interview published by the Zekelman Holocaust Center. |

CHET ח

| CHAIM | [last name not provided] son-in-law of Moshe-Issar, his wife Chaya-Ribah, and the family of his son-in-law Muti, his wife Sheindel and family. | |

TET ט

TEITELMAN	Freida and the family	Most of the Teitelmans descended from Asher Teitelman and his wife Sura Alta. They had six children. Freida married their son Mordechai Teitelman. According to descendants, Freida's original family name was Twerky which was changed to Horowitz to avoid conscription of a son. Freida and Mordechai had seven children. A tribute to her son Avraham-Shlomo appears on page 259. A photo two surviving children Sarah and Naftali Hertz ("Herzl") on p. 503 with additional notes. Another brother Meir also escaped but died fighting in the Russia Army. Child survivor Batya Kaptshik recalls meeting Freida and three daughters among the tombstones in the nearby cemetery where they were hiding, p. 374.
TEITELMAN	Yehoshua, his daughter Mania.	Yehoshua Teitelman was grandson of Asher Teitelman and Sura Alta. His parents were Abraham Teitelman and Rivka (Halperin).
TEITELMAN	Nahman, and his wife Sheindel	

TEITELMAN	Chaim-Meir, his son Mordechai with his wife Chava and their daughter, his son Avraham-Yaakov, his wife and their son.	Chaim Meir was also a son of Asher Teitelman and Sura Alta.
TEITELMAN	Avraham-Shlomo, his wife Belumah and the children, and his brother Yosef-Leibish.	Avraham Shlomo was son of Freida and Mordechai (see first Teitelman entry above). A tribute to him appears on page 259.
TEITELMAN	Yaakov-Yosef, his wife Sarah, their daughter Chana, their son Yisrael, and their daughters Sheindel and Luba.	Grandson of Asher Teitelman and Sura Alta. Son of Abraham Teitelman and Rivkah Halperin.
TEITELMAN	Shmuel, his wife Syrelle, and their daughters and their son.	Grandson of Asher Teitelman and Sura Alta. Shmuel was son of Freida and Mordechai (see Teitelman entry 1). He married his cousin Syrelle Teitelman.
TREPER	Feibish, his wife and his son.	

KAF כ

KATZ	Shmuel (the rav), his wife Tzinah, his son Moshe and his daughters.	Possibly the man remembered by descendants of Katz family as Shloimeh Katz, son of Yankel Volf Katz and Ronya Leah (Wurtzel). Of their nine children, five emigrated to Canada and the US.

LAMED ל

LAKRITZ	Baruch, his wife Ester [nee Finkelshtein] and the family.	alt. spelling Lakric. Baruch was the son of Yisrael and Stisi. Photo of Rachel Likritz on p. 479.
LIKHTER	Eta, her son Baruch and the family.	Possibly the mother and brother of Leye Veyner-Likhter, contributor to this volume, p. 382, with additional notes.
LITZMAN	Moshe, his wife Sima, his son Dov, his son Pesach and his wife Freida, and their daughters and families.	Photo of an Avigdor Litzman p. 479.

MEM מ

MARGULIS	Hersh-Leib and his sister Raisel.	alt. spelling Margolis. Photo of Hersh and Raisel, p. 457, with notes
MALER	Moshe, his wife and their children, and his son Mordechai and his wife with their daughter who was born in the ghetto.	alt. spelling Malar, Meiler.

NUN נ

NACHTELMAN	Yitzhak, his wife Rosi and the family.

[Page 443]

		Editor's notes
NUDLER	Yosef, his wife and his son; his sister Chana and her husband.	
NUDLER	Yeshayahu, his wife and the family.	
NEITER	Moti, his wife Chava and their daughters.	
NEITER	Shimon, his wife [Golda] and his sons.	Shimon was son of Yaakov and Yakhid. He was sister of Pnina (Neiter) who married a Blinder. Pnina's daughter, Batya, a child survivor, contributed an essay, pp. 374–379. Their sister Roza married Yankev Zelig Muravitsky.
NEITER	Hirsch, his son Dov and his daughter…	
NAISHTEIN	Chaim, his wife [Raisel Margulis] and his son, his sister Reizl Gonik, her husband and her son.	alt. spelling Neishtein, Naisztein. Photo of Chaim and family with notes p. 457.

PE פ

PARIZHAK	Shamai His wife Rachel, her mother Chaya, relative Faiga and her husband Motil.
FISHMAN	Yeshayahu, his wife and the family.
FEIN	Zeev, his wife Henia, his son…

FISTEL	Pinchas, his wife and the family.	See photo 479.
FLEISHER	Yechiel, his wife Hanah and hteir son daughter Yocheved, their son-in-law Aharon Kalir and his wife and the family.	Perhaps related to the family of Isaac Isadore Fleisher/Flaisher who married Sorke Wurtzel from Mervits and who both migrated to Philadelphia.
FLEISHER	Yusif and his fatmily	
FELDMAN	Yosef and his wife Neli and his brother Mordechai.	The parents of child survivor Aviva Feldman who was rescued by the Steinberg family. See account p. 395.
PERLUCK	Yudal, his wife and the family.	Perhaps related to the family of Gedaliah Preluck and his wife Golda who migrated to Rhode Island before WWI and whose last residence was Mervits.
FRIDMAN	Yeshayahu, a man from Dorohostai.	

QOF ק

KOBRIK	Devorah [née Gruber] and her huabnd Meir-Shmuel and the family.	alt. spelling Kibrik
KLEINBURD	Fishel, his wife Gitel, their daughters Sarah and Leah, his son Zelig.	alt. spelling Kleinberg. Appears to be man remembered as Fishel Kleinberg who married Gitel Wurtzel. Fishel's father was Azriel Kleinberg. His mother was Leah (Gruber), daughter of Mordechai and Perel Gruber. According to Teitelman family trees Fishe's wife Gitel was his first cousin (their mothers Rachel and Soorah were sisters).

RESH ר

ROSENBLAT	Yaako, his wife and his daughters.	
RAIKHMAN	Shmuel	alt. spelling Raichman.
RAIKHMAN	Nute, his wife Feiga, their sons Moshe and Mordechai, their daughters Mamtzi and Beracha, Yose andf Yusif and the family.	Photo of daughter Beracha on p. 478.

SHIN ש

[Page 444]

		Editor's notes
SVARTZ	David and the family.	alt. spelling Schwartz.
SVARTZ	Zeev his wife Mirel	alt. spelling Schwartz.
SHVARTZMAN	Moshe and his wife, his daughter Shifra, and his son.	
SHTEINSHNEID	Menashe [and wife Gitel], his daughter and his son Shlomo and his wife.	alt. spelling Shteynshnayd; See p. 237.
SHIKHMAN	Yaakov, his wife Chaika [Gruber], their daughters, Peril and Sara, their sons Mordekhai, Shimon, Asher, Yosef and Azriel.	alt. spelling Shichman; Chaika was granddaughter of Mordechai and Pearl Gruber. Her parents were Yosef Moshe Gruber and Shifra (Teitelman). Her siblings included Sonia (Gruber) Teitelman, Rachel (Gruber) Teitelman, both contributors and well as the teacher Ben-Tzion Gruber (see above). A daughter Sara did survive and became Sara Vinokur.
SHIKHMAN	Yenta [née Teitelman], her sons Zelig and Yitzhak, Chana Sara and her family, Batya, Gitel and Sheindel	alt. spelling Shichman; Based on descendants' testimony, Yenta Shichman was born Yenta Teitelman and was a sister of Nahum Teitelman, a contributor to this volume. Yenta married Yehuda Shichman who survived, which is why he is not listed. They had six children. Bracha-Bronia, Scheindel, Chaya, Pinchas, Zelig, and Yitzchak. In addition to Yehuda, two daughters, Bracha and Khaya, survived. Yehuda and Bracha made aliya and Khaya went to the states and became Charlotte Bryl. Bracha married Morechai Vizel and they had a son Avraham.

[Page 445]

List of Martyrs from Sokoliki near Turka who arrived here in the War period and dwelled in Stomorhy

See the essay "Murder of the Sokoliki Refugees," pp. 384–385 with notes.

Translated and edited by Howard I. Schwartz, PhD

		Editor's notes
BET ב		
BRAIER	Yosef and his two children.	alt. spelling Breyer, Brejer; A child Shloyme Breyer survived but died from tuberculosis four months after the liberation, p. 385.
BEK	Benish, Freida Bek with their daughter.	
GIMEL ג		
GLEIKHER	Sheindel, Moshe Gleikher.	alt. spelling Glajkher.
GERSTEL	Nechama with daughters and sons. Yehoshua Gerstel, Zisel Gerstel and two children.	alt. spelling Gershtel.
DALET ד		
DELINGER	Solomon, Gitel Delinger, and her daughter.	
HE ה		
HANS	Yaakov, his wife, two of his daughters and son-in-law.	

HOFTMAN	Mendel and his wife, two of his children and mother-in-law	alt. spelling Gojkhtman.

VAV ו

VOLF	Hersh. Rivkah Volf.	alt. spelling Wolf, Vulf.

TET ט

TEIKHMAN	Mendel, Freida Teichman, Avraham Teichman, Moshe Teichman his wife and children.	alt. spelling Tejkhman.

LAMED ל

LAUFER	Tzarna, with her son Salek.	alt. spelling Loifer.
LOEWENTAL	Rivkah [nee Rozenberg], Salke Levental, Mendel Levental, Breindl Levental, with six children.	alt. spelling Levental.

NUN נ

NANEF	Shmuel and Bluma. Faivel Nanef with wife and children. Moshe Nanef with wife and daughter. Roiza Nanef.	
NEISHTEIN	Meir, Shprintze Neishtein, with four of their children.	alt. spelling Nejshtejn, Neinstein.

PEH פ

FRAM	Moidel, Leib Fram, Freida Fram, Yehudit Fram, Yisrael Fram, Rivkah Fram and her husband.	alt. spelling From/Frum. Leib Fram was killed July 13, 1941.

QOF ק

KUPFERBERG	Shimon, Yitzhak Kupferberg, Tzvia Kupferberg [nee Treiber], Yoel Kupferberg, Solke with two children, Rela Kupferberg, Dzhinie [Andzia] Kupferberg, Chaia Kupferberg.	alt. spelling Kuperberg. See account by Frida Kupferberg, pp 384–385.
KELLER	Shimon, Freida Keller with four children, Ruchtzia Keller, [Zeev] Wolf Keller, Beirish Keller, Hersh Keller, Shimon Keller, Mendel Keller, Chana Keller with her son.	alt. spelling Keler. Death of Volf Keler and his sons, p. 384, this volume.

RESH ר

ROSENBERG	Rivkah with husband and a son.	alt. spelling Rozenberg.

SHIN ש

SHMERLER	Reizl	alt. spelling Shmereler.
SHTEMERMAN	Yisrael, Kersil Shtemerman with two children.	alt. spelling Shtimerman.

[Page 446]

		Editor's notes
BRODMAN	Shmuel	alt. spelling Bratman; From Sokoliki, lived in Stomorhy, killed with Mlynov ghetto.
BRODMAN	Rize	alt. spelling Bratman; From Sokoliki, lived in Stomorhy, killed with Mlynov ghetto.
GELOBTER	Berche	alt. spelling Galabter; Acccount of Gelobter murder, p. 384.
GELOBTER	Rivkah	
GELOBTER	Yosef	
HOLTZMAN	Hertz with his wife and their son	alt. spelling Holtsman.
LAUTERMAN	Malka	alt. spelling Loitermann.

| ROSENBERG | Yisrael, with his wife and six children. | alt. spelling Rozenberg. |

Martyrs of Nearby Villages

		Editor's notes
BERMAN	Yitzhak, Batya his wife (Smordva). Moshe, Aharon, and Leah (Smordva)	
GRINSHPAN	Perel, widow of Berel; Yenta their daughter (from the village Kosareve); their son Zelig is living in Israel, their daughter Gitel is in Brazil.	alt. spelling Grenspun and Greenspun.
GRINSHPAN	Yoel-Leib (from Parmilovka [Peremylivka]); Rachel his wife passed away. Yitzhak their son, Bat-Sheva their daughter, Ribah their daughter (a son in Israel, a daughter Tovah in Israel; their son Micael in France and their daughter Mania in Canada).	alt. spelling Grenspun and Greenspun; A photo of Bat-Sheva appears among a group of young people, p. 203 with notes.

[Page 447]

Names of Residents of our Town
Who Passed Away in Our Land [Israel]

Translated and edited by Howard I. Schwartz, PhD

	Editor's notes
The poet Yitzhak Lamdan	See Lamdan's poem on page 83 with notes.
Lipa Halperin	Contributed a number of essays to this volume.
Moshe Fishman	Contributed to this volume, p. 60 with notes.
The shochet and kosher examiner Yehuda Shichman	alt. spelling Shikhman. Yehuda Shichman married Yenta (Teitelman). See the Mervits matyr list, p. 444, for Yenta with additional notes.
Moshe Chizik	See a photo of the family on top of page 457 with notes.
Reuben Goldreich	A photo of a Goldreich family on page 463.

Yosef Mandelkern	A tribute to Joseph Mandelkern p. 448.
Yukal Liberman	
Chaia Gershtein	
Sarah [Teitelman] Vinokur	A photo of Sarah page 479 with notes.
Tova [Genut] Teitelman	A photo p. 478, wife of Asher Teitelman.
Abisch Rosenberg his wife Rachel and their son Lamel	

Fallen Soldiers

Translated and edited by Howard I. Schwartz, PhD

	Editor's notes
Hanich [Hanoch] Goldseker, of blessed memory	Photo, p. 455, tribute by his sister, 420-421.
Tzvi Linkes, of blessed memory	Photo p. 455.
Israel Halperin	Photo p. 455 with notes.

<u>Addendum / Addition</u>

[Page 448][1]

Translated and edited by Howard I. Schwartz, PhD **with** Hanina Epstein

This is the Gateway...

to a photo section for many Mlynov-Mervits residents, [including those] who were murdered by the Nazi enemy in the disaster (shoah) of the Second World War; [and those] who were gathered to their people [i.e., passed away] before the destruction; and also the photos of those who left the town alive — may they live until 120 — in the United States.

This section was submitted by the Mandelkern brothers, Shmuel[2] and his wife Malcah (from the Lamdan line), and Yitzhak Mandelkern and his wife Fania — in memory of their brother Joseph Mandelkoren who died in Haifa on the 26 of Shevat 5723 (1963).

Joseph Mandelkoren

[Page 448b]

From Story of his Life:

Our brother Joseph, of blessed memory, was born in Mlynov in 1907 to our parents Menachem [which means "to comfort"] and Nechama [which means "consolation"] (their names portray their character). He received his education in the Tarbut school in Mlynov and was considered among the outstanding students.

After finishing his studies, our brother expressed the desire to make aliyah to the Land of Israel, but in line with my advice, he agreed first to prepare himself in Mlynov for a career in carpentry together with other pioneers. For the "tuition" to the master craftsmen, we, the men of "The Pioneer" (HeHalutz) [youth group] found ourselves hired as civil night guards, a role that was bestowed on us; this despised work which had been done before that time in Mlynov by outsiders only.

And thus, after some time, our brother was granted authorization with us for aliyah from the center in Rovno. However, for technical reasons I [Shmuel] and my wife went first, and he remained at home. This was 1925. The year of mass aliyah, after which there was a shocking paucity of work and many of the pioneers "left" [lit. "went down"] from the Land. This "emigration" [lit. descent] resulted in heavy damage to the Zionist work in the Diaspora.

In the meantime, the authorization for aliyah expired in the hands of our brother and the time came to be conscripted in the Polish army. However, after he was liberated from his military service, he began trying again to make aliyah to the Land. The situation in the Polish Diaspora was deteriorating — and all roads pointed towards [the necessity] of making aliyah. But the difficulties in obtaining authorization to make aliyah were significant and numerous. Since our brother was without any party affiliation, he had to run from organization to organization to beg for "righteousness and fairness" which one could not always find … and when he finally succeeded in making aliyah he arrived here broken in body and spirit.

In Haifa, he was inducted into the association of building workers, and here too one needed "righteousness" in order to receive a day of exhausting work. Since he was weak and limited in strength for labor — his path was not strewn with roses. He lived with the perpetual nightmare lest, God forbid, he needed to rely on people. This idea depressed him and hastened his end. He died in Haifa on the 26th of Shevat, 1963.

May his memory be blessed.

Written S. M. [Shmuel Mandelkern]

Editor's footnotes:

1.   The pages of the original book are misnumbered.
2.   Shmuel Mandelkern is the contributor of two essays to this volume, 116–145 and 208–219 with additional notes. A photo of Shmuel and his wife Malcah is on page 482.

[Page 449]

Nazi Crimes in the Volyn Neighborhood

by Sore Shichman-Vinokur[1]
daughter of Khayke, Yosel Gruber's [daughter]

Translated from the Yiddish by Hannah B. Fischthal, PhD

Edited by Howard I. Schwartz, PhD

In May 1942, the Germans chose the smallest and dirtiest street, encircled it with wire, and made the Jewish ghetto inside. If the Nazis allowed a Jew to bring a few things into the ghetto, they did not allow any food whatsoever inside. Hunger started immediately. I still see small, hungry children in front of my eyes.

Yom Kippur [Sept. 21, 1942],[2] the same year, Jews learned that the Ukrainians were digging graves not far from Mlynov, and that the graves were being prepared for the Jews in the ghetto. All the people wanted to save themselves. But how? Ukrainian police were guarding the ghetto. The Ukrainian inhabitants were quite happy that the Jews were going to be killed. They would also benefit from Jewish goods. Our Shichman family consisted of nine people: two girls, their father and mother, and five boys. We decided that I, Sore, should get work as a maid for a farmer, and maybe thereby I might have an opportunity to get my family out of the ghetto.

It took practically our entire fortune to secure a position for me as a maid in a neighboring shtetl for Master Bialkovsky.[3] With his help we did manage to get not only my whole Shichman family out of the ghetto in a wagon covered with straw, but also my Uncle Nute Gruber[4] with his wife and two children. We paid a Ukrainian farmer, Rituk from the village of Kutsa, to hide everyone until we would be liberated.[5] Rituk dug a large ditch under his stable, and that became the grave we lived in. During the day we could never go out of the ditch so that nobody, God forbid, should see us. Only at night would someone go outside to the farmer to cook something to eat for the next day. Every day the Ukrainian would come down into the ditch and ask for something: a dress, a shoe, a blanket, money. Wanting to live, everyone complied.

[Page 450]

We had some very small children about five years old among us. After two weeks, on a Shabbes evening, my mother became ill, and she started to faint. She declared that she had a feeling that a tragedy will befall us. The children comforted their mother, but she cried silently a whole night (Jews were not permitted to cry, because someone might hear them). The next day, Sunday, there was nothing to eat. The Ukrainian's daughter came down and asked me to take off my shoes and give her my coat because she wanted to go to church. It was hard for me to take off my only pair of shoes in the cold winter, and to give away my only coat, but I was afraid to say no, fearing for our lives. I gave away my shoes and coat to the Christian.

After she left, my five-year-old little brother started to bawl. He cried so terribly that we could not quiet him down. Finally, the little boy got tired, and suddenly we heard somebody walking on our earthen hut. I was sitting at the opening to the bunker, and through a crack I saw that it was the Ukrainian police. I became petrified. Someone screamed that all Jews should get out of the bunker, and at the same time someone shot bullets into the ditch. I fainted. When I came to, nobody was left in the bunker. I only heard noise and talking outside: "Killed all the Jews." I understood that they had missed me. I started to think. I covered myself completely with straw, and I determined to wait until night and then run away to Poles or Czechs that I knew. Barely covered with straw, I heard how several Ukrainians were going down into the ditch, saying that since the police had not yet entered, they would be able to plunder the better things. The daughter who had taken my shoes and coat told her sister how she had modelled for the police.

After taking our possessions, the Christians, or better said, the murderers of Jews, left the ditch. It was clear to me that I must get out of there, but where should I go? I was barefoot, without a coat, and wearing a summer dress. But the battle for life is strong. I got out of the ditch only to step on my father's dead body.

[Page 451]

Near it was my brother's body. It occurred to me that maybe they just fainted. I grabbed my brother, but he fell out of my arms. He was already cold, stiff. I broke two boards from our side of the stable, and I went out. I ran barefoot through the deep snow. The police saw me, and they started to shoot at me. I ran through the fields, through ditches, through rivers. The police could not catch up to me. I saw a small house. I understood that if I would go straight inside, my bare feet would leave tracks. So I ran around the house a few times and then I went inside.

A poor Polish woman whom I knew lived there. Recognizing me, she began to cross herself:

"My God, you are alive?"
She saw my swollen hands and feet, and she brought me a pail of water, and told me to put my feet into the water. And then I saw how the police were driving over. I acted as though nothing bothered me. The farmers, however, became white as chalk. But the police did not go into the house. They just asked through the window if a *zhidowka* [Jewish woman] was in the house. Something like an angel protected me. The woman answered, "No," and I, meanwhile, disappeared.

I stayed by the woman until evening. She gave me a rag for my head, and rags for my feet, and I went out again. It was very cold. The rags on my feet quickly fell off, and I walked through the snowy fields. I had bad luck that it was not a dark night. I saw a man across from me who was screaming, "Halt!"

I started to run.

I heard again, "Halt! If not, I will shoot!"

I stood still. The mayor of the village Dobryatyn came over to me. He recognized me right away and he explained that according to the law, he had to give me over to the Germans; but he will not do it. He told me to hide, and he let me go. I felt bad in my heart because the Pole, by whom I wanted to hide, was Mayor Vorotshik 's neighbor. However, I had no other choice.

By various means I came to Zawodsky the Pole. I went to the window and saw that he had a guest. That meant that I had to still be outside.

[Page 452]

I tried to warm up a little in the stable, but the pigs started to scream. Therefore, I had to go out of the stable. There was a large haystack outside. I dug a hole, crept inside, covered up the hole, and immediately fell asleep.

When I got up it was still dark. I crawled out and went to the window. I saw the Polish woman heating the oven. I knocked and went inside. She clapped her hands:

"You are alive?! Akh, what kind of feet you have! Sit down!"
And she immediately gave me something to eat and water to wash with.

I learned that I had slept in the straw three days and three nights. The Zovodsky family had sympathy for me. They started to heal my frozen feet and hands. They kept me on the stove the entire time, blocked off with a bread kneading trough.

A few weeks later the same Mayor Vorotshik went to Zovodsky's vestibule. A while later Zovodsky came back; I saw through a crack that Zovodsky had become different. He called his wife over and I heard him tell her that the mayor knows that I am hiding there, and he even promised to help Zovodsky: "A pity on the Jew."

They were afraid of Mayor Vorotshik. He was, after all, a Ukrainian! That was in 1943. The roars of the Russian Katyusha rocket launchers were already heard. I crawled to my aunt and uncle, Sonia and Mendel Teitelman, who were hidden in a bunker until 1944, when the Red Army entered and liberated us.

How much I endured hunger, cold — that is indescribable. I was in danger every minute of every day. Even after we fell asleep, we used to be awakened by horrible nightmares. But a person is stronger than iron. A person can endure everything. While there is life, there is hope. And I survived with my aunt and uncle; we were saved by the Red Army.

Translator's and editor's footnotes:

1. The writer, Sore Sarah (Shichman) Vinokur (? – 1957) was the daughter of Khayke (or Chaika) (Gruber) and Yaakov Shichman. This Shichman family from Mervits, who spelled their last name with a yod, was not related to the Shechman/Schuchman family from Mlynov who did not have a yod in their name, according to Schechman descendants. Sore was one of seven children in her immediate family, the rest of whom did not survive and are listed in the Mervits martyrs (p. 444). Sore's mother Khayke was a sister of Rachel (Gruber) Teitelman and Sonia (Gruber) Teitelman, survivors and contributors to this volume, all children of Yosel Moshe Gruber and Shifra (Teitelman). –HS

2. Erev Yom Kippur that year was September 20, 1942. – HS

3. A photo on page 429 shows farm workers, including one Jewish man named Fishel Kleinberg, outside the house of a man named Bialkovsky, probably the same man mentioned here in whose house Sore secured work as a maid and who helped her family escape. Fishel Kleinberg's presence in that photo suggests the link since he was first cousin of this writer's mother, Khaye (Gruber) Shichman. – HS

4. Nute Gruber was another sibling of Sore's mother and a son of Yosel/Yosef Gruber and Shifra (Teitelman). Nute's wife was Miriam (Sherman). One of their children's names was Shifra. – HS

5. The book length survival story of Asher Teitelman, published on the Mlynov website, pp. 27ff, also contains an account of their separation from Sore's family and what they learned of her survival. – HS

[Page 453]

Photographs of Our Martyrs

Translated by Howard I. Schwartz, PhD

Rabbi Yehuda Gordon, z"l
**Last head rabbi of the Mlynov Community
(kehill**

Rabbi Yehuda-Leib Lamdan[2]

Moshe Lamdan (the poet's brother) murdered by Denikin's[1] gangs in 1919

Motel Litvak and his wife Riva [Lamdan] z"l[3]

[Page 455]

Fallen While Defending in Israel

Hanoch Goldseker, z"l[4]

Tzvi Linkes, z"l

Yisrael Halperin z"l[5]

Fallen While Defending in Israel

**Yochai Givol
(from the line of Rachel Shapovnik)**[6]

**? Mandelkern, z"l
Zelig Pichniuk, z"l
Herschel Grin, z"l
Abraham Goldseker, may he be distinguished for a long life**

[Page 456]

Mr. Ben-Tzion Meren, z"l (the teacher) his wife[7] and daughter Seril, z"l

The teacher Shurin and his wife, z"l

[Page 457]

The teacher Motel Chizik [also spelled Tzizik] and his family.[8] May his son Meir (left) be distinguished for a long life. The son Moshe (on the right) died in Israel. Original courtesy of Hagar Lipkin

The teacher Ben-Tzion Gruber and his family, z"l [left].[9] Chaim Naishtein[10] with his family, z"l [center]. Hersh-Leib Margulis (first from the right), [next to him] his sister Raisel [Naishtein (nee Margulis)] and their brother Efraim (is in Russia) [and not present in the photo]

[Page 458]

Lipa Halperin died in Israel[11]

*[Lipa's mother] Rivkah [Shrentzel]
Halperin (seated)
and [her sister] Sorke (Shrentzel)
Gertnich z"l*

*Moshe Gertnich,[12] his wife Sorke [Shrentzel],
their son Shmuel, their daughter Faiga [bottom
left], and to be distinguished for a long life, Yosef
(Koiftze) [Ganon]*

*[Lipa's maternal grandfather] Mordechai Meir
Shrentzel z"l[13]*

[Page 459]

A postcard sent from the Mlynov ghetto by Rivkah Halperin to Lipa Halperin in the Land [of Israel], via Portugal[14]

Translator's and editor's footnotes:

1.   Referring to the army of Anton Denikin, (1872–1947) a Russian Lieutenant General in the Imperial Russian Army (1916) who then led White forces against the Bolsheviks in the Civil War. During that period, the White Army was associated with a percentage of the attacks on 50,000 Jews who perished in pogroms and was responsible for propaganda campaigns against the Jews whom they associated with communism.

2.   The father of the poet, Yitzhak Lamdan.

3.   The parents of Yosef Litvak, a contributor to this volume.

4.   Hanoch (1930–1948), a Shoah survivor, was son of Yankel, son of Moshe, son of Abraham Holtzeker. After his escape, he joined his sisters on Kibbutz Negba. He died on May 5, 1948, in the battle for Negba against the Egyptian army.

5.   Israel was son of Lipa Halperin, born April 11, 1950. He fell in battle as a fighter in a commando unit during the War of Attrition (June 11, 1970).

6.   Yochai Givol's mother, Rachel Shapovnik, was born in Mlynov, and appears in the photos on page 9 and page 460 as a member of the Zionist Youth Group, Hashomer Hatzair. Rachel's father, Abisch Shapovnik, was born in Luck in 1882 and married Khaia Fridman. The family came to live in Mlynov by the 1920s.

7.   Ben-Tzion Meren was the father of Boruch Meren who contributed to this volume. Ben-Tzion was married to Miriam Goldseker, daughter of Hirsh Goldseker. Boruch tells the story about his father becoming a teacher in "The Treasure That Ran Out," pp. 272–276, and writes a poem about him, "My Father Ben-Tzion," p. 255.

8.   Motel (Mordechai) Chizik (or Tzizik) was born in 1882 and married a woman named Rut. Their daughter Luba Leah stayed in Mlynov with her parents and they perished in the liquidation. Their son, Moshe, married Mlynov-born Rosa Berger (sister of Aaron Harari) in Palestine after they both made aliyah. Moshe (1909–1959) tragically died of a poisonous snake bite in 1959. His brother Meir (1907–1996) was drafted in the Polish army in 1922 and made aliyah after his brother in the 1930s; they both lived in Kibbutz Beit Alfa. Meir married and had five children.

9.   The people in this photo were all Mervits residents and all related. A short reflection by Eliyahu Gelman in this volume called "The Two of Them" (p. 241) provides some memories about Ben-Tzion Gruber and Hersch Leib Margulis, who both left Mlynov for larger cities but then returned to settle down and raise families.
On the left is Ben-Tzion Gruber (1900–1942), the son of Yosef Moshe Gruber and Shifra (Teitelman). He was the brother of Sonia and Rachel Teitelman who are both survivors and contributors to this volume. Ben-Tzion's wife was Gitel Tovah (Margulis) which explains why the other Margulises are in the photo. Ben-Tzion and Gitel had a daughter Yehudit. All of them perished in Lutzk.
On the right are Gitel's siblings, Hersch-Lieb Margulis and Reizl (Margulis) Naishtein (1910–1942), who are also listed among the martyrs of Mervits (p. 442). Based on Yad Vashem records, their brother Efraim Margulis (1920–1941) was in Kiev before WWII and thus is not in the photo. He served in the Soviet army and was reported as missing in action in July 1941.

10.   Chaim Naishtein (1902–1942) (or Naisztein, Neinstein) is third from the right in the photo. He married Reizl (Margulis). Based on Yad Vashem records, he was son of Moshe and a textile merchant. In the Mervits list of martyrs (p. 443), Chaim and Reizl have a son, presumably the young man standing in front of Chaim. The martyr list indicates Chaim's sister was Reizl (Naishtein) Gonik. She, her husband and son perished as well.
It is conceivable that this Chaim Naishtein was first cousin to Bernard Neinstein, the well-known Chicago politician. Bernard's father Paul Neinstein (1881–1949) married Eva (Chava) Berger from Mlynov and migrated to Chicago in 1910. He arrived under the name of "Pinchus Neustein" was listed as a tailor, and was headed when he first arrived to a cousin Moshe Fishman in Baltimore who was from Mlynov/Mervits. Pinchus Neustein's manifest appears to indicate he was born in Mervits. Paul's son Bernard Neistein went on to be the well-known Chicago politician.

11.   Lipa Halperin (1907–1969) was one of five children of Israel Halperin and Rivkah (Shrentzel also spelled Shrentzil). The family had a haberdashery in Mlynov. Growing up, Lipa was involved in the Zionist Youth Groups, and he made aliyah in 1937. The rest of his family perished. Lipa was on the Book Committee for this volume and contributed a number of essays recalling his childhood memories including "The Mill," pp. 13–15, and "When I Was a Lad, pp. 153–155."

12. Moshe Gertnich (or Gertnikh) (1900–1942) married Sara (Shrentzel) (1906–1942). Their son Yosef (called Kuftzia and Ganon) made aliyah and contributed the essay "Memories of Home," 262–263 in this volume.

13. Mordechai Meir Shrentzel was the father of Rivkah [Shrentzel] Halperin and Sura [Shrentzel] Gertnich. Lipa credits this grandfather with the story about how the Ikva got its name in his essay, "The Mill."

14. The postcard was written by Lipa's mother, Rivkah Halperin to Lipa in Mandate Palestine. It is the last postcard he received. It poorly written German and appears to be a translation from Yiddish to evade censorship. No one knows how the postcard was sent out of Portugal. The postcard is dated July 7, 1942. It reads, "We received your letter from January 28th, 1942. We thank you. Our whole family is healthy. We all live in our house. Your three sisters and your brother work in town. Father and I are at home. Write to us at the previous address. We greet Tola and the little son. R.H." I'd like to thank Lipa's daughter, Miriam Aharoni, for the postcard's background and help with the translation as well as Leah Heymann and Viviane Heymann-Knops for their help translating the old German/Yiddish.

[Page 460]

Photographs of Our Martyrs (cont.)

Translated by Howard I. Schwartz, PhD

The group, HaTikvah ("The Hope") [a group of] "Hashomer Hatzair" in Mlynov[III]

Members of [Zionist Youth Group] HeHalutz ["The Pioneer"], Mlynov

[Page 461]

*[original caption is confused][2] **Shlomo Schechman [first from left],[3] Yidel Liberman, z"l [third from left],[4] Avraham Goldseker [standing second from right],[5] Avraham Goldseker [=Chuna Goldsker,[6] seated front], and to be distinguished for a long life, Pinchas Klaper[7] [first from right] and Pesach Mandelkern [second from left][8]***

Original courtesy of Irene Fishman and Audrey Goldseker Polt

Graduation of Grade 7 in the government school (1938). May he be distinguished for a long life the teacher Barshtchovko Alexander (in the middle above)

[Page 462]

Hannah [Schuchman] Golisuk, Gershon's [daughter],[9] her son Shmuel and daughter Tzvia, z"l

Rivitz Pesia z"l[10] (daughter of Aizik Wolf from Shalbia)

Sherman Moshe, his wife Etel [Golisuk] z"l[11]

[Page 463]

Pesich Golisuk z"l.

Yosel Golisuk z"l.

Motia Golisuk z"l

Bunia [Steinberg] Upstein and her mother [Hanah (Lerner) Steinberg]

Mendel and Faiga Upstein [Steinberg][12]

Moshe and Zalman Zider and their families,[13] z"l

Fania Grinberg[14] [right] and Batia Holtzeker[15]   *Goldreich family (from the refugees of Turka)[16]*

Editor's footnotes:

1.   Four persons have been identified in this photo: Rachel (Shapovnik) Givol, standing left, also appears in the photo on page 8 from 1933. Her son's photo is among those who fell defending Israel (p. 455) with notes about the family. Rosa Berger appears first row right. Two of the boys in this photo appear again in the photo of the six young men (on the next page 461). Chuna Goldseker (son of Shimon Goldseker) stands 3rd from the right. Pesach Mandelkern stands in the back center. Some of the same individuals appear in the 1927 photo of the Youth Group on page 71. See subsequent notes for more detail.

2.   The caption on this photo is confusing and misleading. The names are listed here in English in the order they appear in the Hebrew suggesting the order is right to left. However, the names don't match the names of the same boys who appear older in the photo on page 227. A comparison of the two photos and captions is reproduced below for convenience. Confirmation from several descendants helped to clarify identities, thanks to Morris Schechman, Orit Nahmias (Mandelkern descendant) and Audrey Goldseker Polt.

3.   Shlomo Schechman (1910–1969) son of Noach Moshe Schechman/Schuchman and Faiga Beshe ("Batya") Wolk. Noach Moshe was the brother of Joseph Schuchman from Mlynov who migrated to Baltimore. Noach Moshe and Faiga Beshe had five children, who had families themselves, including Shlomo's siblings: Aharon Shmuel, Yitzhak, Shimon and Bentzion. Shimon Schechman is recalled briefly in Aaron Harari's recollections from his visit back to Mlynov in 1937–1938. Shlomo Schechman, pictured here, on the left of the photo, was the only offspring of the family to survive the Shoah. He fought with the partisans, was shot several times in the back and side and lost a toe and finger.

After the war, he met and married Liza Zabirowicz (1920—2007) in Lutzk and they had two sons, Morris, who was born in 1945 in a train on the way to the displaced persons camp of Föhrenwald and Rueben who was born in 1952. The family eventually connected with family of Shlomo's mother in Waterbury, Connecticut. After moving there and feeling isolated, the family later moved to Baltimore where Shlomo's paternal uncle Joseph Schuchman and family had settled before the war.

4.   It seems likely that the Yidel Liberman in these photos may be the one known from the martyr list as son of Mordechai Lieberman and his wife Bracha. Yad Vashem records submitted by Yosef (Teitelman) Tomer, son of Rachel (Gruber) and Nachum Teitelman, refer to him as Aidel (Idl /Yehuda) and identifies Yidel's mother Bracha as born to the Gruber family and a sister of Yosef's mother, Rachel (Gruber) Teitelman. This entire Liberman family perished including Yidel's siblings: Asher, Rivka, Miriam and Chaya. The fate of Yidel Liberman is mentioned in the essay by Yehudit (Mandelkern) Rudolf, p. 88, indicating Yidel was accidentally included in a German sweep of 10-15 individuals suspected of being active in Polish political parties, which took place, a month to six weeks after the occupation in June 1942. There is another photo of an "Aidel Liberman," first name spelled with an aleph, who appears on page 280, who may be the same boy here grown to a young man in 1938.

5.   There were quite a few Avraham Goldsekers (Holtzekers), great-grandsons named after the patriarch of the family. The patriarch Avraham had five sons (Hirsch, Moishe, Yankel, Shimon, Yoel) and four of them had at least one grandson (and sometimes two) named Avraham after the patriarch. It is unknown which Avraham this is, though it might be a good guess that it is the Avraham in the martyr list who is listed as still alive in Israel, explaining why he has no z"l following his name in this caption. This Avraham thus appears to be the grandson of Yankel (one of the five original sons to come to Mlynov). Yankel had a son, Moishe, who named a son Avraham. This Avraham was the brother of the contributor to this volume, Yankev/Yaakov Goldseker. Yankel also had another son, Yehoshua, who named a son Avraham. There were several other Avraham Goldsekers in the same generation. Hirsch's son, Yitzhak, named a son Avraham. Yoel's son, Pinchas, named a son Avraham. Moishe's son Yaakov/Yankel named a son Avraham.

6.   Seated first on the right is Chuna Goldseker, not Avraham Goldseker, according to a handwritten note on this original photo that came from Irene Siegel, daughter of Eta (Goldseker) Fishman in Baltimore. Chuna followed other Mlynov boys to Buenos Aires in 1929 where he married, settled and had children.

7.   Pinhas Klaper was presumably from the Klaper (or Klapir) family listed among the Mlynov martyrs (p. 438) and in Yad Vashem records. The father, Bentzion Klaper, married a woman named Tsherna or Charna

[surname unknown] (1880–1942), daughter of Shmuel and Liba. They and their following children and their families perished: Avraham (1900–1942) a merchant, Reuven (1908–1942) a blacksmith, Mendel (1904–1942) a blacksmith, Chaia (1907–1942), Hana (1911–1942) a seamstress and Zwi (1912–1942). Avraham, Reuven and Mendel were married.

8.   Pesach Mandelkern (1911–1987) was one of seven children of Avraham Mandelkern and Rivkah (Nudler) (see the list of martyrs p. 436). Two of his sisters, Faiga / Fania (Mandelkern) Burnstein (1917-?), and Yehudit (Mandelkern) Rudolf (later Rom) (1930–2005) contributed their collective memories of the German occupation and survival in this volume (pages 287–299). Pesach, Eliyahu (1921–2009) and Gedaliah (1915–2005) made it to Israel at some point. The parents and two of the siblings, Moishe (1913–1943) and Rosa (also called Shoshana) (1927–1943) perished.

9.   Hannah Golisuk was daughter of Gershon and Shaindel Bluma Schuchman. She was widowed. She had seven children, five of whom appear in photos to follow. In addition to those whose photos appear here, there was also a child named Buka in the list of martyrs. Hannah's daughter, Etel, pictured below, married Moshe Sherman. Their son Yechiel survived in the Russian army and is a contributor to this volume. Their son, Ezra Sherman, was visiting his grandmother, Hannah, in Mlynov in 1942 when the ghetto was erected. You can listen to Ezra describe his escape from the ghetto and survival wandering alone as a young boy in the countryside on the Mlynov website.

10.   What we know of this family comes from Yad Vashem records submitted by Bat Sheva (Ribitz) Ben Eliyahu, who is author of the dirge that appears on pages 263–265 and who was a cousin of the family. Pesia Rivitz (alternative spellings: Riwic and Ribitz) (~1928–1942) was born in Luck, the daughter of Aisik (also Yitzhak) Wolf and Sarah Rivitz. Before the War, the family was involved in agriculture and living in a village outside of Luck, perhaps the unidentified "Shelbia" mentioned in the caption. During the War, they were in Mlynov where they perished. Pesia had a brother Mordechai. It seems very plausible this family was related to Ida and David Rivitz from Mlynov who were children of Mordechai Rivitz. Both David and Ida married and migrated to Baltimore. Ida married Getzel Fax, both becoming the pioneers to the US and David married Pesia Demb and they became David and Bessie Hurwitz in Baltimore. See more of the Fax and Demb stories on the Mlynov website.

11.   Etel Golisuk is the daughter of Hannah (Schuchman) Golisuk who appears in the above photo. Etel married Moshe Sherman and they are the parents of survivors Ezra Sherman and Yechiel Sherman, the latter a contributor to this volume. Etel died prematurely from an injury sustained in a fall she had taken before the Russian occupation.

12.   The caption on this photo is incorrect. The surname of Mendel and Faiga was Steinberg, not Upstein. Mendel Steinberg is a contributor to this volume, p. 358. They were siblings of survivor Bunia (Steinberg), who appears in the adjoining photo and who later married Yitzhak Upstein from Mervits. Faiga Steinberg married Falek Shtival and moved to Varkovychi where she, her husband and two children were murdered. Bunia, Mendel and their brother Getzel survived the Shoah. Getzel and Mendel also appear in later family photos below on page 505. The other Steinberg siblings, Chanan, Tsvi Herschel, and Eliaykim (Yukal) perished.

13.   According to the martyr list, Moshe Zider was living in Mervits and was married to Frida. Zalman Zider (see also photo p. 475) was from Mlynov and married to Zelda. One of the sons, Zelig, was part of the Jewish police set up after the German occupation and was involved with other young people in trying to organize a resistance, as told in the account by Yehudit (Mandelkern) Rudolf, "Life Under the Occupying German Government," pp. 288–290.

14.   Perhaps the woman in Yad Vashem records called Faiga Rakhel Grinberg (nee Ingerman) (1878–1942) who was born in Mlynov and who married David Moshe Grinberg and lived in Demydivka during the War.

15.   It is not known which of the several Batia Holtzekers is in the photo: Batia, daughter of Yaakov (and Ratzia), Batia daughter of Yaakov Holtzeker, son of Hirsch, or 3) Batia, daughter of Moshe son of Yoel.

16.   On the refugees from Turka, see the essay in this volume by Frida Kuperberg, "Murder of the Sokoliki Refugees," pp. 384–386.

[Page 464]

Photographs of Our Martyrs (cont.)

Translated by Howard I. Schwartz, PhD

Nute Iskiewicz,[1] his sister [Devorah (Iskiewicz) Grin] (on the right), his wife [Rachel, center] and daughter Zlata, of blessed memory (on the left)

Eliezer Iskiewicz,[2] his wife Faiga [Grin] and their children: Shlomo, Sheindel [center], Raizel [front], and Moshe, may he live a long life. The grandmother of Eliezer, Yenta Barshof, of blessed memory.

Shlomo Iskiewicz[3] and his wife Sheindel

[Page 465]

Pesia Grin (Meirzon)[4] of blessed memory

Herschel Grin,[5] of blessed memory, died in service in the Polish army 1926

Abraham Grin[6] and his wife [Rachel] Kutzka,
of blessed memory

Ben-tzion Grin,[7] his wife Zlata [Kwasgalter], and
their son Mend

[Page 466]

[Chaim] Monik Kwasgalter[8] and his cousin Faivel

Meir Kwasgalter[9] and his wife
Shentzi [Gonik], of blessed memory

Hantzia [Szteinsznaid née Kwasgalter][10]
and her son Feiveli

[Page 467]

Zelig Kwasgalter,[11] *Chaya Gershtein*
from the Kwasgalter line (left)

Wolf Berger,[12] *his wife Golda, their daughter Hannah [left], of*
blessed memory. Distinguished for a long life: Reizel [Rosa] their
daughter [center] and Ahron [Harari] their son.

[right to left] Shlomo Iskiewitz,[13] Zalman Sheidman[14] blessed memory. Distinguished for a long life Rubin Kozak[15]

Shlomo Nekunchinik,[16] Hershel Gertnich,[17] of of blessed of blessed memory . Distinguished for a long life Berel Rabinovitch[18] [front right] and Yitzhak Mandelkern

Translator's and editor's footnotes:

1.   Nute Iskiewicz (alternative spelling Isakovich) was born in about 1872 in Mlynov. He had two siblings, Dvora (in this photo) and Shlomo (photo below). Nute was a housewares trader living in Lutsk before the War and he and his daughter, Zlata, were killed in Lutsk. Zlata's Yad Vashem record indicates her mother's name was Rachel. The martyr list (p. 431) indicates that the couple also had a daughter, Sarah, living in Israel and a son Avigdor in Canada.

Nute's sister, Devorah, married Lieb Grin. Their daughter Khaia Faiga Grin married Shlomo's son (her first cousin) Eliezer Iskiewicz. Their family photo below.

2.   Eliezer Iskiewicz (alternative spelling Isakovich) (1896–1942) was son of Shlomo and Sheindel. He married his first cousin Faiga Khaia Grin, daughter of Lieb Grin and Dvorah (Iskiewicz). They were the parents of Moshe Iskiewicz, author of essay, "Impressions and Memories" in this volume, pp. 88–89, who appears as a young boy in this photo. Another photo of the Eliezer / Leazar appears on page 477. The other children in this photo are Shlomo (1921–1942), Raizel (1927–1942), and Sheindel (1935–1942). Shlomo (1921–1942) was apparently named for his grandfather, Shlomo, in the photo to the right. He also appears as a school lad in the photo on p. 467. According to the martyr list (431), Shlomo disappeared in the battle of Stalingrad in 1942.

3.   This Shlomo Iskiewicz, was the brother of Nute and Devora who appear in the photo above. He and his wife, Sheindel, are the parents of Eliezer Iskiewicz and grandparents of Moshe Iskiewicz, the contributor to this volume.

4.   Pesia (Grin) Meirzon (1900–1942) was also a daughter of Lieb Grin and Dvora (Iskiewicz). Photos of other siblings follow. She married Aba Meirzon. Pesia died in the German bombing of the airfield in June 1941, when the Germans attacked the Soviets who had occupied the eastern side of Poland.

5.   Herschel Grin was also a son of Leib Grin and Devorah (Iskiewicz).

6.   Avraham Grin (1900–1942), was also a son of Leib Grin and Devorah (Iskiewicz). Avraham's wife was Rachel Kutzkeh, a daughter of Moshe Melamed (the teacher).

7.   Ben-tzion (1894–1942) was also a son of Leib Grin and Devorah (Iskiewicz). His wife Zlata (Kwasgalter) (1900–1942) was the daughter of Yaakov and Rivka, according to Yad Vashem records submitted by Moshe Iskiewicz. Their son Arieh and his family also perished. Zlata's brother Menahem Mendel Kwasgalter is remembered in the bunkers near Berehy by Fania (Mandelkern) Bernstein, "In the Valley of Death," p. 294.

8.   Chaim Monik (1895–1942) was the son of Meir and Sheintzi Kwasgalter (their photo to the right). His cousin Faivel is not identified but he is probably the same Feivel in the photo below.

9.   Meir Kwasgalter (1896–1942) was son of Faivel (1894–1942) and Leah. He was a pharmacist and married Sheintzi /Sheina (Gonik/ Genik) (1900–1942) from Rovno. They had two children. Their son Chaim Monik (1931–1942) perished. Their daughter Rachel (Kwasgalter) Rabinovitch (1925–?) survived in hiding with a Czech farmer. Meir and Rachel were among the Mlynov Jews in the bunkers near Berehy mentioned in the account by Fania (Mandelkern) Bernstein, "In the Valley of Death," p. 295, 303. According to survivor Helen (Fixler) Nudler, Rachel Kwasgalter married Berel Rabinovitch, the man who organized the commemoration in Mlynov after the War.

10.   Hentzia (also called Encia) Szteinsznaid (alternative spellings Steinshneid, Sztajnsznajd) (1895–1942) was born in Dubno to Faivel and Leah Kwasgalter. She was a sister of Meir Kwasgalter whose photo is above. She married Motel Szteinsznaid and they were in Mlynov at the liquidation of the ghetto.

11.   This line of the family is unidentified.

12.   One of the Berger families from Mlynov. Aaron (Berger) Harari contributed a number of the essays and photos to this volume. Aaron's parents and sister Hannah perished in the Shoah. Aaron's younger sister, Reizel/Rosa (1910–1994) made aliyah in 1933 and married Moshe Chizik (1909–1959) from Mlynov. Two of Aaron's older brothers, Sol (1898–1977) and Kalman/Karl (1906-1990), migrated to Chicago. Another brother, Shaul, was in the Russia army (1901–1976) and survived. Another photo of Wolf, Golda and Hannah appears in Aaron's essay on "Jewish Farmers in Mlynov," p. 76, taken during his visit to Mlynov in the winter of 1937/1938.

13.   Shlomo Iskiewicz (alternative Isakovich) was son of Eliezer Iskiewicz and Chaia Faiga (Grin). See their photos and notes on 465. Shlomo was the brother of Moshe Iskiewicz, a contributor of "Memories and Impressions," pp. 88–89.

14.   Zalman Sznaidman (alternative spellings Shneidman / Snaidman) (1921–1942) was born in Mlynov to Aharon Yitzhak Sznaidman (~1892–1942) and Sara (~1894–1942). He was single and a dental technician. He was one of six siblings to perish.

15.   Rubin Kozak (1922– ~2016) was the son of Icek Kozak (1899–1994) and Fayge / Chava (Bichman) (1903–1991). Icek contributed "What My Family Endured" to this volume. Icek snuck his whole family, one by one, out of the Mlynov ghetto and they survived. After the displaced persons camp, they migrated to Philadelphia where Icek's brother had settled earlier. Rubin's siblings were Morris Kozak (1924–2012), Jean (Genia) Litz (1928–1998), and Karen (Kreina) Lowenthal (1931–). Another child Kalman died before the War. A later photo of the family appears on page 506.

16.   Shlomo Nekunchinik (alternative spellings Nakonechnik, Nakonechnyuk) his wife Ester from Trovits; Fania Mandelkern remembers Shlomo as one of the men at the head of a group organizing resistance and securing weapons in the early days of the Mlynov ghetto. She recalls Shlomo and his brothers, Yitzhak and Yaakov, were later in bunkers near Berehy. In a book length account, Asher Teitelman who was in the bunkers near Smordva (which is close to Berehy) reports meeting Shlomo Nekunchinik in the bunkers (p. 29) and indicates that Shlomo was shot when the Ukrainians discovered the bunkers and starting shooting (p. 34). Asher's book length story is published on the Mlynov website.

17.   Herschel (which means "deer") Gertnich (alternative spelling Gertnikh) is probably the man identified as Tzvi (which means "deer") Gertnich in the list of Mlynov martyrs, p. 433. His father was Yitzhak called "the glazier" (1883–1942) and his mother Tehila was from Trovits. His brother Moshe was a kosher butcher (shochet) in Demydivka. This family was related to the Gertnich family who appear in the photo on page 458.

18.   Berel Rabinovitch (alternative spellings Rabinovitsh, Rabinovitz, Rabinowitz) survived the Shoah. He is remembered in Mlynov after the liberation by survivors Nahum Teitelman, "In the Depths of Hell," 341, and Mendel Steinberg in "The Terror of Annihilation," p. 367. David Bernstein, p. 309, credits Berel with being the initiator of the commemorative monument erected in Mlynov after the liberation for those who perished. Berel stands in the front of the photo taken on that occasion (p. 313). As the Nuremberg trials drew near, Bernstein indicates that Rabinovitch was involved with a local committee documenting Nazi atrocities. In the list of Mlynov martyrs, p. 433, his siblings, Mania and Gitel, are listed under the surname "Geler Rabinovitz." Also listed is a Chaim Geler Rabinovitz with his wife Dvorah and children, Shlomo and Zysl.

19.   Yitzhak Mandelkern was the brother of Shmuel Mandelkern, who contributed essays to this volume. Yitzhak with his young son Gerhson, one of six children, was with group from Mlynov in the bunkers in the forests near Karolinka and Berehy, as described by the writers of "During the Shoah," pp. 291, 294, 299, 301. After their bunker was discovered, Yitzhak led the group as they headed to the forests and bunkers near Uzhynets'. He eventually found a hiding place for himself and his son with a Czech farmer (p. 302) and the two of them were among the survivors who reappeared after the liberation (p. 310). He made aliyah after the War.

[Page 468]

Photographs of Our Martyrs (cont.)

Translated by Howard I. Schwartz, PhD

Mr. Anshel Teitelman,[1] his wife, Zelda and their son, Asher [Zelig], of blessed memory. (Parents of the writer Tamari)

Shika Teitelman,[2] of blessed memory and distinguished for a long life, Yaakov Shuchman[3]

Mutia (called staroste[4]) and Yehekiel Liberman[5] and their families, of blessed memory

[Page 469]

Moshe Fishman[6] and his sister Sarah Schwartz (Peretz's [mother]) of blessed memory
Original Courtesy of Audrey Goldseker Polt

Chaya Fishman, wife of Moishe, of blessed memory

Abush Rosenfeld[7] and his family, of blessed memory. First to make aliyah to Haifa

Daughters[8] of Mlynov, of blessed memory Original Courtesy of Ted Fishman and Neena Schwartz

Translator's and editor's footnotes:

1.   This is the family of Moshe (Teitelman) Tamari who wrote the essay "In the Presence of Yitzhak Lamdan in Mlynov." His parents were Anshel Teitelman (1880–1942) and Zelda (Paken) (1880–1942). His father, Anshel, was an older brother of Nahum Teitelman, another contributor to this volume (both sons of Efraim Fishel Teitelman and Chaya Bakowietzky). Ashel and Zelda's son Moshe made aliyah in 1933. The rest of his immediate family perished.

2.   Probably Yehoshua Teitelman (1902–1942), since "Shika" appears elsewhere as a nickname for Yehoshua.

3.   No one by the name of Yaakov Schuchman who survived has been identified. However, keeping with the Teitelman theme of this page, it is possible this person is another Teitelman relative, Yaakov Schichman/Schechman (the surname spelled with a yod in the list of martyrs but as Shukhman in Yad Vashem records). Yaakov Schichman/Schuchman married Chaika (Gruber), daughter of Yosef Gruber and Shifra (Teitelman) and a sister of Nahum Teitelman's wife, Rachel (Gruber) and Mendel Teitelman's wife, Sonia (Gruber). Nahum Teitelman in his essay, "In the Depths of Hell," p. 315, refers to Yaakov Shuchman as his brother-in-law and describes hurrying to his house in Mervits at the end of town on July 11, 1941, and hiding with him the day a number of Mlynov residents were murdered. More of the family's story is recounted in a book

length story of survival by Asher Teitelman on the Mlynov website. Their daughter Sara (Shichman) Vinokur, was the only member of the family to survive and a contributor of "Nazi Crimes in the Volyn Neighborhood" to this volume. The family is listed among the Mervits martyrs (p. 444), including Yaakov, his wife, Chaika (Gruber) their sons Mordechai, Shimon, Asher and Yosef and Azriel and their daughters, Perel and Sarah, the latter who is mistakenly identified as having perished.

4.   "Starosta" is a term of Slavic origin denoting a community elder whose role was to administer the assets in a range of civic and social contexts. The family surname is uncertain but, in line with the Teitelman theme of the page, probably refers to Mordechai Motel Teitelman (~1902/1905–1942) from Mervits, son of Chaim Meir Teitelman (1867–1942). Mordechai married Chava and they had four children according to Yad Vashem records.

5.   From the Mlynov martyr list, page 435, Yehezkiel Liberman (1897–1942), Doba his wife, and daughter Rachel (1924–1942) all perished. A son Herschel was living in Canada when the volume was published. A Yad Vashem record submitted by Yosef (Teitelman) Tomer suggests this family was related to the Teitelmans but the precise relationship is unknown.

6.   Moshe Fishman is a contributor of the essay "Mlynov in the Past." He created a fuss in Mlynov when he made aliyah in 1921 with his wife, Chaya (Gilden) (1880–1927) (see adjoining photo) and two children (David Fishman, also a contributor to this volume, and Chuva). They soon settled in Moshav Balfouria. The story of their aliyah is recounted in this volume by Boruch Meren's "The First Aliyah from the Shtetl." Standing with him is Moshe's sister Sarah Fishman (1878–1963) who had married Israel Schwartz (1874–1935) and settled in Baltimore before WWI with their son Peretz (Paul) Schwartz (1902–1956) and daughter Irene (Ida) Edelstein (1900–1975). This photo was taken in 1952 when Moshe came to Baltimore to see his sons and grandchildren.

7.   The history of this family is unknown.

8.   Seated center is Yetta (Demb) Schwartz, great-grandmother of Howard Schwartz, the editor of this volume. She was born in Mlynov in 1870. She married Chaim Schwartz (brother of Israel Schwartz) and migrated to Baltimore with her husband and her two younger sons in 1912. She was one of six children of Israel Jacob Demb and Rivka (Gruber) who ended up in Baltimore. Yetta returned to Mlynov for a visit in 1930 when this photo was taken with cousins from the Tesler family. Liba Tesler, who stands behind her, survived the Shoah, in a story told by David Sokolsky, *Monument: One Woman's Courageous Escape from the Holocaust.* Also in the photo are Liba's sisters, Hinda (seated left), and Golda (seated right), neither of whom survived. Back left is Rivka (Schwartz) Grintzveig, a niece of Chaim Schwartz. The woman standing back right is unidentified. A photo of Yetta with her husband Chaim Schwartz later in Baltimore appears on page 503.

[Page 470]

Photographs of Our Martyrs (cont.)

Translated by Howard I. Schwartz, PhD

The Rivitz Family, of blessed memory, to be distinguished for a long life their daughter Bat Sheva[1] (on the left)

[Toba née Guz] Fisher (the mother in the middle) her son Shmuel, of blessed memory. Distinguished for a long life, Yafa[2][Sheindel Fisher] from the Fisher line.

463

Tzvi Fisher (1908–1942)[1] and his wife Rivka[4] [Holtzeker, daughter of Moshe Nahmanis Holtzeker], of blessed memory

Esther Fisher,[5] of blessed memory

[Page 471]

Shmuel Gruber[6] and his wife Charna [Goldseker] [in front], of blessed memory

*Baila (Goldseker) Kulisz[7] wife of
Pesach, of blessed memory
Original courtesy of Irene Siegel
and Audrey Goldseker Polt*

*Beni Kulisz[8] [standing back is in fact Chuna
Goldseker] may he be distinguished for a long life, with
the children of Pesach Kulisz, his brother [seated front],
may their memory be a blessing
Original courtesy of Irene Siegel
and Audrey Goldseker Polt*

[Page 472]

*Rivkah Mandelkern[9] and Raisi, of blessed memory.
Distinguished for a long life, Faiga and Itka.*

Mlynov-Muravica Memorial Book

Shika Goldseker[10] (front) and his daughter [Batia], of blessed memory. To be distinguished for a long life, their son Pinchas.

Moshe Goldseker (right)[11] and his wife Luba, of blessed memory, distinguished for a long life their son Yoel

[Page 473]

Benyomin Grenspun[12] and his family. His father Motel Tesler, of blessed memory.

Yankel Preziment and his wife Chana Gittel[13] (Gelberg) and their children, of blessed memory

Pesach Gelman,[14] his wife Raizi and their daughters, ster and Yentil. Distinguished for a long life, Eliyahu. Photo courtesy of Rachel Gordon

Translator's and Editor's Folotnotes:

1. Bat-Sheva Ben Eliyahu made aliyah in 1939 and contributed the essay, "The Home That was Lost," pp. 263–265 that includes details about her family. The caption on this photo seems to suggest that Bat Sheva is the little girl on the left.

2. Yafa Dayagi Dashut (1916–1998) was born Sheindel Fisher. She contributed the essay "Home and Youth Movement in Mlynov," pp. 247–250, which discusses her family and experiences growing up. She made aliyah in 1939 following several of her sisters. Another sister, Rachel, survived the Shoah.

3. Tzvi Fisher (1908–1942) is one Sheindel's brothers who perished (see note 2).

4. Tzvi Fisher's wife, Rivka (Holtzeker), is described as the daughter of "Moshe Nahman's" (pronounced Moshe Nahmanis). She is the sister of Yehoshua Holtzeker who is also described as son of "Moshe Nahman's" in the list of martyrs (p. 432) and Yad Vashem records. It seems probable that "Moshe Nahman's" refers to the Moshe remembered as one of five brothers in the first generation of Holtzekers who came to Mlynov. This identification is consistent with the family tree recorded by the Baltimore Goldsekers, which lists both a Rivka and a Yeshea (=Yehoshua) as the children of the Moshe in the first generation. It should be noted, however, that normally, the Yiddish expression "Moshe Nahman's," which is possessive, implies that Moshe was the son (or grandson of Nahman), although there is one example in this volume where it is used to describe a father-in-law. Although we don't know of any Nahman in the prior Holtzeker generation, we do know that Moshe (one of the five brothers to come to Mlynov) had a grandson named Nahman (suggesting there might have been a Nahman in an earlier generation). It is also possibly significant that the martyr list indicates that a "Nahman from the Gelberg line," was living in the household of Yehoshua Holtzeker (one of Moshe's sons) and was related to Yehoshua's wife Sima. Perhaps for some reason this same Nahman Gelberg was the source of the name "Moshe Nahman's."

5.   Ester Fisher (1918–1942) a sister of Yafa Dayagi (Sheindel Fisher) who perished. See note 2.

6.   Shmuel Gruber (?-1943) was grandson of Perel and Mordechai Gruber and son of Israel Gruber. He was thus a first cousin of Rachel (Gruber) and Sonia (Gruber) (their fathers were brothers). Shmuel married Charna Goldseker (1898–1943), daughter of Shimon Goldseker and Anna (Fishman), and sister of the Goldseker siblings who migrated to Baltimore. Shmuel helped create bunkers in the forest near Karolinka and he, his brother Hanoch, and his wife and children escaped to the bunkers just before the ghetto liquidation. They all perished "During the Shoah," (pp. 291, 294, 301) as told in the joint testimony of the Yehudit and Fania Mandelkern and David Bernstein.

7.   Baila Goldseker (1897–1942) was also daughter of Shimon Goldseker and Anna (Fishman) and sister of Charna in the photo above. She married Peisach Kulisz (alternative spellings Collidge, Kulish) whose photo is to the right with three of their five children.

8.   The original caption on this photo is incorrect based on handwritten notes on the photo from the Baltimore Goldseker family. Standing in the back is Chuna Goldseker (1909–1972), the brother of Charna (in photo above) and Baila (Peisach's wife) and the Goldsekers siblings who migrated to Baltimore. This photo was taken not long before Chuna left Mlynov in 1929 and made his way to Buenos Aires where he became Juan Golceker, married, settled down and had a family. Seated in the front row is his brother-in-law, Peisach Kulisz (husband of Baila Goldseker) with three of their children in descending age: Moishe (1923–1942), Henia (~1925–1942), and Shimon (1927–1942). Two younger children, Golda and Ben-Zion perished as did Pesach's sister Yenti and his mother Chana.

9.   Two of the Mandelkern sisters, Fania and Yehudit (Itka) survived in bunkers to tell their survival story in the essay "During the Shoah," pp. 287–313. Their mother Rivka perished with two of their other siblings, Moishe and Rosa (Riisi). Three brothers Pesach (1911–1987), Eliyahu (1921–), and Gedaliah (1915–2005) all made it to Israel at some point. Pesach's photo appears on page 227.

10.   A record submitted to the Yad Vashem database by Moshe Isakovich (alternative spelling Iskiewicz) a contributor to this volume, identifies this photo with Yehoshua Goldseker, son of "Moshe Nahman's." "Shika" thus appears to be a nickname for Yehoshua, a sibling of Rivka (Holtzeker) Fisher whose photo appears on the previous page (page 470). For reasons discussed there, their father Moshe Nahman's is assumed to be the Moshe in the first generation of the five Holtzeker brothers who came to Mlynov. According to the Yad Vashem record, Yehoshua's wife was Sima (née Gelberg) who was born in Mlynow and daughter of the mill owner Yosef Gelberg and his wife Sara Dvora. The list of martyrs (p. 432) indicates their children Avraham, Yosef, and Batia (who is in the photo), also perished, as did "Nahman from the Gelberg family" who was apparently a relative of Sima's and living in their household. The list indicates that Yehoshua and Sima's son, Pinchas Holtzeker, (who appears to be in a military uniform in the photo) was in fact living in Russia at the time of this volume's original publication.

11.   Vad Vashem records submitted by Moshe Isakovich, identifies these photos with Moshe Holtzeker (~1902–1942) who was son of Yoel Holtzeker, one of the original five brothers who came to Mlynov. Moshe married a woman named Luba (also spelled Liuba) (~1904–1942) who was born in Dubno. Their children Batia (age 15), Mordechai (age 12), and Chaya (age 8) perished. A son Yoel was living in Russia when this volume was originally published.

12.   This photo of the Grenspun family from Mervits (alternative spellings Grinshpun, Greenspun, Grenspun) is remembered as the family of survivor Sheindel (Grenspun) Steinberg (1912–1978), wife of survivor Mendel Steinberg, who contributed, "Terror of Annihilation" in this volume. Sheindel's father was Benyomin Grenspun who married Sura (Tepler) from Trochenbrod. The essay by Sheindel's husband, Mendel, recalls how he got Sheindel and their son Anshel out of the ghetto and how they survived. Sheindel's grandfather, the older man on the right of the photo called "Motel Tesler" ("carpenter"), is remembered as the first to be killed in Mervits, in the synagogue, on July 12, 1941, as told by Nachum Teitelman, "In the Depths of Hell," (p. 316). Sheindel's brother, Joe (Yosel) Greenspun (1918–1985), also survived and came to Cleveland to live, which is also where Sheindel and her husband Mendel Steinberg settled after leaving the displaced persons camp.

13.   Yankel Preziment married Chana Gitel (Gelberg) (~1890– ~1942) who was the third oldest of seven children of Labish (or Leibish) Gelberg (1860- ~1915) and Eta Leah (Schuchman) (~1856-?). Chana Gitel and two of her older siblings, Pinchus Gelberg (1874–1935) and Esther (Gelberg) Malar (1888– ~1942) and most of their immediate families perished. A son of Ester's, David Malar, survived and later came to America. Several of the younger Gelberg siblings migrated to the US just before and shortly after WWI, and settled in New York and Baltimore, with their families including Moishe Goldberg (1875–1967), Ida (Gelberg) Gevantman (1893–1949), Sarah (Sura Gelberg) Spector (1894–1941), and George (Gershon Joe) Goldberg (1896–1984). For more on Gelberg / Goldberg story, see the Mlynov website.

14. Eliyahu Gelman (1913–2008), the young boy in this photo, contributed several essays to this volume including "My Father's Home," p. 259, which provides details about his family.

[Page 474]

Photographs of Our Martyrs (cont.)

Translated by Howard I. Schwartz, PhD

Bilah and her husband Kesselman from Mervits, of blessed memory

Benyumekah Teitrelbaum [1] and his wife, Rivkeh, of blessed memory

69

Mlynov-Muravica Memorial Book

Gershon Upstein[2] and his sisters, Faiga and Chaya, of blessed memory, from Mervits

Beautiful women of Mlynov. From the right, Chaya Holtzeker,[3] Gitel Holtzheker,[4] Tzipa Tilimzejger[5]

[Page 475]

The home of Shamai and Rachel Parizak[6] in Mervits, of blessed memory

Faiga Bermeister and her husband Motel from Mervits, of blessed memory

Moshe, Yosef, and Yizrael Wurtzel,[7] of blessed memory. And Zalman son of Mr. Meir Hirsch Zider[8]

Translator's and editor's footnotes:

1.   Beyumekah Teitelbaum (alternative spellings Teitelboim, Tatelbaum and Ferteybaum) is listed among the martyrs with his wife Rivkah (née Khinkes) and their two children Yitzhak and Silka. It seems probable that Beyumekah is the son of "Icek Starote" and Malia Ferteybaum, who are described in several essays in this volume as the maternal grandparents of contributor, Sylvia (Silka) Barditch-Goldberg. In her essay "Visiting My Grandparents," pp. 266–271, Sylvia recalls how "my mother's younger brother Benimke, who was the same age as my older brother, but who treated me a lot better, showed me around the small garden," and offered to pay for treats. In 1921, Silka, her mother Bassa Borodacz (later Bessie Barditch), and her siblings followed her father to America after WWI. Silka's other maternal uncle Usher (Harry Tatelbaum), traveled to Baltimore in March 1911 with two other men from Mlynov.
Rivkah, the wife of Benimke, was born with the surname Khinkes. A man named Tzvi Zeev Khinkes is listed among the martyrs, p. 435, and is likely her brother.

2.   These three Upstein siblings (alternative spelling Epshtein) were nieces and nephews of Yitzhak Upstein (1910–2004). Yitzhak survived the War in the Red Army in Siberia. He returned to Mlynov to find his whole family had perished. He soon married Bunia Steinberg (1912–1995) who had survived with her brothers Getzel and Mendel. Their story is recounted by Bunia in a book length account now available in English on the Mlynov website.

3. Possibly one of two Chaya Hotzekers. This woman resembles later photos of Chaya (Ida) Goldseker (1888–1968), daughter of Shimon Goldseker, one of the five brothers who originally came to Mlynov. Ida migrated to Baltimore in 1912 after marrying her uncle Meyer Fishman. She later married Benjamin Gresser. Alternatively, this could be Chaya Holtzeker, the daughter of Basa and Yoel Holtzeker, the latter one of the other original five Holtzeker brothers to come to Mlynov. In the family tree documented by Baltimore descendants, this daughter is called "Chaiyz" and is called "Chaya" in the list of martyrs (p. 432). A Yad Vashem record submitted by Tania Feldman from LA identifies Chaika daughter of Yoel Holtzeker as a cousin as well as several Goldsekers from Dubno, suggesting that the Dubno line of Goldsekers was related to the Mlynov line.

4. Gitel is the daughter of Hirsch Holtzeker, also one of the five original Holtzeker brothers. Gitel is remembered as a beautiful daughter in an essay by Shmuel Mandelkern which describes a prank carried out on the home of Hirsch Holtzeker by the young men involved in "Self Defense in Mlynov," p. 134.

5. It seems probable that Tzipa Tilimzeiger belongs to the Tilimzeiger family known from the martyr list (p. 435, spelled there with the Hebrew "tet") and Yad Vashem records submitted by Bat Sheva Ben Eliyahu, who wrote "The Home That Was Lost." The Tilimzeiger household included Ezra Tilimzeiger, a butcher, and his wife, Chana, and their two children Chaim and Yeshayahu. Yeshayahu was married to Chava from Ostrozhets. They had three children: Brakha, Ezra and Golda.

6. Records submitted by Brakha (Grinberg) Shochet, a niece of the family, indicate Shame/Shamai Parizak (1895–1942) was born in Dubno and lived in Mervits with his wife Rachel (1897–1942).

7. The Wurtzel brothers (alt. spelling Vortsel) were sons of Zelig "Ulinik" Wurtzel and Sooreh (Gruber). Their sister Pessia (1907–1994) married Getzel Steinberg and survived with her husband and son Gerry. Their Wurtzel paternal grandparents were Doovid and Meerel Wurtzel. Their maternal grandparents were Mordechai and Perel Gruber. The Wurtzel brothers and their sisters, Ester who married Yosel Duvid Milhalter, and Gitel who married Fishel Kleinberg, perished with their families.

8. In the Mlynov martyr list (p. 435), Zalman Zider is listed with his wife Zelda and sons, Zelig and Avraham-Aharon.

[Page 476]

Photographs of Our Martyrs (cont.)

Translated by Howard I. Schwartz, PhD

Family of Zahvil [Shmuel Zeev] Katz [and Brakha Katz, née Gelberg[1]], of blessed memory

A group of young people, of blessed memory

[Page 477]

Leazar Iskiewicz,[2] of blessed memory

la Gelman from Mervits,[3] of blessed memory

Gedaliah Gelman [Alman] and Rikel Gelman,[4] of blessed memory

The daughters of Tola Gelman, Sarah, Rivkah, and Mania, of blessed memory

Editor's footnotes:

1. Yad Vashem records submitted by the daughter, Batya (Katz) Mohel, indicate her father Zanvil (Shmuel Zeev) Katz (~1877–1944) and her mother Brakha (Gelberg) (~1879–1944) perished with Batya's brothers: Tzvi, Arieh, Moshe, and Avraham and their families. Batya, survived with her husband, Yitzhak Mohel, who contributed the essay "A Murdered Family" to this volume. A photo of Batya sitting in the window of the Mohel house appears on page 411 of this volume. Batya and Yitzhak fled East from Mlynov at the German invasion and survived in Uzbekistan, as told by Dani Tracz (Issachar Mohel) in *Riva and Yehuda: Life Story of Trancman, Mohel, Tracz and Ben-Eliezer Families*, 2015. Batya's brother Arieh Katz (1910–1942), who was a hatter, was married to Feiga (Bik) from Kremenets (1910–1942) and had a daughter Soma, age 7. Her brother, Abraham Katz (1906–1942), was born in Dubno, was a tailor and married to Pesia. They had two children, Pesa and Yankele (1936–1942). It is unknown if this Katz family was related to the Mervits family of Yankel-Volf Katz, who married Ronya Leah Wurtzel, and whose five of seven children migrated to Canada and the US.

2. Leazar or Eliezer Iskiewicz (also spelled Isakovich) was the father of Moshe Iskiewicz who contributed the essay "Impressions and Memories," 88-89 to this volume. A photo of Eliezer and family appears on page 464. Additional details on the family are provided there.

3. Tola Gelman's genealogy is not known. It seems plausible he was related to Gedaliah Gelman whose photo appears next. It is not known how or if the Gelmans in these photos were related to Mervits family of Eliyahu Gelman described in his essay "My Father's Home" in this volume.

4. Gedaliah Gelman (1876–1951) and Rikel (Gruber) (1881–1952) became Joseph and Rebecca Alman in Springfield, Massachusetts. Gedaliah arrived in the US in 1913 and was joined by Rikel and several of their daughters in 1921. Rikel was the daughter of Perel and Mordechai Gruber and was probably born in Mervits. The only US record found that unambiguously indicates the family's connection to Mervits is a 1923 passenger

manifest of their eldest daughter, Beatrice (Gelman) Steinberg (appearing as "Bejla Stzejnberg") which indicates she was born in "Morovice." After the Shoah, the Alman family was responsible for sponsoring Rikel's niece, Pesia (Wurtzel) Steinberg, to come to the US with her husband Getzel (George) and son Zelig (Gerald) Steinberg. There are conflicting family memories regarding how many siblings were in Rikel Gruber's family. According to Etti Natiiv, a granddaughter of Rikel's sister, Ester (Gruber) Borenstein, there were four sisters in the family: Rikel (Gruber) Alman, Sooreh (Gruber) Wurtzel, Rachel (Gruber) Feldman, and Ester (Gruber) Boronstein. A more expansive list of nine siblings is recorded in the Teitelman family tree put together by other descendants of Mordechai and Perel Gruber: Yaakov Gruber, Yosef Moshe Gruber (who married Shifra Teitelman, parents of Rachel and Sonia Teitelman), Bracha Gruber (who married Mordechai Liberman), Yisrael Gruber (who married Tova), Hanah Gruber (who married Shimon Weisfeld), Rikel Gruber (who married Gedalia Gelman/Alman), Sooreh Gruber (who married Zelig Wurtzel), Miriam Gruber (who married Moshe Pelichov), and Leah Gruber who married Azriel Kleinberg.

[Page 478]

Photographs of Our Martyrs (cont.)

Translated by Howard I. Schwartz, PhD

Avraham (Peretz's)[1] [Tesler], of blessed memory.
Grandfather of Sorah Gitlas [Mutter] and Liba [Tesler]

Yitzhak-Yukal (Peretz's) [Tesler] (Liba's brother)

Yankel (Jacob) Tesler (Peretz's), of blessed memory.

Beinish Schwartz,[2] of blessed memory

*Shlomo Schechman,[3]
of blessed memory*

Beracha Raikhman from Mervits[4]

*Eliezer Hochberg,[5]
the teacher from Boremel*

*Tova[Genut]
Teitelman[6]*

*Chaim Rabinovitch,[7]
of blessed memory*

[Page 479]

Perel Mandelkern,[8] of blessed memory

Pinkhas Fistel, of blessed memory (from Mervits)

The brothers Shlomo and Fishel Teitelman,[9] of blessed memory

Peretz [Paul] Schwartz,[10] of blessed memory
(grandson of Moshe Holtzeker)

Moshe Wurtzel[11] from Mervits.

Pesach Goldseker,[12] of blessed memory

*Sheyke Berger
(daughter of Chaim Berger[13])*

Avraham Pikhniuk[14]

Sarah Vinokur,[15] of blessed memory

Aba Goldseker,[16] of blessed memory

Rachel Likrits,[17] of blessed memory (sister of Shmuel)

Avigdor Litzman,[18] of blessed memory (son of Moshe Maklas)

Translator's and editor's footnotes:

1.   Avraham Tesler was born Avraham Kotel in Ostroh according to the story recounted by his granddaughter, Liba Tesler, who survived the Shoah and narrated her life story to her step-grandson, David Sokolsky. For reasons not understood, Avraham is called "Peretz's Avraham" perhaps because he had a father Peretz after whom he named one of his sons. According to Liba, her grandfather Avraham left Ostroh when it was time to be conscripted and adopted the name Avraham Tesler ("carpenter") which was on a passport he had gotten from another conscript who was deceased. With his assumed identity, he came to Mlynov to avoid detection and married a woman named Hannah through an arranged marriage. They had two children: Yankel and Baila (Clara).

Their son Yankel (Jacob) Tesler (1878–1942), whose photo appears in this row, married Bluma Woskobojnic in 1903. They had three daughters (Hinda, Liba and Golda) and two sons (Itzhak and Peretz). Only Liba survived the Shoah in a story recounted in David Sokolsky's book, *Monument*. Liba and her two sisters appear in the photo on page 469, labeled "Daughters of Mlynov."

Avraham and Hannah's daughter Baila (Clara) Tesler (1881–1951) married Isaac Marder (1876–1942) from Mlynov. They had three children before migrating to Baltimore. Their eldest was "Sora Gitlas" Marder (1903–1991) (who married David Mutter in Baltimore). The other two children became Pauline Bargteil (1905–1986) and Nathan Marder (1909–1992) in Baltimore. Isaac migrated to Baltimore before WWI and was joined by his wife and children in June 1920 when they traveled to Baltimore with the Mlynov families of Aaron Demb, Joseph Lerner, and the young Benjamin Fishman.

2.   The list of Mlynov martyrs (p. 439) includes Beinish Schwartz (alternative spelling Svartz), son of Sheintzi. He perished with his wife Faiga, who was the daughter of Yitzchak Rabinovitch, and their daughter Nusia. Yiddish inscriptions on the back of postcards with Benish and Feigas photo are addressed to "uncle Israel and aunt Sarah" (Israel Schwartz and Sarah [Fishman]) that remain in a collection preserved by Eugene Schwartz, grandson of Israel and Sarah. According to Eugene's recollection, there were five Schwartz brothers in the generation of his grandfather, Israel Schwartz, though we know the names of only four who came to Baltimore (see Mlynov website). It seems probable that Beinish is the son of the fifth Schwartz brother whose name is no longer remembered. Another photo in the same collection which refers to "uncle Israel and Aunt Sarah" is from a Rivkah (Schwartz) Grintzveig or Gruntzweig (alternative spelling Gruntsvayg) who may have been Beinish's sister. Beinish is described as a prospering business man in an essay on page 97, and his home is mentioned along the road where the young Mlynov men trained in self-defense, (p. 122) after WWI.

3.   Shlomo Schechman, a Shoah survivor, was the son of Noach Moshe Schechman, p. 246. Other photos of Shlomo as a young man appear on pages 227 and 461 with additional notes there. He is mentioned among those met by others after the liberation on pages 311 and 341. He married after the War and eventually settled with his wife and two children in Baltimore.

4.   A family by the name of Raikhman is listed among Mervits martyrs though it is not known how this Beracha relates to them.

5.   From online trees, it appears Eliezer Hochberg was a son of Golda (Lender) and Shlomo Hochberg from Boremel.

6.   Tova Genut, from Transylvania, became the wife of Mlynov born Asher Teitelman, a contributor of the essay "The Massive Disaster," pp. 38–40. The two young people met after their liberation in the Displaced Persons camp of Bad Gastein. In 1947, they were able to get on an illegal ship bound for Palestine with Asher's parents but were then turned back to Cyprus by the British. There in the British internment camps, they got married. Finally in April 1948, they were permitted to land in what had by then become the State of Israel. After having two children, Tova tragically died of preeclampsia in 1956. The story of Asher and Tova is recounted in Dinah Tomer's book about Asher's life, *Happy is the Man*, published on the Mlynov website.

7.   A Chaim "Geler Rabinovitz" appears in the Mlynov martyr list (p. 433) married to a Devorah with two children, Shlomo, and daughter Zysl. Chaim is described earlier as a prospering businessman in an essay on page 97. In Yad Vashem records submitted by Pinhas Berger, Chaim's wife, Devorah Rabinovitz (1903–1942), was daughter of Malka and Yosef Berger; It appears she had a sibling, Shimon Berger, who also perished.

8. Perel Mendelkern was the wife of Yitzhak Mandelkern. As discussed in the essay, "Life Under the Occupying German Government," p. 290, she went to Dubno seeking a work certificate to support her sister-in-law and was swept up in a German roundup. According to a Yad Vashem record, she was born Perel Klotz (1912–1943) to Nakhman and Rakhel Leah in the Dubno region. Prior to WWII she lived in Mlynov. She died in 1943 in the Belzec Extermination Camp.

9. The two young sons of Nahum and Rachel Teitelman who left the ghetto without permission of authorities shortly before the liquidation. They were captured, killed, and the first to be thrown into the pit that had been dug. See their father, Nahum's account, "In the Depths of Hell," p. 322.

10. Paul Schwartz (1902–1956) son of Israel Schwartz (1874–1935) and Sarah (Sore) Fishman (1878–1963) one of at least three first cousins named Paul (Peretz) Schwartz. who came to America. This Paul arrived in 1912 with his mother and sister Chaia (Irene Edelstein) (1900–1975). What is not understood is how Paul Schwartz could be the grandson of Moshe Goldseker, as this caption indicates.

11. Moshe's photo with his brothers also appears on 475 with additional notes there. His sister, Pessia (Wurtzel) Steinberg, survived with her husband Getzel and son Zelig (Gerald).

12. A Pesach Goldseker who was killed in the Russian military service is listed among the martyrs of Mlynov (p. 432). He is the son of Ben-Tzion Goldseker and Ester-Mania Feldman, daughter of Pesach Feldman from Boremel. Also listed are two siblings: Avraham and Rivkah. Pesach's brother Avraham was the one who led the resistance effort before the liquidation, mentioned in the essay, "Life Under the Occupying German Government," p. 291. It appears that Pesach's grandfather was Moshe Holtzeker, one of the five original brothers who came to Mlynov. His father "Ben-Tzion" was the one listed as "Bene" in the Goldseker family tree documented by Baltimore descendants.

13. Not much is known about Sheyke Berger or her father Chaim's family. Chaim is mentioned as helping with the establishment in 1920 of "The Youth Movement, Hashomer Hatzair" (p. 69) by hosting a young Zionist visitor from Rovno. Chaim's home is also mentioned as being near the synagogue where the young men practiced "Self-Defense in Mlynov," p. 136. Another daughter of Chaim's named Rachel is listed in the Vad Vashem records married to Yosef Wurtzel.

14. Avraham Pikhniuk (1922–1942) (alternative spellings Pikhniuk Pikhnyuk) was son of Yaakov (1892–1942) and Gitel Pikhniuk (1892–1942). His siblings included Chaim (1912–1942), Rachel (1918–1942), Feiga (1920–1942) and Zelig (1920–1942). His brother Zelig appears in the photo on 455.

15. Sarah Vinokur was born Sara Shichman (?–1957), daughter of Chaika (Gruber) and Yaakov Shichman. She contributed the essay "Nazi Crimes in the Volyn Neighborhood," 449–452 which includes additional notes about her family and her survival.

16. In the list of Mlynov martyrs (p. 432), Aba Holtzeker is listed as son of Aisik (or Isaac) Holtzeker and Perel Shochet, the daughter of R. Itzi Shochet. It thus appears that Aba was the grandson of Hirsch Holtzeker, the eldest of the original five Holtzeker brothers to come to Mlynov. Aba had a number of siblings. One of the siblings, Micael made aliyah before the War. There he adopted the last name Givoni (Gibeon in English), picking the name of the biblical people identified as "hewers of wood" (Joshua 9.27) which is the original meaning of the surname Holtzeker.

Based on information from Micael's granddaughter, it appears there were 11 siblings who perished as well as children of theirs. Micael begged his family to make aliyah but they didn't think the Nazis would come to Mlynov. They were hiding in a bunker and executed upon capture. The names of known siblings of Aba and Micael were: Avraham, Yaakov, and Israel (Srul / Shurlik), Malka and Bailah. From records, we know that Israel/Srul (1906–1942) married Shifra Kotel (1915–1942) and they had two children, Rachel age 5 and a one-year-old child. From the martyr list (p. 439), we know that Malka Holtzeker married Mordechai Shefer (alternative spelling Shiper).

It also seems plausible that these children's mother, called "Perel Shochet, daughter of R. Itzi Shochet," (p. 432) may actually have been from the Gelman line and the sister of Pesach Gelman since he is called a shochet and called the son of Itzi Shohet (p. 433).

17. Rachel Lakritz (alternate spelling Lakic or Lakrits) is perhaps related to the Lakritz family documented in Yad Vashem submitted by Meir Teitelman, a contributor to this volume. The parents were Baruch (1889–1942) son of Israel and Stisi. Baruch was a blacksmith and married to Ester Finkelsthtein. Their children were Malka, Miriam, Pinkhas and Ben.

18. A Litzman family is included among the Mervits martyrs (p. 442): Moshe Litzman, his wife Sima, his son Dov, his son Pesach and his wife Freida, and their children and families.

_____

[Page 480]

Photographs of Our Martyrs (cont.)

Translated by Howard I. Schwartz, PhD

Feiga Veiner,[1] of blessed memory

Shmuel Kobrik,[2] of blessed memory

Dvorah [Gruber] Kobrik,[3] of blessed memory

Baruch Teper[4]

NoahGrinberg,[5]
of blessed memory (Mervits)

Rivkah Veiner,[6] of blessed memory

Boruch and Reizel Likhter,[7] of blessed memory

Baruch Likhter,[8]
Mutka Malar,[9]
of blessed memory

Pesach[10]
of blessed memory

Pesach Fishman,[11]
of blessed memory

Yisrael Freeman[12] (cantor)
of blessed memory

[Page 481]

Arieh Katz[13] and his family, of blessed memory

[Avraham] son of [Shmuel] Zanvil Katz[14] and his wife [Pesa], of blessed memory

Sarah Nudler, Fania Neiter,[15] Freida Nudler,[16] of blessed memory

Sarah and [husband] Boka [Baruch] Kugal, of blessed memory

A group of young girls [with a sewing machine],[17] of blessed memory

[Page 482]

R. Nahum Teitelman his wife Rachel [Gruber],[18] his grandson Ben-Tzion, may they be distinguished for a long life

Shmuel Mandelkern,[19]
may he be distinguished for a long life

Malcah Lamdan[20] *(from the Lamdan line),*
may she be distinguished for a long life

Translator's and editor's footnotes:

1.   Feiga was sister of Sunny Veiner, who contributed "Poems," p. 251, which includes additional family notes. They were children of Yaakov and Brendl. Their siblings include Khaia Leah, Henia, Mordechai and Rivka (whose photo is below).

2.   Identified as "Meir-Shmuel" Kibrik in the list of Mervits martyrs (p. 441) and married to Devorah [Gruber], next photo. A Kibrik family with many members was living in Boremel according to Yad Vashem records.

3.   Devorah Kibrik [née Gruber] appears in the list of Mervits martyrs (p. 441) with her husband Meir-Shmuel (previous photo) and family. In Yad Vashem records, she is identified by nephew Asher Teitelman, as born in Mervits in 1917, the daughter Yosef Moshe Gruber and Shifra (Teitelman). A sister-in-law, named Rachel Meiri, identifies her as born in 1914 in Boremel as daughter of Yosef Moshe Gruber and his second wife Tzirel, which is consistent with versions of the family tree from the Teitelman family.

4.   Possibly the son of Feibish Teper who is listed with a wife and child in the Mervits martyrs (p. 442).

5.   Probably Noah Grinberg (1909–1942) brother of Feiga Grinberg (1913–1942) both children of Yehoshua and Reizel. A sister, Brakha (Grinberg) Shokhet, submitted Yad Vashem records indicating they both were born in Boremel though Feiga was a student in Muravica during the War. Noah and his wife Ester had a daughter Shoshana. Noah was taken out and shot according to the essay "Tragic Tales," p. 332, by Mendel and Sonia Teitelman.

6.   Rivkah was the sister of Feiga Veiner whose photo is above. See note 1.

7.   Boruch is probably the brother of Leye (Leah) Veyner-Likhter, a contributor of "In Fear and Pain," pp. 382–383, which mentions her brother Baruch and describes the fate of her family. This photo is probably placed here because Boruch's sister, Leah, married Yehuda Veiner, a relative of the other Veiners in the photo here.

8.   See prior note about Boruch Likhter. Boruch is probably the one on the right.

9.   Probably Moshe Malar (alt. spelling Meler or Meiler) (1880–1942) a butcher born in Mervits in 1880 to Barukh Malar, is listed in the Mervits martyrs (p. 442) and Yad Vashem records with his wife and children. His children were Mordechai, Yosef, Barukh, and Chaim. The son Mordechai and his wife had a newborn in the ghetto. It is possible the son Yosef Malar is the man remembered as Yossel Malar who married Ester Gelberg/Goldberg, daughter of Labish and Eta Leah (Schuchman).

10.   It appears that this Pesach is the same as the one in the next photo.

11.   Possibly the Pesach Fishman listed as son of Kalman Fishman and Chaya in the Mlynov martyrs, p. 437, along with siblings David, Shimon, Asher Yosel. Kalman Fishman is mentioned as a coachman on p. 217. A Yad Vashem record submitted by Yaakov Goldseker, another contributor to this volume, indicates that Kalman's son, David, married Nuna Shkolnick (1912–1942) from Mlynov daughter of Chaim Shkolnick and Liba (Goldseker); Liba was daughter of Yoel Goldseker (one of the original five Goldseker brothers who came to Mlynov). David and Nuna and their children, Avraham, Hasia, Eliyahu, Batia, all perished.

12.   Possibly the man listed as Israel "Fridman" (not Freeman) among the Mervits martyrs, p. 437, with his father Nahum, son of Yosil Shichnas from Mervits "the educator of most of the children of Mlynov, Mervits and Lutzk in Torah and haskalah (enlightenment)," Pesia his mother, and brother Yosef.

13.   Arieh is the young man standing behind his father in the Katz family which appears on page 476 with notes about the family. Here, Arieh (1910–1942) who was born in Dubno is with his wife Feiga (Bik), who was born in Kremenets, and their daughter Soma. During the War they lived in Mlynov where Arieh was a hatter. His brother Avraham is in the next photo. His sister, Batia (Katz) married Yitzhak Mohel and they survived.

14.   Avraham Katz is the brother of Arieh (photo to the left). Avraham appears as the son in the back left in the family photo on page 476. Avraham (1906–1942) was born in Dubno and is here with his wife Pesa who was born in Mlynov. They had a son Yankele/ Yaakov, age 6.

15.   There are Neiter families (alt. spelling Neyter) in both the Mlynov and Mervits martyr lists, though Fania is not mentioned. Sore Neiter is the person who wrote to Yitzhak Mohel to notify him what happened to his family, p. 410. Pnina (Neiter) Blinder is the mother of Batia (Blinder) Kopchak who contributed an essay, p. 374.

16.   Freida Nudler is perhaps one of two women known as Feiga Nudler in the Mlynov martyr list. One Feiga Nudler was daughter of Khaikyl Nudler, the ladies' tailor, who owned the gramophone that disappeared one day in Mlynov, p. 199. There was also a Feiga Nudler, who was daughter of Metayahu Nudler and Chaika from the Mandelkern line.

17.   Appears to be the same four girls as in photo above but at a younger age.

18.   Nahum Teitelman (1890–1976) is a contributor to this volume, p. 314, as is his wife Rachel (Gruber), (1894–1980), p. 380, and their son, Asher (1922–2009), p. 38, with additional notes there. Rachel was a sister of Sonia (Gruber) Teitelman, also a contributor to this volume. A photo appears earlier, p. 479, of Nahum and Rachel's sons, Fishel and Shlomo, who were the first to be thrown into the pit dug for the liquidation.

19.   Shmuel Mandelkern is the contributor of two essays to this volume (p. 116 and p. 208), which include additional notes on his family. Mandelkern was remembered as a prankster in town in an essay by Boruch Meren (p. 190), and as the initiator in the early 1920s behind the creation of the Zionist Youth groups in Mlynov, as described by Aaron Harari in his essay on culture and education, p. 66. Another photo with Shmuel and Malcah among a group of young people appears there. Shmuel and his wife Malcah (next photo) made aliyah in 1924.

20.   Malcah was the daughter of Yehuda Leib Lamdan (see photo p. 454) and sister of Yitzhak Lamdan, famous for his Hebrew poem, "Masada." See the essay in this volume about Lamdan's return visit to Mlynov, by Moshe Teitelman (p. 32). Malcah is described as a teacher in Mlynov, p. 66. She married Shmuel Mandelkern (previous photo) and they made aliyah in 1924.

[Page 484]

Writers and Poets

Writers and Poets

Dr. Shlomo Mandelkern[1]

Translated and edited by Howard I. Schwartz, PhD with Hanina Epstein

Shlomo Mandelkern was born at daybreak on the second day of Passover 5606 (1846), in the small town of Mlynov close to the district town of Dubno ("The Greater Dubno," Volhynia). His father R. Simha Dov, tried to make him a Torah scholar (talmid chacham) and hired the top-notch teachers in the town for him. And indeed, already by the age of six years old, the small Shlomo was already an expert in the Five Books of Moses and by the age of ten already knew many pages of Gemara by heart and was a student of Rabbi Pinchas, Av Beit Din ("chief justice") in Targowica [Trovits][2] which was also in the district of Dubno.

Dr. Shlomo Mandelkern, of blessed memory

[Page 485]

When he reached 16 years old, in 1862, he lost his father. He then went to study Torah in Dubno. There he learned Torah from the lips of the Gaon R. Tzvi Rapaport HaCohen, the author of "Ezrat Cohanim" and "Tosefet Ha-Ezrah" on the Sifra. From the lips of his brother-in-law, R. Rabbi Yitzchak Eliyahu Landa, the author of interpretations of the Mekhilta, the Tana Devei Eliyahu, the Hebrew Bible, and the established liturgy, who was at the end of his days Maggid Mesharim in Vilna. Subsequently, the young Mandelkern expanded his study of Talmud and its commentaries with another sharp teacher, Rabbi Yehoshua Cahana. But he was not satisfied exclusively with Talmud: he also studied Zohar,[3] Tanya[4] and other books of Kabbalah. And earlier he made a pilgrimage to the "Rebbe," Rabbi Menachem Mendel from Kotzk[5] Polonia [Kock, Poland] and he studied Kabbalah and Hasidism especially with R. David [Morgenstern], the son of the Rebbe.

When he returned to Dubno, which was full of sages and Hebrew writers, he abandoned Talmud and began a diligent study of Hebrew grammar, Hebrew Bible, literature of the Middle Ages and the new literature.

As a young man of about 18, in 1864, his relatives married him to a woman as required in Ethics of the Fathers.[6] The young woman was homely and very religious. After a year, they had a son. But his heart longed for Torah — and he fled from his religious wife and infant son to the rabbinical seminary in Zhytomyr. But he didn't retain his position — certainly because of his "easy"[7] personality. He, therefore, transferred to the rabbinical seminary in Vilna and here he started a new period in his life.

About the year 5628 (1868), Mandelkern completed his rabbinical studies and received certification, which enabled him to be a Crown rabbi.[8] He returned to Dubno and divorced his wife from whom he had grown more distant the more he studied, while she remained a plain observant Jewish woman. Subsequently, he also forgot about his first born son, "a simple and crude young man, who didn't read nor study, and his father neither worried about him nor bothered to grace him with his presence."[9]

In Dubno, the enlightened members (maskilim) of the city wanted to appoint him as Crown rabbi. But he still desired Torah study. He traveled to Petersburg, entered the university in the Department of Eastern Languages, became friendly with Prof Chwolson[10] and finished his studies as a candidate (equivalent to our[11] humanities degree). His dissertation was on interpretation of the Hebrew Bible according to the translation of the seventy (=Septuagint[12]), and the Arabic Peshitta of Rav Saadia Gaon, along with a paleographic investigation of the places that diverged from the Hebrew Bible, for which he earned a gold medal from the faculty.

His writings:

First his writing in Hebrew in chronical order:

Teshu'at Melekh Rav, Ode to Czar Alexander II, on the day God saved the Tzar righteous Alexander II from the hands of violent men [assassination attempt], the second day of the new month of Iyyar (5666) (assassination attempt by [Dmitry] Karakozov on April 4, 1866) Vilna 5666.

[Page 486]

"Bat Sheva or Craziness of David," a love poem in six parts and 120 stanzas (Vilna 5626 [1865-1866]; Second edition, Leipzig, 5656 [1895-1896].

Witty Sayings, *Ḥiẓẓim Shenunim*; 75 original translated epigrams and at their end "Rose of the North," two romances translated from Russian, Vilna 5626 [1865-1866].

"*Ezra ha-Sofer*," a story set in the days of Achashverosh King of Persia by Ludwig Philippson, translated [from the German] by Shlomo Mandelkern, Vilna 5626 [1865-1866]; Second Edition, Leipzig, 5661.

A poem "Greeting for Montefiore," Petersburg 5632 [1872-73] (one large page). "Song of Greeting to [Sir Moses] Montefiore," Petersburg 5632 (One large page).

"*Dibre Yeme Russiya*,"[13] [a history of Russia] 3 Vols. From the beginning of the Russian people until the rule of Alexander II. (Warsaw, 5635) [1874-1875].

Shirei Sefat Ever. [Poems in Hebrew], 3 vols., Vol. 1, Leipzig 5642 [1881-1882]; Vol. 2, ibid., 5649 [1888-1889]; and Volume 3, ibid. 5661 [1900-1901].

Shirei Yeshurun, translation of Hebrew Melodies of [Lord] Byron. Published the English source and the Hebrew translation side by side, Leipzig, 5650 [1889-1890]; Second edition, also there, 5661 [1890-1891].

Heikhal ha-Kodesh [Holy Temple] , Hebrew and Aramaic Concordance, Leipzig 5656 [1865–1866]; (preceded by the notebook, which showed the failings of the earlier concordances, in combination with the official authorization of the new concordance by 15 sages of Israel and of the nations, ibid. (5644) [1883–1884]); Second edition, corrected and improved, Schocken Publishing, 5696 [1935-1936].

Tavnit Heikhal, abridged edition of the concordance, Leipzig, 5656 [1865–1866].

Mapot Shel Russiya [Maps of Russia], Mandelkern prepared for a book, "Studies in the Land of Russia" of Kalman Shulman. His many Hebrew writers were found in every Hebrew daily, weekly newspaper, monthly Hebrew [journal] and Hebrew annual.

In *Ashkenazi-Jewish*, I know[14] only of Mandelkern's story "Resurrection of the Dead" (techiyat hametim), Vilna, 5620 [1859-1860].

He also translated a great deal to Russian and German:

To Russian, he translated "Yeven Mezulah" [The Abyss of Despair, Psalm 69:3] of Rabbi Nathan Neta Hanover[15] (second edition, Leipzig, 1883) and Lessing's Fables, in which the pages have the source German and Russian translation opposite each other (Leipzig 1885).

To German, he published the translation of [Mapu's] Ahavat Zion under the title Tamar in 1885, as an original story and only hinted at the original author (see above, page 287[16]).

[Page 487]

He compiled a Russian language grammar in two volumes (ibid., 1884) and published "Bat Kol meRussiya" [A divine echo from Russia) in 1888 and a Russian-German dictionary for this volume "Bat Kol" in 1895. He also translated to German, the famous Russian stories called "The Blind Musician" and "Day of Atonement" from the important Russian storyteller Vladmir Korolenko,[17] and he published many articles in German with all the scientific questions and literature.

It is self-evident, that there is not sufficient space to speak of his essays and translations in Russian and German. Nor about his Hebrew essays, which are worth discussing in detail. To a greater or lesser degree, it is worthwhile to analyze "Bat Sheva" or "*Shirei Sefat Ever*" and the epigrams of his, which are found in *Ḥiẓẓim Shenunim*, and in all three volumes of "*Shirei Sefat Ever*," and Dibrye Yemei Russia and his "Holy Temple" [Concordance].

He died in 1902.

(According to "History of New Hebrew Literature," by Dr. Yosef Klausner[18])

Translator's and editor's footnotes:

1. Solomon Mandelkern was born in Mlynov in 1846 and died in Vienna in 1902. A poem of his with additional notes appears on p. 146 of this volume.
2. Also known as Torhovytsia today and Trovits in Yiddish.
3. Foundational work of Kabbalah, Jewish mystical literature.
4. A foundational book for Hasidism written in 1797 by Rabbi Schneur Zalman of Liadi, founder of Chabad Hasidism.
5. Also known as the Kotzker Rebbe (1787–1859), Rabbi Menachem Mendel Morgensztern attracted young, brilliant aspiring youth.
6. Referring to the Pirkei Avot 5:21 which specifies the appropriate ages for marriage at the age of 18.
7. It is not clear what an "easy" personality implies here but may be related to his recurring changes of heart.
8. The Crown Rabbi was a position in the Russian Empire given to a member of a Jewish community appointed to act as an intermediary between his community and the Imperial government, to perform certain civil duties such as registering births, marriages, and divorces. Because the main job qualification was fluency in Russian, Crown rabbis were typically considered agents of the state by members of their own communities, rather than true rabbis, and they often had no education in or knowledge of Jewish law.
9. The source of the quote is not known.
10. Daniel Abramovich Chwolson (or Khvolson) (1819–1911) was a Russian Jewish orientalist.
11. The narrator is Yosef Klausner who was a professor at Hebrew University.
12. The Septuagint is the earliest Greek translation of the Hebrew Bible and is the oldest complete translation made by the Jews. It is called the translation of seventy because tradition suggested seventy scholars were involved in the translation.
13. Written for the Society for the Promotion of Culture Among Russian Jews; for which he was honored by the Tzar.
14. The "I" refers to the original author, Yosef Klausner.
15. Not much is certain about the birthplace and early background of R. Nathan ben Moses Hannover. His life in Volynia came to an end with the Chmielnicki massacres in 1648–49 recorded in the work that Mandelkern translated.
16. This reference belongs to the original essay which was part of a larger work and does not reference a page in this volume.
17. Korolenko (1853–1921), born in Zhytomyr, Ukraine then part of the Russian Empire. He was a human rights activist, a journalist, and a storyteller calling for social justice in the Russian empire. The Blind Musician (1886) was his masterpiece novel and made him an internationally renowned writer.
18. Yosef Klausner (1874–1958) a Jewish historian and professor of Hebrew Literature. Born near Vilna. He went to Palestine in 1919 and taught at Hebrew University 1925–1950.

Yitzhak Lamdan[1]

Translated and edited by Howard I. Schwartz, PhD with Hanina Epstein

Yitzhak Lamdan [was born in Mlynov,] November 7, 1899 (5th day of Kislev, 5660) — [and died in] Tel Aviv, November 16, 1954 (20th Heshvan 5715). He received his Hebrew and general education, and during the years of the First World War, he and his brother were separated from the family and they were wandering all over Ukraine and Russia. He was there through the period of upheaval and afterward during the bloody riots [or pogroms][2] which killed his brother (the dedication to his brother in the preface to "Masada": "[This shall be] a memorial candle to the soul of my brother, upright and kind-hearted, who fell on the soil of Ukraine during the slaughter in Israel, and shall be a marker for his grave, the location of which I do not know"). After the Russian Revolution, he volunteered for the Red Army and afterwards fled during the mayhem and riots and by an unconventional route reached the Land [of Israel] in 1920. During his first years in the Land, he worked paving roads and in agriculture in Samaria[3] in the lower Galilee, in the Jezreel Valley and Judah (finally in Ben Shemen) and also in the Cultural Department of the Histadrut.[4] From the second half of the 1920s, [he was engaged in] literary efforts.

He began his writing in children's newspapers ("The Flowers" and "The Jordan") and afterwards he began publishing his poems in HaShiloah[5] (5678) [1917-1918]. In the Land [of Israel], he began taking his first steps in "Echoes" (Hedim)[6] under the supervision of A. [Asher] Barash and Yaakov Rabinowitz and this was the publisher he was most attached to and regarded as a model, even if in other [later] circumstances, [it would be] his [monthly] Gilyonot.[7] The editors of "Echoes" also published his first literary work, the poem "Masada" (5687) [1926–1927]. There have been many editions until our present day), in which he expressed the faint whisper of his generation whose world was devoured by the threat of the riots [or pogroms] on his way to Masada, and the path "from which he could not turn away," while maintaining the continuity of the chain [i.e., the continuity of the tradition].

[Page 488]

Brenner[8] described here [in Masada poem by Lamdan as a "wallower":] ("you monk of Masada, who have strengthened with your sorrow and contempt – for your hatred was love, and your anger – comfort") was among the most influential of his well-known and lesser known influences, and thus he was regarded with the small number whose creativity was in poetry and prose with the closest affinity to life and challenges of the generation.

After this followed collections of poetry: "The Threefold Harness," (Berlin-Tel-Aviv, 5690 [1929–1930], "Mispar HaYamim" ["Number of Days"] (5700 [1939–1940], "Be-Ma'aleh Akrabbim" ["On Scorpions' Pass"] (5705) [1945]; He also brought out an episode in the show "Akiba" called Mahnaiim 5704 [1943–1944]. [He was involved for] many years of activity in the Writer's Association and their different institutions (Gnazim and others).

In 5694 (1933–1934) he started the publishing house Gilyonot, his own publishing house, which he stamped with his personal style, and which ended only with his death. (The last publication was published posthumously and dedicated to his memory. It was designated volume 31. (Heshvan-Kislev 5715).

Yitzhak Lamdan, of blessed memory

[Page 489]

He did much here [in Gilyonot] as a publicist (in major articles and minor responses) in which he assumed a maximalist line with a tie to the Labor Zionism of Eretz Yisrael. He also encouraged creative forces of up and coming (including here the first steps in literature – S. Yizhar[9]). In Gilyonot, he also dedicated a lot of attention to the creation of Hebrew creativity outside of the Land [of Israel] (Poland, the United States, and dedicated to them special editions). In addition, he got involved in the domain of anthologies, publishing and translation. He published the anthology "Hebrew Stories" (a collection of stories from our new literature from its inception until our day, or: Smolenskin until Bialik (5707) [1946–1947] and he translated: "Two stories" of G. D'Annunzio[10] (5787). Two stories of Jack London "Between Islands" (5687) [1926-1927], "In the Forests of the North," (1928), "Reubeni Prince of the Jews," of Max Brod (5689) [1929], "The Army Behind the Iron Thorns (Siberian Diary) by Edwin Erich Dwinger (5690) [1929-30], "Nine in Trimidor," by L. Aldenov, (5691) [1930–31], "We ascend the Himalayas," by Parnak (5692) [1931–32], "Freya of the Seven Islands," by Conrad (about 5692) [1931–32], "Letter from Uriah," by A. Cohen[11] (5695) [1934–35], "Bibi" by Michaelis (about 1944), he translated, collected and edited a collection of stories and legends: "We Will Tell and We Will listen" (5704) (1943–1944), "Treasure of the Zodiac" (5716) [1955–56], "Palace of Ramses" (5716), "King of Avion" (5716), "The Trustee," (5716), "The Wise Judge" (5716), "Moses the Judge," (5716) and more. He was among the editors of the Writer's Association literary collection: "Sedarim," (from the generation of poets) (5712) [1951–52], "Writers Words," (with A. Barash, (5704) [1943–44], and weekly "Dorot," (1949. A number of Gilyanot also were published). Also, he edited "A Book of Responses," to World War II (5709) (1948–49). In addition, he participated in newspapers and periodicals, before "Gilyanot" and less frequently during its appearance. A large collection of his letters from the period of "Echoes," was published in a collection "Archives (Gnizim Alef)".

(From "Lexicon of Hebrew Literature" by Getzel Kressel)[12]

Translator's and editor's footnotes:

1.   Yitzhak Lamdan became famous for the Hebrew poem, "Masada," which he published in 1927 after he made aliyah. Yitzhak was born in Mlynov, son of Yehuda-Leib Lamdan and Liba Lamdan. His father Yehuda-Leib is mentioned throughout this volume as a beloved and well-respected member of the town. See Yehuda-Leib's artful resolution to the "event in the shtetl," p. 193. Photos of Yitzhak's father, his brother Moshe, whose death is discussed below, and his sister Rivkah-Devorah (who married Motel Litvak), appear on page 454. Another sister, Malcah married Shmuel Mandelkern, a contributor to this volume, and their photos appear on p. 482. Yitzhak was one of the youthful collaborators with Shmuel Mandelkern on the early failed attempt to send Yaakov-Yosi to the Land of Israel, pp. 208–218. See also the interesting essay on Yitzhak's visit back to Mlynov in 1932, by Moshe Tamari, "In the Presence of Yitzhak Lamdan in Mlynov," pp. 32–37. Yitzhak's own poem in this volume "Internal Turmoil," p. 83, which imagines a difficult conversation between Yitzhak and his father in which he cannot bring himself to reveal how difficult life is in Palestine.

2.   The period is referring to the chaos and civil wars that followed the Russian Revolution which included pogroms.

3.   A biblical name for the central region of the ancient Land of Israel.

4.   The first unified organization of workers or Zionist trade union founded in 1920 in Haifa. The Cultural Department provided a number of services for members including films, publications, courses in Hebrew, geography, Bible, dancing and the arts.

5.   Ha-Shiloah, published between 1896 and 1926, was the leading Hebrew-language literary journal at the beginning of the 20th century.

6.   A literary journal published in the Palestine between 1922–1930 in the form of small booklets.

7.   Gilyonot was an independent literary monthly founded and edited by Yitzhak Lamdan, from 1934 to 1954.

8.   Yosef Haim Brenner (1881–1921) was a Russian-born Hebrew language writer and one of the pioneers of modern Hebrew literature. He is one of the poets that Lamdan figuratively encounters and questions in his poem, Masada. Brenner had a gloomy outlook which Lamdan questions. But Brenner has no answer. See discussion by Leon Yudkin, *Isaac Lamdan*, pp. 65–66 and translation 225.

9.   Pen name for Yizhar Smilansky, known by his pen name S. Yizhar.

10.   Uncertain if refers to Gabriel D'Annunzio, a prolific Italian writer who also became an ultranationalist.

11.   Other sources list this work by Emil Bernhard.

12.   Kressel (1911–1986) was a bibliographer and Hebrew writer from Galicia who settled in Palestine in 1930. His most important work "Lexicon of Hebrew Literature in Recent Times" was published 1965–1967.

Aleph Katz

Translated from the Yiddish by Hannah B. Fischthal, PhD

Edited by Howard I. Schwartz, PhD

Aleph Katz (Mlynov 1898–United States 1969) learned in cheder, after which he finished Russian elementary school in Mlynov. At the end of 1913, together with his mother and a part of his family, he came to America.[1] His father and older sister had already been in the United States since 1906.[2] In New York, Aleph Katz started to write Hebrew poems. He was a founder and secretary of the Hebrew Youth Club "Bnei Am Chai." He worked in shops, stores, laundries, and offices.

[Page 490]

In the evenings he studied in night schools, then in City College. He published poems and wrote a column for the English language college journal *Owl.* One of his poems was included in the college anthology *Poets of the Future* (Editor: Henry T. Schnittkind, Boston, 1824–1922).

Aleph Katz made his Yiddish debut with a poem in *Der groyser kundes,* New York, 28 December 1917. Since then, he has published his poetry in New York in *In Zich, Oyfkum, Fraye arbiter-shtime, Di vokh, Zangen, Dos yudishe folk, Tsukunft, Idisher kemfer, Di feder,* and *Getseltn.* In Philadelphia he published in *Idishe velt.*

Aleph Katz z"l

[Page 491]

In Chicago: in *Idisher kuryer.* In children's publications in New York: *Kinder-zhurnal, Kinderland, Kinder-velt, Kinder-tsaytung.* In Warsaw: *Kinder-fraynd.* In Buenos Aires: *Argentiner beymelekh.* In Chile: Zid-Amerike. Also *Havaner lebn; meksikaner shrift; der shpigl.* Also in Buenos Aires: *Di prese un idishe tsaytung.* In Montreal: *keneder odler.* In Toronto: *Idisher zshurnal.* And others.

His publications in books: *A mayse fun yam un andere lider* [Story of the Sea and other poems], Zangen, NY 1925, 59 pp.; *Akertsayt* [Plowing season], Biderman, NY 1929, 80 pp.; *Dos telerl fun himl, poeme, mit ilustratsyes fun Yosl Kotler* [Plate from heaven, poem, with illustrations by Yosl Kotler], Matones, NY, 30 pp.; *Fun alef biz tof,* a poem about the alphabet, illustrated by Yoysef Shor, Alef, NY, 32 pp.; *Amol iz geven a mayse* [There once was a story], poems, sold principally by Matones, NY, 96 pp.; *Gut morgn* [Good morning], Alef, first published in Tsukunft, NY, March 1946. Later it was presented in DP camps in Germany and by various troupes in other countries. It was published in book-form as *Gut morgn Alef, Purim shpil un Yosele, tsvey shpiln un a mayse* [Two plays and a story], NY, 1950, 64 pp. It was praised by the Yiddish critics.

The small Yiddish letters are living creatures for Aleph Katz: Alef, beys, giml, lamed and vov, nun and samekh are the heroes and play parts in this drama. . . The tragic drama of the Yiddish letters became a symbol of the tragedy of the Jewish people, the people of writing, the people of the letter.—Shmuel Niger

On his sixtieth birthday, his *Kholem aleykhem* [Dream about you], play and poems, was published by Medinas Yiddish, NY, 1958, 160 pp. On the same occasion, many articles about the poet came out in the Yiddish press for a special celebration in his honor in New York.

Aleph Katz lived in New York, where he was editor of the Jewish division of the Jewish Telegraphic Agency since 1925. He composed the news and edited the JTA syndicated column, "Literary news." He worked with the linguistic journal *Yidishe shprakh* and he helped prepare the *Great Dictionary of the Yiddish Language*, NY. Music was composed for several of his poems and plays. The songs were sung at concerts by Yiddish choirs and societies in New York and other cities.

[Page 492]

His poems appeared in: Joseph Leftwich's anthology of Yiddish poetry in English, *The Golden Peacock,* London, 1939; Y. Kisin's anthology *Lider fun der milkhome* [Poems from the war], NY, 1943; *Hemshekh-antologye fun M. Shtarkman* [Continued anthology by M. Shtarkman], NY, 1945; the Russian anthology of Yiddish poetry by L. Feinberg, *Yevreiskaya poezye* [Jewish poetry], NY, 1947; *Antologye lider fun gezang un pyane* [Anthology of songs for singing and piano] by Heynekh Kohn, NY, 1947; M. Basin's *Antologye fun yidisher poezye oyf amerikaner motivn* [Anthology of Yiddish poetry on American themes] (Mimeographed), distributed by the Congress for Yiddish Culture, NY, 1955; and Shimshon Meltser's Hebrew anthology of Yiddish poems *Al naharot [By the rivers],* Jerusalem, 1956. His poems were also included in readers for Yiddish schools. His book *Gut morgn, Alef!* Received the Abel Shaban prize from the Congress for Yiddish Culture in 1955.

Reading Katz one has the impression that the poet stands at the head of a group of "Broder singers"[3] who travel with him . . . to entertain the Jewish audience and console its sadness with song and story. . . Aleph Katz belongs in the category of pure creators. The language of the famous playwright is always at hand for depicting lyrical moments with his poetic lines and his poetic words. – Dr. Sh, Bikl

His "extravaganza" *Reb Alter Fish* appeared In *Almanakh Yiddish* published by the Congress for Yiddish Culture, NY, 1961, pp. 267–275.

(From *Leksikon fun der nayer yidisher literature* [Leksikon of new Yiddish literature], vol. 4.)

Translator's and editor's footnotes:

1.   Originally born Moshe Katz in 1898 in Mlynov, "Aleph" as he came to be known as a Yiddish poet, came to the US in 1913 with his mother and two of his siblings. His mother was known as "Henia Arelas," the daughter of Aaron [Hirsch], and one of several Hirsch siblings to come to America. For a time, Aleph worked at Standard Laundry the business of the Hirsch family. A photo of Aleph's mother, Henia Arelas, appears on p. 500 of this volume. See the Hirsch family story on the Mlynov website. – HS

2.   Aleph's father was Chaim Yeruchem Katz born in Chelm. Accompanied by his eldest daughter, Shifre (later Sophie Cohen,) he arrived in 1907 in New York as "Jerichem Girsch," using the surname of his wife. – HS

3.   Famed brothers from Brod who were essentially troubadors. "Broder singers" became a generic term for secular entertainers popular until the 1930s. – HS

_____

[Page 493]

Over the Ocean

Page 494]

**Sylvia[Barditch]
Goldberg[1]
[With
George Goldberg]**

The Yizkor Book for Mlynov-Mervits

Translated from the Yiddish by Hannah B. Fischthal, PhD

Edited by Howard I. Schwartz, PhD

This is a monument for the murdered martyrs from both shtetls. Destroyed: The respected Jews, the scholars, the enlightened intelligentsia, famous writers, cantors. They are no longer there.

The important world of famous people that the small shtetl Mlynov produced floats in front of my eyes: Dr. Solomon Mandelkern,[2] who became eternal through his Concordance of the Bible, *Hekhal ha-kodesh,* and also with his creative work in Hebrew poetry; Yitzhak Lamdan,[3] the Hebrew poet who earned praise for his "*Masada*" ; Aleph Katz,[4] the renowned poet; Berele the Blacksmith's [son], famous singer in the Tłomackie Synagogue[5] in Warsaw; Moyshe Arele's [son],[6] artist.

I hear the voice of my grandfather Itse the Staroste.[7] He says to me: "My child, record this for the coming generations; may they know that Mlynov-Mervits was a holy community (kehilla) in beautiful, rich Volhyn. And may they know that the shtetls of Mlynov-Mervits no longer exist, but they will be included in the pantheon of eternity, under the wings of the Divine Presence."

We, the remaining sparks of the great fire, will never forget the precious martyrs. We will extend the golden chain of former Mlynov-Mervits.

[Page 495]

We will continue to further their ideals for the existence of our people in our holy land of Israel. We pay tribute to their memories with great honor and respect.

Translator's and editor's footnotes:

1.   Sylvia (Barditch) Goldberg was the only woman on the Book Committee of Eight responsible for bringing out the Memorial Book. She was born Silka Borodacz in the town of Lutzk, one of five children. She always had a soft spot in her heart for Mlynov, which is where her grandparents Itcik and Malia Ferteybaum lived. Sylvia would visit her grandparents in Mlynov on holidays and summer vacations and she wrote about her sweet memories of those times in her essays in this volume including "Visiting My Grandparents," an essay about her grandfather Icek Statorste, called "Stoliner Hasidism," and a "Wedding in Mlynov." Sylvia arrived with her mother and siblings in Baltimore in 1921. The family subsequently moved to New York after her brother was killed in a hit and run accident in Baltimore. In New York, she subsequently married George/Gershon Goldberg from Mlynov. Sylvia also appears in a photo on page 500 in this volume. – HS

2.   For background on Solomon Mandelkern, see p. 484. – HS

3.   For background on Yitzhak Lamdan, see 487. – HS

4.   For background on Aleph Katz, see p. 489. – HS

5.   The Great Synagogue on Tłomackie Street in Warsaw was one of the grandest synagogues constructed in Poland, built in 1878 and became a site of cultural flourishing. It was one of the few "reform" or "German" synagogues in Poland. During the important services and festive holidays, the Grand Synagogue was frequented by prominent Polish musicians, singers, clergy, and government officials. The Mlynov born singer mentioned here has not been identified. – HS

6.   Referring to Moshe Hirsch son of Aaron. See the Hirsch family story. – HS

7.   See Sylvia's essay about her grandfather, called "Stoliner Hasidism." – HS

Jews from Baltimore Assisted their Home Shtetl Mlynov

by Eta [Goldseker] Fishman[1], Baltimore

Translated from the Yiddish by Hannah B. Fischthal, PhD

Edited by Howard I. Schwartz, PhD

After the First World War, many from our shtetl Mlynov went to America.[2] They mostly were the unhappy women and children who had been dying of starvation in eastern Europe during wartime, when their husbands and fathers slaved in the American factories but were unable to send any money to their families. When the happy day of peace arrived in the world, these were the first families to leave their former homes.

All the new arrivals labored very hard the first few years. They stood in small businesses (their workday was 17–18 hours) and in the factories (10 hours), and yet they did not forget their sisters, brothers, and relatives back in Mlynov. They saved as much as they could from their hard work so that they could send something back home.

* * *

In 1925 the Mlynov Verein [Society] was founded with the purposes of meeting every month and also of doing something for the community in Mlynov.[3]

When my dear husband David Fishman z"l and I came to Baltimore in 1927, my sister Ida, who is no longer among the living, said to us: "Children, we have a gathering of the Mlynov Society this Sunday. Come with me. I am certain that you will be able to help with something."

We did not disappoint her. After residing a little while in Baltimore, I accepted the position of Secretary of the Society, and I held this office until the end.

[Page 496]

I always used to write letters to the Mlynov Committee; we still have, thank God, a living witness, Nakhum Teitelboym,[4] who was on the Committee. Here in Baltimore, we came together every month. We used to pay a fee and we also made a lot of additional money.

In 1929 bad times came to America. Our Mlynovers here were burdened from the waves of Depression, like everyone else. But nobody gave up Society work. All members united to do their duty to help those in Mlynov.

We used to send out quite meaningful sums of money, because the number of poor in Mlynov kept increasing. Yesterday's rich man was today a poor man. We also sent money for necessary expenses, like erecting fences for the cemetery, the bath, and the mikvah, which everyone in the kehilla needed. We also sent money to buy a machine that bakes matzas.[5] We used to get a list indicating how the money was distributed.

With tears in our eyes, every one of us mourned the situation of our Mlynovers. Nobody could imagine that a terrible fog was rushing over our poor Jews, and that they all would be killed. (My own loss: three sisters and their families, Perel, Baila, Charna,[6] and practically the entire large Goldseker family). From 1939–1944 European Jewry was torn from us.[7] We learned the real truth of our general Jewish tragedy from the few remaining Jews from Mlynov and Mervits.

[Page 497]

Then our assistance renewed. We sent some money directly to everyone in the camps.[8] We also sent packages to people who were in Poland and Italy. At the same time, we also, as the Mlynov Society, supported Palestine with quite large sums.

With that, the chapter of the Mlynov Society ended,[9] because the majority of the Mlynovers were already in their eternal resting place. Very few survived. The children, the grandchildren, were no longer from Mlynov.

Mlynov-Mervits Landsmen
Who Died in the United States

Translated and edited by Howard I. Schwartz, PhD

Aleph Katz [the Yiddish poet, born Moshe Avraham Katz, 1898–1969]
Efraim Gitelman

Gedaliah and Rikel Gelman [became Joseph and Rebecca Alman in Springfield, MA]
Simha Zutelman
Efraim Zutelman [became Frank Settleman in Baltimore, 1901–1967]
Rivka Yamshtok
Shmuel Katz [brother of Yiddish poet, 1895–1969]
Mollie Roskes [born Mollie Demb, arrived in Baltimore in about 1908, left Baltimore for aliyah later in life and died in Israel, 1876–1963]
Shlomo Schechman [survivor, son of Noach Moshe Schechman, eventually settled in Baltimore, 1910–1969]
Hertz Shulman [son of Tsodik and Pearl (Demb) Shulman, became Harry Shulman in Baltimore, 1894–1964]
Pesach Steinberg [married Beatrice, daughter of Gedaliah and Rikel Gelman/Alman, became Harry Steinberg in Springfield, MA, 1895–1964)
Sheindel Iskiewicz

[Page 498]

Photos of Mlynov Immigrants and Survivors in the US

Sylvia [Barditch] Goldberg's brother, Chaim-Meyer[10]

Sylvia [Barditch] Goldberg's parents [Isadore and Bessie Barditch][11]

*Usher [Harry] Tatelbaum[12] (the Staroste's son)
with wife Feiga [Fanny Hornstein]*

*Baila [Karla/Clara]
Marder (Sarah Gitla's mother)[13]*

[Page 499]

*Gershon (George / Joe) Goldberg[14]
with his sister Sorke [Sarah Spector]*

*Chaya Goldberg [Ida Gevantman],[15]
Gershon's sister [with Gershon]*

Chultzia,[16] with her man Leazar with Bassa Barditch

Shimon [Samuel][17] with Sophie Berger

[Page 500]

Hirsh [Holtzeker] Slobadar's grandchildren:[18]
[Kalman Carl Gaynor (center) and two sisters (either side) and a cousin (back)]

Moishe Goldberg[19] with his brother.
[Gershon Joe Goldberg]

Bassa [Barditch],[20] the Starosta's daughter (left)
with Henia Ahrelas [née Hirsch] (Aleph Katz's mother)
[center] right: Sylvia Goldberg [Marilyn (Jacobs) Israel front center]

[Page 501]

*Simha [Samuel] Spector family
with his wife Sorke [Sarah],[21]
(Gershon Goldberg's youngest sister*

*Chaya [Ida Gevantman] with
her husband Benjamin
(daughter of Labish [Gelberg])[22]*

Mamtze [Teitelman] Genut[23] with her husband [Israel] and child

{page 502]

Yussel and Esther Malar [née Gelberg][24] and their children [David and Gissie]

The father Yosel [Joseph]
Schuchman[25]
husband of Chissa [née Klepatch]

Chissa Schuchman [née Kleptach],
[with nephew] Moshe Goldberg[26]
of blessed memory

Chaim with [his wife]   Yenta [née Demb] Schwartz[27]

Pinchus Gelberg[28] [seated] (lived in Klevan)
[Gershon Joe Goldberg his brother stands back left]

The Rabbi [Yisrael] Feldman [right]
with his wife Sarah (Teitelman)[29] and her brother Herzl Teitelman

Translator's and editor's footnotes:

1.   Eta Goldseker (1896–1989) was born in Mlynov to Shimon Goldseker (1867–1926) and Anna (Fishman). Three of her siblings migrated to Baltimore between 1912 and 1923: Ida (Goldseker) Fishman Gresser, Morris Goldseker, and Samuel Goldseker. Eta is remembered in the family as traveling deep into Russia and smuggling goods back to Mlynov in a teapot which she carried with her on the train following the custom of the day. An allusion to Eta's travels to Kursk appears in this volume in a humorous story told my Shmuel Mandelkern, "Self-Defense in Mlynov," p. 134. In 1926, Eta left Mlynov for Mandate Palestine to marry her first cousin, Mlynov-born, David Fishman, son of Moshe Fishman, both contributors to this volume. Their daughter "Shimonette Anna" (Selma Ann) was born in Palestine in 1926. Life was dangerous and difficult in Palestine at the time, and they left for the United States in 1927. Their daughter Irene (Fishman) Siegel, who was a family historian, was born in 1929 in Baltimore. – HS

2.   See the detailed record of those Mlynov families coming to America on the Mlynov website. A number of husbands had arrived in Baltimore before WWI and when the War intervened their families had been stranded in Mlynov. In 1920–1921, arriving in Baltimore were the family of Aaron Demb, Isaac Marder, Joseph Lerner, the Shulman family, Pesach Zutelman (Paul Shulman) among others. – HS

3.   Records from the Mlynov Verein are available online at the Jewish Museum of Maryland in Baltimore.

4.   Nahum Teitelman is intended. – HS

5.   On making of matza in Mlynov and Mervits, see Sonia and Mendel Teitelman's essay, "Baking Matzas." The matza machine funded from America is recalled in the book length narrative about Asher Teitelman's life.

6.   Siblings and their families who did not survive were: Perl Goldseker (1893–1942) married Meyer Ben Zion Pressman. They had two children: Hanoch (1921–1942) and Moishe (1926–1945). Baila Goldseker (1897–1942) married Peisach Collidge (or Kulisz) and their children: Ben-Zion (1923–1942), Moishe (1925–1942), Shimon (1927–1942), Gilda (?–1942) and Henya (?–1942). Charna Goldseker (1898–1942) who married Shmuel Gruber and their sons Shimon 1930-1942 and Yisrael (1934–1942). – HS

7.   Jews in Europe were being slaughtered until 8 May 1945. – HBF

8.   DP [Displaced persons] camps. – HBF

9.   The Mlynov Verein morphed into the Maryland Free Loan Society. – HS

10. Chaim-Meyer Barditch (originally Borodacz) was tragically killed in a hit and run automobile accident in Baltimore in 1922 at the age of 15. He had arrived in America only six months earlier with his mother in November 1921. This photo of the young Meir was cut from the original photo which appears below with his mother, Bessie Barditch (Bassa Teitelbaum). Chaim-Meir's sister, Sylvia ("Silke") Barditch Goldberg, later became the only woman on the Book Committee for this volume to which she contributed a number of essays about her mother's hometown of Mlynov and her grandparents who lived there. Her sister, Shirley (Barditch) Jacobs contributed "A True Event In Mlynov," pp. 196–197. The Barditch parents appear in the next photo. Out of grief over Chaim-Meyer's death, the Barditch parents moved with three of their children to New York where Sylvia later married George Goldberg, also from Mlynov (see their photo on p. 494), who is also a contributor to this volume and whose photo appears below. A longer version of Sylvia's story appears on the Mlynov Website. – HS

Courtesy of Andrea Kerker Zanzuri

11.   Sylvia's (Barditch) Goldberg, as noted in the previous note, was on the Book Committee that put together this volume. Her photo with her husband George Goldberg appears on page 494. She was the daughter of Isadore (Yehiel) Barditch (Jechiel Borudocz) (1873–1953), who was born in Lutzk, and Bassa Ferteybaum (aka Bessie Teitelbaum) (1876–1960) who was born in Mlynov. Bassa's photo appears in a group photo below. Isidore arrived in Baltimore in 1910. He was joined by his wife and children only in 1921 after WWI. Sylvia's maternal grandfather who lived in Mlynov was "Icik Staroste," "starosta" being a term of Slavic origin denoting a community elder who had an administrative role. Sylvia describes him as a Stolin Hasid in her essay, "Stoliner Hasidism in Mlynov," pp. 80–82. She also describes both her maternal grandmother, Malia, and grandfather in her essay "Visiting My Grandparents," pp. 266–271. Sylvia later married George Goldberg from Mlynov after the family moved to New York. – HS

12.   Usher (later Harry) Teitelbaum/ Tatelbaum (1888–1955) was an uncle of Sylvia Barditch Goldberg and the brother of her mother, Bessie (see prior photos and notes). Usher arrived in Baltimore in 1911 traveling with two other Mlynov men, Israel Schwartz and Nathan Chaim Fishman. He is here in a photo with his wife Fannie (Hornstein) who was born in Maryland to Romanian parents. – HS

13.   The woman labelled here as "Baila" Marder was in fact Klara (Clara) Marder, born in Mlynov as Klara Tesler, sister of Yankel (Jacob) Tesler (photo and notes on page 478). Clara married Isaac Marder and had three children in Mlynov before she traveled to join her husband in Baltimore with two other Mlynov families in June 1920. Her daughter Sarah ("Sore Gitlas") married David Mutter in Baltimore. A daughter of theirs (Sheila [Mutter] Mandelberg) recalls that they were relatives of the Barditch family who appear in the prior photos, probably explaining why these photos are together on the same page. The exact relationship is no longer recalled. – HS

14.   In 1927, Gershon (George/Joe) Gelberg/Goldberg married Sylvia Barditch whose family is in the previous photos. Gershon (1896–1984) was born in Mlynov, son of Labish Gelberg and Eta Leah (Schuchman). In 1921, he arrived in New York with his sister-in-law and her children. He contributed the essay in this volume "Our Former Way of life in Mlynov," 156-158. See more about the Goldberg family story on the Mlynov website. – HS

15.   Ida (Gelberg) Gevantman (1893–1949), with her brother Gershon (Joe) Goldberg, children of Labish Gelberg and Eta Leah (Schuchman). She and her husband arrived in New York in June 1921 headed to the home of her sister Sarah Spector. Before leaving they had been living in Trovits, her husband's hometown. They soon settled in Baltimore.

16.   Chultzie Gelberg (1903–1989), later called Helen Dishowitz and Helen Lederer, was the eldest daughter of Moshe Goldberg (1875–1967) and Gitel (Weitzer). Her father Moshe arrived in New York in December 1911. Chultzie and her family were refugees from Mlynov during WWI and she wrote about the experience in the essay, "In Pain From the First World War," pp. 147–148. In April 1921, she arrived in

New York to join her father with her mother and siblings and her uncle Gershon (Joe) Gelberg. She subsequently married Louis Dishowitz and later remarried and became Helen Lederer.

17. Samuel Symon Berger (1894–1986) with his wife Sophie (Selkoff). Born in Mlynov, he was the son of Ben Zion Berger (1865–1912) and Zelda (Hirsch) (1865–1938). On the Berger side, he was first cousin with Aaron Harari (born Berger) who is a contributor to this volume. Through his mother, he was related to the Hirsch family that migrated to Jersey City. Symon arrived in Baltimore in June 1913 and then headed to Chicago to join his brother Nathan Berger who had arrived in 1912. Read more about the Berger and the Hirsch families on the Mlynov website. – HS

18. Four grandchildren of Hirsh (Holtzeker), nicknamed Slobadar, the eldest of the five Holtzeker brothers who came to Mlynov from the nearby town of Sloboda. Sloboda, which appears on old maps slightly northeast of Mlynov, is now incorporated into today's town of Uhzynets'. Kalman (aka Carl) Gaynor and his two sisters in the front row were children of Hirsch's daughter, Leah. She married Elia Aron Gaynor (whose mother may have been a sister of Labish Gelberg, according to handwritten notes recorded by Edith Geller in the Goldberg family). The cousin in the back row has not been identified. A photo of Carl's mother, Leah, and his larger family appears below on page 504 below. Carl came to America via Trieste, Italy in September 1913 and settled in New York. Another of Hirsh's grandsons, Boruch Meren, is a contributor of several essays to this volume. – HS

19. Moishe Goldberg, born in Mlynov (1875–1967), son of Labish Gelberg and Eta Leah (Schuchman), was the first of their children to arrive in the US in 1911, where he settled in New York City. He was joined in New York by his sister, Sarah, before WWI. His wife Gitel and their children arrived in 1921. His siblings Gershon (Joe) and Sarah Spector appear in a photo the previous page (p. 499) with additional notes there. – HS

20. Bassa (Bessie) Barditch (née Teitelbaum) (left) is with her daughter Sylvia (Barditch) Goldberg (right). Sylvia was a contributor to this volume and the only woman on the Book Committee who put together this volume. See Bessie's photo also on page 498 with additional notes. Bessie's granddaughter Marilyn (Jacobs) Israel is the foreground. She is the daughter of Bessie's other daughter, Shirley (Barditch) Jacobs. They are with the Anna Katz ("Henia Arelas" née Hirsch, center), the mother of Aleph Katz. Anna came with her children to the US in 1913. – HS

21. Sarah also appears with her brother Gershon (Joe) on p. 499 with notes. Sarah arrived in the US around 1914 and married Samuel Spector, a distant cousin, whom she had met back in Dubno. He had fallen in love with her there at first sight. After he migrated to the New York in 1912, he had worked to bring her to the US. After Sarah arrived, she fell in love with and became engaged to another man. But then she had a dream in which her father appeared and told her to marry Sam. Being a provincial, superstitious girl, she did. They were married New Year's Eve 1918. In the photo are their two eldest daughters, Frances (standing) (later Frances Goldberg / Rosen) and Edith (later Edith Geller), who shared with me her family story. – HS

22. Ida (Gelberg) Gevantman appears in a photo on p. 499 with additional notes there. – HS

23. Mamtze Teitelman (1917–1985) was a survivor and the sister of Mendel Teitelman, the prolific contributor to this volume, who mentions her in one of his essays, p. 325. She met her husband Israel Genut in the Föhrenwald displaced persons camp. Asher Teitelma's book length survival Story, published on the Mlynov website, includes information about Mamtze's survival ordeal as well. Mamtze appears in the photo of survivors on page 313.

24. Esther Gelberg (1888–1942) was born in Mlynov, the eldest daughter of Labish Gelberg and Eta Leah (née Schuchman). She was a sibling of the other Gelbergs/ Goldbergs whose photos appear on pages 498–500. She married Yussel (Josef) Malar (1883–1942) who was born in Dubno. They and their daughter Gissie perished. Their son David (1910–2004) survived the Holocaust and came to the US. – HS

25. Joseph Schuchman (1874–1958) was born in Mlynov to Gershon and Shaina Bluma Schuchman. He married Chissa (aka Jessie) Klepatch (1876–1947) (see her in the next photo). Joseph's siblings include Eta Leah (Schuchman) who married Labish Gelberg and was mother of Moshe Gelberg/Goldberg who appears in the next photo as well as Ester (Gelberg) Malar who appears above. Her siblings include Noach Moshe Schuchman (the subject of an essay in this volume, p. 246), Hanah (Schuchman) Golisuk, whose photo is on p. 462. – HS

26. Chissa (Klepatch) Schuchman was the daughter of Yitzhak Leib and Chana Yenta (Klepatch) and wife of Joseph Schuchman (in the photo to the left). The story of her niece, "Chana Klepatch–A Mlynov

Tragedy," includes additional notes on the family. Chissa is sitting here with her nephew, Moshe Goldberg, who was a son of her husband's sister: Eta Leah Gelberg (née Schuchman). Moishe (1875–1967) was the first of Labish and Eta Leah's children to arrive in New York in 1911. Several of his siblings appear in photos on this and the previous page. He married Gitel (Weitzer or Weizer) in Mlynov and was joined in New York by her and their four children in 1921. His eldest daughter, Helen Lederer, contributed the essay "In Pain from the First World War," pp. 147–48. – HS

27.   Chaim (later Hyman) Schwartz (1863–1946) married Yenta Demb (1870–1962), daughter of Israel Jacob Demb and Rivka Gruber. They had three sons in Mlynov before coming to Baltimore: Benjamin, Norton and Paul H. Benjamin came to Baltimore in 1910 and was followed by the rest of the family in 1912. Paul H. is the grandfather of Howard Schwartz, the editor and one of the translators of this volume's English version. Read more about the Schwartz and Demb family stories on the Mlynov website. – HS

28.   Pinchus Gelberg (1874–1935) was the eldest child of Labish Gelberg and Eta Leah (Schuchman) and a sibling of the other Gelbergs/Goldbergs whose photos appear on this and the preceding page. According to family memories, Pinchus had become an educated man and married Chaia Rive in Klevan, was well-off with his leather goods store, and had two sons. He died in 1935. His wife and sons were later killed during WWII. – HS

29.   Sarah Teitelman (1924–1983) and her brother Herzl (~1912/1915–2002) were born in Mervits, one of seven children of Mordechai Teitelman and Freida (Horowitz), five of whom perished. Their other brother is remembered in "Mr. Avraham-Shlomo Teitelman," p. 259. The siblings were first cousins of Nahum and Meir Teitelman, contributors to this volume. Sarah and a brother Moshe Lipa each separately escaped the ghetto. They met later and went to a partisan camp. Moshe Lipa enlisted in the Russian army in 1944 and was killed in Russia in the last week of the war. Sarah's other brother Naftali Hertz Teitelman, known affectionately in the family as Herzl, was taken by the Russians to a work camp and eventually was drafted into the Russian Army. He was wounded and sent to a hospital in the Ural Mountains. His sister only learned that he was alive in the last days of the war. Sarah survived and married Rabbi Yisrael Feldman in the displaced persons camp of Bad Gastein. Sarah and her brother Herzl subsequently settled in Milwaukee in the US. Herzl later moved to Brooklyn and was later buried in Israel. – HS

[Page 504]

Photos of Mlynov Immigrants and Survivors in the US (cont.)

Efraim Gitelman, Rachel Faiveshe's son[1]

Mollya Roskes, of blessed memory[2]

To my dear son Kalman [Carl Gaynor][3] from your dear mother Leah Gaynor (nee Holtzeker)

[Page 505]

Mendel with Sheindel (Grenspun) Steinberg[4] with their daughter Sarah

Getzel [George] with Pessia [Paula] Steinberg[5] with their son [Zelig/Gerald] (and Aviva Feldman [who was rescued])

[Page 506]

Family of Yitzhak Kozak[6]

Morris Newman (Iskiewicz)[7] *with his wife Rachel with son David Shlomo*

[Page 507]

Udiya (Yenta Brendle's Sister)[8]

Gitel Goldberg[9] *Pessie Khoylye's daughter*

Yosef [Joseph] Shargel[10]

Yenta Brendels (Shargel)[11]

Luba Schwartz[12]

Avraham Goldberg[13]

Mutel Schwartz[14]

Tsipe wife of long / tall Moyshe[15]

Kalman (Carl) Gaynor[16]

Translator's and editor's footnotes:

1.   Likely a brother of Moshe Gitelman who is also called Rachel Faivesh's [son] p. 127 and is described as the one who procured bullets for the self-defense units in Mlynov. Moshe Gitelman is in the list of Mlynov martyrs with his wife Sal and their daughter Yehudit (born circa 1926). It is unknown when Efraim came to America or what became of him. – HS

2.   Mollie Roskes (1876–1963 in Israel) was born Molya Demb, the daughter of Israel Jacob Demb and Rivka (Gruber). She married Samuel Roskes from Lutsk. Samuel migrated to Baltimore in 1901 and Mollie followed with her eldest son David in 1908. She was the second of the five Demb children to migrate to Baltimore. Her siblings who also came to Baltimore include: Bessie (Demb) Hurwitz, Pearl Malka (Demb) Shulman, Yetta (Demb) Schwartz, Aaron Demb, and Max Demming. Later in life, Mollie made aliyah. Read more of the Demb family story on the Mlynov website. – HS

3.   See also the photo of Carl Gaynor and two of his sisters on page 500 with additional notes on the family there. His mother Leah was daughter of Hirsch Holtzeker, the eldest of the Holtzeker brothers who came to Mlynov. – HS

4.   Mendel Steinberg and his wife Sheindel (Grenspun) and son Anshel survived the Shoah in the essay told by Mendel "The Terror Of Annihilation," pp. 358–369. They appear in the commemoration photo of survivors, p. 313. Their daughter Susie in this photo was born in the Lechfeld displaced persons camp. – HS

5.   Getzel (George) Steinberg, the brother of Mendel Steinberg from the previous photo, survived the Shoah with his wife Pessia (Paula) (Wurtzel), and son Zelig (Gerald) Steinberg. They appear in the commemoration photo of survivors, p. 313 with additional notes about the family and the rescue story of Aviva Feldman who was adopted for a time into their family. See the Steinberg family story on the Mlynov website. – HS

6.   Icek Kozak (1899–1994) managed to get his entire family out of the Mlynov ghetto as recounted in his essay, "What My Family Endured," pp. 354–57 with additional notes. The family settled later in Philadelphia. Icek's wife Chava Bichman (also spelled "Bickmouiu") (1903–1991) is in this photo with their four surviving children: Rubin (1922– ~2016), Morris (Moshe) (1924–2012), Jean Litz (Genia / Genendal Vidravnik) (1928–1998) and Karen Lowenthal (Kreina Kozak) (1931–). Another son died before the War. – HS

7.   US records indicate that "Maurice" / Morris Abraham Newman (1900–1984) arrived in the US in April 1924 with his wife "Rachil." His US records also indicate his family surname was originally Iskiewicz. Their son, David, was born in 1931 in Philadelphia. It seems probable that this Maurice Newman (Iskiewicz) was related to the contributor called "Moshe Iskiewicz" from Haifa who contributed "Impressions and Memories," pp. 88-89. See additional notes there about the Iskiewicz family. – HS

8.   Sister of Yenta / Yetta Breindl Shargel, who appears in the photo below this one with additional notes.

9.   Gitel Goldberg (née Weitzer or Weizer) (1880–1939) was the wife of Moishe Goldberg whose photo appears on p. 500 with notes there. Gitel arrived in New York with their children in 1921 to join her husband who came before WWI. The name of Gitel's father was Aaron Weitzer/Weizer and her mother is referred to here as "Pessie Khoylye's (daughter)," a name also used in an essay by her daughter, Helen Lederer, "In Pain from the First World War." The meaning of "Khoylye" is not certain. It is possible there is a relationship between her and Abraham Khollis who is mentioned, p. 60, as the man who watched over the eternal light in the memorial for the Rebbe from Stolin who died in Mlynov. – HS

10.   Yosef / Joseph Shargel (1870–1954) was a son of Yisrael Shargel. He married Yetta Breindl (1870–1954) whose photo is below in the next row with notes about her family. Joseph and Yetta came to Baltimore in April 1925. Two of their eldest children came to the US before WWI: Mollie (Shargel) Feingold (1891–1976) and Julius Shargel (1897–1970). Several of their other children arrived in Baltimore in the late 1920s after a stay in Mexico: Bernard Shargel (1906–1979), Amelia "Milka" (Shargel) Meren (1910–2005), and Earl (Israel) Shargel (1912–1981). A daughter Elka (Shargel) Yakobovitz (1908–?) remained in Russia. A son, Itzik (Shargel) Rom, settled in Mexico. – HS

11.   Yenta (also Yetta) Breindl Shargel (1870–1954) was the wife of Yosef/Joseph Shargel (photo in previous row). She was the daughter of Baba (Mandelkern), the sister of the famous Solomon Mandelkern. Her father's name was Yisrael Yitzhak and it seems likely his family name was Weiner based on the fact

that two of Yenta Breindl's children were headed to an uncle with the last name of Weiner on their passenger manifests. Sylvia Barditch Goldberg recalls meeting Yetta and her husband and some of their children in Mlynov in her essay "Visiting My Grandparents," page 268. A funny story (p. 32) indicates that when the famous Solomon Mandelkern came back to Mlynov one day from Vienna, his sister didn't recognize him because he had shaved his beard. – HS

12. Unknown. – HS

13. Abraham Goldberg (1908–1954) was the son of Moishe (Morris) Golberg and Gitel (Weitzer/Weizer). He arrived with his mother and siblings in the US in 1921. He later married his first cousin Frances Spector (1920–2008) the daughter of his father's sister, Sarah/Sura (Gelberg) Spector and her husband Samuel. – HS

14. Unknown. – HS

15. Unknown. – HS

16. Carl Gaynor (1896–1958) with his wife Fannie (Domb) Gaynor (1896–1982) in New York. Carl appears in a photo with his family on page 500 above with additional notes there. – HS

————————————

Name Index

Kheim, 404
Khinkes, 404, 405, 471
Kholis, 139, 302
Khollis, 55, 523
Khorwits, 92
Kiniver, 162
Kipergluz, 20, 21, 49, 53, 69, 90, 141, 198, 204, 269,
    270, 273, 302, 311, 312, 314, 320, 321, 378, 379,
    411
Kisin, 501
Klaper, 248, 274, 322, 323, 324, 411, 412, 445, 450
Klausner, 28, 33, 496
Kleeman, 69, 274, 320, 379, 411
Kleinburd, 220, 421
Kleinman, 411
Klepatch, 117, 134, 258, 259, 261, 411, 512, 516
Kleper, 211
Kleynbord, 162
Kline, 261, 399, 400
Klingbeil, 403
Kobrik, 421, 484
Koftziav, 322
Kohn, 501
Koler, 312
Kolton, 101, 118
Koltun, 410, 411
Komarinitz, 279
Koretky, 316
Korman, 369
Korolenko, 495, 496
Kosciuszko, 48, 53
Koval, 97, 127, 202, 331
Kozak, 42, 52, 219, 221, 318, 321, 322, 325, 330, 333,
    364, 367, 456, 457, 520, 523
Kozlavsky, 315
Kozlovsky, 316
Krasitsky, 10
Krave, 335
Kravets, 333, 334, 336, 338
Kravits, 339
Kreimer, 126, 136, 270, 274, 403, 411
Kreitzer, 274, 402
Kressel, 498, 499
Kritser, 101, 219, 306
Kritzer, 411
Kubal, 123
Kubilensky, 91
Kugal, 411, 415, 488
Kugul, 312
Kulish, 312, 410, 467
Kulisz, 410, 464, 467, 514
Kupferberg, 288, 291, 293, 294, 298, 353, 354, 425
Kuptsik, 349

Kwasgalter, 94, 121, 135, 278, 282, 285, 286, 288,
    292, 317, 320, 339, 341, 454, 455, 457
Kwasgalter, 410

L

Lahav, 355, 356
Lakritz, 419
Lamdan, 28, 29, 30, 32, 33, 34, 37, 42, 45, 46, 47, 50,
    52, 54, 61, 62, 70, 71, 75, 82, 86, 87, 111, 112, 132,
    133, 147, 148, 149, 173, 175, 176, 181, 186, 187,
    191, 192, 200, 201, 202, 221, 222, 225, 268, 308,
    371, 372, 376, 378, 406, 413, 426, 429, 436, 442,
    460, 490, 491, 497, 498, 499, 504, 505
Lamden, 220
Landa, 151, 494
Laufer, 424
Lauterman, 425
Lederer, 137, 138, 243, 254, 515, 517, 523
Leftwich, 501
Lerner, 197, 209, 224, 239, 366, 406, 448, 482, 514
Levental, 424
Liberman, 219, 263, 270, 272, 274, 275, 304, 322, 325,
    406, 427, 445, 450, 459, 461, 476
Lieberman, 112, 211, 450
Likhter, 220, 298, 312, 319, 324, 352, 353, 419, 485,
    486, 491
Likrits, 481
Linkes, 427, 437
Lipkin, 7, 67, 148, 439
Litsman, 312, 359
Litvak, 47, 52, 58, 154, 155, 176, 222, 223, 225, 265,
    268, 270, 273, 274, 314, 321, 376, 377, 378, 379,
    386, 406, 413, 436, 442, 499
Litz, 41, 42, 333, 457, 523
Litzman, 419, 481, 484
Loewental, 424
Lokrits, 101, 162, 313
Lomar, 406
Lovshis, 191, 202
Lumer, 94, 312

M

Maisler, 191, 192, 193
Maizlish, 55, 61, 65, 123, 350
Maklas, 481
Malar, 165, 288, 302, 420, 467, 486, 491, 512, 516
Maler, 420
Mandelkern, 28, 37, 50, 54, 57, 61, 62, 63, 65, 108,
    132, 134, 136, 137, 148, 149, 151, 176, 177, 186,
    187, 188, 191, 196, 201, 202, 203, 212, 222, 239,
    254, 261, 263, 269, 271, 272, 273, 274, 275, 276,
    277, 281, 282, 285, 286, 292, 294, 298, 304, 309,